AUSTRALIAN CONSTITUTIONAL LAW

CONCEPTS & CASES

SECOND EDITION

An understanding of the *Australian Constitution* as a framework for government in Australia is critical for any law student interested in ensuring that the rule of law is upheld. *Australian Constitutional Law: Concepts & Cases* provides an accessible and coherent introduction to Australian constitutional law, integrating theory and doctrine.

This book provides clear explanations and carefully selected case extracts that are structured conceptually, rather than chronologically, to enable students to understand both the current state of constitutional law doctrine and how to engage in constitutional reasoning. Discussion questions at the end of each chapter encourage students to consider how the law has evolved and how it can be applied to hypothetical legislation.

Now in its second edition, the text has been comprehensively updated to include commentary on significant recent High Court decisions, such as *Chetcuti v Commonwealth of Australia* (2020) 272 CLR 457, *Love v Commonwealth; Thoms v Commonwealth* (2020) 270 CLR 152, *Ruddick v Commonwealth* [2022] HCA 9 and *Alexander v Minister for Home Affairs* [2022] HCA 19, and a new chapter that examines the scope of the Commonwealth's power to impose taxation.

Written by leading constitutional law scholar Luke Beck, *Australian Constitutional Law* remains an invaluable resource for law students.

Luke Beck is Professor of Constitutional Law at Monash University. He is a leading scholar of Australian constitutional law and the leading expert on religious freedom under the *Australian Constitution*. His research has been cited by the High Court of Australia and he regularly provides expert advice to parliamentary committees. He is also a regular media commentator.

AUSTRALIAN CONSTITUTIONAL LAW

CONCEPTS & CASES

SECOND EDITION

Luke Beck

CAMBRIDGE
UNIVERSITY PRESS

CAMBRIDGE
UNIVERSITY PRESS

Shaftesbury Road, Cambridge CB2 8EA, United Kingdom

One Liberty Plaza, 20th Floor, New York, NY 10006, USA

477 Williamstown Road, Port Melbourne, VIC 3207, Australia

314–321, 3rd Floor, Plot 3, Splendor Forum, Jasola District Centre,
New Delhi - 110025, India

103 Penang Road, #05–06/07, Visioncrest Commercial, Singapore 238467

Cambridge University Press is part of Cambridge University Press & Assessment,
a department of the University of Cambridge.

We share the University's mission to contribute to society through the pursuit of education, learning and research at the highest international levels of excellence.

www.cambridge.org
Information on this title: www.cambridge.org/highereducation/isbn/9781009326605

First published 2020
Second edition 2024

Cover designed by Bec Yule, Red Chilli Design
Typeset by Lumina Datamatics Ltd

A catalogue record for this publication is available from the British Library

A catalogue record for this book is available from the National Library of Australia

ISBN 978-1-009-32660-5 Paperback

Additional resources for this publication at www.cambridge.org/highereducation/isbn/9781009326605/resources

Please be aware that this publication may contain several variations of Aboriginal and Torres Strait Islander terms and spellings; no disrespect is intended. Please note that the terms 'Indigenous Australians', 'Aboriginal and Torres Strait Islander peoples' and 'First Nations peoples' may be used interchangeably in this publication.

CONTENTS

PREFACE

The *Australian Constitution* provides a framework for government in Australia. It establishes the Commonwealth of Australia as a federation, distributing powers and functions between the Commonwealth and the States. It enables and facilitates the exercise of all public power in Australia, and limits and constrains the exercise of that power.

There is rarely, if ever, an objectively correct interpretation of a constitutional provision. Interpretative choices are necessarily made, and they can be, and are, remade over time. It is therefore essential that students learn not only the current state of constitutional law doctrine but also how to do constitutional law and how to engage in constitutional reasoning.

Before the writing of the first edition of this book, market research undertaken by Cambridge University Press found a need in the Australian book landscape for a constitutional law book that combines the best features of a casebook and the best features of a textbook. *Australian Constitutional Law: Concepts and Cases* responds to that need, providing a clear and methodical overview of Australian constitutional law. This second edition continues that approach with revised and updated chapters and a new chapter on taxation powers.

This book was written with two related guiding principles in mind. The first guiding principle is that constitutional law topics should be structured conceptually. Each chapter, with its focussed case extracts, is structured by concepts or elements of the relevant constitutional doctrine, rather than merely being presented as a chronological sequence of cases. The principal aim is to make it easy for students to understand the state of the law, including uncertainties and debates about particular concepts. The second guiding principle is that complex ideas can and should be explained in clear language. Clear explanations enable students to understand and engage with constitutional law, including its complexity and nuance. Students are not left by themselves to derive the relevant principles from case extracts or to synthesise cases in order to put together an understanding of the current state of the law. Easy-to-follow commentary guides students through Australian constitutional law, explaining what the law is and why various interpretations have been adopted.

Studying constitutional law is essential for any student who intends to be admitted to the legal profession. Truly understanding constitutional law and how to do constitutional law is essential for any lawyer interested in ensuring that the rule of law is upheld, that abuses of power are restrained and remedied, and that the ultimate sovereignty of the Australian people is maintained. Constitutional law is essential to good government.

Luke Beck
Melbourne, May 2023

ACKNOWLEDGEMENTS

The authors and Cambridge University Press would like to thank the following for permission to reproduce material in this book.

Extract from Jeffrey Goldsworthy, 'Constitutional Cultures, Democracy, and Unwritten Principles' (2012) (3) *University of Illinois Law Review* 683: Reproduced with permission.

Extract from Constitutional Commission, *Final Report of the Constitutional Commission* (Australian Government Printing Service, 1988) vol 1: © Parliament of Australia. Reproduced under Creative Commons Attribution-NonCommercial-NoDerivs 3.0 Australia (CC BY-NC-ND 3.0 AU) licence: https://creativecommons.org/licenses/by-nc-nd/3.0/au/.

Extract from Hans Kelsen, *Pure Theory of Law* (trans: Max Knight, first published 1934, University of California Press, 1967) © University of California Press Books. Reproduced with permission.

Extract from Helen Irving, 'Indigenous Recognition and Constitutional Myths', *Constitutional Critique Blog*, 9 June 2015: Reproduced with permission of Professor Helen Irving.

Extract from *Uluru Statement of the Heart* © Commonwealth of Australia 2017. Licenced under Creative Commons Attribution 4.0 International licence: https://creativecommons.org/licenses/by/4.0/legalcode.

Extract from Robert French (Chapter 3): Reproduced with permission of Mr Robert French AC.

Extracts from *Final Report of the Referendum Council* (Department of Prime Minister and Cabinet, 2017); *Recognising Aboriginal and Torres Strait Islander Peoples in the Constitution: Report of the Expert Panel* (Department of Families, Housing, Community Services and Indigenous Affairs, 2012): © Commonwealth of Australia. Reproduced under Creative Commons Attribution-NonCommercial-NoDerivs 3.0 Australia (CC BY-NC-ND 3.0 AU).

Extracts from Fiona Wheeler, 'Original Intent and the Doctrine of the Separation of Powers in Australia' (1996) 7(2) *Public Law Review* 96; Commonwealth Law Reports (CLR); Federal Court Reports (FCR); Federal Law Reports (FLR); South Australian State Reports (SASR): reproduced with permission of Thomson Reuters (Professional) Australia Limited, legal.thomsonreuters.com.au.

Extracts from Australian Law Reports: originally published by LexisNexis.

Extracts from High Court of Australia (HCA): © Commonwealth of Australia.

Extracts from New South Wales Law Reports (NSWLR): reproduced with permission from the Council of Law Reporting for New South Wales.

Extracts from Family Court of Australia (FamCA): reproduced with permission.

Extracts from Commonwealth legislation: sourced from the Federal Register of Legislation and reproduced under Creative Commons Attribution 4.0 International (CC BY 4.0). For the latest information on Australian Government law please go to https://www.legislation.gov.au.

Extracts from South Australian legislation: sourced from the South Australian Legislation website in May 2023. For the latest information on South Australian Government legislation, please go to www.legislation.sa.gov.au/. Reproduced under Creative Commons Attribution 4.0 International Licence (CC BY 4.0): https://creativecommons.org/licenses/by/4.0/.

Extracts from Victorian legislation: © State of Victoria, Australia. Copyright in all legislation of the Parliament of the State of Victoria, Australia, is owned by the Crown in right of the State of Victoria, Australia. DISCLAIMER: This product or service contains an unofficial version of the legislation of the Parliament of State of Victoria. The State of Victoria accepts no responsibility for the accuracy and completeness of any legislation contained in this product or provided through this service.

Every effort has been made to trace and acknowledge copyright. The publisher apologises for any accidental infringement and welcomes information that would redress this situation.

TABLE OF CASES

TABLE OF STATUTES

COMMONWEALTH

Australian Capital Territory

New South Wales

Northern Territory

Queensland

South Australia

Tasmania

Victoria

Western Australia

UNITED KINGDOM

UNITED STATES OF AMERICA

PAPUA NEW GUINEA

INTERNATIONAL INSTRUMENTS

PART 1

INTRODUCTION

INTRODUCTION TO AUSTRALIAN CONSTITUTIONAL LAW

1

1.1 Overview

This chapter presents an introduction to Australian constitutional law. It begins by examining the various forms a Constitution can take and the purposes a Constitution may serve. The *Australian Constitution* is a written document that is difficult to change and functions principally to establish institutions of government and distribute powers between the Federal and State levels of government.

This chapter also examines the process by which Australia achieved constitutional independence from the United Kingdom. When the *Australian Constitution* came into force on 1 January 1901, Australia was subject to the repugnancy doctrine, which limited the powers of the Federal and State Parliaments to enact legislation inconsistent with British laws, and to Imperial parliamentary supremacy, which enabled the Imperial Parliament to enact legislation having effect as part of Australian law. The key steps towards constitutional independence were the adoption of the *Statute of Westminster 1931* and the *Australia Act 1986*. These statutes abolished, in stages, those doctrines as part of Australian law.

This chapter considers the more conceptual questions of why the *Australian Constitution* was binding in 1901 and why the *Australian Constitution* is binding today. This chapter also considers a number of key principles underlying the *Australian Constitution*: the rule of law, federalism, responsible government, and parliamentary supremacy. This chapter concludes with a consideration of the place of Aboriginal and Torres Strait Islander Australians in Australian constitutionalism.

Key concepts considered in this chapter include:

- constitution
- repugnancy doctrine
- imperial supremacy
- independence
- *grundnorm*
- rule of law
- federalism
- responsible government
- constitutional conventions
- parliamentary supremacy
- constitutional recognition.

1.2 What is a 'Constitution'?

Constitutions are not all the same in form.

Most national constitutions are codified. Codified constitutions are documents usually called 'the Constitution', but sometimes given other names such as 'the Basic Law' (as in Germany), with all other laws and the actions of public officials are subordinate to these documents. However, some constitutions are in uncodified form. The United Kingdom, New Zealand, and Israel have uncodified constitutions. In those countries, there is no single document called 'the Constitution' or similar, and to which all other laws and the actions of public officials are subordinate. Those countries nevertheless have sophisticated sets of written and unwritten rules governing law-making and the organisation of the State.

Some codified constitutions are rigid and some are flexible. Rigid constitutions are difficult to change because of the rules governing constitutional change. For example, Article V of the *United States Constitution* provides that the *United States Constitution* can be altered only with the approval of three-quarters of all State legislatures. Flexible constitutions are relatively easy to change, sometimes requiring only ordinary legislation to make a change. For example, sections 13 and 14 of the *Constitution of Papua New Guinea* provide that the *Constitution* can be altered by legislation, provided that the legislation is approved for a second time by the Papua New Guinea Parliament at least two months after the legislation is first passed.

Constitutional law in Australia consists of a written constitution called the *Australian Constitution*, unwritten rules called 'constitutional conventions', and a number of statutes of constitutional significance. The legal relationship between the written Constitution and the unwritten constitutional conventions is considered below. The most important statutes of constitutional significance are the various State Constitution Acts (considered in Chapter 2), and the *Statute of Westminster 1931* and the *Australia Act 1986* (considered below).

Constitutions are not all the same in respect of the purposes they serve.

The Australian constitutional theorist Jeffrey Goldsworthy explains that national constitutions can serve very different purposes, and serve similar purposes in different ways. His explanation relies on a tripartite understanding of the purposes served by the *United*

States Constitution articulated by the American constitutional theorist Jack M Balkin in *Living Originalism* (Belknap Press, 2011).

Jeffrey Goldsworthy, 'Constitutional Cultures, Democracy, and Unwritten Principles' (2012) (3) *University of Illinois Law Review* 683

Reading Balkin's account brought home to me some major differences between the US and Australian constitutional traditions. He distinguishes between the functions of a constitution as a "basic law" (a foundational or supreme law "that trumps other law to the contrary"), a "higher law" ("a source of inspiration and aspiration, a repository of values and principles"), and "the people's law" ("our achievement and the product of our efforts as a people, which involves a collective identification with those who came before us and with those who will come after us").

It is notable that some constitutions do not have all or possibly any of these functions. Britain's largely unwritten, customary constitution, and New Zealand's written constitution, are not "basic laws" because they do not trump other laws: they can be changed by statutes enacted by their parliaments in the ordinary way. Neither of them serves as a "higher law" either, although the British Constitution might be regarded by the British people as "their law."

The Australian Constitution is a basic but not a higher law, and might not qualify as "the people's law." Compared with its US counterpart, it is "a prosaic document expressed in lawyer's language." Consisting almost entirely of structural and power-conferring provisions, it lacks the grand and inspirational declarations of national values or principles that are found in a "higher law." It includes a handful of provisions designed to suppress regional favouritism and to curb the power of the federal Parliament, but no bill of rights. Its status as "the people's law" is dubious because, in 1992, no less than one-third of Australians were found not to know that they even have a written constitution, let alone anything about its contents. It establishes the basic legal framework for their democratic and federal governance, but remains largely in the background and only occasionally attracts a modicum of public attention due to some dispute (usually a federal one) about its meaning.

In Australia, public commitment to and debate over principles of political morality are largely left to the political realm ...

According to Balkin, the success and legitimacy of the US Constitution stem from its serving as a higher law rather than merely as a basic law. I am not sure why. The lack of grand, inspirational principles in their Constitution does not undermine Australians' attachment to their political and legal system. Their Constitution apparently enjoys legitimacy because, as a basic law providing a "framework for politics and lawmaking," it gives them access to a fair and democratic political process through which they can pursue their political aspirations. It appears unnecessary for it also to function as a "higher law" that gives authoritative expression to those aspirations.

Balkin also regards it as "central" to Americans' attachment to their Constitution that its status as "their law" provides them with "a constitutive narrative through which [they] imagine themselves as a people, with shared memories, goals, aspirations, values, duties, and ambitions." Australians, on the other hand, seem perfectly able to identify themselves as a historically continuing people, characterized by some basic shared values and commitments, without their Constitution playing a large part in the narrative, except as the essential legal device by which federation was attained. The common values and commitments that define them as a people can be left unwritten – the Constitution can take them for granted, and vice versa – while serving the functions that Balkin emphasizes (providing a collective narrative, binding different generations together, and so on).

Indeed, the British have for many centuries enjoyed a high regard for themselves as a historically continuous people, whose distinctive cultural virtues have enabled them to play a vital role in European and world history, although they lack any written constitution at all. Admittedly, appeal to a largely fictional "Ancient Constitution," embodied in custom rather than written law, was for centuries a standard gambit in English political rhetoric, which played much the same role that Balkin sometimes attributes to the US Constitution ...

The whole idea of the Constitution as an object of quasi-religious veneration, inspiration, and redemption is alien to Australians, although an increasing number would like to amend the Constitution so that it could play a more "educative" role in spreading a "human rights culture." In Australia, what Balkin calls "redemption" of social injustice is the responsibility of the political realm, not the constitutional one ...

1.3 The *Australian Constitution*

The document called the *Australian Constitution* is not a stand-alone document. It is found in an Act of the Parliament of the United Kingdom acting in its imperial capacity. Section 9 of the *Commonwealth of Australia Constitution Act 1900* (Imp) states that 'The Constitution of the Commonwealth shall be as follows: [...]'. The first eight sections of that statute are usually referred to as 'covering clauses', rather than sections, in order to avoid confusion with the sections of the *Constitution*.

Commonwealth of Australia Constitution Act 1900 c 12 (Imp)

Section 3 Proclamation of the Commonwealth

It shall be lawful for the Queen, with the advice of the Privy Council, to declare by proclamation that, on and after a day therein appointed, not being later than one year after the passing of this Act, the people of New South Wales, Victoria, South Australia, Queensland, and Tasmania, and also, if Her Majesty is satisfied that the people of Western Australia have agreed thereto, of Western Australia, shall be united in a Federal Commonwealth under the name of the Commonwealth of Australia. But the Queen may, at any time after the proclamation, appoint a Governor-General for the Commonwealth.

Section 4 Commencement of Act

The Commonwealth shall be established, and the Constitution of the Commonwealth shall take effect, on and after the day so appointed. But the Parliaments of the several colonies may at any time after the passing of this Act make any such laws, to come into operation on the day so appointed, as they might have made if the Constitution had taken effect at the passing of this Act.

Section 9 Constitution

The Constitution of the Commonwealth shall be as follows:

Chapter I – The Parliament

Part I – General

Part II – The Senate

Part III – The House of Representatives

Part IV – Both Houses of the Parliament

Part V – Powers of the Parliament

Chapter II – The Executive Government

Chapter II – The Judicature

Chapter IV – Finance and Trade

Chapter V – The States

Chapter VI – New States

Chapter VII – Miscellaneous

Chapter VIII – Alteration of the Constitution

The Schedule

On 17 September 1900, Queen Victoria issued a proclamation providing that the Commonwealth of Australia would come into existence on 1 January 1901.

Proclamation Uniting the People of New South Wales, Victoria, South Australia, Queensland, Tasmania, and Western Australia in a Federal Commonwealth

At the Court at Balmoral,

The 17th day of September, 1900.

Present:

The Queen's Most Excellent Majesty in Council.

The following Draft Proclamation was this day read at the Board and approved:

– A. W. FITZROY.

By The Queen

PROCLAMATION

WHEREAS by an Act of Parliament passed in the sixty-third and sixty-fourth years of Our Reign intituled, "An Act to constitute the Commonwealth of Australia," it is enacted that it shall be lawful for the Queen, with the advice of the Privy Council, to declare by proclamation that, on and after a day appointed, not being later than one year after the passing of this Act, the people of New South Wales, Victoria, South Australia, Queensland, and Tasmania, and also, if Her Majesty is satisfied that the people of Western Australia have agreed thereto, of Western Australia, shall be united in a Federal Commonwealth under the name of the Commonwealth of Australia:

And whereas We are satisfied that the people of Western Australia have agreed thereto accordingly:

We, therefore, by and with the advice of Our Privy Council, have thought fit to issue this Our Royal Proclamation, and We do hereby declare that on and after the first day of January, One thousand nine hundred and one, the people of New South Wales, Victoria, South Australia, Queensland, Tasmania, and Western Australia shall be united in a Federal Commonwealth under the name of the Commonwealth of Australia.

Given at Our Court at Balmoral, this seventeenth day of September, in the year of Our Lord One thousand nine hundred and in the sixty-fourth year of Our Reign.

God Save The Queen!

Although found in a British statute, the *Australian Constitution* was drafted by Australians and approved by the Australian people (although in the 1890s when it was approved not all Australian adults had the right to vote and could participate in the approval process).

The Australasian Federal Convention was held between 1897 and 1898. Its task was to draft a Constitution. Delegates to the Convention were elected from the colonies of New South Wales, Victoria, South Australia, Western Australia and Tasmania. Queensland did not participate. The Federal Convention met for its first session in Adelaide in March 1897. The draft Constitution Bill produced at Adelaide was then referred to the parliaments of the various colonies for their consideration and suggestions. The Federal Convention met for its second session in Sydney in September 1897 to consider the draft Constitution Bill further. The Federal Convention met for its final session in Melbourne between January and March 1898, where a finalised draft Constitution Bill was produced.

In January 1899, the Premiers of the various colonies agreed to make minor amendments to the draft Constitution Bill. The modified draft Constitution was subsequently approved by referenda held in New South Wales, Victoria, Queensland, South Australia and Tasmania.

A delegation of Australian political leaders then travelled to London to lobby for the Imperial Parliament to pass legislation to give effect to the Constitution. After the *Commonwealth of Australia Constitution Act 1900* (Imp) was passed by the Imperial Parliament on 9 July 1900, but before Queen Victoria issued the proclamation that the Constitution should take effect, the people of Western Australia voted in a referendum to join the federation as one of the original States.

1.4 Australian constitutional independence

Federation of the Australian colonies was not an independence movement and the *Australian Constitution* did not give Australia independence from the United Kingdom. The preamble to the *Commonwealth of Australia Constitution Act 1900* (Imp) reflects the intention of Australians that the Commonwealth of Australia would be a subordinate part of the British Empire.

Commonwealth of Australia Constitution Act 1900 c 12 (Imp)

WHEREAS the people of New South Wales, Victoria, South Australia, Queensland, and Tasmania, humbly relying on the blessing of Almighty God, have agreed to unite in one indissoluble Federal Commonwealth under the Crown of the United Kingdom of Great Britain and Ireland, and under the Constitution hereby established ...

Imperial supremacy and the repugnancy doctrine

Both before and after Federation, the Australian States (or colonies, as they were before Federation) were subject to two important and related legal doctrines: imperial supremacy and the repugnancy doctrine. On its establishment, the Commonwealth of Australia also became subject to these doctrines.

Imperial supremacy was the idea that the Imperial Parliament can legislate by paramount force for Australia (and other components of the British Empire). Imperial legislation applying by paramount force was *part of* Australian law in the same way that legislation passed by the Federal or State Parliaments is part of Australian law. In simple terms, the Imperial Parliament could enact legislation expressed to apply in a particular State and that legislation would be effective notwithstanding any State or federal legislation to the contrary. Equally, the Imperial Parliament could enact legislation applying to the whole of Australia and that legislation would be effective notwithstanding any federal legislation or provision of the *Australian Constitution* to the contrary.

The repugnancy doctrine was a doctrine of the common law that was later clarified and given a statutory foundation by the *Colonial Laws Validity Act 1865* (Imp). The repugnancy doctrine operated as a limitation on the scope of the legislative power of any colonial or dominion parliament within the British Empire (such as those of the Australian colonies/States and the Federal Parliament). Notwithstanding the powers of such a parliament, no legislation would be valid that was repugnant to (in the sense of inconsistent with) United Kingdom laws expressed to apply in the relevant territory.

Colonial Laws Validity Act 1865 c 63 (Imp)

Section 2 Colonial Law when void for Repugnancy.

Any colonial law which is or shall be in any respect repugnant to the provisions of any Act of Parliament extending to the colony to which such law may relate, or repugnant to any order or regulation made under authority of such Act of Parliament, or having in the colony the force and effect of such Act, shall be read subject to such Act, order, or regulation, and shall, to the extent of such repugnancy, but not otherwise, be and remain absolutely void and inoperative.

There are examples of Australian federal statutes being struck down as invalid for breaching the repugnancy doctrine. In ***Union Steamship Co of New Zealand Ltd v Commonwealth***, the High Court held that provisions of the *Navigation Act 1912* (Cth) were repugnant to provisions of the *Merchant Shipping Act 1894* (Imp), which applied throughout the British Empire. The legal result was that the federal legislation was void to the extent of the repugnancy.

Union Steamship Co of New Zealand Ltd v Commonwealth (1925) 36 CLR 130

Isaacs J

I have already said that inherently the Constitution by ss 51 (i) and 98 empowers the Commonwealth Parliament to pass such an enactment as the *Navigation Act* provisions now under consideration. If there were no Imperial Act those provisions would be fully operative. But, in presence of the Imperial provisions, have the Australian provisions any legal force?

...

Given, then, the repugnancy between an existing Imperial Act and an existing Commonwealth Act, what is the consequence? It seems to me plain that the constantly speaking s 2 of the *Colonial Laws Validity Act 1865* determines the matter. It declares that the *Navigation Act* "shall be read subject to" the *Merchant Shipping Acts 1894 to 1906,* and "shall to the extent of such repugnancy, but not otherwise, be and remain absolutely void and inoperative." The case falls within the plain words of s 2 ...

The principles applicable to working out whether an Australian law is repugnant in the *Colonial Laws Validity Act* sense no longer matter.

Imperial supremacy and the repugnancy doctrine were abolished in stages.

The *Statute of Westminster*

The *Statute of Westminster 1931* (Imp) marked an important development in the evolution of Australia's constitutional independence, and the independence of other dominions within the British Empire such as Canada and New Zealand. It was enacted by the Imperial Parliament following a conference of the leaders of various parts of the British Empire to discuss the constitutional status of the dominions within the Empire.

The Statute made two key changes to Australia's constitutional position. Section 2 abolished the repugnancy doctrine in respect of federal laws. Section 4 provided that the Imperial Parliament could not legislate for Australia without the request and consent of the Federal Parliament, thereby effectively abolishing imperial supremacy in respect of the Commonwealth.

Statute of Westminster 1931 c 4 (Imp)

Section 1 Meaning of "Dominion" in this Act

In this Act the expression "Dominion" means any of the following Dominions, that is to say, the Dominion of Canada, the Commonwealth of Australia, the Dominion of New Zealand, the Union of South Africa, the Irish Free State and Newfoundland.

Section 2 Validity of laws made by Parliament of a Dominion

(1) The *Colonial Laws Validity Act, 1865,* shall not apply to any law made after the commencement of this Act by the Parliament of a Dominion.

(2) No law and no provision of any law made after the commencement of this Act by the Parliament of a Dominion shall be void or inoperative on the ground that it is repugnant to the law of England, or to the provisions of any existing or future Act of Parliament of the United Kingdom, or to any order, rule or regulation made under any such Act, and the powers of the Parliament of a Dominion shall include the power to repeal or amend any such Act, order, rule or regulation in so far as the same is part of the law of the Dominion.

Section 4 Parliament of the United Kingdom not to legislate for Dominion except by consent

No Act of Parliament of the United Kingdom passed after the commencement of this Act shall extend, or be deemed to extend, to a Dominion as part of the law of that Dominion, unless it is expressly declared in that Act that that Dominion has requested, and consented to, the enactment thereof.

The Statute did not abolish the repugnancy doctrine in respect of the Australian States. The Statute abolished that doctrine only in respect of dominions: the Commonwealth of Australia was a dominion but the individual States were not. Section 9 of the Statute also expressly preserved imperial legislative supremacy in respect of all matters within the authority of the States that were not matters within the authority of the Federal Parliament.

Statute of Westminster 1931 c 4 (Imp)

Section 9 Saving with respect to States of Australia

(1) Nothing in this Act shall be deemed to authorize the Parliament of the Commonwealth of Australia to make laws on any matter within the authority of the States of Australia, not being a matter within the authority of the Parliament or Government of the Commonwealth of Australia.

(2) Nothing in this Act shall be deemed to require the concurrence of the Parliament or Government of the Commonwealth of Australia, in any law made by the Parliament of the United Kingdom with respect to any matter within the authority of the States of Australia, not being a matter within the authority of the Parliament or Government of the Commonwealth of Australia, in any case where it would have been in accordance with the constitutional practice existing before the commencement of this Act that the Parliament of the United Kingdom should make that law without such concurrence.

(3) In the application of this Act to the Commonwealth of Australia the request and consent referred to in section four shall mean the request and consent of the Parliament and government of the Commonwealth.

Section 10 of the Statute provided that its key provisions would not take effect in respect of Australia unless and until adopted by the Federal Parliament. Australia adopted the *Statute of Westminster* in 1942 with the passing of the *Statute of Westminster Adoption Act 1942* (Cth), which backdated the date of commencement to 1939 for the purpose of ensuring the validity of certain war-time legislation.

The *Australia Act*

Full constitutional independence was not achieved until the introduction of the *Australia Act 1986* (Cth).

The *Australia Act* made a number of important of changes to Australia's constitutional position. Section 1 abolished imperial legislative supremacy completely: no British statute can apply by paramount force as part of Australian law. Section 3 abolished the repugnancy doctrine in respect of the States. Section 11 abolished all rights of appeal from decisions of Australian courts to the Privy Council.

Australia Act 1986 (Cth)

Section 1 Termination of power of Parliament of United Kingdom to legislate for Australia

No Act of the Parliament of the United Kingdom passed after the commencement of this Act shall extend, or be deemed to extend, to the Commonwealth, to a State or to a Territory as part of the law of the Commonwealth, of the State or of the Territory.

Section 3 Termination of restrictions on legislative powers of Parliaments of States

(1) The Act of the Parliament of the United Kingdom known as the Colonial Laws Validity Act 1865 shall not apply to any law made after the commencement of this Act by the Parliament of a State.

(2) No law and no provision of any law made after the commencement of this Act by the Parliament of a State shall be void or inoperative on the ground that it is repugnant to the law of England, or to the provisions of any existing or future Act of the Parliament of the United Kingdom, or to any order, rule or regulation made under any such Act, and the powers of the Parliament of a State shall include the power to repeal or amend any such Act, order, rule or regulation in so far as it is part of the law of the State.

Section 11 Termination of appeals to Her Majesty in Council

(1) ... [N]o appeal to Her Majesty in Council lies or shall be brought, whether by leave or special leave of any court or of Her Majesty in Council or otherwise, and whether by virtue of any Act of the Parliament of the United Kingdom, the Royal Prerogative or otherwise, from or in respect of any decision of an Australian court.

There are eight versions of the *Australia Act:* each State enacted legislation requesting that the Federal Parliament enact the *Australia Act,* the Federal Parliament enacted the *Australia Act 1986* (Cth), and the United Kingdom Parliament enacted a version of the legislation.

The High Court has explained that it was the Federal Parliament's *Australia Act 1986* (Cth) that is the effective legislation. That legislation is valid as a matter of Australian law because it falls within the Federal Parliament's power under section 51(xxxviii) of the *Constitution* – this is the power to make laws with respect to 'the exercise within the Commonwealth, at the request or with the concurrence of the Parliaments of all the States directly concerned, of any power which can at the establishment of this Constitution be exercised only by the Parliament of the United Kingdom'. The United Kingdom legislation has relevance only for the law of the United Kingdom, and has no force or effect as part of the law of Australia. The United Kingdom legislation was not necessary for the *Australia Act 1986* (Cth) to take effect.

Sue v Hill (1999) 199 CLR 462

The issue in this case was whether the United Kingdom was a 'foreign power' for the purpose of section 44(iv) of the* Constitution*, which disqualifies citizens of foreign powers from holding seats in Federal Parliament.

Gleeson CJ, Gummow and Hayne JJ

Section 1 of the *Australia Act* does not purport to exclude, as a matter of the law of the United Kingdom, the effect of statutes thereafter enacted at Westminster. Rather, it denies their efficacy as part of the law of the Commonwealth, the States and the Territories. Section 51(xxx–viii) extends to the actual execution within this country of a power of the sort described in that paragraph. The scope of the phrase "within the Commonwealth" in s 51(xxxviii) includes the exercise of legislative power with effect upon the political structures with authority over the geographical area of the Commonwealth, the States and the Territories and the areas provided for in the *Seas and Submerged Lands Act* (Cth): see *New South Wales v Commonwealth* (1975) 135 CLR 337. It follows that s 1 of the *Australia Act* was validly enacted under that paragraph ...

The expression in s 1 of the 1986 UK Act "[n]o Act of the Parliament of the United Kingdom passed ... shall extend, or be deemed to extend" was used in s 4 of the *Statute of Westminster 1931* (UK). Provisions such as s 1 may present doctrinal questions for the constitutional law of the United Kingdom. The effect in the United Kingdom of any amendment or repeal by the United Kingdom Parliament of s 1 would be for those adjudicating upon the constitutional law of that country. But whatever effect the courts of the United Kingdom may give to an amendment or repeal of the 1986 UK Act, Australian courts would be obliged to give their obedience to s 1 of the statute passed by the Parliament of the Commonwealth.

Royal Assent to the *Australia Act 1986* (Cth) was given by the Governor-General in the usual way. In recognition of the importance of the Act, Queen Elizabeth II travelled to Australia and, at a ceremony at Government House in Canberra in her capacity as Queen of Australia, issued a proclamation that the Act would come into force on 3 March 1986 at 4pm Australian Eastern Standard Time. It was at that point that the United Kingdom ceased to have any legal powers in respect of Australia.

The United Kingdom ceasing to have any legal powers in respect of Australia may be a slightly different thing to Australia achieving full independence, independence being a less precise and more political concept. ***Chetcuti v Commonwealth*** includes discussion by three judges of the High Court about the exact date at which Australia became independent of the United Kingdom. At first instance, Nettle J identified the coming into effect of the *Statute of Westminster Adoption Act 1942* as the relevant date. On appeal, Edelman J considered that there is 'no magic date' and Steward J identified the coming into effect of the *Nationality and Citizenship Act 1948* (Cth) on 26 January 1949 as the relevant, albeit somewhat fictitious, date. The other members of the Court did not seek to identify a precise date.

Chetcuti v Commonwealth (2020) 272 CLR 457

This case involved the question of whether a British subject who migrated to Australia in 1948 but who had not become an Australian citizen was an 'alien' for constitutional purposes. Justice Nettle sitting alone at first instance held that such a person fell within the concept of 'alien'. Chapter 7 deals with the substantive matter.

Nettle J

I am not persuaded that either the Balfour Declaration or the *Statute of Westminster* was sufficient of itself, or as an indication of the intra-Empire relational developments it reflected, to constitute Australia an independent sovereign nation in the sense that has since been recognised as characterising the United Kingdom as a foreign power. And while the Statute of Westminster declared novel constitutional conventions that "affect[ed] the basal conceptions of the legal system under which the Empire was governed", its permissive provisions did not manifest in legal and political reality in Australia until the Statute was incorporated into Australian law. I do accept, however, that, at least by reason of the enactment of the *Statute of Westminster Adoption Act*, Australia became sufficiently independent of the United Kingdom to be regarded as an independent sovereign nation and that the relevant constitutional conception of the Crown (as opposed to the statutory description of it which persisted until the *Royal Style and Titles Act 1973* (Cth)) thereupon became the Crown in right of Australia.

... And such vestigial legislative powers as the United Kingdom Parliament retained with respect to the States until the enactment of the *Australia Act* ought not be seen as detracting from the independence that the Commonwealth as such, as opposed to its constituent States, acquired by Australia's adoption of the *Statute of Westminster* with effect from 1939. For, as Barwick CJ observed in *New South Wales v The Commonwealth*, it was the Commonwealth that became "the nation state, internationally recognized as such and independent", and "[o]nly the Commonwealth has international status". Neither the colonies nor the States ever held that status.

Chetcuti v Commonwealth (2021) 272 CLR 609

An appeal from Nettle J's decision on the substantive matter to a full bench of the High Court was dismissed.

Edelman J

There is no magic date when, like Cinderella at midnight, all British subjects who had no other connection to Australia which was capable of taking them outside s 51(xix) suddenly became capable of being treated as aliens in Australia. Rather, the process of Australian independence from the United Kingdom, as the special case before the primary judge pointed out in painstaking detail, involved incremental development marked by a number of significant political and legal steps following Federation in 1901.

The incremental development was, in large part, political ...

... [T]he incremental development of Australian sovereignty over this period also included: the *Nationality Act 1920* (Cth); the *Commonwealth Public Service Act 1922* (Cth); the *Statute of Westminster 1931* (UK); and the *Aliens Deportation Act 1946* (Cth). These legislative steps to complete independence were arguably not wholly concluded until the passage of the *Australia Acts 1986* (Cth and UK).

Steward J

At some point following federation, British subjects, not born in Australia, became aliens of this country. That is because they owed allegiance to the Crown in right of the United Kingdom as opposed to the Crown in right of Australia. This occurred when the indivisible Imperial Crown manifested itself as the Crown in right of Australia. It is impossible to identify any bright line as to when this took place; in fact, it took place over time ...

> Nonetheless, in *Shaw v Minister for Immigration and Multicultural Affairs* a bright line was identified by this Court. A date was chosen. It was 26 January 1949. On that day, the *Nationality and Citizenship Act 1948* (Cth) ('the 1948 Citizenship Act') came into effect. That Act created, for the first time, the statutory concept of Australian citizenship. From that date, a British subject arriving in Australia did so as an alien ...
>
> With very great respect to the learned primary judge, it should not be accepted that the Imperial Crown was transformed, relevantly into the Crown in right of Australia, from the enactment of the *Statute of Westminster Adoption Act* in 1942. It may be accepted that Australia's adoption of the Statute of Westminster was a pivotal step towards Australia's independence; but it was not the step that completed that process. The preamble to the Statute of Westminster affirms that the British Dominions remained "united by a common allegiance to the Crown". The *Statute of Westminster* legally affirmed what probably already existed (due to the forbearance of the Imperial Parliament), namely, the relationship of equality that existed as between each British Dominion Parliament and the Parliament at Westminster. But, critically, it did not alter the constitutional relationship between each British Dominion and the Crown. That relationship was expressed to be one of "common allegiance". That quality of commonality is not consistent with a divided Crown; indeed, it is entirely inconsistent with it.
>
> ...
>
> Australia's independence as a sovereign power was not the product of any one specific legislative change; nor was it the product of any declaration or international meeting. Rather, it was a gradual process comprising political and cultural changes that the law over time, and following these changes, came to recognise as fulfilled ...
>
> Nonetheless, as already mentioned, the plurality in *Shaw* drew a bright line by selecting 26 January 1949 as the date by which the Imperial Crown relevantly divided. That bright line is a necessary and convenient constitutional fiction which should not now be disturbed.

Identifying the precise date on which Australia achieved full constitutional independence is unlikely to be a necessary step in deciding any substantive legal question and, for that reason, it is unlikely the High Court will ever need to finally decide the issue.

The monarch of Australia

The Crown was previously understood to be 'indivisible' in the sense that there was one Crown, and therefore one monarch, for the entire British Empire and therefore for all of the dominions within it. The result was that there could be no such thing as King or Queen of Australia: there was only the King or Queen of the United Kingdom. That was the legal position for much of the twentieth century, but it is no longer the position.

In ***Nolan***, the High Court explained that the Crown is now understood to be divisible. The position of monarch of Australia is entirely distinct from the positions of monarch of the United Kingdom, monarch of Canada, monarch of New Zealand and so on, despite the fact that the same person holds each of these positions. Although there was no such thing as the Queen of Australia when the *Australian Constitution* came into operation, every reference to 'the Queen' in the *Australian Constitution* is now understood to be a reference to the Queen of Australia. The *Constitution* was drafted during the reign of Queen

Victoria with the result that various provisions refer to 'the Queen'. Covering clause 2 states that 'The provisions of this Act referring to the Queen shall extend Her Majesty's heirs and successors'. In other words, constitutional references to 'the Queen' should be read as referring to the reigning monarch.

Nolan v Minister for Immigration and Ethnic Affairs (1988) 165 CLR 178

Mason CJ, Wilson, Brennan, Deane, Dawson and Toohey JJ

The transition from Empire to Commonwealth and the emergence of Australia and other Dominions as independent sovereign nations within the Commonwealth inevitably changed the nature of the relationship between the United Kingdom and its former Colonies and rendered obsolete notions of an indivisible Crown ... It became accepted as a "truism" that, although "there is only one person who is the Sovereign ..., ... in matters of law and government the Queen of the United Kingdom ... is entirely independent and distinct from" the Queen of (for example) Canada or Australia (per May LJ, *R v Foreign Secretary, Ex parte Indian Association* (1982) QB 892, at p 928) ...

It was submitted on behalf of the plaintiff that the references to the "Crown of the United Kingdom" in the preamble and (in an expanded form) in covering cl 2 of the *Commonwealth of Australia Constitution Act 1900* (Imp) and to "subject of the Queen" in the Constitution itself (see ss 34(ii) and 117) were inconsistent with the notion that any subject of the Queen, be he citizen of the United Kingdom or of some other country of the Commonwealth which recognizes the Queen as Head of State (eg, Canada, Jamaica or Mauritius), could be an "alien" in so far as this country is concerned. It is unnecessary to pursue that point beyond saying that those references cannot alter, or avoid the consequences of, the emergence of Australia as an independent nation, the acceptance of the divisibility of the Crown which was implicit in the development of the Commonwealth as an association of independent nations and the creation of a distinct Australian citizenship. Those developments necessarily produced different reference points for the application of the word "alien". Inevitably, the practical designation of the word altered so that, while its abstract meaning remained constant, it encompassed persons who were not citizens of this country even though they might be British subjects or subjects of the Queen by reason of their citizenship of some other nation. We would add that, to the extent that there would otherwise be inconsistency in the use of the words "subject of the Queen" in the Constitution, it should be resolved by treating those words as referring, in a modern context, to a subject of the Queen in right of Australia ...

The word 'dominion' is usually no longer used to describe countries like Australia, Canada and New Zealand within the Commonwealth of Nations that have the British monarch as their head of state. Instead, in circumstances where the word 'dominion' would previously have been be used, the word 'realm' is now used to reflect those countries' independent and sovereign status. The monarch's Australian title is confirmed by statute.

Royal Style and Titles Act 1973 (Cth)

Section 2 Assent to adoption of new Royal Style and Titles in relation to Australia

(1) The assent of the Parliament is hereby given to the adoption by Her Majesty, for use in relation to Australia and its Territories, in lieu of the Style and Titles set forth in the Schedule to the *Royal Style and Titles Act 1953*, of the Style and Titles set forth in the Schedule to this Act, and to the issue for that purpose by Her Majesty of Her Royal Proclamation under such seal as Her Majesty by Warrant appoints.

Schedule – Royal Style and Titles

Elizabeth the Second, by the Grace of God Queen of Australia and Her other Realms and Territories, Head of the Commonwealth.

Acts Interpretation Act 1901 (Cth)

Section 16 References to the Sovereign

In any Act references to the Sovereign reigning at the time of such Act, or to the Crown, shall be construed as references to the Sovereign for the time being.

1.5 Why is the *Australian Constitution* binding?

The *Australian Constitution* is binding. But why?

The answer in 1901, and for most of the twentieth century, was straightforward and uncontroversial: because the Imperial Parliament exercised its legislative powers and imposed the *Constitution* by paramount force. Covering clause 5 of the *Commonwealth of Australia Constitution Act 1900* (Imp) makes this clear.

Commonwealth of Australia Constitution Act 1900 c 12 (Imp)

Clause 5 Operation of the Constitution and laws

This Act, and all laws made by the Parliament of the Commonwealth under the Constitution, shall be binding on the courts, judges, and people of every State and of every part of the Commonwealth, notwithstanding anything in the laws of any State ...

However, with the reality of Australia's independence from the United Kingdom, the supremacy of the Imperial Parliament can no longer be an explanation for why the *Australian Constitution* is binding.

Geoffrey Lindell has suggested that the *Australian Constitution* is binding today for two related reasons: because nothing has happened to alter the inability of the Federal and State Parliaments to legislate inconsistently with the *Constitution* and because the *Constitution* can be changed by the people, who have chosen to do so only in limited respects.

Geoffrey Lindell, 'Why is Australia's Constitution Binding? – The Reasons in 1900 and Now, and the Effect of Independence' (1986) 16 *Federal Law Review* 29

The points made in this article can be conveniently summarised in the form of the following propositions. *First,* the fundamental or legally binding character of the Constitution, when, first enacted as part of a British statute, could be explained by reference to the status accorded to those statutes as an original source of law in Australia and also because of the supremacy accorded to such statutes. *Secondly,* nothing happened or has happened to change the status of that particular statute, ie to change the pre-existing inability of the Parliaments of the Commonwealth and the States to legislate inconsistently with the Constitution, whatever changes may have occurred in relation to the ability of those Parliaments to enact legislation which is inconsistent with other British Acts of Parliament. This approach to the problem was referred to as the "historical explanation" for the status of the Constitution as a higher law. *Thirdly,* the developments which culminated in the enactments of the Statute of Westminster and the Australia Acts and which have enabled Australia to attain the status of an independent nation (from both a domestic and international point of view) make it appropriate to supplement the historical explanation. This can be done by recognising that the status of the Constitution as a fundamental law is now derived from the authority of the Australian people.

Another response to the question of why the *Constitution* is binding is to reply that the question is not a legal question at all. This response relies on the Austrian legal philosopher Hans Kelsen's idea of the *grundnorm* (German for 'basic norm'). In Kelsenian terms, the idea that the *Australian Constitution* is binding is (now) the *grundnorm* of the Australian legal system: the idea that the *Australian Constitution* is binding is (now) the starting premise (or 'presupposed norm' in Kelsen's terms) of all Australian legal analysis. To ask why the *grundnorm* of a legal system is the *grundnorm* of that system is not a legal question.

Hans Kelsen, *Pure Theory of Law* (trans: Max Knight, first published 1934, University of California Press, 1967)

The norm system that presents itself as a legal order has essentially a dynamic character. A legal norm is not valid because it has a certain content, that is, because its content is logically deducible from a presupposed basic norm, but because it is created in a certain way – ultimately in a way determined by a presupposed basic norm. For this reason alone does the legal norm belong to the legal order whose norms are created according to this basic norm ... If by the constitution of a legal community is understood the norm or norms that determine how (that is, by what organs and by what procedure – through legislation or custom) the general norms of the legal order that constitute the community are to be created, then the basic norm is that norm which is presupposed when the custom through which the constitution has come into existence, or the constitution- creating act consciously performed by certain human beings, is objectively interpreted as a norm-creating fact; ...

The basic norm is the presupposed starting point of a procedure: the procedure of positive law creation. It is itself not a norm created by custom or by the act of a legal organ; it is not a positive but a presupposed norm so far as the constitution-establishing authority is looked upon as the highest authority and can therefore not be regarded as authorized by the norm of a higher authority.

[I]f we ask for the reason of the validity of the historically first constitution, then the answer can only be (if we leave aside God or 'nature') that the validity of this constitution – the assumption that it is a binding norm – must be the presupposed norm if we want to interpret (1) the acts performed according to it as the creation and application of valid general legal norms; and (2) the acts performed in application of these general norms as the creation or application of valid individual legal norms.

Since the reason for the validity of a norm can only be another norm, the presupposition must be a norm: not one posited (ie, created) by a legal authority, but a presupposed norm ... formulated as follows: coercive acts ought to be performed under the conditions and in the manner which the historically first constitution, and the norms created according to it, prescribe. (In short: One ought to behave as the constitution prescribes.) The norms of a legal order, whose common reason for their validity is this basic norm are not a complex of valid norms standing coordinatedly side by side, but form a hierarchical structure of super- and subordinate norms ...

The *grundnorm* of Australian law was not always the *Australian Constitution*. Before Australia achieved full independence from the United Kingdom, the *grundnorm* of the Australian legal system was the supremacy of the Imperial Parliament. It was never a legal question to ask why the Imperial Parliament's enactments were binding: the assumption that they were binding was the starting premise of all Australian legal analysis.

In ***Egan v Willis and Cahill***, Mahoney P explained that the *Australia Act 1986* (Cth) marked the point in time at which the *grundnorm* of the Australian legal system changed from the supremacy of the Imperial Parliament to the *Australian Constitution*.

Egan v Willis and Cahill (1996) 40 NSWLR 650

Mahoney P

The Chief Justice, in his judgment, has referred to the effect of the *Australia Act 1986.* The effect and, indeed, the purpose of the legislation of that time was (to follow the language of Kelsen) to alter the *grundnorm* of the Australian legal system.

1.6 Principles underlying the *Australian Constitution*

There are a number of key principles underlying the text and structure of the *Australian Constitution.* Among the most important of these are the rule of law, federalism, responsible government, and parliamentary supremacy.

The rule of law

The English constitutional theorist A V Dicey, in an influential book called *Introduction to the Study of the Law of the Constitution,* explained that the concept of the rule of law in the traditional English sense has three key elements: non-arbitrariness, legal equality, and law being a consequence of the rights of individuals.

A V Dicey, *Introduction to the Study of the Law of the Constitution* (Macmillan, 10th ed, 1959)

The 'rule of law,' then, which forms a fundamental principle of the constitution, has three meanings, or may be regarded from three different points of view.

It means, in the first place, the absolute supremacy or predominance of regular law as opposed to the influence of arbitrary power, and excludes the existence of arbitrariness, of prerogative, or even of wide discretionary authority on the part of the government. Englishmen are ruled by the law, and by the law alone; a man may with us be punished for a breach of law, but he can be punished for nothing else.

It means, again, equality before the law, or the equal subjection of all classes to the ordinary law of the land administered by the ordinary Law Courts; the "rule of law" in this sense excludes the idea of any exemption of officials or others from the duty of obedience to the law which governs other citizens or from the jurisdiction of the ordinary tribunals.

The 'rule of law,' lastly, may be used as a formula for expressing the fact that with us the law of the constitution, the rules which in foreign countries naturally form part of a constitutional code, are not the source but the consequence of the rights of individuals, as defined and enforced by the Courts; that, in short, the principles of private law have with us been by the action of the Courts and Parliament so extended as to determine the position of the Crown and of its servants; thus the constitution is the result of the ordinary law of the land ...

In ***Plaintiff S157/2002***, Gleeson CJ explained that the rule of law is reflected in the *Australian Constitution* ensuring the availability of judicial review. Judicial review is the power of the courts to rule on the lawfulness or validity of government action and on the validity of legislation enacted by Parliament.

Plaintiff S157/2002 v Commonwealth (2003) 211 CLR 476

Gleeson CJ

[T]he *Australian Constitution* is framed upon the assumption of the rule of law (*Australian Communist Party v Commonwealth* (1951) 83 CLR 1 at 193 per Dixon J). Brennan J said (*Church of Scientology v Woodward* (1982) 154 CLR 25 at 70):

> Judicial review is neither more nor less than the enforcement of the rule of law over executive action; it is the means by which executive action is prevented from exceeding the powers and functions assigned to the executive by law and the interests of the individual are protected accordingly.

The logic underlying judicial review is often expressed by the metaphorical aphorism that a stream cannot rise higher than its source. In the United Kingdom, where the constitutional *grundnorm* is parliamentary sovereignty, there is no judicial review of legislation: legislation enacted by the United Kingdom is necessarily valid. In Australia, where the *grundnorm* is the *Australian Constitution,* there must be judicial review of legislation to ensure that Parliament does not breach the *Australian Constitution.*

Australian Communist Party v Commonwealth (1951) 83 CLR 1

In this case, the High Court held that the* Communist Party Dissolution Act 1950 *(Cth) fell outside the scope of federal legislative power and was therefore invalid.

Fullagar J

[A]n elementary rule of constitutional law ... has been expressed metaphorically by saying that a stream cannot rise higher than its source ...

It should be observed at this stage that nothing depends on the justice or injustice of the law in question. If the language of an Act of Parliament is clear, its merits and demerits are alike beside the point. It is the law, and that is all. Such a law as the Communist Party Dissolution Act could clearly be passed by the Parliament of the United Kingdom or of any of the Australian States. It is only because the legislative power of the Commonwealth Parliament is limited by an instrument emanating from a superior authority that it arises in the case of the Commonwealth Parliament.

The nature of constitutional invalidity is considered in Chapter 3.

Federalism

Australia is a federation. John Quick and Robert Garran explained that the idea of federalism has a number of different elements.

John Quick and Robert Garran, *The Annotated Constitution of the Commonwealth of Australia* (Angus & Robertson, 1901)

The Federal idea, therefore, pervades and largely dominates the structure of the newly-created community, its parliamentary executive and judiciary departments. "Federal" generally means "having the attributes of a Federation." By usage, however, the term Federal has acquired several distinct and separate meanings, and is capable of as many different applications ...

These meanings may be here roughly generalized as a preliminary to a separate analysis: –

1. As descriptive of a union of States, linked together in one political system.
2. As descriptive of the new State formed by such a union.
3. As descriptive of a dual system of government, central and provincial.
4. As descriptive of the central governing organs in such a dual system of government.

The first, and oldest, of these meanings directs attention emphatically to the preservation of the identity of the States; the second implies a division of sovereignty – a State composed of States; the third asserts that the duality is a matter of government, not of sovereignty; whilst the fourth asserts nothing, but is merely a convenient form of nomenclature ...

In the primary sense of the word "federal", therefore, the Constitution of the Commonwealth is a remarkable compound of the federal and national elements. It is not wholly National, it is not wholly Federal, but a compound of both. In the sources from which the ordinary powers of government are drawn, people and States, it is partly federal and partly national; in the operation of its laws on individuals it is national and not federal; in the appointment and tenure of its Executive it is national and not federal; in the wide jurisdiction of its judiciary it is more national than federal; in its guarantee of State rights it is federal; in its imposition of disabilities on States it is federal; and finally in the authoritative mode of carrying amendments by requiring a majority of all votes, as well as majorities of the people voting in the majority of States, it is partly federal and partly national ...

In a wide-ranging report making a large number of recommendations for constitutional reform, the Constitutional Commission observed that most of the federal elements of the *Australian Constitution* were borrowed from the *United States Constitution*.

Constitutional Commission, *Final Report of the Constitutional Commission* (Australian Government Printing Service, 1988) vol 1

Federal features in the Australian Constitution

In the nineteenth century, the Constitution of the United States was seen by many as the pre-eminent model of federal government. Our Framers looked mainly to it as a guide to the sort of governmental system they were seeking to establish. While they rejected the presidential system of government and a comprehensive Bill of Rights, in other respects they found, in the American system, what Sir Owen Dixon described as "an incomparable model". The federal features of that country's Constitution that we followed were:

(a) the establishment of a central (or Federal) Government and State Governments, each with its own governmental institutions;

(b) a distribution of authority between the Federal and State Governments that confined the former to express enumerated subjects, while leaving the undefined residue to the States;

(c) a judicial authority, appointed by the Federal Government, to determine whether either level of government had exceeded its legislative, executive or judicial powers;

(d) the supremacy of federal laws over State laws in cases of inconsistency; and

(e) an entrenchment of these features by a rigid constitutional framework that is difficult to alter.

It would seem that the minimal essential features of a federal system as it has come to be understood in Australia are a high degree of autonomy for the governmental institutions of the Commonwealth and the States, a division of power between these organisations, and a judicial "umpire".

There are other aspects of the Constitution which, while not creating a federal state, reflect its federal nature. Some of these are concerned with ensuring that the Commonwealth behaves fairly to each State as compared with other States. These include section 51(ii) which restricts the taxation power "so as not to discriminate between States or parts of States"; section 51(iii) and section 88 which require bounties and customs duties, respectively, to be "uniform throughout the Commonwealth"; and section 99 which provides that "the Commonwealth shall not, by any law or regulation of trade, commerce, or revenue give preference to one State or any part thereof over another State or any part thereof".

Similarly there are provisions relating to the respect and fairness owed by a State to the Government and people of other States. Section 117 is aimed at preventing a State (and perhaps the Commonwealth) from discriminating against non-alien residents of other States. Section 118 requires that "full faith and credit" be given throughout the Commonwealth to "the laws, the public Acts and records and the judicial proceedings of every State". Discrimination against the trade and commerce of another State is prohibited, and the entry of its people is protected, by section 92, guaranteeing that "trade, commerce and intercourse among the States shall be absolutely free", and by section 102 dealing with State railway rates which are "undue and unreasonable or unjust to any State".

Another feature of the Constitution which has, in the courts and in public political debate, been closely associated with the federal principle in Australia is representation in the Senate. The people of the Original States are guaranteed equal representation (section 7). The founding fathers were divided on the desirability of an upper House of this nature (usually depending on whether they came from the larger or smaller colonies). Many of the delegates seem to have approved the adoption of this principle on the practical ground that otherwise union would have been impossible, rather than on the basis of federal principle. This is perhaps borne out by the fact that the right of equal representation in the Senate was not granted to any new State which might be admitted to the Commonwealth, but was, in section 121, made to depend on the will of the Federal Parliament.

The federal nature of the *Australian Constitution* – the fact that the *Constitution* establishes a Commonwealth government and a series of separately organised State governments and requires their continued existence as independent or separate entities – gives rise to limitations on the powers of the Federal and State Parliaments aimed at preserving federalism known as the 'intergovernmental immunities doctrine' (see Chapter 23).

Responsible government

One of the most important principles underlying and reflected in the *Australian Constitution* is responsible government. The key principle of responsible government is that the Executive Government is responsible, or accountable, to the popularly elected lower House of Parliament.

In ***McCloy***, Gageler J explained how the text of the *Australian Constitution* reflects notions of responsible government.

McCloy v New South Wales (2015) 257 CLR 178

Gageler J

Chapter II of the Constitution establishes and sustains the Executive Government of the Commonwealth. Section 61 vests the executive power of the Commonwealth in the Queen, and makes that executive power "exercisable by the Governor-General as the Queen's representative". Section 64 empowers the Governor-General to appoint officers to administer departments of State for the Commonwealth, who are to be Ministers of State for the Commonwealth. Tying the structure of the Executive Government to the structure of the Parliament, s 64 adds the centrally important qualification that "no Minister of State shall hold office for a longer period than three months unless he is or becomes a senator or a member of the House of Representatives".

The link made in that qualification in s 64 – between the structure of the Parliament established and sustained by Ch I and the structure of the Executive Government established and sustained by Ch II – makes plain the design of those chapters to facilitate the application of the particular system of representative government, known as "responsible government", to the "indissoluble Federal Commonwealth" established by the Constitution. That system had developed in the second half of the nineteenth century in each of the six colonies which, on federation, became the Australian States. Evatt J was not inaccurate in stating that "prior to the establishment of the Commonwealth of Australia in 1901, responsible government had become one of the central characteristics of our polity" (*Victorian Stevedoring and General Contracting Co Pty Ltd and Meakes v Dignan* (1931) 46 CLR 73 at 114). And Isaacs J did not exaggerate in proclaiming that "the Constitution is for the advancement of representative government" (*Federal Commissioner of Taxation v Munro; British Imperial Oil Co Ltd v Federal Commissioner of Taxation* (1926) 38 CLR 153 at 178) and that responsible government "is part of the fabric on which the written words of the Constitution are superimposed" (*Commonwealth v Kreglinger & Fernau Ltd and Bardsley* (1926) 37 CLR 393 at 413).

For the most part, responsible government operates by adherence to constitutional conventions. For example, a key convention of responsible government in Australia is that only the person commanding the confidence of the House of Representatives is entitled to be commissioned by the Governor-General as Prime Minister. There are no provisions in the *Australian Constitution* requiring this approach or even referring to the Prime Minister at all. The matter is governed by convention. Similarly, the Cabinet is one of the most significant bodies in the Federal Executive Government but is not mentioned at all in the *Australian Constitution*. Its existence and operation is a matter of convention.

A V Dicey in *Introduction to the Study of the Law of the Constitution* explained that constitutional conventions are not laws in the strict sense but are binding as a matter of political morality.

A V Dicey, *Introduction to the Study of the Law of the Constitution* (Macmillan, 10th ed, 1959)

The other set of rules consist of conventions, understandings, habits, or practices which, though they may regulate the conduct of the several members of the sovereign power, of the Ministry, or of other officials, are not in reality laws at all since they are not enforced by the Courts. This portion of constitutional law may, for the sake of distinction, be termed the "conventions of the constitution," or constitutional morality ...

To put the same thing in a somewhat different shape, "constitutional law," as the expression is used in England, both by the public and by authoritative writers, consists of two elements. The one element, here called the "law of the constitution," is a body of undoubted law; the other element, here called the "conventions of the constitution," consists of maxims or practices which, though they regulate the ordinary conduct of the Crown, of Ministers, and of other persons under the constitution, are not in strictness laws at all.

In ***Re Resolution to Amend the Constitution***, the Supreme Court of Canada explained that constitutional conventions cannot be enforced by the courts because they often conflict with the express terms of the written Constitution.

Re Resolution to Amend the Constitution [1981] 1 SCR 753

The Canadian Parliament requested that the United Kingdom Parliament enact certain legislation that would 'patriate' the British North America Act *by renaming it the* Constitution Act *and placing it under the full authority of Canada. The Supreme Court held that whether that request contravened a Canadian convention that requests for the United Kingdom legislature to alter Canada's Constitution would not be made without the consent of the provincial legislatures was not a matter for the courts and was not relevant to the validity of the Canadian Parliament's request.*

Martland, Ritchie, Dickson, Beetz, Chouinard and Lamar JJ

In contradistinction to the laws of the constitution, they are not enforced by the courts. One reason for this situation is that, unlike common law rules, conventions are not judge-made rules. They are not based on judicial precedents but on precedents established by the institutions of government themselves. Nor are they in the nature of statutory commands which it is the function and duty of the courts to obey and enforce. Furthermore, to enforce them would mean to administer some formal sanction when they are breached. But the legal system from which they are distinct does not contemplate formal sanctions for their breach.

Perhaps the main reason why conventional rules cannot be enforced by the courts is that they are generally in conflict with the legal rules which they postulate and the courts are bound to enforce the legal rules. The conflict is not of a type which would entail the commission of any illegality. It results from the fact that legal rules create wide powers, discretions and rights which conventions prescribe should be exercised only in a certain limited manner, if at all.

So while section 64 of the *Australian Constitution* gives the Governor-General a broad discretion as to the appointment of Ministers, the conventions of responsible government conflict with that broad discretion by restricting its exercise. Convention requires that the person who commands the confidence of the House of Representatives (who will usually be leader of the party with a majority of seats) be appointed Prime Minister and that other Ministers be appointed on the advice of the Prime Minister.

In ***Miller***, the Supreme Court of the United Kingdom referred to ***Re Resolution to Amend the Constitution*** and explained that any sanction for breaches of constitutional conventions must be found in the political arena.

R (on the application of Miller and another) v Secretary of State for Exiting the European Union [2017] UKSC 5

The United Kingdom Government gave notice to the European Union of its intention to withdraw from the European Union treaties. Among other things, the Supreme Court held that whether that action contravened a British convention known as the 'Sewel Convention' governing the relationship between the United Kingdom Parliament and the devolved legislatures of Wales, Scotland and Northern Ireland was not a matter for the courts and was not relevant to the lawfulness of the Government's action.

Lord Neuberger, Lady Hale, Lord Mance, Lord Kerr, Lord Clarke, Lord Wilson, Lord Sumption and Lord Hodge

It is well established that the courts of law cannot enforce a political convention. In *Re Resolution to Amend the Constitution* [1981] 1 SCR 753, the Supreme Court of Canada addressed the nature of political conventions ...

Martland, Ritchie, Dickson, Beetz, Chouinard and Lamer JJ made the same point at pp 882 to 883:

> It is because the sanctions of convention rest with institutions of government other than courts ... or with public opinion and ultimately, with the electorate, that it is generally said that they are political.

Judges therefore are neither the parents nor the guardians of political conventions; they are merely observers. As such, they can recognise the operation of a political convention in the context of deciding a legal question (as in the Crossman diaries case – *Attorney General v Jonathan Cape Ltd* [1976] 1 QB 752), but they cannot give legal rulings on its operation or scope, because those matters are determined within the political world. As Professor Colin Munro has stated, "the validity of conventions cannot be the subject of proceedings in a court of law" – (1975) 91 LQR 218, 228 ...

In reaching this conclusion we do not underestimate the importance of constitutional conventions, some of which play a fundamental role in the operation of our constitution.

The Sewel Convention has an important role in facilitating harmonious relationships between the UK Parliament and the devolved legislatures. But the policing of its scope and the manner of its operation does not lie within the constitutional remit of the judiciary, which is to protect the rule of law.

Parliamentary supremacy

The traditional British conception of parliamentary sovereignty is reflected in Australia in a weaker form known as 'parliamentary supremacy'. A V Dicey defined parliamentary sovereignty as the principle that parliament can make or unmake any law whatsoever. The only limitations of the power of a sovereign parliament are non-legal: the possibility that the people will rebel, and the good conscience of members of Parliament.

A V Dicey, *Introduction to the Study of the Law of the Constitution* (Macmillan, 10th ed, 1959)

The sovereignty of Parliament is (from a legal point of view) the dominant characteristic of our political institutions ...

The principle of Parliamentary sovereignty means neither more nor less than this, namely, that Parliament thus defined has, under the English constitution, the right to make or unmake any law whatever; and, further, that no person or body is recognised by the law of England as having a right to override or set aside the legislation of Parliament

As to the actual limitations on the sovereign power of Parliament the actual exercise of authority by any sovereign whatever, and notably Parliament, is bounded or controlled by two limitations. Of these the one is an external, the other is an internal limitation.

The external limit to the real power of a sovereign consists in the possibility or certainty that his subjects, or a large number of them, will disobey or resist his laws ...

The internal limit to the exercise of sovereignty arises from the nature of the sovereign power itself. Even a despot exercises his powers in accordance with his character, which is itself moulded by the circumstances under which he lives, including under that head the moral feelings of the time and the society to which he belongs.

Australia's Federal and State Parliaments cannot be completely sovereign. Each Australian Parliament is subordinated to the *Constitution*, which limits their law-making powers. The United Kingdom Parliament is not subordinated to any written constitution and the *grundnorm* of the British legal system is parliamentary sovereignty. Because the Australian situation is necessarily different to the British situation, the expression 'parliamentary supremacy' is usually used in Australia.

Kruger v Commonwealth ('Stolen Generations Case') (1997) 190 CLR 1

Dawson J

Those who framed the Australian Constitution accepted the view that individual rights were on the whole best left to the protection of the common law and the supremacy of parliament. Thus the Constitution deals, almost without exception, with the structure and relationship of government rather than with individual rights. The fetters which are placed upon legislative action are, for the most part, for the purpose of distributing power between the federal government on the one hand and State governments on the other, rather than for the purpose of placing certain matters beyond the reach of any parliament.

Parliamentary supremacy is reflected in the High Court's consistent position that the courts have no role in passing judgment on the wisdom or justice of legislation.

Kuczborski v Queensland (2014) 254 CLR 51

Crennan, Kiefel, Gageler and Keane JJ

[I]t is not part of this Court's function to pass judgment on the political wisdom of the impugned laws. As explained by Brennan CJ in *Nicholas v The Queen* (1998) 193 CLR 173 at 197:

> It is for the Parliament to prescribe the law to be applied by a court and, if the law is otherwise valid, the court's opinion as to the justice, propriety or utility of the law is immaterial. Integrity is the fidelity to legal duty, not a refusal to accept as binding a law which the court takes to be contrary to its opinion as to the proper balance to be struck between competing interests.

Faith in parliamentary supremacy and responsible government is largely responsible for the lack of American-style guarantees of individual rights in the *Australian Constitution*.

Australian Capital Television Pty Ltd v Commonwealth (1992) 177 CLR 106

Mason CJ

The framers of the Constitution accepted, in accordance with prevailing English thinking, that the citizen's rights were best left to the protection of the common law in association with the doctrine of parliamentary supremacy (Sir Anthony Mason, "The Role of a Constitutional Court in a Federation", (1986) 16 *Federal Law Review* 1, at p 8).

So it was that Professor Harrison Moore, writing in 1901, was able to say of the Constitution (*The Constitution of the Commonwealth of Australia*, 1st ed (1902), p 329):

> The great underlying principle is that the rights of individuals are sufficiently secured by ensuring, as far as possible, to each a share, and an equal share, in political power.

To make such an implication would run counter to the prevailing sentiment of the framers that there was no need to incorporate a comprehensive Bill of Rights in order to protect the rights and freedoms of citizens. That sentiment was one of the unexpressed assumptions on which the Constitution was drafted.

Despite the absence of a Bill of Rights, the *Australian Constitution* is not completely without guarantees of personal liberty.

Street v Queensland Bar Association (1989) 168 CLR 461

Deane J

It is often said that the Australian Constitution contains no bill of rights. Statements to that effect, while literally true, are superficial and potentially misleading. The Constitution contains a significant number of express or implied guarantees of rights and immunities. The most important of them is the guarantee that the citizen can be subjected to the exercise of Commonwealth judicial power only by the "courts" designated by Ch III (s 71). Others include: the guarantee that the trial on indictment of any offence against any law of the Commonwealth shall be by jury (s 80); the guarantees against discrimination between persons in different parts of the country in relation to custom and excise duties, and other Commonwealth taxes and bounties (ss 51(ii), 51(iii), 86, 88 and 90); the guarantee of freedom of inter-State trade, commerce and intercourse (s 92); the guarantee of direct suffrage and of equality of voting rights among those qualified to vote (ss 24 and 25); the guarantee of the free exercise of religion (s 116); and the guarantee against being subjected to inconsistent demands by contemporaneously valid laws (ss 109 and 118).

All of those guarantees of rights or immunities are of fundamental importance in that they serve the function of advancing or protecting the liberty, the dignity or the equality of the citizen under the Constitution. Some of them, such as ss 71, 90, 92, 109 and 118, are also integral parts of the very structure of the federation.

1.7 Australian constitutionalism and Indigenous Australians

Aboriginal and Torres Strait Islander Australians and the text of the *Australian Constitution*

The *Australian Constitution* in its original form treated Aboriginal and Torres Strait Islander Australians differently to other Australians. Two provisions referred to Indigenous Australians in a negative way.

Australian Constitution

Section 51 Legislative powers of the Parliament

The Parliament shall, subject to this Constitution, have power to make laws for the peace, order, and good government of the Commonwealth with respect to:

...

(xxvi) the people of any race, other than the aboriginal race in any State, for whom it is deemed necessary to make special laws;

....

Section 127 Aborigines not to be counted in reckoning population

In reckoning the numbers of people of the Commonwealth, or of a State or other part of the Commonwealth, aboriginal natives shall not be counted.

The *Constitution Alteration (Aboriginals) 1967* did two things. It deleted the words 'other than the aboriginal race in any State' from section 51(xxvi) and repealed section 127 entirely.

Constitution Alteration (Aboriginals) 1967 (Cth)

Be it enacted by the Queen's Most Excellent Majesty, the Senate, and the House of Representatives of the Commonwealth of Australia, with the approval of the electors, as required by the Constitution, as follows:-

Section 1

This Act may be cited as the *Constitution Alteration (Aboriginals) 1967.*

Section 2

The Constitution is altered by omitting from paragraph (xxvi) of section 51 the words ", other than the aboriginal race in any State,".

Section 3

The Constitution is altered by repealing section 127.

Section 51(xxvi) is examined in Chapter 9. Despite common misconceptions, section 127 was not about excluding Aboriginal and Torres Strait Islander peoples from the census or from the right to vote. Section 127 was about excluding Aboriginal and Torres Strait Islander peoples from population counts where population is relevant to other provisions of the *Constitution.* The key example is section 24, which makes State population numbers relevant to the determination of the number of members of the House of the Representatives to which each State is entitled.

Helen Irving, 'Indigenous Recognition and Constitutional Myths, *Constitutional Critique Blog,* 9 June 2015

2. Aboriginals to be counted

Secondly, following the 1967 referendum, section 127 of the Constitution was removed. This section said: *In reckoning the numbers of the people of the Commonwealth, or of a State or other part of the Commonwealth, aboriginal natives shall not be counted.*

It is a common myth that the section excluded Aboriginal people from being counted in the census, and that the 1967 referendum meant that they would henceforth be counted. It did not. The Aboriginal people have always been counted, from the very first Commonwealth census in 1911. In fact, census statistics specifically recorded the populations of Aboriginal Australians. "Half-blood" Aborigines were considered to be white and were included in the general census.

The purpose of section 127 (admittedly, not obvious from its words) was to guide the calculation of the numbers of parliamentary representatives per State and also to determine certain

State financial entitlements and obligations, based on State populations. When these calculations were made, the numbers of Aboriginal people, as counted, were excluded.

The right to vote

Another common myth is that the 1967 referendum gave the Aboriginal people the right to vote. This is incorrect. The 1967 referendum had nothing to do with this right (or "equal rights" or rights at all).

Aboriginal people were able to vote in all States and in the Commonwealth by 1967. From 1949 they could vote in Commonwealth elections if they were enrolled to vote in NSW, Victoria, South Australia or Tasmania. Indigenous people who had been in military service also had the right to vote. In 1962, all other Aboriginal people became entitled to vote in Commonwealth elections.

At the State level, Aboriginal people were able to vote in South Australia, NSW, Tasmania and Victoria throughout the 20th century. In Western Australia and Queensland they gained the State vote, respectively, in 1962 and 1965.

It should also be noted that the official definition of Aboriginal has changed over time, and voting rights of individuals have therefore changed accordingly. Many Aboriginal people today would not have been excluded from the right to vote under the former laws.

In any case (with the exception of a now-spent transitional provision - section 41), neither eligibility to vote nor the franchise is mentioned in the Constitution. The right to vote is a matter for ordinary legislation. The Constitution did not need to be altered for Aboriginal people to gain the right to vote.

Citizenship

A further common myth is that the 1967 referendum gave citizenship to the Aboriginal people. This is incorrect. Between 1788 and 1949, everyone born in Australia (or any other part of the British Empire) acquired the legal status of "British subject" ("subject" was the term used for British nationality at that time). In 1949, under new legislation every person born in Australia, regardless of race or colour, became simultaneously a British subject and Australian citizen. Subsequent changes in legislation meant that Australians are no longer British subjects.

Eligibility for Australian citizenship has changed over the years. Citizenship laws, however, have never differentiated between Aboriginal and non-Aboriginal persons.

Again, citizenship is not defined in the Constitution. A referendum would not be required to amend the citizenship law.

State constitutional recognition of Aboriginal and Torres Strait Islander Australians

The Constitution Act of each of the States includes text 'recognising' Indigenous Australians. Victoria was the first State to adopt such text in 2004.

The States adopt one of two methods for constitutional recognition of Aboriginal and Torres Strait Islander peoples. Victoria, New South Wales and South Australia have added recognition sections to their Constitution Acts.

Constitution Act 1975 (Vic)

Section 1A Recognition of Aboriginal people

1. The Parliament acknowledges that the events described in the preamble to this Act occurred without proper consultation, recognition or involvement of the Aboriginal people of Victoria.
2. The Parliament recognises that Victoria's Aboriginal people, as the original custodians of the land on which the Colony of Victoria was established –
   (a) have a unique status as the descendants of Australia's first people; and
   (b) have a spiritual, social, cultural and economic relationship with their traditional lands and waters within Victoria; and
   (c) have made a unique and irreplaceable contribution to the identity and wellbeing of Victoria.
3. The Parliament does not intend by this section –
   (a) to create in any person any legal right or give rise to any civil cause of action; or
   (b) to affect in any way the interpretation of this Act or of any other law in force in Victoria.

Constitution Act 1902 (NSW)

Section 2 Recognition of Aboriginal people

1. Parliament, on behalf of the people of New South Wales, acknowledges and honours the Aboriginal people as the State's first people and nations.
2. Parliament, on behalf of the people of New South Wales, recognises that Aboriginal people, as the traditional custodians and occupants of the land in New South Wales:
   (a) have a spiritual, social, cultural and economic relationship with their traditional lands and waters, and
   (b) have made and continue to make a unique and lasting contribution to the identity of the State.
3. Nothing in this section creates any legal right or liability, or gives rise to or affects any civil cause of action or right to review an administrative action, or affects the interpretation of any Act or law in force in New South Wales.

Constitution Act 1934 (SA)

Section 2 Recognition of Aboriginal peoples

1. The Parliament on behalf of the people of South Australia acknowledges that –
   (a) the Parliament of the United Kingdom in 1834 passed a Bill called An Act to empower His Majesty to erect South Australia into a British Province or Provinces and to provide for the Colonisation and Government thereof and that by Letters Patent dated 19 February 1836 His Majesty established the Province of South Australia; and

(b) the making of the above instruments and subsequent constitutional instruments providing for the governance of South Australia and for the making of laws for peace, order and good government occurred without proper and effective recognition, consultation or authorisation of Aboriginal peoples of South Australia.

2. Following the Apology given on 28 May 1997, the Parliament, on behalf of the people of South Australia –
   (a) acknowledges and respects Aboriginal peoples as the State's first peoples and nations; and
   (b) recognises Aboriginal peoples as traditional owners and occupants of land and waters in South Australia and that –
      (i) their spiritual, social, cultural and economic practices come from their traditional lands and waters; and
      (ii) they maintain their cultural and heritage beliefs, languages and laws which are of ongoing importance; and
      (iii) they have made and continue to make a unique and irreplaceable contribution to the State; and
   (c) acknowledges that the Aboriginal peoples have endured past injustice and dispossession of their traditional lands and waters.
3. The Parliament does not intend this section to have any legal force or effect.

Queensland, Western Australia and Tasmania have added statements of recognition in the preamble to their Constitution Acts.

Constitution of Queensland 2001 (Qld)

Preamble

The people of Queensland, free and equal citizens of Australia –

...

(c) honour the Aboriginal peoples and Torres Strait Islander peoples, the First Australians, whose lands, winds and waters we all now share; and pay tribute to their unique values, and their ancient and enduring cultures, which deepen and enrich the life of our community; and ...

Constitution Act 1889 (WA)

Preamble

... And whereas the Parliament resolves to acknowledge the Aboriginal people as the First People of Western Australia and traditional custodians of the land, the said Parliament seeks to effect a reconciliation with the Aboriginal people of Western Australia.

Constitution Act 1934 (Tas)

Preamble

... And whereas the Parliament, on behalf of all the people of Tasmania, acknowledges the Aboriginal people as Tasmania's First People and the traditional and original owners of Tasmanian lands and waters; recognises the enduring spiritual, social, cultural and economic importance of traditional lands and waters to Tasmanian Aboriginal people; and recognises the unique and lasting contributions that Tasmanian Aboriginal people have made and continue to make to Tasmania ...

These statements of recognition are symbolic and have no substantive legal effect. The symbolism is not intended to be tokenistic. In moving the adoption of legislation to recognise Aboriginal people in the *Constitution Act 1902* (NSW), the then Premier of New South Wales, Kristina Keneally, explained that symbols matter.

New South Wales, *Parliamentary Debates,* Legislative Assembly, 8 September 2010

Ms Keneally (Heffron - Premier)

It is humbling to have the opportunity to put before this House legislation to recognise our first people, our Aboriginal people, in the New South Wales Constitution Act ...

Today we are enshrining fundamental truths: the truth that our Aboriginal people are the first inhabitants of New South Wales; the truth of the spiritual, cultural and economic ties that bind our Aboriginal people to their traditional lands and waters; and the truth in the diverse and unique contributions that our many Aboriginal nations, cultures and communities make to the life, the economy and the character of our State.

Some may say that this legislation is just symbolic, but I trust that those who do also know the importance of symbols and their power to inspire and to shape our attitudes and actions. I trust they understand that the icons of our national and cultural identity are of themselves merely symbols, and I ask them to consider how they might feel if they had to live their lives in absence of these symbols, in the absence of the recognition they proclaim, and in the absence of the identity they publicly provide.

I ask them to consider that in all our cultures and in all human history there are symbols, and then there are the meanings that we attach to them ...

So while our commitment to true equality of opportunity in our State is expressed primarily in practical actions, our symbols do matter, especially those that reside in our pre-eminent legal framework. So I am grateful to be here today as our Parliament brings forward necessary and positive change. I commend the bill to the House.

Federal constitutional recognition of Aboriginal and Torres Strait Islander Australians

On 30 June 2017, a Referendum Council that had been appointed by the then Prime Minister, Malcolm Turnbull, delivered its Final Report. The Council was tasked with advising the Prime Minister and the Leader of the Opposition on progress and next steps towards a successful referendum to recognise Aboriginal and Torres Strait Islander peoples in the *Australian Constitution*. That Report was the result of a public consultation process, including a series of First Nations Regional Dialogues and a 'National Constitutional Convention' held at Uluru in May 2017.

The result of the meeting at Uluru was the *Uluru Statement from the Heart.*

Uluru Statement from the Heart

We, gathered at the 2017 National Constitutional Convention, coming from all points of the southern sky, make this statement from the heart:

Our Aboriginal and Torres Strait Islander tribes were the first sovereign Nations of the Australian continent and its adjacent islands, and possessed it under our own laws and customs. This our ancestors did, according to the reckoning of our culture, from the Creation, according to the common law from 'time immemorial, and according to science more than 60,000 years ago.

This sovereignty is a *spiritual notion: the ancestral tie between the land, or 'mother nature', and the Aboriginal and Torres Strait Islander peoples who were born therefrom, remain attached thereto, and must one day return thither to be united with our ancestors. This link is the basis of the ownership of the soil, or better, of sovereignty.* It has never been ceded or extinguished, and co-exists with the sovereignty of the Crown.

How could it be otherwise? That peoples possessed a land for sixty millennia and this sacred link disappears from world history in merely the last two hundred years?

With substantive constitutional change and structural reform, we believe this ancient sovereignty can shine through as a fuller expression of Australia's nationhood.

Proportionally, we are the most incarcerated people on the planet. We are not an innately criminal people. Our children are aliened from their families at unprecedented rates. This cannot be because we have no love for them. And our youth languish in detention in obscene numbers. They should be our hope for the future.

These dimensions of our crisis tell plainly the structural nature of our problem. *This is the torment of our powerlessness.*

We seek constitutional reforms to empower our people and take *a rightful place* in our own country. When we have power over our destiny our children will flourish. They will walk in two worlds and their culture will be a gift to their country.

We call for the establishment of a First Nations Voice enshrined in the Constitution.

Makarrata is the culmination of our agenda: *the coming together after a struggle.* It captures our aspirations for a fair and truthful relationship with the people of Australia and a better future for our children based on justice and self-determination.

We seek a Makarrata Commission to supervise a process of agreement-making between governments and First Nations and truth-telling about our history.

In 1967 we were counted, in 2017 we seek to be heard. We leave base camp and start our trek across this vast country. We invite you to walk with us in a movement of the Australian people for a better future.

In March 2023, the Constitution Alteration (Aboriginal and Torres Strait Islander Voice) 2023 was introduced into the House of Representatives to commence the process of amending the *Constitution* to give effect to the *Uluru Statement from the Heart*'s call for a Voice. The Constitution Alteration (Aboriginal and Torres Strait Islander Voice) 2023 would have inserted a new chapter and section into the *Constitution* but was not approved by voters in the October 2023 referendum.

Chapter IX – Recognition of Aboriginal and Torres Strait Islander Peoples

129 Aboriginal and Torres Strait Islander Voice

In recognition of Aboriginal and Torres Strait Islander peoples as the First Peoples of Australia:

(i) there shall be a body, to be called the Aboriginal and Torres Strait Islander Voice;

(ii) the Aboriginal and Torres Strait Islander Voice may make representations to the Parliament and the Executive Government of the Commonwealth on matters relating to Aboriginal and Torres Strait Islander peoples;

(iii) the Parliament shall, subject to this Constitution, have power to make laws with respect to matters relating to the Aboriginal and Torres Strait Islander Voice, including its composition, functions, powers and procedures.

1.8 DISCUSSION QUESTIONS

1. Why is the *Australian Constitution* found in a British statute?
2. What was the repugnancy doctrine and how was it abolished?
3. What was Imperial parliamentary supremacy and how was it abolished?
4. What are constitutional conventions and why are they not enforceable by the courts?
5. Policy question: Do proposals for constitutional recognition of Aboriginal and Torres Strait Islander peoples suggest that Goldsworthy is not entirely accurate when he observes that the *Australian Constitution* functions only as a basic law and not also as a higher law and people's law?

PART

2

LEGISLATIVE POWERS

STATE LEGISLATIVE POWERS

2

2.1 Overview

This chapter examines the legislative powers of the States. The chapter explains that the legislative powers of the States pre-date the *Australian Constitution*, were made subject to the *Australian Constitution* but otherwise continued in force at Federation, and were confirmed by the *Australia Act 1986*.

In general terms, the States possess plenary legislative power allowing them to make and unmake any laws they want. That power extends to amending State Constitution Acts by ordinary legislation. The plenary power of the States is subject to the possibility of restrictive procedures that regulate the way in which certain types of laws must be passed, but which do not prohibit the passing of those laws. The States also have power under the *Australian Constitution* to refer power to make laws to the Commonwealth Parliament and thereby expand the practical scope of federal legislative power.

Key concepts addressed in this chapter include:

- legislative power
- plenary power
- fundamental common law rights
- manner and form procedure
- double entrenchment
- referral of power.

2.2 The source of State legislative power

Before Federation, the six States existed as colonies with their own Constitutions, Parliaments and laws. On coming into force, the *Australian Constitution* transformed the colonies into States and made provision for their Constitutions, legislative powers and laws to continue in force subject to the demands of the *Australian Constitution*.

Australian Constitution

Section 106 Saving of Constitutions

The Constitution of each State of the Commonwealth shall, subject to this Constitution, continue as at the establishment of the Commonwealth, or as at the admission or establishment of the State, as the case may be, until altered in accordance with the Constitution of the State.

Section 107 Saving of Power of State Parliaments

Every power of the Parliament of a Colony which has become or becomes a State, shall, unless it is by this Constitution exclusively vested in the Parliament of the Commonwealth or withdrawn from the Parliament of the State, continue as at the establishment of the Commonwealth, or as at the admission or establishment of the State, as the case may be.

Section 108 Saving of State laws

Every law in force in a Colony which has become or becomes a State, and relating to any matter within the powers of the Parliament of the Commonwealth, shall, subject to this Constitution, continue in force in the State; and, until provision is made in that behalf by the Parliament of the Commonwealth, the Parliament of the State shall have such powers of alteration and of repeal in respect of any such law as the Parliament of the Colony had until the Colony became a State.

Imperial legislation had established Parliaments in each of the colonies and, over time, granted those Parliaments plenary legislative powers. The formula used in the Imperial legislation referred to power to 'make laws for the peace, welfare, and good government of the said colonies in all cases whatsoever' or 'make laws for the peace, order, and good government of the said colonies in all cases whatsoever'.

The formulae of 'peace, welfare, and good government' or 'peace, order, and good government' continue to be used in some State Constitutions and in the *Australia Act 1986*, confirming the legislative powers of the States.

Australia Act 1986 (Cth)

Section 2 Legislative powers of Parliaments of States

(1) It is hereby declared and enacted that the legislative powers of the Parliament of each State include full power to make laws for the peace, order and good government of that State that have extra-territorial operation.

(2) It is hereby further declared and enacted that the legislative powers of the Parliament of each State include all legislative powers that the Parliament of the United Kingdom might have exercised before the commencement of this Act for the peace, order and good government of that State but nothing in this subsection confers on a State any capacity that the State did not have immediately before the commencement of this Act to engage in relations with countries outside Australia.

Constitution Act 1902 (NSW)

Section 5 General legislative powers

The Legislature shall, subject to the provisions of the Commonwealth of Australia Constitution Act, have power to make laws for the peace, welfare, and good government of New South Wales in all cases whatsoever.

Constitution Act 1975 (Vic)

Section 16 Legislative power of Parliament

The Parliament shall have power to make laws in and for Victoria in all cases whatsoever.

Constitution of Queensland 2001 (Qld)

Section 8 Law-making power

The Constitution Act 1867, section 2 provides for law-making power in Queensland.

Constitution Act 1867 (Qld)

Section 2 Legislative assembly constituted

Within the said Colony of Queensland Her Majesty shall have power by and with the advice and consent of the said Assembly to make laws for the peace welfare and good government of the colony in all cases whatsoever.

Constitution Act 1934 (SA)

Section 5 Powers of the Parliament

The Legislative Council and House of Assembly shall have and exercise all the powers and functions formerly exercised by the Legislative Council constituted pursuant to section 7 of the Act of the Imperial Parliament, 13 and 14 Victoria, Chapter 59, entitled "An Act for the better Government of Her Majesty's Australian Colonies".

Australian Constitutions Act 1850 (UK) 13 & 14 Vic c 59

Section 14

That the Governors of the said Colonies of *Victoria, Van Diemen's Land, South Australia*, and *Western Australia* respectively, with the Advice and Consent of the Legislative Councils to be established in the said Colonies under this Act, shall have Authority to make Laws for the Peace, Welfare, and good Government of the said Colonies respectively ...

Constitution Act 1889 (WA)

Section 2 Legislature to be constituted in Western Australia

(1) There shall be, in place of the Legislative Council now subsisting, a Legislative Council and a Legislative Assembly: and it shall be lawful for Her Majesty, by and with the advice and consent of the said Council and Assembly, to make laws for the peace, order, and good Government of the Colony of Western Australia and its Dependencies: and such Council and Assembly shall, subject to the provisions of this Act, have all the powers and functions of the now subsisting Legislative Council.

Constitution Act 1934 (Tas)

Preamble

Whereas by an Act of Council intituled an *Act to establish a Parliament in Van Diemen's Land and to grant a Civil List to Her Majesty* (known as the *Constitutional Act* and later as the *Constitution Act*) passed in the eighteenth year of the reign of Her Majesty Queen Victoria by the Governor and Legislative Council of the Colony of Van Diemen's Land in pursuance of the provisions of an Imperial Act called the *Australian Constitution Act 1850*, it was enacted for the purpose of securing the peace, welfare, and good government of the said Colony that in Place of the said Legislative Council there should be one Legislative Council and one House of Assembly, constituted as therein provided, which should exercise all the powers and functions of the then existing Legislative Council, and that the Governor and Legislative Council and House of Assembly together should be called the Parliament of Van Diemen's Land ...

2.3 The scope of State legislative power

The High Court explained in ***Union Steamship Co of Australia v King*** that, as a general proposition, the legislative power of each of the States is 'plenary'. The States can make and unmake any law they want. This is a close approximation of the British idea of parliamentary sovereignty.

In that case, the High Court held that it is not open to argue that a State law is invalid because it does not promote the peace, welfare or good government of a State. The words 'peace, welfare and good government' and 'peace, order and good government' are a grant of plenary legislative power and are not words of limitation. The High Court noted that throughout the British Empire those words had long been recognised as signifying plenary power.

Union Steamship Co of Australia v King (1988) 166 CLR 1

This case concerned an argument that New South Wales legislation concerning workers compensation for seamen working on ships that may have had only limited connections to New South Wales was outside the legislative power of the New South Wales Parliament. One argument was that the New South Wales Parliament did not possess plenary legislative power and that for a law to be valid the law had to actually secure the peace, welfare or good government of the State.

Mason CJ, Wilson, Brennan, Deane, Dawson, Toohey and Gaudron JJ

The power to make laws "for the peace, welfare, and good government" of a territory is indistinguishable from the power to make laws "for the peace, order and good government" of a territory. Such a power is a plenary power and it was so recognized, even in an era when emphasis was given to the character of colonial legislatures as subordinate law-making bodies. The plenary nature of the power was established in the series of historic Privy Council decisions at the close of the nineteenth century: *R v Burah* (1878) 3 AppCas 889; *Hodge v The Queen* (1883) 9 AppCas 117; *Powell v Apollo Candle Company* (1885) 10 AppCas 282; *Riel v The Queen* (1885) 10 AppCas 675. They decided that colonial legislatures were not mere agents or delegates of the Imperial Parliament.

Lord Selborne, speaking for the Judicial Committee in *Burah*, said (at p 904) that the Indian Legislature "has, and was intended to have, plenary powers of legislation, as large, and of the same nature, as those of Parliament itself". Later, Sir Barnes Peacock in *Hodge*, speaking for the Judicial Committee, stated (at p132) that the legislature of Ontario enjoyed by virtue of the *British North America Act 1867* (Imp): "authority as plenary and as ample within the limits prescribed by sect 92 as the Imperial Parliament in the plenitude of its power possessed and could bestow. Within these limits of subjects and area the local legislature is supreme, and has the same authority as the Imperial Parliament ...". In *Riel* Lord Halsbury LC, delivering the opinion of the Judicial Committee, rejected (at p 678) the contention that a statute was invalid if a court concluded that it was not calculated as a matter of fact and policy to secure the peace, order and good government of the territory. His Lordship went on to say (at p 678) that such a power was "apt to authorize the utmost discretion of enactment for the attainment of the objects pointed to". In *Chenard and Co v Joachim Arissol* (1949) AC 127, Lord Reid, delivering the opinion of the Judicial Committee, cited (at p 132) *Riel* and the comments of Lord Halsbury LC with evident approval. More recently Viscount Radcliffe, speaking for the Judicial Committee, described a power to make laws for the peace, order and good government of a territory as "connot(ing), in British constitutional language, the widest law-making powers appropriate to a Sovereign": *Ibralebbe v The Queen* (1964) AC 900, at p 923.

These decisions and statements of high authority demonstrate that, within the limits of the grant, a power to make laws for the peace, order and good government of a territory is as ample and plenary as the power possessed by the Imperial Parliament itself. That is, the words "for the peace, order and good government" are not words of limitation. They did not confer on the courts of a colony, just as they do not confer on the courts of a State, jurisdiction to strike down legislation on the ground that, in the opinion of a court, the legislation does not promote or secure the peace, order and good government of the colony. Just as the courts of the United Kingdom cannot invalidate laws made by the Parliament of the United Kingdom on the ground that they do not secure the welfare and the public interest, so the exercise of its legislative power by the Parliament of New South Wales is not susceptible to judicial review on that score. Whether the exercise of that legislative power is subject to some restraints by reference to rights deeply rooted in our democratic system of government and the common law (see *Drivers v Road Carriers* (1982) 1 NZLR 374, at p 390; *Fraser v State Services Commission* (1984) 1 NZLR 116, at p 121; *Taylor v New Zealand Poultry Board* (1984) 1 NZLR 394, at p 398), a view which Lord Reid firmly rejected in *Pickin v British Railways Board* (1974) AC 765, at p 782, is another question which we need not explore.

The proposition that a State Parliament possesses plenary legislative power and can make and unmake any law it wants extends to possessing power to enact a law that is inconsistent with the State Constitution itself. State Constitutions are ordinary statutes and can be amended in the ordinary way. A State Parliament cannot give up or abdicate its plenary legislative power. In ***McCawley v The King***, the Privy Council explained that when a State Parliament enacts legislation that is inconsistent with the State's Constitution Act, that legislation is not only valid but also amends the State's Constitution Act through the ordinary doctrine of implied repeal.

McCawley v The King (1920) 28 CLR 106

Section 15 of the* Constitution Act 1867 *(Qld) provided that Supreme Court judges had life tenure subject to good behaviour. The* Industrial Arbitration Act 1916 *(Qld) created a Court of Industrial Arbitration comprising a President and other judges who were to hold office for renewable seven-year terms. Section 6 of the Act allowed the President to be appointed to the Supreme Court. Section 6 had been interpreted to mean that the President would be a judge of the Supreme Court for only seven years. It was argued that s 6 was inconsistent with the* Constitution Act 1867 *and therefore invalid.

Lord Birkenhead LC

It is of the greatest importance to notice that where the Constitution is uncontrolled the consequences of its freedom admit of no qualification whatever. The doctrine is carried to every proper consequence with logical and inexorable precision. Thus when one of the learned Judges in the Court below said that, according to the appellant, the Constitution could be ignored as if it were a Dog Act, he was in effect merely expressing his opinion that the Constitution was, in fact, controlled. If it were uncontrolled, it would be an elementary commonplace that in the eye of the law the legislative document or documents which defined it occupied precisely the same position as a Dog Act or any other Act, however humble its subject matter ...

It was not the policy of the Imperial Legislature, at any relevant period, to shackle or control in the manner suggested the legislative powers of the nascent Australian Legislatures. Consistently with the genius of the British people, what was given was given completely, and unequivocally, in the belief, fully justified by the event, that these young communities would successfully work out their own constitutional salvation ...

[W]hen legislation within the British Empire which is inconsistent with constitutional instruments of the kind under consideration comes for examination before the Courts, it is unnecessary to consider whether those who were responsible for the later Act intended to repeal or modify the earlier Act. If they passed legislation which was inconsistent with the earlier Act, it must be presumed that they were aware of, and authorized, such inconsistency ...

The legislature of Queensland is the master of its own household, except in so far as its powers have in special cases been restricted. No such restriction has been established, and none in fact exists, in such a case as is raised in the issues now under appeal. It follows, therefore, that sec 6 of the *Industrial Arbitration Act of 1916* was not ultra vires. The Legislature was fully entitled to vary the tenure of the judicial office.

The reasoning in ***McCawley v The King*** means that legislative efforts such as the *Constitution Amendment (Fracking Ban) Act 2021* (Vic) – which inserted a new section 99 into the *Constitution Act 1975* (Vic), purporting to deprive the Victorian Parliament of power to repeal, alter or vary certain statutory provisions banning a mining practice known as fracking – are legally ineffective. While legally ineffective, provisions such as this might have political effectiveness in discouraging politicians from seeking to change the law.

Another line of argument to challenge the validity of State legislation has been to argue that a State Parliament cannot legislate to abrogate fundamental common law rights. In the ***BLF Case***, a majority of the New South Wales Court of Appeal came to the same conclusion about the scope of a State's plenary legislative powers as the Privy Council did in ***McCawley***. In that case, Kirby P in the majority also explained in detail why the plenary legislative powers of the States are not subject to a limitation prohibiting interference with fundamental common law rights. In the final lines of the above extract from ***Union Steamship Co v King***, the High Court deliberately avoided dealing with that issue. President Kirby explained that the idea is inconsistent with the accepted understanding of plenary legislative power, is inconsistent with constitutional history showing the supremacy of Parliament, and would be undemocratic.

Building Construction Employees and Builders' Labourers Federation of New South Wales v Minister for Industrial Relations ('BLF Case') (1986) 7 NSWLR 372

Kirby P

Formulations of the omnipotence of Parliament are derived, in this State, from statements about the Parliament at Westminster which have profoundly affected our approach to the powers of the Parliaments of Australia, modelled as they are on the Westminster Parliament ...

[T]he BLF urge that there should be implied into the constitutional arrangements of New South Wales, a common law right so deep that the legislature could not invade it. This right assured the subject unimpeded pursuit of the entitlement to have a case before the Court determined according to law. In particular the right could not be destroyed by ad hominem legislation directed specifically and only at the termination of the right and, as well, at the termination of the entitlement to costs accrued in the normal way ...

The appeal to natural law and to a principle higher than parliamentary sovereignty is certainly out of line with the mainstream of current constitutional theory as applied in our courts. In *Liyanage* the attempt to argue that there are certain fundamental principles which inhibit legislative supremacy (the operations of the *Colonial Laws Validity Act 1865* apart) was specifically rejected by the Privy Council (op cit at 284): see also *Ibralebbe v The Queen* [1964] AC 900. Furthermore, Lord Reid in *British Railways Board v Pickin* [1974] AC 765 at 782 rejected the notion of any such right so deep, declaring it to be a notion incompatible with historical and constitutional facts:

> In earlier times many learned lawyers seem to have believed that an Act of Parliament could be disregarded in so far as it was contrary to the law of God or the law of nature or natural justice, but since the supremacy of Parliament was finally demonstrated by the Revolution of 1688 any such idea has become obsolete.
>
> ...

I agree with Lord Reid's conclusion. I do so in recognition of years of unbroken constitutional law and tradition in Australia and, beforehand, in the United Kingdom. That unbroken law and tradition has repeatedly reinforced and ultimately respected the democratic will of the people as expressed in Parliament. It has reflected political realities in our society and the distribution of power within it. I also do so in recognition of the dangers which may attend the development by judges (as distinct from the development by the people's representatives) of a doctrine of fundamental rights more potent than Parliamentary legislation. Such extra-constitutional notions must be viewed with reservation not only because they lack the legitimacy that attaches to the enactments ultimately sanctioned by the people. But also because, once allowed, there is no logical limit to their ambit. They may thereby undermine a rule of law and invite the only effective substitute, viz the rule of power. In the end, it is respect for long standing political realities and loyalty to the desirable notion of elected democracy that inhibits any lingering judicial temptation, even in a hard case, to deny loyal respect to the commands of Parliament by reference to suggested fundamental rights that run so deep that Parliament cannot disturb them.

This conclusion does not leave our citizens unprotected from an oppressive majority in Parliament. The chief protection lies in the democratic nature of our Parliamentary institutions ...

But if the legislation is clear, and though the judge considers it to be unjust or even oppressive, it is not for him to substitute his opinion for that of the elected representatives assembled in Parliament. In *Taylor v New Zealand Poultry Board*, Cooke J suggested that I do not think that literal compulsion, by torture for instance, would be within the lawful powers of Parliament. Yet imprisonment, solitary confinement as a punishment and other severe physical and financial restraints have clearly been considered, even in recent times, to be within the power of Parliament. Substituting judicial opinion about entrenched rights for the lawful powers of Parliament, unless anchored in a Bill of Rights duly enacted, inevitably runs into the difficulties of defining what those common law rights are and of explaining how they are so basic that they cannot be disturbed. The developments in legislation on capital and corporal punishment illustrate the fact that perceptions of such "basic rights" are likely to vary in place and over time.

It is not necessary for me to consider in this case whether a power is reserved to the judiciary by the *Constitution Act of 1902*, s 5, to declare invalid a manifestly arbitrary and unjust law as repugnant to the Constitution on the grounds that it could not conceivably be, as the *Constitution Act 1902*, s 5, requires, a law for the peace, welfare and good government of New South Wales. Those words have hitherto been seen as an ample grant of power "in all cases whatsoever". By their history, purpose and language these words may not be apt to provide a limitation on what the legislature may enact.

In ***Durham Holdings Pty Ltd v New South Wales***, the High Court again avoided giving a definitive answer as to whether the legislative powers of the States are subject to a limitation prohibiting interference with fundamental common law rights. In that case, the High Court was able to avoid the issue by finding that the right allegedly breached by the New South Wales legislation was not a fundamental common law right.

Durham Holdings Pty Ltd v New South Wales (2001) 205 CLR 399

The New South Wales Parliament enacted legislation that vested ownership of coal found in certain land in the Crown and provided for compensation payable to the affected landowners. However, the compensation was less than full compensation. Durham Holdings Pty Ltd was an affected landowner. Durham Holdings argued that a right to receive fair compensation was firmly rooted in the common law and that a State Parliament had no power to abrogate such rights.

Gaudron, McHugh, Gummow and Hayne JJ

The question that the applicant posed for the Court of Appeal thus was whether or not the right to receive "just" or "properly adequate" compensation is such a "deeply rooted right" as to operate as a restraint upon the legislative power of the New South Wales Parliament. What the Court of Appeal said is true of the application to this Court, namely:

> The [applicant] was unable to point to any judicial pronouncements, let alone a decided case, which indicated, at any time, that any such principle existed in the common law of England, or of the colonies of Australasia, or of Australia. It advocated the development of the common law, by the recognition of such a principle for the first time in this case.

... Undoubtedly, having regard to the federal system and the text and structure of "[t]he Constitution of each State of the Commonwealth" (the phrase used in s 106 of the *Constitution*), there are limits to the exercise of the legislative powers conferred upon the Parliament which are not spelled out in the constitutional text. However, the limitation for which the applicant contends is not, as a matter of logical or practical necessity, implicit in the federal structure within which State Parliaments legislate. Further, whatever may be the scope of the inhibitions on legislative power involved in the question identified but not explored in *Union Steamship*, the requirement of compensation which answers the description "just" or "properly adequate" falls outside that field of discourse.

2.4 Restrictive procedures for enacting legislation

McCawley v The King demonstrates the point that a Parliament cannot bind itself. Whatever law Parliament makes, even if that law purports to bind Parliament itself, Parliament can unmake.

An exception to this basic proposition arises from the fact that the State Parliaments are subject to the demands of higher laws such as the *Australian Constitution* and, in earlier times, Imperial legislation applicable to the State by paramount force.

A State Parliament can pass a law that prescribes a special or restrictive procedure for enacting certain types of laws. Future Parliaments must comply with those procedures. Restrictive procedures of this kind do not limit the types of law a State Parliament can enact; they merely impose a special process for enacting certain types of law. The power to impose restrictive procedures came from the *Colonial Laws Validity Act 1865* until 3 March 1986, and from that time comes from the *Australia Act 1986*.

Colonial Laws Validity Act 1865 (Imp)

Section 5

... every Representative Legislature shall, in respect to the Colony under its Jurisdiction, have, and be deemed at all Times to have had, full Power to make Laws respecting the Constitution, Powers, and Procedure of such Legislature; provided that such Laws shall have been passed in such Manner and Form as may from Time to Time be required by any Act of Parliament, Letters Patent, Order in Council, or Colonial Law for the Time being in force in the said Colony.

Australia Act 1986 (Cth)

Section 6

... a law made after the commencement of this Act by the Parliament of a State respecting the constitution, powers or procedure of the Parliament of the State shall be of no force or effect unless it is made in such manner and form as may from time to time be required by a law made by that Parliament, whether made before or after the commencement of this Act.

There is a key difference between these two provisions. The *Colonial Laws Validity Act* provision denied power to enact a law in a manner that did not comply with an applicable restrictive procedure. A law that did not comply with an applicable restrictive procedure was invalid. The *Australia Act* provision does not deny power. The *Australia Act* provision denies force and effect to any law enacted in a manner that does not comply with an applicable restrictive procedure. In other words, the law is valid but of no effect. In theory, this is to ensure that there is no gap in law-making power. In practice, there may be little difference: a law that is invalid can be ignored and a law that is of no force or effect can be ignored.

Restrictive procedures under the *Australia Act* apply only to the process of State Parliaments making *laws* and not to the process of engaging in non-legislative action such as governments entering into contracts. ***Mineralogy v Western Australia*** emphasises this point.

Mineralogy Pty Ltd v Western Australia [2021] HCA 30

A mining agreement between a company and the State Government, which had later been given a statutory footing, included a procedure through which the company and government might agree to variations of the agreement. Without following that procedure, the

Parliament of Western Australia enacted legislation with the practical effect of cancelling the agreement. The High Court held that manner and form issues did not arise for decision because there had been no attempt to restrict the procedure by which the State Parliament makes laws.

Kiefel CJ, Gageler, Keane, Gordon, Steward and Gleeson JJ

[Section] 6 of the *Australia Act* is confined to ensuring compliance with requirements which an existing law of the Parliament of a State imposes upon a process of making a law *by* the Parliament of that State.

Determinative for the purpose of s 6 of the Australia Act is that cl 32 of the State Agreement says nothing about any process by which the Parliament of Western Australia might make any law, including any law affecting any right which may have accrued under the State Agreement or affecting the operation of the State Act or the Government Agreements Act.

Neither in form nor in substance does cl 32 of the State Agreement prescribe a requirement as to the manner or as to the form in which a law is to be made by the Parliament of Western Australia. Rather, cl 32(1) prescribes the parameters within which the parties to the State Agreement may agree to a variation of the State Agreement.

There are three key elements to an effective manner and form restrictive procedure:

1. There is the entrenched provision (that is the provision that cannot be changed without following a restrictive procedure), which must be doubly entrenched to protect the restrictive procedure itself against being repealed.
2. There is the manner and form restrictive procedure, which must be genuinely about the manner and form of making laws.
3. There is the amending law that seeks to amend the entrenched provision, which needs to comply with the manner and form procedure only if it is a law about the constitution, powers or procedure of the Parliament.

Double entrenchment

Attorney-General (NSW) v Trethowan demonstrates that to be effective a restrictive procedure needs to be 'doubly entrenched', otherwise a Parliament can simply repeal the provision to avoid needing to comply with it. The case also demonstrates that requiring a referendum of all electors is a true manner and form procedure.

In 1929, section 7A was inserted into the *Constitution Act 1902* (NSW) to prevent the abolition of the Legislative Council, the upper house of the New South Wales Parliament, without a referendum of the people. Sub-section (1) provided that the Legislative Council could not be abolished except in accordance with s 7A. Sub-section (2) set out the referendum requirement. Sub-section (6) sought to doubly entrench the referendum requirement by providing that '[t]he provisions of this section shall extend to any Bill for the repeal or amendment of this section'. In other words, sub-section (6) sought to prevent a future

Parliament repealing section 7A to get rid of the referendum requirement for abolishing the Legislative Council by also requiring a referendum to repeal or amend section 7A.

After a change of government in 1930, two Bills were passed without a referendum, relying on the theory that Parliament can make and unmake any laws it wants. The first Bill purported to repeal section 7A. The second Bill purported to abolish the Legislative Council. The High Court confirmed that the procedure set out in section 7A was an effective manner and form restriction within the meaning of section 5 of the *Colonial Laws Validity Act* and that the Bills were ineffective due to their non-compliance with the manner and form requirement.

The double entrenchment of the manner and form requirement by sub-section (6) was key to the outcome. That sub-section prevented the reasoning in ***McCawley v The King*** from applying. Without sub-section (6), Parliament could have repealed the manner and form requirement. Indeed, Parliament could have impliedly repealed the manner and form requirement simply by passing legislation to abolish the Legislative Council. There would have been no need to enact a Bill repealing section 7A before enacting a Bill to abolish the Legislative Council.

Whether a manner and form requirement is doubly entrenched can be tested by asking this question: Is the manner and form requirement *itself* protected against being amended or repealed in the ordinary way? The answer is 'yes' where there is a second protecting provision (as in ***Trethowan***) or where the provision protects itself (as in ***Attorney-General (WA) v Marquet***: see further below).

Attorney-General (NSW) v Trethowan (1931) 44 CLR 394

Dixon J

[Section 5 of the *Colonial Laws Validity Act*] provides: " ... every representative legislature shall, in respect to the Colony under its jurisdiction, have, and be deemed at all times to have had, full power to make laws respecting the constitution, powers, and procedure of such legislature; provided that such laws shall have been passed in such manner and form as may from time to time be required by any Act of Parliament, letters patent, order in council, or colonial law for the time being in force in the said Colony." This provision both confers power and describes the conditions to be observed in its exercise. It authorizes a representative legislature to make laws respecting its own constitution, its own powers and its own procedure. This authority does not extend to the executive power in the constitution. But it is plenary save in so far as it may be qualified by a law which falls within the description of the proviso. The power to make laws respecting its own constitution enables the legislature to deal with its own nature and composition. The power to make laws respecting its own procedure enables it to prescribe rules which have the force of law for its own conduct. Laws which relate to its own constitution and procedure must govern the legislature in the exercise of its powers, including the exercise of its power to repeal those very laws. The power to make laws respecting its own powers would naturally be understood to mean that it might deal with its own legislative authority. Under such a power a legislature, whose authority was limited in respect of subject matter or restrained by constitutional checks or safeguards, might enlarge the limits or diminish or remove the restraints. Conversely, the power might be expected to enable a legislature to impose constitutional restraints upon its own authority or to limit its power in respect of subject matter ...

I have arrived at the conclusion that such a provision [as s 7A] is properly described as requiring a manner in which the law shall be passed, within the category allowed by the proviso [to s 5 of the *Colonial Laws Validity Act*]. The language of the proviso may be susceptible of an interpretation which confines its application to the procedure by and the form in which a Bill is to be dealt with in the Chambers of the Legislature and possibly by the Sovereign and his representative. Those who contend for this interpretation emphasize the word "pass," to which they give a meaning more restricted than would be expressed by the word "made." It could not be denied that submission to and approval by the electorate, if required in order that a proposal may become law, would aptly and properly be described as part of the manner in which the law must be made.

Justice McTiernan dissented in part on the basis that he did not think that requiring a referendum concerned the procedure – the 'manner and form' – for enacting laws. He thought that such a requirement was an abdication of power to a body of persons external to Parliament.

Manner and form restrictive procedures

Only restrictive procedures prescribing the manner and form in which laws may be passed – in the sense of the process and procedure for passing laws – may be imposed.

South-Eastern Drainage Board (SA) v Savings Bank of South Australia highlights the distinction between a law prescribing the manner and form for passing laws and a law prescribing the substantive content of laws. Only the former kind of restrictions, if they concern the constitution, powers or procedure of the Parliament, are binding.

That case involved section 6 of the *Real Property Act 1886* (SA), which provided that land subject to regulation by the Act could not be subject to regulation by any future law passed by Parliament unless that law used the words 'Notwithstanding the provisions of the Real Property Act 1886'. The *South-Eastern Drainage Amendment Act 1900* (SA) purported to regulate land subject to the *Real Property Act* but did not include the words 'Notwithstanding the provisions of the Real Property Act 1886'. The High Court held that the requirement to use the words 'Notwithstanding the provisions of the Real Property Act 1886' was not a requirement about the manner and form of passing laws. It was a requirement about the content of laws.

Demonstrating the complexity of manner and form rules, the High Court made a significant error in another part of its reasoning. The High Court also held that the requirement to use specified words was ineffective as a manner and form requirement because the *Real Property Act* was not a law concerning the constitution, powers or procedure of Parliament. While this is true, it is irrelevant for the purposes of section 5 of the *Colonial Laws Validity Act* (and now section 6 of the *Australia Act*). It is the later amending law that must be about the constitution, powers or procedure of Parliament in order for it to be subject to manner and form requirements. The correct reasoning should have been that the *Drainage Amendment Act* was not a law concerning the constitution, powers or procedure of Parliament.

South-Eastern Drainage Board (SA) v Savings Bank of South Australia (1939) 62 CLR 603

Latham CJ

It was urged that s 6 of the *Real Property Act* was a law which prescribed a manner and form for the passing of Acts of parliament and that therefore an Act passed not in such manner and form was not valid. But the proviso with respect to manner and form applies only to laws respecting the constitution of the legislature, the powers of the legislature, and the procedure of the legislature. Sec. 6 is plainly not a provision affecting in any way the constitution of the legislature. Nor does it affect the powers of the legislature. It only purports to prescribe the contents of an Act which the legislature has power to pass. Nor does the section relate to any part of the procedure of the legislature in passing statutes. Accordingly, in my opinion s 6 of the *Real Property Act* cannot operate to deprive of effect any subsequent legislation of the South Australian Parliament which, upon the natural construction of its terms, enacts a provision which is inconsistent with the *Real Property Act 1886*.

West Lakes Ltd v South Australia also demonstrates the distinction between prescribing a manner and form requirement for enacting laws and restricting the substance of law-making power. In this case, a requirement to obtain the consent of a commercial entity for amendments to a statute was held not to be a manner and form requirement. A requirement to obtain the consent of an extra-parliamentary entity is an abdication of power.

In this case, South Australian legislation set out building regulations relating to the development of a new suburb that had been designed by the government in consultation with the developer corporation. The legislation also provided that those regulations could not be altered 'without the prior written consent of the Corporation'. Legislation amending the building regulations was later enacted without the consent of the corporation. The Full Court of the Supreme Court of South Australia held (1) that the amending legislation did not concern the constitution, powers or procedure of the Parliament; and (2) that the requirement to obtain the corporation's consent was not a manner and form requirement.

West Lakes Ltd v South Australia (1980) 25 SASR 389

King CJ

I think, however, that it is quite clear that the bill under consideration is not a proposed law respecting any of the topics enumerated in s 5 of the *Colonial Laws Validity Act* ...

A question might arise as to whether a particular statutory provision is truly a manner and form provision, which must be observed (at least as to legislation which falls within s 5 of the *Colonial Laws Validity Act*) as a condition of the validity of the Act, or whether it is a limitation or restraint of substance, which would not invalidate legislation inconsistent with the limitation or restraint. ... There must be a point at which a special majority provision would appear as an attempt to deprive the parliament of powers rather than as a measure to prescribe the manner or form of their exercise. This point might be reached more quickly where the legislative topic which is the subject of the requirement is not a fundamental constitutional provision. ...

Trethowan's case, however, concerned a requirement that an important constitutional alteration be approved by the electors at a referendum. Such a requirement, although extra-parliamentary in character, is easily seen to be a manner and form provision because it is confined to obtaining the direct approval of the people whom the "representative legislature" represents. If, however, parliament purports to make the validity of legislation on a particular topic conditional upon the concurrence of an extra-parliamentary individual, group of individuals, organisation or corporation, a serious question must arise as to whether the provision is truly a law prescribing the manner or form of legislation, or whether it is not rather a law as to substance, being a renunciation of the power to legislate on that topic unless the condition exists ...

A provision requiring the consent to legislation of a certain kind, of an entity not forming part of the legislative structure (including in that structure the people whom the members of the legislature represent), does not, to my mind, prescribe a manner or form of lawmaking, but rather amounts to a renunciation *pro tanto* of the lawmaking power. Such a provision relates to the substance of the lawmaking power, not to the manner or form of its exercise. ... It follows, in my view, that ... [the statute] does not prescribe a manner or form of legislation and Parliament may legislate inconsistently with it. Parliament may therefore validly enact the bill which is under attack.

The constitution, powers or procedures of Parliament

Only laws concerning the constitution, powers or procedure of Parliament need to be enacted in compliance with restrictive procedures. Laws concerning other subject-matters do not need to comply with restrictive procedures, even if they are genuine restrictive procedures that are doubly entrenched.

South-Eastern Drainage Board (SA) v Savings Bank of South Australia (considered above) is a case demonstrating the point that only laws concerning the constitution, powers or procedure of Parliament need to follow restrictive procedures (as well as a case explaining what are genuine manner and form restrictive procedures).

Attorney-General (WA) v Marquet concerned the meaning of the 'constitution ... of the Parliament' and whether legislation concerning electorate boundaries fell within the scope of that concept. The High Court held that laws about electorate boundaries were indeed laws concerning the constitution – in the sense of the composition – of Parliament.

Attorney-General (WA) v Marquet (2003) 217 CLR 545

The* Electoral Distribution Act 1947 *(WA) set out a scheme for the distribution of electorate boundaries in Western Australia. Section 13 required an absolute majority in both Houses of the Western Australian Parliament for 'any Bill to amend this Act'. (This restrictive procedure provision is doubly entrenched because it protects itself against being amended or repealed in the ordinary way: a Bill amending section 13 would be a Bill amending 'this Act'.) Two Bills were passed by ordinary majorities rather than absolute majorities. The Electoral Distribution Repeal Bill 2001 would repeal the 1947 Act. The Electoral Amendment Bill 2001 would set out a new electoral distribution scheme.

Gleeson CJ, Gummow, Hayne and Heydon JJ

The "constitution" of a State Parliament includes (perhaps it is confined to) its own "nature and composition". The Attorneys-General for New South Wales and Queensland, intervening, both submitted that s 6 of the *Australia Act* should be read strictly and that, accordingly, the "constitution" of a State Parliament should be understood as referring only to the general character of the legislature rather than the rules pursuant to which members are returned to a chamber.

For some purposes, the nature and composition of the Western Australian Parliament might be described sufficiently as "bicameral and representative". But the reference in s 6 of the *Australia Act* to the "constitution" of a State Parliament should not be read as confined to those two descriptions if they are understood, as the submissions of the Attorneys-General for New South Wales and Queensland suggested, at a high level of abstraction. That is, s 6 is not to be read as confined to laws which abolish a House, or altogether take away the "representative" character of a State Parliament or one of its Houses. At least to some extent the "constitution" of the Parliament extends to features which go to give it, and its Houses, a representative character. Thus, s 6 may be engaged in cases in which the legislation deals with matters that are encompassed by the general description "representative" and go to give that word its application in the particular case. So, for example, an upper House whose members are elected in a single State-wide electorate by proportional representation is differently constituted from an upper House whose members are separately elected in single member provinces by first past the post voting. Each may properly be described as a "representative" chamber, but the parliament would be differently constituted if one form of election to the upper House were to be adopted in place of the other ...

The Amendment Bill, if it came into force, would have provided for 57 electoral districts and six electoral regions, but they would have been differently drawn from the way for which the *Electoral Distribution Act* provided. The criteria to be applied in drawing electoral boundaries under the Amendment Bill would have differed according to whether the electoral district had an area of less than 100,000 square kilometres. The tolerance in the smaller districts would have been reduced from 15 per cent to 10 per cent; in the larger districts the formula was more complicated, but again the tolerance was changed from 15 per cent. In addition, and no less significantly, under the Amendment Bill, the number of members of the Council would have been increased, from the 30 specified by s 5 of the *Constitution Acts Amendment Act* 1899, to 36. The Amendment Bill was for a law respecting the constitution of the Parliament of Western Australia.

2.5 Key limitations on State legislative power

Sections 106 and 107 of the *Australian Constitution* make the powers of the State Parliaments subject to any limitations found elsewhere in the *Australian Constitution*. The proposition that State Parliaments possess plenary legislative power and can make and unmake any laws they want is therefore qualified. The *Australian Constitution* imposes three main types of limitations on the powers of the States.

First, the *Australian Constitution* vests power to make laws on certain topics exclusively in the Commonwealth Parliament. If law-making power with respect to a particular subject-matter is vested exclusively in the Commonwealth Parliament, it follows that the State Parliaments do not have power to make laws on that subject-matter. Section 52 is the principal provision about exclusive federal powers.

Australian Constitution

Section 52

The Parliament shall, subject to this Constitution, have exclusive power to make laws for the peace, order, and good government of the Commonwealth with respect to:

(i) the seat of government of the Commonwealth, and all places acquired by the Commonwealth for public purposes;

(ii) matters relating to any department of the public service the control of which is by this Constitution transferred to the Executive Government of the Commonwealth;

(iii) other matters declared by this Constitution to be within the exclusive power of the Parliament.

Secondly, the *Australian Constitution* includes provisions that expressly limit the powers of the States. Some of these provisions are set out below.

Australian Constitution

Section 114

A State shall not, without the consent of the Parliament of the Commonwealth, raise or maintain any naval or military force, or impose any tax on property of any kind belonging to the Commonwealth, nor shall the Commonwealth impose any tax on property of any kind belonging to a State.

Section 115

A State shall not coin money, nor make anything but gold and silver coin a legal tender in payment of debts.

Thirdly, the powers of the States are limited by implications arising from the *Australian Constitution*. Two examples are the implied freedom of political communication (see Chapter 12) and the requirement not to impair the institutional integrity of State courts (see Chapter 19).

2.6 Power to refer legislative power to the Commonwealth Parliament

The *Australian Constitution* gives the States power to enlarge the scope of federal legislative power. The *Constitution* does this by providing that the Commonwealth Parliament may make laws with respect to matters referred to it by the States.

Australian Constitution

Section 51

The Parliament shall, subject to this Constitution, have power to make laws for the peace, order, and good government of the Commonwealth with respect to:

...

(xxxvii) matters referred to the Parliament of the Commonwealth by the Parliament or Parliaments of any State or States, but so that the law shall extend only to States by whose Parliaments the matter is referred, or which afterwards adopt the law;

...

The States have a broad discretion as to the nature of the matters they may refer to the Commonwealth Parliament. A State may refer power in respect of a broad subject-matter. Alternatively, a State may refer power to enact a particular statute, with the full text of that statute set out in a schedule to the State legislation.

In ***R v Public Vehicles Licensing Appeal Tribunal (Tas); Ex parte Australian National Airways Pty Ltd***, the High Court confirmed that a State can put a time limit on referrals of power to the Commonwealth. A State can refer power with respect to a matter for a specified time period or make the referral subject to termination by the State. The High Court also suggested, but did not expressly hold, that a State can revoke a referral of power.

R v Public Vehicles Licensing Appeal Tribunal (Tas); Ex parte Australian National Airways Pty Ltd (1964) 113 CLR 207

Tasmania enacted a statute referring power to the Commonwealth in respect of air transport. The statute made the referral of power subject to termination by the State Governor. There was argument about whether section 51(xxxvii) of the Australian Constitution *permitted a State to put time limits on referrals of power.*

Dixon CJ, Kitto, Taylor, Menzies, Windeyer and Owen JJ

The simplest approach, however, to the problem is simply to read the paragraph and to apply it without making implications or imposing limitations which are not found in the express words. ... on reading it, why should there be found in the words "matters referred to the Parliament of the Commonwealth by the Parliament or Parliaments of any State or States" any implications concerning the period of reference? It is plain enough that the Parliament of the State must express its will and it must express its will by enactment. How long the enactment is to remain in force as a reference may be expressed in the enactment. It none the less refers the matter. Indeed the matter itself may involve some limitation of time or be defined in terms which involve a limitation of time. ... There is no reason to suppose that the words "matters referred" cannot cover matters referred for a time which is specified or which may depend on a future event even if that event involves the will of the State Governor-in-Council and consists in the fixing of a date by proclamation. The question which was discussed at length before us as to whether when the Parliament of a State has made a reference it may repeal the reference does not directly arise in this case. It forms only a subsidiary matter which if decided might throw light on the whole ambit or operation of the paragraph. We do not therefore discuss it or express any final opinion upon it. We think that the Tasmanian Act as framed is fairly within the paragraph and does refer a matter. But it must be remembered that the paragraph is concerned with the reference by the Parliament or Parliaments of a State or States. The will of a Parliament is expressed in a statute or Act of Parliament and it is the general conception of English law that what Parliament may enact it may repeal.

The idea that a State could not revoke a referral of legislative power is inconsistent with the idea that the States possess plenary legislative power and can make *and unmake* any law they want.

2.7 DISCUSSION QUESTIONS

1. Is there any basis to think that the High Court might one day hold that the legislative powers of the States are subject to a limitation that a State cannot abrogate fundamental common law rights?
2. It is often argued that the power to impose restrictive procedures for enacting legislation is not inconsistent with the nature of plenary power because restrictive procedures do not limit the substantive powers of a State Parliament. Do you agree?
3. In ***West Lakes***, it was suggested that an overly onerous manner and form restrictive procedure might be seen as an attempt to deprive the Parliament of legislative power rather than setting out a procedure for exercising those powers. What principles should guide the assessment of whether a restrictive procedure is too onerous?
4. Why is double entrenchment important for an effective manner and form restrictive procedure?
5. Problem question: Would a statute that has an incidental effect of limiting the jurisdiction of the Victorian Supreme Court need to comply with section 85(5) of the *Constitution Act 1975* (Vic)?

Constitution Act 1975 (Vic)

85 Powers and jurisdiction of the [Supreme] Court

(1) Subject to this Act the [Supreme] Court shall have jurisdiction in or in relation to Victoria its dependencies and the areas adjacent thereto in all cases whatsoever and shall be the superior Court of Victoria with unlimited jurisdiction.

...

(5) A provision of an Act, other than a provision which directly repeals or directly amends any part of this section, is not to be taken to repeal, alter or vary this section unless

- (a) the Act expressly refers to this section in, or in relation to, that provision and expressly, and not merely by implication, states an intention to repeal, alter or vary this section; and
- (b) the member of the Parliament who introduces the Bill for the Act or, if the provision is inserted in the Act by another Act, the Bill for that other Act, or a person acting on his or her behalf, makes a statement to the Council or the Assembly, as the case requires, of the reasons for repealing, altering or varying this section; and
- (c) the statement is so made
  - (i) during the member's second reading speech; or
  - (ii) after not less than 24 hours' notice is given of the intention to make the statement but before the third reading of the Bill; or
  - (iii) with the leave of the Council or the Assembly, as the case requires, at any time before the third reading of the Bill.

3 CONSTITUTIONAL METHOD

Interpretation, characterisation and invalidity

3.1 Overview

This chapter examines key aspects of constitutional method. First, this chapter considers constitutional interpretation, which is concerned with working out what the terms and provisions of the *Constitution* mean and how they apply. Secondly, this chapter considers the technique of characterisation, which is concerned with working out whether a law is one with respect to a head of legislative power or a prohibition on legislative power. Finally, this chapter considers the nature and consequences of constitutional invalidity.

Key concepts considered in this chapter include:

- constitutional interpretation
- reserved State powers doctrine
- engineers doctrine
- characterisation
- sufficient connection
- dual characterisation

- invalidity
- reading down
- disapplication
- severance.

3.2 Constitutional interpretation and construction

Constitutional interpretation is the process of working out the meaning of the words and provisions of a written Constitution and how they apply. Constitutional theorists sometimes explain that interpretation has two components: interpretation and construction.

Interpretation is the process of working out the semantic meaning of words in a written Constitution. For example, section 119 of the *Australian Constitution* requires the Commonwealth to protect the States 'against domestic violence'. Deciding whether the term 'domestic violence' is used in the sense of violence within a family or in the sense of insurrection or rebellion involves interpretation.

Construction is the process of developing doctrine to articulate what a constitutional provision means and guide the evaluative reasoning necessary to apply it. Some constitutional provisions require more evaluative judgment and the development of more doctrine than others. For example, section 7 of the *Australian Constitution* provides, in part, that there shall be the same number of Senators from each original State. Not much doctrine is needed to explain what this rule means and not much evaluative judgment is needed to apply it in practice. By contrast, section 116 of the *Australian Constitution* provides, in part, that 'The Commonwealth shall not make any law for establishing any religion'. To explain what this provision means requires the development of doctrine, and applying it in practice requires a considerable amount of evaluative judgment.

Judges often do not distinguish between interpretation and construction in the senses just explained, and will also often use the words interchangeably. This is not important. What is important is recognising that both processes take place.

The *Australian Constitution* itself does not set out any rules governing *how* to decide the semantic meaning of the words used or *how* to develop constitutional doctrine. Every time a judge engages in constitutional interpretation and construction, the judge is necessarily making choices about what are legitimate approaches to these processes and what are not legitimate approaches to these processes. Is it relevant how the framers of the *Constitution* expected a provision to apply? Is the underlying purpose of a constitutional provision relevant? Should grants of power be interpreted narrowly or broadly? Reasonable people can disagree about the answers to these types of questions, and there is an enormous body of scholarly writing debating them. Judges engaging in constitutional interpretation and construction necessarily adopt answers to these types of questions. Sometimes judges acknowledge they are adopting a particular approach or methodology of constitutional interpretation and construction; sometimes they do not.

Some judges and many scholars discuss and propose various theories of constitutional interpretation. These theories are often given names ending in '-ism' and articulate approaches for deciding the semantic meaning of the words used in the *Constitution* and developing doctrine. The High Court tends to reject the utility of such 'isms'.

Chief Justice Robert French, 'Theories of Everything and Constitutional Interpretation' (Speech given at the Gilbert & Tobin Centre of Public Law 2010 Constitutional Law Conference Dinner, Sydney, 19 February 2010)

In constitutional law, there is a considerable list of interpretive theories ...

There is a general question about the purpose and utility of interpretive theories. Some set out what their proponents say is a legitimate way or perhaps the only legitimate way of approaching constitutional interpretation. Others simply classify under some general label what particular constitutional judges or particular courts do in particular cases or generally. They may be descriptive of a methodology. With these, I have no difficulty. It is a good thing to reflect upon the unstated assumptions and perhaps unconsciously adopted methods that inform our thinking about particular constitutional problems. Is one acting according to silent principles? If so, are they universally applicable? In any event should they be stated? ...

Speaking for myself, I see little evidence of "isms" in the current methodology of the Court. One looks to the words of the Constitution and to their possible meanings and application. The interpretive choices or choices of application presented will be informed by principles developed in previous decisions of the Court. They will also be informed by the history and historical context of the words or phrases in issue and by their functions within the structure of the Constitution. The way in which these and other factors present themselves for consideration will depend upon the nature of the case which falls for decision ...

At a recent function in Chicago somebody from Australia, a graduate of the University of New South Wales teaching at Chicago University Law School, told me that I am a functionalist. That observation was made without rancour, so I do not take it to have been by way of condemnation. Perhaps it was inspired by the reference to multi-factorial evaluation in *Clarke*. Needless to say, I eschew stereotypes. I also eschew theories of everything. That having been said, both normative and classificatory discussion of constitutional interpretation can help us all to shine a light on our own thought processes. And that is a good thing.

The judgment of six justices in the ***Same Sex Marriage Case*** made the same point.

Commonwealth v Australian Capital Territory ('Same Sex Marriage Case') (2013) 250 CLR 441

In this case, the High Court held that the word 'marriage' in section 51(xxi) of the Australian Constitution *was capable of including unions between persons of the same sex.*

French CJ, Hayne, Crennan, Kiefel, Bell and Keane JJ

The utility of adopting or applying a single all-embracing theory of constitutional interpretation has been denied. This case does not require examination of those theories or the resolution of any conflict, real or supposed, between them. The determinative question in this case is whether s 51(xxi) is to be construed as referring only to the particular legal status of "marriage" which could be formed at the time of federation (having the legal content which it had according to English law at that time) or as using the word "marriage" in the sense of a "topic of juristic classification". For the reasons that follow, the latter construction should be adopted. Debates cast in terms like "originalism" or "original intent" (evidently intended to stand in opposition to "contemporary meaning") with their echoes of very different debates in other jurisdictions are not to the point and serve only to obscure much more than they illuminate ...

Justice Callinan observed in his dissenting judgment in the ***WorkChoices Case*** that the High Court has never embraced any overarching approach to working out what the words of the *Constitution* mean and how they apply.

New South Wales v Commonwealth ('WorkChoices Case') (2006) 229 CLR 1

Callinan J

The truth is that there has been little sustained unanimity on the part of the 46 Justices who have constituted this Court during its 103 years of existence as to how the Constitution should be interpreted: whether strictly textually, by reference to history, purposively, as an exercise in "originalism", flexibly, according to a particular judge's perceptions of contemporary conditions, contextually, by searching for implications emerging from the text and structure, or, as a combination of one or more of these. Each of the approaches has had its proponents at times but none has universally prevailed. No doubt each judge has been convinced of his or her correctness of approach, even descending on occasions to unedifying accusations of "heresy" on the part of predecessors or colleagues, no matter how learned and experienced they may have been. Sir Garfield Barwick in retirement even descended to saying, for publication, that the reasoning of the Court in *Cole v Whitfield* was "laughable" and "terrible tosh". Equally, Justices of this Court on occasions appear to have discouraged the adoption of settled universal principles of constitutional construction. Sir Garfield, for example, on the one hand spoke of the *Engineers' Case* as if it were an eleventh commandment, but on the other, in *R v Joske; Ex parte Australian Building Construction Employees & Builders' Labourers' Federation* expressed a wish to overturn the *Boilermakers' Case*.

The truth is ultimately that if a judge [has] a subjective preference for a particular interpretative approach, somewhere a dictum to support it can usually be found. The reality is that no judge can claim to stride the high ground of exclusive interpretative orthodoxy. In *SGH Ltd v Federal Commissioner of Taxation*, Gummow J said this:

> Questions of construction of the Constitution are not to be answered by the adoption and application of any particular, all-embracing and revelatory theory or doctrine of interpretation. Nor are they answered by the resolution of a perceived conflict between rival theories, with the placing of the victorious theory upon a high ground occupied by the modern, the enlightened and the elect.
>
> ...

Despite its general reluctance to embrace any overarching theory of constitutional interpretation, the High Court employs various principles and techniques in the processes of deciding the semantic meaning of the words used in the *Constitution* and developing doctrine. Some of the key principles and techniques are considered below.

3.3 Reserved State powers doctrine and its rejection

D'Emden v Pedder established a principle of constitutional interpretation that came to be known as the 'reserved State powers doctrine'. The doctrine held that the various heads of federal legislative power should be interpreted in a way that does not authorise federal laws to intrude upon of areas of legislative competence supposedly reserved to the States.

D'Emden v Pedder (1904) 1 CLR 91

The High Court held that the effect of section 107 of the* Australian Constitution, *which continues the powers of the colonial Parliaments in the State Parliaments unless withdrawn by the* Constitution, *was to reserve certain areas of legislative power to the States.

Griffith CJ

It was not disputed by the respondent's counsel that the exclusive power of the Federal Parliament extended to authorize the enactment of these provisions; but it was said that the powers reserved to the States by s 107 of the *Constitution* extended to direct taxation, that the imposition of stamp duty upon receipts given on the payment of money is an ordinary form of direct taxation, that a federal officer giving such a receipt for his salary is in no different position from any other recipient of money from a debtor in the State, and that the provisions of the Constitution as to the exclusive authority of the Commonwealth Parliament ought to be read subject to this power of the States, whether regarded as a power expressly reserved, or as one impliedly reserved from the nature and necessity of the case ...

It must, therefore, be taken to be of the essence of the Constitution that the Commonwealth is entitled, within the ambit of its authority, to exercise its legislative and executive powers in absolute freedom, and without any interference or control whatever except that prescribed by the Constitution itself. There is, however, a large class of cases with respect to which a similar power is for a time reserved to the States ...

The ***Engineers' Case*** overruled the reserved State powers doctrine. The *Engineers' Case* explained that the doctrine was flawed because it approached the process of working out what the words and provisions of the *Constitution* mean and how they apply with preconceived ideas about the proper scope of federal legislative power. There is nothing in the *Constitution* that expressly reserves any area of legislative power to the States.

Amalgamated Society of Engineers v Adelaide Steamship Co Ltd ('Engineers' Case') (1920) 28 CLR 129

The issue in this case was whether federal legislation enacted under the power in section 51(xxxv) of the Australian Constitution *to make laws with respect to the conciliation and arbitration of industrial disputes extending beyond the limits of any one State could apply to such disputes where a State agency was an employer involved in the dispute.*

Knox CJ, Isaacs, Rich and Starke JJ

The chief contention on the part of the States is that what has been called the rule of *D'Emden v Pedder* justifies their immunity from Commonwealth control in respect of State trading ...

It is an interpretation of the Constitution depending on an implication which is formed on a vague, individual conception of the spirit of the compact, which is not the result of interpreting any specific language to be quoted, nor referable to any recognized principle of the common law of the Constitution, and which, when started, is rebuttable by an intention of exclusion equally not referable to any language of the instrument or acknowledged common law constitutional principle, but arrived at by the Court on the opinions of Judges as to hopes and expectations respecting vague external conditions. This method of interpretation cannot, we think, provide any secure foundation for Commonwealth or State action, and must inevitably lead - and in fact has already led - to divergencies and inconsistencies more and more pronounced as the decisions accumulate ...

The ordinary meaning of the terms employed in one place may be restricted by terms used elsewhere: that is pure legal construction. But, once their true meaning is so ascertained, they cannot be further limited by the fear of abuse. The non-granting of powers, the expressed qualifications of powers granted, the expressed retention of powers, are all to be taken into account by a Court. But the extravagant use of the granted powers in the actual working of the Constitution is a matter to be guarded against by the constituencies and not by the Courts ... The one clear line of judicial inquiry as to the meaning of the Constitution must be to read it naturally in the light of the circumstances in which it was made, with knowledge of the combined fabric of the common law, and the statute law which preceded it, and then *lucet ipsa per se* [allow it to shine with its own light] ...

Applying these principles to the present case, the matter stands thus: s 51(xxxv) is in terms so general that it extends to all industrial disputes in fact extending beyond the limits of any one State, no exception being expressed as to industrial disputes in which States are concerned: but subject to any special provision to the contrary elsewhere in the Constitution. The respondents suggest only section 107 as containing by implication a provision to the contrary. The answer is that s 107 contains nothing which in any way either cuts down the meaning of the expression "industrial disputes" in s 51(xxxv) or exempts the Crown in right of a State, when party to an industrial dispute in fact, from the operation of Commonwealth legislation under s 51(xxxv). Section 107 continues the previously existing powers of every State Parliament to legislate with respect to (1) State exclusive powers and (2) State powers which are concurrent with Commonwealth powers.

But it is a fundamental and fatal error to read s 107 as reserving any power from the Commonwealth that falls fairly within the explicit terms of an express grant in s 51, as that grant is reasonably construed, unless that reservation is as explicitly stated. The effect of State legislation, though fully within the powers preserved by s 107, may in a given case depend on s 109. However valid and binding on the people of the State where no relevant Commonwealth legislation exists, the moment it encounters repugnant Commonwealth legislation operating on the same field the State legislation must give way ...

3.4 Interpreting constitutional provisions broadly

A general principle of constitutional interpretation is that words and phrases in the *Constitution* should be interpreted with all the generality with which the words used will admit. In other words, constitutional expressions should not be given narrow interpretations. Justice O'Connor in ***Jumbunna*** appears to be the first member of the High Court to articulate this principle.

Jumbunna Coal Mine v Victorian Coal Miners' Association (No 2) (1908) 6 CLR 309

O'Connor J

[I]t must always be remembered that we are interpreting a Constitution broad and general in its terms, intended to apply to the varying conditions which the development of our community must involve.

For that reason, where the question is whether the Constitution has used an expression in the wider or in the narrower sense, the Court should, in my opinion, always lean to the broader interpretation unless there is something in the context or in the rest of the Constitution to indicate that the narrower interpretation will best carry out its object and purpose. ...

The generality principle means that the scope of individual heads of federal legislative power may overlap. ***Pidoto v Victoria*** holds that it is wrong to adopt an interpretation of one head of federal legislative power for the purpose of avoiding overlap within another head of federal legislative power.

Pidoto v Victoria (1943) 68 CLR 87

The* National Security (Industrial Peace) Regulations *were enacted under the* National Security Act 1939–1940*, which had been enacted in reliance on the power in section 51(vi) of the* Australian Constitution *to make laws with respect to the naval and military defence of the Commonwealth and of the several States.

Latham CJ

The first objection to the Regulations submitted by the State of Victoria is based upon s 51(xxxv) of the *Constitution*, which confers upon the Commonwealth Parliament power to make laws with respect to "conciliation and arbitration for the prevention and settlement of industrial disputes extending beyond the limits of any one State." It is contended that this provision implies a negative – that it means, not only that the Commonwealth Parliament shall have power to legislate in relation to the industrial disputes there defined and in the manner there prescribed, but also that the Commonwealth Parliament shall not have power to deal with any other industrial matter or with any industrial dispute in any other manner. In my opinion this argument cannot be supported.

Section 51(xxxv) is a positive provision conferring a specific power. The particular terms in which this power is conferred are not, in my opinion, so expressed as to be capable of being so construed as to impose a limitation upon other powers positively conferred. Further, if s 51(xxxv) were construed so as to prevent the Parliament from dealing with industrial matters except under that specific provision, similar reasoning would lead to the conclusion that the Commonwealth Parliament could not (under any legislative power) provide for the use of conciliation and arbitration in relation to any other matter than inter-State industrial disputes. It must, I think, be conceded, for example, that the Commonwealth Parliament can, in legislating with respect to the public service of the Commonwealth (*Constitution*, s 52(ii)), provide for conciliation and arbitration in relation to matters such as wages, conditions and hours, whether or not any dispute about those matters is industrial, and whether or not it extends beyond the limits of any one State.

In my opinion the objection to the Industrial Peace Regulations based upon s 51(xxxv) of the *Constitution* must be rejected, because it finds no support in the words of this provision for the implied prohibition suggested ...

There was a period during which the High Court held that the generality principle did not apply to prohibitions on power. An example is provided by the ***DOGS Case*** considering the prohibition in section 116 of the *Australian Constitution* on laws for establishing any religion.

Attorney-General (Vic) ex rel Black v Commonwealth ('DOGS Case') (1981) 146 CLR 559

Wilson J

The plaintiffs' plea for a broad construction overlooks the fact that we are dealing with a clause which does not grant power, but denies it. While it is true that a constitutional grant of plenary legislative power should be construed with all the generality which the words used will admit, carrying with it whatever is incidental to the subject matter of the power, the same is not true of a provision which proscribes power ...

The High Court now accepts that the generality principle applies to prohibitions on power. One example is provided by ***Street v Queensland Bar Association*** in relation to the prohibition in section 117 of the *Australian Constitution* against a State discriminating against residents of other States.

Street v Queensland Bar Association (1989) 168 CLR 461

This case concerned an argument that rules governing who could practise as lawyers in the Queensland courts discriminated against lawyers residing in other States.

Deane J

It is a long-settled general principle of construction that the provisions of a national constitution must be broadly interpreted and applied: their substance should not be confounded by narrow technicality or legalism (see, eg, *Jumbunna Coal Mine, No Liability v Victorian Coal Miners' Association; Reg v Coldham; Ex parte Australian Social Welfare Union* (1983) 153 CLR 297, at p 314). In particular, a constitutional guarantee, such as that contained in s 117, calls for "a generous interpretation ... suitable to give to individuals the full measure of the fundamental rights and freedoms referred to" ...

The ***Plain Packaging Case*** provides another example of the generality principle applying to a prohibition on power. This case concerned the prohibition on federal laws acquiring property otherwise than on just terms.

JT International SA v Commonwealth ('Plain Packaging Case') (2012) 250 CLR 1

***This case considered an argument that federal legislation requiring tobacco products to have plain packaging acquired property otherwise than on just terms was contrary to section 51(xxxi)* of the Australian Constitution.**

French CJ

Section 51(xxxi) embodies a constitutional guarantee of just terms "and is to be given the liberal construction appropriate to such a constitutional provision." ...

The principle that constitutional provisions should be read with all the generality which the words used will admit now has acceptance as a general principle of constitutional interpretation.

The Grain Pool of Western Australia v Commonwealth (2000) 202 CLR 479

Gleeson CJ, Gaudron, McHugh, Gummow, Hayne and Callinan JJ

The general principles which are to be applied to determine whether a law is with respect to a head of legislative power such as s 51(xviii) are well settled. They include the following. First, the constitutional text is to be construed "with all the generality which the words used admit" ...

The generality principle is just a principle. It cannot by itself lead to a complete interpretative answer. It always remains necessary to work out just how much generality the words used will actually admit.

3.5 Interpretation by reference to the Convention Debates and drafting history

The process of constitutional interpretation can have regard to the underlying purposes of a provision and to the original public meaning of the language used in a provision.

This was not always the case. For almost a century, the High Court adopted a rule of interpretation prohibiting any reference to what was said during the Constitutional Convention that drafted the *Constitution*.

Tasmania v Commonwealth (1904) 1 CLR 329

O'Connor J

I do not think it can be too strongly stated that our duty in interpreting a Statute is to declare and administer the law according to the intention expressed in the Statute itself. In this respect the Constitution differs in no way from any Statute of the Commonwealth or of a State ...

In considering the history of the law, you may look into previous legislation, you must have regard to the historical facts surrounding the bringing the law into existence. In the case of a Federal Constitution the field of inquiry is naturally more extended than in the case of a State Statute, but the principles to be applied are the same. You may deduce the intention of the legislature from a consideration of the instrument itself in the light of these facts and circumstances, but you cannot go beyond it. If that limitation is to be applied in the interpretation of an ordinary Act of Parliament, it should at least be as stringently applied in the interpretation of an instrument of this kind, which not only is a statutory enactment, but also embodies the compact by which the people of the several colonies of Australia agreed to enter into an indissoluble union ...

The rule led to at least one ridiculous exchange during argument in the High Court.

Strickland v Rocla Concrete Pipes Ltd ('Concrete Pipes Case') (Transcript of Proceedings, High Court of Australia); extracted in Leslie Zines, 'Book Review' (1972) 5 *Federal Law Review* 159

MR LYONS: Your Honour, with respect, I know we are not permitted to construe para (xx) by reference to what is in the Convention Debates, but the Convention Debates show – this is the only way I can answer your Honour's questions – that it was not so much that the framers thought that special problems arose out of trading and financial corporations, but that they originally had all corporations and they wished to exclude special kinds ...

WINDEYER J: Then it was made trading, I think, and then financial was added at one of the Conventions.

MR LYONS: Yes, they were; those words were inserted your Honour ...

WALSH J: If you were looking at this ground which you say is probably impermissible, this historical thing ...

MR LYONS: I did not say historical is impermissible, your Honour ...

WALSH J: You get that the earlier form of it was that it related to status, then they changed it.

MR LYONS: Yes. I said it was impermissible to look at the Convention Debates, your Honour, but not impermissible to look at surrounding statutory history which ...

OWEN J: What if they changed the status quo? I suppose that's an impermissible question.

MR LYONS: Certainly it is the fact, your Honour, that it is first said ...

OWEN J: Do not answer it; it is quite irrelevant ...

MR ELLICOTT QC: My friend Mr Lyons did refer to the Convention Debates as if they might support the view for which he contended. That reference, of course, was not permissible; but all I want to say is that if they were looked at, one would find the contrary.

MENZIES J: That too is impermissible.

MR ELLICOTT: No doubt your Honours will not look at them.

Cole v Whitfield abolished the rule that reference to the Convention Debates is not permissible in constitutional interpretation. In that case, the High Court made extensive use of the drafting history of section 92, which guarantees freedom of inter-State trade and commerce, and discussion of that provision in the Convention Debates in the process of interpreting that provision. As explained in Chapter 13, the section 92 case law before *Cole v Whitfield* was complex and confusing. Reference to the Convention Debates enabled the High Court to develop a more workable jurisprudence.

Cole v Whitfield allows the process of constitutional interpretation to have regard to three features:

- the underlying purposes of a provision
- the original public meaning of the language used in a provision
- the drafting history or textual evolution of a provision.

Cole v Whitfield (1988) 165 CLR 360

Mason CJ, Wilson, Brennan, Deane, Dawson, Toohey and Gaudron JJ

Reference to the history of s 92 may be made, not for the purpose of substituting for the meaning of the words used the scope and effect – if such could be established – which the founding fathers subjectively intended the section to have, but for the purpose of identifying the contemporary meaning of language used, the subject to which that language was directed and the nature and objectives of the movement towards federation from which the compact of the Constitution finally emerged ...

Cole v Whitfield does not authorise attempts to substitute the original intentions of the framers of the *Constitution* for the meaning of particular constitutional provisions. The contemporary meaning of the language used is sometimes referred to as 'original public meaning'. The idea is that it is permissible to have regard to what people generally (or, at least, lawyers generally) would have understood the words to mean at the time the words were written. Original public meaning can be contrasted with original intentions, which is a concept concerned with the subjective intentions of the people who actually wrote the words of the *Constitution.*

In the ***WorkChoices Case***, the High Court rejected the idea that any original intention was even capable of being found. The High Court pointed out that the early judges of the High Court were all involved in writing the *Constitution* and often disagreed about what the words of the *Constitution* meant and how they applied. The High Court also pointed out that in respect of many provisions, the framers of the *Constitution* may not have given the precise meaning much thought at all. For these reasons, original intentions cannot be the key to constitutional interpretation.

New South Wales v Commonwealth ('WorkChoices Case') (2006) 229 CLR 1

Gleeson CJ, Gummow, Hayne, Heydon and Crennan JJ

There are at least two reasons why it is important to examine what was said about s 51(xx) in *Huddart Parker*. First, the decision is important for what it reveals concerning assertions made about what the framers of the Constitution intended ...

Huddart Parker was argued in October 1908 and March 1909, little more than five years after the Court first sat in October 1903. The membership of the Court had been increased in 1906, with the appointments of Isaacs and Higgins JJ, but all five members of the Court had been leading participants in the Constitutional Conventions. All are properly seen as among the framers of the *Constitution* although, of course, each played a different part in that work ...

The five members of the Court gave separate reasons for judgment. The headnote writer for the Commonwealth Law Reports rightly records that four separate views of s 51(xx) are to be identified in the reasons ...

This examination of *Huddart Parker* reveals several matters of present relevance. First, no one view of the meaning of s 51(xx) commanded the assent of even a majority of the Court. These differences of opinion deny that there was then any settled understanding, accepted by these framers of the Constitution, of what meaning or effect was to be given to s 51(xx) ...

To pursue the identification of what is said to be the framers' intention, much more often than not, is to pursue a mirage. It is a mirage because the inquiry assumes that it is both possible and useful to attempt to work out a single collective view about what now is a disputed question of power, but then was not present to the minds of those who contributed to the debates. And even if a statement about the framers' intention can find some roots in what was said in the course of the Convention Debates, care must be taken lest, like the reserved powers doctrine, the assertion assumes the answer to the very question being investigated: is the law in issue within federal legislative power? For the answer to that question is not to be found in attempting to attribute some collective subjective intention to all or any of those who participated in the Convention Debates. And when it is said that a particular construction of the constitutional text does, or does not, accord with the framers' intention, the statement compares competing constructions of the Constitution, both of which must be based in its text, interpreted in accordance with accepted principles ...

3.6 Constitutional implications

Sometimes the *Australian Constitution* constrains governmental power by implication. Chapter 12 dealing with the implied freedom of political communication provides a significant example.

Gerner v Victoria provides a recent reaffirmation that the fundamental task of constitutional interpretation is working out what the words of the *Constitution* mean and how they apply. So-called constitutional implications can arise only from the text and structure of the *Constitution* and not from general philosophical and political ideas about concepts such as federation.

Gerner v Victoria (2020) 270 CLR 412

This case concerned various challenges to a rule limiting the movement of individuals living in Melbourne to a five-kilometre radius of their home, imposed as a COVID-19 pandemic public health measure under Victorian public health legislation. The High Court rejected

a claim that the rule contravened a constitutionally implied freedom of movement because there is no basis in the text and structure of the* Constitution *for such an implication.

Kiefel CJ, Gageler, Keane, Gordon and Edelman JJ

The plaintiffs argued that the restriction on the legislative power of the Commonwealth and the States for which they contend springs from the fact that Federation produced "one people, one nation, where there had been several peoples and several colonies". Freedom to move wherever one wishes for whatever reason was said to follow, it being the essence of being a community or society or nation that the people can know each other.

...

Contrary to the plaintiffs' submission, the question is not, "what is required by federation". It is now well settled that what the *Constitution* implies depends on "what ... the terms and structure of the Constitution prohibit, authorise or require". That is because federation is not a "one size fits all" proposition; the kind of federation that is created depends on the text and structure of its constitutive instrument. So, just as the *Constitution* "gives effect to the institution of 'representative government' only to the extent that the text and structure of the *Constitution* establish it", the legal nature and effect of the federation established by the *Constitution* can be known only from the terms and structure of the *Constitution* itself.

The legislative powers of the States as members of the federation established by the *Constitution* are expressly preserved by s 106 of the *Constitution*. The proposition that those powers are necessarily limited by the freedom of movement for which the plaintiffs contend draws no support in the text or structure of the *Constitution* ...

The plaintiffs argued that the restriction on legislative power for which they contend may be discerned by a process of reasoning akin to that adopted in *Leeth v The Commonwealth* by Deane and Toohey JJ. In that case, their Honours suggested that "specific provisions of the *Constitution* which reflect or implement some underlying doctrine or principle are properly to be seen as a manifestation of it and not as a basis for denying its existence by invoking the inappropriate rule of *expressio unius* [the expression of one thing excludes others]". This approach to the interpretation of the *Constitution* did not find favour with the majority of the Court in that case. Nor, for that matter, did it command the support of a majority in any subsequent decision of this Court. It is not difficult to understand why. To seek to discern, by a process of induction from the presence in the *Constitution* of specific express restrictions upon legislative power, the existence of a broader limitation upon legislative power is distinctly inconsistent with the orthodox approach to constitutional interpretation established by the *Engineers' Case*.

3.7 Constitutional law and the doctrine of precedent

The doctrine of precedent applies in constitutional law cases. Lower courts are bound to follow the decisions of higher courts in the ordinary way.

There are no fixed rules about when the High Court will overrule a constitutional case. In ***Wurridjal***, French CJ summarised a number of principles that are relevant to whether to overrule a constitutional case.

Wurridjal v Commonwealth (2009) 237 CLR 309

French CJ

The operation of *stare decisis* in constitutional cases was considered in the *Second Territory Senators Case*. Aickin J undertook a review of the authorities and set out some general considerations to assist in deciding whether a previous constitutional decision regarded as erroneous should be overruled. In summary, these considerations were

1. Whether the error of the prior decision had been made manifest by later cases which had not directly overruled it.
2. Whether the prior decision went with "a definite stream of authority" and did not conflict with established principle.
3. Whether the prior decision could be confined as an authority to the precise question which it decided or whether its consequences would extend beyond that question.
4. Whether the prior decision was isolated as receiving no support from other decisions and forming no part of a stream of authority.
5. Whether the prior decision concerned a fundamental provision of the Constitution or involved a question of such vital constitutional importance that its consequences were likely to be far reaching, although not immediately foreseeable in detail.

... Another important factor distinguishing constitutional cases from others is that the effect of constitutional decisions cannot generally be remedied by legislative amendment ...

It is apparent from the authorities that the question whether the Court will overrule one of its earlier decisions is not to be answered by the application of a well-defined rule. Nor is it simply to be answered by the application of such visceral criteria as "manifestly" or "clearly" wrong. Rather it requires evaluation of factors which may weigh for and against overruling. That evaluation will be informed by a strongly conservative cautionary principle, adopted in the interests of continuity and consistency in the law, that such a course should not lightly be taken.

3.8 Characterisation of laws

Characterisation is the process of working out whether a law answers the description of a law with respect to one or more heads of power or answers the description of a type of law prohibited by the *Constitution*.

A federal law that can be characterised as a law with respect to a head of power will be within the scope of federal legislative power, unless it breaches a limitation on federal legislative power. A federal statute might be supported by more than one head of power, and different provisions of a single federal statute might be supported by different heads of power. A law that can be characterised as answering the description of a type of law prohibited by the *Constitution* is beyond legislative power.

Street v Queensland Bar Association (1989) 168 CLR 461

Brennan J

Characterisation is a useful and familiar process when the validity of a law depends on the grant of, or restriction on, legislative power ...

For a time, the High Court adopted the view that a law could only have one character and the process of characterisation was concerned with identifying that one true character. This approach is now rejected.

New South Wales v Commonwealth ('WorkChoices Case') (2006) 229 CLR 1

Gleeson CJ, Gummow, Hayne, Heydon and Crennan JJ

In particular, it is necessary to give effect to the well-established proposition that a law may be characterised as a law with respect to more than one of the subject-matters set out in s 51. To describe a law as "really", "truly" or "properly" characterised as a law with respect to one subject-matter, rather than another, bespeaks fundamental constitutional error. That error is compounded if the conclusion which is reached about the one "real" or "true" or "proper" character of a law proceeds from a premise which assumes, rather than demonstrates, a particular division of governmental or legislative power ...

It is now accepted that a law may be about multiple subject-matters and therefore have multiple characters. This is often called 'dual characterisation' or 'multiple characterisation'.

Murphyores provides an example of dual characterisation. A law that made export licences conditional upon environmental considerations was a law with respect to the subject-matter of 'trade and commerce with other countries' within the meaning of section 51(i) of the *Australian Constitution*, even though the law had effects on the subject-matter of the environment, which is not a head of legislative power.

Murphyores Inc Pty Ltd v Commonwealth ('Fraser Island Case') (1976) 136 CLR 1

Mason J

The point here is that by imposing a conditional prohibition on exportation, a prohibition which may be relaxed according to the exercise of a discretion, the law is dealing with exportation of goods, a matter at the heart of trade and commerce with other countries. It is not to the point that the selection may be made by reference to criteria having little or no apparent relevance to trade and commerce; it is enough that the law deals with the permitted topic and it does not cease to deal with that topic because factors extraneous to the topic may be taken into account in the relaxation of the prohibition imposed by the law. It is now far too late in the day to say that a law should be characterized by reference to the motives which inspire it or the consequences which flow from it ...

It is one thing to say that the trade and commerce power does not enable the Commonwealth to regulate and control directly matters standing outside the subject matter of power, such as the environmental aspects of mining in Queensland. It is quite another thing to say that the Commonwealth cannot in the exercise of that power make laws which have a consequential and indirect effect on matters standing outside the power, even by means of prohibiting conditionally engagement in trade and commerce with other countries. It is no objection to the validity of a law otherwise within power that it touches or affects a topic on which the Commonwealth has no power to legislate ...

Fontana Films provides an example of multiple characterisation. A law prohibiting secondary boycotts was held to be a law with respect to the subject-matter of trading corporations within the meaning of section 51(xx) of the *Australian Constitution*, even though the law could also be fairly described as a law with respect to other subject-matters outside of federal legislative power.

Actors and Announcers Equity Association v Fontana Films Pty Ltd (1982) 150 CLR 169

Stephen J

The law contained in s 45D(1)(b)(i) is composed of three elements: the existence of conduct by persons in concert which impedes a dealing in goods or services; the fact that that dealing is a dealing to which those persons are not themselves parties, and the presence of resultant and intended actual or likely detriment to one of the parties to the dealing, it being a corporation. It would no doubt be possible to describe the law by reference to any one of these elements, the conduct, the dealing or the detriment suffered by a corporation, ignoring in each instance the two other elements. The law could thus be described as one about concerted action affecting dealings, about dealings in goods or services or about detriments to corporations ...

To recognize that a law may possess a number of quite disparate characters is, then, to accept reality. Few laws will involve only one element ...

Once it is recognized that a law may possess several distinct characters, it follows that the fact that only some elements in the description of a law fall within one or more of the grants of power in s 51 or elsewhere in the Constitution will be in no way fatal to its validity. So long as the remaining elements, which do not fall within any such grant of power, are not of such significance that the law cannot fairly be described as one with respect to one or more of such grants of power then, however else it may also be described, the law will be valid. If a law enacted by the federal legislature can be fairly described both as a law with respect to a grant of power to it and as a law with respect to a matter or matters left to the States, that will suffice to support its validity as a law of the Commonwealth ...

It follows that in testing validity ... [i]t will be enough if the law fairly answers the description of a law "with respect to" one given subject matter appearing in s 51, regardless of whether it may equally be described as a law with respect to other subject matters. This will be so whether or not those other subject matters appear in the enumeration of heads of legislative power in s 51 ...

To describe [s 45D(1)(b)(i))] as a law with respect to trading corporations seems entirely apt; it does no more than recognize what is the manifest purpose and direct effect of the law. The connexion with corporations forms a crucial component of the law, making wholly inappropriate any description of that connexion as being merely "so incidental as not in truth to affect its character" ...

The process of dual or multiple characterisation has an important limitation. There are a number of heads of power that include express restrictions or limitations on the scope of federal legislative power. These include:

- section 51(xiii) 'banking, other than State banking'
- section 51(xiv) 'insurance, other than State insurance'
- section 51(xxxi) 'the acquisition of property on just terms from any State or person for any purpose in respect of which the Parliament has power to make laws'.

Positive restrictions on legislative power expressed in one head of legislative power apply to all other heads of legislative power. ***Bourke v State Bank of New South Wales*** held that federal legislation answering the description of a law with respect to 'State banking' is not within the scope of federal legislative power simply because the legislation also answers the description of a law with respect to 'financial corporations' within the meaning of section 51(xx). Accepting such a proposition would entail contradicting an express command of the *Constitution*.

Bourke v State Bank of New South Wales (1990) 170 CLR 276

Mason CJ, Brennan, Deane, Dawson, Toohey, Gaudron and McHugh JJ

It is of course well settled that the various paragraphs of s 51 are not to be construed in a narrow or pedantic manner, but are plenary grants of legislative power to be construed with all the generality which the words used will admit. That principle is naturally subject to such express limitations upon Commonwealth legislative power as the Constitution contains, as well as to certain implied restrictions which have been recognized by this Court. It is the extent of any restriction in relation to State banking with which this case is concerned.

In this context, some qualification must be made to the general principle that a law with respect to a subject-matter within Commonwealth power does not cease to be valid because it affects a subject outside power or can be characterized as a law with respect to a subject-matter outside power. The principle cannot apply when the second subject-matter with respect to which the law can be characterized is not only outside power but is the subject of a positive prohibition or restriction. If a limitation is found to be of general application, then the fact that it is contained within one of the paragraphs of s 51 does not deny it a wider operation; the remaining paragraphs are then to be construed as being subject to the limitation ...

It is therefore necessary in the first instance to determine whether the words "other than State banking" in s 51(xiii) impose a general limitation upon Commonwealth legislative power or are merely intended to confine the ambit of the banking power itself. The immediate difficulty with the second of these alternatives is that s 51(xx) confers power with respect to financial corporations formed within the limits of the Commonwealth. If the words "other than State banking" do not restrict the scope of s 51(xx), then the State banks themselves are subject to Commonwealth power and their activities are in the same position as those of other financial corporations over which the Commonwealth has power. That would be an extraordinary result ...

Bourke was affirmed in the ***WorkChoices Case***.

New South Wales v Commonwealth ('WorkChoices Case') (2006) 229 CLR 1

Gleeson CJ, Gummow, Hayne, Heydon and Crennan JJ

There is a further general proposition that "a law with respect to a subject-matter within Commonwealth power does not cease to be valid because it affects a subject outside power or can be characterized as a law with respect to a subject-matter outside power". That proposition, however, does not apply when, as it was put in *Bourke v State Bank of New South Wales*, "the second subject-matter with respect to which the law can be characterized is not only outside power *but is the subject of a positive prohibition or restriction*" (emphasis added). That positive prohibition or restriction may merely confine the ambit of the particular head of legislative power within which it is found, or it may be of general application. If the latter, then the other paragraphs in s 51 are to be construed as subject to the limitation ...

In other words, dual characterisation cannot be used to get around *express* restrictions on legislative power.

The process of characterisation involves determining whether there is a *sufficient connection* between the law and the subject of the grant or restriction on legislative power. The sufficient connection test is usually attributed to Kitto J's judgment in ***Herald and Weekly Times Ltd v Commonwealth***.

Herald and Weekly Times Ltd v Commonwealth (1966) 115 CLR 418

***Federal legislation provided for the grant of television broadcast licences and provided that licences were subject to various conditions. As a free market measure, federal legislation also made it an offence for a person to have a 'prescribed interest' in three or more licences. It was argued that 'prescribed interest' was given such a broad definition that the offence did not answer the description of a law with respect to 'postal, telegraphic, telephonic, and other like services' in section 51(v)* of the Australian Constitution.**

Kitto J

The main attack, however, is directed against so much of Div 3 as, if valid, creates offences consisting of certain kinds of conduct on the part of persons who are not the holders of television licences. Plainly enough, the attack must succeed unless the conduct which is thus made unlawful is so relevant to the subject of television services that a law forbidding it is a law with respect to that subject.

The central provisions of the division so far as offences by non-licenceholders are concerned, are to be found in ss 92 and 92C. The former begins by providing that a person contravenes the section if, and so long as, he has a "prescribed interest" in each of three or more licences, in each of two or more licences for stations in a Territory, or in each of two or more licences for stations in a State and within a radius of thirty miles of the General Post Office in the capital city of the State: sub-s (1) ...

The division goes thus far by providing that for the purposes of the division a person has "a prescribed interest" in a licence (a) if he is the holder of the licence; or (b) if he is in a position to exercise control, either directly or indirectly, of the licence, that is to say if he is in a position to exercise control of the company that holds the licence, of the operations conducted under or by virtue of the licence, of the management of the licensed station, or of the selection or provision of the programmes to be televised by the station: see s 91(2)(a) and (b) and s 92A(1) ...

We have been given in the course of the argument a number of striking illustrations of the possible working of these provisions, and with their aid the contention has been strongly pressed upon us that a law which would be on the subject of television services if its operation were limited by reference to proprietary interests or to real control, but is expressed to operate by reference to situations where there is or probably is neither proprietary interest nor actual control, should be held not to be a law with respect to television services at all ...

It is unnecessary here to describe the challenged provisions in greater detail. One need only read them to agree with the plaintiffs that they cast a net so wide as to cover many a concrete case that may be imagined, where it is most unlikely that the person concerned would find himself in a position to exercise any form or degree of control, or even of influence, in relation to any television licence or television station. But it does not follow that for this reason they are beyond power, unless the assumption be accepted which the plaintiffs' argument in truth made, that a law cannot be with respect to television services unless there can be seen, in every kind of case that it covers, some likelihood of there being an opportunity of influence or control in respect of a television service. The assumption, in my opinion, unduly limits the notion of substantial connexion upon which the *Constitution* insists when it uses the expression "with respect to".

Undoubtedly it is right to scrutinize minutely the effect of a challenged law in all the variety of cases to which it applies according to its term; but when that has been done the broader inquiry remains: what, then, is the law really doing by the operation which the scrutiny reveals that it has? For it is the answer to that question that shows whether the law is really one "with respect to" the relevant subject matter of power. The answer to it here surely is that the offence provisions are setting up a barrier against, not indeed the probability, but the possibility that a person who may be able, by reason of any of a number of legal or business relationships, to influence the exercise of the rights conferred by one television licence may be able, by reason of such a relationship, to influence the exercise of the rights conferred by another television licence. If it were correct to say of any of the relationships that in no case could it carry with it a special opportunity to exert such an influence, the relevant provision would no doubt lack the necessary connexion with the subject matter of power. But this cannot be said of any of the relationships which the division describes. Each gives rise to a situation which according to ordinary experience may, in some cases at least, support an endeavour to effect the control or management of a television station or its operation under its licence. And, as everyone knows, even the faintest of voices may sometimes carry the day.

Thus the provisions in question operate as part of a legislative plan to insulate the control and management of activities connected with the exercise of a television licence against the possibility of influence by a person who may occupy any of the specified positions of potential influence over like activities in relation to another such licence. It necessarily follows that the provisions are laws upon the subject of television licences and therefore upon the subject of television services ...

Spence v Queensland provides an example where the claimed connection between the operation of a law and a head of power was found not to be sufficient because any connection was insubstantial, tenuous or distant.

Spence v Queensland (2019) 268 CLR 355

The Commonwealth has legislative power in respect of federal elections (including related matters such as political donations for federal political campaigns) under Constitution *section 51(xxxvi) read with sections 10 and 31. One issue in this case was whether this legislative power supported a provision in the* Commonwealth Electoral Act 1918 (Cth) *authorising any person to make donations to political entities where the donation 'may be' (and therefore might never be) used for federal election campaigns. The effect of the provision was to override State prohibitions on property developers making political donations: property developers could make donations to political parties so long as the donations were not made expressly for the purpose of State or local government elections (where the State ban would continue to operate). The High Court held that the provision had too tenuous a connection to federal elections.*

Kiefel CJ, Bell, Gageler and Keane JJ

The connection between the operation of the section and the actual deployment of funds by a political entity in a federal electoral process cannot be described as more than insubstantial, tenuous and distant. The connection between the operation of the section and the subject matter of legislative power, in other words, is at best remote. To adapt one of the examples used rhetorically by Dixon CJ in the *Second Uniform Tax Case*, the connection between the operation of the section and the subject matter of s 51(xxxvi) in its application to ss 10 and 31 of the Constitution is no closer than would exist between the subject matter of "telephonic" services within s 51(v) of the Constitution and a law immunising a person who is a user of a telephone service from payment of all State taxes. The fact that the immunity would serve to provide the person with a greater source of funds from which the person could choose to pay a telephone bill might be said to constitute some connection with the subject matter of the power. The connection, however, would be insubstantial and tenuous, if not unreal.

The Grain Pool outlines the step-by-step process to be undertaken in determining whether there is a sufficient connection between a law and a head of legislative power.

The Grain Pool of Western Australia v Commonwealth (2000) 202 CLR 479

The issue in this case was whether the **Plant Variety Rights Act 1987** *(Cth) and the* **Plant Breeder's Rights Act 1994** *(Cth) creating new forms of intellectual property were laws with respect to 'patents of inventions' within the meaning of section 51(xviii) of the* **Australian Constitution.**

Gleeson CJ, Gaudron, McHugh, Gummow, Hayne and Callinan JJ

The general principles which are to be applied to determine whether a law is with respect to a head of legislative power such as s 51(xviii) are well settled. They include the following.

First, the constitutional text is to be construed "with all the generality which the words used admit". Here the words used are "patents of inventions". This, by 1900, was "a recognised category of legislation (as taxation, bankruptcy)", and when the validity of such legislation is in question the task is to consider whether it "answers the description, and to disregard purpose or object".

Secondly, the character of the law in question must be determined by reference to the rights, powers, liabilities, duties and privileges which it creates.

Thirdly, the practical as well as the legal operation of the law must be examined to determine if there is a sufficient connection between the law and the head of power.

Fourthly, as Mason and Deane JJ explained in *Re F; Ex parte F*:

> In a case where a law fairly answers the description of being a law with respect to two subject-matters, one of which is and the other of which is not a subject-matter appearing in s 51, it will be valid notwithstanding that there is no independent connexion between the two subject-matters.

Finally, if a sufficient connection with the head of power does exist, the justice and wisdom of the law, and the degree to which the means it adopts are necessary or desirable, are matters of legislative choice.

The sufficient connection test of characterisation is not the only test of characterisation. The sufficient connection test applies to those heads of federal legislative power that are subject-matter powers, which is almost of all of them. The sufficient connection test does not apply to grants of purposive legislative powers. There are two key purposive powers: section 51(vi) 'the naval and military defence of the Commonwealth and of the several States, and the control of the forces to execute and maintain the laws of the Commonwealth'; and the component of section 51(xxix) 'external affairs' concerned with the domestic implementation of Australia's international legal obligations.

The test of characterisation applicable to purposive legislative powers is proportionality. This test requires asking whether the law is proportionate – or reasonably appropriate and adapted – to pursuing the purpose of the legislative power. Chapter 6 explains this test in detail in dealing with the external affairs power.

3.9 Constitutional invalidity

The nature of invalidity

A law that is not supported by a constitutional grant of legislative power or that violates a constitutional prohibition on power is void *ab initio*. The concept of void *ab initio*, meaning void 'from the beginning', can be contrasted with the concept of voidable, whereby an act ceases to exist from the time of a judicial ruling that the act is invalid. In other words, an unconstitutional law was never really a law at all.

This principle is often explained with reference to the famous American case of ***Marbury v Madison***.

Marbury v Madison, 5 US 137 (1803)

***This case is usually taken as the authoritative statement of the power of the American courts to declare legislative and executive actions void for breach of the* United States Constitution.**

Marshall CJ

Certainly all those who have framed written constitutions contemplate them as forming the fundamental and paramount law of the nation, and consequently the theory of every such government must be, that an act of the legislature repugnant to the constitution is void.

This theory is essentially attached to a written constitution, and is consequently to be considered by this court as one of the fundamental principles of our society. It is not therefore to be lost sight of in the further consideration of this subject.

If an act of the legislature, repugnant to the constitution, is void, does it, notwithstanding its invalidity, bind the courts and oblige them to give it effect? Or, in other words, though it be not law, does it constitute a rule as operative as if it was a law? This would be to overthrow in fact what was established in theory; and would seem, at first view, an absurdity too gross to be insisted on. It shall, however, receive a more attentive consideration.

It is emphatically the province and duty of the judicial department to say what the law is. Those who apply the rule to particular cases, must of necessity expound and interpret that rule. If two laws conflict with each other, the courts must decide on the operation of each.

So if a law be in opposition to the constitution: if both the law and the constitution apply to a particular case, so that the court must either decide that case conformably to the law, disregarding the constitution; or conformably to the constitution, disregarding the law: the court must determine which of these conflicting rules governs the case. This is of the very essence of judicial duty.

If then the courts are to regard the constitution; and the constitution is superior to any ordinary act of the legislature; the constitution, and not such ordinary act, must govern the case to which they both apply.

Those then who controvert the principle that the constitution is to be considered, in court, as a paramount law, are reduced to the necessity of maintaining that courts must close their eyes on the constitution, and see only the law.

This doctrine would subvert the very foundation of all written constitutions. It would declare that an act, which, according to the principles and theory of our government, is entirely void, is yet, in practice, completely obligatory. It would declare, that if the legislature shall do what is expressly forbidden, such act, notwithstanding the express prohibition, is in reality effectual. It would be giving to the legislature a practical and real omnipotence with the same breath which professes to restrict their powers within narrow limits. It is prescribing limits, and declaring that those limits may be passed at pleasure ...

In ***Kable (No 2)***, Gageler J summarised how the principle operates in Australia.

New South Wales v Kable (No 2) (2013) 252 CLR 118

Gageler J

Within the framework of the *Australian Constitution*, there has never been any doubt that application of the law to produce a final judicial order in the exercise of judicial power can permit and require the making of a judicial determination of the constitutional validity or invalidity of a statute. That principle, and its application to the determination by a court of the constitutional invalidity of a statute purporting to confer jurisdiction or power on the court itself, was established 100 years before the establishment of the High Court, in *Marbury v Madison*. The principle as so established "in our system ... is accepted as axiomatic, modified in varying degree in various cases (but never excluded) by the respect which the judicial organ must accord to opinions of the legislative and executive organs": *Australian Communist Party v Commonwealth* (1951) 83 CLR 1 at 262–263.

Within the framework of the *Australian Constitution*, and consistently with the justification for that principle stated in *Marbury v Madison*, there has never been any doubt that a purported law that is determined in the exercise of judicial power to be invalid, as beyond legislative power or as infringing an express or implied constitutional prohibition, is no law at all and is therefore of no legal force.

The notion that a law may be invalid only prospectively from the time of the making of a judicial order has been firmly rejected on the basis that "it would be a perversion of judicial power to maintain in force that which is acknowledged not to be the law". A judicial determination of validity or invalidity is a determination of what the law applicable to the rights or duties of the persons or classes of persons in controversy is or is not – not of what the law is to be. The settled position is captured in the explanation given by Latham CJ in *South Australia v Commonwealth*. After pointing out that "[c]ommon expressions, such as: 'The courts have declared a statute invalid', sometimes lead to misunderstanding", he said:

> A pretended law made in excess of power is not and never has been a law at all. Anybody in the country is entitled to disregard it. Naturally he will feel safer if he has a decision of a court in his favour – but such a decision is not an element which produces invalidity in any law. The law is not valid until a court pronounces against it – and thereafter invalid. If it is beyond power it is invalid ab initio.

The general consequence of constitutional invalidity is that actions and decisions taken under a statute that turns out to be constitutionally invalid are also invalid because there was never any lawful authorisation for those actions and decisions.

Kable (No 2) demonstrates an important qualification to this principle. Orders made by a superior court of record under legislation that turns out to be constitutionally invalid are not void *ab initio*. This is a result of a doctrine that it is in the nature of a superior court of record that its orders are always legally effective until set aside.

New South Wales v Kable (No 2) (2013) 252 CLR 118

French CJ, Hayne, Crennan, Kiefel, Bell and Keane JJ

A State Act empowered the State's Supreme Court to order the preventive detention of Gregory Wayne Kable if satisfied that otherwise he would probably commit a serious act of violence. The Supreme Court ordered Mr Kable's detention for six months. After the six months had elapsed, the detention order was set aside on appeal to this Court and the State Act held invalid. Did the detention order provide lawful authority for Mr Kable's detention?

... The central question in the appeal to this Court was whether the order made by Levine J, until it was set aside, had provided lawful authority for Mr Kable's detention. There was (and could be) no dispute that the Supreme Court of New South Wales is a "superior court of record". There was (and could be) no dispute that the [State] Act was invalid ...

The State, and the interveners, submitted that the order made by Levine J was made by a superior court of record and accordingly was effective until it was set aside. Because the order was not set aside until after Mr Kable's release from detention, it followed, so the State submitted, that the order provided lawful authority for Mr Kable's detention.

By contrast, Mr Kable submitted that the bases on which this Court held the Act invalid required not only the conclusion that the Act was invalid, but also the conclusion that the Supreme Court could not make (and had not made) a "judicial" order requiring his detention. He submitted that it followed that the principle requiring that effect be given to an order of a superior court until it was set aside was not engaged. Either the order made by Levine J was "void ab initio" or, when set aside by order of this Court, the order was "annulled ab initio". On either footing, the argument continued, the order provided no lawful authority for Mr Kable's detention ...

It is now firmly established by the decisions of this Court that the orders of a federal court which is established as a superior court of record are valid until set aside, even if the orders are made in excess of jurisdiction (whether on constitutional grounds or for reasons of some statutory limitation on jurisdiction). It was not submitted that any of these decisions should be reopened and there would be powerful reasons not to disturb such a long-established stream of authority. Nor was it submitted that these principles did not apply equally to the judicial orders of a State Supreme Court ...

There must come a point in any developed legal system where decisions made in the exercise of judicial power are given effect despite the particular decision later being set aside or reversed. That point may be marked in a number of ways. One way in which it is marked, in Australian law, is by treating the orders of a superior court of record as valid until set aside.

Were this not so, the exercise of judicial power could yield no adjudication of rights and liabilities to which immediate effect could be given. An order made by a superior court of record would have no more than provisional effect until either the time for appeal or review had elapsed or final appeal or review had occurred. Both the individuals affected by the order, and in this case the Executive, would be required to decide whether to obey the order made by a court which required steps to be taken to the detriment of another ...

As a judicial order of a superior court of record, the order of Levine J was valid until set aside. It was not "void ab initio" ...

The extent of invalidity: Reading down, severance and disapplication

The Interpretation Act of each jurisdiction requires the application of the techniques of severance, reading down and disapplication to avoid constitutional invalidity as much as possible. Explanations of these techniques were given by Edelman J in ***Clubb v Edwards***.

Clubb v Edwards (2019) 267 CLR 171

Edelman J

[I]it is necessary to distinguish three different concepts. The labels that can be used, which most closely fit the underlying principles, are "reading down", "severance", and "partial disapplication". The labels of "severance" and "reading down" have, on different occasions, been used to describe each of the three different concepts. A clear vocabulary is needed because, despite the overlap in the concepts, the principles underlying each are different and the consequences can be different.

"Reading down" is a long-recognised part of the process of interpretation at common law, sometimes justified in cases of potential invalidity by the Latin maxim *ut res magis valeat quam pereat* ["It is better for a thing to have effect than to be made invalid"]. The process of reading down in such cases involves the court preferring an interpretation of a statutory provision that renders a provision constitutionally valid over one which would render it invalid. This is part of the process of ascertaining the essential meaning of the words of the provision ...

Where reading down is not possible, the common law also recognises a different doctrine commonly described as "severance". The doctrine of severance, where it applies, permits a court to strike down part of a statute that is beyond power, leaving the remainder of the statute operative. An entire section or sections of a statute can be struck out under the doctrine of severance. Even part of a section can be struck out, commonly where it can be "blue pencilled". The common law doctrine of severance can only be applied if the part of the statute to be severed is independent of the remainder of the statute. Further, severance is not possible where "the Statute with the invalid portions omitted would be substantially a different law as to the subject matter dealt with by what remains from what it would be with the omitted portions forming part of it"...

Reading down is the exercise of an interpretative power to expound meaning. Severance is the exercise of a power to recognise the invalidity of, and to sever, a substantially independent part of a statute or provision. In the process of severance, it is not relevant that the legislature might have preferred partial operation of the statute in place of no operation "if [it] had applied [its notional] mind to the subject". As Griffith CJ explained, what a legislature "would have done in a state of facts which never existed is a matter of mere speculation". In both cases of reading down and cases of severance, the essential meaning of the statutory text as read down or as severed is applied to the facts.

Unlike reading down or severance, the partial disapplication technique under s 2(2) of the *Navigation Act*, as recognised in *Newcastle and Hunter River Steamship Co Ltd*, does not apply the essential meaning to all of the facts or circumstances before the court. The essential meaning of "the coasting trade" in that case could not be read down to mean "the inter-State coasting trade". Nor could any part of the 'one collective expression' used in the relevant provisions be severed from a valid remainder. Instead, the provisions concerning ships engaged in the coasting trade were disapplied to ships engaged in the intra-State coasting trade.

The underlying premise of the partial disapplication approach in *Newcastle and Hunter River Steamship Co Ltd* was the statutory command in s 2(2) that, in order to preserve constitutional validity, the essential meaning of statutory words which cannot be read down or severed is not applied generally to all facts and circumstances that would otherwise have been encompassed.

Without a statutory command, evidencing a statutory intention for partial disapplication, that approach would not have been possible ...

The powers of reading down, severance, and partial disapplication were all given a generalised application in 1930 when the Commonwealth Parliament enacted s 15A of the *Acts Interpretation Act 1901* (Cth). Section 15A has been described as a "direction to every Court" to exercise those powers unless a contrary intention appears in the impugned legislation ... Equivalent provisions were subsequently enacted, and remain in existence, in each State and Territory.

Acts Interpretation Act 1901 (Cth)

15A Construction of Acts to be subject to Constitution

Every Act shall be read and construed subject to the Constitution, and so as not to exceed the legislative power of the Commonwealth, to the intent that where any enactment thereof would, but for this section, have been construed as being in excess of that power, it shall nevertheless be a valid enactment to the extent to which it is not in excess of that power.

The equivalent State and Territory provisions are *Interpretation Act 1987* (NSW) s 31, *Interpretation of Legislation Act 1984* (Vic) s 6, *Acts Interpretation Act 1954* (Qld) s 9, *Acts Interpretation Act 1915* (SA) s 22A, *Interpretation Act 1984* (WA) s 7, *Acts Interpretation Act 1931* (Tas) s 3, *Legislation Act 2001* (ACT) s 120 and *Interpretation Act 1978* (NT) s 59.

These techniques mean that is rarely necessary for a court to declare that an entire statute is invalid.

In the ***Industrial Relations Act Case***, the High Court explained two general limitations applicable to the techniques of severance, reading down and disapplication. First, these techniques cannot be used to contradict a clear legislative intention. Secondly, these techniques do not authorise the courts to act as legislators and redraft legislation.

Victoria v Commonwealth ('Industrial Relations Act Case') (1996) 187 CLR 416

Federal industrial relations legislation was expressed to bind the States. The legislation would be unconstitutional if it applied to the employment of senior State officials. The High Court read down the legislation so that it did not apply to employment of senior State officials.

Brennan CJ, Toohey, Gaudron, McHugh and Gummow JJ

Section 15A of the Interpretation Act may fall for application in two distinct situations. It may fall for application in relation to "particular clauses, provisos and qualifications, separately expressed, which are beyond legislative power". It may also fall for application in relation to general words or expressions. It is well settled that s 15A cannot be applied to effect a partial validation of a provision which extends beyond power unless "the operation of the remaining parts of the law remains unchanged". Nor can it be applied to a law expressed in general terms if it appears that "the law was intended to operate fully and completely according to its terms, or not at all".

Where a law is expressed in general terms, it may be more difficult to determine whether Parliament intended that it should, nonetheless, have a partial operation. And there is an additional difficulty if it "can be reduced to validity by adopting any one or more of a number of several possible limitations". It has been said that if, in a case of that kind, "no reason based upon the law itself can be stated for selecting one limitation rather than another, the law should be held to be invalid".

The limitation by reference to which a law is to be read down may appear from the terms of the law or from its subject-matter. Thus, a law which is "clearly made with the intention of exercising the power to make laws with respect to trade and commerce" can be read down "so as to limit its application to inter-State and foreign trade and commerce". Similarly, where a law is intended to operate in an area where Parliament's legislative power is subject to a clear limitation, it can be read as subject to that limitation ...

Heydon J in ***Public Service Association of South Australia v Industrial Relations Commission of South Australia*** explained these limitations in relation to the technique of reading down.

Public Service Association of South Australia Inc v Industrial Relations Commission of South Australia (2012) 249 CLR 398

Heydon J

A statute is to be construed bearing in mind the constitutional limits on the powers of the relevant legislature. If the impugned statute is capable of bearing two meanings, one which would render it invalid and the other which would render it valid, the latter is to be preferred. "[S]o far as different constructions ... are available, a construction is to be selected which, so far as the language ... permits, would avoid, rather than result in, a conclusion that the section is invalid". But the meaning compatible with validity must be "available". It is wrong to take words which bear only one meaning, which meaning leads to invalidity, and to rewrite them to create another meaning leading to validity. It is not for the Court to stand in the shoes of the legislature and purport to enact legislation within power which is different from the statute which the legislature actually enacted ...

Davis provides an example of where severance is possible. Legislation made it an offence to use certain expressions on consumer goods without permission of a government agency. The High Court held that the offence was constitutionally invalid in respect of some but not all of the expressions. The High Court held that it was possible to sever the invalid parts of the legislation leaving the remaining parts of the legislation to operate.

Davis v Commonwealth (1988) 166 CLR 79

Mason CJ, Deane and Gaudron JJ

At this point it is necessary to consider the relief sought by the plaintiff. The statement of claim seeks, amongst other things, a declaration that ss 22 and 23 are invalid. That declaration is sought on the footing that the first plaintiff intends selling, offering for sale and has in his possession for intended sale articles of clothing to which the name of the Authority and/or a prescribed symbol or a prescribed expression has been applied (par 45 of the amended statement of claim).

The general thrust of the plaintiffs' case is that ss 22 and 23 are invalid in their entirety. However, it is apparent that the validity of the two sections is not an all or nothing question. The invalidity of s 22(1) in its application to prescribed expressions, along with s 22(6)(d)(i) and (ii), would necessarily raise questions of severability. As these questions have not been debated in argument, it is proper to confine the plaintiffs' claim for relief so that the declaration of invalidity relates to the particular prescribed expression for the use of which the consent of the Authority was required, yet refused, that is, the expression "200 years". The plaintiffs have not made out a case for a declaration of invalidity in respect of prescribed symbols.

In the result we would overrule the demurrer so far as it asserts that the plaintiffs lack standing to challenge ss 22 and 23 and that s 22(6)(d)(i) is valid to the extent that it relates to the expression "200 years". Otherwise we would allow the demurrer. We would declare that s 22(6)(d)(i) is invalid to the extent that it refers to the expression "200 years".

Bell Group provides an example of where severance is not possible. In this case, the constitutionally invalid provisions were central to the operation of the legislation as a whole. As a result, it was not possible to sever those provisions and the legislation was declared invalid in its entirety.

Bell Group NV (in liq) v Western Australia (2016) 260 CLR 500

French CJ, Kiefel, Bell, Keane, Nettle and Gordon JJ

Although s 109 invalidates the Bell Act only so far as it is inconsistent with a law of the Commonwealth, the Bell Act presents as a package of interrelated provisions which appears intended to operate fully and completely according to its terms. The evident purpose of it is to provide a comprehensive regime for dealing with all the relevant property of the WA Bell Companies and to give the Authority and the Governor complete discretion as to how all the liabilities of the WA Bell Companies are to be determined and as to any payments to be made (or property to be transferred) in respect of those liabilities.

That is not to say that there are not some provisions of the Bell Act which, if standing alone, would not be inconsistent with the Tax Acts. But, as parts of a regime for dealing with all the relevant property of the WA Bell Companies and giving the Authority and the Governor complete discretion in the determination of liabilities, those provisions assume the valid operation of the provisions of the Bell Act that vest the WA Bell Companies' property in the Authority and give the Authority and the Governor complete discretion as to how the liabilities of the WA Bell Companies are to be determined and paid. Consequently, severance of the provisions of the Bell Act that have been identified as inconsistent with provisions of the Tax Acts would result in a radically different and essentially ineffective residue. The offending provisions are so fundamental to the scheme of the Bell Act and thus so bound up with the remaining provisions that severance of the offending provisions would leave standing a residue of "provisions which the State Parliament never intended to enact" ...

It should be concluded, therefore, that the Bell Act is invalid in its entirety.

Wilson v Minister for Aboriginal and Torres Strait Islander Affairs provides an example of disapplication. The decision was explained as reading down the statutory expression 'a person' to effectively mean 'a person other than a federal judge'. On Edelman J's taxonomy the decision is better explained as disapplying the expression 'any person' to persons who are federal judges. However one labels what the Court did, the result was that a particular decision purportedly made under the provision was not in fact authorised by the provision and was void for that reason.

Wilson v Minister for Aboriginal and Torres Strait Islander Affairs (1996) 189 CLR 1

Brennan CJ, Dawson, Toohey, McHugh and Gummow JJ

The success of the challenge must turn on the meaning to be attributed to the phrase in s 10(1)(c) which speaks of a report to be made by "a person nominated by him", that is, by the Minister. If the function of reporting is constitutionally compatible with the holding of office as a Ch III judge, there is no reason why any restriction should be read into the connotation of the term "person". On that hypothesis, the Minister had authority to nominate any person, whether a Ch III judge or not, to make a report. But if the function of reporting is constitutionally incompatible with the holding of office as a Ch III judge, s 10(1)(c) must be read down so as to preclude the Minister's nomination of a person who holds office as a Ch III judge. So construed, s 10(1)(c) would afford no authority to the Minister to nominate Justice Mathews and consequently would deny to Justice Mathews the capacity to accept any purported nomination. If s 10(1)(c) be so construed, it matters not whether the Minister thinks it desirable to nominate a judge to report ...

A person affected by constitutionally invalid laws or actions is not entitled to damages

In the United States, a person adversely affected by constitutionally invalid laws or actions is sometimes entitled to damages, known as ***Bivens*** damages after a case of that name.

Bivens v Six Unknown Named Agents of Federal Bureau of Narcotics, 403 US 388 (1971)

Brennan J for the Court

The Fourth Amendment provides that: "The right of the people to be secure in their persons, houses, papers, and effects, against unreasonable searches and seizures, shall not be violated."

In *Bell v Hood*, 327 US 678 (1946), we reserved the question whether violation of that command by a federal agent acting under color of his authority gives rise to a cause of action for damages consequent upon his unconstitutional conduct. Today we hold that it does ...

The High Court has always rejected the notion that a similar doctrine could operate in Australia. In ***James v Commonwealth***, Dixon J explained that damages are not available for a breach of the *Australian Constitution* because the *Australian Constitution* does not create private rights.

James v Commonwealth (1939) 62 CLR 339

A person whose business was harmed by laws he said violated the guarantee of freedom of interstate trade and commerce in section 92 of the Australian Constitution *sued for damages.*

Dixon J

Prima facie a constitution is concerned with the powers and functions of government and the restraints upon their exercise. There is, in my opinion, no sufficient reason to regard s 92 as including among its purposes the creation of private rights sounding in damages. It gives to all an immunity from the exercise of governmental power. But to find whether a governmental act be wrongful the general law must be applied. Section 92 will do no more than nullify an alleged justification. The plaintiff cannot, therefore, recover damages under s 92 independently of any tort by the Commonwealth ...

In ***British American Tobacco v Western Australia,*** Kirby J was alone in holding that a breach of the *Constitution* could give rise to a claim for damages independently of any general law cause of action.

British American Tobacco Australia Ltd v Western Australia (2003) 217 CLR 30

***A company sued for the refund of money paid under a State law that imposed excise duties contrary to section 90 of the* Australian Constitution. *The company succeeded under the general law cause of action of money had and received. Justice Kirby was alone in holding that the company could have succeeded if it framed its case as seeking* Bivens *damages for breach of the* Constitution.**

Kirby J

So far, this Court has not adopted a view of the enforcement of the *Constitution* that extends to implying from its terms (even language as emphatic and exclusory as s 90) an implied constitutional cause of action enjoyed by a party for redress in the case of a breach of a constitutional prohibition. In *Kruger v Commonwealth* (1997) 190 CLR 1 four members of the Court ... held that the *Constitution* did not contain any right, as alleged in that case, breach of which would give rise to a right of action sounding in damages. ... The Court's approach was said by Brennan CJ to follow from a view of the *Australian Constitution* as an instrument of government and one "concerned with the powers and functions of government and the restraints upon their exercise".

It is, with respect, an invalid leap of logic from the identification of the suggested character of the *Constitution* (even accepting it for the moment to be accurate and complete) to a conclusion that the instrument "reveals no intention to create a private right of action for damages for an attempt to exceed the powers it confers or to ignore the restraints it imposes". Alike with the majority of the Supreme Court of the United States in *Bivens*, I see no reason to infer such a restrictive "intention". "Intention" is a judicial fiction. It can only be given content according to the *Constitution's* purposes, express or implied. Where the applicable purpose is to prohibit a State Parliament from imposing a duty of excise my view is that the "intention" of the *Constitution* is to permit the right in those from whom the invalid "duty of excise" has been extracted to sue to obtain repayment of the sum ...

Whatever dispute there may be about the provision of damages for implied constitutional torts (as upheld in *Bivens* and rejected in *Kruger*), a constitutional claim for reimbursement of an invalidly exacted tax is a much clearer case. In effect, it is no more than a constitutional means of upholding the "important constitutional value" mentioned earlier in these reasons. The fact that there may presently be other common law and equitable remedies is irrelevant. Where the *Constitution* speaks clearly in terms of a prohibition, its words necessarily carry the power of its own vindication and enforcement ...

3.10 DISCUSSION QUESTIONS

1. What is the effect of the ***Engineers' Case*** on constitutional interpretation?
2. Explain the concept of dual characterisation and its limitations.
3. Outline the differences between the techniques of reading down, severance and disapplication.
4. When is it possible and when is it not possible to sever an invalid provision from a statute?
5. Policy question: Does the High Court's decision in ***Kable (No 2)*** undermine the supremacy of the *Constitution*?

4 TRADE AND COMMERCE POWER

4.1 Overview

This chapter examines the trade and commerce power. Section 51(i) of the *Australian Constitution* grants the Federal Parliament power to make laws with respect to two subject-matters: (1) international trade and commerce; and (2) inter-State trade and commerce.

Australian Constitution

Section 51 Legislative Powers of the Parliament

The Parliament shall, subject to this Constitution, have power to make laws for the peace, order, and good government of the Commonwealth with respect to:

(i) trade and commerce with other countries, and among the States;

...

Under this head of power, the Commonwealth Parliament can enact laws to regulate these types of trade and commerce and to participate in these types of trade and commerce.

Key concepts addressed in this chapter include:

- trade and commerce
- inter-State trade and commerce

- intra-State trade and commerce
- incidental power.

4.2 The meaning of 'trade and commerce'

Section 98 of the *Constitution* includes a partial definition of the concept of trade and commerce.

Australian Constitution

Section 98 Trade and commerce includes navigation and State railways

The power of the Parliament to make laws with respect to trade and commerce extends to navigation and shipping, and to railways the property of any State.

Section 98 is not a full definition. In ***W & A McArthur Ltd v Queensland***, the High Court gave a broad interpretation to the words 'trade and commerce'. The concept includes the acts of buying and selling as well as all of the things related to buying and selling such as the production of goods, commercial negotiations, and supply chain logistics.

W & A McArthur Ltd v Queensland (1920) 28 CLR 530

***Queensland legislation made it unlawful to sell certain products above prices set by the government. A Sydney-based company had agents travelling in Queensland selling its products at prices above the set price. The High Court found that the Queensland legislation was invalid for breaching section 92 of the* Constitution*, which provides that 'trade, commerce, and intercourse among the States, whether by means of internal carriage or ocean navigation, shall be absolutely free'. The High Court gave an explanation of trade and commerce that applies equally to section 51(i) of the* Constitution.**

Knox CJ, Isaacs and Starke JJ

The terms "trade, commerce, and intercourse" are not terms of art. They are expressions of fact, they are terms of common knowledge, as well known to laymen as to lawyers, and better understood in detail by traders and commercial men than by Judges. But as Judges we are taken to know and do in fact in this instance know the general import of the words. The particular instances that may fall within the ambit of the expression depend upon the varying phases and development of trade, commerce and intercourse itself. Aviation and wireless telephony have lately added to the list of instances, but the essential character of the class remains the same. "Trade and commerce" between different countries – we leave out for the present the word "intercourse" – has never been confined to the mere act of transportation of merchandise over the frontier. That the words include that act is, of course, a truism. But that they go far beyond it is a fact quite as undoubted. All the commercial arrangements of which transportation is the direct and necessary result form part of "trade and commerce." The mutual communings, the negotiations, verbal and by correspondence, the bargain, the transport and the delivery are all, but not exclusively, parts of that class of relations between mankind which the world calls "trade and commerce." ...

It is therefore impossible to limit the "trade and commerce" either "among the States" or "with other countries" to the mere act of transportation over the territorial frontier. The notion of a person or a thing, tangible or intangible, moving in some way from one State to another is no doubt a necessary part of the concept of "trade, commerce, and intercourse among the States." But all the commercial dealings and all the accessory methods in fact adopted by Australians to initiate, continue and effectuate the movement of persons and things from State to State are also parts of the concept, because they are essential for accomplishing the acknowledged end. Commercial transactions are multiform ...

4.3 The distinction between inter-State and intra-State trade and commerce

Section 51(i) is limited in its terms to international and inter-State trade and commerce. It does not, in terms, extend to intra-State trade and commerce; that is, trade and commerce that occurs wholly within a single State.

The High Court has held on multiple occasions that the distinction between inter-State and intra-State trade and commerce must be maintained. However, because – in the words of Dixon CJ in *Wragg v New South Wales* (1953) 88 CLR 353 – a grant of legislative power over a subject-matter 'contains within itself authority over whatever is incidental to the subject matter of the power' (sometimes referred to as an 'implied incidental power'), section 51(i) authorises regulation of intra-State trade and commerce in limited circumstances.

In ***R v Burgess; Ex parte Henry***, the High Court emphasised that 'trade and commerce ... among the States' does not extend to intra-State trade and commerce; that is, trade and commerce within a State. That case concerned federal laws authorising the making of regulations 'for the control of air navigation in the Commonwealth'. Regulations were made purporting to regulate the safety of all aircraft operating within Australia, including by introducing a pilot licensing scheme. An unlicensed pilot was prosecuted for flying without a licence and challenged the legislation. The High Court held that the legislation was invalid because it was not limited to international and inter-State aviation.

R v Burgess; Ex parte Henry (1936) 55 CLR 608

Latham CJ

This appeal raises the question whether the Commonwealth Parliament has power to legislate with respect to flying operations carried on within the limits of a single State ...

If the rules, eg, for landing upon an aerodrome, are not uniform, so that one pilot lands in a clockwise direction while another pilot, in the same place, obeying another set of rules, lands in an anti-clockwise direction, there is very grave risk of serious accident. Upon these and similar considerations the argument is based that in order to deal effectively with the subject of aircraft flying between the States or between Australia and other countries the Commonwealth Parliament must also have the power to deal with aircraft flying only within the limits of one State which use, as a matter of absolute necessity, the same air, and as a matter of practical necessity, the same aerodromes.

... Considerations of wisdom or expediency cannot, however, control the natural construction of statutory language. The Constitution gives to the Commonwealth Parliament power over inter-State and foreign trade and commerce and does not give to it power over intra-State trade and commerce, although these subjects are obviously in many respects very difficult to separate from each other. On several occasions the argument has been pressed upon this court that, where inter-State or foreign and intra-State maritime trade and commerce are so intermingled that it is practically essential to control all of them as one subject matter, the Commonwealth Parliament has power under s 51(i) and s 98 of the *Constitution* to deal with intra-State navigation and shipping. ... This argument, however, has always been rejected by the court ... Although foreign and inter-State trade and commerce may be closely associated with intra-State trade and commerce, the court has uniformly held that the distinction drawn by the Constitution must be fully recognized, and that the power to deal with the former subject does not involve an incidental power to deal with the latter subject ...

The decisions of this court ... have therefore left the problem which is indicated by the illustrations above given ... to be solved by some form of co-operation between the Commonwealth and the States. A new problem would be raised if in any given case it were established by evidence in respect of a particular subject matter that the intermingling of foreign and inter-State trade and commerce with intra-State trade and commerce was such that it was impossible for the Commonwealth Parliament to regulate the former without also directly regulating the latter. No such evidence, however, has been presented in this case, and it will be necessary to deal with such a question only when it is directly raised.

Dixon J

In reference to air navigation, as to broadcasting, the suggestion has been made that its control does not admit of the distinction between what is inter-State and what is confined to one State; that to regulate inter-State flying effectively air navigation must be controlled as a whole. The inconvenience and difficulty of maintaining the distinction needs no demonstration. But the legislative power is to make laws with respect to inter-State commerce, and, under the power, the domestic commerce of a State can be affected only to the extent necessary to make effectual its exercise in relation to commerce among the States ...

No one doubts that, like every other legislative power expressly conferred, the power to make laws with respect to trade and commerce with other countries and among the States carries with it legislative authority over whatever is incidental to the subject matter to which the power is addressed. Everything that is incidental to the main purpose of a power is contained within the grant. But I think it would be a matter of regret if the application of this principle to s 51(i) of the *Commonwealth Constitution* led to the adoption of so indefinite a standard of validity as that enunciated in these passages. The express limitation of the subject matter of the power to commerce with other countries and among the States compels a distinction however artificial it may appear and whatever interdependence may be discovered between the branches into which the Constitution divides trade and commerce. This express limitation must be maintained no less steadily in determining what is incidental to the power than in defining its main purpose.

Evatt and McTiernan JJ

It is impossible to accept the theory of the Commonwealth that its power to legislate with respect to inter-State trade necessarily extends to all aircraft engaged solely in intra-State trade, by reason of the possible "commingling," in air routes and air ports, of the aircraft proceeding intra-State with the aircraft proceeding inter-State. No doubt, by virtue of s 109 of the *Constitution*, State laws or regulations of transport may be invalidated by valid Commonwealth laws or regulations dealing with the subject matter of transport. Moreover, the rejection of the "commingling" theory does not deny that there may be occasions when parts of intra-State aviation will be seen to occupy so direct and proximate a relationship to inter-State aviation that the agents and instruments of the former will be drawn within the ambit of the Federal power, for otherwise the particular Commonwealth regulation of inter-State commerce would be entirely frustrated and nullified. But this does not mean that the Commonwealth Parliament is legislating with respect to intra-State trade but only that legislation with respect to inter-State trade may operate in respect of or against persons, matters and things which, though not themselves directly involved in inter-State trade, are brought into a sufficiently proximate relationship with such trade.

R v Burgess does not hold that intra-State trade and commerce can never be regulated under section 51(i). Justices Evatt and McTiernan observed that some elements of intra-State trade and commerce might have 'a sufficiently proximate relationship' with inter-State trade and commerce as to be within the scope of section 51(i).

The ***Second Airlines Case*** demonstrates that a sufficiently proximate relationship with inter-State trade and commerce exists where regulation of intra-State trade and commerce serves the purpose of protecting inter-State trade and commerce from physical harm or interference.

Airlines of New South Wales Pty Ltd v New South Wales (No 2) ('*Second Airlines Case*') (1965) 113 CLR 54

Federal legislation established a regulatory scheme for the licensing of aircraft operating within Australia. In the case of an aircraft that was to operate entirely within a single State, decision-making as to whether to issue a licence was limited 'to matters concerned with the safety, regularity and efficiency of air navigation and to no other matters'. 'Efficiency'

referred to operational matters rather than economic concerns. The High Court held that this licensing scheme for intra-State trade and commerce was supported by section 51(i) of the* Australian Constitution *because it operated to protect inter-State trade and commerce from physical danger.

Kitto J

[T]he licensing system in its application to wholly intra-State air services is limited so as to serve only the purpose of aiding and protecting the safety, regularity and efficiency of air navigation generally. It is at this point that the crucial question arises. In so far as regs 198 and 199 aid and protect the safety, regularity and efficiency of intra-State air navigation, have they the character of a law with respect to any subject or subjects of federal legislative power? ...

This Court is entrusted with the preservation of constitutional distinctions, and it both fails in its task and exceeds its authority if it discards them, however out of touch with practical conceptions or with modern conditions they may appear to be in some or all of their applications ...

It is, I think, a question as to whether, when the factual situation in which the law operates is understood, the law by its operation upon the intra-State section of the relevant form of commerce is seen to operate also upon the actual conduct of an activity or collection of activities in respect of which federal power exists, eg, the actual carrying on of activities forming part of the overseas and inter-State sections of that form of commerce. Where the intra-State activities, if the law were not to extend to them, would or might have a prejudicial effect upon matters merely consequential upon the conduct of an activity within federal power, e.g. where the profit or loss likely to result from inter-State commercial air navigation would or might be affected, that mere fact would not suffice, in my judgment, to make the law a law "with respect to" that activity itself. But, by contrast, where the law, by what it does in relation to intra-State activities, protects against danger of physical interference the very activity itself which is within federal power, the conclusion does seem to me to be correct that in that application the law is a law within the grant of federal power ...

[A] federal law which provides a method of controlling regular public transport services by air with regard only to the safety, regularity and efficiency of air navigation is a law which operates to protect against real possibilities of physical interference the actual carrying on of air navigation, and therefore is, in every application that it has, a law "with respect to" such air navigation as is within federal power, and none the less so because it is also legislation with respect to that intra-State air navigation which is not within the power.

In my opinion regs 198 and 199 are for these reasons valid laws of the Commonwealth, even in their application to regular public transport operations conducted wholly within the borders of a single State.

The ***Western Australia Airlines Case*** demonstrates that a law concerning intra-State trade and commerce will not be incidental to inter-State trade and commerce if its purpose is simply to make inter-State trade and commerce more profitable, at least in circumstances where the trade and commerce in question is trade and commerce undertaken by the Commonwealth.

Attorney-General (WA) v Australian National Airlines Commission ('Western Australia Airlines Case') (1976) 138 CLR 492

***Federal legislation established a government-operated commercial airline that operated inter-State routes. Amending legislation later authorised the government airline to operate intra-State routes 'for the purposes of the efficient, competitive and profitable conduct of the business'. The High Court held that the amending legislation was not supported by section 51(i) of the* Australian Constitution.**

Stephen J

Does, then, s 51(i), by its grant of legislative power over interstate trade and commerce, incidentally include a grant of power to legislate for intrastate trade and commerce when its only relationship to interstate trade and commerce lies in the fact that the purpose of engagement in such intrastate activity is to conduce to the efficiency, competitiveness and profitability of the interstate activity?

The authorities in this Court on the scope of that implied incidental power which attaches to each specific grant of power as to subject matter provide, in my view, a clear negative answer to the question posed. It is primarily to decisions upon s 51(i) that attention must be directed since, as Dixon CJ pointed out in *Victoria v Commonwealth*; (1957) 99 CLR 575, at p 614 the nature and subject of the particular head of power in question will be critical in determining what is incidental to that particular power ...

The effect of this constitutional division of power over trade and commerce between the Commonwealth and the States has led to a quite narrowly confined ambit being given to the incidental power in the case of s 51(i), at least where what is in question is possible intrusion into the field of intrastate trade and commerce.

In *R v Burgess; Ex parte Henry*, Latham CJ said that merely to discover that it was expedient to include intrastate trade within the ambit of Commonwealth control would not bring it within the incidental power under s 51(i), although if it were "impossible" to regulate some aspect of interstate trade without regulating intrastate trade that might call for a different conclusion. Dixon J said that intrastate trade could be affected, under the Commonwealth's power, "only to the extent necessary to make effectual its exercise in relation to commerce among the States". In their joint judgment Evatt and McTiernan JJ. spoke of the need for "so direct and proximate a relationship" of a part of intrastate aviation to interstate aviation as would bring the former into such "a sufficiently proximate relationship" as would justify control of it as incidental to the power under s 51(i) ...

In *Airlines of New South Wales Pty Ltd v New South Wales (No 2)* Barwick CJ, having affirmed earlier rejections of the notion that any commingling of the two divisions of trade and commerce could enlarge the subject matter of Commonwealth legislative power, said that nevertheless Commonwealth power might include within its sweep intrastate trade and commerce if that were necessary for the Commonwealth law to be "effective" as to interstate trade. The Chief Justice went on to say that the fact that international or interstate carriage by air may profit by, or to a significant degree depend upon, the level of intrastate carriage by air did not warrant the conclusion that the Commonwealth might stimulate and encourage the latter so as to foster the former. Kitto J drew a distinction between a law protecting from the danger of physical interference an activity within power and one which prevents prejudice to matters merely consequential to such an activity, as for instance the profitability of interstate commercial air. Only the former, he said, would be within power. Taylor J adopted as a test of extent of power whether its exercise was necessary to the safety and efficiency of interstate air navigation. Menzies J did likewise; he spoke of power to control intrastate air navigation if "necessary for the effectual control" of interstate air navigation; was it, he asked, "necessary to make effectual" the latter? Windeyer J would have required some imperilling of the safety of interstate air navigation before intrastate air navigation could come within Commonwealth competence.

In the light of the foregoing it is apparent that the permitted exercise of the power conferred by s 19B, and which is described in sub-s (2) as "incidental", extends beyond the ambit of that incidental power which s 51(i) carries with it.

Justice Murphy dissented in the ***Western Australia Airlines Case***. He thought that the majority decision had the illogical effect of making commercial considerations such as profit irrelevant to a power that was all about commerce. Justice Murphy would have upheld the legislation. In his view, the legislation did not ignore the distinction between intra-State and inter-State trade and commerce because the legislation authorised intra-State activity only for the purpose of supporting the inter-State activity.

Attorney-General (WA) v Australian National Airlines Commission ('Western Australia Airlines Case') (1976) 138 CLR 492

Murphy J (dissenting)

This legislation does not regulate intrastate non-government air transport. It is an authorization of government air transport which meets the stated criteria of connexion with interstate government air transport services. The criteria are obviously connected with protection of the revenues and expenditures of the Commonwealth, as well as with the promotion of trade and commerce among the States.

The sections in question authorize intrastate transport for the purposes of efficient competitive and profitable conduct of the interstate transport of the Commission. These criteria adopted by Parliament are well within the scope of the commerce power. It is permissible for Parliament to take account of commercial effects in legislating under the commerce power. It would be as illogical to exclude commercial considerations from the construction of the commerce power as it would be to exclude defence considerations from the defence power (s 51(vi)) or industrial considerations from the industrial power (s 51(xxxv)). I find no basis in the *Constitution* for the distinction that Kitto J drew between physical and economic effects upon "interstate commercial air navigation" in *Airlines of New South Wales v New South Wales (No 2)*.

In ***Pape v Commissioner of Taxation***, three members of the High Court held that a law authorising the payment of money to individuals for the purpose of stimulating consumer spending throughout Australia and thereby increasing trade and commerce activity was not supported by section 51(i) of the *Australian Constitution*. Even though it might be expected that some of the boost to trade and commerce would be a boost to inter-State and international trade and commerce, there was not a sufficient connection between the law and any such activity to allow the law to be characterised as a law with respect to inter-State trade and commerce.

Pape v Commissioner of Taxation (2009) 238 CLR 1

The Tax Bonus for Working Australians Act 2009 *(Cth) formed part of the Commonwealth's response to the Global Financial Crisis and provided taxpayers with one-off sums of money to stimulate consumer spending. The Commonwealth argued that the Act was supported by section 51(i) of the* Australian Constitution. *The Act was held to be valid on other grounds. The three judges who considered the section 51(i) argument rejected it.*

Hayne and Kiefel JJ

It may be accepted that the Impugned Act was promoted and passed with the hope that many recipients would spend the sum paid. Those who do spend the money may spend it in a way that constitutes international or interstate trade and commerce. But neither the legal nor the practical effect of the Impugned Act is such as to make it a law with respect to either or both of international or interstate trade and commerce.

The Commonwealth did not press for any reconsideration of the accepted doctrine of the Court about the trade and commerce power. The Commonwealth submitted that the question critical to the engagement of s 51(i) in this case was one about the practical effect of the Impugned Act. In particular, would the Impugned Act have "a substantial economic effect on the flow of commercial transactions, goods, services, money, credit, among the States?"

It is not necessary to decide whether an affirmative answer to the question posed by the Commonwealth would suffice to show that the Impugned Act is a law supported by s 51(i). It was not submitted that the material in the Special Case directly answered the factual question posed by the Commonwealth.

Heydon J

[Section 51(i)] compels a distinction between trade and commerce with other countries, and among the States, on the one hand, and other forms of trade and commerce, on the other. It does not permit an argument that trade and commerce in Australia is one indivisible whole. Nor does it permit an argument that any legislation having an effect on trade and commerce in Australia must inevitably have an effect on trade and commerce with other countries, and among the States. While it may not be necessary to demonstrate that the Tax Bonus Act is exclusively related to trade and commerce with other countries, and among the States, it is necessary to show at least that it has some definable relationship with that class of trade and commerce ...

The Tax Bonus Act does not reveal a purpose of having an impact on trade and commerce with other countries, and among the States, as distinct from other kinds of trade. This point demonstrates weakness in the defendants' second submission on s 51(i) as well.

The second submission advanced by the defendants ... was that "[i]t can reasonably be anticipated that the spending generated by the payments made under the Act will have a material effect on the amount of" trade and commerce with other countries, and among the States.

The silence of the Tax Bonus Act. As South Australia pointed out, nothing in the provisions of the Tax Bonus Act reflects any criterion ensuring that particular recipients are more likely to make expenditures, if they make expenditures at all, in trade and commerce with other countries, and among the States. The Act is structured so as to target a class – persons with taxable incomes between nil and $100,000, divided into three subclasses. The class as a whole is not inherently likely to favour trade and commerce with other countries, and among the States, as the object of their expenditures. The same is true of each subclass.

Sufficient practical connection? The defendants accepted that the payments were "not focused on interstate trade and commerce", but were focused on trade and commerce in general. However, they submitted that the desired effect on gross domestic product gave the payments a sufficient practical connection with trade and commerce with other countries, and among the States. That submission must be rejected. It ignores a necessary distinction. It fails to bridge a gap not otherwise bridged. It could not be correct unless s 51(i) were rewritten by leaving out the last seven words.

4.4 Participation in inter-State and international trade and commerce

The trade and commerce power allows the Commonwealth to participate in international and inter-State trade and commerce. In the ***ANA Case***, the High Court held that a law establishing a government-owned corporation to engage in inter-State trade and commerce answers the description of a law with respect to section 51(i) of the *Australian Constitution*.

Australian National Airways Pty Ltd v Commonwealth ('ANA Case') (1945) 71 CLR 29

Among other things, the Australian National Airlines Act 1945 *(Cth) created a corporate body called the Australian National Airlines Commission. The Commission had the function of establishing and operating commercial airline services for the transport of passengers of goods on inter-State routes. In the High Court, it was argued that section 51(i) of the* Australian Constitution *empowered the Commonwealth to regulate inter-State trade and commerce but did not empower the Commonwealth to engage in inter-State trade and commerce. The High Court disagreed.*

Latham CJ

It is further argued, however, that the power to make laws with respect to trade and commerce does not include a power to prescribe the persons who may engage in trade and commerce, and, more particularly, does not include a power to create a corporation for the purpose of engaging in trade and commerce ...

Under the power to legislate with respect to "(vii) lighthouses, lightships, beacons and buoys" Parliament may authorize the Commonwealth to establish lighthouses &c. So also under (viii) "astronomical and meteorological observations" the Commonwealth Parliament may legislate, as in fact it has done, for the actual making and control of such observations. Similarly, under (xi) "census and statistics" the Commonwealth itself can take a census. Under (xiii) "banking other than State banking" the Commonwealth Parliament can create a bank, as in fact it has done in the case of the Commonwealth Bank. It is unnecessary to extend the illustrations beyond those already given. There can be no reason in law why the power to make laws with respect to trade and commerce with other countries and among the States should not include a power to make laws enabling the Commonwealth itself, or a body established by the Commonwealth, to take part in such trade and commerce.

Dixon J

It is convenient, however, to consider first whether ... the leading provisions of the *Airlines Act* can be regarded as an exercise of the commerce power. It is objected that they cannot be supported under that power because it contemplates the legislative regulation of overseas and inter-State trade and commerce and not the entry of the Government itself into that field of activity. ... The power, it is said, on its bare reading is but a power to make laws for the regulation of these activities, not to undertake them. ...

I am of opinion that this argument ought not to be accepted. It plainly ignores the fact that it is a Constitution we are interpreting, an instrument of government meant to endure and conferring powers expressed in general propositions wide enough to be capable of flexible application to changing circumstances. It confuses the unexpressed assumptions upon which the framers of the instrument supposedly proceeded with the expressed meaning of the power. A law authorizing the government to conduct a transport service for inter-State trade, whether as a monopoly or not, appears to me to answer the description, a law with respect to trade and commerce amongst the States. It is only by importing a limitation into the descriptive words of the power that such a law can be excluded.

4.5 Regulation of inter-State and international trade and commerce

The trade and commerce power, particularly in combination with the incidental power, encompasses a wide ability to regulate matters connected with inter-State or international trade and commerce.

Re Maritime Union of Australia demonstrates that the trade and commerce power can be used to regulate the wages and conditions of people working in businesses engaged in international or inter-State trade and commerce.

Re Maritime Union of Australia (2003) 214 CLR 397

The Maritime of Union of Australia sought orders in the Australian Industrial Relations Commission to have the wages of foreign sailors working on a foreign-owned and registered cargo ship operating in Australian waters comply with the relevant Australian industrial award. Section 5(3) of the Workplace Relations Act 1996 *(Cth) provided that the Commission had jurisdiction to determine matters concerning the relationship between employers and maritime employees, insofar as those matters relate to trade and commerce between Australia and a place outside Australia or between the Australian States. The foreign shipowner argued that the law was not a law with respect to international or inter-State trade and commerce because it purported to apply to employers not present in Australia and to workers who do not live in Australia. The High Court held that section 5(3) of the* Workplace Relations Act 1996 *(Cth) was valid.*

Gleeson CJ, McHugh, Gummow, Kirby, Hayne, Callinan and Heydon JJ

It is also well settled that, in the exercise of the trade and commerce power, the Parliament can validly regulate the conduct of persons employed in those activities which form part of trade and commerce with other countries and among the States. A ship journeying for reward is in commerce; those who co-operate in the journeying of the ship are in commerce and the wages of those persons and the conditions of their employment relate to that commerce ...

[T]he commerce power is attracted by the engagement of the employees in interstate and overseas trade. The Attorney-General correctly stressed in his submissions that it is not to the point that the party responsible for payment of the wages of those employees and owning the ship in question is not itself also plying that ship for commercial reward.

The trade and commerce power can be used to regulate the production of commodities for export, including prohibiting the production of a commodity for export or permitting the production of a commodity for export in only limited circumstances or subject to conditions. In ***O'Sullivan v Noarlunga Meat***, the High Court upheld legislation that regulated in detail the operations of abattoirs for meat for export.

O'Sullivan v Noarlunga Meat Ltd (1954) 92 CLR 565

An abattoir operator faced fines under South Australian law for failing to comply with South Australian meat slaughter regulations. In an attempt to avoid the fines, the abattoir operator argued that the South Australian laws were inoperative under section 109 of the Constitution *for being inconsistent with Commonwealth regulations. The Commonwealth regulations prohibited the export of meat unless the abattoir where it was slaughtered was registered and met various requirements. Assuming there was in fact an inconsistency, the inconsistency argument could only succeed if the Commonwealth regulations were valid. Justice Fullagar gave the leading judgment on the validity of the Commonwealth regulations.*

Fullagar J

So far the general structure [of the Commonwealth law], though somewhat complex and very elaborate in detail, seems clear enough. The export of meat is prohibited unless it was slaughtered in a registered establishment, and an establishment cannot be registered unless it complies with the prescribed conditions. The export of meat is also prohibited unless certain other prescribed conditions as to treatment, storage and so on, are complied with ...

The Commonwealth is legislating to ensure that only meat of a certain grade and quality shall be exported, and the law is clearly a law with respect to trade and commerce with other countries. The power given by s 51(i) extends to authorizing the total prohibition of the export of any commodity, and a fortiori it includes a power to prohibit the export of any commodity except upon compliance with prescribed conditions. ...

But the position originally was, and still is, that reg 5 prohibits the use of premises for slaughter for export unless the premises are registered, and they cannot be registered unless they comply with a large number of prescribed conditions which descend to meticulous detail. The question which emerges is whether the Commonwealth power with respect to trade and commerce with other countries extends to authorizing legislation regulating and controlling the slaughter of meat for export. In my opinion it does so extend. ...

It is true that the Commonwealth possesses no specific power with respect to slaughter-houses. But it is undeniable that the power with respect to trade and commerce with other countries includes a power to make provision for the condition and quality of meat or of any other commodity to be exported. Nor can the power, in my opinion, be held to stop there. By virtue of that power all matters which may affect beneficially or adversely the export trade of Australia in any commodity produced or manufactured in Australia must be the legitimate concern of the Commonwealth. Such matters include not only grade and quality of goods but packing, get-up, description, labelling, handling, and anything at all that may reasonably be considered likely to affect an export market by developing it or impairing it. It seems clear enough that the objectives for which the power is conferred may be impossible of achievement by means of a mere prescription of standards for export and the institution of a system of inspection at the point of export. It may very reasonably be thought necessary to go further back, and even to enter the factory or the field or the mine. How far back the Commonwealth may constitutionally go is a question which need not now be considered, and which must in any case depend on the particular circumstances attending the production or manufacture of particular commodities. But I would think it safe to say that the power of the Commonwealth extended to the supervision and control of all acts or processes which can be identified as being done or carried out for export. The "slaughter for export" of stock is such an act or process, and, in my opinion, the Commerce (Meat Export) Regulations are within the legislative power conferred upon the Commonwealth by s 51(i).

In ***O'Sullivan v Noarlunga Meat,*** the regulations in issue prohibited a particular form of trade and commerce unless there was compliance with certain conditions. ***Murphyores Inc Pty Ltd v Commonwealth*** is another case where the High Court upheld a federal law prohibiting a particular form of trade or commerce unless there was compliance with certain conditions. In ***Murphyores,*** the underlying intention of the federal law concerned environmental protection. ***Murphyores*** demonstrates that the conditions attaching to a licence for export need not be about trade and commerce.

Murphyores Inc Pty Ltd v Commonwealth (1976) 136 CLR 1

The* Customs Act 1901 *(Cth) included a power to make regulations prohibiting exports completely, prohibiting exports to a specified place, and prohibiting exports unless there is compliance with prescribed conditions. The* Customs (Prohibited Exports) Regulations *(Cth) prohibited the export of zircon and rutile concentrates, which are obtained by sand mining, unless the Minister granted an approval. The* Environment Protection (Impact of Proposals) Act 1974 *(Cth) required that, in making any decision, a Minister had to consider the environmental aspects of a matter, and authorised environmental inquiries to be undertaken for this purpose. An applicant for export approval argued that the Act was invalid and could not affect export approval decisions.

Mason J

The power conferred by s 51 (i) enables the Parliament to prohibit, regulate and control the importation and exportation of goods, matters which lie at the heart of trade and commerce with other countries. ...

The power to legislate with respect to trade and commerce with other countries, including as it does power to prohibit and regulate the exportation of goods from Australia, necessarily comprehends the power to select and identify the persons who engage in, and the goods which may become the subject of, that activity ... It is then for Parliament in its wisdom or for the person to whom Parliament delegates the power to decide who may export and what goods may be exported. The means and the criteria by which this choice is to be made are for Parliament to decide. There is nothing in the subject matter of the constitutional power which justifies the implication of any limitation on Parliament's power of selection. It does not follow, for example, that because the subject of the power is trade and commerce, selection of the exporter or of the goods to be exported must be made by reference to considerations of trading policy.

It is enough that the law operates on the topic of trade and commerce with other countries. A law which absolutely or conditionally prohibits exportation of goods is a law that operates on that topic. It is not a law which ceases to deal with that topic because it confers a discretion, unlimited in scope, to permit exportation of particular goods ...

The point here is that by imposing a conditional prohibition on exportation, a prohibition which may be relaxed according to the exercise of a discretion, the law is dealing with exportation of goods, a matter at the heart of trade and commerce with other countries. It is not to the point that the selection may be made by reference to criteria having little or no apparent relevance to trade and commerce; it is enough that the law deals with the permitted topic and it does not cease to deal with that topic because factors extraneous to the topic may be taken into account in the relaxation of the prohibition imposed by the law. ...

It is one thing to say that the trade and commerce power does not enable the Commonwealth to regulate and control directly matters standing outside the subject matter of power, such as the environmental aspects of mining in Queensland. It is quite another thing to say that the Commonwealth cannot in the exercise of that power make laws which have a consequential and indirect effect on matters standing outside the power, even by means of prohibiting conditionally engagement in trade and commerce with other countries. It is no objection to the validity of a law otherwise within power that it touches or affects a topic on which the Commonwealth has no power to legislate.

The concept of trade and commerce with other countries and among the States includes exporting goods from Australia to another country or from one State to another State. ***O'Sullivan v Noarlunga Meat*** and ***Murphyores*** concerned laws regulating pre-export matters.

The concept of trade and commerce also includes the inverse of export, being the importation of goods from another country into Australia or from one State into another State. Laws regulating post-import dealings with goods have been upheld as being incidental to international or inter-State trade and commerce.

In ***Burton v Honan***, a federal law that provided for the forfeiture of goods that had been imported unlawfully, even when those goods had been on-sold, was upheld as being incidental to the trade and commerce power.

Burton v Honan (1952) 86 CLR 169

Section 229 of the Customs Act 1901 *(Cth) provided that goods which are prohibited imports shall be forfeited to the Crown. Prohibited imports included goods that had been imported under a licence that had been obtained as a result of false information. Doyle applied for and was granted a licence to import cars from the United States but had made a number of misrepresentations in applying for the licence. Doyle was convicted in relation to his misrepresentations. Doyle sold an imported car to Honan who later sold it to Burton. Honan and Burton were ordinary purchasers. The car was a prohibited import under section 229 and was seized by the Crown from Burton. The question for the High Court was whether the law authorising the forfeiture of the car was a valid law.*

Dixon CJ

The authority of the Commonwealth Government to impose forfeitures may be said to arise directly from ... the scope of the substantive power to deal with ... importation under the commerce power. But another view of the matter is to treat the power to impose a forfeiture in the case of offences as something which is incidental to the main power. There has in this Court been some discussion as to the use of par (xxxix) of s 51 in cases where the extent of the subject matter of a substantive power of the Commonwealth is involved, and the question is whether a provision in a statute may be supported as directed to carrying out the main power by providing for a matter incidental to the subject matter. The view which I personally have expressed is that everything which is incidental to the main purpose of a power is contained within the power itself so that it extends to matters which are necessary for the reasonable fulfilment of the legislative power over the subject matter ...

It is said that goods which might be forfeited under the words of the provision to which I have referred are exposed to forfeiture notwithstanding that they go into home consumption and are released from the control of the Customs for that purpose, and that they may be found in the hands of persons who have dealt with them quite honestly and have acquired apparent title to them as the last of a line of successive people all dealing in perfect bona fides and for value.

The preliminary question with which we are concerned is whether those two features of the operation of the provisions drive it beyond the application of the incidental power ... These matters of incidental powers are largely questions of degree, but in considering them we must not lose sight of the fact that once the subject matter is fairly within the province of the Federal legislature the justice and wisdom of the provisions which it makes in the exercise of its powers over the subject matter are matters entirely for the Legislature and not for the Judiciary ...

So far as the powers to make laws on matters incidental to trade and commerce, or to taxation, are concerned, it appears to us that it is fairly within the legislative power they confer to provide that conviction shall operate as a condemnation of the goods involved.

In ***R v Smithers; Ex parte McMillan***, legislation providing that a person who deals in narcotics that had been illegally imported into Australia must pay a pecuniary penalty to the Commonwealth equal to the value of any benefit derived from that dealing was held to be valid. The law was valid under section 51(i) of the *Australian Constitution* because the liability to pay the pecuniary penalty arose directly as a result of import activity.

R v Smithers; Ex parte McMillan (1982) 152 CLR 477

Gibbs CJ, Mason, Murphy, Wilson, Brennan, Deane and Dawson JJ

The prosecutor concedes that the Parliament has power, certainly under s 51(i), to prohibit the importation of narcotic goods, to make it an offence to have possession of them or to deal with them when they have been imported in contravention of the Act and to make them liable to seizure and forfeiture. These steps may be taken legitimately in the exercise of the power because they are incidental to the enforcement of the prohibition against importation which itself falls fairly and squarely within the power. But, says the prosecutor, the denial or deprivation of benefits arising from participation in dealings in a prohibited import is another matter altogether; it relates to transactions which take place after the process of importation has come to an end and it stands outside the range of acts and actions which are incidental to enforcement of the prohibition.

We do not agree. It would be a legitimate exercise of the power - and this is conceded - to make it an offence to engage in dealing in narcotic goods, being prohibited imports, that have been imported in contravention of the Act and to impose severe penalties in respect of that offence. Similarly it would be a legitimate exercise of the power to make that conduct the occasion for liability to a civil action for penalties of the traditional kind. Section 243B, in providing for the imposition of pecuniary penalties of the class provided for in Div 3, stands in no different position. It penalizes dealings in narcotic goods that have been imported in contravention of the Act. In so doing it constitutes a deterrent to importation in breach of the statutory provisions and provides a further sanction with a view to ensuring compliance with the statutory provisions governing importation. Its importance in this respect is that it seeks to deprive the dealing in narcotic goods of the considerable financial rewards which are the chief inducement for importing them into Australia and for dealing in them.

Although section 51(i) of the *Australian Constitution* entails a broad scope to regulate pre-export and post-import activities or dealing with goods, the ordinary rules of characterisation limit the scope of that broad power. A law must have a sufficient connection with international or inter-State trade and commerce to be valid. A law that has only an insubstantial, tenuous or distant connection with international or inter-State trade and commerce will not answer the description of a law with respect to section 51(i). Because a lot of trade and commerce involves corporations, the corporations power in section 51(xx) of the *Constitution* (examined in Chapter 5) can also be used to regulate many aspects of trade and commerce without the need to worry about the distinction between inter- and intra-State trade and commerce.

4.6 DISCUSSION QUESTIONS

1. Is Murphy J correct that the High Court's doctrine concerning the extent to which intra-State trade and commerce falls within section 51(i) has the effect of excluding commercial considerations from the interpretation of the word 'commerce'?
2. Would a law that prohibited the sale of imported tobacco products to persons under 30 years of age be supported by section 51(i)? Would a law that prohibited the importation of tobacco products intended to be marketed to persons under 30 years of age be supported by section 51(i)?
3. Does Heydon J's judgment in ***Pape*** suggest that federal legislation that mainly stimulated inter-State trade and commerce, rather than trade and commerce in general, would be valid? Can this be reconciled with the ***Western Australia Airlines Case***?
4. Would the laws considered in ***O'Sullivan v Noarlunga Meat*** and ***Murphyores*** be valid if they applied to the production of commodities 'for inter-State trade' instead of 'for export'?
5. Problem question: If the Commonwealth can prohibit the export of goods subject to conditions concerning how those goods are produced in Australia, can the Commonwealth equally prohibit the import of goods subject to conditions as to how and to whom those goods are sold in Australia? Answer with reference to the following hypothetical statute.

Cannabis Products Act 2023 (Cth)

(1) This Act may be cited as the *Cannabis Products Act 2023.*

(2) A person commits an offence if:

(i) the person grows, manufactures or makes cannabis or a product that includes cannabis as a component or ingredient, and

(ii) the person intends to export out of Australia that cannabis or product, and

(iii) the person does not provide the Australian Federal Police with his or her name, home address and business address within 7 days of commencing the growing, manufacturing or making process.

Maximum penalty: 1000 penalty units.

(3) A person commits an offence if:

(i) the person sells, gives or otherwise provides cannabis or any product that includes cannabis as a component or ingredient to another person under the age of 18 years, and

(ii) the cannabis or product that includes cannabis as a component or ingredient was imported into Australia.

Maximum penalty: 100 penalty units.

5 CORPORATIONS POWER

5.1 Overview

This chapter examines the corporations power. Section 51(xx) of the *Australian Constitution* grants the Commonwealth Parliament power to make laws with respect to three types of corporations: foreign corporations, Australian trading corporations, and Australian financial corporations. The umbrella term 'constitutional corporations' is sometimes used to refer to all three types of corporation.

Australian Constitution

Section 51 Legislative Powers of the Parliament

The Parliament shall, subject to this Constitution, have power to make laws for the peace, order, and good government of the Commonwealth with respect to:

...

(xx) foreign corporations, and trading or financial corporations formed within the limits of the Commonwealth;

...

The corporations power enables the Commonwealth to regulate a large variety of commercial and economic activities in Australia because corporations are such significant players in Australian commercial and economic life. The corporations power can be used to impose duties and prohibitions on the conduct of people in respect of their activities that affect corporations. The corporations power can also be used to regulate the activities of corporations directly by imposing duties and prohibitions on the conduct of corporations.

Key concepts addressed in this chapter include:

- corporation
- trading corporation
- financial corporation
- foreign corporation
- activities test
- object of statutory command.

5.2 What is a 'corporation'?

In most instances, whether an entity is a corporation will not be controversial.

The ***Queensland Rail Case*** concerned a Queensland statute establishing an entity with the features of a corporation but declaring that the entity was not a corporation. The High Court held that because the entity possessed the features of a corporation the entity was indeed a corporation within the meaning of section 51(xx) of the *Australian Constitution*, and therefore subject to federal laws enacted under the corporations power. The key feature was the entity's separate legal personality with capacity to sue and be sued, own property and enter into contracts.

Communications, Electrical, Electronic, Energy, Information, Postal, Plumbing and Allied Services Union of Australia v Queensland Rail ('Queensland Rail Case') (2015) 256 CLR 171

French CJ, Hayne, Kiefel, Bell, Keane and Nettle JJ

The *Queensland Rail Transit Authority Act 2013* (Q) ("the QRTA Act") established the Queensland Rail Transit Authority ("the Authority"). The Authority is now called Queensland Rail. The Authority can create and be made subject to legal rights and duties, which are its rights and its duties. It can sue and be sued in its name. It can own property.

The QRTA Act provides that the Authority "is not a body corporate". The QRTA Act provides that the Authority does not represent the State, and it follows from this provision, coupled with the provisions which give the Authority separate legal personality, that the Authority is not, and is not a part of, the body politic which is the State of Queensland.

The Authority operates as a labour hire company, providing labour used by Queensland Rail Limited ("QRL") to operate railway services in Queensland. QRL is a company governed by the *Corporations Act 2001* (Cth). Pursuant to s 67 of the QRTA Act, the Authority holds all the shares in QRL.

Is the Authority a "trading or financial corporation formed within the limits of the Commonwealth" within the meaning of s 51(xx) of the *Constitution*? If it is, the relations between the Authority and its employees are governed by federal industrial relations legislation. If it is not, State industrial relations legislation applies ...

For the purposes of deciding this case, it is not necessary to attempt to state exhaustively the defining characteristics of a corporation (whether a "foreign corporation" or a "trading or financial corporation"). Whether the Authority is a trading corporation can be answered without attempting that task.

The QRTA Act creates the Authority as a distinct entity. The Authority can have rights and duties. It is, therefore, a separate legal entity: one of those "basic units" of the legal system which "possess the capacity of being parties to the claim-duty and power-liability relationships" ...

[T]he Authority is created as a separate right and duty bearing entity. It may own, possess and deal with real or personal property. It is an entity which is to endure regardless of changes in those natural persons who control its activities and, in that sense, has "perpetual succession". Its constituting Act provides for mechanisms by which its assumption of rights and duties may be formally recorded and signified. The Authority has "the full character of a corporation" ...

Gageler J

Questions have often arisen as to whether particular entities constituted under State legislation, not disputed to be "corporations formed within the limits of the Commonwealth", answer the constitutional description of "trading or financial" corporations. The anterior question in this case is whether a particular entity constituted under State legislation answers the constitutional description of a "corporation".

That anterior question arises because the *Queensland Rail Transit Authority Act 2013* (Q), despite establishing "Queensland Rail", conferring on it "all the powers of an individual" (specifically including to "enter into contracts", "acquire, hold, dispose of, and deal with property", "employ staff", "appoint agents and attorneys", and "engage consultants"), and providing that it "may sue and be sued in the name it is given", declares that it "is not a body corporate". If effective to prevent Queensland Rail answering the constitutional description of a corporation, that declaration would take Queensland Rail outside the operation of the *Fair Work Act 2009* (Cth), which governs employment by constitutional corporations to the exclusion of State and Territory industrial laws ...

Whatever operation the statutory declaration that Queensland Rail is not a body corporate might have under other Queensland legislation, or on any rule of the common law, that statutory declaration is ineffective to prevent Queensland Rail answering the constitutional description of a corporation. It answers that description because it is an entity established by law with capacity to own property, to contract and to sue ...

The term "corporations" is, and was in 1900, readily capable of encompassing all artificial legal persons; that is to say, all entities, not being merely natural persons, invested by law with capacity for legal relations. There is nothing in the context or in the rest of the *Constitution* to indicate that any narrower interpretation would best carry out the object and purpose of the conferral by s 51(xx) of a national legislative power with respect to both foreign corporations and trading or financial corporations formed within the limits of the Commonwealth. The constitutional context, both structural and historical, points in favour of the application of the broad orthodox historical meaning.

The constitutional reference to foreign corporations encompasses all artificial entities invested with legal personality under other systems of law. The constitutional reference to corporations formed within the limits of the Commonwealth encompasses all artificial entities invested with legal personality under Australian law.

Queensland Rail has legal personality because it is legislatively conferred with capacity to own property, to contract and to sue. It is unnecessary to consider whether any lesser subset of those attributes might suffice. The statutory declaration that Queensland Rail is not a body corporate does not deprive Queensland Rail of any of those attributes.

5.3 Laws regulating the formation of corporations are outside the scope of the corporations power

Section 51(xx) of the *Australian Constitution* does not support laws governing the process of incorporation.

The ***Incorporation Case*** explains that section 51(xx) cannot be used to enact laws regulating the formation of corporations because the terms of the provision refer expressly and only to corporations that have come into existence.

New South Wales v Commonwealth ('Incorporation Case') (1990) 169 CLR 482

Mason CJ, Brennan, Dawson, Toohey, Gaudron and McHugh JJ

The underlying question which is raised by this case is whether s 51(xx) of the Constitution empowers the Commonwealth Parliament to legislate for the incorporation of trading and financial corporations ...

The Commonwealth contention is that the words "formed within the limits of the Commonwealth" serve merely to distinguish local trading or financial corporations from foreign corporations. No doubt the words do serve that function but their plain meaning goes beyond the mere drawing of that distinction. The expressions "trading or financial" and "formed within the limits of the Commonwealth" serve to restrict the classes of domestic corporation which can be the subject of Commonwealth power. To fall within one limb of the power, a corporation must satisfy two conditions: it must be formed within the limits of the Commonwealth and it must be a trading or financial corporation. To fall within the other limb, a corporation must be a foreign corporation, that is, a corporation formed outside the limits of the Commonwealth. The distinction based on the place of formation is obvious, but the basis of the distinction is formation.

The word "formed" is a past participle used adjectivally, and the participial phrase "formed within the limits of the Commonwealth" is used to describe corporations which have been or shall have been created in Australia. (Clearly enough, the phrase is used to describe corporations formed after as well as those formed before federation.) The subject of a valid law is restricted by that phrase to corporations which have undergone or shall have undergone the process of formation in the past, present or future. That is to say, the power is one with respect to "formed corporations". That being so, the words "formed within the limits of the Commonwealth" exclude the process of incorporation itself. Such corporations are distinguished from corporations which have been or shall have been created outside the limits of Australia ...

[T]he generality imported by the words "with respect to" cannot expand a power over existing ("formed") corporations into a power to form corporations. The power conferred by s 51(xx) to make laws with respect to artificial legal persons is not a power to bring into existence the artificial legal persons upon which laws made under the power can operate ...

To overcome the effect of this decision, the States 'referred' power to make laws about the formation of corporations to the Commonwealth. Federal laws about the formation of corporations are therefore supported by the power in section 51(xxxvii) of the *Australian Constitution* to make laws with respect to 'matters referred to the Parliament of the Commonwealth by the Parliament or Parliaments of any State or States'.

5.4 What are 'foreign, trading, and financial corporations'?

Foreign corporations

In the ***Incorporation Case***, the High Court explained that a foreign corporation is 'a corporation formed outside the limits of the Commonwealth'. In the ***Queensland Rail Case***, Gageler J commented that the 'constitutional reference to foreign corporations encompasses all artificial entities invested with legal personality under other systems of law'.

Trading and financial corporations formed within the limits of the Commonwealth

The ***Incorporation Case*** explained that to be a trading or financial corporation formed within the limits of the Commonwealth 'a corporation must satisfy two conditions: it must be formed within the limits of the Commonwealth and it must be a trading or financial corporation'.

Adamson's Case holds that a trading corporation is a corporation that engages in substantial trading activities. Trading activities was defined to mean 'business activities carried on with a view to earning revenue'. In this case, the High Court held that the Western Australian State League, the entity governing the Australian rules football competition in Western Australia, and the West Perth Club, which had a team in that competition, were each trading corporations. Their trading activities included holding sports matches for profit, hiring players for remuneration, selling tickets and selling broadcast rights.

R v Federal Court of Australia; Ex parte Western Australian National Football League ('Adamson's Case') (1979) 143 CLR 190

The Australian rules football professional competition player transfer system would be in breach of the* Trade Practices Act 1974 *(Cth) if the various clubs and the leagues operating the national and State competitions were trading corporations and thus subject to the Act.

Barwick CJ

There can be no doubt that both the prosecutors and, for that matter, the National League are corporations. The first two are registered under the *Associations Incorporation Act, 1895–1969* (WA) ("the Associations Act") and consequently incorporated: see s 3 of the Associations Act. The National League is incorporated under the *Companies Act 1961* (Vic) ...

Whilst it is in a sense true to say that the constitutional power is not a power to legislate with respect to the trading activities of corporations, the constitutional description cannot, in my opinion, properly be limited to the making of laws with respect to corporations which were formed as trading corporations, that is to say, as corporations the sole or predominant purpose of whose incorporation was to trade, however widely that word might be defined ...

The only sure guide to the nature of the company is a purview of its current activities, a judgment as to its nature being made after an overview of all those activities.

I remain of the firm conviction that for constitutional purposes a corporation formed within the limits of Australia will satisfy the description "trading corporation" if trading is a substantial corporate activity. Its activities rather than the purpose of its incorporation will designate its relevant character ... It is the corporation which satisfies the description which is the subject matter of the power ... But once it is found that trading is a substantial and not a merely peripheral activity not forbidden by the organic rules of the corporation, the conclusion that the corporation is a trading corporation is open ...

I now consider what the Club and the State League were in fact engaged in doing. Trade for constitutional purposes cannot be confined to dealing in goods or commodities. Its full parameters may be difficult of definition. But the commercial nature of an activity is an element in deciding whether the action is in trade or trading ...

The central activity of the Club and of the League is the promotion of Australian Rules Football. The major avenue chosen for such promotion is the organization and presentation of competition matches in which the players may be, and I gather mostly are, professionals employed and paid for their participation in those matches which are played on grounds usually under the control of the Club or League, either ad hoc or under some form of tenure ...

It was objected by the prosecutors' counsel that the Club was merely conducting a sport and therefore could not be regarded as being in trade. Of course, football of any code may be a sport, as distinct from a trade, when played solely for its own sake as a pastime upon an amateur footing. But what the Club and the League conduct is far removed from any such concept of sport. The players are professionals employed for wages in the playing of the code ...

Charges are made for admission to the grounds under the control of the Club to view the matches promoted by it: the proceeds of the admission charges are received by the State League but part thereof is distributed to the Club, as the Club expects and intends when conducting the matches. The moneys thus received by the Club, usually from the gate money, form a substantial part of its income. It is true that no part of the income of the Club or League is distributable amongst its members. But considerable profit is made by the Club or by the State League out of which considerable assets are built up.

In my opinion, the presentation of a football match as a commercial venture for profit to the promoting body is an activity of trade ...

Here, however, the commercial activity of the Club is not limited to the promotion of football matches. A diverse range of advertising rights, television rights and sundry other rights are sold in connexion with the presentation of the matches ...

Mason J

"Trading corporation" is not and never has been a term of art or one having a special legal meaning. Nor, as the Chief Justice pointed out, was there a generally accepted definition of the expression in the nineteenth century. Essentially it is a description or label given to a corporation when its trading activities form a sufficiently significant proportion of its overall activities as to merit its description as a trading corporation ...

Not every corporation which is engaged in trading activity is a trading corporation. The trading activity of a corporation may be so slight and so incidental to some other principal activity, viz. religion or education in the case of a church or school, that it could not be described as a trading corporation. Whether the trading activities of a particular corporation are sufficient to warrant its being characterized as a trading corporation is very much a question of fact and degree ...

The prosecutors' case is that the trading activities of the two Leagues are incidental to their main objects which are the promotion and encouragement of the sport as a recreation. This to my mind is an inversion of the true position. To me it seems that the sport is promoted and encouraged as a means of ensuring the receipt of the large financial returns which are associated with it. The financial revenue of the Leagues is so great and the commercial means by which it is achieved so varied that I have no hesitation in concluding that trading constitutes their principal activity. In saying this I treat all their activities which I have listed and which produce revenue as trading activities. I do not limit the concept of trading to buying and selling at a profit; it extends to business activities carried on with a view to earning revenue ...

In ***State Superannuation Board v Trade Practices Commission***, the High Court adopted an equivalent test for determining whether a corporation is a financial corporation. A financial corporation is a corporation that engages in substantial financial activities.

State Superannuation Board v Trade Practices Commission (1982) 150 CLR 282

The State Superannuation Board was established by Victorian legislation to administer a fund to provide pensions for public servants. If the Board was a financial corporation it would be subject to the* Trade Practices Act 1974 *(Cth).

Mason, Murphy and Deane JJ

The appellant is a body corporate constituted by the Superannuation Act 1925 (Vic) and continued in existence by the Superannuation Act 1958 (Vic). It is charged with the administration of the Superannuation Fund established by the first Act and continued by the second Act for the purpose of providing pensions for public servants and other officers and with the investment of the Fund in the manner set out in s 6 of the 1958 Act. In the course of discharging its statutory responsibilities the appellant from time to time invests moneys forming part of the Superannuation Fund in mortgages of land ...

It is our view that the Court's approach to the ascertainment of what constitutes a "financial corporation" should be the same as its approach to what constitutes a "trading corporation", subject to making due allowance for the difference between "trading" and "financial". After all, the two adjectives form part of the general category "and trading or financial corporations formed within the limits of the Commonwealth". The two classes are not mutually exclusive – a corporation may be a financial as well as a trading corporation.

In this respect the decision in *Adamson* is of importance for two reasons. First, the majority of the Court (Barwick CJ, Mason, Jacobs and Murphy JJ), rejecting the argument that the purpose for which a corporation is formed is the sole or principal criterion of its character as a trading corporation, concluded that the relevant character of the football leagues and the football club was to be ascertained by reference to their established activities ...

Secondly, the judgments of the majority in *Adamson* make it clear that, in having regard to the activities of a corporation for the purpose of ascertaining its trading character, the Court looks beyond its "predominant and characteristic activity" ...

The nature and the extent or volume of a corporation's financial activities needed to justify its description as a financial corporation do not call for much discussion in the present case. A finance company is an obvious example of a financial corporation because it deals in finance for commercial purposes, whether by way of making loans, entering into hire purchase agreements or providing credit in other forms, and this activity is not undertaken for the purpose of carrying on some other business.

However, just as a corporation may be a trading corporation, notwithstanding that its trading activities are entered into in the course of carrying on some primary or dominant undertaking, so also with a corporation which engages in financial activities in the course of carrying on its primary or dominant undertaking. Thus a corporation which is formed by an employer to provide superannuation benefits for its employees and those of associated employers may nevertheless be a financial corporation if it engages in financial activities in order to provide or augment the superannuation benefits.

In ***State Superannuation Board***, Gibbs CJ and Wilson J dissented. They held that to be a trading or financial corporation the trading or financial activities of the corporation must be the primary activities of the corporation.

In the ***Tasmanian Dam Case***, the High Court reaffirmed the substantial activities test. A corporation is a trading or financial corporation if the corporation engages in substantial trading or financial activities, even if those activities are not the predominant activities of the corporation and even if those activities are undertaken to enable some other principal undertaking.

Commonwealth v Tasmania ('Tasmanian Dam Case') (1983) 158 CLR 1

The Hydro-Electric Commission of Tasmania was established by Tasmanian legislation to produce hydro-electricity from a dam it was to construct on the Franklin River and to sell that electricity. Federal legislation had the effect of prohibiting a trading corporation from doing those things. The High Court held that, even though the Commission had extensive other activities, the Commission was a trading corporation.

Mason J

The Commission has an important policy-making role. It is the generator of electrical power for Tasmania for distribution to the public and for this purpose it engages on a large scale in the construction of dams and generating plants. In this respect its operations are largely conducted in the public interest.

However, *WA National Football League* demonstrates that these considerations do not exclude the Commission from the category of "trading corporations". The majority judgment in *State Superannuation Board* pointed out ... that the case decided that a trading corporation whose trading activities take place so that it may carry on some other primary or dominant undertaking (which is not trading) may nevertheless be a trading corporation.

The agreed facts show that the Commission sells electrical power in bulk and by retail on a very large scale. This activity in itself designates the Commission as a trading corporation ...

The substantial activities test for determining whether a corporation is a trading or financial corporation cannot be applied in cases where a corporation has no activities. ***Fencott v Muller*** held that where a corporation has no activities, the corporation's character is to be determined by reference to the purposes for which it was established.

Fencott v Muller (1983) 152 CLR 570

Oakland was a 'shelf company' that had not yet engaged in any activities. The High Court held that Oakland was both a trading corporation and a financial corporation because the

purposes for which Oakland was established included undertaking financial transactions and engaging in trading activity.

Mason, Murphy, Brennan and Deane JJ

Oakland has not engaged in trading activities. Nor has it engaged in any financial activity, for it has not hitherto engaged in any financial transactions. And so the question arises whether a corporation with objects and powers appropriate for a trading or financial corporation can bear that character before it engages in any trading or financial activity. That question did not arise for consideration in *Adamson's Case*. The majority judgments in that case which held that the established activities of the football league concluded its character as a trading corporation did not suggest that trading activities are the sole criterion of character.

Absent those activities, the character of a corporation must be found in other indicia. While its constitution will never be completely irrelevant, it is in a case such as the present where a corporation has not begun, or has barely begun, to carry on business that its constitution, including its objects, assumes particular significance as a guide (see *State Superannuation Board (Vic) v Trade Practices Commission* (1982) 150 CLR, at p 304). Oakland's memorandum and articles of association reveal that the objects for which it was established include engaging in financial activities and carrying on a large variety of businesses, though it lay dormant – "on the shelf" – after its incorporation. In the circumstances of the present case, there is no better guide to its character than its constitution and its constitution establishes its character as a trading or financial corporation. It is immaterial whether it is a trading corporation or a financial corporation or which of those characters its future activities may give it.

In the ***WorkChoices Case***, the tests for determining the character of corporations were not in issue and therefore not addressed in any substantive way. However, the judgments appear to leave open the possibility that the High Court may reconsider the tests in a future case.

New South Wales v Commonwealth ('WorkChoices Case') (2006) 229 CLR 1

Gleeson CJ, Gummow, Hayne, Heydon and Crennan JJ

The challenge to the validity of the legislation enacted in reliance on the corporations power does not put in issue directly the characteristics of corporations covered by s 51(xx). It does not call directly for an examination of what is a trading or financial corporation formed within the limits of the Commonwealth. (Plainly, a foreign corporation is a corporation formed outside the limits of the Commonwealth.) No party or intervener called in question what was said about trading and financial corporations in *R v Federal Court of Australia; Ex parte WA National Football League,*

Actors and Announcers Equity Association v Fontana Films Pty Ltd, *State Superannuation Board v Trade Practices Commission* or *Fencott v Muller*.

Callinan J

A question left unanswered in this case is as to which corporations may be characterized as financial and trading corporations, a very big question indeed, and which will occupy, I believe, a deal of the time of the courts in the future. It is not answerable in this case, because of the absence of actual facts to which the decision here will apply ...

Courts routinely apply the substantial activities test. For example in ***ALDI Foods Ltd v Transport Workers Union***, the Full Court of the Federal Court held that the Transport Workers Union was not a trading corporation because the entity's substantial activities were industrial advocacy on behalf of members, which is not a trading or commercial activity.

ALDI Foods Ltd v Transport Workers Union [2020] FCAFC 231

ALDI alleged that the Transport Workers Union had engaged in contraventions of the* Australian Consumer Law, *which is binding on trading corporations, in the course of a union campaign for better conditions for truck drivers who deliver stock to ALDI stores.

Besanko, Bromberg and O'Bryan JJ

As stated by the majority in *Adamson*, the expression "trading corporation" is not a term of art and connotes what is commonly accepted to be trade in accordance with the ordinary meaning of that term. It is a commercial or business activity principally involving the supply of goods or services for reward. We consider that there is a clear distinction between activities which constitute industrial or political (in the broad sense) advocacy by a body on behalf of its members and activities that are trading or commercial ...

No evidence was adduced by ALDI to show that the TWU undertook any material activities beyond those stated in clause 2 of its Rules [concerning industrial advocacy and facilitation of benefits to workers]. The primary judge found that, while some branches of the TWU sold some union merchandise, the sales involved sums of about $1,000 or less.

In our view, the fact that members of the TWU pay membership fees does not convert the TWU's core activities (industrial advocacy) into a commercial or business activity. The advocacy activities of a union cannot be characterised as the supply of a service (advocacy) for reward (membership fees) in a trading or commercial sense because the service (advocacy) lacks a defined content. Such advocacy is incapable of being conceived in a contractual framework which is the foundation and touchstone of trading and commercial activity. That is because the advocacy must respond to the industrial landscape across numerous businesses which inevitably are subject to constant change. The focus and priorities of the union must respond to those changes.

Furthermore, the TWU is subject to democratic control by its members, which means that the focus and priorities of the union will also respond to the governance and direction given by members from time to time. In that context, the description of a service for reward is inapt. That is not to suggest that a union is incapable of conducting a commercial or business activity; for example, a union may provide training or similar services for reward. Our conclusion is limited to the contention advanced by ALDI that the primary activities of the TWU, industrial advocacy, are a commercial or business activity.

5.5 Laws with respect to the activities of constitutional corporations

The corporations power supports laws regulating the activities of constitutional corporations.

One of the first cases considering the scope of the corporations power – ***Huddart, Parker & Co Pty Ltd v Moorehead*** (1909) 8 CLR 330 – relying in part on the now discredited reserved State powers doctrine gave the corporations power a very narrow interpretation. In that case, the High Court held that a federal statute prohibiting constitutional corporations from engaging in anti-competitive conduct was not supported by the corporations power.

Huddart, Parker was overruled in the ***Concrete Pipes Case.*** It is now settled law that the corporations power supports laws regulating the trading activities of constitutional corporations, and by parity of reasoning the financial activities of constitutional corporations.

Strickland v Rocla Concrete Pipes Ltd ('Concrete Pipes Case') (1971) 124 CLR 468

Federal legislation established a register of anti-competitive trade agreements. Any such agreement to which a constitutional corporation was a party had to be registered. The High Court held that the legislation was supported by the corporations power.

Barwick CJ

It is plain enough from a reading of the reasons given by the majority in *Huddart, Parker & Co Pty Ltd v Moorehead* that the influence of the then current reserved powers doctrine was so strong that the Court was driven to emasculate the legislative power given by s 51(xx) and to confine it in substance to the statutory recognition of corporations falling within the terms of the paragraph and the fixing of the conditions upon which they might enter trade in Australia: for the rest, their trading activities in intra-State trade was a matter for the State legislation exclusively ...

I therefore conclude that the reasoning of this Court in *Huddart, Parker & Co. Pty Ltd v Moorehead* was in error and that it ought not be accepted now by this Court ...

[The laws at issue in *Huddart, Parker*] were clearly laws regulating and controlling amongst other things the trading activities of foreign corporations and trading and financial corporations formed within the limits of the Commonwealth. In my opinion such laws were laws with respect to such corporations. They dealt with the very heart of the purpose for which the corporation was formed, for whether a trading or financial corporation, by assumption, its purpose is to trade, trade for constitutional purposes not being limited to dealings in goods ...

I ought to observe that it does not follow either as a logical proposition, or, if in this instance there be a difference, as a legal proposition, ... that any law which in the range of its command or prohibition includes foreign corporations or trading or financial corporations formed within the limits of the Commonwealth is necessarily a law with respect to the subject matter of s 51(xx). Nor does it follow that any law which is addressed specifically to such corporations or some of them is such a law. Sections 5(1) and 8(1), in my opinion, were valid because they were regulating and controlling the trading activities of trading corporations and thus within the scope of s 51(xx) ...

A law requiring the registration of trading agreements restrictive of trade to which a foreign corporation or a trading or financial corporation formed within the limits of the Commonwealth is a party, and requiring the corporation to give particulars of such an agreement under penalty of a fine for failing to do so, appears to me clearly to be a law with respect to corporations of the kind described. As I have said, the making of such an agreement in the course of trade is truly a trading activity. Such a law is a law regulating and controlling the trading activities of such corporations. It would in my opinion clearly be within the legislative power of the Parliament granted by s 51(xx) ...

It is also settled that laws regulating what non-corporations may do with respect to the trading and financial activities of constitutional corporations are laws with respect to constitutional corporations.

Fontana Films considered laws prohibiting secondary boycotts against trading corporations. A secondary boycott is an attempt to influence an entity by applying pressure to another entity. For example, workers might go on strike at a business that provides raw materials to another business in order to harm production at that other business and pressure that other business to change its practices. The High Court held that such laws are supported by the corporations power, even though the legal obligations created by the law are not imposed on corporations. The legal obligations are imposed on people in connection with those people's interactions with trading corporations, and for that reason answer the description of laws with respect to trading corporations.

The judgments in ***Fontana Films*** can be divided into a narrow view and a broader view of the scope of the corporations power. On the narrow view exemplified by Gibbs CJ's judgment, the law was valid because its operation had a sufficient connection with the trading activities of constitutional corporations. On the wider view exemplified by Mason J's judgment, the law was valid because its operation had a sufficient connection with entities answering the description of constitutional corporations. This broader view rejects the need for a nexus with the trading activities of constitutional corporations.

Actors and Announcers Equity Association v Fontana Films Pty Ltd (1982) 150 CLR 169

Gibbs CJ

Section 45D(1)(b)(i) imposes no obligation on a corporation. Its command is directed to persons who need not be corporations. However, what is forbidden is conduct that hinders or prevents the supply of goods or services by a third person to a corporation, or the acquisition of goods or services by a third person from a corporation. The conduct is forbidden only if it is engaged in for the purpose of causing substantial loss or damage to the business of a corporation, and if it would have or be likely to have that effect. The section protects a corporation from certain conduct which is intended and likely to cause substantial loss or damage to its business ...

For present purposes, however, it is enough that it is established by *Strickland v Rocla Concrete Pipes Ltd* that a law which governs the trading activities of trading corporations formed within the limits of the Commonwealth is within the scope of s 51(xx): see especially at pp 490, 508, 525. Of course, the law in the present case does not regulate or govern the activities of trading corporations; it regulates the conduct of others. But the conduct to which the law is directed is conduct designed to cause, and likely to cause, substantial loss or damage to the business of a trading corporation formed within the limits of the Commonwealth. I can see no reason in principle why such a law should necessarily fall outside the scope of s 51(xx). A law may be one with respect to a trading corporation, although it casts obligations upon a person other than a trading corporation ...

Mason J

The judgments in *Strickland*, in *R v Trade Practices Tribunal; Ex parte St George County Council* (1974) 130 CLR 533, esp at pp 542–543, and more recently in *R v Federal Court of Australia; Ex parte WA National Football League*, do not attempt to define the limits of the corporations power. They proceed upon the footing that the power extends to the regulation of the trading activities of foreign corporations and trading and financial corporations formed within the limits of the Commonwealth, without deciding whether it travels further ...

I should not wish it to be thought from what I have said that the corporations power is confined in its application to trading corporations to laws that deal with their trading activities. The subject of the power is corporations – of the kind described; the power is not expressed as one with respect to the activities of corporations, let alone activities of a particular kind or kinds. A constitutional grant of legislative power should be construed liberally and not in any narrow or pedantic fashion ...

Nowhere in the Constitution is there to be found a secure footing for an implication that the power is to be read down so that it relates to "the trading activities of trading corporations" and, I would suppose, correspondingly to the financial activities of financial corporations and perhaps to the foreign aspects of foreign corporations. Even if it be thought that it was concern as to the trading activities of trading corporations and financial activities of financial corporations that led to the singling out in s 51(xx) of these domestic corporations from other domestic corporations it would be mere speculation to say that it was intended to confine the legislative power so given to these activities. The competing hypothesis, which conforms to the accepted approach to the construction of a legislative power in the Constitution is that it was intended to confer comprehensive power with respect to the subject matter so as to ensure that all conceivable matters of national concern would be comprehended. The power should, therefore, in accordance with that approach, be construed as a plenary power with respect to the subjects mentioned free from the unexpressed qualifications which have been suggested ...

The ***Tasmanian Dam Case*** upheld a law that operated to regulate things done by constitutional corporations for the purposes of their trading activities.

Commonwealth v Tasmania ('Tasmanian Dam Case') (1983) 158 CLR 1

The effect of certain provisions of the* World Heritage Properties Conservation Act 1983 *(Cth) was to prohibit trading corporations from damaging certain property without the consent of the Minister. The property protected included the area in which the Tasmanian Hydro-Electric Commission, a trading corporation, intended to construct a dam which would produce hydro-electricity to be sold.

Mason J

The question then is whether the corporations power extends to the regulation of the activities of trading corporations, not being trading activities ...

[I]t has been affirmatively established that the power extends to the regulation and the protection of the trading activities of trading corporations; *Rocla Pipes; Actors & Announcers Equity Association v Fontana Films Pty Ltd; Fencott v Muller.* Whether the power goes further remains to be decided. Barwick CJ, Murphy, Brennan JJ and I have indicated that it does; *Rocla Pipes; Fontana.* It would be unduly restrictive to confine the power to the regulation and protection of the trading activities of trading corporations. After all, the subject matter of the power is persons, not activities ...

There is, certainly, no sound reason for denying that the power should extend to the regulation of acts undertaken by trading corporations for the purpose of engaging in their trading activities ...

[I]t might be said that the power extends to, but does not travel beyond, such aspects of a trading corporation's structure, business and affairs, as have relevance to its character as a trading corporation. This view of the power would, if accepted, enable Parliament to enact legislation regulating (and prohibiting) acts and activities engaged in by a trading corporation for the purpose of engaging in its trading activities.

However, it seems to me that there are three powerful objections to the adoption of this limited construction. The first is that this approach to the scope of the power in its application to the classes of corporations mentioned, though it has some plausibility in the case of trading corporations, has none at all in the case of financial and foreign corporations. It can scarcely have been intended that the scope of the power was to be limited by reference to the foreign aspects of foreign corporations and the financial aspects of financial corporations. And it would be irrational to conclude that the power is plenary in the case of those corporations, but limited in the case of trading corporations.

The second objection is that the interpretation fails to give effect to the principle that a legislative power conferred by the Constitution should be liberally construed. And the final objection is that a power to make laws with respect to corporations (of designated categories), as in the case of a power with respect to natural persons, would seem naturally to extend to their acts and activities.

There is nothing in the context of s 51(xx) which compels the conclusion that the language in which the power is expressed should be given a restricted interpretation. In this respect I mention, without repeating, what I said in *Fontana*. In the result we should recognize that the power confers a plenary power with respect to the categories of corporation mentioned ...

A law which prohibits trading and foreign corporations from doing an act is a law about trading and foreign corporations, notwithstanding that it is also a law about the act which is prohibited. It is a law which imposes obligations on such corporations enforceable by injunctions. Consequently, it is simply impossible to say that the law has no substantial connexion with trading and foreign corporations ...

The decision in the ***Tasmanian Dam Case*** is clearly wider than the narrow view expressed in ***Fontana Films*** – that the corporations power extends only to regulating the trading and financial activities of constitutional corporations. The laws upheld in the *Tasmanian Dam Case* did not regulate the trading activities of constitutional corporations. The laws regulated things done for the purposes of trading activities. The laws could have been upheld by noticing a sufficient connection between the operation of the laws and the trading activities of constitutional corporations, since what the laws regulated were things done for the purposes of trading activities. However, Mason J's judgment upheld the laws by applying the broader view he expressed in *Fontana Films* – that the corporations power extends to regulating any activities undertaken by constitutional corporations.

That broader view commanded majority support in the ***WorkChoices Case***. That case upheld laws singling out constitutional corporations as the object of statutory command.

New South Wales v Commonwealth ('WorkChoices Case') (2006) 229 CLR 1

Gleeson CJ, Gummow, Hayne, Heydon and Crennan JJ

The plaintiffs in the present matters submitted that the analysis made by Dawson J in the *Tasmanian Dam Case*, and subsequently amplified in *Re Dingjan*, embodied the distinctive character test and is the preferable approach to determining whether a law is supported by s 51(xx). It is an approach which would read the power as confined to making laws with respect to the trading activities of Australian trading corporations and the financial activities of Australian financial corporations. But that, of course, is not what s 51(xx) says.

It is an approach that presents a particular difficulty with foreign corporations. The character of a foreign corporation is fixed by its status, not by its activities. The power to legislate with respect to foreign corporations would be very narrow if the law must focus upon the status of the corporation. There is no immediately evident reason for there to be such disconformity between the ambit of legislative power with respect to Australian corporations and the ambit of legislative power with respect to foreign corporations ...

The corporations power can be used to regulate any of the activities of constitutional corporations, even, as in ***Fontana Films***, where constitutional corporations are not the object of statutory command.

5.6 Laws where constitutional corporations are the object of statutory command

The corporations power supports laws that single out constitutional corporations as the object of statutory command – such as provisions providing 'A corporation shall not ... ' or 'A corporation must ... ' – without the need for the law to satisfy any other test.

In ***Huddart, Parker & Co Pty Ltd v Moorehead***, the High Court was emphatic that a law would not be supported by the corporations just because the law singled out corporations as the object of statutory command.

Huddart, Parker & Co Pty Ltd v Moorehead (1909) 8 CLR 330

Higgins J

What, then, has been enacted? Shortly stated, this Act, in secs 4 and 7, forbids, as to Inter-State and foreign trade, certain contracts and combinations, intended to restrain or to monopolize trade, or to destroy Australian industries by unfair competition; and they are forbidden to persons as well as to corporations. These sections are admittedly laws "with respect to" Inter-State and foreign trade within sec 51(i) of the Constitution; and it is only because they do regulate such trade that they are valid. But then come secs 5 and 8 of the Act, under which precisely the same kind of conduct is forbidden as to trade of any kind, whether internal to a State or not, but it is forbidden to corporations only; and we are asked to treat the very same words as were used in secs 4 and 7 as now being legislation, not with respect to trade, but with respect to corporations.

To say the least, this is a startling change of front. Secs 4 and 7 indicate that the Parliament regards all such contracts and combinations as bad, not bad in the case of corporations only; and it is obvious that secs 5 and 8 are confined to corporations merely because the Parliament thinks it has power to legislate with respect to such contracts and combinations in the case of corporations and not in the case of persons. This consideration does not settle the matter, however; for whatever Parliament thought, whatever was Parliament's motive, the question remains, is this a law "with respect to" – that is to say, as I understand it, on the subject of – corporations.

If the argument for the Crown is right, the results are certainly extraordinary, big with confusion. If it is right, the Federal Parliament is in a position to frame a new system of libel laws applicable to newspapers owned by corporations, while the State law of libel would have to remain applicable to newspapers owned by individuals. If it is right, the Federal Parliament is competent to enact licensing Acts, creating a new scheme of administration and of offences applicable only to hotels belonging to corporations. If it is right, the Federal Parliament may enact that no foreign or trading or financial corporation shall pay its employees less than 10s per day, or charge more than 6 per cent interest, whereas other corporations and persons would be free from such restrictions. If it is right, the Federal Parliament can enact that no officer of a corporation shall be an Atheist or a Baptist, or that all must be teetotallers. If it is right, the Federal Parliament can repeal the Statute of Frauds for contracts of a corporation, or may make some new Statute of Limitations applicable only to corporations.

Huddart, Parker was decided before the ***Engineers' Case*** rejected the reserved State powers doctrine and before the High Court came to accept the reality of dual characterisation.

Re Dingjan considered a federal law regulating unfair contracts imposed on independent contractors where the contract related to the business of a constitutional corporation, even if a constitutional corporation was not a party to the contract. A majority of the High Court held that the law was not supported by the corporations power. Justice Gaudron dissented in a judgment which was later adopted by a majority of the High Court in the ***WorkChoices Case***.

Re Dingjan; Ex Parte Wagner (1995) 183 CLR 323

Gaudron J (dissenting)

When s 51(xx) is approached on the basis that it is to be construed according to its terms and not by reference to unnecessary implications and limitations, it is clear that, at the very least, a law which is expressed to operate on or by reference to the business functions, activities or relationships of constitutional corporations is a law with respect to those corporations. In this regard, it is sufficient to note that, although the business activities of trading and financial corporations may be more extensive than their trading or financial activities, those corporations, nonetheless, take their character from their business activities ...

As their business activities signify whether or not corporations are trading or financial corporations and the main purpose of the power to legislate with respect to foreign corporations must be directed to their business activities in Australia, it follows that the power conferred by s 51(xx) extends, at the very least, to the business functions and activities of constitutional corporations and to their business relationships. And those functions, activities and relationships will, in the ordinary course, involve individuals, and not merely individuals through whom the corporation acts, as in *Fencott v Muller*, or the control of whose conduct is directly connected with the regulation or protection of the corporation, as in Actors and Announcers Equity Association ...

Once it is accepted that s 51(xx) extends to the business functions, activities and relationships of constitutional corporations, it follows that it also extends to the persons by and through whom they carry out those functions and activities and with whom they enter into those relationships. And when regard is had to the type of contract with which ss 127A and 127B are concerned, namely, a contract for the performance of work by an independent contractor, it is clear that "a contract relating to the business of a constitutional corporation", as those words are used in s 127C(1)(b) of the Act ... will inevitably have as its other party a person who performs the business functions or carries out the business activities of a constitutional corporation or a person who is in a business relationship with that corporation. That other party is within the reach of the legislative power conferred by s 51(xx) of the Constitution, at least to the extent of those functions and activities or that business relationship ...

The ***WorkChoices Case*** holds that the corporations power supports laws that single out corporations as the object of statutory command. In that case, the High Court upheld legislation prescribing a scheme of industrial relations and employment regulation governing the relationship between corporations and their employees.

New South Wales v Commonwealth ('WorkChoices Case') (2006) 229 CLR 1

Gleeson CJ, Gummow, Hayne, Heydon and Crennan JJ

The plaintiffs' submissions about s 51(xx) were directed principally to identifying what were said to be relevant limits to the power. There were three principal strands to the submissions. First, it was submitted that s 51(xx) permits the making of a law with respect to only the external relationships of constitutional corporations, not their internal relationships, and that the relationship between a constitutional corporation and its employees should be classified as "internal". Secondly, both in amplification of and as an alternative to the first submission, it was submitted that it is insufficient for a law to be characterised as a law with respect to constitutional corporations that the law confers rights or imposes obligations upon them. If a positive test is to be adopted, the preferred test was said to be a distinctive character test – that the nature of the corporation is significant as an element in the nature or character of the laws. Thirdly, as indicated earlier, it was submitted that s 51(xx) is to be read down, or confined in its operation, by reference to s 51(xxxv), with the consequence that the Parliament has no power to legislate with respect to the relationship between a constitutional corporation and its employees except pursuant to s 51(xxxv) ...

A distinction between "internal" and "external" relationships

Adopting a distinction which ... distinguishes between matters internal and external to a corporation approaches the question in a way that distracts attention from the issues that must be considered. Those issues focus upon the text of s 51(xx) and the ambit of the power it confers on the federal Parliament, not upon such matters as whether, for example, a corporation's dealings with persons the corporation hopes will become its unsecured note-holders are "internal" or "external" dealings ...

The course of authority after *Huddart Parker*

The dissenting members of the Court in *Re Dingjan*, Mason CJ, Deane and Gaudron JJ, took a view of the reach of s 51(xx) wider than that of the majority. Particular reference need now be made only to the reasons of Gaudron J (with which Deane J agreed). Her Honour's reasoning proceeded by the following steps. First, the business activities of corporations formed within Australia signify whether they are trading or financial corporations, and the main purpose of the power to legislate with respect to foreign corporations must be directed to their business activities in Australia. Second, it follows that the power conferred by s 51(xx) extends "at the very least" to the business functions and activities of constitutional corporations and to their business relationships. Third, once the second step is accepted, it follows that the power "also extends to the persons by and through whom they carry out those functions and activities and with whom they enter into those relationships".

This understanding of s 51(xx) was subsequently amplified by Gaudron J in her reasons in *Re Pacific Coal Pty Ltd; Ex parte Construction, Forestry, Mining and Energy Union* where her Honour said:

> I have no doubt that the power conferred by s 51(xx) of the Constitution extends to the regulation of the activities, functions, relationships and the business of a corporation described in that sub-section, the creation of rights, and privileges belonging to such a corporation, the imposition of obligations on it and, in respect of those matters, to the regulation of the conduct of those through whom it acts, its employees and shareholders and, also, the regulation of those whose conduct is or is capable of affecting its activities, functions, relationships or business.

This understanding of the power should be adopted. It follows, as Gaudron J said, that the legislative power conferred by s 51(xx) "extends to laws prescribing the industrial rights and obligations of corporations and their employees and the means by which they are to conduct their industrial relations ...

A need to limit s 51(xx)?

... Reference has often been made in the cases to what are said to be the possible consequences of concluding that a law whose object of command is only constitutional corporations is a valid law. In *Huddart Parker*, Higgins J spoke of possibilities that he saw as distorting constitutional arrangements. Reference was made to the possibility of the federal Parliament framing a new system of libel laws applicable to newspapers owned by corporations, and to licensing Acts creating a new scheme of administration and of offences applicable only to hotels belonging to corporations.

In part, reference to such consequences seeks to present possible social consequences that it is said could flow if further legislation is enacted, and which it is said are to be seen as absurd or inconvenient, as a reason to confine the reach of the legislative power. Section 51(xx), like other powers, should not be given a meaning narrowed by an apprehension of extreme examples and distorting possibilities of its application to future laws ...

Thus when it is said that there is a point at which the legislative powers of the federal Parliament and the legislative powers of the States are to be divided lest the federal balance be disturbed, how is that point to be identified? ...

Whether a basis for choosing a point of balance is identified or not, the fundamental question which lies behind the plaintiffs' submissions is: what exactly is the content of the proposition that a particular construction of s 51(xx) would, or would not, impermissibly alter the federal balance? ...

General conclusions

It is convenient to summarise at this point the conclusions that follow from the preceding discussion of the arguments about s 51(xx) ... The distinction between external and internal relationships of corporations proffered by the plaintiffs as a limit to the legislative power conferred by s 51(xx) should be rejected as an inappropriate and unhelpful distinction ... The distinction finds no reflection in the Convention Debates or the drafting history of s 51(xx) and, in any event, is unstable. Adopting it would distract attention from the tasks of construing the constitutional text, identifying the legal and practical operation of the impugned law, and then assessing the sufficiency of the connection between the impugned law and the head of power.

In so far as the plaintiffs contended that a test of distinctive character or discriminatory operation is to be adopted it is enough to say that ... the impugned provisions of the Amending Act which depend upon s 51(xx) either single out constitutional corporations as the object of statutory command (and in that sense have a discriminatory operation) or, like the legislation considered in *Fontana Films*, are directed to protecting constitutional corporations from conduct intended and likely to cause loss or damage to the corporation. In so far as the plaintiffs' contentions required tests of distinctive character or discriminatory operation to be understood as inserting a new or different filter into the process of characterisation those contentions should be rejected. A law which prescribes norms regulating the relationship between constitutional corporations and their employees, or affecting constitutional corporations in the manner considered and upheld in *Fontana Films* or, as Gaudron J said in *Re Pacific Coal*, "laws prescribing the industrial rights and obligations of [constitutional] corporations and their employees and the means by which they are to conduct their industrial relations" are laws with respect to constitutional corporations ...

5.7 DISCUSSION QUESTIONS

1. What is a corporation?
2. How is it determined whether a corporation can be characterised as a trading or financial corporation?
3. Consider the judgment in ***Fencott v Muller***. Can the character of a corporation as a trading or financial corporation change over time?
4. What were the three reasons Mason J gave in the ***Tasmanian Dam Case*** for rejecting the view that the corporations power is restricted to supporting laws with respect to the trading activities of trading corporations and the financial activities of financial corporations?
5. Problem question: Consider the hypothetical statute below and the following scenario.

Economic Regulation Act 2023 (Cth)

1. This Act applies to:
   a. natural persons, and
   b. foreign corporations, and trading or financial corporations formed within the limits of the Commonwealth.
2. It is unlawful to employ a person to provide income tax advice to members of the public or to assist members of the public prepare income tax returns unless the person holds a university degree. Penalty: 150 penalty units.

Your Tax Advisors Pty Ltd runs a financial advice business with outlets in various shopping centres and provides assistance to people in preparing income tax returns. Janice Jones is a soletrader and runs her own small business providing assistance to people in preparing income tax returns.

Your Tax Advisors Pty Ltd hires a person who does not hold a university degree to assist members of the public prepare income tax returns. Janice Jones also hires a person who does not hold a university degree to assist members of the public prepare income tax returns. Both are fined.

Are the fines imposed supported by the corporations power?

6 EXTERNAL AFFAIRS POWER

6.1 Overview

This chapter examines the external affairs power. Section 51(xxix) of the *Australian Constitution* grants the Commonwealth Parliament power to make laws with respect to 'external affairs'.

Australian Constitution

Section 51 Legislative Powers of the Parliament

The Parliament shall, subject to this Constitution, have power to make laws for the peace, order, and good government of the Commonwealth with respect to:

...

(xxix) external affairs;

...

The external affairs power has three key components and is both a subject-matter and purpose power. The external affairs power empowers the Commonwealth to make laws with respect to the subject-matters of:

1. international relations, and
2. matters geographically external to Australia.

The external affairs power also empowers the Commonwealth to make laws for the purpose of:

3. implementing Australia's international legal obligations.

The power has enabled the Commonwealth to regulate matters as diverse as aviation safety standards, racial discrimination and terrorist activity.

Key concepts considered in this chapter include:

- external affairs
- international relations
- geographical externality
- international concern
- international recommendations
- proportionality.

6.2 Terminology and overlap with the Pacific Islands relations power

The external affairs power appears to incorporate the full scope of another head of power. Section 51(xxx) of the *Australian Constitution* gives the Federal Parliament power to make laws with respect to 'the relations of the Commonwealth with the islands of the Pacific'.

The framers of the *Constitution* recognised that the Pacific islands relations power may be redundant in the sense that everything it authorises is also authorised by the external affairs power.

Official Record of the Debates of the Australasian Federal Convention, Melbourne, 21 January 1898

Mr Barton (Leader of the Convention)

It has been suggested that this sub-section is embraced in the preceding one – "External affairs and treaties." That is arguable; it is quite possible that it may be true; but there are a very large number of people who look forward with interest to the Commonwealth undertaking, as far as it can as part of the British Empire, the regulation of the Pacific Islands. It may be, I think, as there is a doubt as to whether the one thing is included in the other, and as there are a large number of people who are interested in this question, that it is better in deference to their views to leave the words as they are. As the subsection may do some good, and can do no harm, I think that the objection should not be pressed.

The High Court has never decided a case on the basis of section 51(xxx).

The choice of terminology in section 51(xxix) was explained by Barwick CJ in the ***Seas and Submerged Lands Case*** as directed at ensuring that relations with other British colonies would fall within the head of power.

New South Wales v Commonwealth ('*Seas and Submerged Lands Case*') (1975) 135 CLR 337

The High Court held that the **Seas and Submerged Lands Act 1973** *(Cth), which provides that the Commonwealth rather than the States has sovereignty in Australia's territorial sea and sovereign rights in Australia's exclusive economic zone and continental shelf, was supported by the external affairs power.*

Barwick CJ

The description of the subject matter of the power and the preference for external affairs rather than foreign affairs in the *Constitution* was doubtless designed to include within the subject matter inter-colonial matters which in Imperial days may not have been regarded as foreign affairs.

6.3 Laws with respect to international relations

One component of 'external affairs' is Australia's political relations with other countries and international legal persons. The external affairs power supports laws with respect to foreign and international relations.

R v Sharkey demonstrates that the external affairs power supports laws with respect to Australia's relations with other countries. In that case, legislation prohibiting a person in Australia exciting disaffection against the government or the Constitution of the United Kingdom or any of the King's Dominions was held to be valid under this aspect of the external affairs power.

R v Sharkey (1949) 79 CLR 121

Sharkey was leader of the Australian Communist Party. He was charged with sedition under federal legislation in relation to various comments including comments welcoming the prospect of a Soviet invasion of the United Kingdom.

Latham CJ

The relations of the Commonwealth with all countries outside Australia, including other Dominions of the Crown, are matters which fall directly within the subject of external affairs, a subject with respect to which the Commonwealth Parliament has power to pass laws - *Constitution*, s 51(xxix). The preservation of friendly relations with other Dominions is an important part of the management of the external affairs of the Commonwealth. The prevention and punishment of the excitement of disaffection within the Commonwealth against the Government or Constitution of any other Dominion may reasonably be thought by Parliament to constitute an element in the preservation of friendly relations with other Dominions.

McTiernan J

Section 24A(1) refers to the Constitutions and Governments of other Dominions. To the extent to which the sections punish the expression in Australia of dissatisfaction of a seditious character with those Constitutions and Governments, I think that the sections are justified by the power vested by s 51(xxix) to legislate with respect to external affairs. This expression has a wider meaning than strictly foreign affairs. It covers the relations between the Government of this country and the Government of another Dominion. These relations could be affected if seditious offences against the Government or Constitution of another Dominion were committed here with impunity. The power to legislate with respect to external affairs extends to the punishment in Australia of such offences ...

In ***Koowarta***, Brennan J explained that the foreign relations component of the external affairs includes power to enact laws affecting Australia's relations with 'other international persons'. International legal persons include states (in the sense of countries) as well as non-state entities such as international organisations like the United Nations.

Koowarta v Bjelke-Petersen (1982) 153 CLR 168

Brennan J

When a particular subject affects or is likely to affect Australia's relations with other international persons, a law with respect to that subject is a law with respect to external affairs. The effect of the law upon the subject which affects or is likely to affect Australia's relationships provides the connexion which the words "with respect to" require.

Those relationships, various in form and significance, are the substance of Australia's external affairs ...

In ***Thomas v Mowbray***, three judges held that laws designed to prevent terrorist acts against foreign countries are supported by the foreign relations component of the external affairs power. Comity with foreign governments and the integrity of foreign states are subject-matters capable of affecting political relations with other countries. Three judges did not address the external affairs power and one dissenting judge held that such laws do not affect Australia's relations with foreign countries.

Thomas v Mowbray (2007) 233 CLR 307

Federal legislation authorised a court to impose a control order on any person for the purpose of preventing a terrorist act. 'Terrorist act' was defined to include coercion or intimidation directed against a foreign government or a foreign public.

Gleeson CJ

I agree with Gummow and Crennan JJ that ... the legislation is supported by ... the external affairs power.

Gummow and Crennan JJ

As remarked earlier, when describing the definition in s 100.1 of the Code of "terrorist act", the object of coercion or intimidation may be the government of a foreign country or of a part thereof and "the public" includes reference to the public of a country other than Australia ...

The pursuit and advancement of comity with foreign governments and the preservation of the integrity of foreign states may be a subject matter of a law with respect to external affairs. In *XYZ v Commonwealth*, Gleeson CJ noted (with evident approval) that it was accepted that the external affairs power at least includes power to make laws in respect to matters affecting Australia's relations with other countries. The commission of "terrorist acts" in the sense defined in s 100.1 of the Code is now, even if it has not been in the past, one of these matters.

In *Suresh v Canada (Minister of Citizenship and Immigration)* [2002] 1 SCR 3 at 50, the Supreme Court of Canada said:

> It may once have made sense to suggest that terrorism in one country did not necessarily implicate other countries. But after the year 2001, that approach is no longer valid.

The Court added:

> First, the global transport and money networks that feed terrorism abroad have the potential to touch all countries, including Canada, and to thus implicate them in the terrorist activity. Second, terrorism itself is a worldwide phenomenon. The terrorist cause may focus on a distant locale, but the violent acts that support it may be close at hand. Third, preventive or precautionary state action may be justified; not only an immediate threat but also possible future risks must be considered. Fourth, Canada's national security may be promoted by reciprocal cooperation between Canada and other states in combating international terrorism.

Kirby J (dissenting)

The Commonwealth argued, however, that the Act was supported by the recognised attribute of s 51(xxix) of the *Constitution* concerning matters that affect Australia's relations with other countries. Whilst I do not doubt that "terrorism" is a matter of concern to the community of nations, I do not accept that declaring Div 104 invalid, if that result were otherwise required, would affect Australia's international relations.

The judgment of Gummow and Crennan JJ points out that the matters capable of affecting Australia's relations with other countries may change over time. The judgment notes that terrorist acts may not have always affected relations between countries but now do. Whether a matter is capable of affecting relations with other international legal persons is a question of fact. Justices Gummow and Crennan relied on the factual analysis provided in a Canadian Supreme Court decision to show that, as a matter of fact, terrorist acts are capable of affecting relations between countries.

In ***Alqudsi v Commonwealth***, the appellant argued that the foreign relations component of the external affairs power is purposive in nature. The effect of this proposition would be that the test of characterisation would not be whether there is a sufficient connection between the operation of a law and the subject-matter of foreign relations. Rather, the test of characterisation would be a test of proportionality that asks whether the operation of law is reasonably capable of being seen as appropriate and adapted to pursuing Australia's foreign relations.

The New South Wales Court of Appeal declined to decide the point having resolved the case on other grounds. The Commonwealth argued that the decided cases demonstrate that the sufficient connection test of characterisation for subject-matter powers applies to this component of the external affairs power.

Alqudsi v Commonwealth (2015) 91 NSWLR 92

Leeming JA

It was common ground that the power conferred by s 51(xxix) was engaged by laws with a sufficient connection to the foreign relations of Australia. However, the parties proffered different tests. Mr Alqudsi submitted that it was necessary for a law to have the discernible purpose of pursuing the foreign relations of Australia. He insisted that it was a purposive power, and involved the application of a test of proportionality.

The Commonwealth maintained that the power was broader. It embraced as a test what Brennan J had said in *Koowarta v Bjelke-Petersen*:

> When a particular subject affects or is likely to affect Australia's relations with other international persons, a law with respect to that subject is a law with respect to external affairs. The effect of the law upon the subject which affects or is likely to affect Australia's relationships provides the connexion which the words "with respect to" require.

Further, the Commonwealth submitted that the position was governed by *The King v Sharkey*, and required, first, identifying a "subject" which "affects or is likely to affect" Australia's international relations, and secondly, assessing whether the law was a law with respect to that subject, which essentially involved an inquiry into the effect upon that subject. Mr Alqudsi submitted that this was an unduly wide reading of *Sharkey*...

The Commonwealth also submitted that the introduction of purposive elements and proportionality into the power was "not consistent with principle. This has not been seen to be a purposive power to date and we would resist that endeavour" ...

Whatever the precise test to be applied for the foreign relations aspect of the external affairs power ... cannot affect the outcome of these appeals ...

6.4 Laws with respect to matters geographically external to Australia

Another component of external affairs is matters, things or persons occurring or situated outside Australia. This component can be referred to as the 'geographical externality component' of the external affairs power.

In ***Polyukhovich***, the High Court held that legislation making it a crime for an Australian citizen to have engaged in a war crime in Europe during World War II was supported by the external affairs power because the law operated on matters, things or persons occurring or situated outside Australia. Some of the judges accepted that mere externality was enough. In dissent, Brennan J required that there also be some nexus with Australia. In this case, Brennan J held that there was no nexus with Australia because the victims were not Australian and the alleged offender was not an Australian at the time of the alleged offending.

Polyukhovich v Commonwealth ('*War Crimes Act Case*') (1991) 172 CLR 501

Brennan J (dissenting)

Under this Act, the plaintiff is charged with offences allegedly committed in 1942 and 1943 in the Ukraine during Germany's occupation of that territory. It is alleged that he wilfully killed a number of people in pursuit of German policies – either a policy of persecuting the Jewish people or those opposed to German policies or a policy of annihilating suspected partisans or communists. The plaintiff was not then an Australian citizen or resident ...

I do not understand the phrase "external affairs" to sweep into Commonwealth power every person who exists or every relationship, set of circumstances or field of activity which exists or occurs outside Australian territory. The "affairs" which are the subject matter of the power are, in my view, the external affairs of Australia; not affairs which have nothing to do with Australia. Although affairs which exist or occur outside Australia may be described as "external" in a geographical sense, I would not hold that the Constitution confers power to enact laws affecting affairs which, though geographically external, have nothing to do with Australia. There must be some nexus, not necessarily substantial, between Australia and the "external affairs" which a law purports to affect before the law is supported by s 51(xxix) ...

It leaves no great lacuna in the plenitude of Australian legislative power to deny the character of a law with respect to external affairs to a law which does no more than affect something or somebody unconnected with Australia occurring or existing outside Australia. To take an extreme example: would a law be properly characterized as a law with respect to external affairs if it imposed a criminal penalty on a person who, being a citizen and resident of France, had dropped litter in a Parisian street forty years ago? The limits of the power conferred by s 51(xxix) are, in a real sense, a guarantee of the immunity from harassment by Australian law of persons who, having no connection with Australia, engage in conduct elsewhere which does not affect Australian interests or concerns ...

Deane J

The first thing to be stressed about s 51(xxix) of the *Constitution* for the purposes of the present case is that its reference to "External affairs" is unqualified. The paragraph does not refer to "Australia's external affairs". Nor does it limit the subject matter of the grant of power to external affairs which have some special connection with Australia. The word "external" means "outside". As a matter of language, it carries no implication beyond that of location. The word "affairs" has a wide and indefinite meaning. It is appropriate to refer to relations, matters or things. Used without qualification or limitation, the phrase "external affairs" is appropriate, in a constitutional grant of legislative power, to encompass both relationships and things: relationships with or between foreign States and foreign or international organizations or other entities; matters and things which are territorially external to Australia regardless of whether they have some identified connection with Australia or whether they be the subject matter of international treaties, dealings, rights or obligations ...

Whatever may have been the position before the emergence of Australia as a fully independent sovereign State, it should now be accepted that any law which can properly be characterized as a law with respect to any matter, thing or person occurring or situate outside Australia is a law with respect to "External affairs" for the purposes of s 51(xxix) ...

To the extent that they provide for the trial and punishment of Australian citizens and residents for acts committed outside Australia and having a specified relationship with the 1939–1945 war or armed conflict which occurred in Europe, the provisions of the Act are clearly a law or laws with respect to matters or things which occurred or were done outside Australia. It follows from what has been said above that, at least to that extent, the Act is a law with respect to "External affairs" within the meaning of that phrase as used in s 51(xxix) ...

Justice Brennan's insistence in ***Polyukhovich*** that the external affairs power supports laws with respect to matters, things and persons geographically external to Australia only where there is also some nexus with Australia was applied by all seven judges in ***Horta***. In *Horta*, it was unnecessary to decide between the mere externality principle and the requirement for an additional nexus with Australia.

The legislation considered in ***Horta*** was enacted to give effect to a treaty between Australia and Indonesia about joint exploration of oil resources in the Timor Gap. The case occurred before East Timor achieved independence from Indonesia. Mr Horta, who was an East Timorese independence leader, argued that Indonesia did not have lawful sovereignty over East Timor and the Timor Gap ocean resources. Mr Horta claimed the legislation was not supported by the external affairs power because the legislation was intended to implement a treaty that was void under international law. The High Court avoided dealing with that issue by holding that the legislation was valid because it was a law about a thing (namely, mineral resources) geographically external to Australia that had a substantial nexus with Australia.

Horta v Commonwealth (1994) 181 CLR 183

Mason CJ, Brennan, Deane, Dawson, Toohey, Gaudron and McHugh JJ

In *Polyukhovich v The Commonwealth*, Mason CJ, Deane J, Dawson J, Gaudron J and McHugh J all expressed the conclusion that a law with respect to a matter which is territorially outside Australia is a law with respect to "External affairs" for the purposes of s 51(xxix) of the Constitution. The other two members of the Court, Brennan J and Toohey J, considered that some additional factor was necessary ...

Regardless of whether the mere fact that a matter or thing is territorially outside Australia is of itself sufficient to bring a matter or thing within the phrase "External affairs" for the purposes of s 51(xxix) or whether one or other of those additional factors is necessary, it is clear that the area of the Timor Gap and the exploration for, and the exploitation of, petroleum resources within that area all fall within that phrase. Each of those matters is geographically external to Australia. There is an obvious and substantial nexus between each of them and Australia. As the enactment of the Act demonstrates, they are all matters which the Parliament recognizes as affecting or touching Australia. That being so, the enactment of a law with respect to one or all of those matters is prima facie within the legislative power conferred by s 51(xxix).

When one examines the provisions of the Act as a whole, it is clear that it can properly be characterized both as a law with respect to the area of the Timor Gap and as a law with respect to the exploration for, and exploitation of, petroleum resources within that area. Accordingly, it is prima facie a law with respect to "External affairs" for the purposes of s 51(xxix). And that is so regardless of whether the provisions of the Act enable the discharge of the obligations of Australia under the Treaty or give effect to provisions of the Treaty. Indeed, it would be so even if there were no Treaty ...

XYZ v Commonwealth confirms that mere externality is enough and that there is no requirement for an additional nexus with Australia. In that case, a law making it a crime for an Australian to have sex with minors overseas was upheld on the basis of the mere externality principle.

XYZ v Commonwealth (2006) 227 CLR 532

Gleeson CJ

The issue in this case concerns the constitutional validity of legislation enacted by the Parliament which makes it a criminal offence, punishable by the law of Australia, for an Australian citizen or resident, while outside Australia, to engage in certain forms of sexual activity involving children. The Court was informed that legislation of that nature (aimed primarily at what is sometimes called "sex tourism") has been enacted by some 34 countries. The power relied upon to support the legislation is that conferred by s 51(xxix) of the Constitution, that is, the power to make laws for the peace, order, and good government of the Commonwealth with respect to external affairs ...

There was a difference between the view of s 51(xxix) taken [in *Polyukhovich*] by Mason CJ, Deane J, Dawson J, Gaudron J and McHugh J, on the one hand, and the views of Brennan J and Toohey J on the other. That difference does not affect the point presently in issue. *Polyukhovich* held that the external affairs power covers, but is not limited to, the matter of Australia's relations with other countries. It also includes a power to make laws with respect to places, persons, matters or things outside the geographical limits of, that is, external to, Australia. That conclusion represents the current doctrine of the Court on the external affairs power, and should be maintained because it is correct ...

Gummow, Hayne and Crennan JJ

In the joint judgment of five members of the Court in the *Industrial Relations Act Case*, it was said:

> The modern doctrine as to the scope of the power conferred by s 51(xxix) was adopted in *Polyukhovich v The Commonwealth.* Dawson J expressed the doctrine in these terms:
>
> > [T]he power extends to places, persons, matters or things physically external to Australia. The word "affairs" is imprecise, but is wide enough to cover places, persons, matters or things. The word "external" is precise and is unqualified. If a place, person, matter or thing lies outside the geographical limits of the country, then it is external to it and falls within the meaning of the phrase "external affairs".
>
> Similar statements of the doctrine are to be found in the reasons for judgment of other Justices: Mason CJ; Deane J; Gaudron J; and McHugh J. They must now be taken as representing the view of the Court.

In the present case, the "matter or thing" which lies outside the geographical limits of Australia is the conduct proscribed by the terms of ss 50BA and 50BC of the *Crimes Act* ("A person must not" and "A person ... contravenes this section if" respectively). The result is that the proscribed conduct falls within the meaning of the phrase "external affairs" and supplies a sufficient "constitutional fact" ...

The reading of s 51(xxix) accepted in the *Industrial Relations Act Case* is correct and denies the reading for which the plaintiff contends in the present case ...

Alqudsi demonstrates that the geographical externality component of the external affairs power is not limited to *tangible* things and matters that are geographically external to Australia. *Intangible* things and matters are included. *Alqudsi* also demonstrates that things and matters situated within Australia are capable of having a sufficient connection with things, matters and persons geographically external to Australia.

The case considered legislation making it an offence for a person in Australia to give money or goods to, or perform services for, another person who intended to enter a foreign state with intent to engage in hostile activity. There were two geographically external elements in this case. First, the accused person's intangible mental state had a sufficient connection with something geographically external to Australia – namely, activities outside Australia carried out by other persons – because that mental state involved an intention to assist those external activities. Secondly, the accused person's tangible conduct within Australia had a sufficient connection with something geographically external to Australia – namely, the carrying out of activities outside Australia by other persons – because the conduct within Australia in fact assists the conduct outside Australia.

Alqudsi v Commonwealth (2015) 91 NSWLR 92

Section 6(1) of the **Crimes (Foreign Incursions and Recruitment) Act 1978** *(Cth) made it an offence to 'enter a foreign state with intent to engage in a hostile activity in that foreign state'. Section 7(1) of the Act made it an offence to 'give money or goods to, or perform services for, any person ... with the intention of supporting or promoting the commission of an offence against section 6'. Mr Alqudsi was charged with contravening section 7(1).*

Leeming JA

Mr Alqudsi recognised that this Court was bound by what had been held in *Polyukhovich, Horta* and *De L* and confirmed in *XYZ*. His submissions focussed on a limitation said to be found in "places, persons, matters or things" *physically* external to Australia. He submitted that what was required was *conduct* outside Australia, and that where, as here, "the only 'external' element of an offence is the offender's state of mind, there is nothing *physically* or *territorially* external to Australia" (original emphasis). He submitted that the power could not extend to intangible concepts ...

I see no reason to confine the subject matter regulated by the power to physical things. The issue is what is meant by "places, persons, matters or things" when that collocation of words was used in *Polyukhovich* and the *Industrial Relations Act Case* to describe the scope of a power to legislate with regard to geographically external affairs. I find it difficult to conceive how in that context those words could be confined to tangibles. The High Court has used a collocation of four unqualified nouns, including two ("matters" and "things") which need not necessarily be confined to tangibles, to explicate a wide constitutional term "affairs". There is no textual or structural basis in the Constitution for discerning such an implied limitation upon power. It would not be sensible to do so. Why would there be power to regulate, say, the movement outside Australia of physical precursors to nuclear or biological weapons, but no power to regulate the dissemination outside Australia of information as to how to construct such a weapon? Why would there be power to regulate, say, overseas transfers by cash or cheque or other negotiable instruments that were associated with organised crime or terrorism, but no power to regulate overseas electronic transfers?

To the contrary, on a fair reading of what Dawson J said in *Polyukhovich*, his Honour was deliberately using open-ended words to make plain that the power extended to laws regulating all manner of things, whether they be tangible or intangible, so long as they were physically external to Australia ...

What is required by s 7(1)(e) is some conduct by the supporter (say, giving money, giving a plane ticket or a false passport, or providing information about routes and contacts) with the supporter having an intention that the conduct will support or promote an offence against s 6(1)(a). It follows that there must be an intention that the conduct will support or promote a militant's entry into a foreign State. Undoubtedly, as the primary judge observed, the mental state has a connection with a matter which is geographically external to Australia (entering into a foreign State with s 6(3) intent). *But so too does the conduct*, if it is to be conduct which is undertaken with the intention of supporting or promoting the commission of an offence against s 6(1)(a).

Fundamentally, I cannot accept Mr Alqudsi's submission that the only external element is an offender's state of mind. The conduct which is undertaken with the intention of supporting or promoting the commission of an offence against s 6 is itself conduct which is linked to a place outside Australia, even if the only physical activities by the supporter take place in Australia. Only if the conduct is intended to support or promote the entry of a militant into a foreign country can the offence against s 6(1)(a) be made out. In other words, what is regulated is conduct intended to support something happening in a foreign State. Consistently with the approach taken in *Thomas v Mowbray*, I think that is sufficient for the law to be one which is with respect to external affairs.

To reiterate, there must be a sufficient connection between the head of power and the practical or legal operation of the law: *Grain Pool of Western Australia v Commonwealth*. I think that conduct which is intended to promote or support an offence under s 6(1)(a) is sufficiently connected with external affairs when it is borne in mind that s 6(1)(a) necessarily involves entry into a foreign State with a hostile intent. It is the combination of the external aspect of the supporter's mental state and the conduct undertaken by the supporter to support or promote an offence against s 6(1)(a) which cause me to conclude that s 7(1)(e) is within the head of power. The supporter's mental state concerns something external to Australia. The offence against s 6(1)(a) sought to be supported or promoted is necessarily an object external to Australia ...

6.5 Laws implementing international legal obligations

The external affairs power supports laws implementing Australia's international legal obligations. This component of the external affairs power is purposive in character, rather than being a subject-matter power. This affects the applicable test of characterisation. A law will be supported under this limb of the external affairs power where the law is capable of being considered reasonably appropriate and adapted to implementing or giving effect to an international law obligation that is: (1) a binding obligation rather than a non-binding commitment or a mere recommendation; and (2) sufficiently specific to direct the general course to be taken.

There are two main sources of international law: treaties and customary international law. International legal obligations may arise under a treaty or under customary international law.

Treaties are binding agreements between two or more international legal persons. The Commonwealth of Australia is a legal person, such that the Federal Government can enter into treaties but the States are not international legal persons and so cannot enter into treaties. Article 38(1) of the *Statute of the International Court of Justice* describes customary international law as 'international custom, as evidence of a general practice accepted as law'. The nature of customary international law was described by Brennan J in ***Polyukhovich***.

Polyukhovich v Commonwealth ('*War Crimes Act Case*') (1991) 172 CLR 501

Brennan J

[T]he custom required to evidence "a general practice accepted as law" must be "extensive and virtually uniform" (North Sea Continental Shelf Cases (1969) ICJR1, at p 43) and "followed on the basis of a claim of right and, in turn, submitted to as a matter of obligation" (MacGibbon, "Customary International Law and Acquiescence", (1957) XXXIII *The British Year Book of International Law* 115, at p 117). In *Nicaragua v United States of America* (1986) ICJR 14, the International Court of Justice accepted (at p 98) that it is "sufficient that the conduct of States should, in general, be consistent with" a postulated rule of international law, but that was a view expressed in conjunction with an inquiry whether there was an opinio juris as to the binding character of the postulated rule (see pp 99–101). An opinio juris supportive of a postulated rule of customary international law must explain and inform the practice of States in order to show that that practice is "accepted as law". The principle is conveniently stated by Dr Akehurst's summary of his article "Custom as a Source of International Law", (1974–1975) XLVII *The British Year Book of International Law* 1, at p 53:

> Opinio juris is necessary for the creation of customary rules; State practice, in order to create a customary rule must be accompanied by (or consist of) statements that certain conduct is permitted, required or forbidden by international law (a claim that conduct is permitted can be inferred from the mere existence of such conduct, but claims that conduct is required or forbidden need to be stated expressly). It is not necessary that the State making such statements believes them to be true; what is necessary is that the statements are not challenged by other States.
>
> ...

R v Burgess; Ex parte Henry demonstrates that the external affairs power can be used to enact laws regulating conduct within Australia for the purpose of carrying out and giving effect to Australia's international legal obligations. In this case, the High Court heard an argument that the external affairs power could not be used to implement international legal obligations *within* Australia because there was nothing *external* involved that could engage the external affairs power. The High Court held that the external affairs power would support legislation giving effect to Australia's obligations under the *Convention Relating to the Regulation of Aerial Navigation*. The High Court held that the parts of the *Air Navigation Act 1920* (Cth) giving effect to the treaty were supported by the external affairs power and that the remaining parts of the Act were invalid because they did not have the purpose of giving effect to the treaty.

R v Burgess; Ex parte Henry (1936) 55 CLR 608

Evatt and McTiernan JJ

The question which next arises is of outstanding importance not only in this case but generally. It is whether the Parliament has power to provide for the carrying out, and giving effect to, the Aerial Navigation Convention of 1919 and its amendments. It is necessary for the Commonwealth, which affirms the existence of the power, to point to an affirmative grant in the Constitution, and the only relevant power is that to legislate "with respect to ... external affairs" (s 51(xxix)) ...

The main argument advanced in denial of the competence of the Commonwealth Parliament to authorize the making of regulations to secure the execution of the Aerial Navigation Convention, was that a perusal of the convention shows that there is nothing "outside" Australia, but only matters, things and persons "within" Australia, which are to be regulated by the Governor-General, and that the inevitable result is to invade the domestic jurisdiction of the States ...

[I]t is true that the Commonwealth law relates to acts, matters, things and persons within the Commonwealth. But there is no necessary antithesis between that and a valid law with respect to "external affairs." So long as a Commonwealth enactment truly relates to a matter specified in s 51 of the Constitution, it is nothing to the point that it relates also to matters not therein specified. Therefore the real question is – what is comprehended by the expression "external affairs." ...

It would seem clear, therefore, that the legislative power of the Commonwealth over "external affairs" certainly includes the power to execute within the Commonwealth treaties and conventions entered into with foreign powers. The legislative power in s 51 is granted "subject to this Constitution" so that such treaties and conventions could not be used to enable the Parliament to set at nought constitutional guarantees elsewhere contained, such, for instance, as ss 6, 28, 41, 80, 92, 99, 100, 116, or 117 ...

No suggestion has been made that the entry into the convention was merely a device to procure for the Commonwealth an additional domestic jurisdiction ...

But it is a necessary corollary of our analysis of the constitutional power of Parliament to secure the performance of an international convention that the particular laws or regulations which are passed by the Commonwealth should be in conformity with the convention which they profess to be executing. In other words, it must be possible to assert of any law which is, ex hypothesi, passed solely in pursuance of this head of the "external affairs" power, that it represents the fulfilment, so far as that is possible in the case of laws operating locally, of all the obligations assumed under the convention ...

Doubtless this requirement does not necessarily preclude the exercise of wide powers and discretions by the Parliament or the Executive of the Commonwealth, for the international convention may itself contemplate that such powers and discretions should be exercisable by the appropriate authority of each party to the convention. Everything must depend upon the terms of the convention, and upon the rights and duties it confers and imposes. But the general requirement must be fulfilled or the Commonwealth will be exceeding its lawful domain ...

On the whole case the conclusions to which we have come are that: –

(1) The Commonwealth Parliament has no general control over the subject matter of civil aviation in the Commonwealth.

(2) The Commonwealth has power both to enter into international agreements and to pass legislation to secure the carrying out of such agreements according to their tenor even although the subject matter of the agreement is not otherwise within Commonwealth legislative jurisdiction.

(3) The subject matters of these agreements may properly include such matters as, eg, suppression of traffic in drugs, control of armament, regulation of labour conditions and control of air navigation.

(4) It is an essential condition of the power to carry out such international agreements that the local legislation should be in conformity with the terms of the agreement.

(5) Sec 4 of the Air Navigation Act is invalid so far as it purports to authorize the Executive to control civil aviation in the Commonwealth, but is valid so far as it authorizes the Executive to carry out within Australia the international air convention.

(6) In their present form, the regulations made by the Commonwealth Executive are invalid because they are not stamped with the purpose of executing the air convention but are stamped with the unauthorized purpose of controlling civil aviation throughout the Commonwealth.

Koowarta involved a three-way division of opinion about what types of treaty obligations would be sufficient to enliven the external affairs power. In this case, a majority of the High Court held that the *Racial Discrimination Act 1975* (Cth) was supported by the external affairs power as carrying out and giving effect to the *International Convention on the Elimination of All Forms of Racial Discrimination.*

Justices Mason, Murphy and Brennan held that the external affairs power supports laws implementing a treaty obligation on any subject-matter.

Koowarta v Bjelke-Petersen (1982) 153 CLR 168

Mason J

Of course, it is of paramount importance that the power is expressed as a legislative power and that, like the other grants of power in s 51, it is plenary with respect to the subject-matter. In accordance with the received canon of constitutional construction it is to be construed liberally, not narrowly and pedantically ...

The power applies to a treaty to which Australia is a party, for it is not in question that such a treaty is an external affair or a matter of external affairs, subject only to the qualification, if it be a qualification, that the treaty is a genuine treaty – a matter to be mentioned later. It would seem to follow inevitably from the plenary nature of the power that it would enable the Parliament to legislate not only for the ratification of a treaty but also for its implementation by carrying out any obligation to enact a law that Australia assumed by the treaty. It is very difficult to see why such a law would not be a law with respect to an external affair, once it is accepted that the treaty is an external affair ...

But the States which challenge the validity of the Act go further and say that the external affairs power is necessarily subject to the special limitation that it will not support legislation which is exclusively domestic in its operation ...

The Constitution does not draw any distinction between external affairs and internal affairs so as to give power over the former but deny all power over the latter. The true position, in accordance with received doctrine, is that a law, which according to its correct characterization is on a permitted topic, does not cease to be valid because it also happens to operate on a topic which stands outside power. The critical question is whether in the present case the law is with respect to external affairs, not whether it is with respect to internal affairs ...

Nor is there a solid foundation for implying a restriction that the treaty must relate to a matter which is international in character or of international concern, if the suggested restriction is intended to convey more than that the treaty is a genuine treaty. It is difficult to perceive why a genuine treaty, especially when it is multi-lateral and brought into existence under the auspices of the United Nations or an international agency, does not in itself relate to a matter of international concern and is not in itself an external affair. It is scarcely sensible to say that when Australia and other nations enter into a treaty the subject-matter of the treaty is not a matter of international concern – obviously it is a matter of concern to all the parties ...

Agreement by nations to take common action in pursuit of a common objective evidences the existence of international concern and gives the subject-matter of the treaty a character which is international. I speak of course of a treaty which is genuine and not of a colourable treaty, if that can be imagined, into which Australia has entered solely for the purpose of attracting to the Commonwealth Parliament the exercise of a legislative power over a subject-matter not specifically committed to it by the Constitution ...

Justice Stephen held that the external affairs power supports laws implementing treaty obligations only where the treaty is on a subject of international concern. Justice Stephen considered that the elimination of racial discrimination was a subject of international concern, and agreed that the legislation was valid.

Koowarta v Bjelke-Petersen (1982) 153 CLR 168

Stephen J

What I have described as the natural contextual meaning of par (xxix) includes, although it extends rather further than, what may be called the highest common factor to be deduced from the judgments in this Court concerning the meaning of the paragraph: namely, a power to implement by legislation within Australia such treaties, on matters international in character and hence legitimately the subject of agreement between nations, as Australia may become party to ...

The real issue in these cases is confined to the question whether this power to implement treaty obligations is subject to any and if so what overriding qualifications derived from the federal nature of our Constitution. It is such qualifications which, in my statement of a highest common factor, have led to the introduction of the phrases "matters international in character" and "legitimately the subject of agreement between nations".

The need for such qualifications is said to arise in this way. Whereas, read in isolation, par (xxix) would seem to authorize legislation to give effect municipally to each and every international obligation which Australia may incur, yet Australia is a federation possessing a constitution which assigns carefully limited legislative power to the federal legislature, leaving the undefined residue of legislative competence to the States. The power of the federal Executive to conclude treaties upon any subject-matter it sees fit is undoubted. If it can thereby at will create such "external affairs" as it wishes and if par (xxix) then confers power upon the federal legislature to legislate with respect to whatever external affair has thus been brought into being, this may place in jeopardy the federal character of our polity, the residuary legislative competence of the States being under threat of erosion and final extinction as a result of federal exercise of the power which par (xxix) confers ...

It will not be enough that the challenged law gives effect to treaty obligations. A treaty with another country, whether or not the result of a collusive arrangement, which is on a topic neither of especial concern to the relationship between Australia and that other country nor of general international concern will not be likely to survive that scrutiny ...

That prohibition of racial discrimination, the subject-matter of the *Racial Discrimination Act*, now falls squarely within the concept I regard as undoubted. That a consequence would seem to be an intrusion by the Commonwealth into areas previously the exclusive concern of the States does not mean that there has been some alteration of the original federal pattern of distribution of legislative powers. What has occurred is, rather, a growth in the content of "External affairs". This growth reflects the new global concern for human rights and the international acknowledgement of the need for universally recognized norms of conduct, particularly in relation to the suppression of racial discrimination.

In dissent, Gibbs CJ, Aicken and Wilson JJ held that the external affairs power supports laws implementing treaty obligations only where the treaty is on a subject that is indisputably international in character. These judges held that the elimination of racial discrimination was not a subject that is indisputably international in character and therefore held that the legislation was invalid.

Koowarta v Bjelke-Petersen (1982) 153 CLR 168

Gibbs CJ (dissenting)

The crucial question in the case is whether under the power given by s 51(xxix) the Parliament can enact laws for the execution of any treaty to which it is a party, whatever its subject-matter, and in particular for the execution of a treaty which deals with matters that are purely domestic and in themselves involve no relationship with other countries or their inhabitants ...

In no case has it been decided whether or not the Parliament has power to give effect to a treaty which deals with a matter that is entirely domestic, and affects only Australians within Australia, and their relations to each other, and does not involve any relationship between Australia or Australians and other countries or their citizens. The question which now falls for decision is therefore an open one ...

There are strong arguments which support the conclusion that s 51(xxix) does not empower the Parliament to give effect in Australia to every international agreement, whatever its character, to which Australia is a party. If the Parliament is empowered to make laws to carry into effect within Australia any treaty which the Governor-General may make, the result will be that the executive can, by its own act, determine the scope of Commonwealth power ...

[T]he executive could, by making an agreement, formal or informal, with another country, arrogate to the Parliament power to make laws on any subject whatsoever. It could, for example, by making an appropriate treaty, obtain for the Parliament powers to control education, to regulate the use of land, to fix the conditions of trading and employment, to censor the press, or to determine the basis of criminal responsibility – it is impossible to envisage any area of power which could not become the subject of Commonwealth legislation if the Commonwealth became a party to an appropriate international agreement. In other words, if s 51(xxix) empowers the Parliament to legislate to give effect to every international agreement which the executive may choose to make, the Commonwealth would be able to acquire unlimited legislative power. The distribution of powers made by the Constitution could in time be completely obliterated; there would be no field of power which the Commonwealth could not invade, and the federal balance achieved by the Constitution could be entirely destroyed ...

I conclude, therefore, that the view of Evatt and McTiernan JJ must be rejected, and that a law which gives effect within Australia to an international agreement will only be a valid law under s 51 (xxix) if the agreement is with respect to a matter which itself can be described as an external affair. I consider that a law which carries into effect the provisions of an international agreement will only have the character of a law with respect to external affairs if the provisions to which it gives effect answer that description ...

It is difficult to suggest any more precise test than ... – was the treaty made in reference to some matter international in character? The addition ... of the adverb "indisputably" [is] intended to do no more than emphasize that a treaty on such a subject would, beyond doubt, be within the power ...

The fact that many nations are concerned that other nations should eliminate racial discrimination within their own boundaries does not mean that the domestic or internal affairs of any one country thereby become converted into international affairs. There may be legitimate international concern as to the domestic affairs of a nation. An Australian law which is designed to forbid racial discrimination by Australians against Australians within the territory of Australia does not become international in character, or a law with respect to external affairs, simply because other nations are interested in Australia's policies and practices with regard to racial discrimination.

The ***Tasmanian Dam Case*** resolved the division of opinion about what types of treaties were capable of enlivening the external affairs power. A majority of the High Court comprising Mason, Murphy, Brennan and Deane JJ held that the external affairs power supports legislation implementing treaty obligations on any subject-matter. In dissent, Gibbs CJ, Wilson and Dawson JJ held that the external affairs power supports laws implementing treaty obligations only where the treaty is on a subject of international concern.

The ***Tasmanian Dam Case*** also outlined the relevant test of characterisation. Because the implementation of the international legal obligations limb of the external affairs is purposive, the test of characterisation is whether the legislation is capable of being considered appropriate and adapted to giving effect to the relevant treaty obligations. The High Court also explained that legislation that only partially implements a treaty obligation will be valid, provided that the legislation is not contrary to the treaty obligation.

Commonwealth v Tasmania ('*Tasmanian Dam Case*') (1983) 158 CLR 1

Section 69(1) of the World Heritage Properties Conservation Act 1983 *(Cth) authorised the making of regulations to give effect to the* Convention for the Protection of the World Cultural and Natural Heritage 1972. *A majority of the High Court held that the provision was capable of being considered appropriate and adapted to giving effect to the treaty. A minority of the High Court held that because the subject-matter of the treaty was not a subject of international concern the treaty could not enliven the external affairs power.*

Deane J

Thus, a law would not properly be characterized as a law with respect to external affairs if it failed to carry into effect or to comply with the particular provisions of a treaty which it was said to execute (see *Burgess' Case; Airlines of NSW (No 2)*) or if the treaty which the law was said to carry into effect was demonstrated to be no more than a device to attract domestic legislative power; *Burgess' Case; Koowarta.* More importantly, while the question of what is the appropriate method of achieving a desired result is a matter for the Parliament and not for the Court, the law must be capable of being reasonably considered to be appropriate and adapted to achieving what is said to impress it with the character of a law with respect to external affairs. In that regard, the purpose which a law operating upon a domestic subject matter is intended to achieve (for example, the carrying into effect of a treaty, the performance of an international obligation or the obtaining of an international benefit) is likely to assume an importance in deciding questions of characterization in relation to s 51(xxix) which is comparable to its importance in characterization in relation to the defence power (s 51 (vi)) since it will commonly be that purpose which, in the factual context, is called in aid to provide the character of a law with respect to external affairs ...

Implicit in the requirement that a law be capable of being reasonably considered to be appropriate and adapted to achieving what is said to provide it with the character of a law with respect to external affairs is a need for there to be a reasonable proportionality between the designated purpose or object and the means which the law embodies for achieving or procuring it. Thus, to take an extravagant example, a law requiring that all sheep in Australia be slaughtered would not be sustainable as a law with respect to external affairs merely because Australia was a party to some international convention which required the taking of steps to safeguard against the spread of some obscure sheep disease which had been detected in sheep in a foreign country and which had not reached these shores. The absence of any reasonable proportionality between the law and the purpose of discharging the obligation under the convention would preclude characterization as a law with respect to external affairs ... The law must be seen, with "reasonable clearness", upon consideration of its operation, to be "really, and not fancifully, colourably, or ostensibly, referable" to and explicable by the purpose or object which is said to provide its character ...

What is claimed, on behalf of the Commonwealth, to enliven the external affairs power and to support the specific statutory provisions is Australia's participation in the *Convention for the Protection of the World Cultural and Natural Heritage* (the Convention) which was adopted by the General Conference of UNESCO on 16th November, 1972, combined with the entry, on the nomination of Australia, of the Wilderness National Parks upon the World Heritage List which is kept pursuant to the provisions of the Convention ...

However loosely such obligations may be defined, it is apparent that Australia, by depositing its instrument of ratification, bound itself to observe the terms of the Convention and assumed real and substantive obligations under them. Apart from the obligation to pay contributions (Art 16), the most clearly defined obligations assumed by Australia under the Convention are those relating to properties, such as the Wilderness National Parks, which have been included, on Australia's nomination, in the World Heritage List ...

Those obligations include the primary "duty of ensuring", among other things, the protection, conservation and presentation of the relevant property (Art 4) and an express undertaking to "endeavour, in so far as possible, and as appropriate for each country", to "take the appropriate legal, scientific, technical, administrative and financial measures necessary for the identification, protection, conservation, presentation and rehabilitation" thereof (Art 5(d)) ...

The scope of the regulation-making power which s 69(1) confers will be considered in greater detail subsequently when consideration is given to the validity of the *World Heritage (Western Tasmania Wilderness) Regulations* purportedly made under the subsection. For immediate purposes, it suffices to say that s 69(1) would only authorize the making of regulations which were capable of being reasonably considered to be appropriate and adapted to giving effect to the Convention. That being so, the provisions of s 69(1) are, in so far as they authorize the making of regulations for and in relation to giving effect to the Convention, a law with respect to external affairs within s 51(xxix) of the Constitution ...

Wilson J (dissenting)

[Section] 51(xxix) empowers the Parliament to enact a law of purely domestic operation on a topic with respect to which it would not otherwise have power provided that the law is directed to the implementation of a treaty obligation on a topic of international concern having the capacity to affect Australia's relations with other countries. It is against this background that the issues in the present case referable to the scope of the external affairs power fall to be considered ...

Richardson v Forestry Commission confirmed the principles applied by the majority in the ***Tasmanian Dam Case***: (1) the external affairs power supports laws implementing a treaty obligation on any subject-matter; and (2) this limb of the external affairs power is purposive in nature, such that the test of characterisation is whether a law is capable of being considered reasonably appropriate and adapted to giving effect to the international law obligation. Justices Wilson and Dawson did not apply the view they expressed in the ***Tasmanian Dam Case*** that only treaty obligations on subjects that are international in character enliven the external affairs and joined the majority.

Richardson v Forestry Commission (1988) 164 CLR 261

Federal legislation established a Commission of Inquiry to assess whether particular areas in Tasmania should be included in the World Heritage List under the Convention for the Protection of the World Cultural and Natural Heritage 1972. *The legislation also prohibited development activities in the relevant areas during the period of the inquiry. The High Court held that the legislation was capable of being considered reasonably appropriate and adapted to implementing obligations under the treaty and was therefore supported by the external affairs power.*

Wilson J

Although I remain convinced of the correctness of the view I expressed in the *Tasmanian Dam Case* – and indeed the argument in the present case has served only to strengthen that sense of conviction – unless and until the decision is reviewed I am obliged to accept its authority ...

There is no point in repeating what I then wrote. The present case must be approached on the basis that the *Tasmanian Dam Case* established both the existence of certain obligations imposed upon Australia by the Convention and the legislative power of the Commonwealth with respect to their observance ...

Dawson J

In the *Commonwealth v Tasmania* (*The Tasmanian Dam Case*), the majority took the view that legislation implementing the *Convention for the Protection of the World Cultural and Natural Heritage* was a valid exercise of the external affairs power contained in s 51(xxix) of the Constitution. That view was taken, as I read the judgments, upon the basis that subject to express constitutional prohibitions, any matters covered by a bona fide international treaty are, by their very inclusion in the treaty, brought within the ambit of the external affairs power. As will be apparent from my reasons for judgment in *The Tasmanian Dam Case*, I am unable to accept that view ...

Precedent must, however, have a part to play, even in the interpretation of a constitution. Considerations of practicality make it necessary that the law should, as far as possible, take a consistent course. The constant re-examination of concluded questions is incompatible with that aim. That is why this Court has adopted the practice of requiring leave to be granted before it will allow a previous decision to be reargued: *Evda Nominees Pty Ltd v Victoria* (1984) 154 CLR 311. The parties in the present case did not seek to question the decision in the *Tasmanian Dam Case*. In these circumstances, and having made my own view clear, it is, I think, proper to proceed upon the same basis as did the argument in this case and to assume the authority of that decision.

The *Tasmanian Dam Case* does, I think, provide an answer in the present case because whatever else it decided, it did decide that the legislative implementation of an international treaty concluded in good faith is within the ambit of the external affairs power ...

The ***Tasmanian Dam Case*** also explains that to enliven this limb of the external affairs power an international legal obligation needs to entail an obligation, although that obligation need not be expressed with a high degree of precision.

Commonwealth v Tasmania ('Tasmanian Dam Case') (1983) 158 CLR 1

Deane J

International agreements are commonly "not expressed with the precision of formal domestic documents as in English law". The reasons for this include the different importance attributed to the strict text of agreements under different systems of law, the fact that such agreements are ordinarily "the result of compromise reached at the conference table" and the need to accommodate structural differences in official languages ...

It is, therefore, not surprising that, in a Convention to which more than seventy States are parties and which was drawn up in no less than five "equally authoritative" official languages (Art 30), the terms in which the obligations of "the States Parties" are defined do not possess the degree of precision which is desirable in a private contract under the common law. That absence of precision does not, however, mean any absence of international obligation. In that regard, it would be contrary to both the theory and practice of international law to adopt the approach which was advocated by Tasmania and deny the existence of international obligations unless they be defined with the degree of precision necessary to establish a legally enforceable agreement under the common law ...

However loosely such obligations may be defined, it is apparent that Australia, by depositing its instrument of ratification, bound itself to observe the terms of the Convention and assumed real and substantive obligations under them. Apart from the obligation to pay contributions (Art 16), the most clearly defined obligations assumed by Australia under the Convention are those relating to properties, such as the Wilderness National Parks, which have been included, on Australia's nomination, in the World Heritage List. Such properties have been specifically identified as properties in respect of which obligations undertaken by parties to the Convention are applicable (see Arts 6(1) and (2), 11 and 13). A main purpose of the provisions relating to establishing and keeping the World Heritage List with its requirement that a property be not entered without the agreement of the State in whose territory it is situated is to identify property which is indisputably subjected to the terms of the Convention. Those obligations include the primary "duty of ensuring", among other things, the protection, conservation and presentation of the relevant property (Art 4) and an express undertaking to "endeavour, in so far as possible, and as appropriate for each country", to "take the appropriate legal, scientific, technical, administrative and financial measures necessary for the identification, protection, conservation, presentation and rehabilitation" thereof (Art 5(d)) ...

Unless one is to take the view that over seventy nations have engaged in the solemn and cynical farce of using words such as "obligation" and "duty" where neither was intended or undertaken, the provisions of the Convention impose real and identifiable obligations ...

To enliven this limb of the external affairs power an international law obligation does not need to be precise but it must not be impermissibly vague. The ***Industrial Relations Act Case*** holds that to enliven the external affairs power a treaty obligation must be sufficiently specific to direct the general course to be taken.

The ***Industrial Relations Act Case*** also confirms the proposition articulated in the ***Tasmanian Dam Case*** that legislation only partially implementing a treaty obligation will be valid, provided that the legislation is not contrary to the treaty obligation.

Victoria v Commonwealth ('*Industrial Relations Act Case*') (1996) 187 CLR 416

Federal legislation prescribed various rules governing employment and working conditions. The Commonwealth argued that the legislation implemented Australia's obligations set out in various conventions Australia had entered into as part of its participation in the General Conference of the International Labour Organisation.

Brennan CJ, Toohey, Gaudron, McHugh and Gummow JJ

In general terms, the provisions of the Act which are challenged in these proceedings allow for the imposition of, or impose, obligations on employers with respect to minimum wages, equal pay, termination of employment, discrimination in employment and family leave, and provide as well for collective bargaining and the right to strike ...

The Commonwealth claims that many of the provisions in question were enacted pursuant to its power with respect to external affairs. This is because a number of these matters are the subject of Conventions which have been adopted by the General Conference of the International Labour Organisation ("the ILO") and ratified by Australia. Some matters are the subject of Recommendations adopted by the General Conference of the ILO. Freedom of association and the right to strike are said to be the subject of customary international law. However, the plaintiff States argue that, contrary to what was said in the judgments of the majority in *Commonwealth v Tasmania* (*The Tasmanian Dam Case*), the power to legislate with respect to external affairs does not extend to the implementation of treaty obligations unless the subject-matter of the treaty is one of international concern. According to their argument, the ILO Conventions and Recommendations on which the provisions in question are based are not concerned with matters of that kind. As well, they argue that the ILO Conventions and Recommendations do not impose obligations or, if they do, the provisions in question are not capable of being viewed as appropriate or adapted to their implementation. In some instances, they say, the provisions are simply not directed to any relevant external affair ...

The difficulty in the path of these submissions is that ... the majority in the *Tasmanian Dam Case* adopted the broader view ...

The legislative implementation of a treaty

There may be some treaties which do not enliven the legislative power conferred by s 51(xxix) even though their subject-matter is of international concern. For example, Professor Zines has suggested that a treaty expressed in terms of aspiration (for example "to promote full employment") cannot support a law which adopts one of a variety of possibly contradictory ways that might be selected to fulfil the aspiration ...

When a treaty is relied on under s 51(xxix) to support a law, it is not sufficient that the law prescribes one of a variety of means that might be thought appropriate and adapted to the achievement of an ideal. The law must prescribe a regime that the treaty has itself defined with sufficient specificity to direct the general course to be taken by the signatory states ...

Where the legislative power is said to be enlivened by a treaty binding on the Commonwealth of Australia, and the law prescribes a regime affecting a domestic subject-matter, a question arises as to the connection which must exist between the law and the treaty. To be a law with respect to "external affairs", the law must be reasonably capable of being considered appropriate and adapted to implementing the treaty. Thus, it is for the legislature to choose the means by which it carries into or gives effect to the treaty provided that the means chosen are reasonably capable of being considered appropriate and adapted to that end. But that is not to say that an obligation imposed by treaty provides the outer limits of a law enacted to implement it. The term "purpose" has been used to identify the object for the advancement or attainment of which a law was enacted. Hence, the statement by Brennan J in *Cunliffe v The Commonwealth* that the external affairs power has "a purposive aspect". As this phrase indicates, care is required in relevant analysis. Where a treaty relating to a domestic subject-matter is relied on to enliven the legislative power conferred by s 51(xxix) the validity of the law depends on whether its purpose or object is to implement the treaty ...

In this context, purpose is not something found in the head of power. Rather, it is a test for determining whether the law in question is reasonably capable of being considered as giving effect to the treaty and therefore as being a law upon a subject which is an aspect of external affairs ...

[T]he basic question ... is whether the law selects means which are reasonably capable of being considered appropriate and adapted to achieving the purpose or object of giving effect to the treaty, so that the law is one upon a subject which is an aspect of external affairs.

Deficiency in implementation of a supporting Convention is not necessarily fatal to the validity of a law; but a law will be held invalid if the deficiency is so substantial as to deny the law the character of a measure implementing the Convention or it is a deficiency which, when coupled with other provisions of the law, makes it substantially inconsistent with the Convention ...

Pape provides an example of an aspirational commitment that is not sufficiently specific to enliven the external affairs power. Because the case was ultimately decided on other grounds, only two judges in the majority and one judge dissenting considered the external affairs power issue. Those three judges all held that a commitment among members of the G-20 group of nations, including Australia, to "[u]se fiscal measures to stimulate domestic demand to rapid effect, as appropriate, while maintaining a policy framework conducive to fiscal sustainability" was not an international legal obligation and, even if it were an obligation, was not sufficiently specific to direct the general course to be taken.

Pape v Commissioner of Taxation (2009) 238 CLR 1

This case concerned legislation providing cash handouts to taxpayers as part of the Commonwealth's economic stimulus program in response to the Global Financial Crisis.

Hayne and Kiefel JJ

The Commonwealth submitted that the Impugned Act is a law with respect to external affairs ... [I]t was submitted that the fiscal stimulus (including the provision of the tax bonus) implements an international agreement or understanding. Neither argument should be accepted ...

It is not shown that Australia has undertaken any international obligation sufficient to found the Impugned Act in the external affairs power. It was submitted that there is an international agreement or understanding to make a co-ordinated international response to a global economic problem. The agreement or understanding was said to have two sources. First, reference was made to a Declaration of the Summit on Financial Markets and the World Economy made by the leaders of the Group of Twenty ("the G-20") on 15 November 2008 in Washington DC. Australia is a member of the G-20. Secondly, reference was made to some recommendations of the IMF and the Organisation for Economic Co-operation and Development ("the OECD"). Australia is a member of each of those organisations.

As was pointed out in *Victoria v Commonwealth* (*Industrial Relations Act Case*) legislation may be supported under the external affairs power if the legislation gives effect to some international obligation. But as also pointed out in that case, what is said to be the legislative implementation of a treaty may present some further questions for consideration, including whether the treaty in question sufficiently identified the means chosen in legislation as one of the ways in which parties to the treaty are to pursue some commonly held aspiration expressed in the treaty. In the present case, however, it is not necessary to examine these questions. It is sufficient to observe that neither the Declaration by the leaders of the G-20, nor the recommendations of either the IMF or the OECD, imposed any obligation on Australia to take action of the kind now in question ...

[T]he relevant obligation was said to be contained in a part of the Declaration that described "Actions Taken and to Be Taken". Under that heading, the Declaration recorded that the nations represented had taken certain actions and would take a number of steps to "restore growth, avoid negative spillovers and support emerging market economies and developing countries". Six steps were set out. One of them was:

> "Use fiscal measures to stimulate domestic demand to rapid effect, as appropriate, while maintaining a policy framework conducive to fiscal sustainability".

Read in the context of the Declaration as a whole it is evident that none of the six steps described was intended to bind the nations whose leaders signed the Declaration to any particular course of action. Rather, the document as a whole made plain (by its use of expressions like "as appropriate") that it was for each nation to chart its own course in responding to the circumstances that have arisen. The Impugned Act was not enacted in fulfilment of any obligation on Australia recorded in the Declaration of the leaders of the G-20 ...

Heydon J

The need for specificity. If legislation is to be validated by recourse to a treaty (or international commitment) that treaty or commitment must set out a regime defined with "sufficient specificity to direct the general course to be taken" by the relevant states. The treaty or commitment need not have the precision necessary to establish a legally enforceable agreement at common law, but it must avoid excessive generality.

The G-20 Declaration – the central passage. The high point of the defendants' argument, and the only matter to which South Australia referred, was the passage quoted above from the G-20 Declaration. That language is no more than aspirational. It does not say which fiscal measures are to be used. What is stated leaves it very much open to individual governments to decide whether to use fiscal measures, and, if so, which ones. That is because of the words "as appropriate". It is also because of the reference to "maintaining a policy framework conducive to fiscal sustainability", which points against deficit spending. As New South Wales submitted, it is a qualified proposition on which governments can agree, but it "commits to nothing, because different views quite reasonably can be taken of what is sufficient to stimulate domestic demand to rapid effect as appropriate, and what is necessary to maintain fiscal sustainability." It is what might be expected of an organisation like the G-20, which concentrates on discussion, dialogue and influence, and which has a diverse membership. It is highly improbable that in the ordinary course the deliberations of such a body would generate obligations in international law. In *Victoria v Commonwealth* it was said that an "external affair" did not exist where all that was stated was a "broad objective with little precise content and permitting widely divergent policies by parties". Yet that is all the G-20 Declaration does ...

The G-20 Declaration falls more into the genre of public relations than the genre of treaties ...

6.6 No power to enact laws with respect to matters of international concern

In ***Richardson v Forestry Commission,*** Dawson J suggested that the effect of the ***Tasmanian Dam Case,*** and especially the reasoning of Stephen J in that case, is that the external affairs power supports laws with respect to matters of international concern, even in the absence of an international legal obligation.

Richardson v Forestry Commission (1988) 164 CLR 261

Dawson J

The *Tasmanian Dam Case* does, I think, provide an answer in the present case because whatever else it decided, it did decide that the legislative implementation of an international treaty concluded in good faith is within the ambit of the external affairs power. True it is that The *Tasmanian Dam Case* appears to have decided more than this. As I read the judgments of the majority, it is enough to attract legislative power if, even though there is no treaty, a subject-matter is of sufficient international concern (pp 129–132 per Mason J; pp 171–172 per Murphy J; p 222 per Brennan J; pp 258–259 per Deane J).

Although the majority did not necessarily place any reliance upon the judgment of Stephen J in *Koowarta v Bjelke-Petersen*, that conclusion flows logically from the view which he expressed that the implementation of a treaty is not automatically an exercise of the external affairs power; the subject-matter of the treaty must also be a matter of international concern. Stephen J saw the requirement of international concern as a restriction upon the power and I was prepared to view it in that way in *The Tasmanian Dam Case*.

But in reality, as the decision in the latter case shows, the fact that a matter is the subject of a bona fide treaty makes it difficult to say that it is not a matter of international concern and, if international concern is the touchstone, why is a treaty necessary at all? Why is international concern over a matter not sufficient of itself to bring it within the external affairs power?

Alqudsi points out that this reading of the ***Tasmanian Dam Case*** is wrong because it is contrary to High Court ratio, and emphasises that there is no power to enact laws with respect to matters of international concern.

Alqudsi v Commonwealth (2015) 91 NSWLR 92

Leeming JA

I do not consider that what Stephen J said in *Koowarta* is of *any* appreciable precedential authority in respect of the proposition that international concern alone is sufficient to engage the power ...

In *Commonwealth v Tasmania* (*Tasmanian Dam Case*) it was the minority (Gibbs CJ, Wilson and Dawson JJ) who adopted Stephen J's "international concern" limitation upon the power ...

But the majority took a broader view, concluding that once a bona fide treaty had been entered into, the Commonwealth had power to implement treaty obligations. One reason for doing so was the difficulty in a court assessing the "international character or concern" of a treaty ...

Thus Stephen J's approach has been overtaken by the broader reasoning of the majority in the *Tasmanian Dam Case* ... It is, with respect, wrong to regard Stephen J's statements as to international concern, made in support of a long-superseded and (as it turns out) unduly narrow view of the scope of the external affairs power, as supportive of yet further expansion of that head of power. The occasion for his Honour's qualification disappeared when a broader view (to which he was opposed) was adopted in the *Tasmanian Dam Case*.

There is another point: Stephen J's view of "international concern" was confined to cases where there was a treaty. It is in the teeth of Stephen J's reasoning to invoke international concern in cases which do not involve a treaty ...

There is no separate "international concern" aspect of the external affairs power

I turn to why I would reject the Commonwealth's alternative submission based on "international concern" ...

At the level of authority, the concept of "international concern" has been forcefully criticised by Mason J in *Tasmanian Dam Case*, Dawson J in *Richardson*, and by Kirby J and Callinan and Heydon JJ in *XYZ*. Such support as may be found in the reasons of Brennan J in *Polyukhovich* recognised the difficulties in the doctrine, and was much more qualified than the concept for which the Commonwealth contended and the primary judge found.

I do not consider that the state of authority *precludes* recognition of the doctrine, but to do so it would be necessary to address the criticisms which have been made in the three decades since *Koowarta*. Although the Commonwealth sought to defend this aspect of the reasons of the primary judge, it did not seek to take that course ...

There are to my mind large difficulties attendant upon a separate aspect of the external affairs power based on "international concern" ... The essential problem is an absence of, to use Mason J's language, "any acceptable criteria or guidelines". How is it to be determined that something which *ex hypothesi* is insufficient to generate the ordinary formal processes of treaty-making nevertheless is sufficient to engage federal legislative power? How is the area of international concern identified? What is the relationship between the content of federal legislative power and the subject? Mr Alqudsi summarised the critique in XYZ concisely:

> The concept of 'international concern' is impermissibly vague. There are no identified limits. Recognition of an 'international concern' power would be inconsistent with the Communist Party Case. It would facilitate the Executive reciting itself into power. If the concept were accepted as a criterion of power 'the concept would ... be virtually limitless and potentially destructive of Australian federal arrangements': XYZ at [124] per Kirby J.
>
> ...

The absence of a principled basis for the doctrine, the weight of High Court authority against it and the fact that the submission involves a misuse of what Stephen J wrote in *Koowarta* lead me to conclude, respectfully, that there is no separate aspect of the external affairs power based on "international concern".

6.7 No power to enact laws implementing international recommendations that are not an implementation of an international legal obligation

There is a history of dicta in the case law suggesting that the external affairs power supports laws implementing recommendations made by international organisations. An example of such dicta is found in ***R v Burgess; Ex parte Henry***.

R v Burgess; Ex parte Henry (1936) 55 CLR 608

Evatt and McTiernan JJ

But it is not to be assumed that the legislative power over "external affairs" is limited to the execution of treaties or conventions; and, to pursue the illustration previously referred to, the Parliament may well be deemed competent to legislate for the carrying out of "recommendations" as well as the "draft international conventions" resolved upon by the International Labour Organization or of other international recommendations or requests upon other subject matters of concern to Australia as a member of the family of nations.

The ***Industrial Relations Act Case*** shows that a law that is capable of being considered reasonably appropriate and adapted to implementing international recommendations will be supported by the external affairs power *if* those international recommendations are themselves capable of being considered reasonably appropriate and adapted to implementing an international legal obligation. This is because the law is in fact implementing the underlying international law obligation. In this case, the High Court declined to decide whether the external affairs power supports laws implementing international recommendations that are not connected to an international law obligation.

Victoria v Commonwealth ('*Industrial Relations Act Case*') (1996) 187 CLR 416

Federal legislation prescribed various rules governing employment and working conditions. The Commonwealth argued that parts of the legislation implemented recommendations issued by the International Labour Organisation.

Brennan CJ, Toohey, Gaudron, McHugh and Gummow JJ

Australia was a foundation member [of the International Labour Organisation] ...

The organs of the ILO are the General Conference, the Governing Body and the International Labour Office (Art 2). The General Conference comprises four delegates from each of the members of the ILO, two representing the government and two representing respectively employers and "workpeople" (Art 3(1)). The General Conference acts by voting on the adoption of International Conventions or Recommendations. A majority of two-thirds of the votes cast by the delegates present must be in favour of the Convention or Recommendation for it to be adopted (Art 19(2)). Neither Conventions nor Recommendations are binding merely as a result of their being adopted by the General Conference. Both Conventions and Recommendations are communicated to members; in the case of Conventions for ratification, in the case of Recommendations for "consideration with a view to effect being given to (them) by national legislation or otherwise" (Art 19(5)(a), 19(6)(a)) ...

The section refers separately to a measure being reasonably regarded as appropriate and adapted for giving effect to Recommendation No 90 or Recommendation No 111. That provision can be supported under s 51(xxix) if, but only if, the terms of these Recommendations themselves can reasonably be regarded as appropriate and adapted to giving effect to the terms of the Conventions to which they relate. In our view, they can be so regarded. Hence measures that fall within the terms of s 170BC(1) and implement the terms of the Recommendations will fall within the terms of s 170BC(3)(b)(i).

On this line of reasoning, the words "can reasonably be regarded as appropriate and adapted to" in s 170BC(3)(b) may be superfluous in relation to the Recommendations but are obviously designed to cover the situation where the Recommendations are relied upon of themselves to support an exercise of the external affairs power. This is a point which, at this stage, it is not necessary to decide.

In ***Pape***, Heydon J in dissent was the only judge to directly consider the issue of international recommendations. Justice Heydon expressly rejected the idea that international recommendations that are not connected to a treaty can enliven legislative power. The reason for this conclusion was that such recommendations do not entail an obligation.

Pape v Commissioner of Taxation (2009) 238 CLR 1

Heydon J

Recommendations by international agencies cannot support the validity of the *Tax Bonus Act*. Any support they can give to a law enacted in reliance on s 51(xxix) exists only where they are pronounced in order to give effect to the terms of a treaty to which they relate. The defendants relied on the following words of Evatt and McTiernan JJ in *R v Burgess; Ex parte Henry*:

> [T]he Parliament may well be deemed competent to legislate for the carrying out of 'recommendations' ... resolved upon by the International Labour Organization or of other international recommendations or requests upon other subject matters of concern to Australia as a member of the family of nations. (emphasis added)

The defendants said that that passage, which was quoted in *Victoria v The Commonwealth*, was actually applied in that case. That is not so. In that case the Court specifically declined to decide whether legislation enacted to carry out the recommendations of international agencies made otherwise than in order to give effect to the terms of a treaty to which they relate could be supported by s 51(xxix). The better view is that it cannot, because mere recommendations do not create international obligations. In any event, even if some recommendations could do so, the recommendations relied on in this case are too vague ...

In ***Alqudsi***, Leeming JA held that the necessary effect of the ***Industrial Relations Act Case*** is to reject the possibility that recommendations that are not connected to a treaty can enliven legislative power.

Alqudsi v Commonwealth (2015) 91 NSWLR 92

Leeming JA

The primary judge also accepted the Commonwealth's submission that s 51(xxix) was engaged by a recommendation of international agencies. Her Honour said:

> [T]he Commonwealth submitted that the recommendations of international agencies such as the UN, in pursuit of international objectives, enlivened the external affairs power. I regard the express approval by the majority in the *Industrial Relations Act Case* at 483 of the dicta of Evatt and McTiernan JJ in *The King v Burgess; ex parte*

> *Henry* as establishing the proposition for which the Commonwealth contended. Thus, it is not, in my view, to the point that, unlike treaties, the 'recommendations' do not necessarily impose legal duties on States to take certain steps and enact laws with a particular effect.

On that basis, her Honour concluded that "the external affairs power authorised the Commonwealth to carry into effect legislation which can be regarded as having as its purpose the implementation of the recommendations in the Friendly Relations Declaration."

I respectfully disagree. I regard this Court as bound to hold to the contrary. The Commonwealth's submission proceeds on a misreading of the *Industrial Relations Act Case* ...

[I]n the reasons of the Industrial Relations Act Case the joint judgment turned to two recommendations made by the ILO which qualified the conferral of power upon the Commission in s 170BC of the *Industrial Relations Act 1988* (Cth) by reference to whether an order was reasonably regarded as appropriate and adapted to giving effect to those recommendations. Unlike the passages on which the Commonwealth relied, the following passage at 509 is squarely directed to whether a recommendation by an international organisation will engage the s 51(xxix) power:

> That provision can be supported under s 51(xxix) if, *but only if*, the terms of these Recommendations themselves can reasonably be regarded as appropriate and adapted to giving effect to the terms of the Conventions to which they relate. In our view, they can be so regarded. Hence measures that fall within the terms of s 170BC(1) and implement the terms of the Recommendations will fall within the terms of s 170BC(3)(b)(i). On this line of reasoning, the words 'can reasonably be regarded as appropriate and adapted to' in s 170BC(3)(b) may be superfluous in relation to the Recommendations but are obviously designed to cover the situation where the Recommendations are relied upon of themselves to support an exercise of the external affairs power. *This is a point which, at this stage, it is not necessary to decide* (emphasis added).

The first sentence emphasised above states a necessary as well as a sufficient condition for legislation to be supported by a recommendation. I do not see how such formal language can be disregarded. It is simply inconsistent with the stated necessary condition to contend, as the Commonwealth submits, or to hold, as the primary judge held, that implementing a recommendation can of itself engage the power. On the current state of authority, that can occur only if the recommendation is itself reasonably regarded as appropriate and adapted to give effect to some Convention.

If there were any doubt about that, it is dispelled by the second emphasised sentence. The High Court was, expressly, not deciding whether a recommendation is relied upon itself, in the absence of a treaty, to support the exercise of the external affairs power. I do not see how one can read general language earlier in the judgment, in a section dealing with the implementation of treaties, as undermining passages which were precisely directed to the particular issue, in that part of the judgment where the issue was determined.

The same reading of the *Industrial Relations Act Case* was advanced by the Commonwealth in *Pape*. It was rejected by Heydon J, for reasons mirroring those I have summarised above.

Moreover, in the same decision, Hayne and Kiefel JJ proceeded on the basis (consistently with the understanding stated above of the effect of the *Industrial Relations Act Case*) that the external affairs power was only engaged if Australia had undertaken an international obligation. Neither French CJ nor Gummow, Crennan and Bell JJ considered the external affairs power.

The view I hold of the effect of the *Industrial Relations Act Case* is thus shared by all three members of the High Court who were asked to determine the same submission in respect of it as has been advanced by the Commonwealth in this appeal ...

It is not open to me to do other than apply what a majority of the High Court has said in the *Industrial Relations Act Case* is a necessary and sufficient condition of a mere recommendation engaging the external affairs power.

I conclude that I am bound to reject the Commonwealth's submission, and bound to conclude that the primary judge was wrong to reason to the contrary.

6.8 DISCUSSION QUESTIONS

1. Which components of the external affairs power are subject-matter powers and which component of the external affairs power is a purposive power? Why does this distinction matter?
2. To what extent can the external affairs power be used to enact laws to give effect within Australia to international law obligations entered into by Australia?
3. To what extent can the external affairs power be used to enact laws to give effect within Australia to recommendations made by international bodies?
4. To what extent can the external affairs power be used to enact laws with respect to matters of 'international concern'?
5. Problem question: Consider the following hypothetical scenario and legal instruments. Australia is a party to the *South Pacific Regional Convention on Economic Cooperation*, which establishes the South Pacific Regional Economic Cooperation Organisation. The Convention provides:

   Article 3 The South Pacific Regional Economic Cooperation Organisation may issue directives setting out economic goals and policies.

   Article 4 Member states are obliged to faithfully implement the directives of the South Pacific Regional Economic Cooperation Organisation to the fullest extent possible taking into account the social, economic and legal conditions of the member state.

   The South Pacific Regional Economic Cooperation Organisation issues the *Ensuring Strong Economic Futures Through Education Directive 2023*, which requires all member states to make attendance at school compulsory from the age of at least seven years to the age of 17 years.

   Shortly after the directive is issued, the Commonwealth Parliament enacts the *School Leaving Age Act 2023*. Section 3 of the Act provides: 'It is the duty of the parent or lawful guardian of a child who is above the age of 6 years and who has not yet attained the age of 17 years to cause the child to be enrolled at, and to attend, a government school or a non-government school established or registered as the case may be in accordance with the law of the State or Territory in which the child ordinarily resides.'

Is section 3 of the Act supported by the external affairs power?

IMMIGRATION AND ALIENS POWERS

7

7.1 Overview

This chapter examines two related heads of power: the immigration power in section 51(xxvii) and the aliens power in section 51(xix) of the *Australian Constitution*.

Australian Constitution

Section 51 Legislative Powers of the Parliament

The Parliament shall, subject to this Constitution, have power to make laws for the peace, order, and good government of the Commonwealth with respect to:

...

(xix) naturalization and aliens;

...

(xxvii) immigration and emigration;

...

Immigration is concerned with the act of a non-Australian entering into Australia and the process of an immigrant becoming absorbed into the Australian community so that they are no longer an immigrant. Whether a person is an immigrant is largely a question of fact.

By contrast, alienage is a legal status. Within the limits of the concept of 'alien', Parliament has power to determine who is and is not an alien. The general contemporary position is that an alien is anyone who is a non-citizen. The aliens power includes the power to take away citizenship so as to turn a citizen into an alien.

The case law shows that all immigrants are aliens but that not all aliens are immigrants. Both heads of power can be used to regulate the conduct of individuals, including providing for their deportation. Because the meaning of the concepts involved is clearer, Parliament nowadays tends to rely on the aliens power to support legislation dealing with migration and related policy areas.

Key concepts considered in this chapter include:

- immigration
- absorption
- alien
- non-alien
- allegiance
- denaturalisation.

7.2 Scope of the immigration power

The constitutional concept of immigration is concerned with the act of a non-Australian entering into Australia and the process of absorbing that person into the Australian community. The case law indicates that the immigration power can be used not only to regulate who may and may not immigrate to Australia but also to regulate immigrants once they are present within Australia.

Who is an 'immigrant'?

Potter v Minahan gives the basic definition of 'immigrant'. A person is an immigrant if, at the time of entry into Australia, they are not a member of the Australian community. It follows that a person returning home to Australia after a period of time away is not an immigrant.

Potter v Minahan (1908) 7 CLR 277

Minahan, whose mother was white and father was Chinese, was born in Victoria in 1876 but was taken to China at the age of five by his father. Twenty-six years later, Minahan returned to Australia. Immigration authorities treated Minahan as an immigrant.

The Immigration Restriction Acts 1901–1905 *(Cth) required immigrants to pass the dictation test. The dictation test, which was a key mechanism for implementing the White Australia Policy, required immigrants to transcribe in a European language chosen by officials a passage of text read to them by an official. Minahan failed the test. Any immigrant who failed the test and remained in Australia for a year or more was guilty of an offence. The question for the High Court was whether Minahan was an immigrant and thus guilty of the offence.*

Griffith CJ

In my opinion the word "immigration" as used in the Constitution does not mean mere physical entry into the Commonwealth although the fact of entry is, if no more appears, sufficient prima facie evidence that the person entering is an immigrant ...

There is no doubt that a British subject coming to the Commonwealth from another part of the British Dominions may be an immigrant within the meaning of the Constitution ...

The return of such a person to his native land after temporary absence has never, so far as I have any acquaintance with the English language, been described as "immigration." That word is not a technical term of art, and when used in s 51(xxvii) of the Constitution must receive its ordinary signification unless the context requires some other meaning to be adopted ...

The respondent is a person who, upon the evidence, was entitled by the circumstances of his birth to regard Victoria as his home. Upon the facts as found by the magistrate he has not himself, nor has anyone by whose acts he is bound, done anything to deprive him of that right, or to confer on him a right to enter or remain in any other part of the world, except so far as his British nationality may confer any such right.

It follows, in my judgment, that, although entry into another part of the British Dominions might and probably would have been immigration, his return to the Commonwealth was not immigration within the meaning of s 51(xxvii) of the Constitution ...

For these reasons I am of opinion that the Acts have no application to the respondent ...

Barton J

He had not made China his home. Victoria was his old home. His return to it was the fulfilment of an oft-expressed desire and intention. Was his return a home-coming? I cannot refuse to say that it was. When he was taken away in 1882 he was a member of this community, and here lay his home. He did not make himself a fresh one in another community. He is entitled to this one. My opinion is that the sense attached to the word "immigration," to denote the legislative power conferred on the Commonwealth, was the ordinary sense. No one describes a man returning home to his own country as an immigrant. He is coming into a country which was a former habitat and which he has not abandoned. Immigration has various but kindred meanings. They all imply that the country which the immigrant seeks to enter is not his home, by any criterion, natural or artificial. He has not migrated thither. He has not come as a new settler. He has not sought admission as a foreigner. I think then that the act of the respondent was not an immigration ...

O'Connor J

Having once established that a country is a man's home in the sense which I have explained, absence, no matter how prolonged, will render it none the less his home if there be always present to his mind the intention to return. A boy, for instance, Australian-born and residing with his parents in Australia, goes to England for purposes of education or the acquirement of business knowledge or a profession, and resides there for many years. He does not thereby change his home provided that he has always persevered in his intention to return to Australia. To describe his return as an "immigration" to Australia would obviously be a misuse of the word "immigrant" in its ordinary sense ...

I therefore agree in the conclusion on the facts that the respondent never did establish his permanent home in China, and that in returning to Australia he was coming back to the home which he had never abandoned. Taking that view of the facts, it follows that in my opinion the respondent was not an "immigrant" within the meaning of the Immigration Restriction Act, that the section under which he was convicted had no application to him ...

Isaacs J

[I]mmigration connotes two facts; the first, that there is an entry into Commonwealth territory, and the second, that the person entering is not in fact at the moment he enters one of the people of the Commonwealth.

The ultimate fact to be reached as a test whether a given person is an immigrant or not is whether he is or is not at that time a constituent part of the community known as the Australian people ...

Higgins J

According to the Standard Dictionary "immigration" is the entrance of settlers from a foreign country; and "immigrate" means to come into a country or region from a former habitat. So that, if the respondent had in fact his habitat in China before he came to Australia, that is enough to make his entry into Australia immigration – at all events where (as in this case) he came to reside here. Looked at in this light the question is merely one of fact – was the respondent's residence or habitat in China before he left China to come to Australia? What constitutes a man's residence may sometimes be difficult to determine; all the circumstances have to be considered; and from the nature of the case no rigid rule can be laid down ...

R v Macfarlane; Ex parte O'Flanagan and O'Kelly stands for three important propositions concerning the scope of the immigration power. First, non-Australian British subjects who enter Australia are immigrants within the meaning of section 51(xxvii) because they are not members of the Australian community. Secondly, the scope of the immigration power extends beyond regulating the act of entry into Australia and includes regulating the conduct of immigrants in Australia. Thirdly, foreign visitors who have no intention of settling in Australia are nevertheless immigrants within the meaning of section 51(xxvii).

R v Macfarlane; Ex parte O'Flanagan and O'Kelly (1923) 32 CLR 518

At the time of this case, Ireland was part of the United Kingdom. Two Irish republicans visited Australia to promote the cause of Irish independence. Both were charged with sedition over speeches they gave. While the charges were pending, both were summoned to appear before a Board established under the* Immigration Act 1901–1920 *(Cth) to show cause why they should not be deported. The High Court held that both men were immigrants and therefore subject to laws enacted under the immigration power.

Knox CJ

The main grounds on which the objection to the validity of this provision was founded were ... that the Commonwealth Parliament has no power to legislate for the exclusion or deportation of British subjects [and] that the power to legislate with respect to immigration does not authorize legislation extending to persons coming into Australia without the intention of settling there ...

The ... ground is covered by the observations of Griffith CJ and O'Connor J and of my brother Isaacs J in *Potter v Minahan*. Griffith CJ says: "There is no doubt that a British subject coming to the Commonwealth from another part of the British Dominions may be an immigrant within the meaning of the Constitution." ... In my opinion this ground of objection entirely fails ...

To hold that absence of intention to settle or reside in the Commonwealth on the part of a person entering is sufficient to prevent his exclusion under a law with respect to immigration would, in my opinion, render nugatory for all practical purposes the power to exclude undesirable immigrants, which is admittedly conferred on the Commonwealth Parliament by s 51(xxvii) of the Constitution. The word "immigration" is undoubtedly capable of meaning entry with the intention of settling or becoming a resident, but it is also capable of the wider meaning which excludes the element of intention ... In my opinion, the word immigration in s 51(xxvii) should not be construed in its narrower sense as connoting the idea of intended settlement or residence, but rather as including the entry into Australia of any person who in so entering is not coming home ...

I do not think it is possible to deny, that the Commonwealth Parliament had power to prohibit absolutely the entry into Australia of any person who is an "immigrant." If this be so, it seems to follow that Parliament may prescribe the conditions on which an "immigrant" may be permitted to enter ...

Isaacs J

There is nothing in either the words of the specific power or any immediate context, or in any other part of the Constitution, to except British subjects who are not Australians from the operation of the power construed in its primary sense. Australia is a distinct constituent unit of the Empire, and the natural law of self-preservation requires that the primary and unqualified sense of the power shall not be cut down ...

[A]n "immigrant" – that is, a person whose original home was elsewhere and who comes to this country for any purpose – remains an "immigrant" as long as he is in Australia. As to him, while in Australia, the rule holds "Once an immigrant always an immigrant," and the Parliamentary power is never abandoned and cannot be abandoned ...

Starke J

[T]he legislative power with respect to immigration extends to every person entering the Commonwealth, whether a British subject or an alien ...

Clearly, as it seems to me, a restrictive power is involved in the authority to make laws with respect to immigration. But restriction must operate upon persons; and if it is to be effective, the Parliament must have authority to refuse, to a person who does not belong to the people of Australia, permission to enter the Commonwealth, or "to annex what conditions it pleases to the permission to enter," and further, to expel or deport from the Commonwealth at pleasure, any such person, if the Parliament considers his presence in Australia "opposed to its peace, order, and good government, or to its social or material interests" or to the welfare of its people ...

Justice Isaacs' aphorism 'once an immigrant always an immigrant' takes a very broad view of the scope of the immigration power. Later case law shows that a person may become absorbed into the Australian community and thereby lose the status of immigrant.

Absorption into the Australian community

In ***Ex parte Walsh and Johnson***, the High Court held that an immigrant who becomes absorbed into the Australian community ceases to be an immigrant.

Re Yates; Ex parte Walsh and Johnson (1925) 37 CLR 36

Walsh (born in Ireland in 1871, arrived in New South Wales in 1893) and Johnson (born in Holland in 1885, arrived in New South Wales in 1910 and naturalised in 1913) led a seamen's strike in 1925. Parliament amended the Immigration Act *to allow the deportation of any person not born in Australia who has been concerned in acts hindering the transport of goods or passengers. The question for the High Court was whether Walsh and Johnson were immigrants and therefore liable to deportation. The High Court held that because Walsh arrived before Federation he was not subject to the immigration power. The High Court also held that because Johnson had been absorbed into the Australian community due to having made Australia his permanent home, he was no longer an immigrant and therefore was no longer subject to the immigration power.*

Knox CJ

The power undoubtedly extends to every person who is, at the relevant time, an immigrant, that is to say, a person coming into Australia who is not at the time of entry a member of the Australian community. If the question be whether he is entitled to enter Australia, the question for decision is whether at that time he is not a member of the Australian community and is therefore subject to the immigration power.

If the question be whether he is entitled to remain in Australia, or, stated otherwise, whether he may be lawfully expelled from Australia under a law made under the authority of this power, and of this power only, the question for decision is whether he is, at the time when it is sought to expel him, a person who is not a member of the Australian community and who is therefore subject to the immigration power. On any given day any person either is or is not a member of the Australian community.

[A] person who has originally entered Australia as an immigrant may, in course of time and by force of circumstances, cease to be an immigrant and become a member of the Australian community. He may, so to speak, grow out of the condition of being an immigrant and thus become exempt from the operation of the immigration power ...

Parliament has authority under this power to expel or deport from the Commonwealth any person who does not belong to the people of Australia, but I can find no reason for extending that authority so as to include within the scope of this power persons who have become members of the Australian community ...

Higgins J

The primary question, therefore, is: Is s 8AA an Act with respect to "immigration"? The answer is surely obvious: that s 8AA is not an Act with respect to immigration at all, but an Act with respect to deportation of residents of Australia, members of the Australian community, who have been immigrants at any time ...

It is a fundamental mistake to treat the power to make laws as to immigration as if it were a power to make laws as to immigrants.

If this view is right – if this is not a law with respect to immigration at all, but a law for the deportation of residents who have been immigrants – s 8AA cannot be valid by virtue of the power conferred by s 51(xxvii) ...

Starke J

Expulsion and banishment of people from a country is not emigration in the ordinary and usual signification of the word. The emigration power will not support s 8AA. Nor is the expulsion of citizens or members of the community from a country ordinarily called immigration ...

Now here, I think, is foreshadowed a clear principle, namely, that those who "originally associated themselves together to form" the Commonwealth and those who are "afterwards admitted to membership" cannot thereafter, upon entering, or crossing the boundary of, Australia, from abroad, be regarded as immigrating into it unless in the meantime they have in fact abandoned their membership. They have never been within, or else have passed beyond, the range of the power: it has never operated, or else has become exhausted. Of course, conditions may be attached to persons immigrating into Australia, upon entry, and so long as they remain within the range of the power ...

Justice Isaacs disagreed with the majority, maintaining his view of 'once an immigrant always an immigrant'.

Re Yates; Ex parte Walsh and Johnson (1925) 37 CLR 36

Isaacs J

It ignores the fundamental principle that it is the original entry, the "immigration," that attracts the power; that all that takes place afterwards takes place by virtue of and flowing from the original permission, and must be based on that permission; that that permission was originally and always remains a matter of law, that the law is an essential element in determining whether or not a man is originally or has become and remains an Australian, having a right to be here (the very argument assumes it), and, lastly, that the law may be altered retrospectively so as to remove from the relevant circumstances that essential element of legal right to be present on Australian territory ...

Again I apply "Once an immigrant always an immigrant." ...

Ex parte Walsh and Johnson indicates that whether a person has become part of the Australian community is (usually) a question of fact.

O'Keefe v Calwell holds that, while absorption into the Australian community takes a person outside the concept of immigrant, legislation can prevent an immigrant being absorbed into the community. In this case, an Indonesian woman married to an Australian man had legal permission to remain in Australia for a designated period. The High Court held that the fact that she had made her home in Australia and had an Australian family did not make her any less an immigrant with permission to remain in Australia for only a designated period. The legal time limit on O'Keefe's permission to remain in Australia meant that, as a matter of law, she could never be absorbed into the Australian community.

O'Keefe v Calwell (1949) 77 CLR 261

O'Keefe was born in Celebes in the Dutch East Indies (now Sulawesi in Indonesia) and lived there until 1942 when she was evacuated by the Royal Australian Navy with her Australian husband and their children to escape advancing Japanese forces. Upon arrival in Australia, O'Keefe was granted a certificate allowing her to remain in Australia for a temporary period, which was extended on a number of occasions. The certificate expired in 1948, making her liable to deportation. Only Latham CJ and Dixon J dealt with the constitutional question of whether O'Keefe was an immigrant within the meaning of section 51(xxvii) of the Australian Constitution.

Latham CJ

It is further argued that the plaintiff has now made her home in Australia and has become a member of the Australian community, so that the *Immigration Act* can no longer be applied to her ...

Laws with respect to immigration may properly control, not only the act of entry into Australia, but also the conditions upon which persons not already members of the Australian community may be permitted to remain in Australia. The basis of s 4 of the Act is that persons may be permitted to remain in Australia for limited periods, which may be extended from time to time, so that as long as they are in Australia under an authorized permit they are not remaining in Australia in contravention of the Act ...

But such persons, expressly allowed to remain for a temporary period, cannot, during that period, become members of the Australian community so as to become entitled to remain here permanently. It is true that the plaintiff has married an Australian husband, has an Australian home, has children who are going to school here, has joined her husband's church, and has her whole life here. But a person cannot become a member of the Australian community by his own act when he has been admitted and has been allowed to remain in Australia only under a temporary permit authorized by statute ...

Admission of any person not already a member of the community may, under a power to make laws with respect to immigration, be allowed or prevented either completely or partially and subject to conditions as Parliament thinks proper. There could be no effective control of the subject of immigration if it were not possible to limit the entry and stay of persons who claimed that they were only making a short visit, or if it were not possible to deport persons who were allowed into the country only for a specified period and who then changed their minds and wished to remain permanently.

Immigration into a country, if completed, involves two elements, (a) entry into the country, and (b) absorption into the community of the country. Both of these elements can be controlled under a power to make laws with respect to immigration ...

Dixon J

Once the plaintiff came under s 4 and received an exemption certificate no attempt on her part to make Australia her permanent home could prevent the operation of the provision. The legislation adopts the machinery of an exemption certificate to prevent persons entering or remaining except by consent and then so long only as the consent continues. If that is within the legislative power with respect to immigration, as I think it is, it is difficult to understand how a person holding an exemption could by nevertheless resolving to make Australia her permanent home and by identifying herself with this country pass from the operation the Constitution allows to the provision.

Ex parte Henry affirmed the proposition that a person who has been absorbed into the Australian community is no longer an immigrant and the proposition that the law can be used to prevent absorption into the Australian community. In this case, the High Court interpreted legislation applying to 'every immigrant child' as not applying to children who had been absorbed into the Australian community.

R v Director-General of Social Welfare (Vic); Ex parte Henry (1975) 133 CLR 369

Barwick CJ

It is implicit in a law made under s 51(xxvii) that, in default of express provisions to the contrary, it does not reach to control a person who has entered as an immigrant beyond the time at which that person ceases to be an immigrant, e.g. by absorption into the Australian community as a member thereof ...

Gibbs J

I consider that a person who has immigrated into Australia will pass beyond the range of the power when the act of immigration is at an end – that is when that person has become a full member of the Australian community. It follows, in my opinion, that the Parliament can attach to the entry of an immigrant who is a child the condition that the child have a suitable guardian and can ensure that the guardianship subsists until the child has been fully absorbed into the Australian community, but cannot validly make a law providing for the guardianship of a child who has become a member of the Australian community ...

Mason J

The immigration power is not confined to regulation of the physical entry of an immigrant into Australia; it may be exercised so as to apply to him at least until he becomes a member of the Australian community ...

[T]he power is not confined to the control of entry and that it extends to control of the absorption of immigrants into the country ...

Justice Jacobs, while agreeing with other members of the majority on the key propositions of law, also suggested that Isaac J's aphorism 'once an immigrant always an immigrant' might have some limited truth to it.

R v Director-General of Social Welfare (Vic); Ex parte Henry (1975) 133 CLR 369

Jacobs J

It does not follow that because a person has entered Australia and been permitted to remain here and to become a member of the Australian community, therefore no law of the Commonwealth whose validity depends upon the immigration power can validly apply to such a person. It is within the immigration power not only to control entry and absorption into the Australian community of persons not born in Australia but also, as an incident of the power, to make laws which so relate to the special needs or special characteristics of immigrants that the subject matter of a law dealing particularly with immigrants may be valid as a law with respect to immigration even where the subject matter generally is not one upon which the Commonwealth has power to legislate. There is truth in the aphorism that the power is in respect of immigration and not immigrants.

But there is truth also in the aphorism "Once an immigrant, always an immigrant". Like most aphorisms in the law they are both no more than half-truths and they solve nothing. In relation to deportation a day comes, it has been held, when an immigrant is absorbed into the Australian community so that he cannot thereafter be deported under the immigration power. But the concept of absorption into the Australian community, though it is a useful consideration in all aspects of the power, has a different content in the context of deportation from that which it has in other contexts of the immigration power. So long as an immigrant has a special need or so long as Australia has a special need from him then so long may the Commonwealth legislate in respect of that special need of the immigrant or the country; and this may be so even if he has become a member of the Australian community in that he can no longer be deported. Of course it could be said that so long as an immigrant has a special need or Australia has a special need from him then he has not been absorbed into the Australian community. But it can only be correct provided that it is then kept clear that the words "absorption into the Australian community" are used in this context with different content and application from those in the context of deportation ...

The complexities and uncertainties around the scope of the concept of absorption into the Australian community have led Parliament to rely principally on the aliens power in section 51(xix) of the *Constitution* to regulate immigration and non-Australians. For example, the aliens power can be used to deport a non-Australian even if that person is not or is no longer an immigrant.

7.3 The naturalisation and aliens power

Section 51(xix) gives Parliament power to make laws with respect to naturalisation and aliens. The *Australian Constitution* does not refer to Australian citizenship. Australian citizenship is not a constitutional concept or status. The relevant constitutional concept is alienage: a person is either an alien or a non-alien.

Until the *Nationality and Citizenship Act 1948* (Cth), there was no legal status of Australian citizen. Australians were all British subjects. That Act instituted the status of Australian citizen and conferred it on a variety of persons living in Australia at the time and prescribed the means by which Australian citizenship could be acquired. The relevant legislation is now the *Australian Citizenship Act 2007* (Cth). These Acts were enacted principally under section 51(xix) of the *Australian Constitution.*

The basic constitutional position from the time the status of Australian citizen was established is that: (1) 'naturalisation' is the legal process by which a non-Australian becomes an Australian citizen; and (2) an 'alien' is any person who is not an Australian citizen.

7.4 Who is an 'alien'?

Alienage is a legal status.

The development of the definition of 'alien' has not been straightforward. The leading case is ***Nolan***, which was overruled in ***Re Patterson; Ex parte Taylor***. ***Re Patterson*** was itself overruled in ***Shaw*** to reinstate the principles in *Nolan*.

The leading case on the meaning of 'alien' is ***Nolan v Minister for Immigration and Ethnic Affairs***. The central holding in *Nolan* is that a person is an 'alien' if the person is not an Australian citizen, and that this includes British subjects who are not Australian citizens.

Nolan v Minister for Immigration and Ethnic Affairs (1988) 165 CLR 178

The Commonwealth intended to deport Nolan, a British subject resident in Australia who was not an Australian citizen and who had committed criminal offences. The question for the High Court was whether a British subject resident in Australia who was not an Australian citizen was an 'alien' within the meaning of section 51(xix) of the* Australian Constitution. *The High Court held that such a person is an alien.

Mason CJ, Wilson, Brennan, Deane, Dawson and Toohey JJ

The primary submission on behalf of the defendants is that the provisions of s 12 [of the *Migration Act 1958* (Cth)], being confined in their application to "non-citizens", come within the power of the Commonwealth to make laws with respect to "aliens" (sub-s (xix)). For the plaintiff, it is submitted that that legislative power cannot validly extend to a person, like himself, who is a subject of the Queen for the reason that such a person is not an "alien" for the purposes of the Constitution regardless of his origins, nationality or citizenship or of the capacity in which the Queen holds his allegiance as a subject.

As a matter of etymology, "alien", from the Latin *alienus* through old French, means belonging to another person or place. Used as a descriptive word to describe a person's lack of relationship with a country, the word means, as a matter of ordinary language, "nothing more than a citizen or subject of a foreign state" (*Milne v Huber* (1843) 17 Fed Cas 403, at p 406 (US)). Thus, an "alien" has been said to be, for the purposes of United States law, "one born out of the United States, who has not since been naturalized under the constitution and laws" (ibid). That definition should be expanded to include a person who has ceased to be a citizen by an act or process of denaturalization and restricted to exclude a person who, while born abroad, is a citizen by reason of parentage. Otherwise, it constitutes an acceptable general definition of the word "alien" when that word is used with respect to an independent country with its own distinct citizenship ...

[Once Australia had acquired status as a sovereign, independent nation], [t]he fact that a person who was born neither in Australia nor of Australian parents and who had not become a citizen of this country was a British subject or a subject of the Queen by reason of his birth in another country could no longer be seen as having the effect, so far as this country is concerned, of precluding his classification as an "alien". It is not that the meaning of the word "alien" had altered. That word is and always has been appropriate to describe the status, vis-a-vis a former colony which has emerged as an independent nation with its own citizenship, of a non-citizen who is a British subject by reason of his citizenship of a different sovereign State ...

So much was recognized by this Court in 1982 in *Pochi v Macphee* (1982) 151 CLR 101 ... The leading judgment was that of Gibbs CJ. His Honour, having traced the alteration in the concept of "British subject" and the development of Australian citizenship, concluded that the plaintiff's argument was "based on a false assumption and must fail" for the reason that, pursuant to the legislative power granted by s 51(xix) with respect to "aliens", "the Parliament can ... treat as an alien any person who was born outside Australia, whose parents were not Australians, and who has not been naturalized as an Australian". Two of the other three members of the Court in *Pochi*, Mason and Wilson JJ, concurred in the judgment of Gibbs CJ. It follows that the basis of the decision in *Pochi* is inconsistent with the plaintiff's argument in the present case to the effect that he is beyond the reach of the legislative power of the Commonwealth with respect to aliens notwithstanding that he was and is, in the words of Gibbs CJ, a "person who was born outside Australia, whose parents were not Australians, and who has not been naturalized as an Australian" ...

[W]e agree with the decision in *Pochi* and with the reasoning of the majority of the Court upon which it was based. It follows that the provisions of s 12 of the Act and their application to the plaintiff are within the legislative competence of the Parliament under s 51(xix) of the Constitution ...

In ***Te***, the High Court again emphasised that alienage is a legal status and not a question of fact. The High Court held that a person's absorption into the Australian community such that they are no longer an immigrant does not transform an alien into a non-alien.

Re Minister for Immigration and Multicultural Affairs; Ex parte Meng Kok Te (2002) 212 CLR 162

Gleeson CJ

Alienage is a legal status. Naturalization is the act in the law by which a person who was formerly an alien ceases to be one. The power conferred by s 51(xix) includes a power to determine legal status ... An alien retains the status of alienage until that status is removed by the process of naturalization. It is for Parliament to decide, from time to time, what that process will involve ...

The concept of absorption into the Australian community, vague as it may be, has been developed as a method of indicating that the activity of immigration in which a person has engaged has come to an end. But it does not mean that the person has lost the status of an alien. Many immigrants become resident aliens. One of the aspects of the power given by par (xix) is a power in the Parliament to determine, by legislation, how an alien may alter that status ...

Gaudron J

[I]t is contended for the prosecutor that, notwithstanding that he is not an Australian citizen, he is not and was not an alien at the time of the deportation order. It is put that he had, by then, ceased to be an alien either by reason of his absorption into the Australian community or by reason that he then owed allegiance to the Queen of Australia and none other ...

Citizenship is a statutory, not a constitutional concept. The relevant constitutional concepts with which this case are concerned are "alien", the singular form of the word used in s 51(xix) of the Constitution, and, by way of constitutional distinction, "non-alien". Thus, the fact that the prosecutor is not an Australian citizen is irrelevant if he is not an alien ...

At least since 1948, the Citizenship Act has exhaustively provided with respect to the circumstances in which persons who are alien born ... may become members of the Australian body politic by the acquisition of Australian citizenship. It cannot be disputed that the prosecutor was alien born and has not obtained Australian citizenship in accordance with the Citizenship Act. He is, therefore, an alien.

McHugh J

Those who enter a common law country as aliens can only acquire citizenship and the status of non-aliens by legislation. For this reason, the applicants' arguments that they are not aliens because they owe allegiance to the Queen or because they were refugees or because they are subject to the laws of Australia must be rejected. Similarly, their claim that they are not aliens because they have become members of the Australian body politic must be rejected. To say that an alien is a member of the body politic is a contradiction in terms ...

Accordingly, the applicants are non-citizens and aliens within the meaning of s 51(xix) ...

Gummow J

[T]he terms "[n]aturalization" and "aliens" do not identify as a head of legislative power conduct or activities associated with movement of persons to or from Australia. Rather, they identify the possession by persons of a particular status (alienage) in the eye of the law and the prescription by law of formalities by which that status is removed ...

The power with respect to "[n]aturalization" is, in a sense, the obverse of that with respect to "aliens". It supports laws which prescribe the process and procedures by which an alien becomes and may remain an Australian national and which give a particular designation or status, here "Australian citizenship", to those former aliens ...

However, the prosecutor submits that under the Australian common law, independently of statute, and by the coming to pass of a state of affairs meeting the criterion of "absorption" and the other metaphors used in authorities construing the reach of the immigration power, an alien may lose that status and so pass beyond the reach of the aliens power. The prosecutor then invites the conclusion of constitutional fact that this is what has happened to him.

There are several answers to this submission. The first is that were there such a common law principle or doctrine, it would be subject, like any part of the common law, to displacement by statute. On this hypothesis, that displacement has occurred by the specific provision made by the Citizenship Act for the granting of Australian citizenship to persons not already Australian citizens. The second is that there has never been any such common law doctrine ...

Hayne J

The status of alien is not lost or altered by the fact that the person in question may have lived in Australia for a long time, or may have cut all the ties which once existed with the body politic of the place where that person was born or with the country of which he or she was formerly a subject or citizen ...

I do not accept that concepts of "absorption", developed in considering the reach of s 51(xxvii) of the Constitution – the immigration and emigration power – have a place in considering who is an alien ...

In ***Re Patterson; Ex parte Taylor*** (2001) 207 CLR 391, a majority of the High Court overruled ***Nolan.*** The High Court held that there were three classes of people: (1) non-aliens who are citizens; (2) non-aliens who are non-citizens but are British subjects resident in Australia who arrived in Australia before the *Australia Act 1986* came into effect; and (3) aliens, which includes everyone else.

Shaw overruled ***Re Patterson; Ex parte Taylor*** and reinstated the principle in ***Nolan*** that a person is either an alien (in the sense of a non-citizen) or a non-alien (in the sense of a citizen). Shaw was born in the United Kingdom to British parents. Shaw came to Australia as an infant but never became a citizen. The High Court held that Shaw was an alien.

Shaw v Minister for Immigration and Multicultural Affairs (2003) 218 CLR 28

Shaw came to Australia as an infant with his parents and had a permanent residency visa. Shaw never became a citizen. Following criminal convictions, Shaw's visa was cancelled, rendering him liable to deportation. The question for the High Court was whether Shaw was an 'alien' and therefore subject to laws, such as the visa cancellation law, enacted under the aliens power.

Gleeson CJ, Gummow and Hayne JJ

The power conferred by s 51(xix) supports legislation determining those to whom is attributed the status of alien; the Parliament may make laws which impose upon those having this status burdens, obligations and disqualifications which the Parliament could not impose upon other persons. On the other hand, by a law with respect to naturalisation, the Parliament may remove that status, absolutely or upon conditions. In this way, citizenship may be seen as the obverse of the status of alienage ...

Much of the applicant's argument proceeded from the premise that, because the expression "British subject" could be applied to him, he was not an alien. That premise is flawed. First, "British subject" is not a constitutional expression; it is a statutory expression. Secondly, and more fundamentally, if "British subject" was being used as a synonym for "subject of the Queen", an expression which is found in the Constitution, that usage would assume that there was at the time of federation, and there remains today, a constitutional and political unity between the UK and Australia which 100 years of history denies ...

[T]he applicant entered Australia as an alien in the constitutional sense. *Re Minister for Immigration and Multicultural Affairs; Ex parte Meng Kok Te* establishes that, this being so, he did not lose that status by reason of his subsequent personal history in this country. Upon the cancellation of his visa, he became an "unlawful non-citizen" within the meaning of the Act.

This case should be taken as determining that the aliens power has reached all those persons who entered this country after the commencement of the Citizenship Act on 26 January 1949 and who were born out of Australia of parents who were not Australian citizens and who had not been naturalised. The scope of any earlier operation of the power does not fall for consideration ...

The decision in *Patterson* does not rest upon a principle carefully worked out in a significant succession of decisions; the contrary, as we have indicated, is the case. Secondly, the treatment of the aliens power in *Patterson* was not necessary for the decision, because there was a clear alternative basis for the decision. Thirdly, the inconvenience flowing from the existence of *Patterson* is indicated by reference to *Long*. Finally, the Minister has moved as quickly as may be in this Court to obtain a reconsideration of *Patterson*. That case henceforth should be regarded as authority for what it decided respecting s 64 of the *Constitution* and the constructive failure in the exercise of jurisdiction by the Minister ...

Consistently with the proposition that alienage is a legal status applying to anyone who is not a citizen, ***Singh*** demonstrates that a person born in Australia may be an alien. In this case, Singh was born in Australia to parents who were Indian citizens but not Australian citizens or permanent residents. Under Indian law, Singh acquired Indian citizenship at birth. Under Australian legislation, a person born in Australia is not automatically a citizen unless other circumstances exist. None of those circumstances existed in this case, with the result that Singh was not an Australian citizen. The High Court held Singh was an alien.

The High Court also held that the constitutional term 'alien' has an outer limit, such that Parliament cannot deem a person falling outside that limit to be an alien. However, Parliament can choose to treat only a narrower class of persons as aliens. For example, Parliament could change the law so that anyone born in Australia, like Singh, is automatically an Australian citizen. The High Court noted that Singh legally owed allegiance to India and did not owe allegiance to Australia. The result was that Singh did not fall outside the limit of the constitutional concept of 'alien'.

Singh v Commonwealth (2004) 222 CLR 322

The Migration Act 1958 *(Cth) provided for the deportation of non-citizens who did not hold a valid visa. The question for the High Court was whether Singh, a young child, was an alien within the meaning of the* Australian Constitution *and therefore liable to deportation.*

Gleeson CJ

To be more precise, the question is whether, in s 51(xix), "aliens" necessarily excludes persons born in Australia, subject to certain presently irrelevant exceptions such as children of foreign diplomats, or of members of visiting armed forces ... Parliament cannot, simply by giving its own definition of "alien", expand the power under s 51(xix) to include persons who could not possibly answer the description of "aliens" in the Constitution. Within the class of persons who could answer that description, Parliament can determine to whom it will be applied, and with what consequences. Alienage is a status, and, subject to the qualification just mentioned, Parliament can decide who will be treated as having that status for the purposes of Australian law and, subject to any other relevant constitutional constraints, what that status will entail ...

The argument for the plaintiff has not been made out. She is a citizen of a foreign state, the child of foreign citizens and, although born in Australia, she is an alien.

Gummow, Hayne and Heydon JJ

As a citizen of India the plaintiff has obligations, "owes allegiance", to a nation other than Australia. She is, therefore, a person within the class referred to in s 51(xix) as "aliens". As will be apparent from what has just been said, the plaintiff does not fall into that class simply because her parents do so ...

A central characteristic of the status of "alien" is, and always has been, owing obligations to a sovereign power other than the sovereign power in question. The plaintiff has that characteristic ...

"Aliens", even if it had once had a fixed legal meaning, did not bear such a meaning by the end of the 19th century. But what did remain unaltered was that "aliens" included those who owed allegiance to another sovereign power, or who, having no nationality, owed no allegiance to any sovereign power ...

It was common ground that the plaintiff is a citizen of India. She is, therefore, a citizen of a foreign state. She is a person within the naturalization and aliens power ...

Koroitamana reaffirms the decision in ***Singh*** that a person born in Australia is not automatically a non alien. The facts of this case are almost identical to the facts of *Singh*. The children in this case were born in Australia but, unlike the child in *Singh*, did not hold any foreign citizenship. However, they were entitled to Fijian citizenship but their parents did not wish to register them for Fijian citizenship. The fact the children were born in Australia and were not citizens of any other country (and therefore effectively stateless) did not mean they were not aliens. Together, this case and *Singh* demonstrate that *absence* of legal allegiance to Australia is a necessary component of the constitutional concept of 'alien'.

Koroitamana v Commonwealth (2006) 227 CLR 31

Gleeson CJ and Heydon J

The present case and *Singh* are not factually identical, and there was argument about the extent to which the decision in *Singh* left open issues of significance for this case. Two things, however, are clear. First, *Singh* decided that birth in Australia does not of itself mean that a person is beyond the reach of the power conferred on the Parliament by s 51(xix). The applicants cannot claim, and do not claim, that, solely because they were born in Australia, it is beyond the power of Parliament to treat them as aliens ...

On the approach that was adopted by the parties, the difference between the present case and *Singh* is that in *Singh* it was common ground in argument that the plaintiff was a citizen of India by descent from her parents whereas the applicants in this case are not citizens of Fiji. The similarity, of course, is that the parents of the applicants, like the parents of the plaintiff in *Singh*, are citizens of a foreign country ...

The power conferred by s 51(xix) is a wide power, under which the Parliament has the capacity to decide who will be admitted to formal membership of the Australian community, which now means citizenship. Within the limits of the concept of "alien" in s 51(xix), it is for Parliament to decide who will be treated as having the status of alienage, who will be treated as citizens, and what the status of alienage, or non-citizenship, will entail. The concept of "alien" does not exclude persons born in Australia, where they are children of parents who are foreign nationals ...

The argument for the applicants was that, in the ordinary understanding of the word "alien", a person born within Australia could not possibly answer the description unless a further characteristic, of which foreign allegiance was the clearest example, could be shown to exist. Hence the significance sought to be attached to the difference from the facts in *Singh* ...

Regard may be had to the variety of circumstances in which a child of foreign nationals may be born in Australia. The parents may be in Australia unlawfully, or for a brief visit, or even unintentionally. They may be in transit to another destination. They may be here for temporary purposes of a business or personal nature. Once one rejects the notion that birth in Australia (except in the case of children of foreign diplomats and members of armed forces) necessarily results in membership of the Australian community, then it is a short step to the conclusion that it is open to Parliament to decide that a child born in Australia of parents who are foreign nationals is not automatically entitled to such membership. It cannot be said of such a person that he or she could not possibly answer the description of alien ...

Gummow, Hayne and Crennan JJ

Singh is authority at least for the propositions that (i) the common law of England respecting alienage as understood in 1900 does not mark the boundaries of the power conferred by s 51(xix); (ii) it is not an essential characteristic of the "aliens" referred to in s 51(xix) of the Constitution that they be born outside Australia; and (iii) the Parliament might treat as an "alien" a person born in Australia with a foreign citizenship derived from that of the parents of that person.

However, the applicants denied that they were within the reach of the legislative power conferred by s 51(xix) of the Constitution for the Parliament to make laws with respect to "Naturalization and aliens". The applicants submitted that (i) a person born in Australia and having then no other "relevant characteristic" cannot be treated by the Parliament as an alien; and (ii) they had no such relevant characteristic ...

The consequence is that, on the terms of their own case, the applicants were born stateless and this was a relevant characteristic then rendering them aliens. That is a sufficient basis to dismiss the appeal ...

7.5 Aboriginal Australians are an exception to the citizen/ alien dichotomy

Love v Commonwealth complicates the citizen/alien binary. A majority of the High Court held that Aboriginal people are not aliens even where they are, like Mr Love (who was born in Papua New Guinea and is a citizen of that country) and Mr Thoms (who was born in New Zealand and is a citizen of that country), non-citizens. For this purpose, the High Court adopted the tripartite test of Aboriginality from the native title case of *Mabo v Queensland (No 2)* (1992) 175 CLR 1: (1) membership of the Aboriginal race; (2) self-identification as an Aboriginal person; and (3) acceptance as a member of an Aboriginal group in accordance with the laws and customs of that group.

Love v Commonwealth (2020) 270 CLR 152

***Love and Thoms had lived most of their lives in Australia but were not Australian citizens. Each had been born overseas and held foreign citizenship. Both men had committed certain crimes. Acting under the* Migration Act 1958 (Cth), *the Commonwealth cancelled the men's visas and intended to remove them from Australia. Both men claimed to be Aboriginal and that this fact meant they were not aliens and therefore beyond the reach of the removal provisions of the* Migration Act.**

Bell J

I am authorised by the other members of the majority to say that although we express our reasoning differently, we agree that Aboriginal Australians (understood according to the tripartite test in *Mabo (No 2)*) are not within the reach of the 'aliens' power conferred by s 51(xix) of the *Constitution*.

There are some common themes in the separate majority judgments of Bell, Nettle, Gordon and Edelman JJ. The first theme concerns the idea that an Aboriginal person's indigeneity, or status as an indigenous person, means that it is impossible to consider them as a foreigner or outsider.

Love v Commonwealth (2020) 270 CLR 152

Gordon J

The constitutional term "aliens" conveys otherness, being an "outsider", foreignness. The constitutional term "aliens" does not apply to Aboriginal Australians, the original inhabitants of the country. An Aboriginal Australian is not an 'outsider' to Australia.

Edelman J

The application of the aliens power and the race power was generally understood to be complementary. The aliens power and the immigration power in s 51(xxvii) included a concern with the conditions of admission to Australia of those who were considered as members of foreign races. The race power was concerned with the treatment of the people considered to be members of those foreign races "who are in the Commonwealth [of Australia]" even if they were granted citizenship ...

In its literal terms, the race power could have applied to all "races" since, as Professor Sawer observed, there is difficulty in seeing why the race power should not be "applicable to the majority 'race' - every person, say, of 'Caucasian origin'". It was effectively the concept of political community, which included Aboriginal people, that limited the application of the race power to "alien races". Hence, even without an express exclusion from the meaning, Aboriginal people would probably not have been within the application of the race power. The express exclusion of them from the meaning of s 51(xxvi) was thus, unsurprisingly, not the subject of debate: "it was simply taken for granted that they should be excluded". There was, however, no need, even for clarity, for the same exclusion from the meaning of s 51(xix), which did not mention race. Aboriginal people simply did not fall within the application of "alien", a foreigner to the political community.

The second theme in the majority judgments is that the spiritual and cultural 'belonging' of Aboriginal people to their traditional lands as recognised by the common law and those traditional lands being part of the Commonwealth of Australia leads to the conclusion that Aboriginal people are necessarily members of the Australian people.

Love v Commonwealth (2020) 270 CLR 152

Bell J

The Commonwealth's concern, that to hold that its legislative power does not extend to treating an Aboriginal Australian as an alien is to identify a race-based limitation on power, is overstated. It is not offensive, in the context of contemporary international understanding, to recognise the cultural and spiritual dimensions of the distinctive connection between indigenous peoples and their traditional lands, and in light of that recognition to hold that the exercise of the sovereign power of this nation does not extend to the exclusion of the indigenous inhabitants from the Australian community.

Gordon J

The sovereignty of the Commonwealth is asserted over territory, territory to which the common law recognises that Aboriginal Australians have a unique connection. And what the common law then acknowledged about Aboriginal Australians is relevant to interpreting the scope of s 51(xix) because the common law may inform the understanding of constitutional concepts. The issue is what follows from the continued two-way connection of Aboriginal Australians with land and waters that *Mabo [No 2]* held could and did survive the assertion of sovereignty.

To speak of a polity or body politic, which in the case of Australia is a nation-state, or the sovereignty exercised by that polity, without considering its territorial dimension is to overlook one of the essential requirements of a polity and of sovereignty ...

The connection recognised by Australian law between Aboriginal Australians and the land and waters of this country therefore cannot be dismissed as irrelevant to membership of the present polity of the Commonwealth of Australia, a polity established on the same land and waters. To assert sovereignty over land or waters where the connection of Aboriginal Australians has not been severed requires that those connected to the land or waters in that way are not classified as aliens, or as 'other' or foreign to the land or waters of the polity.

Edelman J

The identity of Aboriginal people, whether citizens or non-citizens, is shaped by a fundamental spiritual and cultural sense of belonging to Australia. It is that identity which constitutes them as members of the Australian political community. At Federation that identity limited the reach of the aliens power in s 51(xix) of the Constitution, preventing the fragmentation of the political community and the stripping of that Aboriginal identity. It would be bizarre if the evolved application of the aliens power could do so today.

...

A political community is not a thing that exists in space. It is a metaphysical construct that describes a group of people who belong to a defined place or territory, here the land of the Australian state, and who are to be regulated as such belongers.

There were also common themes in the separate dissenting judgments of Kiefel CJ, Gageler and Keane JJ. The first theme was about emphasising the difference between the notion of belonging to traditional lands and the notion of belonging to the Australian body politic.

Love v Commonwealth (2020) 270 CLR 152

Kiefel CJ

[I]t may be said that the common law accepts that members of an Aboriginal group may feel a sense of "belonging" to the land in question and that others may perceive them to "belong" to the land. But that is not the "belonging" spoken of in the constitutional sense. In the constitutional context it refers to a characteristic which a citizen has with respect to the sovereign State of which they are a citizen and which an alien does not. A citizen may be said to belong to their country. A non-citizen or alien does not belong. An alien belongs to the sovereign State of which they are a citizen.

...

In the constitutional context "belonging" refers to the formal legal relationship between a person and the community or body politic in question. In Australia it is apt to describe the connection between a citizen and the body politic. It reflects a conclusion reached about that relationship rather than a premise upon which the relationship may be founded.

Keane J

The plaintiffs' argument confuses the body politic that was brought into existence at Federation with lands and waters, parts of which were occupied by particular Aboriginal groups long before that body politic came into being. The plaintiffs' argument also confuses the spiritual connection of an indigenous person to particular lands and waters with a connection to the body politic that is inconsistent with alienage. In this regard, the plaintiffs' submission is fatally imprecise. If, as is the case here, one is speaking of the body politic being the Commonwealth of Australia, the "Australian community" is not 50,000 years old: the Australian community, the Commonwealth of Australia, was established only at Federation.

The second key theme in the dissenting judgments was that by relying on the *Mabo (No 2)* test of who is an Aboriginal person the majority position has the effect of impermissibly accepting that Aboriginal groups exercise a form of political sovereignty.

Love v Commonwealth (2020) 270 CLR 152

Kiefel CJ

There is a more fundamental difficulty which arises from the plaintiffs' argument. It is that the legal status of a person as a "non-citizen, non-alien" would follow from a determination by the Elders, or other persons having traditional authority amongst a particular group, that the person was a member of that group. To accept this effect would be to attribute to the group the kind of sovereignty which was implicitly rejected by *Mabo [No 2]* – by reason of the fact of British sovereignty and the possibility that native title might be extinguished – and expressly rejected in subsequent cases.

Gageler J

To concede capacity to decide who is and who is not an alien from the perspective of the body politic of the Commonwealth of Australia to a traditional Aboriginal or Torres Strait Islander society or to a contemporary Aboriginal or Torres Strait Islander community, or to any other discrete segment of the people of Australia, would be to concede to a non-constitutional non-representative non-legally-accountable sub-national group a constitutional capacity greater than that conferred on any State Parliament. Yet that would be the practical effect of acceptance of either of the first and second variations of the plaintiffs' argument.

Keane J

[T]o suggest that members of Aboriginal groups have authority to make choices that bind the Commonwealth of Australia is to attribute to those persons a measure of political sovereignty. To assert that the ordinary application of laws made pursuant to s 51(xix) of the *Constitution* to foreign citizens born outside Australia such as the plaintiffs is displaced as a result of recognition by members of the Aboriginal group from which they claim descent, is to assert an exercise of political sovereignty by those persons.

The third key theme in the dissenting judgments was an objection to what was seen as the majority introducing a racial component to what it means to be Australian.

Love v Commonwealth (2020) 270 CLR 152

Kiefel CJ

[R]ace is irrelevant to the questions of citizenship and membership of the Australian body politic.

Gageler J

Nor can I be party to a process of constitutional interpretation or constitutional implication which would result in the inference of a race-based constitutional limitation on legislative power. My objection is one of principle to the judicial creation of any race-based constitutional distinction irrespective of how benign the particular distinction contended for might seem. Creativity of that nature and in that degree is not within the scope of the acknowledged judicial function of ensuring that the structure of government, democratically endorsed through the adoption and amendment of the Constitution, is accommodated to the "changeful necessities and circumstances of generation after generation" as "the nation lives, grows, and expands". It is supra-constitutional innovation.

Keane J

Alienage or citizenship is a status created by law. That status is a relationship between an individual and the sovereign nation. It is not a relationship between an ethnic group and the nation. Nor is it a relationship between an individual and an ethnic group. Australian law does not recognise an entitlement to membership of the Australian body politic independently of the satisfaction of the ordinary legal requirements and qualifications for Australian citizenship. In this regard, membership of a particular race does not afford an entitlement to membership of the Australian body politic under the Constitution or any Act of Parliament. Considerations of race are irrelevant to the requirements for membership of the Australian body politic. As Gaudron J said in *Kartinyeri v Commonwealth*: "[R]ace is simply irrelevant ... to the question of continued membership of the Australian body politic."

There are different ways of looking at the decision in *Love*. One way is to say that *Love* is principally of symbolic significance about the status of Aboriginal people in Australia's constitutional framework and of very limited practical impact. There would be very few Aboriginal individuals who are not Australian citizens, and of that small number even fewer would have circumstances that trigger the *Migration Act*'s removal power.

7.6 The future of the citizen/alien dichotomy

Another way of looking at ***Love*** is to focus on how it highlights problems with the general approach of treating the concept of alien as the antonym of citizen. In ***Chetcuti v Commonwealth***, the joint judgment of Kiefel CJ, Gageler, Keane and Gleeson JJ described ***Love*** as establishing an *exception*, rather than representing a challenge to or unsettling of established principles. However, aspects of the majority reasoning do seem to highlight the lack of settled understanding of the constitutional concept of 'alien'.

Chetcuti reaffirmed the decision in ***Shaw*** that non-citizen British subjects can be considered aliens. The High Court held that British subjects who migrated to Australia before the concept of Australian citizenship was created by legislation with effect from 26 January 1949 and who never obtained Australian citizenship are capable of being considered aliens.

Chetcuti v Commonwealth (2021) 272 CLR 609

Chetcuti was born in 1945 as a British subject in the then British colony of Malta and migrated to Australia in 1948. He never obtained Australian citizenship. After serving a sentence for murder, the Commonwealth sought to remove Chetcuti from Australia under the* Migration Act 1958 (Cth). *Chetcuti argued that he was a non-alien and therefore beyond the reach of the removal provisions of the* Migration Act. *The High Court held that Chetcuti was an alien.

Kiefel CJ, Gageler, Keane and Gleeson JJ

Since 2 April 1984, the Commonwealth Parliament has relied on the legislative power with respect to aliens to sustain the Migration Act. Subject to providing through s 15A of the *Acts Interpretation Act 1901 (Cth)* for the Migration Act to have a distributive and severable operation to the extent of any constitutional overreach, the Parliament has done so treating all non-citizens as aliens ...

...

[T]he appellant does not seek to disturb the settled understanding that the aliens power encompasses both power to determine who is and who is not to have the legal status of an alien and power to attach consequences to that status. Nor does the appellant seek to disturb the settled understanding that, in determining who is and who is not to have the legal status of an alien, it is in general open to the Parliament to "treat as an alien any person who was born outside Australia, whose parents were not Australians, and who has not been naturalized as an Australian".

Seeking to build on the recognition by the majority in *Love v Commonwealth* of an exception in respect of a person who is an Aboriginal Australian according to the tripartite test in *Mabo v Queensland [No 2]*, the appellant argues for recognition of a further exception. The further exception is in respect of a person who was a natural born British subject and who commenced residing permanently in Australia before 26 January 1949. The appellant argues that the status of a non-alien attaches indelibly to a person in that category either by reason of the person having been born within the allegiance of an as yet undivided Imperial Crown or by reason of the Parliament having once and for all determined the person not to be an alien under the Nationality Act.

[T]he answer to the appellant's argument is to be found in the reasons for judgment of the majority in *Shaw v Minister for Immigration and Multicultural Affairs*, from which the holding of the majority in *Love v Commonwealth* does not depart except in respect of an Aboriginal Australian according to the tripartite test in *Mabo v Queensland [No 2]*.

The conclusion of the majority in Shaw was confined in its terms to a determination that "the aliens power has reached all those persons who entered this country after the commencement of [the *Australian Citizenship Act*] on 26 January 1949 and who were born out of Australia of parents who were not Australian citizens and who had not been naturalised". The reasoning employed by the majority to reach that conclusion nevertheless equally supports the conclusion that the aliens power has reached all those persons who entered this country before 26 January 1949 who did not then or did not afterwards become Australian citizens.

The principal significance of ***Chetcuti*** lies in the fact that each member of the Court accepted the possibility that there might be non-citizen non-aliens. The plurality judgment of Kiefel CJ, Gageler, Keane and Gleeson JJ indicates openness to this idea in its reference to the possibility of severing any 'constitutional overreach' in Parliament treating all non-citizens as aliens. Justices Gordon and Edelman in separate majority judgments were more explicit in acknowledging the prospect of non-citizen non-aliens, emphasising that statutory concepts (like citizen) cannot control the meaning of constitutional concepts.

Chetcuti v Commonwealth (2021) 272 CLR 609

Gordon J

[C]itizenship is a matter that is relevant to alienage, but it is not determinative of alienage. "Aliens" is a constitutional term, whereas "citizenship" is a purely statutory concept. "Non-citizen" is not a synonym for "alien". It is not the case that, on and from the commencement of the *Australian Citizenship Act 1948 (Cth)* on 26 January 1949, all persons who have not had the status of Australian citizens have been aliens. Indeed, the majority holding in *Love v Commonwealth* was to the contrary.

It is, however, unnecessary in this case to chart the metes and bounds of the constitutional concept of "alien".

Edelman J

The unchanging, essential meaning of an "alien" in s 51(xix) of the *Constitution* is a foreigner to the Australian political community ...

...

The meaning of "alien" in s 51(xix) does not correspond precisely with the concepts of either (i) non-subjecthood or non-allegiance or (ii) non-citizenship. To set the meaning by reference to either non-allegiance or non-citizenship would be to ascribe too narrow a scope for the evolution of application of that constitutional term.

...

[T]o re-define the essential meaning of "alien" as "non-citizen" would effectively be a judicial amendment to the *Constitution*. It would also be contrary to basic constitutional principle.

In *Love v Commonwealth*, multiple members of this Court acknowledged the existence of a constitutional limit upon the extent to which Parliament could affect the meaning of "alien" by legislation. This limit, which Gibbs CJ (with whom Mason and Wilson JJ agreed) had earlier regarded as clear in *Pochi v Macphee* and which many other members of this Court have reiterated, was that the Commonwealth Parliament cannot "simply by giving its own definition of "alien", expand the power under s 51(xix) to include persons who could not possibly answer the description of "aliens" in the ordinary understanding of the word" ...

In *Love v Commonwealth*, as in this case, the Solicitor-General of the Commonwealth gave an example of a person who, whatever their status under statutory citizenship laws, would be beyond the aliens power due to the strength of that person's connection with the Australian political community. His example, which should be accepted as correct, is a person born in Australia, to two parents who are Australian citizens, who is not a citizen of another country, and who has not renounced their allegiance to Australia. Another example, recognised by a majority of this Court in *Love v Commonwealth*, is Aboriginal Australians.

In *obiter* remarks in ***Alexander v Minister for Home Affairs***, Edelman J strongly criticised the course of authority on the definition of 'alien' and suggested that in an appropriate case 'it will become necessary to confront the correctness of those decisions rather than tip-toeing around them'. Justice Edelman also suggested that in an appropriate case absorption into the community, even without having obtained statutory citizenship, should be accepted as a sufficient basis for a person no longer being alien.

Alexander v Minister for Home Affairs [2022] HCA 19

Edelman J

The [problematic] effect of the decisions of this Court began in 1982, when this Court first held that persons who had been unconditionally absorbed into the Australian political community were still within the reach of the aliens power. From that premise, and case by case, the application of the essential meaning of "alien" – a foreigner to the Australian political community – was extended further and further to apply to persons who had less and less "foreign" connection ...

[A]n overly broad application of the aliens power [has been] adopted in decisions of this Court that, described politely, would strike an ordinary person as very curious. A majority of this Court reasoned in *Shaw v Minister for Immigration and Multicultural Affairs* that the prosecutor in

Re Patterson; Ex parte Taylor, Mr Taylor, was an alien due to his British citizenship despite having been a permanent resident in Australia for more than 30 years from the age of six and on State and federal electoral rolls since the age of 18. This Court concluded in *Falzon v Minister for Immigration and Border Protection* that Mr Falzon was an alien due to his Maltese citizenship, despite his permanent residence in Australia for 61 years after emigrating from Malta at the age of three. This Court also concluded in *Chetcuti v Commonwealth* that Mr Chetcuti was an alien despite his permanent residence in Australia for 69 years, during which he was a voter in local, State and federal elections and a registrant for military service, having arrived from Malta at the age of two as a British subject ...

[O]nce a person is naturalised according to whatever might be the requirements of a Commonwealth law made under s 51(xix), the legislative power over naturalisation is "spent" in relation to that person, subject to any reasonable conditions that are imposed. The naturalisation law might be amended or repealed but a person who has been naturalised is generally beyond the scope of the power.

There are exceptions ... [and] it cannot be denied that s 51(xix) supports laws that regulate some circumstances in which a person can cease to be a member of the political community of the Australian body politic.

7.7 Turning a non-alien into an alien

Nolan, ***Te*** and ***Shaw*** each note that section 51(xix) supports denaturalisation or citizenship stripping laws; that is, section 51(xix) authorises laws that transform a non-alien (i.e. a citizen) into an alien (i.e. a non-citizen). Those cases also indicate that this power is limited by the outer limit of the constitutional concept of 'alien': Parliament cannot deem a person falling outside that limit to be an alien.

In ***Nolan***, Gaudron J disagreed with the majority's definition of alien and adopted the position that briefly gained acceptance in ***Re Patterson; Ex parte Taylor***. Separately to that issue, Gaudron J's judgment in *Nolan* also discussed transforming a non-alien into an alien. Justice Gaudron explained that, whatever definition of 'alien' is adopted, there needs to be some 'relevant change in the relationship' between the non-alien and the Australian body politic in order for section 51(xix) to support legislation transforming that non-alien into an alien.

Nolan v Minister for Immigration and Ethnic Affairs (1988) 165 CLR 178

Gaudron J

The power to legislate with respect to naturalization and aliens seems necessarily to carry with it a power to revoke the grant of naturalization and a power to define the circumstances in which a non-alien may become an alien ...

Nor, in my view, can the Parliament expand the power by constituting a non-alien an alien if there has not been some relevant change in the relationship between that person and the community constituting the body politic of Australia, including, for example, the abandonment of membership of the community, or the acquisition of membership of some other nation community. It seems to me that such was the condition which the common law attached to the transformation from non-alien to alien status ...

As the transformation from non-alien to alien requires some relevant change in the relationship between the individual and the community, it is not, in my view, open to the Parliament to effect that transformation by simply redefining the criterion for admission to membership of the community constituting the body politic of Australia ...

One relevant change in the relationship between a non-alien and the Australian body politic that supports legislation transforming that non-alien into an alien is change in territorial sovereignty. In ***Ex parte Ame,*** the High Court held section 51(xix) supports laws transforming residents of territory that ceases to be part of Australia from non-aliens into aliens. The case concerned legislation taking away Australian citizenship from the people of the former Australian external territories of Papua and New Guinea upon the independence of Papua New Guinea in 1975.

Re Minister for Immigration and Multicultural and Indigenous Affairs; Ex Parte Ame (2005) 222 CLR 439

Gleeson CJ, McHugh, Hayne, Callinan and Heydon JJ

[T]he capacity to acquire an external territory and the power to make laws for the government of that territory necessarily implied a capacity to legislate for the consequences of the cessation of those powers of government. When Papua ceased to be an external territory of Australia, and became part of the sovereign Independent State of Papua New Guinea, the people of Papua owed allegiance to the new sovereign State. Their rights and obligations were declared by the Papua New Guinea Constitution, and the membership of the new nation was defined by the provisions of that Constitution relating to citizenship. It was within the power of the Parliament, cognisant of those provisions, to respond to the change in sovereign rights, and the new realities affecting the relationship between the inhabitants of Papua and their government, by treating those inhabitants as aliens and withdrawing their Australian citizenship. Parliament did this, knowing that the Papua New Guinea Constitution gave them automatic citizenship of the new Independent State.

Another relevant change in the relationship between a non-alien and the Australian body politic that supports legislation transforming that non-alien into an alien is where a person has by their conduct repudiated their membership of the Australian community. ***Alexander*** held that section 51(xix) supports a law taking away Australian citizenship from a person who engages in conduct, such as travelling overseas to fight with terrorist groups, that 'demonstrates that the person has repudiated their allegiance to Australia'.

Alexander v Minister for Home Affairs [2022] HCA 19

Alexander was an Australian citizen from birth and also a Turkish citizen. He travelled to a part of Syria that was under the control of the so-called Islamic State, a declared terrorist group. Australia Security Intelligence Organisation reports indicated that Alexander had joined Islamic State and likely engaged in foreign incursions and recruitment within the meaning of the 'foreigner fighter' provisions of the Criminal Code *(Cth). Alexander was captured by Syrian forces and detained. Section 36B of the* Australian Citizenship Act 2007 *(Cth) empowered the Minister for Home Affairs to make a determination that a person above 14 years of age and who holds citizenship of at least one other country ceases to be an Australian citizen if they are satisfied that the person has engaged in specified conduct (including engaging in foreign incursions and recruitment) demonstrating repudiation of allegiance to Australia. The Minister made such a determination in respect of Alexander. The High Court held that the provision was supported by section 51(xix) of the* Constitution *(but was invalid for contravening limitations on federal legislative power arising from Chapter III of the* Constitution, *discussed in Chapters 16 and 17).*

Kiefel CJ, Keane and Gleeson JJ

There is ample support in authority for the view that the scope of s 51(xix) extends to permit Parliament to "determine the legal basis by reference to which Australia deals with matters of nationality … to create and define the concept of Australian citizenship [and] to prescribe the conditions on which such citizenship may be acquired *and lost*" …

[T]here is nothing fanciful in classifying as an alien – separate from "the people" – an individual who, though previously a citizen, has acted so inimically to Australia's interests as to repudiate the obligations of citizenship on which membership of the people of the Commonwealth depends.

…

Given that citizenship is a status of reciprocal rights and obligations, it is to understand the status of citizenship in an incoherently one sided way to say that s 51(xix) supports a law that specifies the criteria by which a citizen may voluntarily renounce Australian citizenship – as Mr Alexander accepted – but does not support a law that treats voluntary conduct demonstrating a repudiation of allegiance to Australia as an implied renunciation of citizenship.

Mr Alexander argued that voluntary conduct of the kind described in s 36B(5)(h) cannot rationally be treated as a repudiation of allegiance unless it is intended to be so. The facts stated in the special case suggest that it was reasonably open to the Parliament to regard voluntary conduct, as described in s 36B(5)(h), as so reprehensible as to be incompatible with the common bonds of allegiance to the Australian community, even though the person who has engaged in that conduct did not act intentionally to repudiate the bonds of citizenship.

Edelman J

[I]t cannot be denied that s 51(xix) supports laws that regulate some circumstances in which a person can cease to be a member of the political community of the Australian body politic. Such circumstances include: a change in sovereign identity or territory; breach by a naturalised member of the political community of a reasonable condition upon membership; and express or implied renunciation of membership of that political community. Each of these circumstances is a natural cause of the cessation of membership of a political community: a change in the community itself; a failure of an express, and reasonable, condition subsequent to membership of the community; or voluntary abandonment of membership of the community.

The premise of s 36B of the *Australian Citizenship Act* is that a further circumstance exists where, by s 36B(1)(b), a person has engaged in conduct which "demonstrates that the person has repudiated their allegiance to Australia". It is implicit in s 36B that the section will apply irrespective of whether the person's conduct permits an inference that the person wished to renounce their membership of the political community.

I therefore agree with Steward J that the limited class of conduct which might justify loss of citizenship "might include actions which seek to destroy or gravely harm the fundamental and basal features of the nation guarded by its Constitution, such as representative democracy and the rule of law, and actions directed at overthrowing state institutions where such conduct amounts to a clear rejection of allegiance to Australia. Terrorist attacks might also be included."

...

On its proper interpretation, s 36B of the *Australian Citizenship Act* is consistent with this reasoning. The objective conduct caught by ss 36B(1)(a) and 36B(5), involving matters related to terrorism, foreign incursions, and service in the armed forces of a country at war with Australia, provides a baseline for the extreme nature of the conduct required to establish a repudiation of allegiance, albeit divorced from any mental element that would render that conduct an offence.

7.8 Scope of the aliens power

Most of the case law concerning section 51(xix) of the *Australian Constitution* is about the definition of 'alien' in the context of cases involving legislation authorising the deportation of aliens. However, the ordinary rules of characterisation (discussed in Chapter 3) mean that Parliament can make laws having a sufficient connection to aliens. Migration laws regulating which non-citizens are eligible to enter Australia on tourist or work visas and the terms on which such visa-holders may remain in Australia are examples.

The aliens power also supports laws applying to non-aliens where those laws have a sufficient connection with the subject-matter of aliens. ***Cunliffe*** provides an example. In that case, the High Court held that legislation regulating the profession of migration agents, including matters such as admission to the profession and the provision of immigration advice to non-citizens, is supported by the aliens power.

Cunliffe v Commonwealth (1994) 182 CLR 272

Mason CJ

The provision of immigration assistance to aliens, especially by persons who act on their behalf and for them by representing them and giving them advice, is, in my view, at the core of both the aliens power and the immigration power. It can make no difference that the law operates by way of creating rights, duties and privileges on non-aliens in terms of the services they wish to provide to aliens rather than by way of creating rights, duties and privileges on aliens in terms of the services they wish to receive from non-aliens. The point is that Pt 2A seeks to regulate the provision of immigration assistance to aliens and to no one else ...

Thoms provides another example. The aliens power supports laws requiring the detention of both persons who are in fact aliens and persons who are believed to be, even if they turn out not to be, aliens.

Thoms v Commonwealth [2022] HCA 20

Section 189(1) of the* Migration Act 1958 *provides that 'If an officer knows or reasonably suspects that a person in the migration zone ... is an unlawful non-citizen, the officer must detain the person.' Thoms was detained in immigration detention under this provision but was released following the High Court's decision in* Love v Commonwealth; Thoms v Commonwealth. *Thoms sued the Commonwealth for false imprisonment. That claim failed because section 189(1) provided a lawful basis for his detention.

Kiefel CJ, Keane and Gleeson JJ

The applicant's case is that, in its application to him, s 189(1) of the Act is not supported by s 51(xix) of the *Constitution*, the constitutional head of power which includes as its subject matter "aliens"...

The issues raised by the applicant are largely disposed of by the decision of this Court in *Ruddock v Taylor* (2005) 222 CLR 612. Mr Taylor's detention was held by the Court to be validly authorised and required by s 189(1) regardless of whether or not he was an alien. As a matter of construction, the question raised by s 189(1) is whether an officer held a reasonable suspicion that the person to be detained was an unlawful non-citizen, not whether the person in fact had that status. What constitutes reasonable grounds for suspecting a person to be an unlawful non-citizen is to be judged as at the time the detention was effected. There can be no doubt that the constitutional validity of s 189(1) was raised in *Ruddock v Taylor* and that the answer given by the majority was that it was a valid law. That can only have been because it was supported by the aliens power in the *Constitution* ...

While s 51(xix) confers legislative power concerning a class of persons – aliens – it can support any law that has more than an 'insubstantial, tenuous or distant' connection with aliens.

It is capable of supporting a law which affects the rights and obligations of persons who are not aliens. *Cunliffe v The Commonwealth* furnishes an example. There, s 51(xix) was held to support a law with respect to migration agents.

Section 189(1) of the Act may be seen to have a sufficient connection with s 51(xix) of the *Constitution* in its application to persons who are "reasonably suspected" of being aliens without a valid visa. In *Milicevic v Campbell* (1975) 132 CLR 307, a provision of the *Customs Act 1901* (Cth) made it an offence to possess any prohibited imports which were "reasonably suspected of having been imported into Australia" in contravention of the *Customs Act*. It was argued in that case that the trade and commerce power in s 51(i) of the *Constitution* is limited to goods which "are in truth imports". The provision was argued to be invalid because it created an offence for a person to have in his possession goods which in truth had not been imported. It will be observed that the applicant in this case puts a similar argument. In *Milicevic*, the provision was held to be a valid law. Mason J considered that the existence of a reasonable suspicion that goods may have been imported may itself constitute a sufficient nexus with the subject matter of the power in s 51(i).

Moreover, the purpose of s 189(1) is appropriate to provide the necessary connection to s 51(xix). The purpose of a law – the end sought to be achieved – may provide the key to determining whether a law is incidental to the subject matter of a power. The purpose of the detention required by s 189(1) is to keep separate from the community a person who is reasonably suspected of being an unlawful non-citizen until their immigration status is investigated and determined.

7.9 DISCUSSION QUESTIONS

1. What is the definition of 'immigrant'?
2. Why can the law prevent the absorption of a person into the Australian community?
3. Describe the scope of the concept of 'alien'.
4. Could a 'citizenship-stripping' law of the kind considered in ***Alexander*** apply to an Aboriginal person who engages in the same conduct as Mr Alexander?
5. Problem question: Advise whether the following hypothetical legislation is valid.

Citizenship (Expulsion of Criminal Foreigners) Act 2023

1. This Act may be cited as the *Citizenship (Expulsion of Criminal Foreigners) Act 2023*.
2. The Governor-General may by declaration revoke a person's Australian citizenship if all of the following circumstances apply:
   a. The person holds citizenship of another country.
   b. The person is aged at least 18 years.
   c. The person has been convicted of a crime against a law of the Commonwealth, a State or a Territory punishable by imprisonment for 6 months or more.

TAXATION POWER

8

8.1 Overview

This chapter examines the scope of the Commonwealth's power to impose taxation.

Australian Constitution

Section 51 Legislative Powers of the Parliament

The Parliament shall, subject to this Constitution, have power to make laws for the peace, order, and good government of the Commonwealth with respect to:

...

(ii) taxation; but not so as to discriminate between States or parts of States;

...

The tax power enables the Commonwealth to raise revenue, as well as to indirectly regulate behaviour by using taxes to encourage or discourage behaviour. In general terms, a tax is a compulsory exaction of money for public purposes enforceable by law and which is not a fine or pecuniary penalty, a fee for service or a fee for a licence. The *Constitution* imposes special rules about the procedure for enacting federal tax laws, which are not justiciable, and special rules about the content of federal tax laws, which are justiciable.

The *Constitution* also makes the power to impose duties of customs and excise an exclusively federal power, thereby limiting the power of the States to impose taxes on goods.

Key concepts considered in this chapter include:

- tax
- single subject of taxation
- public purposes
- fines and pecuniary penalties
- fees for services
- fees for licences
- customs duties
- excise duties.

8.2 Special rules for legislation imposing taxation

The *Constitution* sets out special rules applicable to legislation imposing taxation. The special rules concern the procedure for enacting that legislation and the content of that legislation.

Procedural rules for tax imposition Bills

In most cases, a Bill may originate in either the House of Representatives or the Senate and may be amended by both Houses. However, section 53 requires that Bills that would impose taxation must commence in the House of Representatives and must not be amended by the Senate. The Senate can pass or reject such Bills, or recommend (rather than make) amendments to the House of Representatives.

Australian Constitution

Section 53 Power of the Houses in respect of legislation

Proposed laws ..., ... imposing taxation, shall not originate in the Senate ...

The Senate may not amend proposed laws imposing taxation ...

The Senate may at any stage return to the House of Representatives any proposed law which the Senate may not amend, requesting, by message, the omission or amendment of any items or provisions therein. And the House of Representatives may, if it thinks fit, make any of such omissions or amendments, with or without modifications ...

Failure to comply with the procedural rules set out in section 53 does not affect the validity of a tax law. As explained in Chapter 21 in respect of the equivalent procedural rules section 53 sets out for Bills appropriating funds to enable government spending, the High Court has held that section 53 is not justiciable. The rationale for this position is that section 53 concerns 'proposed laws' and the internal activities of Parliament rather than actual laws.

Rules about the content of legislation imposing taxation

In most cases, a federal statute may deal with multiple subject-matters. However, section 55 of the *Constitution* provides that a federal law imposing taxation must deal only with the imposition of taxation and must deal with one subject of taxation only.

Australian Constitution

Section 55 Tax Bill

Laws imposing taxation shall deal only with the imposition of taxation, and any provision therein dealing with any other matter shall be of no effect.

Laws imposing taxation, except laws imposing duties of customs or of excise, shall deal with one subject of taxation only; but laws imposing duties of customs shall deal with duties of customs only, and laws imposing duties of excise shall deal with duties of excise only.

The purpose of section 55 is to prevent 'tacking'. This practice, which had occurred sometimes in the United Kingdom and the Australian colonies before Federation, involves provisions about other policy issues being tacked onto a tax Bill in an effort to prevent the Upper House from amending the non-tax provisions.

Mutual Pools & Staff Pty Ltd v Federal Commissioner of Taxation (1992) 173 CLR 450

Deane J

[Section 55 is] aimed at protecting the Senate from possible abuse of the restriction placed upon it by s 53 of the Constitution which provides that the Senate "may not amend proposed laws imposing taxation". The first requirement prevents the tacking of extraneous matters to laws imposing taxation. The second and third requirements prevent the House of Representatives from sending to the Senate a single Bill containing a large number of unrelated taxing laws with the consequence that the Senate, being unable to amend the Bill, could reject the taxing provisions of which it did not approve only by also rejecting those of which it approved. No doubt, as a matter of history, the third requirement also facilitated the distinct accounting procedures in relation to duties of customs and excise which were necessary in the early days of the federation.

Unlike section 53, section 55 is justiciable because it deals with actual laws rather than proposed laws.

The first limb of section 55: Federal laws imposing taxation shall deal only with the imposition of taxation

Section 55 distinguishes between laws imposing taxation, laws dealing with the imposition of taxation, and laws dealing with any other matter.

House of Representatives Practice (Department of the House of Representatives, 7th ed, 2018)

Reflecting the requirements of the *Constitution*, House practice distinguishes between bills dealing with taxation, such as tax assessment bills, and tax bills. Tax assessment bills provide the means for assessing and collecting tax. Tax bills, which impose the burden upon the people, are the bills which have been regarded as imposing taxation, and are therefore not capable of originating in the Senate or of being amended by the Senate. This practice has been recognised by the High Court as carrying out the constitutional provisions on a correct basis. It has also been reviewed and accepted by the House's Standing Committee on Legal and Constitutional Affairs.

A former Chief General Counsel of the Attorney-General's Department advised that bills dealing with taxation can be further categorised as follows:

A. provisions imposing taxation;

B. other provisions dealing with the imposition of taxation (e.g. provisions removing or adding exemptions or deductions, increasing or reducing rates or otherwise defining a taxable amount); and

C. provisions not dealing with the imposition of taxation (e.g. provisions for the assessment, collection and recovery of tax and provisions providing for penalties).

A standard practice is for tax legislation to be split into a statute imposing taxation and a statute governing the assessment and collection of the tax. An example is the *Income Tax Act 1986* (Cth), which imposes the obligation to pay income tax, and the *Income Tax Assessment Act 1997* (Cth), which governs how income tax is assessed and collected.

The practice of splitting tax legislation in this manner is not strictly necessary to ensure constitutional validity under section 55, although the practice remains useful politically for limiting the powers of the Senate under section 53. The category of 'laws imposing taxation' is a subcategory of 'laws dealing with the imposition of taxation'.

In ***Permanent Trustee Australia Ltd v Commissioner of State Revenue (Vic)***, the High Court held that provisions regulating the assessment and collection of a tax are provisions dealing with the imposition of taxation and therefore may, but need not, be included in the same statute as provisions imposing the obligation to pay the tax to which they relate.

Permanent Trustee Australia Ltd v Commissioner of State Revenue (Vic) (2004) 220 CLR 388

This case concerned taxation legislation that did not follow the usual practice of being split into a statute imposing the obligation to pay the tax and a statute setting out provisions on the assessment and collection of that tax. The High Court rejected an argument that including the assessment and collection provisions in the same statute as the provision imposing

the obligation to pay the tax meant that the statute contravened the rule in section 55 of the **Constitution** ***that a law imposing taxation shall deal only with the imposition of taxation.***

Gleeson CJ, Gummow, Hayne, Callinan and Heydon JJ

The other view ... accepts that provisions for the assessment, collection and recovery of tax are provisions which deal with the imposition of taxation. That proposition, with which the above majority disagreed, was accepted by McTiernan J, Taylor J and Menzies J in *Re Dymond* (1959) 101 CLR 11. This conclusion follows from a construction of the words "dealing with" as allowing "the insertion of any provision which is fairly relevant or incidental to the imposition of a tax on one subject of taxation" and the inclusion "in a taxing Act [of] provisions incidental and auxiliary to the assessment and collection of the tax". The former formulation is that of Higgins J in *Osborne* (1911) 12 CLR 321 and the latter that of Starke J in *Munro* (1926) 38 CLR 153.

These formulations by Higgins J and Starke J should be accepted. They are consistent with the evident purpose of s 55, supported by its history, of restraining abuse by the House of Representatives of its powers with respect to taxing measures by the tacking of other measures and so placing the Senate in the invidious position of which Deakin spoke in his argument in *Stephens*. "Tacking" is quite a different matter to the insertion in a taxing statute of provisions for the assessment, collection and recovery of that tax.

To accept these propositions means that a law containing added provisions of this nature is still a "law imposing taxation" to which there attaches the stipulation in s 53 of the Constitution denying to the Senate a power of amendment but enabling a return of Bills with a request, by message, for omission or amendment of any items or provisions therein.

However, the construction of the first limb of s 55 which should be accepted does not foreclose further observance of a practice or convention of splitting Bills between a taxing Act and an assessment Act. An assessment Act of the character of those in the numerous decisions of this Court discussed earlier in these reasons will not be a law imposing taxation with respect to which s 53 will restrict the powers of the Senate.

Section 55 provides that where a law imposing taxation deals also with other matters the provisions dealing with the other matters are of no effect. A complexity arises where an amending statute seeks to insert a provision imposing taxation into an existing statute that deals with other matters. The High Court has held that the amending statute will be invalid in such situations. In pragmatic terms, it would be highly impractical, and not what Parliament intended, to allow the amending statute to take effect and thereby render most of the existing statute of no effect. In legal terms, such an amending statute seeks to bring about a situation expressly forbidden by section 55.

Air Caledonie concerned the *Migration Amendment Act 1987* (Cth), which sought to insert a new provision into the *Migration Act 1958* (Cth) imposing a liability on airlines to collect and pass onto the Commonwealth an immigration clearance 'fee' from each passenger. The Commonwealth had believed that the exaction of money was a fee for service (see below) rather than a tax and therefore outside of section 55's scope. However, the High Court held that the exaction was actually a tax with the result that the Amendment

Act would make the *Migration Act* a law that both imposed taxation and dealt with other matters. The Amendment Act was held to be invalid. This case is significant for its pragmatic holding that the amending statute was invalid, and not the non-tax provisions of the principal statute.

Air Caledonie International v Commonwealth (1988) 165 CLR 462

Mason CJ, Wilson, Brennan, Deane, Toohey and Gaudron JJ

If an amending Act purports to insert a provision imposing taxation in an existing valid Act which contains provisions dealing only with other matters, it seeks to bring about something which the Constitution directly and in terms forbids and which is not within the competence of the Parliament to achieve. In such a case, one cannot disregard the barrier of the constitutional injunction against a law dealing both with the imposition of taxation and other matters on the basis that, once the result which that injunction forbids has been achieved, the second limb will rectify the breach by invalidating all the other provisions of the principal Act. The injunction of the first limb constitutes a restriction on legislative power. Its effect in the present case is to invalidate the relevant provisions of the amending Act and one never reaches the situation where the second limb operates to strike down all of the provisions of the principal Act dealing with matters other than the imposition of taxation.

The High Court followed this approach in ***Australian Tape Manufacturers Association Ltd v Commonwealth*** (1993) 176 CLR 480. The case concerned an amending statute that sought to insert new provisions into the *Copyright Act 1968* (Cth). The Commonwealth had believed that the new provisions created an obligation to pay royalties to copyright owners but the High Court held those provisions actually imposed a tax. The result was that the amending statute was invalid.

The second limb of section 55: Federal laws imposing taxation shall deal with one subject of taxation only

Section 55 also provides that a law imposing taxation must not deal with more than one subject of taxation. In practice, the courts give significant weight to Parliament's view of what constitutes one subject of taxation.

A subject of taxation can be contrasted with the applications of a taxation law. For example, personal income is a subject of taxation. While income tax legislation applies to personal income earned from wages and to personal income earned from returns on financial investments, those are not separate subjects of taxation requiring separate statutes. A subject of taxation can also be contrasted with the objects of taxation – that is, the persons or entities liable to pay the tax.

The principles for identifying a subject of taxation were summarised in ***Austin v Commonwealth***.

Austin v Commonwealth (2003) 215 CLR 185

Gaudron, Gummow and Hayne JJ

In *The Second Fringe Benefits Tax Case* (1987) 163 CLR 329, reference was made in the joint judgment to statements by Isaacs J in *Harding v Federal Commissioner of Taxation* (1917) 23 CLR 119 and by Dixon J in *Resch v Federal Commissioner of Taxation* (1942) 66 CLR 198 for several propositions. They are:

(i) in construing the expression "subject of taxation" in s 55 it is not to be supposed that there exists some recognised classification of taxes according to subject-matter;

(ii) s 55 is not directed to categories concerned with economic consequences or operation upon the creation, transfer and devolution of legal rights;

(iii) rather, s 55 is concerned with political relations and contemplates "broad distinctions between possible subjects of taxation based on common understanding and general conceptions, rather than on any analytical or logical classification";

(iv) it is for the legislature to choose its own subjects of taxation unfettered by existing nomenclature or by categories adopted for other purposes; and

(v) the test is whether, looking at the subject of taxation selected by the Parliament, it can fairly be regarded as a unit rather than a collection of matters necessarily distinct and separate.

The case law provides examples of the breadth with which the High Court understands the concept of one subject of taxation.

Resch v Federal Commissioner of Taxation (1942) 66 CLR 198 held that income tax legislation dealt with the single subject of 'all profits and gains accruing to a taxpayer'. The High Court rejected an argument that income derived as a receipt on capital (in this case, arising from the sale or winding up of a company of which the taxpayer is a shareholder) and income derived as a receipt on income (in this case, distributions paid to the taxpayer as a shareholder in a company that is an ongoing concern) were distinct subjects of taxation.

The *Second Fringe Benefits Tax Case* (1987) 163 CLR 329 held that fringe benefits tax legislation that made a tax payable by an employer in respect of non-wage benefits provided (1) to their employees by the employer, (2) to their employees by a third party, (3) to associates of their employees such as family members by the employer and (4) to associates of their employees such as family members by a third party dealt with a single subject of taxation. The High Court described the single subject as being 'benefits, not being salary or wages, referable to the employment relationship, whether provided by the employer or not and whether received by the employee or not'.

Permanent Trustee Australia Ltd v Commissioner of State Revenue (Vic) (2004) 220 CLR 388 held that the *Commonwealth Places (Mirror Taxes) Act 1998* (Cth) – which made most State taxes applicable in Commonwealth places – dealt with a single subject of taxation. Section 52(i) of the *Constitution* grants the Commonwealth exclusive legislative power in respect of 'all places acquired by the Commonwealth for public purposes' such that State tax laws cannot apply of their own force in Commonwealth places within a State. The case concerned the payment of stamp duties in respect of property transactions connected to the development of a hotel on land forming part of a Commonwealth-owned airport in Victoria. The High Court said that 'the application of State taxation laws to Commonwealth places was a single legislative initiative ... [and] may fairly be regarded within the sense of the authorities as a unit rather than as a collection of distinct and separate matters'.

8.3 What is a tax?

As a general proposition, a tax is a compulsory and non-arbitrary exaction of money by a public authority for public purposes enforceable by law and which is not a fine or pecuniary penalty, a fee for service or a fee for a licence.

Air Caledonie International v Commonwealth (1988) 165 CLR 462

Mason CJ, Wilson, Brennan, Deane, Dawson, Toohey and Gaudron JJ

In *Lower Mainland Dairy Products Sales Adjustment Committee v Crystal Dairy Ltd* (1933) AC 168, 175, the Privy Council identified three features which sufficed to impart to the levies involved in that case the character of a "tax". Those features were that the levies: were compulsory; were for public purposes; and were enforceable by law. In *Matthews v Chicory Marketing Board (Vic)* (1938) 60 CLR 263, 276, Latham CJ adopted those three features as the basis of what has subsequently been recognized in this Court as an acceptable general statement of positive and negative attributes which, if they all be present, will suffice to stamp an exaction of money with the character of a tax:

> a compulsory exaction of money by a public authority for public purposes, enforceable by law, and ... not a payment for services rendered.

... More recently this Court has drawn attention to other criteria, namely, that a tax is not by way of penalty and that it is not arbitrary (see *MacCormick v Federal Commissioner of Taxation* (1984) 158 CLR 622, 639; *Deputy Federal Commissioner of Taxation v Truhold Benefit Pty Ltd* (1985) 158 CLR 678, 684).

There are three comments which should be made in relation to the above general statement of Latham CJ. The first is that it should not be seen as providing an exhaustive definition of a tax. Thus, there is no reason in principle why a tax should not take a form other than the exaction of money or why the compulsory exaction of money under statutory powers could not be properly seen as taxation notwithstanding that it was by a non-public authority or for purposes which could not properly be described as public. The second is that, in *Logan Downs Pty Ltd v Queensland* (1977) 137 CLR 59, 63, Gibbs J made explicit what was implicit in the reference by Latham CJ to "a payment for services rendered", namely, that the services be "rendered to" – or (we would add) at the direction or request of – "the person required" to make the payment. The third is that the negative attribute – "not a payment for services rendered" – should be seen as intended to be but an example of various special types of exaction which may not be taxes even though the positive attributes mentioned by Latham CJ are all present. Thus, a charge for the acquisition or use of property, a fee for a privilege and a fine or penalty imposed for criminal conduct or breach of statutory obligation are other examples of special types of exactions of money which are unlikely to be properly characterized as a tax notwithstanding that they exhibit those positive attributes.

Tax laws do not need to serve a revenue-raising purpose

A law imposing taxation does not lose that characterisation simply because Parliament does not really intend for the law to raise revenue. Imposing a tax on certain conduct can be a useful policy lever to encourage or discourage real-world behaviour. This means that the Commonwealth can use taxation as a means of pursuing public policy goals in respect of subject-matters over which it otherwise lacks direct legislative power.

Northern Suburbs General Cemetery Reserve Trust concerned a law imposing a tax on businesses that did not spend a certain sum on staff skills training. The quantum of the tax was set at the same sum as the Commonwealth wanted each business to spend on staff training. The purpose of the law was to encourage businesses to spend money on training their workforces. The High Court held that the law imposed a tax.

Northern Suburbs General Cemetery Reserve Trust v Commonwealth (1993) 176 CLR 555

Mason CJ, Deane, Toohey and Gaudron JJ

But the fact that the revenue-raising burden is merely secondary to the attainment of some other object or objects is not a reason for treating the charge otherwise than as a tax. One might as well suggest that a protective customs duty is not a tax because its primary object is the protection of a particular local manufacturing industry from overseas competition.

If a law, on its face, is one with respect to taxation, the law does not cease to have that character simply because Parliament seeks to achieve, by its enactment, a purpose not within Commonwealth legislative power. In *Osborne v Commonwealth* (1911) 12 CLR 321, the Court rejected a challenge to the validity of the *Land Tax Act 1910* (Cth) and the *Land Tax Assessment Act 1910* (Cth) which was based on the ground that their object was to prevent residents owning large areas of land or to prevent landholders from residing out of Australia or to prevent absentees from holding land in Australia. Subsequently, in *Radio Corporation Pty Ltd v Commonwealth* (1938) 59 CLR 170, Latham CJ (with whom Rich, Starke and McTiernan JJ agreed) said:

> After *Osborne v Commonwealth*, it is difficult to contend that an Act relating to taxation is invalid because it is designed for the purpose of carrying out a policy of the

Commonwealth Parliament which affects matters which are themselves not directly within the legislative power of the Parliament.

...

Accordingly, the conclusion that the Act and the Administration Act are laws with respect to taxation is unaffected by the omission of the purpose of raising revenue from the statement of legislative objects.

Taxes are exactions for public purposes

The proposition that taxes are exactions of money for public purposes entails the proposition that exactions of money for private purposes are not taxes.

Australian Tape Manufacturers demonstrates that a purpose of resolving a complex policy problem by adjusting the competing interests of two groups in favour of one group is a public purpose. The legislation at issue involved a levy collected on the sale of blank tapes, which were often used to record copyright material without the permission of, and without compensation to, copyright owners. The legislation made the funds payable to a collecting society which would then distribute the funds in accordance with the legislative scheme to copyright owners. The High Court rejected an argument that the levy served a private purpose.

Australian Tape Manufacturers Association Ltd v Commonwealth (1993) 176 CLR 480

Mason CJ, Brennan, Deane and Gaudron JJ

In Australia, the fact that a levy is directed to be paid into the Consolidated Revenue Fund has been regarded as a conclusive indication that the levy is exacted for public purposes ... But neither principle nor Australian authority provides any support for the converse proposition that an exaction is not a tax if it is not to be paid into the Consolidated Revenue Fund.

...

The only possible reason, apart from those already rejected, for holding that the provision in question in this case is not a law imposing taxation is that an expropriation from one group for the benefit of another as an incident of legislative regulation of interests on a subject-matter within power, with a view to bringing about what is conceived to be an equitable outcome, is not an exaction for public purposes and is therefore not a tax. In one sense it may be said that the purpose is private in that it concerns the interests of the two groups only. But, in truth, the legislative solution to the problem proceeds on the footing that it is imposed in the public interest. Indeed, the purpose of directing the payment of the levy to the collecting society for ultimate distribution of the net proceeds to the relevant copyright owners as a solution to a complex problem of public importance is of necessity a public purpose.

...

[T]he compensation of relevant copyright owners arising out of what has been a complex problem of public importance is a public purpose.

The proposition in *Australian Tape Manufacturers* that funds payable into the Consolidated Revenue Fund are taken to serve public purposes is qualified in the limited circumstances where it is shown that the payment serves private purposes.

Lutton v Lessels provides an example of funds payable into the Consolidated Revenue Fund not serving public purposes. The legislative scheme in issue had two key features. First, a parent entitled to child support payments from their child's other parent was able to elect to register that entitlement with the Commonwealth in order to be paid the relevant amount of the child support payment by the Commonwealth rather than by the other parent. Secondly, where such registration had occurred, the other parent would instead be liable to pay the amount to the Commonwealth. The scheme was intended to ensure that child support payments were always made even if the other parent defaulted on payments. The High Court held that the legislative scheme did not involve a tax because the payment to the Commonwealth served private purposes. In effect, the legislative scheme allowed the Commonwealth to take over a private debt and collecting money owed under a private debt is not taxation.

Lutton v Lessels (2002) 210 CLR 333

Gleeson CJ

The Assessment Act creates a private or personal obligation, in the form of a debt payable by the liable parent to the eligible carer. The debt is recoverable by the carer. The creation of a legal obligation, enforceable by private action, in a parent, to pay for the support of a child, is not taxation. It is a scheme for the creation and adjustment of private rights and liabilities. But the existence of the obligation is of significance in considering the aspect of the legislative scheme upon which the plaintiff principally relies, which is in the Registration and Collection Act. What is alleged to be taxation is in substance no more than a mechanism for the enforcement of a pre-existing private liability.

...

The legislation does not have either the purpose or the effect of raising revenue for the Commonwealth. Its purpose is to create, and facilitate the enforcement of, private rights and liabilities. The Assessment Act creates a personal liability in a parent to the carer of a child; the Registration and Collection Act gives the carer the facility, in exchange for extinguishment of the liability to the carer, to have the Commonwealth recover the child support payments assessed and pay an equivalent amount to the carer.

The legislation does not bear the character of taxation.

Gaudron and Hayne JJ

Imposing a financial burden on one group in society for the benefit of another group in society will often constitute a tax. Pointing to some identifiable relationship between the group of payers and the group of recipients or even to some relationship between a particular payer and a particular recipient will not usually require some different conclusion. Under the Registration and Collection Act, however, the obligation to make a payment to the carer of the child is replaced by the obligation to pay the same amount to the Commonwealth. That obligation is coupled with the creation of a new right in the carer to have the Commonwealth pay the carer whatever the payer thereafter gives up – whether by making a payment to the Commonwealth or by suffering a compulsory deduction from salary or wages. The combination of these features – the substitution of a new obligation to the Commonwealth equal to an existing obligation which is terminated, coupled with the substitution of new rights in the carer against the Commonwealth equal to the extent to which the payer performs his or her obligation to the Commonwealth – takes this compulsory exaction outside the description of "taxation".

Roy Morgan is distinguishable from *Lutton v Lessels.* The case involved a legislative scheme intended to incentivise businesses to pay superannuation to their employees. If a business failed to pay an employee the amount to which the employee was legally entitled in superannuation, legislation made a sum equivalent to the shortfall payable to the Commonwealth. Another part of the legislative scheme required the Commonwealth to pay an equivalent sum to the tax collected to the employee's superannuation account. Unlike in *Lutton v Lessels,* the original legal obligation was not terminated and an employee could sue the business for the unpaid superannuation (and thereby end up financially better off due to the extra payment from the Commonwealth). The High Court held that the exaction was for a public purpose (namely, incentivising businesses to comply with superannuation laws) and therefore a tax.

Roy Morgan Research Pty Ltd v Commissioner of Taxation (2011) 244 CLR 97

French CJ, Gummow, Hayne, Crennan, Kiefel and Bell JJ

The submission by the appellant that the Charge is invalid because the legislation confers upon employees a "private and direct benefit" cannot be accepted. Nor does this "linkage" indicate that the Charge is not imposed by the Parliament for "public purposes". It is settled that the imposition of a tax for the benefit of the Consolidated Revenue Fund is made for public purposes. That is not to say that the receipt of funds into the Consolidated Revenue Fund conclusively establishes their character as the proceeds of a tax. But it does establish in the present case that the Charge is imposed for "public purposes" and thus, if other necessary criteria are met, as they are in this case, the Charge is a valid tax.

Moneys received into the Consolidated Revenue Fund are available to be appropriated for any purpose for which the Parliament may lawfully spend money; this is so, whatever the purpose for which those moneys were raised ...

Heydon J

Luton v Lessels is distinguishable because there the obligation created in the Commonwealth was created in substitution for a former obligation of another person which was terminated ... In *Luton v Lessels* the legislation created a new legal obligation to do something in substitution for an existing one. Here the legislation merely creates an incentive to do something, whether or not there was any obligation to do it.

Taxes are exactions usually levied by public authorities

It has generally been considered that a tax is an exaction levied by a public authority, and in practice this is usually the case. Current High Court authority leaves open the possibility that being levied by a public authority is not an essential characteristic of a tax.

Air Caledonie demonstrates that a tax can be understood as levied by a public authority even if the money is collected in the first instance by a private entity to be passed on to the Commonwealth.

Air Caledonie International v Commonwealth (1988) 165 CLR 462

Mason CJ, Wilson, Brennan, Deane, Dawson, Toohey and Gaudron JJ

An obligation to pay a "fee for immigration clearance" in whatever amount might be prescribed by regulation was imposed on airline passengers arriving from overseas who had not been exempted (as a "prescribed passenger") by regulation. The fee was to be collected ("shall be collected") by the relevant "international airline operator" which was made liable to pay the amount of the fee to the Commonwealth regardless of whether the fee had been or could be actually collected from the passenger ...

It is clear that the "fee" purportedly exacted by s 34A possessed all of the positive attributes which have been accepted in this Court as prima facie sufficient to stamp an exaction of money with the character of a tax: ... it was exacted by a public authority (the Commonwealth itself) for public purposes (consolidated revenue: see *Constitution* s 81); ...

There was a suggestion in ***Australian Tape Manufacturers*** that an exaction may be a tax even if it is not levied by a public authority.

Australian Tape Manufacturers Association Ltd v Commonwealth (1993) 176 CLR 480

Mason CJ, Brennan, Deane and Gaudron JJ

It would seem to be a remarkable consequence if a pecuniary levy imposed for public purposes by a non-public authority acting pursuant to a statutory authority falls outside the concept of a tax simply because the authority which imposes the levy is not a public authority, when the amount of the levy is to be expended on public purposes, more particularly, if those purposes are Commonwealth purposes. It is scarcely to be contemplated that the character of the impost as a tax depends upon whether the authority is a public authority, unless it be a case in which the character of the authority will be relevant and influential in deciding whether the purposes on which the moneys raised are to be expended are themselves public. Of course, it is a misnomer to describe an authority as non-public when one of its functions is to levy, demand or receive exactions to be expended on public purposes. To that extent, at least, the authority should be regarded as a public authority. But the better view is that it is not essential to the concept of a tax that the exaction should be by a public authority.

The High Court in ***Roy Morgan*** commented that it remains undecided whether being levied by a public authority is an essential characteristic of a tax.

Roy Morgan Research Pty Ltd v Commissioner of Taxation (2011) 244 CLR 97

French CJ, Gummow, Hayne, Crennan, Kiefel and Bell JJ

The majority in *Tape Manufacturers* suggested that it is not essential to the concept of a tax that the exaction should be by a public authority. That suggestion would constitute a large and controversial step beyond what was said in *Matthews*. As the reasons of the majority in *Tape Manufacturers* show, whether that step could or should be taken depends, at least in part, upon what meaning would be given to the expression "non public" authority if "one of its functions is to levy, demand or receive exactions to be expended on public purposes". It was not necessary to decide that question in *Tape Manufacturers* and the majority in that case did not do so. Nor is it necessary in this case, given the addition of the proceeds of the Charge to the Consolidated Revenue Fund, to pursue that question, or any broader questions about whether it is essential to the concept of a tax that the exaction should be by a public authority.

A tax is not arbitrary

Another key characteristic of a tax is that the exaction is not arbitrary, in the sense that liability to pay the exaction is imposed by reference to criteria and is not incontestable.

Truhold summarises the basic principles for understanding when an exaction is not arbitrary. The case involved complex legislation imposing a 'recoupment tax'. Where a financial transaction had the effect of an entity lacking the funds or assets to pay its company tax liability, the party who ultimately obtained the financial benefit of that transaction was liable to pay a recoupment tax. The High Court rejected an argument that the recoupment tax was arbitrary because the process for identifying the person or entity liable to pay the recoupment tax involved the Commissioner of Taxation forming an administrative opinion on the basis of statutory criteria.

Deputy Commissioner of Taxation v Truhold Benefit Pty Ltd (1985) 158 CLR 678

Gibbs CJ, Mason, Wilson, Deane and Dawson JJ

In *MacCormick v Commissioner of Taxation* (1984) 158 CLR 622 it was held that the recoupment tax, for which the Act provides, answers the usual description of a tax. Amongst the characteristics which were said by the majority to bring it within that description was the fact that the tax is not arbitrary. This was ... a reference to the fact that liability can only be imposed by reference to ascertainable criteria with a sufficiently general application and that the tax cannot lawfully be imposed as a result of some administrative decision based upon individual preference unrelated to any test laid down by the legislation.

...

[The statute has] an overall design to ensure that recoupment tax, when it has become payable, will be paid by some person or persons falling within the description provided by the legislation. If recovery from a company otherwise liable to pay is not possible because it has ceased to exist, or because it is insolvent, or if it is unreasonable by reason of a sale of its shares into different hands, then liability may be passed further along the chain which commences with the transaction which resulted in the stripping of the target company. The Commissioner is to be guided and controlled by the policy and purpose of the enactment and, whatever the width of his discretion, it is not unexaminable should he exceed the limits which may be discerned from its provisions. The legislation does not contemplate the formation of an opinion by the Commissioner in an arbitrary manner and any attack upon it on that ground cannot, in our view, succeed.

Austin v Commonwealth demonstrates that a tax is not arbitrary even though the amount of tax payable is determined in part by complex actuarial calculations which might have different results when performed by different actuaries. Such a tax is based on legislative criteria and the decision-making process is not incontestable.

Austin v Commonwealth (2003) 215 CLR 185

Gaudron, Gummow and Hayne JJ

The plaintiffs complain that different actuaries, all applying SCR 97/1 and SR 371 of 1997, can reasonably differ in working out the amount of their surchargeable contributions under s 9 of the *Protected Funds Assessment Act*. That is because the "eligible actuary" identified in s 9(5) will be making assumptions and judgments on such variables as mortality rates, retirement age, marital status, age differences between spouses and the like. However, the various actuarial assumptions selected by SCR 97/1 supply "the method" mandated by s 9(5).

The submissions by the plaintiffs are foreclosed by what was said by Kitto J in *Giris*:

> There is no need to cite authority for the general proposition that the operation of a law with respect to taxation may validly be made to depend upon the formation of an administrative opinion or satisfaction upon a question, eg, as to the existence of a fact or circumstance, or as to the quality (eg, the reasonableness) of a person's conduct, or even as to the likelihood of a consequence of the operation of the law in an individual case, as in s 265 [of the ITAA] where the question is whether the exaction of an amount of tax will entail hardship.

In such situations there has been no "abdication" of legislative authority. This objection to validity fails.

8.4 Compulsory exactions of money that are not taxes

Not all compulsory exactions of money for public purposes are taxes. Section 53 expressly provides that the following exactions of money are not taxes: fines and pecuniary penalties, fees for licences and fees for services.

The principal significance of whether an exaction of money by federal legislation is characterised as a tax or something else concerns whether the law imposing the exaction of money is subject to the rules set out in sections 53 and 55 of the *Constitution*.

Determining whether an exaction of money is a tax or something else is a question of characterisation.

Lutton v Lessels (2002) 210 CLR 333

Gleeson CJ

To decide whether an exaction of money or the imposition of some other financial obligation is a tax involves an exercise in characterisation.

Fines and pecuniary penalties

Fines and pecuniary penalties are not taxes. Fines and pecuniary penalties are compulsory exactions of money arising as a consequence of contravening a legal obligation.

R v Barger (1908) 6 CLR 41

Isaacs J (during argument)

The difference between a pecuniary penalty and a tax is that the former is a sum required in respect of an unlawful act, and the latter is a sum required in respect of a lawful act.

Proceeds of crimes laws requiring the confiscation of property obtained as a result of criminal wrongdoing are for equivalent reasons taken to not impose taxation.

AD v Commissioner of the Australian Federal Police (2018) 97 NSWLR 588

One issue in this case was whether the Proceeds of Crimes Act 2002 *(Cth) was a law imposing taxation.*

Beazley P (Meagher and Gleeson JJA agreeing)

In my opinion, the scheme for the forfeiture of property does not constitute a tax. ... [T]here are laws that impose fines or pecuniary penalties which, by these features alone, do not impose a tax. The same may be said of a law that requires the forfeiture of property. Nor could such a law be said to be a "compulsory exaction of money for public purposes". Property is forfeited under the Proceeds of Crime Act as part of a legislative regime to deprive persons engaged in criminal activity of the proceeds of crime. That this is the purpose of the forfeiture provisions of the Act is demonstrated by the inclusion in the Act of s 107, which provides that the forfeiture ceases to have effect if the person's conviction is quashed and the forfeiture does not also relate to the person's conviction of other offences that have not been quashed. A compulsory exaction of money for public purposes does not have this characteristic.

Northern Suburbs General Cemetery Reserve Trust emphasises that a tax on conduct the Commonwealth wishes to discourage is different from a penalty for conduct that is unlawful.

Northern Suburbs General Cemetery Reserve Trust v Commonwealth (1993) 176 CLR 555

Mason CJ, Deane, Toohey and Gaudron JJ

[T]he considerations pointing to a tax rather than a penalty are decisive. Neither the Act nor the Administration Act mandates or proscribes conduct of any kind. The legislative provisions do not make it an offence to fail to spend the minimum training requirement; nor do they provide for the recovery of civil penalties for such a failure. Consequently, the charge is not a penalty because the liability to pay does not arise from any failure to discharge antecedent obligations on the part of the person on whom the exaction falls. The fact that the legislature has singled out those who do not spend the minimum training requirement as the class to bear the burden of the charge and to quantify the amount of the liability by reference to the shortfall does not deprive the charge of the character of a tax.

Fees for services

Fees for services are not taxes. As a general proposition, an exaction is a fee for services if: (1) there is some identifiable service provided; (2) a fee is paid for the service; (3) the service is provided to, or at the request or direction of, the person required to make the payment; and (4) the quantum of the fee is reasonably related to the cost of providing the service.

Fees for services in this sense are distinguishable from the totality of benefits and services a person receives from government and towards which a person contributes financially through taxation.

Air Caledonie International v Commonwealth (1988) 165 CLR 462

Mason CJ, Wilson, Brennan, Deane, Dawson, Toohey and Gaudron JJ

In one sense, all taxes exacted by a national government and paid into national revenue can be described as "fees for services". They are the fees which the resident or visitor is required to pay as the quid pro quo for the totality of benefits and services which he receives from governmental sources. It is, however, clear that the phrase "fees for services" in s 53 of the Constitution cannot be read in that general impersonal sense. Read in context, the reference to "fees for services" in s 53 should ... be read as referring to a fee or charge exacted for particular identified services provided or rendered individually to, or at the request or direction of, the particular person required to make the payment.

General Practitioners Society is a case in which an identifiable service was provided to a person at their request. The case demonstrates that a service may be one which is practically necessary if the person wishes to engage in certain conduct.

General Practitioners Society in Australia v Commonwealth (1980) 145 CLR 532

Gibbs J

The provision which is said to impose taxation is s 16C(2), which provides that where an eligible person who wishes to become an approved pathology practitioner gives the appropriate written undertaking together with a fee of $10 or of such other amount as is prescribed, the Minister shall either accept the undertaking, or refer the question to a Medical Services Committee of Inquiry as the case may be. The fee when paid is not required to be used for any particular purpose of the Act; it is not paid into the Health Insurance Fund under s 126 of the Act, but is paid into Consolidated Revenue.

...

[I]t is a fee for services. It is the price which a medical practitioner, who seeks to become an approved pathology practitioner, must pay for the purpose of having his undertaking considered by the Minister, and either accepted or referred for inquiry and report to a Medical Services Committee of Inquiry. In other words, it is a charge for the services performed in dealing with the application. The fact that it is paid into Consolidated Revenue does not prevent it from being a fee for services. The nature of such a payment is not determined by what is done with it after its receipt. Further, the fact that the service for which the fee is charged is one which the practitioner is in effect compelled to obtain does not in my opinion alter the character of the fee or convert it into a tax. An exaction may properly be characterized as a licence fee notwithstanding that the licence is one that must necessarily be obtained.

Air Caledonie demonstrates that a fee for services exists only where an identifiable service is provided. The legislative scheme in issue in this case required that a $10 charge be paid in respect of each airline passenger arriving in Australia on an international flight, including Australians returning home. The High Court held that, despite the statute describing the charge as a fee, the charge was a tax because there was no identifiable service being provided to the passengers in exchange for the charge. The case highlights the distinction between taxes that raise revenue to fund the cost of government operations and fees for identified services to particular individuals.

Air Caledonie International v Commonwealth (1988) 165 CLR 462

Mason CJ, Wilson, Brennan, Deane, Dawson, Toohey and Gaudron JJ

At least in a case of the ordinary Australian citizen returning by air from overseas, the description of the purported impost (see s 34A(1)) as a "fee for immigration clearance of that passenger" did not suffice to make the impost a "fee for services" in any relevant sense. As has been said, such a citizen had, under the law, the right to re-enter the country, without need of any Executive fiat or "clearance", for so long as he retained his citizenship. The subjection of such a citizen to administrative procedures at the point of entry (see Migration Regulations, reg 4) may be necessary, in the public interest, to enable the entry of non-citizens to be prevented or controlled and to enable proper administrative records and procedures to be kept or followed in relation to the arrival and departure of citizens and non-citizens alike. A requirement that a returning citizen submit, in the public interest, to the inconvenience of such administrative procedures at the end of a journey cannot, however, properly be seen as the provision or rendering of "services" to, or at the request or direction of, the citizen concerned. Nor is it possible to find in s 34A (or in any other provision of the Act) any identification of particular services provided or rendered to the individual passenger for which the impost could relevantly be regarded as a fee or quid pro quo. As has been seen, the section neither fixed the amount of the fee nor indicated the considerations to which the Executive was required to pay regard in prescribing it ... Indeed, one need do no more than refer to the second reading speech of the responsible Minister, to which both sides referred the Court, to confirm that the moneys intended to be raised by the purported impost were not related to particular services to be supplied to particular passengers but were intended to provide, when paid into consolidated revenue, a general off-setting of the administrative costs of certain areas of the relevant Commonwealth Department, including, for example, the administrative costs involved in maintaining facilities for the issue of visas in overseas countries and "general administrative overheads". Therefore, the fee which s 34A purported to exact was, at least in so far as it related to passengers who were Australian citizens, a tax.

Airservices Australia v Canadian Airlines shows that the requirement that the quantum of the fee be reasonably related to the cost of providing the service can be met in a number of ways. In this case, the cost of the services was divided among service users but not on the basis of a calculation of the actual cost of providing the services to each individual user.

Airservices Australia v Canadian Airlines (1999) 202 CLR 133

Legislation imposed charges on airline operators to recoup the cost of providing air traffic services, rescue and firefighting services and meteorological services by the Civil Aviation Authority. The total cost of services was divided among users in accordance with the weight of their aircraft rather than by calculating the cost of providing the services to each particular user.

Gleeson CJ and Kirby J

Do charges bear the legal character of taxation because some individual users or consumers pay more than the cost of the particular services which they use? In Australia, postal services, transportation services, educational services, and health services, amongst others, and many facilities, are provided by governments, or government instrumentalities, in circumstances where charges are imposed which take account of such factors as price sensitivity or capacity to pay, or which seek to equalize costs between, for example, rural and urban consumers, or which in some other way exhibit characteristics similar to those of the charges presently in question. It is not to the point that such pricing of services may have an economic effect, equivalent, or similar, to taxation.

...

In this case: the charges were not imposed to raise revenue; the charges were undoubtedly charges for the provision of services and facilities; the charges were imposed to recover the cost of providing such services and facilities across the entire range of users; the charges for categories of services were reasonably related to the expenses incurred in relation to the matters to which the charges related; the services and facilities were, of their nature, part of an activity which must be highly integrated in order to be effective; there was a rational basis for such discrimination between users as existed.

In those circumstances, there is no warrant for concluding that the charges amounted to taxation on the ground that they exceeded the value to particular users of particular services or the cost of providing particular services to particular users.

The obiter comments of Brennan J in ***Cunliffe v Commonwealth***, provide a contrast to the facts of *General Practitioners Society*. Justice Brennan took it as obvious that a $1000 fee payable in connection with applying for registration as a migration agent was so large (in the context of the early 1990s) as to not be a fee for service.

Cunliffe v Commonwealth (1994) 182 CLR 272

Brennan J

The making of an application for registration attracts liability to pay a levy under the *Migration Agents Registration (Application) Levy Act 1992* (Cth) (the Application Act) unless the applicant or his or her employer proposes to give immigration assistance without fee or reward. The renewal of an application for registration attracts liability to pay a similar levy under the *Migration Agents Registration (Renewal) Levy Act 1992* (Cth) (the Renewal Act) unless the applicant or his or her employer gives immigration assistance without fee or reward. The levy is a substantial tax; it is clearly not a fee for service.

Fees for licences

Fees for licences are not taxes. Whether an exaction is a fee for a licence is determined broadly in alignment with the method for determining whether an exaction is a fee for service. The key difference is the distinction between a service and a licence. A licence is a legal permission to engage in conduct, such as conducting a business of a particular kind.

Harper v Minister for Sea Fisheries (1989) 168 CLR 314

The legislation under consideration provided that a person could not harvest abalone from the sea without a licence. The licence fee was a function of the quantity of the abalone the licence-holder was authorised to harvest (as opposed to the quantity actually harvested). The High Court held that the exaction was genuinely a licence fee and as such could not be an excise because it was not a tax.

Dawson, Toohey and McHugh JJ

Whilst the proper conclusion is that the amount paid for a commercial abalone licence is not a tax and, therefore, is not a duty of excise, that conclusion flows from all the circumstances of the case. Most important is the fact that it is possible to discern a relationship between the amount paid and the value of the privilege conferred by the licence, namely, the right to acquire abalone for commercial purposes in specified quantities. In discerning that relationship it is significant that abalone constitute a finite but renewable resource which cannot be subjected to unrestricted commercial exploitation without endangering its continued existence.

However, the conclusion reached by Brennan J by no means carries with it the consequence that no exaction of money can constitute a tax if it is demanded for the purpose of conserving a public natural resource. If such an exaction otherwise exhibits the characteristics of a tax it will properly be seen as such. In particular, if the exaction "has no discernible relationship with the value of what is acquired, the circumstances may be such that the exaction is, at least to the extent that it exceeds that value, properly to be seen as a tax": *Air Caledonie International v. Commonwealth*. This may be so notwithstanding that the exaction is one means of ensuring the conservation of a natural resource; there are, of course, other ways in which such a resource may be protected. Clearly the line between a price paid for the right to appropriate a public natural resource and a tax upon the activity of appropriating it may often be difficult to draw. But what is otherwise a tax is not converted into something else merely because it serves the purpose of conserving a natural public resource.

There is an important body of case law (considered below) concerning whether a purported licence fee is in fact a disguised tax on goods. In respect of State laws, a purported licence fee that is in fact a disguised tax on goods will be invalid for contravening the rule that only the Commonwealth can impose excise duties.

8.5 Exclusive federal power to impose customs and excise duties

While the Commonwealth and States both have power to impose taxation, section 90 of the *Constitution* has the effect that the power to impose customs and excise duties is an exclusively federal power.

Australian Constitution

Section 90 Exclusive power over customs, excise, and bounties

On the imposition of uniform duties of customs the power of the Parliament to impose duties of customs and of excise, and to grant bounties on the production or export of goods, shall become exclusive. ...

In simple terms, customs duties are taxes on the import and export of goods into or out of Australia, excise duties are taxes on goods within Australia, and bounties on production are financial payments to incentivise the production of goods.

The *Customs Act 1901* (Cth) imposed uniform customs duties, triggering the operation of section 90.

Customs duties

Customs duties are a species of tax, such that the general definition of what amounts to a tax applies. Customs duties are taxes on the importation or export of goods into or out of Australia.

Commonwealth Oil Refineries Ltd v South Australia (1926) 38 CLR 408

In this case, the High Court held that a South Australian tax imposed on petrol when sold for the first time on its arrival into South Australia from other countries was in substance a tax on the importation of a commodity and therefore a customs duty.

Starke J

Duties of customs under the Constitution are duties levied upon the importation or exportation of commodities into and out of the Commonwealth.

Excise duties

Excise duties are another species of tax, such that the general definition of what amounts to a tax applies.

A common feature of excise cases is that the impugned State legislation usually purports to impose a licence fee and the issue for decision is whether that exaction is really a disguised excise duty. A narrower definition of excise gives the States more power to raise revenue and a broader definition gives the States less power to do so.

The introduction of the federal goods and services tax (GST) in 2000, and the associated arrangement that the revenue collected will be distributed by the Commonwealth to the States, means that the States now have less need to enact the kinds of laws that have traditionally given rise to section 90 challenges.

Taxes on the production or manufacture of goods

Taxes on the production or manufacture of goods within Australia are excise duties.

Matthews v Chicory Marketing Board concerned a levy payable to the Chicory Marketing Board by chicory (a type of crop) farmers calculated at the rate of £1 per half acre of land planted with chicory. The High Court held that while the levy was not imposed on the commodity itself it was nevertheless in substance a tax on the production of the commodity and therefore an excise.

Matthews v Chicory Marketing Board (1938) 60 CLR 263

Rich J

In the present case the levy is clearly a tax ... planting chicory is an essential step in its production. If you tax according to planting you affect or influence an operation upon which the extent of attempted production depends. The fact that some producers may have to pay the tax although their attempt fails is merely one of the chances and accidents which attend all the pursuits of man and makes it no less true that the tax is aimed at production.

Starke J

It is true that the levy is not imposed "in relation to the quantity or value" of the commodity produced but at the rate of £1 for every half acre or part thereof planted by such producer with chicory. Still, that merely prescribes the basis of the levy, to use the language of s 32, and does not alter the nature of the tax. It remains a tax in respect of the commodity produced for sale. It is not a land tax nor a tax upon the producer irrespective of the production of the commodity.

Dixon J

By adopting area planted as the criterion of the amount of the levy upon each producer the board has taxed the production of the commodity as effectually as if it had selected, for instance, the weight of the chicory gathered in its raw state, the quantity treated or the gross returns. For it has placed upon an essential step in production, namely, planting, an impost computed quantitatively. There is no distinction of substance and scarcely any even of form between levying a tax upon the area planted and levying a tax upon the act of planting the area. The levy is directed to the normal case of a man reaping even as he sows. The fact that the tax would also fall upon a chicory farmer whose expectations are disappointed through some of the mischances of agriculture does not seem to me to make the levy any less a tax upon production.

Gosford Meats provides another example of a licence fee amounting to a tax on the production of goods. The legislation in this case concerned a purported abattoir licence fee calculated by reference to the number of animals slaughtered during the preceding financial year. The slaughter of livestock is a step in the production of meat.

Gosford Meats Pty Ltd v New South Wales (1985) 155 CLR 368

Mason and Deane JJ

[T]he tax is payable by a producer by reason of an essential step (slaughtering of livestock on the premises) in his production process and in an amount ascertained by reference to the quantity of livestock which he processes. Such a tax is, when viewed as a matter of substance, an excise duty notwithstanding that it is payable in the form of a licence fee which the producer is bound to pay in respect of the next following licence period or that the producer may escape the liability to pay it by ceasing to carry on his business on the relevant premises.

Brennan J

The slaughtering of animals in an abattoir is a step in the process of converting livestock into a variety of vendible meat products. A tax on the slaughtering of animals in an abattoir is therefore a duty of excise for it is a tax on a step in production of goods ...

The slaughtering of animals in the abattoir during the relevant period determines the measure of the tax liability. The circumstance that the tax is, and is described as, a fee for a licence to operate an abattoir during the licence period does not deny the tax the character of a duty of excise on the goods produced from the animals slaughtered in the preceding relevant period ...

Hematite Petroleum concerned a yearly $10 million fee for permission to operate a pipeline that transported oil from an oil field where it was extracted to a refinery. The High Court held that the fee was a tax on the production of petroleum and therefore an excise.

Hematite Petroleum Pty Ltd v Victoria (1983) 151 CLR 599

Mason J

[T]he pipeline operation fee payable by the plaintiffs is not a mere fee for the privilege of carrying on an activity; it is a tax imposed on a step in the production of refined petroleum products which is so large that it will inevitably increase the price of the products in the course of distribution to the consumer. The fee is not an exaction imposed in respect of the plaintiffs' business generally; it is an exaction of such magnitude imposed in respect of a step in production in such circumstances that it is explicable only on the footing that it is imposed in virtue of the quantity and value of the hydrocarbons produced from the Bass Strait fields. To levy a tax on the operation of the pipelines is a convenient means of taxing what they convey for they are the only practicable method of conveying the hydrocarbons to the next processing point.

Brennan J

Where a tax which takes the form of a licence fee is exacted not in respect of a business generally but in respect of a particular act done in the business, it is a tax upon the doing of that act; where that act is a step in the production, manufacture or distribution of goods, a tax upon that step is a burden upon production, manufacture or distribution. And that is so whether or not the tax is calculated upon the quantity or value of the goods produced, manufactured or distributed.

Taxes on the sale or distribution of goods

Taxes on the sale or distribution of goods are excise duties.

In ***Parton v Milk Board***, a majority of the High Court held that a tax on the sale or distribution of goods has the same substantive effect as a tax on the production or manufacture of goods and is therefore an excise.

Parton v Milk Board (Vic) (1949) 80 CLR 229

Legislation required milk distributors to pay a levy to the Milk Board to contribute to its operating costs. The levy was set at three quarters of a penny per gallon of milk sold during the financial year.

Rich and Williams JJ

It must be imposed so as to be a method of taxing the production or manufacture of goods, but, the production or manufacture of an article will be taxed whenever a tax is imposed in respect of some dealing with the article by way of sale or distribution at any stage of its existence, provided that it is expected and intended that the taxpayer will not bear the ultimate incidence of the tax himself but will indemnify himself by passing it on to the purchaser or consumer ...

Each of the present levies fulfils these requirements. It is a contribution of a fraction of a penny for every gallon of milk sold or distributed by the taxpayer during a certain period. This affects the goods, that is the milk sold or distributed by these taxpayers as articles of commerce, the basis of assessment is the quantity of the goods sold or distributed, and it is a levy against which it is expected and intended that the taxpayer should indemnify himself at the expense of the persons to whom the milk is sold or distributed.

Dixon J

A tax upon a commodity at any point in the course of distribution before it reaches the consumer produces the same effect as a tax upon its manufacture or production. If the exclusive power of the Commonwealth with respect to excise did not go past manufacture and production it would with respect to many commodities have only a formal significance.

Uncertainties concerning ad valorem licence fees

As ***Harper v Minister for Sea Fisheries*** (considered above) demonstrates, an exaction that is genuinely a licence fee is not a tax and therefore cannot be an excise. However, the case law on working out whether a purported licence fee is genuinely a licence fee rather than a tax is complex and unclear. The cases concern licence fees calculated according to the value (i.e. ad valorem) of goods sold in a period of time that is not contiguous with the period of time in which the licence operates.

Dennis Hotels Pty Ltd v Victoria (1960) 104 CLR 592 is the starting point for much complexity and uncertainty. Victorian legislation required that a person hold a 'victualler's licence' in order to operate a hotel. The fee was set at 6 per cent of the gross value of the alcohol purchased by the hotel for sale in the year to 30 June preceding the licence year. The legislation also required that a person hold a 'temporary licence' in order to operate booths and bars at fairs and sporting events. The fee was set at a flat nominal rate plus 6 per cent of the gross value of the alcohol purchased for sale under the licence. Three judges held that both licence fees were excise duties. Three judges held that neither licence fee was an excise duty. And one judge held that the temporary licence fee was an excise duty but that the victualler's licence fee was not an excise duty. Given these divergent conclusions, no clear principle arises from the case even though the result is binding as a matter of precedent.

Dickenson's Arcade v Tasmania (1974) 130 CLR 177 upheld a Tasmanian licence fee for tobacco retailers on the basis that the legislation could not be distinguished from the legislation considered in *Dennis Hotels*. The fee was calculated by reference to the average monthly value of the tobacco stock held by the retailer in the year ending six months before the commencement of the licence. *HC Sleigh Ltd v South Australia* (1977) 136 CLR 475 upheld a petrol retailer's licence fee, calculated along equivalent lines to the fees in *Dennis Hotels*, again on the ground that the case was indistinguishable from *Dennis Hotels*.

Ha v New South Wales appears to have set a limit on how far *Dennis Hotels*-licence fees will be accepted as not being excise duties. The case concerned a New South Wales fee for a monthly tobacco seller's licence calculated by reference to the value of goods sold in the month ending two months before the current licence period. Unlike the fees considered in the earlier case, the rate was set at 100 per cent of the value of the tobacco sold. A majority of the High Court held that the licence fee was really an excise duty, but did not overrule *Dennis Hotels*.

Ha v New South Wales (1997) 189 CLR 465

Brennan CJ, McHugh, Gummow and Kirby JJ

The principle that an inland tax on a step in production, manufacture, sale or distribution of goods is a duty of excise has been long established. As a criterion of a duty of excise, it was expressed by Kitto J in *Dennis Hotels* and adopted by a unanimous Court in *Bolton v Madsen*. It can be traced back to the judgments in *Parton* and, before that, to the judgment of Dixon J in *Matthews v Chicory Marketing Board (Vic)*. As Brennan J said in *Philip Morris Ltd v Commissioner of Business Franchises (Vic)*:

> If there be any rock in the sea of uncertain principle, it is that a tax on a step in the production or distribution of goods to the point of receipt by the consumer is a duty of excise.
>
> ...

[A]s the present case requires a declaration of the limits of the protection offered by the franchise cases so as to accord with the *Parton* doctrine, it seems right to accede to the defendants' application to reopen the *Parton* line of cases. But the correctness of the doctrine they establish must now be affirmed. Therefore we reaffirm that duties of excise are taxes on the production, manufacture, sale or distribution of goods, whether of foreign or domestic origin. Duties of excise are inland taxes in contradistinction from duties of customs which are taxes on the importation of goods. Both are taxes on goods, that is to say, they are taxes on some step taken in dealing with goods.

...

It is therefore unnecessary to canvass again the question whether the decisions in the franchise cases can be reconciled with the doctrine based on *Parton*. That exercise was undertaken by Brennan J in *Philip Morris* and we agree with the analysis and conclusions in his Honour's judgment. In *Philip Morris*, McHugh J was also in dissent. His Honour rejected the authority of the earlier franchise cases as support for any proposition save the validity of the imposts upheld in those cases. We do not apprehend that, in the result, there is any dissimilarity in the approach taken by the two Justices in dissent. Both Brennan J and McHugh J pointed to the proximity of the relevant period to the licence period, the shortness of the licence period, the size of the tax imposed ad valorem and the fact that it is to be borne only once in the course of distribution as indicia that were inconsistent with the tax being merely a licence fee having – to use the test stated by Kitto J in *Dennis Hotels* – "no closer connexion with production or distribution than that it is exacted for the privilege of engaging in the process at all". Brennan J added a reference to "the revenue raising and non-regulatory purpose of the scheme".

Those factors are present and relevant to the character of the licence fees and the amounts payable under the Act in this case. Moreover, an amount equal to 75 or 100 per cent of the value of tobacco sold during a relevant period is levied by the Act. That amount could not conceivably be regarded as a mere fee for a licence required as an element in a scheme for regulatory control of businesses selling tobacco. The Act contains minimal provisions controlling businesses selling tobacco, chiefly those contained in s 36(2) which authorises the refusal of a licence to a person who has been convicted of an offence under s 59 of the *Public Health Act 1991* (NSW) or, pursuant to s 36(2AA), if the Chief Commissioner is satisfied that "the issue of a licence would be contrary to the public interest". Subject to these provisions, renewal of a licence requires merely the due payment of the fees exacted. The licence fee is manifestly a revenue-raising tax imposed on the sale of tobacco during the relevant period. The licensing system is but "an adjunct to a revenue statute".

...

[T]he decision of this Court is not to overrule *Dennis Hotels* or *Dickenson's Arcade*. They may stand as authorities for the validity of the imposts therein considered. Properly understood, the test of "no closer connexion" as stated by Kitto J in *Dennis Hotels* and explained by Brennan J in *Philip Morris* is maintained.

Underlying the dissenting judgment in *Ha* was a fundamental difference in understanding as to the purpose served by section 90. The dissenting judges took the narrower view that section 90 is intended only to prevent the States from interfering with a single Australian tariff, whereas the majority judges took the broader view that section 90 is intended to prevent the States imposing taxes on goods more generally.

Ha v New South Wales (1997) 189 CLR 465

Dawson, Toohey and Gaudron JJ

[I]t is plainly incorrect to assert that a tax upon a commodity at any point in the course of distribution before it reaches the consumer has the same effect as a tax upon its manufacture or production. Not only is it an incorrect assertion but it fails to comprehend that the purpose of making the power to impose excise duties exclusive to the Commonwealth was to prevent impairment by the States of the common external tariff. A tax upon the manufacture or production of goods increases the cost of those goods without effecting a corresponding increase in the cost of imported goods of the same kind. Any protection afforded by customs duties imposed upon the imported goods is thereby reduced. But a tax imposed upon a step in the distribution of goods which falls indiscriminately upon locally produced and imported goods does not have that effect.

...

A State tax which fell selectively upon imported goods would, of course, be a customs duty and be prohibited by s 90. A State tax which fell selectively upon goods manufactured or produced in that State would be an excise duty and be prohibited by s 90. A State tax which discriminated against interstate goods in a protectionist way would offend s 92 and be invalid. But those three instances do not exhaust the categories of taxes upon goods and do not support, as a legal conclusion, the proposition that the Commonwealth was intended to have an exclusive power to tax commodities. That is a suggestion which appears to be made in this case, but clearly a State tax – a tax upon sale, for example – which does not fall selectively upon imported goods or locally produced or manufactured goods and does not discriminate against interstate goods, offends against none of the prohibitions imposed by the Constitution. In particular, such a tax would not affect freedom of interstate trade because all goods would compete in the State on the same footing: there would be no discrimination of a protectionist kind.

...

It would seem that the argument proceeded on the footing that, had New South Wales chosen to impose a tax on the production or manufacture of tobacco or tobacco products, it would have raised almost the same amount of revenue from practically the same sources as it did by the imposition of the licence fees. To approach the matter in that way is, however, to mistake the purpose of s 90. The purpose of that section was not to restrict the revenue raising capacity of the States. Equally, its purpose was not to secure to the Commonwealth a revenue base: that is the function of s 51(ii). Rather, the purpose of s 90 was to preclude State imposts on goods which would undermine the common external tariff regardless of the revenue which the States would be compelled to forgo by reason of the prohibition. Thus, in these cases it is the nature of the impost and not the revenue involved which is important and it is the fact that the impost falls upon domestic and imported goods alike which is the substance of the matter. It is not to the point that only a small amount of tobacco products sold in New South Wales, or in Australia generally, is imported. Whatever the proportion, the level of protection, if any, which the Commonwealth has chosen to give tobacco products produced or manufactured in Australia remains unaffected.

The decision in *Ha* had the effect that the States could no longer use a mechanism that had previously raised significant revenue. The introduction of the federal goods and services tax (GST) in 2000, and the associated arrangement that the revenue collected will be distributed by the Commonwealth to the States, has made an impact in making up for the lost revenue.

Taxes on the consumption of goods

There is *obiter dicta* in some early cases to the effect that taxes on the consumption of goods amount to excise duties. However, the point has never been decided and was expressly left unresolved by the majority in *Ha*.

Ha v New South Wales (1997) 189 CLR 465

Brennan CJ, McHugh, Gummow and Kirby JJ

In this case, as in *Capital Duplicators (No 2)* (1993) 178 CLR 561, it is unnecessary to consider whether a tax on the consumption of goods would be classified as a duty of excise.

Whether a tax on the consumption of goods is an excise duty will likely turn in part on the view adopted as to the purpose served by section 90 and which underpinned the division between the majority and minority judges in *Ha*.

8.6 Taxation must not discriminate between States or parts of States

Section 51(ii) includes an express prohibition that taxation must not 'discriminate between States or parts of States'. This limitation is echoed in section 99.

Australian Constitution

Section 99 Commonwealth not to give preference

The Commonwealth shall not, by any law or regulation of trade, commerce, or revenue, give preference to one State or any part thereof over another State or any part thereof.

The High Court has held that the section 51(ii) and section 99 limitations overlap. All instances of preference involve discrimination, but not all instances of discrimination involve preference.

Permanent Trustee Australia Ltd v Commissioner of State Revenue (Vic) (2004) 220 CLR 388

Gleeson CJ, Gummow, Hayne, Callinan and Heydon JJ

[W]hile preference necessarily involves discrimination or lack of uniformity, the latter does not necessarily involve the former.

Queensland Nickel Pty Ltd v Commonwealth (2015) 255 CLR 252

Nettle J (French CJ, Hayne, Kiefel, Bell, Gageler, Keane JJ agreeing)

For the purposes of s 99 of the Constitution, the Commonwealth does not give a "preference" by law or regulation to one State over another unless the law or regulation discriminates between those States.

Some basic principles on the discrimination limitation were summarised in ***Fortescue Metals***.

Fortescue Metals Group Ltd v Commonwealth (2013) 250 CLR 548

Hayne, Bell and Keane JJ

Three textual points may then be made about the concluding words of s 51(ii). First, the reference to discriminating between "parts of States" suggests that the concluding words of s 51(ii) are to be read as directed against laws which discriminate between States, or parts of States, on the basis of *geography* or *locality*. "[P]arts of States" must be defined geographically. There is no textual foundation for reading the reference to 'States', as distinct from "parts of States", in any different way. Second, the concluding words of s 51(ii) do not speak of a law that discriminates *against* States or parts of States. The expression used is "so as not to discriminate *between* States or parts of States" (emphasis added). Third, it is necessary to recognise that the words 'but so as not to discriminate' qualify a power to make laws with respect to taxation.

...

There are relatively few decisions about the meaning and application of the limiting words of s 51(ii). The effect of those decisions may be described generally as being that discrimination has been found only when the relevant Act provided for the application of different rules according to locality and has not been established by showing only that application of the Act's provisions yields an assessment which would have been different if, by operating elsewhere, the taxpayer would have incurred different outgoings.

The 'mirror taxes' at issue in ***Permanent Trustee*** did not contravene section 51(ii) (because that limitation did not apply to the head of power under which the mirror taxes were enacted) and did not contravene s 99 because the different outcomes in each State produced by the legislation were not a direct function of geography.

Permanent Trustee Australia Ltd v Commissioner of State Revenue (Vic) (2004) 220 CLR 388

Gleeson CJ, Gummow, Hayne, Callinan and Heydon JJ

It was held in *Allders* (1996) 186 CLR 630 both that s 52(i) included a power to make a law imposing taxation, providing the law was otherwise one with respect to Commonwealth places and, further, that such a law was not subject to the prohibition against discrimination in s 51(ii). The refusal of leave to re-open *Allders* has the consequence that the argument the appellant presents respecting s 51(ii) must fail at the threshold.

...

The appellant accepts that there would be no infringement of s 99 by the imposition by federal law of a stamp duty which applied to all Commonwealth places whatever their location, even though the result could be that within the one State different rates would apply depending on the situation of a locality inside or outside a Commonwealth place in that State. What the appellant does assert is that the Mirror Taxes Act has an effect of preferring one State over another State because different rates of taxation and exemptions from taxation apply depending solely on whether the relevant Commonwealth place is in one State rather than another. The rates of taxation and, indeed, the types of taxes that are imposed by federal law differ from State to State.

...

Where then in the Mirror Taxes Act is there to be found the necessary element of discrimination between one State or any part thereof and another State or any part thereof? The scheme of the Mirror Taxes Act is to treat as relevantly of the same character the whole of the geographic area of each State, including those portions which are Commonwealth places; the taxation laws applying in the Commonwealth places are assimilated with those laws in the surrounding State. The scheme of the Mirror Taxes Act may produce differences in revenue outcomes between States, but that mirrors the differences that exist between the different taxation regimes from State to State. The differential treatment and unequal outcome that is involved here is the product of distinctions that are appropriate and adapted to a proper objective. There is no benefit or advantage enjoyed in or in relation to a Commonwealth place that is not shared by the remainder of the State in which it is located.

Similarly, the different outcomes in each State produced by the tax formula considered in ***Fortescue Metals*** were not a function of geography. The case concerned a 'minerals resource rent tax' payable by miners. The formula for calculating the sum of tax payable involved deducting the sum paid to a State in royalties. This meant that the formula would produce different outcomes for miners operating in different States because the States have differing royalties regimes. The High Court held that this scheme did not discriminate between States.

Fortescue Metals Group Ltd v Commonwealth (2013) 250 CLR 548

French CJ

The stated object of the MRRT Act is to ensure that the Australian community receives an adequate return for its "taxable resources" having regard to their inherent value, their non-renewable nature and the extent to which they are subject to Commonwealth, State and Territory royalties. The Act makes allowance, in fixing the MRRT liability of a miner, for mining royalties payable under State laws. Because the MRRT Act makes those allowances, the liabilities it imposes can vary according to State mineral royalty regimes. That potential for a differential operation from State to State underpins the plaintiffs' argument that the Act discriminates between States contrary to s 51(ii) of the Constitution and gives preference to one State over another contrary to s 99 of the Constitution.

...

As explained earlier in these reasons, the constraints imposed by ss 51(ii) and 99 of the Constitution serve a federal purpose – the economic unity of the Commonwealth and the formal equality in the Federation of the States inter se and their people. Those high purposes are not defeated by uniform Commonwealth laws with respect to taxation or laws of trade, commerce or revenue which have different effects between one State and another because of their application to different circumstances or their interactions with different State legal regimes. Nor are those purposes defeated merely because a Commonwealth law includes provisions of general application allowing for different outcomes according to the existence or operation of a particular class of State law. A criterion for determining whether that category of Commonwealth law discriminates or gives a preference in the sense used in ss 51(ii) and 99 is whether the distinctions it makes are appropriate and adapted to a proper objective.

...

The objective of the impugned provision in that case was non-discriminatory. So too are the objectives of the impugned provisions of the MRRT Act. In general terms, they are those set out in the stated objectives of the Act referred to at the commencement of these reasons. The differences in the operation of the MRRT Act which arise out of its interaction with different royalty regimes serve those objectives. They are proper objectives, to which the impugned provisions are appropriate and adapted.

Hayne, Bell and Keane JJ

The MRRT Legislation does not discriminate between States or parts of States. It has no different application between States. Observing that a miner would pay a different amount of MRRT if that miner conducted identical operations in a different State does not demonstrate discrimination ...

The MRRT Legislation does not discriminate between States. If the States had enacted no provision for royalties or if all States had chosen to exact royalties at identical rates, the plaintiffs' argument of discrimination would evidently be without foundation ...

Neither income tax Act provisions permitting deduction of State taxes from taxable income nor the royalty provisions of the MRRT Act discriminate between States ...

Because the MRRT Legislation does not discriminate between States, there is no preference of one State over another.

Queensland Nickel is another case where the different outcomes were not a function of geography. A tax was payable on greenhouse emissions arising from nickel production. Each nickel producer was allocated tax credits under a 'Jobs and Competitiveness Program' (JCP) to reduce the sum of tax payable. The credits were calculated by reference to the volume of nickel produced and industry averages for greenhouse gas emissions arising from nickel production. This formula disadvantaged Queensland Nickel because its refinery technology produced more pollution than that used by its competitors in other States. In practical terms, this meant Queensland Nickel paid more tax than its competitors would in respect of the same volume of nickel produced. The High Court held that there was no discrimination between States.

Queensland Nickel Pty Ltd v Commonwealth (2015) 255 CLR 252

Nettle J (French CJ, Hayne, Kiefel, Bell, Gageler, Keane JJ agreeing)

[T]he view consistently taken in relation to taxation laws has been that it is not enough, in order to demonstrate discrimination in the relevant sense, to show only that a taxation law may have different effects in different States because of differences between circumstances in those States ...

Construed accordingly, it is apparent that the JCP did not discriminate between States. In terms, it applied equally to eligible persons carrying on the production of nickel regardless of the State of production and, in terms of practical effect, the plaintiff did not suggest that the differences in inputs, production processes and outputs were due to anything other than differences in natural, business and other circumstances as between the States of production ...

[E]ven allowing that there might be cases in which s 99 is attracted to a Commonwealth taxing Act because it produces different consequences in different States as the result of differences between States in natural, business or other circumstances, in this case it does not appear that any of the differences between the plaintiff's and the Western Australian nickel producers' inputs, production processes or outputs were due to differences between Queensland and Western Australia in natural, business or other circumstances.

8.7 DISCUSSION QUESTIONS

1. Why is splitting tax legislation into a tax imposition statute and a tax assessment statute not required by section 55 of the *Constitution* but still of utility under section 53 of the *Constitution*?
2. Explain the requirement that a tax is an exaction of money for public purposes by reference to the facts of ***Lutton v Lessels*** and ***Roy Morgan***.
3. What is the difference between a tax and a fine or pecuniary penalty?
4. Why was the legislation in ***Harper v Minister for Sea Fisheries*** not a tax on the production of a commodity?
5. Problem question: The *Workplace Gender Equality Act 2012* (Cth) established the Workplace Gender Equality Agency and imposes obligations on certain employers to disclose certain information to the agency. Consider this hypothetical amending legislation and scenario. Following its introduction and passage in the Senate and subsequent passage in the House of Representatives, the *Paying for the Gender Pay Gap (Amendment) Act 2023* (Cth) took effect on 1 January 2023.

   The Act introduces a new Division into the *Workplace Gender Equality Act 2012* (Cth) creating a liability on corporations with more than 100 employees to pay a 'gender pay gap fee' to the Workplace Gender Equality Agency if the average pay of its female employees is more than 15 per cent lower than the average pay of its male employees. The rate of the fee is set at twice the value of the total remuneration package of a corporation's chief executive officer or managing director.

   Advise whether the *Paying for the Gender Pay Gap (Amendment) Act 2023* is a valid and effective law under section 51(ii) of the *Constitution*.

CONSTITUTIONAL ALTERATION AND THE RACE POWER

9

9.1 Overview

This chapter examines the process of constitutional alteration and the scope of the race power in section 51(xxvi) of the *Australian Constitution*. The race power was altered by referendum in 1967 and provides a useful case study in the way in which alteration of a constitutional provision affects its meaning.

Section 128 provides that the *Constitution* may be altered only by a law approved by the electors voting in a referendum. The electors' approval must be expressed by way of double majority: any constitutional alteration must be approved by a majority of electors nationwide and by a majority of electors in a majority of States.

In 1967, such a double majority was achieved to alter the scope of the race power by extending its scope to include Aboriginal and Torres Strait Islander Australians. Aboriginal and Torres Strait Islander Australians were originally excluded from the scope of the race power. Contemporary controversy has focused on whether the race power is limited to laws beneficial to the people of any race or whether the race power extends to laws that are detrimental to the people of any race. The most recent case upholds the validity of a law that was detrimental to the people of a race.

Key concepts considered in this chapter include:

- alteration
- referendum
- double majority
- 'people of any race'
- special laws.

9.2 Section 128 and popular sovereignty

Section 128 vests power to alter the *Constitution* ultimately in the Australian people: there can be no alteration to the *Constitution* without the approval of the electors.

Australian Constitution

Section 128 Mode of altering the Constitution

This Constitution shall not be altered except in the following manner:

The proposed law for the alteration thereof must be passed by an absolute majority of each House of the Parliament, and not less than two nor more than six months after its passage through both Houses the proposed law shall be submitted in each State and Territory to the electors qualified to vote for the election of members of the House of Representatives.

But if either House passes any such proposed law by an absolute majority, and the other House rejects or fails to pass it, or passes it with any amendment to which the first-mentioned House will not agree, and if after an interval of three months the first-mentioned House in the same or the next session again passes the proposed law by an absolute majority with or without any amendment which has been made or agreed to by the other House, and such other House rejects or fails to pass it or passes it with any amendment to which the first-mentioned House will not agree, the Governor-General may submit the proposed law as last proposed by the first-mentioned House, and either with or without any amendments subsequently agreed to by both Houses, to the electors in each State and Territory qualified to vote for the election of the House of Representatives.

When a proposed law is submitted to the electors the vote shall be taken in such manner as the Parliament prescribes. But until the qualification of electors of members of the House of Representatives becomes uniform throughout the Commonwealth, only one-half the electors voting for and against the proposed law shall be counted in any State in which adult suffrage prevails.

And if in a majority of the States a majority of the electors voting approve the proposed law, and if a majority of all the electors voting also approve the proposed law, it shall be presented to the Governor-General for the Queen's assent.

No alteration diminishing the proportionate representation of any State in either House of the Parliament, or the minimum number of representatives of a State in the House of Representatives, or increasing, diminishing, or otherwise altering the limits of the State, or in any manner affecting the provisions of the Constitution in relation thereto, shall become law unless the majority of the electors voting in that State approve the proposed law.

In this section, "Territory" means any territory referred to in section one hundred and twenty-two of this Constitution in respect of which there is in force a law allowing its representation in the House of Representatives.

Even in 1901, when the Imperial Parliament could still legislate for Australia by paramount force, it was recognised that vesting power to alter the *Constitution* in the Australian people suggested popular sovereignty; that is, section 128 reflects the notion that all governmental power in Australia stems ultimately from the people.

John Quick and Robert Garran, *The Annotated Constitution of the Commonwealth of Australia* (Angus & Robertson, 1901)

A Federal Legislature is a mere creature of the Federal Constitution; it is mere instrument or servant of a federal community; it is an agent, not a master. The Constitution is the master of the legislature, and the community itself is the author of the Constitution. In this respect a federal legislature differs from a supreme legislature like that of Great Britain, which is the embodiment and essence of the sovereignty of the British nation. Sovereignty resides in that person, or body, or class of persons in whom is ultimately vested the power to amend a Constitution of Government ...

The preparation of a proposed amendment, and its approval by an absolute majority of members in each of the Houses, or by an absolute majority of members twice in one House, is merely a preliminary act in the amending procedure. The principal element in the process is the submission of the proposal to the electors. This process is a concrete exemplification of the political expedient, formerly known as the Plebiscite, now better known as the Referendum. It is an undoubted recognition of the qualified electors as the custodians of the delegated sovereignty of the Commonwealth ...

As at late 2023, there have been 45 proposals submitted to referendum and the *Australian Constitution* has been amended only eight times since it came into force on 1 January 1901. The *Constitution Alteration (Aboriginal and Torres Strait Islander Voice) 2023* was the 45th proposal submitted to referendum.

9.3 What can be altered using the section 128 mechanism?

Section 128 provides the mechanism for amending the *Constitution*. Any part of the *Constitution* may be altered, including section 128 itself. The *Constitution Alteration (Referendums) 1977* altered section 128 to permit electors in the Territories to vote on proposed alterations to the *Constitution*.

As Chapter 1 explained, the *Constitution* is found in section 9 of the *Commonwealth of Australia Constitution Act 1900* (Imp), which states 'The Constitution of the Commonwealth shall be as follows: ...'. Section 128 does not provide for any alteration to the preamble or to the covering clauses, because those are not parts of the *Constitution*.

John Quick and Robert Garran, *The Annotated Constitution of the Commonwealth of Australia* (Angus & Robertson, 1901)

The Constitution can be altered in a certain manner. What is the Constitution? What is an alteration? The Constitution is that part of the Imperial Act comprehended in Clause 9 and divided into chapters, parts, and sections, the sections being numbered from 1 to 128 inclusive. The Schedule also is a part of the Constitution. Clauses 1 to 8 of the Imperial Act are not parts of the Constitution, and cannot be altered except by the Imperial Parliament ...

Quick and Garran's comment that only the Imperial Parliament can amend the preamble and covering clauses, because they are not part of the *Constitution*, is no longer correct. It remains correct that the preamble and covering clauses are not part of the *Constitution* and therefore do not fall within the scope of section 128.

However, the United Kingdom Parliament no longer has power to legislate for Australia. Today, the *Statute of Westminster* and the *Australia Act* (see Chapter 1) together provide a mechanism by which the preamble and covering clauses could be amended. That mechanism involves only legislation and does not require the approval of the electors voting in a referendum.

Anne Twomey, 'The Preamble in Indigenous Constitutional Recognition' (2011) 15(2) *Australian Indigenous Law Review* 4

While the *Statute of Westminster* lifted the application of the *Colonial Laws Validity Act* to Commonwealth laws, section 8 of the *Statute of Westminster* expressly preserved the *Commonwealth of Australia Constitution Act* from amendment by virtue of any power granted by the *Statute*. Hence, the Commonwealth Parliament, through its ordinary legislative powers or section 128 of the Constitution, still had no power to amend the *Commonwealth of Australia Constitution Act*. That position could have been altered by the *Australia Acts*, which could have repealed section 8 of the *Statute of Westminster* if it was desired to do so. However, while other provisions of the *Statute of Westminster* were repealed, section 8 was not. Instead, section 15 was inserted in the *Australia Acts* which established the sole way of altering the *Statute of Westminster*, and hence the means of providing for the amendment or repeal of the *Commonwealth of Australia Constitution Act*, including its Preamble ...

Section 15(1) of the *Australia Acts*, however, sets out a method for amending section 8 of the *Statute of Westminster*, and through it, the Preamble to the *Commonwealth of Australia Constitution Act*. It requires the enactment of Commonwealth legislation passed at the request or with the concurrence of the parliaments of all the states. It further states that, subject to sub-section 15(3), this is the *only* way to amend the *Statute of Westminster*. Hence the safest way of amending the Preamble would be for all the states to enact laws requesting the enactment of a Commonwealth law, which amended section 8 of the *Statute of Westminster* in such a way as to permit the amendment or repeal of the Preamble.

This would mean, however, that the Preamble could be amended without the direct approval of the people through a referendum. This outcome may be politically objectionable as it would deprive the people of their say ...

9.4 The process of constitutional alteration

Section 128 provides for a three-step procedure for altering the *Constitution*:

1. parliamentary approval
2. approval of the electors, and
3. Royal Assent.

Parliamentary approval

The first step in altering the *Constitution* is parliamentary approval. Either House of Parliament may initiate a proposal to alter the *Constitution*.

The text of section 128 suggests that a proposal to alter the *Constitution* that is passed by an absolute majority of both Houses must be submitted to the people: 'the proposed law *shall be* submitted in each State and Territory to the electors'. Section 128 sets a precise timeframe in which the referendum must be held. The referendum must be held between two and six months after the proposal was approved by Parliament.

In practice, proposals to alter the *Constitution* that are passed by an absolute majority of both Houses are not always submitted to the people. For example, the Constitution Alteration (Local Government) Bill 2013 was passed by both Houses of Parliament and would have amended the *Constitution* to permit the Commonwealth to grant financial assistance directly to local government bodies. However, the proposed alteration was never submitted to the people.

A proposal to alter the *Constitution* that has been approved by only one House of Parliament may also be submitted to the people. The steps in this process are:

1. A proposal to alter the *Constitution* is passed by an absolute majority of one House.
2. That proposal is not agreed to by an absolute majority of the other House.
3. After an interval of three months, the first House again passes the proposal by an absolute majority.
4. The proposal may (although need not) be submitted to the people.

There are examples of proposed alterations to the *Constitution* that have been passed only by one House of Parliament being submitted to the people. The Constitution Alteration (Simultaneous Elections) Bill 1973, Constitution Alteration (Democratic Elections) Bill 1973, Constitution Alteration (Local Government Bodies) Bill 1973 and Constitution

Alteration (Mode of Altering the Constitution) Bill 1973 were each passed only by the House of Representatives and submitted to the people. None of the Bills were approved by the people at the 1974 referendum.

Approval of the electors

Section 128 requires the approval of the electors before any alteration to the *Constitution* can be granted Royal Assent and take effect.

In the ordinary case, the approval of the electors is required by way of what is often referred to as a 'double majority'. Section 128 requires a proposed alteration to the *Constitution* to be approved by a majority of electors nationwide *plus* a majority of electors in a majority of States. The votes of Territory electors count only in the overall majority requirement.

The double majority requirement is a function of federalism and political pragmatism. Without the double majority requirement, the much larger populations of New South Wales and Victoria could use their voting power to alter the *Constitution* without regard to the interests of the people of the less populous States.

In three instances, a double majority is not sufficient. Those three instances are set out in the penultimate paragraph of section 128. They are:

1. alterations diminishing the proportionate representation of any State in either House of the Parliament, or the minimum number of representatives of a State in the House of Representatives
2. alterations increasing, diminishing, or otherwise altering the limits of the State
3. alterations in any manner affecting the provisions of the Constitution in relation to a State.

In each of these three circumstances, a majority of electors in the affected State or States must approve the proposed alteration.

Section 128 also states that 'the vote shall be taken in such manner as the Parliament prescribes'. The *Referendum (Machinery) Provisions Act 1984* (Cth) provides for referendum votes to be conducted in a manner similar to federal elections, including the standard features of compulsory voting, paper ballots, pre-polling, and postal voting.

Since 1912, the *Referendum (Machinery) Provisions Act 1984* (Cth) has also required the Electoral Commissioner to send to each address on the electoral roll a pamphlet setting out:

> (1) the arguments for the proposed alteration authorised by the members of Parliament in favour of the proposed alteration; and (2) the arguments against the proposed alteration authorised by the members of Parliament opposed to the proposed alteration. Each set of arguments must not exceed 2,000 words.

Royal Assent

In practice, Royal Assent is a formality. It is improbable that a Governor-General would ever withhold Royal Assent from a proposed alteration to the *Constitution* that has received the approval of a double majority of electors.

Once the *Constitution* is altered in accordance with the procedure set out in section 128, the practical and legal consequences of the alteration arise for consideration. The alteration to the 'race power' in 1967 provides an important case study.

9.5 Alteration of the race power

Section 51(xxvi) of the *Australian Constitution* permits Parliament to make laws with respect to the people of any race. The scope of the power was expanded in 1967 following a referendum conducted under section 128.

Australian Constitution

Section 51 Legislative powers of the Parliament

The Parliament shall, subject to this Constitution, have power to make laws for the peace, order, and good government of the Commonwealth with respect to:

> ...
>
> (xxvi) the people of any race, ~~other than the aboriginal race in any State~~, for whom it is deemed necessary to make special laws;
>
> ...

The words 'other than the aboriginal race in any State' were deleted by the *Constitution Alteration (Aboriginals) 1967*.

Justice Kirby summarised the original purposes of the race power in his dissenting judgment in ***Kartinyeri***. Justice Kirby explained that its original purpose was to enable federal laws discriminating against people of non-white races and to leave the regulation of Indigenous peoples to the States.

Kartinyeri v Commonwealth (1998) 195 CLR 337

Kirby J

Paragraph (xxvi), in its original form, should be understood in the context of attitudes to race and to "White Australia" which were common amongst the settlers represented in the Conventions and constituting the electors of the federating colonies. In the original draft Constitution Bill of 1891, the proposal was for a grant of exclusive legislative power to the Federal Parliament with respect to:

> "The affairs of people of any race with respect to whom it is deemed necessary to make special laws not applicable to the general community; but so that this power shall not extend to authorise legislation with respect to the aboriginal native race in Australia and the Maori race in New Zealand".

There is uncertainty as to the initial purpose of including this power and proposing that it be exclusive to the Federal Parliament. The provision was Sir Samuel Griffith's idea, and it has been suggested that it was based upon the unhappy experiences of Queensland with "blackbirding". This was the practice by which people from the Pacific Islands had been snatched from their homes and sold into a form of slavery in the Queensland sugar farms. Whether its inclusion was out of a concern for the victims of such activities, a desire to exclude the States from control over them or to provide the Federal Parliament with powers, in addition to the proposed power over aliens, to deal with possible unrest and expulsion, is not entirely clear. The Convention Debates, particularly those of the Melbourne Convention of 1898, show that some delegates wanted to retain power for the States, and to permit the Federal Parliament to enact, laws far from beneficial for people of minority races (such as Chinese in factories and shops, "Asiatic or African ... miner[s]" and so on). However, other delegates regarded the prospect of discriminatory legislation on the part of the new federal polity as "disgraceful" and "degrading to us and our citizenship".

As finally adopted, the power in par (xxvi) was not restricted, in terms, to securing the benefit or advancement of the people of a given race. In the historical context of that time such protective purposes would have been possible, eg in the case of the "kanakas" in Queensland. But so also would laws detrimental to, or discriminatory against, such people. The exclusion from the paragraph of power with respect to "the aboriginal race in any State" appears principally to have been designed to leave their regulation to the States. It may have had the effect of protecting them from any risk of the misuse of the race power by the new Federal Parliament ...

Justice Kirby's judgment also summarised the reasoning underlying the 1967 alteration to the race power. The purpose was not simply to permit federal laws applying only to Indigenous peoples. Unlike the original purpose of the race power to permit laws detrimental to the people of non-white races, the amendment to the race power seems intended principally to permit laws beneficial to Indigenous peoples.

Kartinyeri v Commonwealth (1998) 195 CLR 337

Kirby J

[O]n 1 March 1967, a new Prime Minister (Mr Holt) introduced the Constitution Alteration (Aboriginals) Bill 1967 (Cth). He explained that the government had been influenced by the "popular impression" that the words "other than the aboriginal race in any State" in par (xxvi) "are discriminatory". This was a view which the government believed to be erroneous. But it was deeply rooted. It required amendment of the Constitution in a way that would give the Parliament the power to make special laws for Aboriginals which, with cooperation with the States, would "secure the widest measure of agreement with respect to Aboriginal advancement".

The Government's Bill was supported by the Leader of the Opposition (Mr Whitlam). He referred to the many disadvantages which Australian Aboriginals had suffered and which needed positive federal initiatives. It was also supported by Mr Wentworth. He expressed the opinion that some discrimination was necessary in relation to Aboriginals but "it should be favourable, not unfavourable". The Bill passed through the House of Representatives without a single dissenting vote.

In the Senate, the Minister responsible for the Bill (Senator Henty) repeated what had been said by the Prime Minister. The Leader of the Opposition in the Senate, Senator Murphy, met directly the argument that the exclusion of Aboriginals from par (xxvi) had been intended to be beneficial for them. He said:

> The simple fact is that they are different from other persons and that they do need special laws. They themselves believe that they need special laws. In this proposed law there is no suggestion of any intended discrimination in respect of Aboriginals except a discrimination in their favour.

The Bill was also approved by the Senate without a single dissenting vote.

There having been no opposition within the Parliament to the proposed alterations to the Constitution, it was necessary, in the procedures which followed, to prepare only the argument in favour of the proposed law to be distributed in pamphlet form to the electors. The case for the "yes" vote authorised by the Prime Minister, the Leader of the Australian Country Party and the Leader of the Opposition addressed the amendments to par (xxvi) and s 127 which were to be put before the electors as a single proposal. The case, relevantly, argued:

> The purposes of these proposed amendments ... are to remove any ground for the belief that, as at present worded, the Constitution discriminates in some ways against people of the Aboriginal race, and, at the same time, to make it possible for the Commonwealth Parliament to make special laws for the people of the Aboriginal race, wherever they may live, if the Commonwealth Parliament considers this desirable or necessary. ... The Commonwealth's object will be to co-operate with the States to ensure that together we act in the best interests of the Aboriginal people of Australia.
>
> ...

The referendum was put on 27 May 1967. It was overwhelmingly approved. In the history of Australian constitutional referendums, no other such vote has come close to the unique political and popular consensus demonstrated in the 1967 referendum on Aborigines.

The general expectation and intention was that an amended race power would be used in practice to enact laws beneficial to Aboriginal and Torres Strait Islander Australians. However, there was never any intention to prohibit racially discriminatory or detrimental laws. The then Prime Minister, Harold Holt, made this explicit in his Second Reading Speech for the Constitution Alteration (Aboriginals) Bill 1967.

Parliamentary Debates, House of Representatives, 1 March 1967

Mr Holt (Higgins – Prime Minister)

I think I should say a few words about the suggestion that has been made that we should include a constitutional guarantee against discrimination on the ground of race. Such a proposal was put forward, in particular, by the honourable member for Mackellar (Mr Wentworth) in a private member's Bill. The recommendation to include such a guarantee in our Constitution has the obvious attraction of providing evidence of the Australian people's desire to outlaw discriminatory practices of every kind, but the disadvantages of the inclusion of such a guarantee are so substantial that the Government does not believe that it should be pursued. Such a guarantee could provide a fertile source of attack on the constitutional validity of legislation which we, at this point of time, would not consider discriminatory. The extent of litigation that has arisen from section 92 provides a serious warning of the ramifications of an apparently straightforward constitutional guarantee. Moreover, such a guarantee would operate only to limit government action, it would not affect actions by individuals. Racial discrimination, if it exists in a community, is the outward manifestation of beliefs rooted in the hearts and minds of some men and women. I do not believe that such beliefs are to be found on any significant scale in this country; but even if it were otherwise, I do not think the position could be remedied in practice by a constitutional guarantee.

In their judgment in ***Kartinyeri***, Gummow and Hayne JJ noted that the 1967 referendum did no more than include Indigenous Australians within the broad general scope of section 51(xxvi).

Kartinyeri v Commonwealth (1998) 195 CLR 337

Gummow and Hayne JJ

Another interpretation of the events of 1967 is that, whilst the purpose of the 1967 Act was to ensure that the Parliament could legislate beneficially in respect of the indigenous races, this was implemented by including them within the generality of the power in s 51(xxvi) ...

The text is not limited by any implication such as that contended for by the plaintiffs. This is so whether one has regard alone to the terms of the Constitution after the 1967 Act took effect or also to that statute. The circumstances surrounding the enactment of the 1967 Act, assuming regard may properly be had to them, may indicate an aspiration of the legislature and the electors to provide federal legislative powers to advance the situation of persons of the Aboriginal race. But it does not follow that this was implemented by a change to the constitutional text which was hedged by limitations unexpressed therein.

The bill for the 1967 Act did not attract any opposition in Parliament so as to lead to the distribution to each elector of an argument against the proposed law by the Chief Electoral Officer.

Section 6A of the Referendum Act provided for the distribution of "yes" and "no" cases authorised by a majority of those members of both Houses of Parliament who voted for and against the proposed law. Only a "yes" case was authorised and distributed to each elector. It stated that the proposed alteration of s 51(xxvi) would do two things and continued:

> First, it will remove words from our Constitution that many people think are discriminatory against the Aboriginal people.
>
> Second, it will make it possible for the Commonwealth Parliament to make special laws for the people of the Aboriginal race, wherever they may live, if the Parliament considers it necessary.
>
> This cannot be done at present because, as the Constitution stands, the Commonwealth Parliament has no power, except in the Territories, to make laws with respect to people of the Aboriginal race as such.
>
> This would not mean that the States would automatically lose their existing powers. What is intended is that the National Parliament could make laws, if it thought fit, relating to Aboriginals – as it can about many other matters on which the States also have power to legislate. The Commonwealth's object will be to co-operate with the States to ensure that together we act in the best interests of the Aboriginal people of Australia.

The treatment in the "yes" case of the proposed alteration to the power of the Commonwealth legislature emphasised considerations of federalism. It did not speak of other limitations upon the nature of the special laws beyond confirming that they might apply to the people of the Aboriginal race "wherever they may live" rather than be limited to the Territories. Further, the proposed law took its form after the expression of learned opinion that complete repeal of s 51(xxvi) would have been preferable to any amendment intended to extend to the Aboriginals "its possible benefits".

The omission in the 1967 Act of any limitation, making specific reference to the provision of "benefits" to persons of the Aboriginal race, upon the operation of the amended s 51(xxvi), is consistent with a wish of the Parliament to avoid later definitional argument in the legislature and the courts as to the scope of its legislative power. That is the effect of what was achieved.

It appears that there were no federal laws passed under the race power before 1967. There were also no cases decided on the basis of race power before 1967.

9.6 'The people of any race'

The race power permits laws with respect to 'the people of any race'.

The High Court has given a broad definition of the concept of 'race'. The concept of race is broader than simply questions of genetics or biology. The ***Tasmanian Dam Case*** holds that the race power supports laws protecting the cultural heritage of a race of people because the cultural heritage of a people is inseparably connected to that people.

In this case, the High Court upheld provisions of a federal law operating to protect sites of particular historical or cultural significance to Aboriginal people, even though those sites were also of significance to humanity more generally.

Commonwealth v Tasmania ('Tasmanian Dam Case') (1983) 158 CLR 1

Mason J

In essence the argument is that, as a subject matter of the legislative power, the cultural heritage of the people of a race is distinct and divorced from the people of that race, so that a power with respect to the latter does not include power with respect to the former. The answer is that the cultural heritage of a people is so much of a characteristic or property of the people to whom it belongs that it is inseparably connected with them, so that a legislative power with respect to the people of a race, which confers power to make laws to protect them, necessarily extends to the making of laws protecting their cultural heritage.

A law which protects the cultural heritage of the people of the aboriginal race constitutes a special law for the purpose of par (xxvi) because the protection of that cultural heritage meets a special need of that people. However, it is argued that ss 8 and 11 do not answer the description of such a law because the law only protects a site which is of significance to the whole of mankind and to the people of the aboriginal race. This argument fails to acknowledge that something which is of significance to mankind may have a special and deeper significance to a particular people because it forms part of their cultural heritage. Thus an aboriginal archaeological site which is part of the cultural heritage of people of the aboriginal race has a special and deeper significance for aboriginal people than it has for mankind generally. If it be found on the facts that the sites do have a particular significance for them because the sites are part of their cultural heritage, there is a special need to protect the sites for them, a need which differs from, and in one sense transcends, the need to protect it for mankind ...

Brennan J

Though the biological element is, as Kerr LJ pointed out, an essential element of membership of a race, it does not ordinarily exhaust the characteristics of a racial group.

Physical similarities, and a common history, a common religion or spiritual beliefs and a common culture are factors that tend to create a sense of identity among members of a race and to which others have regard in identifying people as members of a race. As the people of a group identify themselves and are identified by others as a race by reference to their common history, religion, spiritual beliefs or culture as well as by reference to their biological origins and physical similarities, an indication is given of the scope and purpose of the power granted by par (xxvi). The kinds of benefits that laws might properly confer upon people as members of a race are benefits which tend to protect or foster their common intangible heritage or their common sense of identity. Their genetic inheritance is fixed at birth; the historic, religious, spiritual and cultural heritage are acquired and are susceptible to influences for which a law may provide. The advancement of the people of any race in any of these aspects of their group life falls within the power.

A law which, on its face, does not discriminate in favour of the people of a race, may nevertheless be valid if it discriminates in favour of those people by its operation upon the subject matter to which it relates. That involves no departure from the ordinary processes of constitutional interpretation. The characterization of a law requires that the operation of the law be ascertained by reference to its terms and their application to the circumstances in which the law operates. If the power under par (xxvi) were restricted to a discriminatory conferring of legal rights or a discriminatory imposition of legal obligations on the people of a race, laws for the general protection of historical memorabilia, of religious or spiritual shrines or of cultural practices which are of particular significance to the people of particular races would not be valid. The things which are a focus of the life of the race would lie outside the boundaries of a power which is expressed to authorize special laws for its people ...

Koowarta explains that the word 'any' means that the race power does not support laws applying to the people of *all* races. In this case, the High Court held that the race power did not support certain provisions of the *Racial Discrimination Act 1975* (Cth) because those provisions prohibited racial discrimination generally. The provisions applied to the people of *all* races rather than to the people of *any* race. The legislation was found to be valid under the external affairs power (see Chapter 6).

Koowarta v Bjelke-Petersen (1982) 153 CLR 168

Gibbs CJ

However ss 9 and 12 are not directed to the protection of people of the Aboriginal race. They prohibit discrimination generally on the ground of race; that is, they protect the persons of any race from discriminatory action by reason of their race. On behalf of the Commonwealth it was sub mitted that the Act is a special law within par (xxvi) because it selects as its subject the people of any race against whom discrimination on racial grounds is, or may be, practised. This argument cannot be accepted, for it gives insufficient weight to the words "for whom it is deemed necessary to make special laws". It is true that in some contexts the word "any" can be understood as having the effect of "all", but it would be self-contradictory to say that a law which applies to the people of all races is a special law. It is not possible to construe par (xxvi) as if it read simply "The people of all races". In the context provided by par (xxvi), the word "any" is used in the sense of "no matter which". The Parliament may deem it necessary to make special laws for the people of a particular race, no matter what the race. If the Parliament does deem that necessary, but not otherwise, it can make laws with respect to the people of that race. The opinion of Parliament that it is necessary to make a special law need not be evidenced by an express declaration to that effect; it may appear from the law itself. However, a law which applies equally to the people of all races is not a special law for the people of any one race. Sections 9 and 12 of the Act deal with discrimination against the people of all races. It is impossible to describe those sections as laws with respect to "the people of any race for whom it is deemed necessary to make special laws".

Kartinyeri explains that the race power will support laws applying to a sub-class of the people of any race rather than applying to all members of the people of a particular race. In this case, the High Court rejected an argument that the *Hindmarsh Island Bridge Act 1997* (Cth) was not supported by the race power because the Act applied only to affect the interests of one particular Aboriginal group – the Ngarrindjeri people – rather than the interests of all Aboriginal people.

Kartinyeri v Commonwealth (1998) 195 CLR 337

Gummow and Hayne JJ

The first submission by the plaintiffs was that the Bridge Act lacked "a sufficient level of generality" to found support by s 51(xxvi). This was because, whilst the Ngarrindjeri people are members of the Aboriginal race, they do not constitute the entirety of that race, and s 51(xxvi) requires a law to answer the description "with respect to ... [t]he people of any race", not with respect to some only of the people of any race.

The construction of s 51(xxvi) for which the plaintiffs contend would cripple the reach of the legislative power to deal with social, economic or other conditions which particularly afflicted certain members or groups of Aboriginals ...

The legislative power is to be construed with all the generality of which the phrase "the people of any race" admits. That being so, why should the phrase "the people ..." be read as if limited to "all the people", rather than as including within the reach of the power any members of that class identified by the expression "the people of" the race in question?

The state of authority in this Court affirms that the phrase is "apposite to refer to any identifiable racial sub-group among Australian Aboriginals": *Commonwealth v Tasmania* (*'Tasmanian Dam Case'*) (1983) 158 CLR 1 at 274. The *Native Title Act Case* was determined on the basis that those for whom the *Native Title Act* (1993) (Cth) was a "special" law were those Aboriginal and Torres Strait Islanders who were holders of native title, and that it was not essential to determine whether the statute conferred a benefit upon all the people of those races.

The first submission by the plaintiffs should not be accepted.

9.7 'For whom it is deemed necessary to make special laws'

The words 'for whom it is deemed necessary to make special laws' have given rise to interesting questions of whether Parliament can enact laws under the races power that are detrimental rather than beneficial to the people of any race.

In the ***Native Title Act Case***, a majority of the High Court held that a law will be a 'special law' if the law confers a right or benefit or imposes an obligation or disadvantage especially on the people of a particular race. The *Native Title Act 1993* (Cth) is a special law on this definition because it confers a benefit on some Aboriginal and Torres Strait Islander people in the form of statutory protection of their native title rights.

Western Australia v Commonwealth ('Native Title Act Case') (1995) 183 CLR 373

Mason CJ, Brennan, Deane, Toohey, Gaudron and McHugh JJ

The constitutional character of the *Native Title Act* may now be examined. The Act removes the common law defeasibility of native title, and secures the Aboriginal people and Torres Strait Islanders in the enjoyment of their native title subject to the prescribed exceptions which provide for native title to be extinguished or impaired. There are only three exceptions: the occurrence of a past act that has been validated, an agreement on the part of the native title holders, or the doing of a permissible future act. The Act confers its protection upon native title holders who, ex hypothesi, are members of a particular race. As "(t)he relationship between the Aboriginal people and the lands which they occupy lies at the heart of traditional Aboriginal culture and traditional Aboriginal life", (*Tasmanian Dam Case* (1983) 158 CLR 1 at 274–275 per Deane J) the significance of security in the enjoyment of native title by the Aboriginal people of Western Australia who hold native title is undoubted ...

"Special" qualifies "law"; it does not relate to necessity. Therefore the special quality of a law must be ascertained by reference to its differential operation upon the people of a particular race (*Koowarta v Bjelke-Petersen* (1982) 153 CLR at 186, 245, 261), not by reference to the circumstances which led the Parliament to deem it necessary to enact the law. A special quality appears when the law confers a right or benefit or imposes an obligation or disadvantage especially on the people of a particular race. The law may be special even when it confers a benefit generally, provided the benefit is of special significance or importance to the people of a particular race ... That was the view of the majority in the *Tasmanian Dam Case*, where the protection of objects of significance to Aboriginal cultural heritage was held to be supported by the races power albeit the same objects were items of cultural heritage under an international treaty the protection of which was supported by the external affairs power ...

Applying these observations, the *Native Title Act* is "special" in that it confers uniquely on the Aboriginal and Torres Strait Islander holders of native title (the "people of any race") a benefit protective of their native title. Perhaps the Act confers a benefit on all the people of those races. The special quality of the law thus appears.

The ***Native Title Act Case*** also explains that it is for Parliament to deem that special laws are necessary. The High Court cannot decide that, in its own view, special laws are not necessary.

Western Australia v Commonwealth ('Native Title Act Case') (1995) 183 CLR 373

Mason CJ, Brennan, Deane, Toohey, Gaudron and McHugh JJ

If ... the requirement that a law enacted under s 51(xxvi) be special were held to evoke a judicial evaluation of the needs of the people of a race or of the threats or problems that confronted them in order to determine whether the law was, or could be deemed to be, "necessary", the Court would be required to form a political value judgment. Yet it is clear that that judgment is for the Parliament (And was so intended by the Constitutional Conventions of Sydney in 1891 (*Official Report of the National Australasian Convention Debates*, 3 April 1891 at 703–704) and Melbourne in 1898 (*Official Record of the Debates of the Australasian Federal Convention*, 28 January 1898 at 248, 253–254)), not for the Court. If the Court retains some supervisory jurisdiction to examine the question of necessity against the possibility of a manifest abuse of the races power, this case is not the occasion for an examination of that jurisdiction. The removal of the common law general defeasibility of native title by the *Native Title Act* is sufficient to demonstrate that the Parliament could properly have deemed that Act to be "necessary".

The definition of 'special law' in the ***Native Title Act Case*** is not restricted to laws conferring benefits. The majority held that a special law is a law that confers 'a right or benefit or *imposes an obligation or disadvantage* especially on the people of a particular race'. The facts of the *Native Title Act Case* involved a beneficial law. By contrast, ***Kartinyeri*** involved a detrimental law and an argument that the races power could not be used to enact laws that were disadvantageous or detrimental to the people of a particular race.

The *Aboriginal and Torres Strait Islander Heritage Protection Act 1984* (Cth) ('*Heritage Act*') provides for the protection of sites of cultural and spiritual significance to Aboriginal and Torres Strait Islander peoples, including preventing development activity on such sites. In order to facilitate the construction of a bridge, the *Hindmarsh Island Bridge Act 1997* (Cth) ('*Bridge Act*') excluded a particular geographical area from the scope of the *Heritage Act*. This had the effect of removing sites of significance to the Ngarrindjeri people from the protection of the *Heritage Act*. A majority of the High Court held that the *Bridge Act* was supported by the race power, albeit for varying reasons. The result of this case suggests that the race power can indeed be used to enact laws detrimental to the people of any race, at least in circumstances where the detriment involves the withdrawal of a previously granted benefit.

In their judgment, Brennan CJ and McHugh J decided the case on the basis of the proposition that whatever Parliament can enact it can repeal. The *Bridge Act* was merely a partial repeal of the *Heritage Act*, and was therefore supported by the same head of power as that Act. It was uncontroversial that the *Heritage Act* was supported by the race power.

Kartinyeri v Commonwealth (1998) 195 CLR 337

Brennan CJ and McHugh J

The only effect of the Bridge Act is partially to exclude the operation of the Heritage Protection Act in relation to the Hindmarsh Bridge area. The Bridge Act, like Pt IIA of the Heritage Protection Act, limits the area to which Pt II applies. As Pt II of the Heritage Protection Act is a law with respect to the subject matter of s 51(xxvi), a law which governs the area of its operation has a direct connection with that subject matter. In the absence of any constitutional limitation on the power to repeal an earlier law, the true principle is stated by Dawson J in *Kirmani v Captain Cook Cruises Pty Ltd [No 1]*:

> A law which effects the repeal of another law is not a law with respect to repeal; its subject-matter is the subject-matter of the law which is repealed.

Thus the Bridge Act is itself a law with respect to the subject matter of s 51(xxvi).

Justice Gaudron accepted that the race power authorises detrimental laws, but doubted that there would be many detrimental laws that would satisfy the test she proposed for when a special law could be deemed necessary. Justice Gaudron held that the words 'for whom it is deemed necessary to make special laws' has the effect that the race power supports only laws reasonably capable of being viewed as appropriate and adapted to some difference affecting a race of people which the Parliament might reasonably judge to exist. Like Brennan CJ and Mason J, Gaudron J held that the *Bridge Act* was a partial repeal of the *Heritage Act*. For Gaudron J, the amended *Heritage Act* was still supported by the race power with the result that the *Bridge Act* must be valid.

Kartinyeri v Commonwealth (1998) 195 CLR 337

Gaudron J

Were s 51(xxvi) simply a power to legislate with respect to "the people of any race", there would, in my view, be no doubt that Parliament might legislate in any way it chose so long as the law in question differentiated in some way with respect to the people of a particular race or dealt with some matter of "special significance or importance to the[m]". However, the words "for whom it is deemed necessary to make special laws" must be given some operation. And they can only operate to impose some limit on what would otherwise be the scope of s 51(xxvi) ...

Clearly, it is for the Parliament to deem it necessary to make a law of that kind. To form a view as to that necessity, however, there must be some difference pertaining to the people of the race involved or their circumstances or, at least, some material upon which the Parliament might reasonably form a political judgment that there is a difference of that kind. Were it otherwise, the words "for whom it is deemed necessary to make special laws" would have no operation and s 51(xxvi) would simply be a power to make laws for the people of any race.

Once it is accepted that the power conferred by s 51(xxvi) may only be exercised if there is some material upon which the Parliament might reasonably form a judgment that there is a difference necessitating some special legislative measure, two things follow. The first is that s 51(xxvi) does not authorise special laws affecting rights and obligations in areas in which there is no relevant difference between the people of the race to whom the law is directed and the people of other races ...

The second matter which flows from the requirement that there be some matter or circumstance upon which the Parliament might reasonably form the judgment that there is some difference pertaining to the people of a particular race which necessitates some special law is that the law must be reasonably capable of being viewed as appropriate and adapted to the difference asserted ... Unless the law in question is reasonably capable of being viewed as appropriate and adapted to the difference which is claimed, it could not be concluded that the Parliament formed the view that there was such a difference.

Notwithstanding that it is difficult to envisage circumstances in which a law which operated to the disadvantage of the people of a racial minority might validly be enacted under s 51(xxvi) of the Constitution, the test of constitutional validity is not whether it is a beneficial law. Rather, the test is whether the law in question is reasonably capable of being viewed as appropriate and adapted to a real and relevant difference which the Parliament might reasonably judge to exist. It is the application of that test to today's circumstances, so far as they are known, that leads to the conclusion that prima facie, at least, s 51(xxvi) presently only authorises laws which operate to the benefit of Aboriginal Australians ...

[Section] 51(xxvi) not only authorises the Heritage Protection Act but, also, authorises its partial repeal ... the Heritage Protection Act as amended by the Bridge Act remains a law for the protection and preservation of areas and objects of significance in accordance with Aboriginal tradition and, for the reasons already given, continues to be a valid enactment under s 51(xxvi).

In their judgment, Gummow and Hayne J relied on the statement of principle in the ***Native Title Act Case*** and upheld the *Bridge Act* on the reasoning that it singled out the people of a race for differential treatment.

Kartinyeri v Commonwealth (1998) 195 CLR 337

Gummow and Hayne JJ

As just indicated, "differential operation" is that which gives to any law based upon s 51(xxvi) its character as a "special" law. Once it is accepted, as it has been, that a law may make provision for some only of a particular race, it follows that a valid law may operate differentially between members of that race. That is the situation with the Bridge Act. Moreover, as was said in the joint judgment in the *Native Title Act Case*:

> A special quality appears when the law confers a right or benefit or imposes an obligation or disadvantage especially on the people of a particular race.

Here, the Bridge Act imposes a disadvantage, of the nature identified above, with respect to areas and objects within the Hindmarsh Island bridge area and the pit area. The disadvantage is in the contraction of the field of operation of the Heritage Protection Act, itself a law which is to be taken as supported by s 51(xxvi) ...

In dissent, Justice Kirby held that the race power, at least since its amendment in 1967, does not permit laws detrimental to the people of a race. Justice Kirby considered that the *Bridge Act* was detrimental and therefore invalid on his view of the race power.

Kartinyeri v Commonwealth (1998) 195 CLR 337

Kirby J

I have concluded that the race power in par (xxvi) of s 51 of the Constitution does not extend to the enactment of laws detrimental to, or discriminatory against, the people of any race (including the Aboriginal race) by reference to their race ...

Whatever the initial object of the original exception to par (xxvi), by the time that the words were removed, the amendment did not simply lump the Aboriginal people of Australia in with other races as potential targets for detrimental or adversely discriminatory laws. It was the will of the Australian Parliament and people that the race power should be significantly altered. If the Constitution were not to be changed to provide the power to make laws with respect to the advancement of Aboriginal people and to forbid discrimination on racial grounds (as Mr Wentworth had proposed), it was to be altered, at least, to remove their exclusion from the Parliament's law-making power in order that the Parliament might have the power to make special laws with respect to them. To construe the resulting power in par (xxvi) as authorising the making of laws detrimental to, and discriminatory against, people on the ground of race, and specifically Aboriginal race, would be a complete denial of the clear and unanimous object of the Parliament in proposing the amendment to par (xxvi) ...

The Bridge Act itself is, in substance, detrimental to all Aboriginals, as it removes their opportunity of making an application under the Heritage Protection Act in regard to the Hindmarsh Island Bridge area. This has a particularly telling impact on the Ngarrindjeri people, and hence on the plaintiffs ...

The Bridge Act does not answer to the description of a law with respect to the people of any race for whom it is deemed necessary to make special laws. It is a special law; that is true. But it is detrimental to, and adversely discriminatory against, people of the Aboriginal race of Australia by reference to their race. As such it falls outside the class of laws which the race power in the Australian Constitution permits.

9.8 Future reform of the race power

Questions about further alterations to the race power feature in ongoing discussions about constitutional recognition of Aboriginal and Torres Strait Islander peoples.

Expert Panel on Constitutional Recognition of Aboriginal and Torres Strait Islander Peoples

In January 2012, an Expert Panel on Recognising Aboriginal and Torres Strait Islander Peoples in the Constitution, which had been appointed by the then Prime Minister, Julia Gillard, recommended replacing the race power with a new Aboriginal and Torres Strait Islander peoples power.

Recognising Aboriginal and Torres Strait Islander Peoples in the Constitution: Report of the Expert Panel (Department of Families, Housing, Community Services and Indigenous Affairs, 2012)

[T]he recommendation of the Panel is that section 51(xxvi) be repealed but that Parliament continue to have power under section 51A to legislate with respect to Aboriginal and Torres Strait Islander peoples. Based on legal advice, the Panel has concluded that such an approach would ensure that existing laws applicable to Aboriginal and Torres Strait Islander peoples would continue to operate. It would remove unacceptable references to 'race', and provide a broad Commonwealth competence – consistent with the aspirations of the Australian people in 1967 – to legislate with respect to Aboriginal and Torres Strait Islander peoples ...

The Panel's recommendation is for a new 'section 51A' consisting of operative language to grant and define legislative competence. The Panel recommends that such express conferral of legislative power should extend to the making of laws 'with respect to Aboriginal and Torres Strait Islander peoples'.

A significant issue raised during the course of the Panel's consultations, and in submissions to it, is whether such power ought be textually confined to laws 'for the benefit of' or 'for the advancement of' Aboriginal and Torres Strait Islander peoples, or the like. At present, the power given by section 51(xxvi) is 'to make special laws' for the 'people of any race for whom it is deemed necessary' – 'laws for the peace, order, and good government of the Commonwealth'. The High Court has held, very clearly, that the deeming is for the Parliament, not for the High Court, except in possible but as yet undemonstrated cases of extremity or abuse.

The unsuccessful arguments in *Kartinyeri* included an attempt to require that a section 51(xxvi) law be 'for the benefit and/or advancement of Aborigines', and the successful argument asserted that it allowed 'adverse laws' and remained 'a power with an element of prejudice inherent'.

In relation to section 51(xxvi), there is little reason to doubt that the far-reaching judicial deference to the legislative judgment of Parliament concerning the merit of proposed laws, including their supposed beneficial effect in favour of Aboriginal and Torres Strait Islander peoples, is very likely to be followed for the foreseeable future.

Would the new 'section 51A' invite the courts to a significantly greater engagement with 'the merits' of legislation in determining whether it is authorised by the proposed new legislative power? There is clearly strong support for qualifying any new power to make laws for Aboriginal and Torres Strait Islander peoples so that its beneficial purpose is clear.

Inevitably, to confine the power in this way may require a court to make judgments as to the purpose or effect of a law. Based on the Panel's legal advice, the preambular language proposed by the Panel for 'section 51A' would make it clear that a law passed pursuant to that power would be assessed according to whether, taken as a whole, it would operate broadly for the benefit of the group of people concerned, rather than whether each and every provision was beneficial or whether each and every member of the group benefited. The Panel does not believe that this would create any particular difficulty or uncertainty for Parliament, or create any real risk of excessive court challenges ...

Recommendations

2 The Panel recommends that section 51(xxvi) be repealed, and that a new 'section 51A' be inserted after section 51 consisting of preambular or introductory language (italicised below – see Chapter 4) and operative language along the following lines:

Section 51A Recognition of Aboriginal and Torres Strait Islander peoples

Recognising *that the continent and its islands now known as Australia were first occupied by Aboriginal and Torres Strait Islander peoples;*

Acknowledging *the continuing relationship of Aboriginal and Torres Strait Islander peoples with their traditional lands and waters;*

Respecting *the continuing cultures, languages and heritage of Aboriginal and Torres Strait Islander peoples;*

Acknowledging *the need to secure the advancement of Aboriginal and Torres Strait Islander peoples;*

the Parliament shall, subject to this Constitution, have power to make laws for the peace, order and good government of the Commonwealth with respect to Aboriginal and Torres Strait Islander peoples.

3 The Panel further recommends that the repeal of section 51(xxvi) and the insertion of a new head of power, 'section 51A', be proposed together, that is, in a single referendum question.

The Expert Panel's recommendation was not taken up by Parliament.

Referendum Council

Chapter 1 discussed the Referendum Council whose final report in 2017 included the *Uluru Statement from the Heart*. The Referendum Council's final report also considered whether the race power should be altered again. The Referendum Council did not recommend making any additional alterations to the race power.

Final Report of the Referendum Council (Department of Prime Minister and Cabinet, 2017)

Section 51(xxvi) is the essential achievement of the 1967 referendum. Delegates to the First Nations Regional Dialogues were conscious of this. Many expressed the view that, as archaic as the term 'race' might be according to contemporary standards, the triumph of 1967 and the mostly beneficial legislation that has flowed from it, argues against the deletion of this historically important provision.

Delegates placed focused attention on the discriminatory potential of section 51(xxvi). The three most frequently cited examples used in the dialogues were the amendments to the Native

Title Act, the Hindmarsh Island Bridge amendments and the Northern Territory Emergency Response, the latter enacted under the Territories power.

However proposed solutions aimed at removing or ameliorating this discriminatory potential were assessed as equivalent to maintaining the head of power in its current form.

Amending or deleting the race power was ranked low in many Dialogues and rejected in other Dialogues. Delegates understood there was no iron clad guarantee that Parliament could be prevented from passing discriminatory laws that single out Aboriginal and Torres Strait Islander peoples for adverse treatment.

Many participants at the dialogues felt it was too risky to amend section 51(xxvi) because it could not be assured that the judicial interpretation of words such as 'benefit' or 'advancement' would accord with the desires and aspirations of the affected peoples.

Delegates were concerned that section 51 (xxvi) had empowered significant legislation in cultural heritage protection, land rights and native title that may be placed at risk. Similar concerns were raised by the Joint Select Committee in relation to the implications of altering or deleting section 51(xxvi) upon the Native Title Act.

There was no significant appetite for removing the word 'race'. Dialogues understood that although the concept of 'race' was a social construction, removing the word 'race' and inserting 'Aboriginal and Torres Strait Islander Peoples' does not alter the adverse discriminatory potential of the race power. Therefore, removing the word 'race' was not regarded as an improvement on the status quo of the people affected.

9.9 DISCUSSION QUESTIONS

1. What are the three key steps for altering the *Constitution*?
2. In what time frame must a referendum be held if a proposed alteration to the *Constitution* has been passed by Parliament?
3. In which three circumstances will a double majority not be sufficient to constitute the necessary approval of the electors for an alteration to the *Constitution*?
4. Does the race power support laws that are detrimental to the people of any race?
5. Policy question: Compare the Expert Panel's proposal to alter the race power with the Referendum Council's proposal to leave the race power unaltered. How does the underlying reasoning for each proposal differ? What are the strengths and weakness of each proposal?

PART

3

LIMITATIONS ON POWERS

ACQUISITION OF PROPERTY ON JUST TERMS

10

10.1 Overview

This chapter examines section 51(xxxi) of the *Australian Constitution*, which functions as: (1) a head of federal legislative power empowering the Commonwealth to compulsorily acquire property from individuals and States; and (2) as a limitation on federal legislative power restricting the power of the Commonwealth to acquire property otherwise than on just terms.

Australian Constitution

Section 51 Legislative powers of the Parliament

The Parliament shall, subject to this Constitution, have power to make laws for the peace, order, and good government of the Commonwealth with respect to:

...

(xxxi) The acquisition of property on just terms from any State or person for any purpose in respect of which the Parliament has power to make laws;

...

The High Court has given a broad interpretation of the concept of 'property', which includes the full range of property rights recognised by the general law, such as real and personal property, intellectual property, and choses in action. The High Court has also given a broad interpretation to the concept of 'acquisition', but has emphasised that mere deprivation or taking of property without some countervailing benefit accruing to another does not amount to an acquisition.

Key concepts considered in this chapter include:

- property
- acquisition
- deprivation of property
- adjustment of competing interests in property
- property rights inherently susceptible to variation
- just terms
- incongruous with the notion of just terms.

10.2 Section 51(xxxi) as a head of power and a limitation on power

Section 51(xxxi) of the *Australian Constitution* is both a head of federal legislative power and a limitation on federal legislative power. In ***Grace Brothers v Commonwealth***, Dixon J explained that section 51(xxxi) was included in the *Constitution* to ensure that the Commonwealth had power to acquire property as needed. Justice Dixon also explained that the requirement for just terms was intended to prevent arbitrary exercises of that power. Section 51(xxxi) was not intended primarily as a guarantee of individual property rights.

Grace Brothers Pty Ltd v Commonwealth (1946) 72 CLR 269

Dixon J

The argument invoking these grounds appears to me to proceed from the assumption that s 51(xxxi) of the Australian Constitution has the same effect as the last paragraph of the Fifth Amendment of the American Constitution, and that the case law upon that and upon analogous constitutional provisions of the American States should be applied in Australia.

I am not able to assent to such an assumption. The material part of the Fifth Amendment says "nor shall private property be taken for public use, without just compensation." It follows the due process clause, repeated in reference to the States in the Fourteenth Amendment, which has been construed as producing the same effect in protecting the proprietary interests of the citizen when the power of eminent domain is exerted. The clause of the Fifth Amendment concerning just compensation cannot be dissociated from the due process clause nor, indeed, from the general principles of American constitutional law animating what is called the Bill of Rights. The framers of the Australian Constitution preferred to leave those principles, in the main, to constitutional convention and tradition, as they have been left in England, rather than to follow the American course of expressing them in the paramount law ...

The power conferred by s 51(xxxi) is express, and it was introduced as a specific power, not, like the Fifth Amendment, for the purpose of protecting the subject or citizen, but primarily to make certain that the Commonwealth possessed a power compulsorily to acquire property, particularly from the States. The condition "on just terms" was included to prevent arbitrary exercises of the power at the expense of a State or the subject ...

Section 51(xxxi) empowers the Commonwealth to make laws acquiring property on just terms. It also limits the scope of other heads of legislative power by abstracting from them power to make laws acquiring property otherwise than on just terms.

Bank of New South Wales v Commonwealth ('Bank Nationalisation Case') (1948) 76 CLR 1

Dixon J

Section 51(xxxi) serves a double purpose. It provides the Commonwealth Parliament with a legislative power of acquiring property: at the same time as a condition upon the exercise of the power it provides the individual or the State, affected with a protection against governmental interferences with his proprietary rights without just recompense. In both aspects consistency with the principles upon which constitutional provisions are interpreted and applied demands that the paragraph should be given as full and flexible an operation as will cover the objects it was designed to effect. Moreover, when a Constitution undertakes to forbid or restrain some legislative course, there can be no prohibition to which it is more proper to apply the principle embodied in the maxim *quando aliquid prohibetur, prohibetur et omne per quod devenitur ad illud* ["when something is forbidden, everything which leads to the same result is also forbidden"]. In requiring just terms s 51(xxxi) fetters the legislative power by forbidding laws with respect to acquisition on any terms that are not just.

10.3 What is 'property'?

The High Court has given the term 'property' a very broad meaning. It covers the full range of property rights recognised by the general law.

Minister of State for the Army v Dalziel (1944) 68 CLR 261

Rich J

The facts are simple and not in dispute. Certain vacant land in the City of Sydney is owned, so far as land is susceptible of private ownership, by a bank. It was let by the bank to one Dalziel upon a weekly tenancy at a rental of £8 per week. Dalziel carried on upon it the business of a parking station for motor cars, out of which he made a net profit of about £15 a week. The Minister for the Army, purporting to act under reg 54 of the *National Security (General) Regulations*, took possession of this land for defence purposes ...

The meaning of property in such a connection must be determined upon general principles of jurisprudence, not by the artificial refinements of any particular legal system or by reference to Sheppard's Touchstone. The language used is perfectly general. It says the acquisition of property. It is not restricted to acquisition by particular methods or of particular types of interests, or to particular types of property. It extends to any acquisition of any interest in any property ...

Starke J

Property, it has been said, is *nomen generalissimum* and extends to every species of valuable right and interest including real and personal property, incorporeal hereditaments such as rents and services, rights of way, rights of profit or use in land of another, and choses in action. And to acquire any such right is rightly described as an "acquisition of property." On the other hand a mere personal licence such as is not assignable would not be rightly described as property ...

McTiernan J

The word "property" in s 51(xxxi) is a general term. It means any tangible or intangible thing which the law protects under the name of property. The acquisition of the possession of land is an instance of the acquisition of property ...

Victoria v Commonwealth ('Industrial Relations Act Case') (1996) 187 CLR 416

Brennan CJ, Toohey, Gaudron, McHugh and Gummow JJ

It is well established that the guarantee effected by s 51(xxxi) of the Constitution extends to protect against the acquisition, other than on just terms, of "every species of valuable right and interest including ... choses in action": *Minister of State for the Army v Dalziel*. It has been held to prohibit the extinguishment of vested causes of action: *Georgiadis v Australian and Overseas Telecommunications Corporation*. At least that is so if the extinguishment results "in a direct benefit or financial gain ... and the cause of action is one that arises under the general law": *Georgiadis v Australian and Overseas Telecommunications Corporation* ...

10.4 What amounts to an 'acquisition of property'?

As a general proposition, an acquisition of property occurs where a property owner is deprived of the substance of proprietary interests and a countervailing benefit accrues to another person or entity.

Section 51(xxxi) applies to laws with respect to acquisition of property by the Commonwealth and by other persons and entities

Section 51(xxxi) prohibits laws for the acquisition of property otherwise than on just terms. It does not matter who has acquired the property for a law to be characterised as one with respect to the acquisition of property. The provision applies where the property in question has been acquired by the Commonwealth. The provision also applies where the property in question has been acquired by some other entity or person.

Trade Practices Commission v Tooth & Co Ltd (1979) 142 CLR 397

The effect of a federal statute was to compel a property owner to grant a lease to another person unless certain conditions applied. The High Court held that there was an acquisition of property within the meaning of section 51(xxxi) of the **Australian Constitution.**

Barwick CJ

Section 51(xxxi) is a very great constitutional safeguard, not confined to the protection of the citizen from confiscation of his property by the State. It ensures that no one may, by virtue of a Commonwealth statutory provision, acquire his property except upon just terms ...

Gibbs J

Further, s 51(xxxi) is not limited to acquisitions by the Commonwealth ...

Mason J

There is nothing in the wide and general language of s 51(xxxi) which gives support to the view that the "acquisition of property" to which it refers is limited to acquisition for the "use and service of the Crown", a conception which is in itself by no means precise and certain in scope.

The interpretation thereby suggested is at variance with the policy which underlies par (xxxi) and the protection which it gives to the citizen against compulsory acquisition of his property otherwise than on just terms. As a matter of policy and protection it makes very little sense to say that the Commonwealth cannot pass laws for its acquisition of the citizen's property without giving just terms but it can pass laws for the acquisition of the citizen's property by others without giving any compensation at all ... Accordingly, I agree that s 51(xxxi) extends to laws for the acquisition of property by persons other than the Commonwealth or an agency of the Commonwealth ...

Aicken J

It would be a serious gap in the constitutional safeguard which is the manifest policy of par (xxxi) if the Parliament could legislate for compulsory acquisition of property without just terms by statutory bodies which were not the Commonwealth itself or its agents or by persons or bodies having no connexion with the government. Neither the words of s 51 nor the context require the adoption of so anomalous a view ...

ICM Agriculture Pty Ltd v Commonwealth (2009) 240 CLR 140

In this case, a State was said to have acquired property as a consequence of federal legislation.

French CJ, Gummow and Crennan JJ

[I]t is settled since *Trade Practices Commission v Tooth & Co Ltd* that s 51(xxxi) is not confined to the acquisition of property by the Commonwealth or its instrumentalities ...

Hayne, Kiefel, Bell and Heydon JJ

[Section] 51(xxxi) can be engaged where there is an acquisition of property by the Commonwealth or by another ...

Whether an acquisition of property has occurred is a question of substance

Whether an acquisition of property has occurred is a question of substance rather than simply a question of legal form. For example, a law giving the Commonwealth possession and control of property, but not legal or equitable title to that property, is a law with respect to the acquisition of property.

In ***Minister of State for the Army v Dalziel***, a majority of the High Court rejected the proposition that acquisition involves acquiring full legal ownership of property. In that case, the Commonwealth took possession of – but not legal or equitable title to – commercial land for defence purposes. In dissent, Latham CJ adopted a formalistic view of the concept of acquisition. Chief Justice Latham held that because the Commonwealth had not become the legal or equitable owner of either the fee simple or the leasehold over the land, it had not acquired the property.

Minister of State for the Army v Dalziel (1944) 68 CLR 261

Latham CJ (dissenting)

Under this regulation the Minister may, on behalf of the Commonwealth, take possession of any land for defence purposes and if he does so the land may be used for defence purposes as fully as if he, the Minister, had an unencumbered interest in fee simple in the land. The validity of this regulation has not been challenged. It is indeed obvious that the defence of the country may make it necessary or expedient for the defence authorities to take possession of and to use land ...

The Commonwealth cannot be said to have acquired land unless it has become the owner of land or of some interest in land. If the Commonwealth becomes only a possessor but does not become an owner of land, then, though the Commonwealth may have rights in respect to land, which land may be called property, the Commonwealth has not in such a case acquired property ...

In contrast, the majority judges held that the Commonwealth had, in substance, acquired a right to possess and use the land, which right was proprietary in nature.

Minister of State for the Army v Dalziel (1944) 68 CLR 261

Rich J

In the case now before us, the Minister has, *in adversum*, assumed possession of land of which Dalziel was weekly tenant. With all respect to the argument which has been addressed to us to the contrary, I am quite unable to understand how this can be said not to be an acquisition of property from Dalziel within the meaning of the placitum. Property, in relation to land, is a bundle of rights exercisable with respect to the land. The tenant of an unencumbered estate in fee simple in possession has the largest possible bundle. But there is nothing in the placitum to suggest that the legislature was intended to be at liberty to free itself from the restrictive provisions of the placitum by taking care to seize something short of the whole bundle owned by the person whom it was expropriating ... Not only is a right to possession a right of property, but where the object of proprietary rights is a tangible thing it is the most characteristic and essential of those rights ...

If the argument which has been addressed to us on behalf of the Minister were allowed to prevail, the Commonwealth Parliament could authorize the Executive to take possession of not only all or any of the private property of citizens but also the property of the States and keep it indefinitely without paying a farthing of compensation to anyone. To accede to this argument would be in effect to strike placitum xxxi out of the Constitution ...

McTiernan J

The primary question, therefore, is whether the executive action, which is authorized by reg 54, is in its nature an acquisition of property ...

Reg 54 empowers the Commonwealth to take possession of land and, while the land is in its possession, to use it, or authorize it to be used, for the purposes which are specified.

The word "property" in s 51(xxxi) is a general term. It means any tangible or intangible thing which the law protects under the name of property. The acquisition of the possession of land is an instance of the acquisition of property ...

Williams J

It is true that the entry into possession by the Commonwealth does not determine any estate or interest in the land, so that in the present case the Bank of New South Wales continues to be the owner of the land in fee simple and the respondent continues to be a tenant of the Bank of New South Wales from week to week, but the rights of the bank and of the respondent only continue to exist subject to the statutory right of the Commonwealth to take possession of the land and to use it for the purpose authorized by the regulation. Under the regulation, therefore, the Commonwealth acquires by compulsion a right for an indefinite period to the possession and use of land previously vested in some person (in the present case the respondent) by virtue of some estate or interest in the land which that person owns at common law ...

The focus on substance over form also means that the property right acquired need not be identical to the property right lost. In ***Georgiadis***, legislation extinguished a vested common law cause of action, which is recognised to be a chose in action and therefore a species of property. Extinguishing the cause of action had the effect of releasing the defendant from liability to pay damages. The High Court held that the defendant had acquired property from the plaintiff.

Georgiadis v Australian and Overseas Telecommunications Corporation (1994) 179 CLR 297

Georgiadis was injured at work while an employee of Telecom, a Commonwealth entity. At the time of his injury, legislation gave injured employees the option of suing for damages at common law or claiming statutory workers compensation. Legislation was later enacted extinguishing any common law cause of action and requiring injured employees to pursue statutory workers compensation. The High Court held that by extinguishing the common law cause of action, which was a chose in action, Telecom had acquired a release from liability to pay damages.

Mason CJ, Deane and Gaudron JJ

Clearly, a right to bring an action for damages for negligence is a valuable right ...

Thus, the question in this case is whether s 44 is a law with respect to the acquisition of that right for a purpose in respect of which the Parliament has power to make laws within s 51(xxxi).

Telecom and the Commonwealth, intervening, resisted the claim that s 44 involves an acquisition of property within s 51(xxxi) in two ways. First, they argued that, so far as the issue in this case is concerned, s 44 does no more than extinguish a cause of action which was not sued upon before the new compensation scheme came into effect.

In this context, it was pointed out that, whatever else happened, neither Telecom nor anyone else acquired the cause of action which Mr Georgiadis lost. The second argument was that s 44 did no more than modify the limitation period applicable to a cause of action which vested before the new scheme came into operation ...

"[A]cquisition" directs attention to whether something is or will be received. If there is a receipt, there is no reason why it should correspond precisely with what was taken. That is particularly so with "innominate and anomalous interests". Thus, the fact that neither Telecom nor anyone else now has the cause of action which was previously vested in Mr Georgiadis is not conclusive of the question whether there has been an acquisition of property for the purposes of par (xxxi).

Telecom and the Commonwealth relied on the difference between a taking and an acquisition to argue that the extinguishment of a cause of action cannot constitute an acquisition. Of course, it will often be the case that it does not, as, for example, where the cause of action is extinguished by judgment or by the effluxion of time ...

Accordingly, "acquisition" in s 51(xxxi) extends to the extinguishment of a vested cause of action, at least where the extinguishment results in a direct benefit or financial gain (which, of course, includes liability being brought to an end without payment or other satisfaction) and the cause of action is one that arises under the general law. The position may be different in a case involving the extinguishment or modification of a right that has no existence apart from statute. That is because, prima facie at least and in the absence of a recognized legal relationship giving rise to some like right, a right which has no existence apart from statute is one that, of its nature, is susceptible of modification or extinguishment. There is no acquisition of property involved in the modification or extinguishment of a right which has no basis in the general law and which, of its nature, is susceptible to that course ...

The legislation considered in ***Georgiadis*** extinguished the general law cause of action immediately upon the legislation coming into force. The legislation considered in ***Smith v ANL Ltd*** did not, in terms, extinguish any general law cause of action. The legislation provided that a vested general law cause of action could only be sued on within six months of the legislation coming into force. The High Court held that, in substance, this legislation effected an acquisition of property: the plaintiff's right to bring an action had been reduced in scope and the defendant thereby acquired a countervailing benefit.

Smith v ANL Ltd (2000) 204 CLR 493

Gleeson CJ

The legislation, it was contended, did not take away the appellant's right of action; at most it diminished its value by requiring that it be exercised, if it were to be exercised at all, within six months. Correspondingly, the only benefit conferred upon the respondent was an assurance that, if it were to be sued at all, that had to occur within six months ...

The legislation did not operate immediately to divest the appellant of his right of action against the respondent. However, it had the effect that, after the expiration of a further six months, he did not have a right to bring an action against the respondent for damages for a work-related injury. Section 54 removed the right of action. Section 13 provided that, despite s 54, the respondent had a right to bring such an action within a further six months. The combined legal effect of the two provisions, which were intended to be read together, was that the appellant's pre-existing common law right was modified; and a corresponding benefit was conferred on the respondent. Once it is accepted, as the authorities establish, that a chose in action is a species of property to which s 51(xxxi) applies, and that the constitutional guarantee is not to be narrowly confined, then modification of a right to bring an action, in circumstances where a corresponding advantage accrues to the party against whom action may be brought, would ordinarily involve an acquisition of property ... The extent of the disadvantage may be a material matter in deciding whether just terms have been provided. The circumstance that the appellant could have avoided the adverse consequences of the legislation by taking action within six months does not, in my view, mean that there was no acquisition. The appellant did not consent to the modification of his right. It is, however, a matter to be taken into account in considering whether, in the circumstances, there was a failure to provide just terms ...

Kirby J

If, as this Court has held, the requirements of s 51(xxxi) of the Constitution address attention to substance and not merely form, depriving a person such as the appellant of the effective right to prosecute his claims at common law may amount to an acquisition of those entitlements from him. Confirmation that this was so in the present context lies in the fact that the effect of the impugned legislation was to accord a real financial benefit to the respondent. After the periods successively provided for in the impugned legislation, the respondent could write off its contingent liability to a person such as the appellant. That person, by the terms of s 54 of the Seafarers Act, thereafter did "not have a right to bring an action". It is true that the fact that the descent of the final statutory disentitlement was, by s 13 of the Transitional Provisions Act, postponed for six months. This delayed the "acquisition". But it did not make it any less an "acquisition" when that time expired and the statutory bar descended ...

To characterise the impugned legislation solely as a limitations provision is once again to focus attention on form rather than substance. From the point of view of the person whose "property" (in the form of choses in action) is denuded of practical enforceability, and thus of real content, it matters not that the means chosen were those of imposing an abridged limitations period. The Parliament cannot "by statutory modification or change of rights", in this way, "do by circuitous means what it could not successfully do directly" ...

This Court has repeatedly held that exact equivalence between the "modification" of property rights and the "benefits" gained by those deemed to have "acquired" those rights need not be shown. It is sufficient that the beneficiary gains "some identifiable and measurable countervailing benefit or advantage". By effectively curtailing, in some cases significantly, the time within which a person with a vested common law right might prosecute that right against an employer said to be liable to that person in negligence and in contract, it is obvious that the employer gains an "identifiable and measurable ... benefit or advantage" ...

Newcrest provides another example of what is acquired being different to what is lost. A mining company owned mining rights over land, some of which was later created as a national park with ownership of the fee simple of the national park land vested in a statutory entity. The federal law creating the national park also prohibited mining within the national park to a depth of 1,000 metres.

The High Court held that, in substance, the mining company had lost the benefit of its mining rights because those rights were now practically impossible to exercise: the mining company lost the right to mine to a depth of 1000 metres and mining only below that depth was practically impossible. Countervailing benefits accrued to the legal owner of the national park, in the form of the ownership of the land no longer being subject to the company's mining rights.

Newcrest Mining (WA) Ltd v Commonwealth (1997) 190 CLR 513

Newcrest owned the right to mine certain minerals in certain parcels of land in the Northern Territory. Federal legislation established the Kakadu National Park covering some of the land over which Newcrest owned mining tenements. The federal legislation:

(1) prohibited mining operations on the surface of the national park and to a depth of 1000 metres below the surface; (2) vested ownership of minerals to that depth in the Commonwealth; and (3) vested ownership of the land of the national park in a Director of National Parks.

Gummow J

None of the provisions relied upon by the appellants is expressed in direct language as effecting an acquisition of any property. However, the question is whether, even if not formally, the appellants effectively have been deprived of "the reality of proprietorship" by the indirect acquisition, through the collective operation of the provisions of the Conservation Act, of "the substance of a proprietary interest" ...

The appellants say that, in substance, the Commonwealth and the Director acquired identifiable and measurable advantages. In the case of the Director, those advantages were the acquisition of the land freed from the rights of Newcrest to occupy and conduct mining operations thereon and, in the case of the Commonwealth, the minerals freed from the rights of Newcrest to mine them. In accordance with the authorities, that is sufficient derivation of an identifiable and measurable advantage to satisfy the constitutional requirement of an acquisition.

There is no reason why the identifiable benefit or advantage relating to the ownership or use of property, which is acquired, should correspond precisely to that which was taken ...

Here, there was an effective sterilisation of the rights constituting the property in question. That this is so is only emphasised upon a consideration of the contrary submission made by the Commonwealth and the Director. It is true, as they submit, that the mining tenements were not, in terms, extinguished. It is true also that Kakadu extended only 1,000 metres beneath the surface. But, on the surface and to that depth, s 10(1A) of the Conservation Act forbade the carrying out of operations for the recovery of minerals. The vesting in the Commonwealth of the minerals to that depth and the vesting of the surface and balance of the relevant segments of the subterranean land in the Director had the effect, as a legal and practical matter, of denying to Newcrest the exercise of its rights under the mining tenements.

Kirby J

Whilst it is true that the first appellant's interests were not expressly acquired or extinguished by, or under, any federal law, it is also true that the creation and extension of the Kakadu National Park by federal law – encompassing, in the areas acquired, some 1,000 metres beneath the surface of the land – effectively deprived the first appellant of the benefit of its property in the mining tenements, principally the right to recover minerals. A notional possibility that the first appellant could tunnel more than 1,000 metres below the surface to win the mineral product without disturbing the surface of the Park can be ignored as unrealistic.

The issue was thus presented whether such prohibition against the recovery of minerals amounted in law, as it did in effect, to an acquisition of the first appellant's property ... The outcome of the prohibition on "operations for the recovery of minerals" in the Kakadu National Park was, in my view, an acquisition of the first appellant's remaining mining tenements ...

Wurridjal demonstrates that the policy purpose underlying an acquisition of property is irrelevant to whether section 51(xxxi) is engaged. In this case, federal legislation imposed leases in favour of the Commonwealth over land owned by Aboriginal Land Trusts. This was done to enable the Commonwealth to exercise its rights as lessee to improve facilities on the land and for other regulatory and service-provision purposes. The High Court rejected the argument that the regulatory purposes involved meant that creation of the leases could not be described as an 'acquisition' of property. Leasehold title is property and the Commonwealth had acquired that property. The regulatory purposes involved could not change that fact.

Wurridjal v Commonwealth (2009) 237 CLR 309

This case arose out of the Commonwealth's 'Intervention' in Northern Territory Aboriginal communities. The **Northern Territory (Aboriginal Land Rights) Act 1976** *had vested the fee simple to various parcels of land in an Aboriginal Land Trust. The* **National Emergency Response Act 2007** *granted leasehold title over the same land to the Commonwealth.*

French CJ

At the centre of the plaintiffs' challenge is s 31 of the [National Emergency Response] Act, which provides, inter alia, in sub-s (1):

> "A lease of the following land is, by force of this subsection, granted to the Commonwealth by the relevant owner of the land ... "

The land referred to is that described in Sched 1 to the Act and land prescribed by regulation. The terms of leases granted under s 31(1) are set out in s 31(2) which is to be read with s 32 ...

The Commonwealth's substantive submission was that the legislative scheme of the Land Rights Act had always been subject to adjustment of the interests necessarily involved. These were matters of regulation susceptible to parliamentary variation. Legislative amendments to give effect to such variations could be done without the need to pay compensation to the holder of the fee simple estate or anyone else ...

The fee simple estate in the Maningrida land granted to the Land Trust lay well within the class of "property" to which s 51(xxxi) applies ...

It may be accepted that the creation of the s 31 leases was intended to facilitate Commonwealth control of townships so that additional accommodation and other services could be provided to the relevant Aboriginal communities. In a broad sense the s 31 lease granted over the Maningrida land might be described as a legal device adopted for regulatory purposes. However, its legal effect was to diminish the ownership rights conferred by the grant of the fee simple estate so far as they related to the Maningrida township. By operation of s 35 of the NER Act the statutory lease conferred upon the Commonwealth the essential rights of a lessee abstracted from the fee simple estate. It also conferred the right to vary the area covered by the lease and to terminate the lease early. An acquisition of property is no less an acquisition of property because it also has a regulatory or other public purpose. The grant of the lease was an acquisition of property from the Land Trust ...

Kirby J

"Property" clearly includes an estate in fee simple such as that granted to the Land Trust. The holder of such an estate enjoys rights akin to full ownership, including the right to exclude others from the subject land and to decline a leasehold interest in that land to a stranger. On this basis, the statutory imposition upon the Land Trust of a five-year lease in favour of the Commonwealth constitutes the "acquisition", although temporary, of defined "property".

Mere deprivation, extinguishment or devaluation of property does not involve any acquisition

A law that does no more than deprive a person of property or that has the result of devaluing property is not an acquisition of property. An acquisition requires another person or entity to receive some identifiable and measurable advantage.

Mutual Pools & Staff Pty Ltd v Commonwealth (1994) 179 CLR 155

Deane and Gaudron JJ

Nonetheless, the fact remains that s 51(xxxi) is directed to "acquisition" as distinct from deprivation. The extinguishment, modification or deprivation of rights in relation to property does not of itself constitute an acquisition of property ...

For there to be an "acquisition of property", there must be an obtaining of at least some identifiable benefit or advantage relating to the ownership or use of property. On the other hand, it is possible to envisage circumstances in which an extinguishment, modification or deprivation of the proprietary rights of one person would involve an acquisition of property by another by reason of some identifiable and measurable countervailing benefit or advantage accruing to that other person as a result. Indeed, the extinguishment of a chose in action could, depending upon the circumstances, assume the substance of an acquisition of the chose in action by the obligee ...

The legislation considered in the ***Plain Packaging Case*** had the practical effect of prohibiting the use of various trademarks and get-up, potentially rendering those intellectual property rights valueless. The legislation under challenge required all tobacco products to be sold in plain packaging as an anti-smoking measure. The High Court explained that while there might have been a loss or deprivation of property, there was no *acquisition* of property by the Commonwealth or anyone else.

JT International SA v Commonwealth ('Plain Packaging Case') (2012) 250 CLR 1

French CJ

The *Tobacco Plain Packaging Act 2011* (Cth) ("the TPP Act") imposes significant restrictions upon the colour, shape and finish of retail packaging for tobacco products. It prohibits the use of trade marks on such packaging, other than as permitted by the TPP Act, which allows the use of a brand, business or company name for the relevant tobacco product. Pre-existing regulatory requirements for health messages and graphic warnings remain in place and include, under a recent Information Standard, a requirement for the inclusion of the Quitline logo of the Victorian Anti-Cancer Council and a telephone number for the Quitline service.

In two proceedings which were heard by this Court in April this year, the plaintiffs, tobacco companies JT International SA ("JTI") and members of the British America Tobacco Group ("BAT") argued that, subject to a reading down provision, the TPP Act effected an acquisition of their intellectual property rights and goodwill on other than just terms, contrary to s 51(xxxi) of the Constitution ...

Taking involves deprivation of property seen from the perspective of its owner. Acquisition involves receipt of something seen from the perspective of the acquirer: *Georgiadis v Australian Overseas Telecommunications Corporation*. Acquisition is therefore not made out by mere extinguishment of rights. In an observation quoted and approved by the majority in *Australian Tape Manufacturers Association Ltd v Commonwealth*, Mason J said in the *Tasmanian Dam case*:

> To bring the constitutional provision into play it is not enough that legislation adversely affects or terminates a pre-existing right that an owner enjoys in relation to his property; there must be an acquisition whereby the Commonwealth or another acquires an interest in property, however slight or insubstantial it may be.

Importantly, the interest or benefit accruing to the Commonwealth or another person must be proprietary in character. On no view can it be said that the Commonwealth as a polity or by any authority or instrumentality, has acquired any benefit of a proprietary character by reason of the operation of the TPP Act on the plaintiffs' property rights. In this respect I agree with the reasons of Gummow J and the reasons of Hayne and Bell JJ ...

In summary, the TPP Act is part of a legislative scheme which places controls on the way in which tobacco products can be marketed. While the imposition of those controls may be said to constitute a taking in the sense that the plaintiffs' enjoyment of their intellectual property rights and related rights is restricted, the corresponding imposition of controls on the packaging and presentation of tobacco products does not involve the accrual of a benefit of a proprietary character to the Commonwealth which would constitute an acquisition ...

Gummow J

JTI submits ... the pursuit of the legislative purposes in s 3 of the Packaging Act confers the requisite advantage upon the Commonwealth to satisfy the requirement of an "acquisition" ... [P]ursuit of the legislative objectives stated in s 3 of the Packaging Act does not yield a benefit or advantage to the Commonwealth which is proprietary in nature ...

However, as Hayne and Bell JJ explain in passages in their reasons with which I agree, to characterise as "control" by "the Commonwealth" compliance with federal law which prescribes what can and cannot appear on the retail packaging of tobacco products diverts attention from a fundamental question presented by s 51(xxxi) of the Constitution. Compliance with the federal law does not create a relationship between "the Commonwealth" and the packaging which is proprietary in nature ...

Hayne and Bell JJ

There can be no acquisition of property without "the Commonwealth or another acquir[ing] an interest in property, however slight or insubstantial it may be". Giving a liberal construction to "acquisition" and "property" does not, and must not, erode the bedrock established by the text of s 51(xxxi): there must be an acquisition of property ...

Though variously expressed, the tobacco companies submitted that the TPP Act gives the Commonwealth the use of, or control over, tobacco packaging because the Commonwealth or the TPP Act (the submissions did not clearly identify which) required certain things to be done or not done on the packaging. But the requirements of the TPP Act are no different in kind from any legislation that requires labels that warn against the use or misuse of a product, or tell the reader who to call or what to do if there has been a dangerous use of a product. Legislation that requires warning labels to be placed on products, even warning labels as extensive as those required by the TPP Act, effects no acquisition of property ...

By prescribing what can and cannot appear on retail packaging the TPP Act affects that packaging and those who produce and sell the tobacco products. But to characterise this effect as "control" diverts attention from the fundamental question: does the TPP Act give the Commonwealth a legal interest in the packaging or create a legal relation between the Commonwealth and the packaging that the law describes as "property"? Compliance with the TPP Act creates no proprietary interest ...

Statutory requirements for warning labels on goods will presumably always be intended to achieve some benefit: usually the avoidance of or reduction in harm. But the benefit or advantage that results from the tobacco companies complying with the TPP Act is not proprietary. The Commonwealth acquires no property as a result of their compliance with the TPP Act ...

ICM Agriculture considered legislation that cancelled licences to access groundwater and replaced those with new licences with less generous groundwater access rights. The plaintiffs claimed that the State had acquired the benefit of control of additional water resources. The High Court held that the State had always had full control of all water resources. Therefore, even though the licence-owners might have lost property, the State had acquired nothing.

ICM Agriculture Pty Ltd v Commonwealth (2009) 240 CLR 140

Legislation had the effect of abolishing groundwater bore licences and replacing them with aquifer access licences. The rights granted under the new species of licence were less generous than under the old species of licence. The High Court held that no property had been acquired.

French CJ, Gummow and Crennan JJ

[W]hatever the proprietary character of the bore licences, s 51(xxxi) speaks, not of the "taking", deprivation or destruction of "property", but of its acquisition ...

However, in the present case, and contrary to the plaintiffs' submissions, the groundwater in the [Lower Lachlan Groundwater System] was not the subject of private rights enjoyed by them. Rather, and as these reasons have sought to demonstrate, it was a natural resource, and the State always had the power to limit the volume of water to be taken from that resource. The State exercised that power from time to time by legislation imposing a prohibition upon access to and use of that natural resource, which might be lifted or qualified by compliance with a licensing system. The changes of which the plaintiffs complain implemented the policy of the State respecting the use of a limited natural resource, but that did not constitute an "acquisition" by the State in the sense of s 51(xxxi). Nor can it be shown that there has been an acquisition in the necessary sense by other licensees or prospective licensees. They have at best the prospect of increasing or obtaining allocations under the new system applying to the [Lower Lachlan Groundwater System] ...

Hayne, Kiefel and Bell JJ

The acquisition of property of which the plaintiffs complain is alleged to have been effected by the replacement of their bore licences by aquifer access licences with smaller extraction entitlements. (In argument the plaintiffs often referred to this process as a "cancellation" of their bore licences and the issue of the new licences. Nothing turns on the accuracy of this description.) ...

It may readily be accepted that the bore licences that were cancelled were a species of property. That the entitlements attaching to the licences could be traded or used as security amply demonstrates that to be so. It must also be accepted, as the fundamental premise for consideration of whether there has been an acquisition of property, that, until the cancellation of their bore licences, the plaintiffs had "entitlements" to a certain volume of water and that after cancellation their "entitlements" were less. Those "entitlements" were themselves fragile. They could be reduced at any time, and in the past had been. But there can be no acquisition of property unless some identifiable and measurable advantage is derived by another from, or in consequence of, the replacement of the plaintiffs' licences or reduction of entitlements. That is, another must acquire "an interest in property, however slight or insubstantial it may be".

The only possible recipient of an advantage in this matter is the State. Did it derive some advantage from replacing the bore licences or reducing water entitlements?

The four considerations set out earlier in these reasons (the replaceable and fugitive nature of groundwater; that the licences in issue are a creature of statute and inherently fragile; that groundwater has not hitherto been thought to be a subject of property; and that the rights vested in the State are statutory rights for the purpose of controlling access to a public resource) all point towards the conclusion that the State gained no identifiable or measurable advantage from the steps that have been taken with respect to the plaintiffs' water licences and entitlements.

Since at least 1966 no landowner in New South Wales has had any right to take groundwater except pursuant to licence. The rights the plaintiffs had under their bore licences (in particular, their right to extract certain volumes of water) did not in any sense "return" to the State upon cancellation of the licences. The State gained no larger or different right itself to extract or permit others to extract water from that system. It gained no larger or different right at all ...

Mere adjustment of competing interests in relation to property is not an acquisition of property

A law that does no more than adjust competing rights in relation to property does not amount to an acquisition of property, even where the adjustment benefits one party and disadvantages another party.

The creation of a new species of intellectual property rights in relation to circuit layouts provides an example of an adjustment of competing interests in property that does not amount to an acquisition of property.

Nintendo Co Ltd v Centronics Systems Pty Ltd (1994) 181 CLR 134

Centronics imported video game machines that used circuit layouts designed by Nintendo. The Circuit Layouts Act 1989 *(Cth) later came into effect giving Nintendo intellectual property rights in respect of the circuit layouts. The effect was that Centronics would breach Nintendo's intellectual property rights by selling the imported machines if it did not obtain a licence from Nintendo to do so. Centronics argued that the effect of the legislation was that Nintendo acquired proprietary rights in what was previously entirely Centronics' property.*

Mason CJ, Brennan, Deane, Toohey, Gaudron and McHugh JJ

As a defence of last resort, Centronics invoked the implied guarantee of just terms contained in s 51(xxxi) of the Constitution. It was submitted on its behalf that, to the extent that the Act operated to confer, upon Nintendo, the exclusive right of commercial exploitation of the Spica circuits contained in the Entertainment Units which were already owned by Centronics at the commencement of the Act, the Act purported to effect an "acquisition of property" on other than the "just terms" which s 51(xxxi) guarantees ...

The cases also establish that a law which is not directed towards the acquisition of property as such but which is concerned with the adjustment of the competing rights, claims or obligations of persons in a particular relationship or area of activity is unlikely to be susceptible of legitimate characterisation as a law with respect to the acquisition of property for the purposes of s 51 of the Constitution ...

The Act is a law of that nature. It cannot properly, either in whole or in part, be characterised as a law with respect to the acquisition of property for the purposes of that section. Its relevant character is that of a law for the adjustment and regulation of the competing claims, rights and liabilities of the designers or first makers of original circuit layouts and those who take advantage of, or benefit from, their work. Consequently, it is beyond the reach of s 51(xxxi)'s guarantee of just terms ...

Mutual Pools considered legislation governing the refund of taxes paid under a tax law that later turned out to be invalid. The 'taxes' had been paid by pool builders, who therefore had a right of action against the Commissioner of Taxation for a refund. Legislation was passed providing that refunds would be paid to the builders only if they had not passed on the cost of the 'tax' to their customers. The legislation also provided that where the cost of the 'tax' had been passed on to a customer, the Commissioner of Taxation would pay the refund to the customer.

The High Court held that although the legislation reduced the value of the builders' chose in action against the Commissioner of Taxation, there was no acquisition of property by the Commissioner. The legislation did not simply reduce the value of a chose in action to the financial benefit of a defendant like in ***Georgiadis***. The legislation in this case adjusted competing interests in the refunds. The Commissioner was still required to refund the full value of the 'taxes' paid to those who ultimately incurred the cost of those 'taxes'.

Mutual Pools & Staff Pty Ltd v Commonwealth (1994) 179 CLR 155

Mason CJ

A law with respect to taxation which regulates competing claims and interests is not a law for the acquisition of property. And here there is no additional element in the Refund Act which would enable the Court to say that, though it is a law with respect to taxation, it is also a law for the acquisition of property ...

Because in this case the tax has been passed on to the pool owners, that is, the pool owners have borne the burden of the tax, they too have an interest in the refund of the taxes collected. Thus, notwithstanding the Commonwealth's contractual arrangements with the pool builder, the Refund Act is in essence a legislative measure directed to achieving a genuine resolution of the competing claims of pool builders, pool owners and the Commonwealth in relation to the refund of moneys in respect of the tax that was invalidly levied. As such, for the reasons discussed above, extinguishment of the cause of action does not constitute an acquisition of property within the meaning of s 51(xxxi) ...

Deane and Gaudron JJ

It is now common ground that, subject to the effect of the Refund Act, the defendant Commonwealth is under a contractual obligation to repay to the plaintiff ("Mutual Pools") the amount of $1,522 paid in respect of Mr and Mrs Chaplin's in situ swimming pool pursuant to the agreement between the Swimming Pool and Spa Association of Australia Limited and the Commonwealth. In circumstances where Mutual Pools has passed on that amount to Mr and Mrs Chaplin and has not made any refund of it to them, the effect of the Refund Act, if it is valid, is to extinguish Mutual Pools' contractual right against the Commonwealth to recover that amount ...

Both generally and in its application to the present case, the Refund Act is a law defining and regulating the entitlement of persons with possibly competing claims (ie builders and owners of in situ swimming pools) to a refund of amounts paid to the Commonwealth on account of taxes in circumstances where no tax was, in fact, payable. Its operation is designed to ensure that any refund of amounts so paid is made to a person who has in fact truly borne the burden of the payment. In defining and regulating entitlement to receive such refunds, the Refund Act necessarily affects any rights to a refund which would have existed if it had not been enacted. In some cases, such pre-existing rights are transformed into rights under the Refund Act. In other cases, they are modified or extinguished, without compensation, in favour of some competing claim, such as the claim of a pool owner who has borne the burden of payment and received no refund from the builder who has merely made the actual payment. In the present case where Mr and Mrs Chaplin had borne the burden of the tax, the Refund Act extinguished Mutual Pools' right to receive a refund of the amount paid in respect of Mr and Mrs Chaplin's pool.

Any such modification or extinguishment of pre-existing rights without compensation was, however, but an incident of the operation of the law as a law defining and regulating rights of refund and does not impart to any of the provisions of the Refund Act a distinct additional character. It follows that, even if such an extinguishment or modification of some pre-existing right does constitute or bring about an "acquisition of property" within the meaning of those words as used in s 51(xxxi), that incidental operation of the Refund Act does not impart to all or any of its provisions the character of a law with respect to the acquisition of property. It follows that the Refund Act is not within the reach of the guarantee of just terms contained in s 51(xxxi) of the Constitution ...

Dawson and Toohey JJ

[W]e do not regard the Refund Act as effecting an acquisition of property by the Commonwealth or anyone else. No doubt the right of action on the part of the plaintiff to recover from the Commonwealth the amount paid by way of sales tax upon the Chaplins' pool is extinguished. But that has not resulted in any acquisition of property by the Commonwealth, even if the Commonwealth has acquired a financial advantage or benefit (although the Commonwealth is obliged to refund moneys under the Refund Act) ...

A variation to a property right inherently susceptible to variation does not involve an acquisition of property

Some property rights, especially those created by statute, are inherently susceptible to variation. A variation of such a property right does not involve an acquisition of property. Both before and after the variation the owner retains a property right inherently susceptible to variation. The property owner has not lost any part of that right, even though the financial value of the right might have changed. The case law provides examples. The cases demonstrate the need to identify with precision the nature of the property interest in question.

Chaffey involved a change in statutory rights to workers compensation. The plaintiff was injured at work in circumstances giving rise to a right to monetary compensation under legislation to be calculated 'as is prescribed' by the legislation. At the time of the injury, the calculation was prescribed to be by reference to the worker's salary and superannuation entitlements. The legislation was later changed to prescribe that the calculation be by reference to only the worker's salary. The worker claimed that this reduction in the value of compensation involved a countervailing benefit to the employer, and was therefore an acquisition of property.

The High Court held that the nature of this particular statutory right to compensation was inherently susceptible to legislative variation, with the result that a variation would not amount to an acquisition of property. At all times, the worker retained his full right to compensation to be calculated 'as is prescribed'.

Attorney-General (NT) v Chaffey (2007) 231 CLR 651

This case arose under a provision the **Northern Territory (Self-Government) Act 1978** *(Cth) prohibiting the Northern Territory Parliament from 'making of laws with respect to the acquisition of property otherwise than on just terms'. The* **Self-Government Act** *further provided that this provision had the same meaning as section 51(xxxi) of the* **Australian Constitution.**

Gleeson CJ, Gummow, Hayne and Crennan JJ

[C]ontraction in what otherwise would be the measure of liability in respect of a cause of action or other "right", may constitute an "acquisition" of property for the purposes of s 51(xxxi). Hence the change brought about by the 2004 Act in the content of the "remuneration" by reference to which the right of Mr Chaffey to compensation had been measured since 2003 could, all else being equal, constitute an "acquisition" of property in the necessary sense. But these appeals do not turn upon the notion of "acquisition". They depend upon the identification of the "property" to which s 50 of the Self-Government Act is said to apply ...

It is too broad a proposition, and one which neither party contended for in these appeals, that the contingency of subsequent legislative modification or extinguishment removes all statutory rights and interests from the scope of s 51(xxxi). *Newcrest Mining (WA) Ltd v Commonwealth* is an example to the contrary ...

The appellants' construction of s 53 of the Work Health Act as it stood at the time of the injury suffered by Mr Chaffey is correct. The consequence is that his rights to compensation under that statute were of a nature which rendered them liable to variation by a provision such as that made by the 2004 Act. Once this nature of the "property" involved is understood it is apparent that there was no "acquisition"...

Kirby J

[T]he particular provision of the Act, concerning the property right allegedly acquired by the removal of the superannuation component in the computation of the respondent's compensation benefits (s 53), contains a triple indication of the impermanency of the benefits accorded by the Act.

The three indications of this susceptibility are shown in the critical section, reproduced as it was in force at the time, with appropriate emphasis:

> *Subject to this Part*, where a worker suffers an injury within or outside the Territory and that injury results in or materially contributes to his or her –

(a) death;
(b) impairment; or
(c) incapacity,

there is payable by his or her employer to the worker or the worker's dependants, *in accordance with this Part*, such compensation *as is prescribed*.

Each of the emphasised phrases indicates, from the text of the statute, the impermanency and variability of the entitlement in question, and the necessity to read the statutory compensation "right", as it was provided by law from time to time. The right was, and is, therefore, a "right" inherently susceptible to variation. It follows that a law fulfilling the predicted variation was not a law with respect to the "acquisition" of property, nor was the "right" that was varied "property" that was susceptible to acquisition for "just terms" purposes ...

Cunningham is a similar case. Former members of Parliament were entitled under legislation to retirement allowances calculated by reference to the parliamentary allowance. Legislative and administrative changes altered the value of the parliamentary allowance, with a flow-on effect to the value of the retirement allowances. The High Court held that the former politicians had lost nothing. At all times, they retained their entitlement to retirement allowances calculated by reference to the parliamentary allowance. Like in ***Chaffey***, the method by which the financial value of the right was determined was always susceptible to variation.

Cunningham v Commonwealth (2016) 259 CLR 536

French CJ, Kiefel and Bell JJ

The question which arises from s 51(xxxi) is therefore whether the 2011/12 amendments are laws with respect to the acquisition of property. This enquiry necessitates a close analysis of the "property" which is said to have been acquired. Both enquiries – as to the rights making up the property and the character of the law changing them – require, in the first place, consideration of the nature of the entitlement to retiring allowances under the Superannuation Act.

The plaintiffs' case is that they became entitled, upon retirement, to receive a benefit, payable fortnightly during their lifetime, by way of retiring allowances. Each of the retiring allowances was defined by reference to a specified percentage of the parliamentary allowance and, where relevant, parliamentary office holder allowance and ministerial salary which was for the time being payable. The plaintiffs' statutory right, arising under the Superannuation Act, to receive money is a presently existing debt and it is therefore property. Further, the plaintiffs contend that they each have a vested chose in action to recover monies from the Commonwealth on account of the contributions made by them under the Superannuation Act.

The plaintiffs' argument then proceeds, that the 2011/12 amendments and the Determinations made thereafter effected a substantial modification to that property, by reducing the amount which might be payable by way of retiring allowances and at the same time giving a corresponding advantage to the Commonwealth. They point out that it is not necessary that property be extinguished in order to effect an acquisition. It is sufficient that a corresponding advantage, of a proprietary nature, accrues to the Commonwealth, such as where the Commonwealth's liability as a debtor is reduced ...

The plaintiffs' comparison of their entitlements under the Superannuation Act with a debt which is reduced, which is to say partially extinguished, implies that their entitlements have at all times been of a fixed and certain kind and that these entitlements were, to an extent, taken away. This description is apt to mislead. The 2011/12 amendments do not purport to reduce the plaintiffs' entitlements to retiring allowances. They operate to alter the method by which the quantum of the retiring allowances is calculated ...

The point made in *Chaffey* was that the method by which the amount of compensation payable was derived was liable to change. That would be so regardless of the means by which the change was effected ...

The plaintiffs take issue with descriptions which have been given to statutory rights of this kind, as "inherently susceptible" to modification and extinguishment, or "inherently unstable". They argue that such phrases should be deprecated because they are misleading and circular. All statutory provisions are liable to amendment and all are subject to s 51(xxxi), they contend.

The plaintiffs' submissions overlook that these descriptions identify within particular statutory rights a feature which is critical to their nature as "property" for the purposes of the application of s 51(xxxi). If a right or entitlement was always, of its nature, liable to variation, apart from the fact that it was created by statute, a variation later effected cannot properly be described as an acquisition of property. The Commonwealth does not as a result of an amendment effecting a variation receive a release from an existing liability and therefore acquire property, as the plaintiffs contend. The Commonwealth's liability corresponds with the variation made ...

10.5 What amounts to 'just terms'?

Where a federal law effects an acquisition of property, the law will be invalid unless the acquisition is made on 'just terms'. The High Court has not given a clear indication of what criteria must be satisfied for just terms to exist. Early case law suggests that less than full compensation may be acceptable, taking into account the public interest. More recent case law suggests that full compensation is required.

In ***Grace Brothers***, the High Court held that, because section 51(xxxi) is a grant of power, Parliament has some discretion in determining what amounts to 'just terms' and may take into consideration questions of fairness between the property owner and the Australian community. Terms will be just provided that a court cannot describe them as unjust. The fact that more just terms could be imagined will not lead to invalidity. In this case, compensation for compulsorily-acquired land calculated by reference to the value of the land as at 1 January the year before the acquisition occurred was held to amount to just terms.

Grace Brothers Pty Ltd v Commonwealth (1946) 72 CLR 269

Latham CJ

The *Lands Acquisition Act 1906–1936* was enacted under the power conferred upon the Federal Parliament by the Constitution, s 51(xxxi), to make laws with respect to the acquisition of property on just terms from any State or person for any purpose in respect of which Parliament has power to make laws. It is contended by the plaintiff that the Act does not provide just terms for the acquisition of land and therefore is invalid ...

It is contended for the plaintiff that the Act fails to provide just terms for the acquisition of property for four reasons. In the first place, s 29 requires compensation to be assessed according to the value of the land on the 1st day of January last preceding the date of acquisition. It is argued that an expropriated owner must, if he is treated justly, be entitled to obtain the value of his property as at the date of acquisition ...

I do not think that the terms of s 51(xxxi) entitle the Court to declare a statute providing a general method for the acquisition of property invalid because in particular cases it was possible to devise a more just scheme. The Court should not, in my opinion, hold such legislation to be invalid unless it is such that a reasonable man could not regard the terms of acquisition as being just.

Justice involves consideration of the interests of the community as well as of the person whose property is acquired. In some cases the announcement of the intention of the Government to acquire land might itself put up the value of the land. It is at least not obviously unjust to make provision against the community being compelled to pay higher prices for such a reason.

Section 29 takes the 1st January in the year of acquisition as the date of valuation as being on the whole a reasonable basis for adjusting the interests of the individual and of the community. In my opinion this is a not unfair provision. I am not prepared to hold that it is so obviously unjust as to invalidate the Act ...

Dixon J

Under that paragraph the validity of any general law cannot, I think, be tested by inquiring whether it will be certain to operate in every individual case to place the owner in a situation in which in all respects he will be as well off as if the acquisition had not taken place. The inquiry rather must be whether the law amounts to a true attempt to provide fair and just standards of compensating or rehabilitating the individual considered as an owner of property, fair and just as between him and the government of the country. I say "the individual" because what is just as between the Commonwealth and a State, two Governments, may depend on special considerations not applicable to an individual ...

In deciding whether any given law is within the power the Court must, of course, examine the justice of the terms provided. But it is a legislative function to provide the terms, and the Constitution does not mean to deprive the legislature of all discretion in determining what is just. Nor does justice to the subject or to the State demand a disregard of the interests of the public or of the Commonwealth ...

Comments in more recent cases suggest that the concept of 'just terms' involves full compensation and that there is no role for balancing the interests of the community in the analysis. In ***Georgiadis***, Brennan J said that just terms means full compensation.

Georgiadis v Australian and Overseas Telecommunications Corporation (1994) 179 CLR 297

Brennan J

The purpose of the guarantee of just terms is to ensure that the owners of property compulsorily acquired by government presumably in the interests of the community at large are not required to sacrifice their property for less than its worth. Unless it be shown that what is gained is full compensation for what is lost, the terms cannot be found to be just. Section 44 purports to extinguish a plaintiff's cause of action without compensation; it does not provide just terms for the extinguishment ...

In ***Smith***, Gleeson CJ approved Brennan J's comment in ***Georgiadis*** but suggested the full compensation need not necessarily be financial. Justice Kirby appears to have adopted a similar position.

Smith v ANL Ltd (2000) 204 CLR 493

Gleeson CJ

The extent of the disadvantage may be a material matter in deciding whether just terms have been provided. The circumstance that the appellant could have avoided the adverse consequences of the legislation by taking action within six months does not, in my view, mean that there was no acquisition. The appellant did not consent to the modification of his right. It is, however, a matter to be taken into account in considering whether, in the circumstances, there was a failure to provide just terms. So is the fact that the legislative scheme provided certain other benefits in place of the common law rights which it affected. However, it is the position of the appellant, not other injured seafarers considered collectively, or the public generally, that is to be addressed. As Brennan J said of the corresponding legislation in *Georgiadis*:

> If a worker is entitled at common law to a lump sum award in damages, it is not within the power of the Commonwealth under s 51(xxxi) to limit the amount which it or a statutory authority may have to pay the worker or to delay the worker's entitlement to payment. In determining the issue of just terms, the Court does not attempt a balancing of the interests of the dispossessed owner against the interests of the community at large. The purpose of the guarantee of just terms is to ensure that the owners of property compulsorily acquired by government presumably in the interests of the community at large are not required to sacrifice their property for less than its worth. Unless it be shown that what is gained is full compensation for what is lost, the terms cannot be found to be just.

The guarantee contained in s 51(xxxi) is there to protect private property. It prevents expropriation of the property of individual citizens, without adequate compensation, even where such expropriation may be intended to serve a wider public interest. A government may be satisfied that it can use the assets of some citizens better than they can; but if it wants to acquire those assets in reliance upon the power given by s 51(xxxi) it must pay for them, or in some other way provide just terms of acquisition ...

Kirby J

Once it is accepted that the appellant's property has been acquired under the impugned legislation, "just terms" would necessitate the provision to a person such as the appellant, in a case such as the present, of legal means of securing entitlements approximately equivalent to those which the appellant had lost by virtue of the legislation ...

By contrast, in ***Smith***, Gaudron and Gummow JJ approved ***Grace Brothers***.

Smith v ANL Ltd (2000) 204 CLR 493

Gaudron and Gummow JJ

The question thus becomes whether just terms were provided, bearing in mind that s 51(xxxi) involves a compound concept of "acquisition of property on just terms". It is trite that the decisions of this Court allow to the Parliament a measure of latitude in such matters. ANL relied upon *Grace Brothers Pty Ltd v Commonwealth* in which the validity of certain provisions of the *Lands Acquisition Act 1906* (Cth) was upheld. In *Grace Brothers*, Dixon J said of s 51(xxxi):

> Under that paragraph the validity of any general law cannot, I think, be tested by inquiring whether it will be certain to operate in every individual case to place the owner in a situation in which in all respects he will be as well off as if the acquisition had not taken place. The inquiry rather must be whether the law amounts to a true attempt to provide fair and just standards of compensating or rehabilitating the individual considered as an owner of property, fair and just as between him and the government of the country.
>
> ...

The standard position is that just terms is concerned with monetary compensation. In ***Wurridjal***, the High Court avoided deciding whether just terms might require *more* than monetary compensation. In this case, the claim was that acquisition of rights relating to Aboriginal sacred sites could not be compensated for in money. The High Court held that no such rights had been acquired. Justice Kirby was sympathetic to the proposition that monetary compensation may not amount to just terms were such a case actually to arise, while other judges were sceptical of the idea.

Wurridjal v Commonwealth (2009) 237 CLR 309

Kirby J

By contrast, however, an acquisition of legal interests in property belonging to traditional Aboriginals, even if only temporary, is not of such a character. Such interests are, or may be, essential to the identity, culture and spirituality of the Aboriginal people concerned. The evidence might ultimately show in this case that they do indeed love their traditional "property" interests in a way that conventional "property" is rarely if ever cherished in the general Australian community. This might oblige a much more careful consultation and participation procedure, far beyond what appears to have occurred here. As stated by Dixon J, the "terms" which s 51(xxxi) guarantees are "concerned with fairness" and potentially the inquiry is a wide one. It is enlivened by the type of Aboriginal "property" affected in consequence of the impugned legislation. As such, the "just terms" requirement of the Constitution arises for consideration. Its application would depend upon evidence, including evidence as to the way the Commonwealth went about the process of "acquisition". Such evidence could only be considered at trial. It is not met by a statutory obligation to pay monetary compensation ...

Heydon J

[T]he law can provide compensation for money losses even though there is no market for the thing lost and even though the attraction of the thing lost to the person who lost it rests on non-financial considerations. Secondly, a good example of things for which there is no market and which have non-financial aspects is native title rights. Yet in *Griffiths v Minister for Lands, Planning and Environment* a majority of the Court assumed that it was possible to extinguish native title on just terms ...

The plaintiffs submitted that "just terms" could require more than the provision of monetary compensation. An appeal was made to "the equitable maxim that one who suffers a wrong shall not be without a remedy, which applies where damages would be an inadequate remedy", and to cases recognising a right to the specific performance of contracts. The plaintiffs submitted that a particular example of the extension of "just terms" beyond monetary compensation might arise where the acquisition of traditional Aboriginal rights and interests in land was under consideration, in view of their "sui generis nature". The plaintiffs relied on a proposition that "the determination of just terms must take into account the particular value of the property to the former owner in circumstances where it ... cannot be readily replaced, nor readily compensated for by the payment of money". They attributed this proposition to Latham CJ in *Johnston Fear & Kingham & The Offset Printing Co Pty Ltd v Commonwealth* ...

In any event, the appeal which the plaintiffs make to the authorities is defective in two respects. First, the cases applying the principles relating to specific performance do not suggest any relevant analogy with the present controversy. Secondly, the point of Latham CJ's reasoning in the *Johnston Fear* case was not that just terms for the acquisition of some interests could include matters other than money; rather it was that if monetary payments were not truly compensatory, the acquisition was invalid ...

Kiefel J

The remaining aspect of the plaintiffs' case concerning just terms which requires consideration focuses upon the special value which particular areas may have. Sacred sites were identified in this regard. It was said that it may not be possible to attribute a market value to such sites, implying that a loss of or interference with rights exercised in relation to these places is not compensable by money. Such a proposition should not be readily accepted ...

The requirement for just terms can be satisfied by prescribing a mechanism for calculating compensation

It is not necessary that the law effecting an acquisition of property prescribe the just terms to which the property owner is entitled. It is enough that the law provides a mechanism for calculating just terms compensation.

In ***Wurridjal***, the legislation included what is sometimes called a 'historic shipwrecks clause', which provides for compensation only if it turns out the legislation does in fact effect an acquisition of property. The legislation provided that the Commonwealth 'is liable to pay a reasonable amount of compensation' to property owners. Where agreement could not be reached between the Commonwealth and the property owner on the quantum of compensation, the property owner had a right to 'institute proceedings in a court of competent jurisdiction for the recovery from the Commonwealth of such reasonable amount of compensation as the court determines'. The High Court held that this mechanism satisfied the requirement for just terms.

Wurridjal v Commonwealth (2009) 237 CLR 309

French CJ

In my opinion, however, the compensation provisions of the NER Act, to which reference was made earlier, afforded just terms for the acquisition of the Land Trust property. Heydon J has provided detailed reasons in support of that conclusion and I agree with them ...

Gummow and Hayne JJ

The plaintiffs stigmatise s 60 as creating what are but "contingent" rights. That is not so ... Section 60 is an example of prudent anticipation by the Parliament that its law may be held to attract the operation of s 51(xxxi) and of the inclusion of provision for compensation in that event, thereby avoiding the pitfall of invalidity. Moreover, the right to compensation is absolute if it transpires that s 51(xxxi) is engaged.

The provision for payment of "reasonable compensation" determined, in the absence of agreement, by exercise of the judicial power of the Commonwealth, satisfies the requirement of "just terms" with respect to the Maningrida Five Year Lease. The phrase "reasonable compensation" is apt to include provision for interest to reflect delay occasioned by recourse to adjudication in the absence of agreement. The submissions to the contrary by the plaintiffs raise a false alarm. Another false alarm is the contention that, when s 61 requires in that adjudication the taking into account of amounts of rent and other matters specified in that section, no other matters may be taken into account even where failure to do so would deny "just terms" ...

Heydon J

[I]t is a misuse of language to call the right to compensation "contingent" by reason of any delay involved, or by reason of the possible need to go to court. The need to vindicate rights in court does not make those rights "contingent", and the process of doing so is not unfair. It should not take long to establish that the Commonwealth will not agree with the amount of compensation claimed by the person seeking it. Thereafter the controversy is committed to the court of competent jurisdiction, and in modern conditions such a court will endeavour to give a speedy remedy to a claimant who is not tardy in using the court's procedures. A claimant of that kind does not fall within the category stated by Deane J in *Commonwealth v Tasmania* of those who "will be forced to wait years before [they are] allowed even access to a court, tribunal or other body which can authoritatively determine the amount of the compensation which the Commonwealth must pay." As Black CJ and Gummow J said of similarly worded legislation:

> It is not correct to say that in such circumstances the right to compensation is conditional rather than absolute; the right is absolute if upon a proper analysis the law effects an acquisition of property.

And even if there is delay, its effects can be overcome by orders for interest ...

Kiefel J

A provision such as s 60(2) appeared in the *Historic Shipwrecks Act 1976* (Cth) and has been incorporated in legislation since then. Such a provision was considered in *Minister for Primary Industry and Energy v Davey* (1993) 47 FCR 151 where it was held that it suffices to comply with s 51(xxxi). As Black CJ and Gummow J there said, "[i]t is possible for the Parliament legislatively to anticipate that a law might be held to constitute an acquisition of property otherwise than on just terms, and to provide in that event for compensation, in order to avoid a legislative vacuum". It is not necessary that "just terms" be dealt with explicitly, as a precondition to validity.

The provision of compensation, expressed as an amount that is fair and reasonable in all the circumstances, prima facie complies with the requirement of s 51(xxxi) ...

Some procedures for the calculation of just terms compensation might be designed in a way that is so unfair as to not satisfy the requirement for just terms. In the ***Tasmanian Dam Case,*** Deane J discussed one example. A procedure that was designed to involve considerable delay in resolving the quantum of just terms to the disadvantage of a property owner unless the property owner agreed with the Commonwealth's proposed offer of compensation was held not to satisfy the requirement for just terms.

Commonwealth v Tasmania ('Tasmanian Dam Case') (1983) 158 CLR 1

Deane J

The relevant provisions of s 17 of the Act are set out in the judgment of the Chief Justice. In summary, their effect is as follows. Where a person (the claimant) considers that the operation of the Act or of the Regulations has resulted in an acquisition of property from him, he may give notice in writing to the Minister requesting the Minister to pay a specified amount of compensation (the claimed amount) in respect of the acquisition (s 17(3)). If, within three weeks, the Minister gives notice advising that he does not consider that there has been such an acquisition, the claimant may apply to the High Court for a declaration that there has been (s 17(4)). If the Minister does not give such a notice within three weeks, the operation of the Act or the Regulations shall be taken to have resulted in such an acquisition (s 17(5)). If the Minister has given such a notice and the High Court subsequently declares that there has been such an acquisition, the Commonwealth is then liable to pay such compensation as is agreed or, failing agreement, "as is determined in accordance with the succeeding provisions of this section" (s 17(6)). The procedure established for determining the amount of compensation varies according to whether the amount claimed is less than $5 million. If the amount claimed is less than $5 million, the claimant may apply to the Federal Court to "determine the compensation that is fair and just in respect of the acquisition" (s 17(14)(a)). If the amount claimed is equal to or more than $5 million, the Act establishes a compulsory waiting period of six months in which agreement as to the amount might be reached. After that waiting period without agreement, the Governor-General shall, after fourteen days' notice, establish a Commission of Inquiry (s 17(7)(b)). The Commission of Inquiry shall, before the expiration of twelve months after its establishment, report in writing to the Governor-General setting out its "recommendation" as to the compensation that is "fair and just in respect of the acquisition" (s 17(10)). Within three months of the receipt of those recommendations, the Governor-General shall "if the person and the Commonwealth have not reached agreement as to the compensation payable, having regard to the report of the Commission and to such other matters as the Governor-General considers relevant, determine the compensation that the Governor-General considers to be fair and just in respect of the acquisition" (s 17(12). If the claimant considers that the amount determined by the Governor-General is not fair and just, he may then apply to the Federal Court to "determine the compensation that is fair and just in respect of the acquisition" ...

[W]here the Parliament does not specify the amount of compensation but provides a procedure for determining what is fair and just, the Court will examine the nature and extent of the entitlement of a claimant under the procedure established and the nature of the procedure itself in deciding whether the acquisition for which the law provides is "on just terms" ...

There is not, of course, anything intrinsically unfair in the Parliament providing a procedure for determining the quantum of compensation outside the ordinary judicial process. There is however something intrinsically unfair in a procedure which, in effect, ensures that, unless a claimant agrees to accept the terms which the Commonwealth is prepared to offer, he will be forced to wait years before he is allowed even access to a court, tribunal or other body which can authoritatively determine the amount of the compensation which the Commonwealth must pay ...

10.6 When are laws not subject to the guarantee in section 51(xxxi)?

Some acquisitions of property do not require just terms compensation. In other words, section 51(xxxi) does not apply to every law effecting an acquisition of property. Obvious examples are laws requiring the payment of taxes and laws confiscating property as punishment for a crime.

In ***Mutual Pools***, Deane and Gaudron JJ explained that there are two key bases on which section 51(xxxi) will not apply to a federal law effecting an acquisition of property. First, some heads of legislative power authorise acquisitions of property otherwise than on just terms: section 51(xxxi) operates a general limitation on legislative power only by a process of construction and therefore has no application where a contrary outcome is manifest from the terms or content of another head of legislative power. Secondly, some acquisitions of property are 'antithetical to the notion of just terms', 'inconsistent or incongruous with the notion of just terms' or may be 'of a kind that does not permit of just terms'.

Mutual Pools & Staff Pty Ltd v Commonwealth (1994) 179 CLR 155

Deane and Gaudron JJ

The presence of the words "just terms" indicates that the acquisitions to which the grant of legislative power is directed are acquisitions of a kind which permit of just terms. There are some kinds of acquisition which are of their nature antithetical to the notion of just terms but which were plainly intended to be permissible under laws made pursuant to one or more of the grants of power contained in s 51. An example of those kinds of acquisition is the compulsory forfeiture to the Commonwealth of money or specific property as punishment for breach of some general rule of conduct prescribed by a valid law of the Commonwealth.

Such an acquisition stands apart from the kinds of "acquisition of property" which constitute the subject-matter of s 51(xxxi) and such laws are beyond the reach of the paragraph's guarantee of just terms. Indeed, a law providing for an acquisition of property of a kind which is inconsistent or incongruous with the notion of just terms could validly be enacted pursuant to par (xxxi) itself. An example is a law providing for the payment of a pecuniary penalty for a corrupt breach of a statutory duty imposed by a valid law with respect to the acquisition of property on just terms.

It is because s 51(xxxi) operates only indirectly to confine other powers in s 51, and, then, only within the area in which it operates, that the following laws involving acquisition of property without the provision of just terms have been held or indicated, in judgments in the Court, to be supported by a grant of legislative power other than that contained in s 51(xxxi): the imposition of a tax (*Australian Tape Manufacturers Association Ltd v Commonwealth* (1993) 176 CLR at 508–510.); the imposition of a liability to pay moneys in advance of an actual taxation liability (ie provisional tax) (*Commissioner of Taxation v Clyne* (1958) 100 CLR 246 at 263, 270; *Federal Commissioner of Taxation v Barnes* (1975) 133 CLR 483 at 494–495.); the forfeiture of illegally imported goods in the hands of an innocent third party *Burton v Honan* (1952) 86 CLR 169 at

180–181. See also *Cheatley v The Queen* (1972) 127 CLR 291 at 307–308.); the imposition of a pecuniary penalty by way of civil proceedings (*Reg v Smithers; Ex parte McMillan* (1982) 152 CLR 477 at 487–489.); the acquisition by the Controller of Enemy Property of the property of subjects of a former enemy to be applied to reparations payable by an enemy State (*Attorney-General (Cth) v Schmidt* (1961) 105 CLR at 373, 376–377.); the vesting of a bankrupt's estate in an Official Receiver or Trustee (ibid at 372.); and, the condemnation of prize (ibid at 372–373.).

In such cases, the law in question is either (or both) clearly within the intended scope of another legislative power so that it is manifest that the rule of construction which gives s 51(xxxi) its operation as a guarantee of just terms does not operate to deny authority to make that law, or it is a law of a kind that does not permit of just terms in the sense we have explained and, thus, stands outside s 51(xxxi) ...

The cases do not always carefully distinguish between these bases for the non-application of section 51(xxxi), and some cases of the non-application of section 51(xxxi) can be justified by reference to either or both of these bases. Some cases where these explanations may be invoked can also be explained by reason of there being no acquisition at all because, for example, there is only an adjustment of competing interests in relation to property. In ***Airservices Australia v Canadian Airlines***, Gaudron J explained that this happens because the grounds on which section 51(xxxi) does not apply overlap.

Airservices Australia v Canadian Airlines (1999) 202 CLR 133

Gaudron J

The laws which stand apart from the guarantee in s 51(xxxi) of the Constitution do not constitute discrete categories of exception. Thus, for example, a law which is not properly characterised as a law for the acquisition of property because it is a law adjusting competing rights and interests may also be a law enacted under a head of power which clearly authorises the acquisition of property other than on just terms. Whatever the precise relationship between the various categories of exception, however, a law under s 51 of the Constitution which operates to vest a person's property in another for a purpose for which the Commonwealth has power to make laws and which does not fall within one of those exceptions is a law to which the guarantee in s 51(xxxi) of the Constitution applies ...

Lawler demonstrates that forfeitures of property used in the commission of criminal offences are not protected by section 51(xxxi), even where the property owner is entirely innocent. Forfeiture of property used in the commission of a criminal offence is an acquisition of property that does not permit of just terms.

The case considered legislation providing that any boat used in the commission of the offence of using an unlicensed boat for commercial fishing in designated waters is forfeited to the Commonwealth upon conviction. Lawler owned a boat that had been leased to another person and that other person was convicted of using an unlicensed boat for commercial fishing in designated waters. The High Court held that the acquisition of Lawler's property was an acquisition of property that does not admit of just terms.

Re Director of Public Prosecutions; Ex parte Lawler (1994) 179 CLR 270

Brennan J

A law which imposes a penalty or sanction for breach of a provision prescribing a rule of conduct and which, apart from its imposition of the penalty or sanction, is a law with respect to a head of power other than s 51(xxxi) cannot be classified as a law with respect to the acquisition of property within s 51(xxxi). To place it within the s 51(xxxi) category would be to annihilate the penalty or sanction and thus to weaken, if not destroy, the normative effect of the prescription of the rule of conduct. The irrelevance of s 51(xxxi) to the imposition of fines and forfeitures is trite law ...

[T]he provision for forfeiture contained in s 106(1)(a) of the Act authorizing, as it does, the forfeiture of vessels owned by persons who are or might be innocent of any complicity in the offence which creates the liability to forfeiture is appropriate and adapted to the enforcement of the offence-creating provision. The forfeiture provision is therefore properly characterized as a law with respect to fisheries supported by s 51(x) of the Constitution. That power is not to be read down in order to protect the rights of private owners ...

Deane and Gaudron JJ

The applicants contend – and it is their only contention – that, in so far as s 106(1)(a) of the Act authorizes an order for the forfeiture of the property of persons referred to in argument as "innocent third parties", it is invalid by reason that it authorizes an acquisition of property other than on just terms as required by s 51(xxxi) of the Constitution ...

There are two reasons why some laws stand outside s 51(xxxi). The first is the nature of the guarantee effected by s 51(xxxi). As we explain in *Mutual Pools and Staff Pty Ltd v Commonwealth* it is an indirect guarantee which comes about in consequence of a rule of construction and that rule is subject to any contrary intention that is manifest from the terms or content of the other legislative powers conferred by s 51. Thus, its guarantee of just terms does not apply to laws clearly encompassed in another power as, for example, a law imposing a tax or a law vesting a bankrupt's estate in an Official Receiver or Trustee. The second is that there is no guarantee of "just terms" outside the area in which s 51(xxxi) operates as a grant of power ...

However, the power conferred by s 51(xxxi) is one with respect to "acquisition of property on just terms". That phrase must be read in its entirety and, when so read, it indicates that s 51(xxxi) applies only to acquisitions of a kind that permit of just terms. It is not concerned with laws in connection with which "just terms" is an inconsistent or incongruous notion. Thus, it is not concerned with a law imposing a fine or penalty, including by way of forfeiture, or a law effecting or authorizing seizure of the property of enemy aliens or the condemnation of prize. Laws of that kind do not involve acquisitions that permit of just terms and, thus, they are not laws with respect to "acquisition of property", as that expression is used in s 51(xxxi). It follows that a law which effects or authorizes forfeiture of property in consequence of its use in the commission of an offence against the laws of the Commonwealth stands outside s 51(xxxi).

The validity of a law that effects or authorizes forfeiture of property in consequence of its use in the commission of an offence depends on whether it can be characterized as a law with respect to some matter concerning which the Commonwealth Parliament has power to make laws ...

McHugh J

The complete answer to the contention of the prosecutors is that an order made under s 106 does not effect an acquisition of property for the purposes of s 51(xxxi). An order made under s 106 is a drastic but incidental measure whose purpose is to facilitate compliance with those provisions of the Act which regulate commercial fishing in Australian waters. When the forfeiture of property is a reasonably proportional consequence of a breach of a law passed under a power conferred by s 51 of the Constitution, no acquisition of property for the purpose of s 51(xxxi) takes place. The notion of paying fair compensation to the owner of property which is validly forfeited to the Crown for a breach of the law is simply absurd. In the case of the forfeiture of property to the Commonwealth for breach of a law of the Parliament, the question is whether the forfeiture is reasonably incidental to the exercise of a power other than s 51(xxxi). If it is not, the forfeiture is invalid. If it is, s 51(xxxi) has no operation ...

Theophanous is another forfeiture case. The legislation in this case provided that a member of Parliament who is convicted of corruption offences forfeits their entitlement to retirement and superannuation benefits to which retired members of Parliament are otherwise entitled. The High Court acknowledged that the concept of 'incongruous' involves questions of degree and judgment but insisted that it is a workable test.

Theophanous v Commonwealth (2006) 225 CLR 101

Gummow, Kirby, Hayne, Heydon and Crennan JJ

It may be complained that the boundary marked to the "just terms" requirement of s 51(xxxi) by reference to its application being "inconsistent" or "incongruous" states a criterion that may require difficult questions of judgment. But to mark the boundary to the application of the "just terms" requirement in this way is grounded in the realisation that to characterise certain exactions of government (such as levying of taxation, imposition of fines, exaction of penalties or forfeitures, or enforcement of a statutory lien) as an acquisition of property would be incompatible with the very nature of the exaction ...

The operation of Pt 2 of the CSB Act in respect of the benefits and interests of the plaintiff and his wife, vested or contingent, manifests one of the adverse consequences of his conviction for corruption offences. The corruption offences in question were committed whilst the plaintiff was a member of the House of Representatives. They involved abuse of that position and were committed for a corrupt purpose.

The provision of benefits to legislators, whether by salary, allowance or retirement benefit, has long been regarded as made to lessen the risk of and temptation to corruption and abuse of office. Legislation such as Pt 2 of the CSB Act, in its application to the situation of the plaintiff, vindicates the public interest in denying to those who succumbed to that temptation the benefits provided to encourage probity in legislators. To require the provision of "just terms" in such circumstances would indeed, in the sense of the authorities, be incongruous.

For these reasons, s 51(xxxi) has no operation with respect to the application of Pt 2 of the CSB Act to the plaintiff ...

Emmerson followed the reasoning in ***Theophanous***. In *Emmerson*, legislation provided that 'all or any property that is owned or effectively controlled by' a person convicted of three or more drug trafficking offences is forfeited. The High Court held that this acquisition of property constituted punishment for criminal offending and was therefore incongruous with the notion of just terms. The High Court also held that in cases of forfeiture of property as punishment it is not necessary that the extent of the forfeiture be proportionate to the seriousness of the offence or to any other purposes of forfeiture.

Attorney-General (NT) v Emmerson (2014) 253 CLR 393

French CJ, Hayne, Crennan, Kiefel, Bell and Keane JJ

First, because the forfeiture worked by the Forfeiture Act is imposed as punishment for crime, the impugned provisions do not amount to an acquisition of property other than on just terms. Second, whether that punishment fits the crime (in this case, the repeated commission of certain crimes) is a matter for the legislature. It is irrelevant (and wrong) for the courts to attempt to determine whether any forfeiture which may be worked by the Forfeiture Act (or which is worked in this particular case) is proportionate to the stated objectives ...

It was accepted that several authorities in this Court have found, in s 51 of the Constitution, heads of legislative power in respect of which just terms "is an inconsistent or incongruous notion." This development was traced in *Theophanous v Commonwealth*. Marking the boundary of "just terms", by reference to the application of a requirement that an exaction is "inconsistent" or "incongruous" with them, may admittedly involve difficult questions of degree and judgment. Notwithstanding such difficulties, marking the boundary in that way is:

> grounded in the realisation that to characterise certain exactions of government (such as levying of taxation, imposition of fines, exaction of penalties or forfeitures, or enforcement of a statutory lien) as an acquisition of property would be incompatible with the very nature of the exaction.

The first respondent did not urge any reconsideration or overruling of authorities illustrative of that proposition ...

The proper inquiry, however, is the subject matter of the statutory scheme. The question is whether the statutory scheme can be properly characterised as a law with respect to forfeiture, that is, a law which exacts or imposes a penalty or sanction for breach of provisions which prescribe a rule of conduct. That inquiry must be answered positively, which precludes any inquiry into the proportionality, justice or wisdom of the legislature's chosen measures ...

Nintendo provides an example of law enacted under a head of power that authorises acquisitions of property without requiring just terms. The creation of a new species of intellectual property under the intellectual property power in section 51(xviii) of its nature necessarily involves the creation of new proprietary rights at the expense of someone.

Nintendo Co Ltd v Centronics Systems Pty Ltd (1994) 181 CLR 134

The High Court held that the enactment of the* Circuit Layouts Act 1989 *(Cth) was not subject to section 51(xxxi) for two independent reasons: (1) because the legislation merely adjusted competing interests in property (see the extract of this case above); and (2) because the head of power under which the legislation was enacted evinces an intention to authorise acquisitions of property otherwise than on just terms such that the rule of construction by which section 51(xxxi) limits other heads of power does not apply.

Mason CJ, Brennan, Deane, Toohey, Gaudron and McHugh JJ

The grant of Commonwealth legislative power which sustains the Act is that contained in s 51(xviii) of the Constitution with respect to "Copyrights, patents of inventions and designs, and trademarks". It is of the essence of that grant of legislative power that it authorises the making of laws which create, confer, and provide for the enforcement of, intellectual property rights in original compositions, inventions, designs, trademarks and other products of intellectual effort. It is of the nature of such laws that they confer such rights on authors, inventors and designers, other originators and assignees and that they conversely limit and detract from the proprietary rights which would otherwise be enjoyed by the owners of affected property. Inevitably, such laws may, at their commencement, impact upon existing proprietary rights. To the extent that such laws involve an acquisition of property from those adversely affected by the intellectual property rights which they create and confer, the grant of legislative power contained in s 51(xviii) manifests a contrary intention which precludes the operation of s 51(xxxi) ...

Airservices Australia v Canadian Airlines is a case in which some judges found that the acquisition of property involved was incongruous with the notion of just terms. Other judges found that there was no acquisition of property at all but merely an adjustment of competing interests in property.

Legislation provided that airlines operating commercial routes within Australia had to pay fees to the Civil Aviation Authority in respect of each aircraft operated by the airline to contribute to the cost of civil aviation safety services provided by the Authority. The legislation also imposed liens over each aircraft to secure payment of those fees.

An airline operating aircraft leased from another company collapsed, owing the Authority fees. The owner of the aircraft argued that the liens effected an acquisition of its property otherwise than on just terms. Gleeson CJ, Kirby and McHugh JJ rejected the owner's argument by holding that the statutory liens were acquisitions of property that were incongruous with the notion of just terms.

Airservices Australia v Canadian Airlines (1999) 202 CLR 133

Gleeson CJ and Kirby J

It was argued on behalf of the respondents, although not decided in the Federal Court, that, even assuming the charges and penalties in question to have been validly imposed upon Compass, the provisions of the Act relating to statutory liens (ss 68 to 75) were invalid for the reason that, although they were laws for the acquisition of property for a purpose in respect of which the Parliament has power to make laws, they did not provide for the just terms required by s 51(xxxi) of the Constitution ...

Having regard to the relationship between the services provided by the CAA and the safety of the aircraft concerned, the reasonableness of a system which provides that those who operate aircraft must pay charges which, in totality, will defray the cost of providing the services, the possibility that operators will have few assets in the jurisdiction apart from aircraft, the mobility of aircraft, and the desirability of providing adequate security for liabilities incurred, it is at least as easy to draw a conclusion supportive of the legislation as it was in *Ex parte Lawler* ...

We accept that s 51(xxxi) of the Constitution must not, in accordance with the authority of this Court, be given a pedantic or narrow construction. We also accept that the taking of property under a federal law is not removed from "acquisition" simply because it is described as "forfeiture". It is not the name, but the character of the taking, that controls the outcome of constitutional characterization. But, in this case, the statutory liens are valid ... They were provided to secure the effectiveness of charges relating to aircraft which, of their very nature, could otherwise leave Australia with substantial debts unpaid and with no effective means for their recovery ...

McHugh J

The conclusion that the charges which the liens secured are "fees for services" and not taxation is important to the resolution of this question. It means that the debt secured by the lien was the quid pro quo accruing to the Authority as the result of its prior supply of valuable services to the aircraft operator. The lien was used to secure an existing indebtedness and it was only in force until that indebtedness was discharged. The subject matter of the lien is one that is arguably within the power conferred on the Parliament by s 51(i) and s 51(xxix) of the Constitution.

If "fair compensation" were to be paid to those having a proprietary interest in an aircraft upon the imposition of a lien, it would mean that the Authority would have an interest in the aircraft which on sale could be realised to satisfy the operator's previously incurred debt to the Authority, but on the other hand the Authority would incur a liability to pay "fair compensation" to those having a proprietary interest in the aircraft. The amount of this liability for "fair compensation" would be at least equal to the amount secured by the lien (as the "fair value" of the lien in the sense of the amount required to be paid before it will be discharged), and may be greater than the amount secured by the lien (if fair compensation involved an amount for loss of profits consequent upon the loss of use of the aircraft).

Thus, the entire purpose of the lien would be frustrated as the Authority would be no better off, and indeed may be worse off, in terms of net recovery of the charges levied as a quid pro quo for the provision of the services. Accordingly, in my opinion, the imposition of a statutory lien in these circumstances is irrelevant to or incongruous with the notion of fair compensation in the sense adverted to by me in *Mutual Pools*. Fair compensation would not be incongruous or irrelevant if there were no services provided. But that is not this case.

Gummow and Hayne JJ rejected the owner's argument by holding that the statutory liens merely adjusted interests in the property of the aircraft since the owner had benefited from the safety services provided in respect of the aircraft it owned but which had been operated by another company.

Airservices Australia v Canadian Airlines (1999) 202 CLR 133

Gummow J

The statutory lien provisions are part of the regulatory scheme for civil aviation safety created by the Act. The lien provisions adjust the respective interests of those who own, lease or operate the aircraft and of the provider of services necessary for commercial operations of the aircraft in Australia. The interests of security holders are, to the extent discussed above, not displaced. The services were provided by the Authority to the aircraft, in the sense that it was particular operations using the aircraft which provided the incident for the attraction of the charges ...

The bundle of rights and remedies held by the Authority constituted the exchange for the provision of the services. In the events that occurred, the services were provided, but the charges and penalties were not recouped to the Authority. For the Authority then to assert its rights and remedies against the respondents is not to compulsorily acquire property from the respondents with an attendant obligation of fair compensation to the respondents from the Authority. The lien provisions are not invalid as laws which must answer the condition imposed by s 51(xxxi) of the Constitution in order to be valid ...

Hayne J

The charges which may be satisfied by sale of an aircraft under these provisions of the Act may not have been (and were not, in these cases) incurred by the owner of the aircraft. Thus the security interest, for the creation of which the Act provides, attaches in this case to the property of one person to satisfy the debt of another. That fact might suggest that the law providing for creation of the security interest is not concerned with the adjustment of the competing rights, claims or obligations of persons in a particular relationship or area of activity. It is necessary to recall, however, that the lien is a lien over the aircraft which was used in ways that gave rise to the imposition of the charge; it is not a lien over any other property of the owner of the aircraft. That being so, for the reasons given by Gummow J, the statutory lien provisions are not properly characterised as a law with respect to the acquisition of property on just terms from any person for any purpose in respect of which the Parliament has power to make laws ...

10.7 DISCUSSION QUESTIONS

1. What is 'property' for the purposes of section 51(xxxi)?
2. Why does section 51(xxxi) operate as a limitation on power?
3. Make a list of four cases considered in this chapter in which the High Court held there was no acquisition of property effected. For each case, make a brief note of what happened to the property in question and why that did not amount to an acquisition.
4. Why is it acceptable under section 51(xxxi) for legislation effecting an acquisition of property to provide a mechanism for calculating just terms compensation?
5. Problem question: Consider the following hypothetical legislation and scenario. The Commonwealth Government has decided to implement a domestic violence awareness campaign making use of National Rugby League ('NRL') and Australian Football League ('AFL') logos. To implement the policy, the following legislation is passed:

Awareness Campaigns (Domestic Violence) Act 2023

1. This Act may be cited as the Awareness Campaigns (Domestic Violence) Act 2023.
2. Notwithstanding any other law, the Minister may use or cause to be used any logo specified in the schedule to this Act for any purpose in connection with any domestic violence public awareness campaign.
3. A logo specified in the schedule to this Act must not be used for any purpose in connection with advertising alcoholic beverages.

The Schedule includes the NRL and AFL logos.

Provide advice to the NRL and AFL about whether the *Awareness Campaigns (Domestic Violence) Act 2023* violates the limitation provided in section 51(xxxi) of the *Australian Constitution*.

FREEDOM OF RELIGION

11

11.1 Overview

This chapter examines an important limitation on federal power: the limited guarantee of religious freedom provided by section 116 of the *Australian Constitution.*

Australian Constitution

Section 116 Commonwealth not to legislate in respect of religion

The Commonwealth shall not make any law for establishing any religion, or for imposing any religious observance, or for prohibiting the free exercise of any religion, and no religious test shall be required as a qualification for any office or public trust under the Commonwealth.

Section 116 prohibits federal laws, but not State laws, for: (1) establishing any religion; (2) imposing any religious observance; and (3) prohibiting the free exercise of any religion. Section 116 also prohibits religious tests for holding any office or public trust under the Commonwealth, whether that religious test is imposed by law or otherwise. There are very few cases considering section 116, with the consequence that the case law is not well developed.

Section 116 was included in the *Australian Constitution* to ensure that the Federal Parliament would not be able to pass laws in respect of religion. There had been a concern from some religious minorities that federal laws might be enacted requiring people to participate in mainstream Christian observances.

Luke Beck, *Religious Freedom and the Australian Constitution: Origins and Future* (Routledge, 2018)

What might be called the "standard account" of Higgins' argument for section 116 tends to be presented as follows: The insertion of the words "humbly relying on the blessing of Almighty God" in the preamble to the Commonwealth of Australia Constitution Bill (Imp) might give rise to an implication that, notwithstanding the absence of an express power to legislate with respect to religion, the Commonwealth was indeed empowered to legislate with respect to religion. A provision such as section 116 is therefore necessary to prevent any such implication being drawn or to counteract any such implication ...

Higgins told the Convention that the Seventh Day Adventists were "exceedingly troubled over the fact that through putting the words in question in the preamble there may be an attempt to enforce the observance of Sunday upon them." Higgins explained that his amendment was necessary because:

> [t]here will be in the preamble of this Constitution a declaration of a religious character, from which, as experience shows, a number of corollaries will be deduced, and upon which attempts will be made, from time to time, to pass legislation of a character which I do not think we intend to give the Federal Commonwealth power to pass.

The Convention seems to have been under the impression that the reason why it was necessary to insert this denial of power was because of the possibility an implied power to legislate in respect of religion might arise from constitutional recognition of God in the preamble. In reality, the source of the power to legislate in respect of religion identified by Higgins was the various express powers granted to the Commonwealth.

What Higgins labelled an exercise of "inferential powers" is better understood as an instance of what would now be described as a law with multiple characterisations ...

Key concepts considered in this chapter include:

- religion
- establishing any religion
- religious observance
- free exercise of religion
- religious test
- under the Commonwealth
- purpose.

11.2 What is a 'religion'?

The leading case on the legal definition of 'religion' is the ***Scientology Case***, a case about exemptions from Victorian payroll tax available to religious organisations. The various judgments offer slightly different, although all broad, definitions of religion. The High Court held that Scientology was a religion.

Church of the New Faith v Commissioner of Pay-Roll Tax (Vic) ('Scientology Case') (1983) 154 CLR 120

Mason ACJ and Brennan J

The chief function in the law of a definition of religion is to mark out an area within which a person subject to the law is free to believe and to act in accordance with his belief without legal restraint. Such a definition affects the scope and operation of s 116 of the Constitution and identifies the subject matters which other laws are presumed not to intend to affect. Religion is thus a concept of fundamental importance to the law. Moreover, although this case does not arise under s 116 of the Constitution or under any part of its fourfold guarantee of religious freedom, it is inevitable that the judgments in the Supreme Court [of Victoria], so long as they stand without consideration by this Court, will influence the construction placed upon s 116 of the Constitution by other Australian courts ...

We would therefore hold that, for the purposes of the law, the criteria of religion are twofold: first, belief in a supernatural Being, Thing or Principle; and second, the acceptance of canons of conduct in order to give effect to that belief, though canons of conduct which offend against the ordinary laws are outside the area of any immunity, privilege or right conferred on the grounds of religion. Those criteria may vary in their comparative importance, and there may be a different intensity of belief or of acceptance of canons of conduct among religions or among the adherents to a religion. The tenets of a religion may give primacy to one particular belief or to one particular canon of conduct. Variations in emphasis may distinguish one religion from other religions, but they are irrelevant to the determination of an individual's or a group's freedom to profess and exercise the religion of his, or their, choice ...

To restrict the definition of religion to theistic religions is to exclude Theravada Buddhism, an acknowledged religion, and perhaps other acknowledged religions. It is too narrow a test. We would hold the test of religious belief to be satisfied by belief in supernatural Things or Principles and not to be limited to belief in God or in a supernatural Being otherwise described ...

Wilson and Deane JJ

There is no single characteristic which can be laid down as constituting a formularized legal criterion, whether of inclusion or exclusion, of whether a particular system of ideas and practices constitutes a religion within a particular State of the Commonwealth. The most that can be done is to formulate the more important of the indicia or guidelines by reference to which that question falls to be answered. Those indicia must, in the view we take, be derived by empirical observation of accepted religions ...

One of the more important indicia of "a religion" is that the particular collection of ideas and/or practices involves belief in the supernatural, that is to say, belief that reality extends beyond that which is capable of perception by the senses. If that be absent, it is unlikely that one has "a religion". Another is that the ideas relate to man's nature and place in the universe and his relation to things supernatural. A third is that the ideas are accepted by adherents as requiring or encouraging them to observe particular standards or codes of conduct or to participate in specific practices having supernatural significance. A fourth is that, however loosely knit and varying in beliefs and practices adherents may be, they constitute an identifiable group or identifiable groups. A fifth, and perhaps more controversial, indicium is that the adherents themselves see the collection of ideas and/or practices as constituting a religion ...

None of the case law considering section 116 directly has involved any doubt about whether a 'religion' was involved. The cases have all involved recognisable religions.

11.3 The establishment clause

The first clause of section 116 provides: 'The Commonwealth shall not make any law for establishing any religion'. The case law on the establishment clause is not well developed.

The only case about the establishment clause considered by a full bench of the High Court is the ***DOGS Case***. A majority of the High Court rejected an argument that federal legislation providing for public funding of religious primary and secondary schools amounted to laws for establishing any religion.

The majority judges gave slightly different definitions of the concept of establishing any religion. The common thread in the majority judgments is that the establishment clause prohibits federal laws intending to set up a single national official religion.

Attorney-General (Vic) ex rel Black v Commonwealth ('DOGS Case') (1981) 146 CLR 559

The Association for the Defence of Government Schools (DOGS) sued the Commonwealth on the relation of the Victorian Attorney-General, arguing that federal legislation providing for public funding of religious schools amounted to laws for establishing any religion.

Barwick CJ

Before turning to the interpretation of the language of s 116, having regard to the various submissions made as to its meaning, I wish to say something as to the use in that connexion of material extraneous to the text itself. First, as to the use of the Convention debates: the settled doctrine of the Court is that they are not available in the construction of the Constitution: and, in my opinion, rightly so ...

I have now to deal with the meaning of the operative words of s 116 before applying them to the statute under challenge in this case.

As I have already indicated, I find no ambiguity in the language of s 116 ... In my opinion, as used in an instrument brought into existence at the turn of the century, establishing a religion involves the entrenchment of a religion as a feature of and identified with the body politic, in this instance, the Commonwealth. It involves the identification of the religion with the civil authority so as to involve the citizen in a duty to maintain it and the obligation of, in this case, the Commonwealth to patronize, protect and promote the established religion. In other words, establishing a religion involves its adoption as an institution of the Commonwealth, part of the Commonwealth "establishment" ... Thus what s 116 forbids is the passage of a law which will erect a religion into such a relationship to the body politic of the Commonwealth as I have attempted to describe ...

Here, the impugned legislation in substance appropriates, and authorizes the disbursement of, part of the consolidated revenue of the Commonwealth for the financial support of the education of Australians by and according to the regiment of non-government schools, including such schools as are owned and conducted by bodies professing and practising the Christian religion, albeit according to the doctrines of a particular church. The financial aid is expressly limited to the educational activities of such schools ...

A law which in operation may indirectly enable a church to further the practice of religion is a long way away from a law to establish religion as that language properly understood would require it to be if the law were to be in breach of s 116.

Gibbs J

The primary argument submitted for the plaintiffs is that the relevant words of s 116 – "the establishment clause" – prohibit the Commonwealth from making any law which provides any recognition, aid or support (financial or otherwise) to one or more religions or to religion generally, and that the legislation in question provides financial assistance to the religions which conduct, or are closely associated with, the schools that receive the moneys. Alternatively it was submitted that s 116 should be construed as prohibiting the giving of recognition, aid or support to one or more religions in preference to other religions, and that the legislation is invalid within that test, because it does not prohibit the Minister from giving preference to some non-government schools over others on account of their religious affiliation, and because in the nature of things some religions must benefit more than others from the assistance provided under the Acts, because more schools are conducted by, or associated with, some denominations than by others. A further alternative submission was that the legislation, and in particular the *Schools Commission Act 1973*, requires the Commonwealth to be excessively involved in religion and that that is a contravention of s 116.

Whether any of these arguments can succeed depends in the first place on the proper meaning of the expression "establishing any religion" in s 116 ... The natural meaning of the phrase "establish any religion" is, as it was in 1900, to constitute a particular religion or religious body as a state religion or state church ...

It is strongly argued on behalf of the plaintiffs that since s 116 was closely modelled on part of the First Amendment to the Constitution of the United States it must be taken to have been intended to have the same meaning as that which had been attributed to the First Amendment in the United States before 1900 when the Constitution was enacted, and further that the United States decisions since that date provide a useful guide to the meaning of the section. In deference to this argument I shall turn to some of the American authorities, but it is necessary to notice that there are a number of differences between s 116 and the First Amendment to the American Constitution. The First Amendment is in the following terms:

"Congress shall make no law respecting an establishment of religion, or prohibiting the free exercise thereof; or abridging the freedom of speech, or of the press; or the right of the people peaceably to assemble, and to petition the Government for a redress of grievances."

More importantly, the words of s 116 did not reproduce verbatim those of the First Amendment. The latter speaks of a law "respecting an establishment of religion" and those words appear wider than those of s 116 which refer to "any law for establishing any religion" – words which look to the purpose of the law rather than to its relationship with a particular subject matter, and which suggest that it is the establishment of one particular religion rather than of religion generally that is proscribed ...

It was submitted on behalf of the plaintiffs that the words of s 116 should be given as broad and liberal a construction as possible ... There is no reason to give such a provision a liberal interpretation ...

I consider that the words "The Commonwealth shall not make any law for establishing any religion", where they appear in s 116, mean that the Commonwealth Parliament shall not make any law for conferring on a particular religion or religious body the position of a state (or national) religion or church.

It may be a question of degree whether a law is one for establishing a religion. However, on no view of the evidence in the present case can it be said that any of the laws in question infringes s 116, if that section is given the meaning which I have attributed to it ...

However, it is impossible to say, on any view of the statutory provisions in question or of the evidence in the case, that the challenged legislation has the purpose or effect of setting up any religion or religious body as a state religion or a state church, even for limited purposes only. None of the laws in question is a law for establishing religion within s 116.

Stephen J

What it is which constitutes "establishing any religion" has, of course, been central to the debate in this case. The plaintiffs say that "establishing" in s 116 includes the provision by the Commonwealth of funds to schools associated with churches. The predominant view of the various defendants and intervenors is, I think, that "establishing" means the constituting of a religion as an officially recognized State religion ...

It is that meaning which the Shorter Oxford English Dictionary alone gives to it when specifically related to religion, namely "to place (a church or a religious body) in the position of a state church". This I have no doubt is the meaning of the verb "establish" and of its present participle according to common usage when used with reference to a church or religion ...

Mason J

I agree with Wilson J that the first clause in the section forbids the establishment or recognition of a religion (and by this term I would include a branch of a religion or church) as a national institution. Quick and Garran in *Annotated Constitution of the Australian Commonwealth* say of s 116 (p 951): "by the establishment of religion is meant the erection and recognition of a State Church, or the concession of special favours, titles, and advantages to one church which are denied to others." With one qualification, I agree with this statement. The qualification is that to constitute "establishment" of a "religion" the concession to one church of favours, titles and advantages must be of so special a kind that it enables us to say that by virtue of the concession the religion has become established as a national institution, as, for example, by becoming the official religion of the State ...

[T]he principal obstacle to an acceptance of the plaintiffs' argument lies in the words "any law for establishing any religion". It is altogether too much to say that a law which gives financial aid to churches generally, to be expended on education, is a law for establishing religion. The mere provision of financial aid to churches generally, more particularly when that aid is genuinely linked to expenditure on education, falls short of "establishing" a "religion" as we understand the expression. By it we mean the authoritative establishment or recognition by the State of a religion or a church as a national institution ...

Wilson J

I infer a legislative intent to adopt a narrow notion of establishment, namely, that which requires statutory recognition of a religion as a national institution. The precise status, responsibility and privileges that attend such establishment may vary a good deal, and it is not necessary to consider its features in detail; the point to be made is that establishment involves the deliberate selection of one to be preferred from among others, resulting in a reciprocal relationship between church and state which confers and imposes rights and duties upon both parties ...

It identifies a relationship which goes much deeper than financial assistance, whether casual or regular, from time to time, because it is expressive of a duty to maintain and support, or, in other words, a duty to "promote religion" as embodied in the doctrine and standards of the Church ...

On the reasoning of the majority, a federal law providing that a particular religion is the official religion of one or more Territories would not breach section 116. It is not clear why such law would not answer the description of a law 'for establishing any religion' simply because the law establishes only a sub-national religion. The United Kingdom has examples of sub-national established religions. The Church of England, sometimes referred to in legislation as 'the Church of England as by law established', is a sub-national established church in the United Kingdom. The Church of England is established only in England; it was never the official church in Scotland (where the Church of Scotland, which practises Presbyterianism, has official status) and it was disestablished in Wales and Northern Ireland by statute.

Justice Murphy dissented, holding that the establishment clause prohibits federal laws providing any support of religion.

Attorney-General (Vic) ex rel Black v Commonwealth ('DOGS Case') (1981) 146 CLR 559

Murphy J (dissenting)

Three meanings of "establishing" in s 116 have been advanced. The first and narrowest means establishing one national church or religion. The second ("preferential") means preferring, by sponsorship or support, any religion over others (and therefore includes the first). The third ("separation") means any sponsorship or support of religion (and therefore embraces the first two). These meanings are therefore not mutually exclusive. The separation interpretation of the clause means that it forbids not only a national church, and any preference to one religion over others, but also sponsorship or support (including financial support) of any religion. The ordinary principle that constitutional provisions should be read not narrowly, but "with all the generality which the words admit", strongly supports the adoption of the more general reading, that is, the separation interpretation ...

To read s 116 as prohibiting only laws for establishing one religion or church, but permitting laws for establishing a number of religions or churches is inconsistent with the comprehensive terms of the prohibition. There is no warrant for reading "any religion" as "any one religion"; yet this is necessary if "establishing" refers only to the recognition or setting up of one national church or religion. Such a reading trivializes the section. It would allow laws for sponsoring and supporting (financially and otherwise) a number of religions (even in the most discriminatory and preferential way) as long as the laws stopped short of setting up one national church or religion. The same objection applies to the adoption of the "preferential" interpretation. It requires that the prohibition against laws for establishing "any" religion be read down so that "any" means "only one or some", instead of "every", or "all". This distorts the meaning of the section. It would forbid preference such as financial assistance to any one religion over others (and presumably to some but not all) but would permit such preference or assistance to all religions over no religion. If a law for financial support for one or more religions but not all (that is, a preferential or discriminatory law) violates the prohibition against "any law for establishing any religion", it follows irresistibly that a law for financial support for all religions also violates the prohibition. There is not the slightest hint in the words used in the establishment clause that it forbids only discriminatory or preferential laws. The preferential interpretation would convert the clause into one permitting laws for establishing all religions. This would make a farce of the section and would deny that s 116 is a guarantee of freedom from religion as well as of religion. This reading is repelled by the emphatic use of "any" ...

The argument that the aid to church schools is only of minor assistance to the religious aspect of the schools and its major impact is to aid the secular aspects is no answer to the plaintiffs' challenge ...

The fact is that under the Commonwealth laws vast sums of money are being expended for the support of church schools. The result of the capital grants Acts is that great and increasing sums are being given to churches to acquire property, which can then lawfully be used for religious purposes apart altogether from schooling ...

The effect of the Grants Acts is that the wealth of the churches is increased annually by many millions of dollars of taxpayers' moneys. They have the effect of establishing religion. As Douglas J observed "In common understanding there is no surer way of 'establishing' an institution than by financing it" (*Wheeler v Barrera* (1974) 417 US 402, at p 430) ...

The ongoing authority of the definitions given in the ***DOGS Case*** is open to doubt. The New South Wales Court of Appeal pointed out in ***Hoxton Park*** that the *DOGS Case* was decided when the rules about constitutional interpretation were different to what they are now. The Court of Appeal noted two important changes in the High Court's approach to constitutional interpretation. First, the High Court now adopts the approach that constitutional provisions should not be given narrow or restrictive interpretations. Secondly, the High Court now permits reference to the Convention Debates in interpreting constitutional provisions.

Hoxton Park Residents Action Group Inc v Liverpool City Council (No 2) (2011) 256 FLR 156

A single judge of the New South Wales Supreme Court struck out proceedings arguing federal laws under which public funding was provided to a particular religious school, allegedly for both educational and religious purposes, breached the establishment clause. The single judge held that the case had no prospects of success given the decision in the DOGS Case. *The Court of Appeal overturned the strike-out decision.*

Basten JA (Allsop P and Beazley JA agreeing)

The question, not in terms identified by the primary judge, was whether the applicants could present a tenable argument for distinguishing current authorities on s 116, or suggesting that a supportable approach to Constitutional interpretation might achieve a different result in the present case ...

While it may be accepted that the term "establishing" in s 116 was given a restrictive meaning, which would not cover the grant of financial aid directly to churches for religious purposes, unless the purpose was to set up the religion "as an institution of the Commonwealth" - Barwick CJ at 583 - other members of the Court expressed the concept differently, though to similar effect ...

There are other issues which may warrant permitting the applicants to proceed with their claim. For example, there are differences in approach in *Black* as to the legitimacy of reference to convention debates and United States cases dealing with the First Amendment to the US Constitution ...

While, in respect of the establishment limb of s 116, the applicants must confront the approach adopted in *Black*, there are two factors (at least) which would permit a contrary approach to be presented. First, as pleaded, the applicants' case alleges direct funding of a religious institution for religious purposes, a matter which was not in issue in *Black*. Secondly, developments in constitutional law since *Black* was decided in 1981 may allow submissions to be made supporting a more flexible approach to the constraints on legislative power expressly identified in s 116 ...

When the substantive matter came again to the New South Wales Court of Appeal some years later, the plaintiffs were unsuccessful. The Court of Appeal considered itself bound by the rules of precedent to follow the ***DOGS Case***. The Court of Appeal also had no real opportunity to reconsider the reasoning in the *DOGS Case* because the plaintiffs failed to advance any substantive arguments based on the Convention Debates.

Hoxton Park Residents Action Group Inc v Liverpool City Council (2016) 310 FLR 193

Beazley P (MacFarlan JA agreeing)

The appellants contended that notwithstanding the view of Barwick CJ in *Ex rel Black*, at 578 that it was not appropriate to seek to construe the provisions of the Constitution by reference to the constitutional debates, the High Court has subsequently altered its view on the appropriateness of recourse to the constitutional debates: see, for example, *Cole v Whitfield* at 385–392.

Accepting that to be so, the appellants did not refer the Court to any aspect of the Convention debates that was relevant to the construction of s 116 or to the present case. In my view, it is inappropriate for the Court to embark upon an examination of the debates without being directed to specific aspects of the debates and without any adequate submission explaining the import of the debates to the issue ...

There is no reference whatsoever in the terms of the *Australian Education Act* and the Regulation to religion in general or any particular religion. There is no reference to the promotion of a religion, to the teaching of a religion, or to the recognition of a religion. Importantly, there is no provision directed, intended or designed to set up the Islamic religion "as an institution of the Commonwealth" per Barwick CJ at 582–583; "setting up ... a national church" or "favouring ... one church over another" per Stephen J at 610; or recognising a church "as a national institution" per Mason J at 616. There is no "reciprocal relationship" between the Commonwealth and the Islamic religion: per Wilson J at 653.

Rather, the impugned Acts provide for the expenditure of Commonwealth funds for educational purposes, including by provision to schools that require of their students the observance of religious practices whilst those children are at school. This does not serve to create a reciprocal relationship with the Commonwealth. Indeed, *Ex rel Black* is authority that the Commonwealth may provide support, including financial support, to such entities. To explicate upon the matter further would simply be to reiterate in my own words the various statements made by the High Court to the effect that such payments are permissible in the sense of not being contrary to the first limb of s 116. Having set out the relevant passages above, it is not necessary to do so.

Finally, there is no basis upon which to distinguish *Ex rel Black* on the basis that there had been no submission in that case that the effect of the funding was to establish a particular religion as distinct from a particular denomination in Australia. This submission was not supported by any ground of appeal. Ground 6 of the appeal was confined to a contention that the primary judge erred in his interpretation and application of *Ex rel Black*. Nonetheless, I would reject the argument.

As I have already explained, the question in *Ex rel Black* was whether the impugned legislation, which made provision for the funding of non-government schools, infringed s 116. That is the same issue that arises in this case, although challenged through the prism of a school that practices, or observes the Islamic faith. There is no relevant point of distinction between the issue in this case as compared to *Ex rel Black*.

Basten JA

Thus the concept of establishment accepted in *Black* involves the preferential treatment, arguably to the extent of creating a "state religion" directed to one particular religion or denomination or division, to the exclusion of others. By contrast, the regime established under the *Australian Education Act* (and its predecessors) is neutral and non-discriminatory as between secular and other religious institutions and as between different faiths. The appellants' submission cannot succeed without departing from this aspect of *Black*, a course which is not open to this Court ...

A broader definition of 'establishing any religion' would not necessarily mean that the laws at issue in the ***DOGS Case*** or in **Hoxton Park** would be found unconstitutional. Nor would a broader definition of 'establishing any religion' necessarily mean that Murphy J's dissenting position in the *DOGS Case* would be the correct interpretation.

11.4 The religious observances clause

The second clause of section 116 provides: 'The Commonwealth shall not make any law ... for imposing any religious observance'. The High Court has never decided a case based on the religious observances clause.

Justice Murphy's dissenting judgment in ***R v Winneke; Ex parte Gallagher*** held that a law requiring a person to take an oath before giving evidence before a Royal Commission was a law for imposing a religious observance. Justice Murphy held that an oath is a religious observance and that the fact an oath was *required* of witnesses involved an imposition. The section 116 issue did not arise for the majority judges.

R v Winneke; Ex parte Gallagher (1982) 152 CLR 211

Murphy J (dissenting)

An oath is a religious observance, "A solemn appeal to God (or to something sacred) in witness that a statement is true, or a promise binding" (Shorter Oxford English Dictionary). In Australia, there is now a great variety of old and new religions and a considerable number of persons who profess no religion. At common law, witnesses are required to take that form of oath which binds their conscience in their religious belief (see *Omychund v Barker* (1744) 1 Atk 22, at pp 29, 45; *Atcheson v Everitt* (1775) 1 Cowp 382; *Miller v Salomons* (1852) 7 Exch 475) no matter how bizarre it may appear to non-believers. The form is not confined to words; it includes other rituals such as kissing of books or other objects, tying ropes around the body, snuffing out candles, smashing saucers and even the killing of cocks. (See Bolan and Sayer, *Oaths and Affirmations*, 2nd ed (1961); *Wigmore on Evidence*, 3rd ed (1940), vol 6) (at p227) ...

[T]he provisions of the *Royal Commissions Act*. Any of the Commissioners may administer an oath to any person appearing as a witness before the Commission and may examine the witness upon oath: s 3. Where any witness to be examined before the Commission conscientiously objects to take an oath, he may make an affirmation that he conscientiously objects to take an oath, and that he will state the truth, the whole truth, and nothing but the truth to all questions that may be asked him: s 4(1). Every person who refuses to be sworn or to make an affirmation is guilty of an offence: s 6.

The *Constitution*, s 116 provides, "The Commonwealth shall not make any law for establishing any religion, or for imposing any religious observance, or for prohibiting the free exercise of any religion ..." It is a broad guarantee that the Commonwealth shall not make any law impairing freedom of religion or freedom from religion. (See Latham CJ in *Adelaide Company of Jehovah's Witnesses Inc v Commonwealth* (1943) 67 CLR 116, at p 123; also *Attorney-General (Vic) v Commonwealth* (1981) 146 CLR 559). As a law of the Commonwealth, the *Royal Commissions Act* must comply with s 116 of the *Constitution*. It does not. Its provisions which deal with oath-taking infringe the constitutional prohibition. The mandate against laws imposing any religious observance protects believers as well as non-believers; it may be a more serious interference with the freedom of religion to impose a religious observance on believers than on non-believers.

No law of the Commonwealth may compel a person to take an oath, whether his objections are conscientious or not. Whatever his reason, or even if he has no reason for declining to take an oath, he cannot constitutionally be required to do so. The provision in s 4 of the *Royal Commissions Act* which relieves a person from taking an oath if he conscientiously objects and makes an affirmation that he conscientiously objects therefore does not avoid the constitutional prohibition. It extends only to conscientious objection. Further, it requires the person (as a condition of being relieved from taking an oath) to affirm that he conscientiously objects. This interferes with the free exercise of religion. Consistently with s 116 no one can be required by any law of the Commonwealth to state or explain his reasons for declining to take an oath; his religious beliefs or lack of belief cannot be examined and he cannot be called upon to state, explain or justify them, as conscientious or otherwise. In short, s 116 guarantees that a person cannot be required by or under any law of the Commonwealth to take an oath or to state that he conscientiously objects to taking an oath. A witness before a Royal Commission under the Act may lawfully decline to take an oath and lawfully decline to state why he declines to take an oath ...

In ***Hoxton Park***, the New South Wales Court of Appeal rejected an argument that federal laws providing public funding to a religious school that required its students to participate in various religious observances were laws for imposing religious observances.

It was accepted that the school required its students to participate in religious observances. The Court of Appeal held that since the federal laws simply provided public funding to non-government schools, including religious non-government schools, there was no basis to characterise that legislation as a law for imposing any religious observance.

Hoxton Park Residents Action Group Inc v Liverpool City Council (2016) 310 FLR 193

Beazley P (MacFarlan JA agreeing)

That pupils at the School are required to comply with certain religious observances may be accepted. However, as the primary judge correctly observed, at [67]:

> Neither Act has the purpose or effect of requiring any person to attend the School or its Hoxton Park campus or to engage in any religious observance or practice

Nor, as the primary judge also correctly noted, at [68]:

> ... has any of the funding provided ... had the purpose or effect of requiring any person to attend the School or its Hoxton Park campus or to engage in any religious observance or practice.

There is no basis for either Act to be characterised as a law for imposing religious observance. Each Act made provision for Commonwealth funding of education, by means of state-mediated grants, subject to certain safeguards and requirements. Funding under the Acts was not limited to religious schools. Even in allowing for the funding of religious schools, the purpose of the Acts, both in their objects and in their specific provisions, was the funding of education and not the imposition of any religious observances incidental to the religious character of a recipient school ...

In ***Eagleton v Eagleton***, the Family Court held that any legislation empowering a court or other body to compel a person to participate in a religious practice would be a law for imposing a religious observance contrary to section 116. For that reason, the Family Court held that its governing statute did not grant it power to order the mother of children to do all things necessary to facilitate the children's baptism in the religion shared by the mother and father.

Eagleton v Eagleton [2018] FamCA 623

McClelland J

The father seeks further orders for the children to be baptised in his faith. The father states at paragraph 51 of his Affidavit that the parties had spoken in the past of their intention to baptise the children. The father says that he practices his faith and that the mother is of the same faith, but not practising ...

The father contended that the orders sought by him should be made on the basis that there is no dispute between the parties that the children should be baptised into, and bought up in, his faith. The mother did not challenge the father' contention regarding the children's religious upbringing, but maintained that she did not wish for the children to be baptised at this time, given the current level of disputation between the parties and the less than pleasant environment that would likely exist at such a baptism, on what would, otherwise, be a day of celebration ...

I note there is doubt as to whether the Court has power to make such an order ... That prohibition on the Parliament of Australia enacting any legislation that would impose religious observance necessarily applies to enacting legislation that would empower any other body, including a court or tribunal, to make an order imposing religious observance ...

It is common for the Court to make orders giving one parent responsibility to make decisions in relation to a child's religion. The father's application is not, however, for such an order. The father's application seeks an order in the nature of a mandatory injunction, requiring the mother to "do all acts and things and sign all documents necessary to facilitate the children's baptism in [his] faith". As such, the proposed order would impose upon the mother an obligation to participate in a religious observance, namely the baptism of the children.

As such, while I have rejected the father's application on the basis of his failure to establish why such an order is in the best interests of the children, it is also my view that the order he seeks is beyond the power of the Court ...

11.5 The free exercise clause

The third clause of section 116 provides: 'The Commonwealth shall not make any law ... for prohibiting the free exercise of any religion'. The High Court has considered only a small number of cases involving the free exercise clause. The High Court has not articulated clear principles for applying the free exercise clause.

The first case to come before the High Court was ***Krygger v Williams***. The impugned legislation required all teenage boys to undertake military training. Krygger, a Jehovah's Witness, said that his religion prohibited the taking of human life and that he therefore could not participate in military training. With very limited reasoning, the High Court held: (1) that undertaking military training did not prevent Krygger practising his religion; and (2) that the free exercise clause is not engaged in cases where a law requires a person to do something prohibited by the person's religion.

Krygger v Williams (1912) 15 CLR 366

Griffith CJ

I will deal first with the suggested constitutional objection. Section 116 of the Constitution provides that "the Commonwealth shall not make any law for ... prohibiting the free exercise of any religion" – that is, prohibiting the practice of religion – the doing of acts which are done in the practise of religion. To require a man to do a thing which has nothing at all to do with religion is not prohibiting him from a free exercise of religion. It may be that a law requiring a man to do an act which his religion forbids would be objectionable on moral grounds, but it does not come within the prohibition of s 116, and the justification for a refusal to obey a law of that kind must be found elsewhere. The constitutional objection entirely fails ...

Barton J

The charge is laid under s 135, for failure to render personal service, without lawful excuse. The first provision to which I wish to refer is s 125, which makes all male inhabitants of Australia, except those who are exempted under the Act, liable to be trained; and the appellant is within clause (b) of that section; being between the ages of 14 and 18 years ...

As to the constitutional objection, the Defence Act is not a law prohibiting the free exercise of the appellant's religion, nor is there any attempt to show anything so absurd as that the appellant could not exercise his religion freely if he did the necessary drill. I think this objection is as thin as anything of the kind that has come before us ...

The idea that the exercise of religion cannot involve abstaining from certain conduct is difficult to accept. On the reasoning of the High Court in *Krygger*, a federal law requiring Jews and Muslims to eat pork (eating pork is prohibited on most interpretations of Judaism and Islam) would not raise any free exercise clause issues.

In the ***Jehovah's Witnesses Case***, the High Court held that the free exercise of religion is not absolute and that only *undue* infringements on freedom of religious exercise are prohibited. The High Court did not articulate any clear test for determining when a burden on the free exercise of religion would be undue. In this case, the High Court held that laws applying during World War II to dissolve subversive associations and confiscate their property, even where those associations were religious, did not infringe section 116 because the laws were directed to the preservation of the community.

Adelaide Company of Jehovah's Witnesses Inc v Commonwealth ('Jehovah's Witnesses Case') (1943) 67 CLR 116

The Adelaide Company of Jehovah's Witnesses Incorporated was found to be a subversive organisation operating to prejudice the war effort during World War II. The legislation challenged in this case authorised the Governor-General to dissolve such organisations and confiscate their property.

Latham CJ

The principal questions which arise in the case are: – Does s 116 prevent the Commonwealth Parliament from legislating to restrain the activities of a body, the existence of which is, in the opinion of the Governor-General, prejudicial to the defence of the Commonwealth or the efficient prosecution of the war, if that body is a religious organization? Is the answer to this question affected by the fact that the subversive activities of such a body are founded upon the religious views of its members? Can such a body be suppressed? ...

The section refers in express terms to the exercise of religion, and therefore it is intended to protect from the operation of any Commonwealth laws acts which are done in the exercise of religion. Thus the section goes far beyond protecting liberty of opinion. It protects also acts done in pursuance of religious belief as part of religion ...

Section 116 does not merely protect the exercise of religion, it protects the free exercise of religion. The word "free" is vague and ambiguous ...

In the Constitution of the United States there is a provision which is very similar to that contained in s 116 of our Constitution. The first amendment of the Constitution of the United States provides that "Congress shall make no law respecting an establishment of religion, or prohibiting the free exercise thereof". In the United States the problems created by this provision have been solved in large measure by holding that the provision for the protection of religion is not an absolute, to be interpreted and applied independently of other provisions of the Constitution ...

[T]he general protection given by the Constitution to the freedom in question leaves it to the court to determine whether a particular measure which in fact limits complete freedom involves an "undue" infringement of that freedom. It is upon this principle that many cases have been decided in the American Courts ...

But the cases which I have cited do show that in 1900 it had been thoroughly established in the United States that the provision preventing the making of any law prohibiting the free exercise of religion was not understood to mean that the criminal law dealing with the conduct of citizens generally was to be subject to exceptions in favour of persons who believed and practised a religion which was inconsistent with the provisions of the law. The result of this approach to the problem has been the development of the principle which has been applied in the later cases, to which I have already referred, according to which it is left to the court to determine whether the freedom of religion has been unduly infringed by some particular legislative provision. This view makes it possible to accord a real measure of practical protection to religion without involving the community in anarchy.

There is, therefore, full legal justification for adopting in Australia an interpretation of s 116 which had, before the enactment of the Commonwealth Constitution, already been given to similar words in the United States. This interpretation leaves it to the court to determine whether a particular law is an undue infringement of religious freedom. It is possible, however, in my opinion, to decide the present case upon a narrower principle which escapes the criticisms to which that interpretation may be open ...

But I think it must be conceded that the protection of any form of liberty as a social right within a society necessarily involves the continued existence of that society as a society. Otherwise the protection of liberty would be meaningless and ineffective. It is consistent with the maintenance of religious liberty for the State to restrain actions and courses of conduct which are inconsistent with the maintenance of civil government or prejudicial to the continued existence of the community. The Constitution protects religion within a community organized under a Constitution, so that the continuance of such protection necessarily assumes the continuance of the community so organized ...

Rich J

As to the relevant part of the prohibitions I cannot believe that the suppression of the plaintiff corporation prohibits the free exercise of any part of the religious faith ascribed by the case stated to the individual corporators ... Any regulations, therefore, which empower the Government to prevent persons or bodies from disseminating subversive principles or doctrines or those prejudicial to the defence of the Commonwealth or the efficient prosecution of the war do not infringe s 116. The peace, good government and order of the Commonwealth may be protected at the same time as the freedom of religion is safeguarded. Freedom of religion is not absolute. It is subject to powers and restrictions of government essential to the preservation of the community. Freedom of religion may not be invoked to cloak and dissemble subversive opinions or practices and operations dangerous to the common weal. Any competition between governmental powers and liberty under the Constitution can be reconciled and made compatible. They co-exist without invasion of their respective spheres of action. Accordingly I consider the Regulations in question do not infringe the section ...

Starke J

The liberty and freedom predicated in s. 116 of the Constitution is liberty and freedom in a community organized under the Constitution. The constitutional provision does not protect unsocial actions or actions subversive of the community itself. Consequently the liberty and freedom of religion guaranteed and protected by the Constitution is subject to limitations which it is the function and the duty of the courts of law to expound. And those limitations are such as are reasonably necessary for the protection of the community and in the interests of social order. Therefore there is no difficulty in affirming that laws or regulations may be lawfully made by the Commonwealth controlling the activities of religious bodies that are seditious, subversive or prejudicial to the defence of the Commonwealth or the efficient prosecution of the war.

The critical question is whether the particular law, as in this case, is reasonably necessary for the protection of the community and in the interests of social order. In my opinion the present Regulations, if they had been within power, would not have transcended those limits ...

McTiernan J

Does the Constitution deprive the Executive in war-time of the power to secure the safety of the Commonwealth against invasion by suppressing a body whose existence is prejudicial to the defence of the Commonwealth and the efficient prosecution of the war? The provisions of s 116 that the Commonwealth shall not make any law for prohibiting the free exercise of any religion must obviously be limited in their legal effect by necessity and accommodated, at least, to the powers with which the Constitution arms the Commonwealth to defend itself against invasion. In my opinion s 116 does not according to its true interpretation extend to the executive action which has been taker to suppress the plaintiff. I agree with the reasons which the Chief Justice has given for denying that the words of s 116, on which the plaintiff relies, create an absolute guarantee of the free exercise of any religion ...

Williams J

The right to the free exercise of religion conferred by the Constitution postulates a continuous right to such freedom in a Commonwealth which will survive the ordeal of war. When, therefore, the safety of the nation is in jeopardy, so that the right to such free exercise can only survive if the enemy is defeated, laws which become necessary to preserve its existence would not be laws for prohibiting the free exercise of religion ... It is impossible, in my opinion, to impute to the framers of the Constitution an intention that the phrase "the free exercise of religion" should confer an absolute right to propagate a belief that the system of government created by the Constitution was of a satanic nature, the functioning of which, in spheres which the common sense of the community generally would regard as entirely secular, was not to be judged on its merits or demerits as worldly legislation, but to be condemned in every instance as an emanation of Satan ...

If the Regulations only conferred such powers as were reasonably required to prevent bodies disseminating principles and doctrines prejudicial to the defence of the Commonwealth during the war, they could not be impeached under s 116, even if they interfered incidentally with activities that some persons in the community considered to be the free exercise of religion, because in its popular sense such principles and doctrines would not be considered to be religion, but subversive activities carried on under the cloak of religion. The attack on the Regulations as an infringement of s 116 therefore fails ...

One possible future direction for free exercise clause case law is the adoption of freedom of political communication-style analysis (see Chapter 12) for determining when a law unduly infringes the free exercise of religion. On that style of analysis, a law that burdens the free exercise of religion will be valid only if it is reasonably appropriate and adapted, or proportionate, to achieving some non-religious purpose. This would be consistent with Gaudron J's comments in the ***Stolen Generations Case.*** Justice Gaudron's judgment in that case suggests that a law will breach the free exercise clause in two circumstances: (1) if the law has a purpose of prohibiting the free exercise of religion; or (2) if the law has a disproportionate effect on the free exercise of religion in the pursuit of a non-religious purpose.

Kruger v Commonwealth ('Stolen Generations Case') (1997) 190 CLR 1

This case concerned legislation authorising the removal of Aboriginal children from their families in the Northern Territory, leading to the creation of what is now called the 'Stolen Generations'. It was argued that removing children from their families had the effect of preventing the children learning and participating in traditional Aboriginal religious practices.

Gaudron J

The use of the word "for" indicates that purpose is the criterion and the sole criterion selected by s 116 for invalidity ...

[I]n the absence of some overriding social or humanitarian need – and none is asserted – it might well be concluded that one purpose of the power conferred by s 16 of the Ordinance was to remove Aboriginal and half-caste children from their communities and, thus, prevent their participation in community practices. And if those practices included religious practices, that purpose necessarily extended to prohibiting the free exercise of religion ...

As with the implied freedom of political communication ..., a law will not be a law for "prohibiting the free exercise of any religion", notwithstanding that, in terms, it does just that or that it operates directly with that consequence, if it is necessary to attain some overriding public purpose or to satisfy some pressing social need. Nor will it have that purpose if it is a law for some specific purpose unconnected with the free exercise of religion and only incidentally affects that freedom. It is not pleaded in the present case either that the Ordinance was necessary for the protection or preservation of Aboriginal people or that its purpose was a purpose unconnected with the free exercise of religion ...

Were the Commonwealth to further amend its Defence to assert that the purpose of protecting and preserving Aboriginal people was unconnected with the purpose of prohibiting the free exercise of religion, a question might arise, if the plea were to be made good, whether the interference with religious freedom, if any, effected by the Ordinance was appropriate and adapted or, which is the same thing, proportionate to the protection and preservation of those people. And as the purpose of a law is to be determined by reference to "the facts with which it deals", that question would necessarily have to be answered by reference to the conditions of the time in which it operated. However, the answer to the question depends on an analysis of the law's operation, not on subjective views and perceptions ...

Whether the Ordinance was invalid on that account is not a matter that can presently be determined ...

11.6 The religious tests clause

The religious tests clause provides: 'no religious test shall be required as a qualification for any office or public trust under the Commonwealth'. The clause is different from the other three clauses of section 116 because it is not connected to the words 'The Commonwealth shall not make any law ...'. The case law on the religious tests clause is not well developed.

Section 116 invalidates religiously discriminatory qualifications for federal offices, whether the discriminatory qualifications are imposed by law or otherwise.

Attorney-General (Vic) ex rel Black v Commonwealth ('DOGS Case') (1981) 146 CLR 559

Stephen J

The first three [clauses of s 116] prohibit the making of laws of particular kinds, laws "for" the doing of certain things. The fourth prohibits the imposition, whether by law or otherwise, of religious tests for the holding of Commonwealth office ...

There have been few cases considering the religious tests clause. In ***Crittenden v Anderson***, a single justice of the High Court held that to disqualify a person from Parliament simply because the person was a Catholic would amount to imposing a religious test for an office under the Commonwealth.

Crittenden v Anderson (High Court of Australia, Fullagar J, 23 August 1950)

Section 44(i) of the **Constitution** *disqualifies a person under any acknowledgment, obedience or allegiance to a foreign power from being a Member of Parliament.*

Fullagar J

I will deal with the first ground stated. It is particularised in the petition as follows:-

The said Gordon Anderson was, at the times of his nomination and election, a professed member of the Roman Catholic Church. As such he, as in the case of all members of that Church in all countries, is under "acknowledgement of Adherence, Obedience or Allegiance to a Foreign Power" – the Papal State. He is therefore incapable of being chosen or of sitting as a Member of the House of Representatives.

... [T]he root of the matter, to my mind, lies in the fact that the petitioner really seeks to revive a point of view which was abandoned in England in 1829, when s 2 of Act 10 Geo IV, c 7, enacted that any person professing the Roman Catholic religion might lawfully sit and vote as a member of either House of Parliament, if in other respects duly qualified.

Section 116 of our own Constitution was, of course, not enacted by men ignorant or unmindful of history, and it is, in my opinion, s 116, and not s 44(i) of our Constitution which is relevant when the right of a member of any religious body to sit in Parliament is challenged on the ground of his religion. Effect could not be given to the petitioner's contention without the imposition of a "religious test". In my opinion, the view put forward by ground 1 of the petition is quite untenable ...

Woodward was another decision of a single justice of the High Court. The case was poorly pleaded. The plaintiffs argued that the Director-General of the Australian Security Intelligence Organisation had imposed a religious test for offices under the Commonwealth by advising Ministers that applicants for public service jobs were security risks by reason of being Scientologists. The plaintiffs should have argued that the Commonwealth had imposed religious tests by refusing to hire them because they were Scientologists. Had the case been pleaded properly, it would have been necessary for the High Court to decide to what extent it is possible to take a person's religion into account in hiring decisions for federal government positions without amounting to imposing a religious test for an office under the Commonwealth.

Church of Scientology Inc v Woodward (High Court of Australia, Aickin J, 9 November 1979)

Aickin J

Paragraph 15 alleges that by causing and permitting ASIO to act as aforesaid the defendant has caused or permitted ASIO to require a religious test as a qualification for an office or public trust of the Commonwealth contrary to s 116 of the Constitution. Particulars under that paragraph state that in making security assessments for the purpose of advising Ministers as to the requirements of security with respect to persons employed or proposed to be employed by the Commonwealth and in communicating such assessments ASIO has characterized the second plaintiff and other members of the first plaintiff as "security risks" by reason of their membership and by reason of their being practising adherents of Scientology religion ...

[T]he allegation, so it was argued for the defendant, is not one that ASIO itself applied a religious test in relation to appointment of its own officers or that the defendant as the Director-General did so. The allegation, as spelt out in the particulars, seems really to be that the Commonwealth itself required a religious test, but that does not particularize the allegation in par 15 itself. The plaintiffs' argument in par 15 appears untenable on its face. The provision of information to a prospective employer cannot be regarded as the imposition of a religious test by the provider of the information ...

The ***School Chaplains Case*** was decided by focusing on the meaning of 'office under the Commonwealth'. The High Court appears to have decided that direct control or direct employment is necessary for an office to be considered 'under the Commonwealth'. In this case, the Commonwealth entered into a contract with a service provider. The contract provided that the service provider could hire only religious people to perform the contracted work. The High Court held that the people hired by the service provider did not hold offices under the Commonwealth.

Williams v Commonwealth (No 1) ('School Chaplains Case') (2012) 248 CLR 156

The Commonwealth entered into a contract with an organisation called Scripture Union Queensland. The Commonwealth would pay SUQ to place a worker in a public school to provide student welfare services. The contract specified the selection criteria that SUQ would use in hiring the worker. The selection criteria included religious criteria. The High Court rejected an argument that a religious test had been required as a qualification for an office under the Commonwealth.

Gummow and Bell JJ

Section 116 of the Constitution states that "no religious test shall be required as a qualification for any office or public trust under the Commonwealth". The plaintiff contends that the "school chaplain" is an "office ... under the Commonwealth" and that the definition of "school chaplain" in the Guidelines imposes a religious test for that office. To qualify as a "school chaplain", a person must be recognised "through formal ordination, commissioning, recognised qualifications or endorsement by a recognised or accepted religious institution or a state/territory government approved chaplaincy service".

However, the plaintiff's case under s 116 fails at the threshold. Questions 2(b) and 4(b) presented by the Special Case should be answered accordingly.

The chaplains engaged by SUQ hold no office under the Commonwealth. The chaplain at the Darling Heights State Primary School is engaged by SUQ to provide services under the control and direction of the school principal. The chaplain does not enter into any contractual or other arrangement with the Commonwealth. That the Commonwealth is a source of funding to SUQ is insufficient to render a chaplain engaged by SUQ the holder of an office under the Commonwealth.

It has been said in this Court that the meaning of "office" turns largely on the context in which it is found, and it may be accepted that, given the significance of the place of s 116 in the Constitution, the term should not be given a restricted meaning when used in that provision. Nevertheless, the phrase "office ... under the Commonwealth" must be read as a whole. If this be done, the force of the term "under" indicates a requirement for a closer connection to the Commonwealth than that presented by the facts of this case ...

The practical effect of the ***School Chaplains Case*** appears to be that the Commonwealth can impose religious tests for jobs, provided the Commonwealth outsources the jobs rather than hires workers directly.

11.7 The role of purpose in section 116 analysis

The current weight of authority indicates that the word 'for' in section 116 means 'for the purpose of'. In other words, the current weight of authority indicates that a law that has the *effect* of establishing a religion, imposing a religious observance, or prohibiting the free exercise of religion will not breach section 116. Only laws that have the *purpose* of doing one of those things will be invalid.

In the ***Jehovah's Witnesses Case***, Latham CJ said that the purpose of an impugned law could be taken into account.

Adelaide Company of Jehovah's Witnesses Incorporated v Commonwealth ('Jehovah's Witnesses Case') (1943) 67 CLR 116

Latham CJ

The word "for" shows that the purpose of the legislation in question may properly be taken into account in determining whether or not it is a law of the prohibited character ...

In later cases, the idea that purpose was a relevant factor was transformed into the proposition that only laws with a prohibited purpose will infringe section 116.

Attorney-General (Vic) ex rel Black v Commonwealth ('DOGS Case') (1981) 146 CLR 559

Barwick CJ

The divergence in language to which I have earlier referred is apparent from the use of the word "respecting" in the American text and the word "for" in s 116. What the former may fairly embrace, quite clearly the latter cannot: and that is so, in my opinion, even without placing critical significance on the purposive nature of the Australian expression and the lack of such an element in the American text.

However, in the interpretation and application of s 116, the establishment of religion must be found to be the object of the making of the law. Further, because the whole expression is "for establishing any religion", the law to satisfy the description must have that objective as its express and, as I think, single purpose ...

Gibbs J

More importantly, the words of s 116 did not reproduce verbatim those of the First Amendment. The latter speaks of a law "respecting an establishment of religion" and those words appear wider than those of s 116 which refer to "any law for establishing any religion" – words which look to the purpose of the law ...

Wilson J

Furthermore, it seems to me that the words "for establishing" are not comparable with the words "respecting an establishment". The former words convey the sense of "in order to establish", and speak quite specifically of the purpose of the law in terms of the end to be achieved ...

Mason J

We speak of any "law for establishing" any religion. The Americans speak of a law "respecting an establishment" of religion. In *Lamshed v Lake* (1958) 99 CLR 132, at p 141, Dixon CJ, when referring to s 122, equated "for" with "with respect to" in its application to the government of the Territory. Here, however, we are dealing, not with a grant of legislative power, but with a prohibition against the exercise of legislative power. In such a context "for" is more limiting than "respecting"; "for" connotes a connexion by way of purpose or result with the subject matter which is not satisfied by the mere circumstance that the law is one which touches or relates to the subject matter. In this respect the first prohibition in s 116 is narrower than its American counterpart ...

Kruger v Commonwealth ('Stolen Generations Case') (1997) 190 CLR 1

Brennan CJ

To attract invalidity under s 116, a law must have the purpose of achieving an object which s 116 forbids. None of the impugned laws has such a purpose ...

Toohey J

The question should therefore be asked: was a purpose of the Ordinance to prohibit the free exercise of the religion of the Aboriginals, to whom the Ordinance was directed? It may well be that an effect of the Ordinance was to impair, even prohibit the spiritual beliefs and practices of the Aboriginal people in the Northern Territory, though this is something that could only be demonstrated by evidence. But I am unable to discern in the language of the Ordinance such a purpose ...

Gaudron J

In *Adelaide Company of Jehovah's Witnesses Inc*, Latham CJ observed in relation to s 116 that "[t]he word 'for' shows that the purpose of the legislation in question may properly be taken into account in determining whether or not it is a law of the prohibited character." In my view, that is not entirely accurate. The use of the word "for" indicates that purpose is the criterion and the sole criterion selected by s 116 for invalidity. Thus, purpose must be taken into account. Further, it is the only matter to be taken into account in determining whether a law infringes s 116 ...

Gummow J

The use of the preposition "for" in the expression in s 116 of the Constitution "for prohibiting the free exercise of any religion" directs attention to the objective or purpose of the law in issue. The question becomes whether the Commonwealth has made a law in order to prohibit the free exercise of any religion, as the end to be achieved. "Purpose" refers not to underlying motive but to the end or object the legislation serves ...

Whether this authority is still good law is not clear. Interpreting the word 'for' to mean 'for the purpose of' rather than 'with respect to', which the High Court accepts is an open interpretation, is clearly inconsistent with the High Court's holding in the ***School Chaplains Case*** that the words of section 116 should not be given restrictive meanings. If a non-restrictive meaning of section 116 is adopted then laws with the effect of establishing a religion, imposing a religious observance, or prohibiting the free exercise of religion would breach section 116.

11.8 DISCUSSION QUESTIONS

1. What are the key characteristics or indicia of a 'religion'?
2. What is the reasoning in ***Krygger***? Is it persuasive?
3. What is the role of purpose in determining whether a federal law breaches section 116?
4. Is the definition of 'establishing any religion' given in the ***DOGS Case*** settled law?
5. Problem question: Mr F and Mr S have been convicted of conspiring to do acts in preparation for, or planning, a terrorist act, contrary to sections 11.5(1) and 101.6(1) of the *Criminal Code* (Cth). The terrorist act in question was detonating a bomb at the Holsworthy army barracks in Sydney. The intention was to advance Islam by violence for the purposes of coercing or influencing the Australian Government by intimidation, or alternatively to intimidate the public or a section of the public. A third man, Mr A, had a role in the conspiracy to seek a fatwa (a religious ruling from Muslim muftis as to whether it was permissible in Islam [halal] or impermissible [haram]) to carry out the proposed terrorist act, and to assist Mr S also to seek a fatwa for the proposed terrorist attack. Fatwas were obtained from (extremist) clerics in Somalia, indicating that the planned attacked was permissible in Islam.

   Mr F and Mr S appeal against their convictions on the ground that the relevant provisions of the *Criminal Code* prohibit the free exercise of their religion. Advise whether that ground of appeal has reasonable prospects of success.

12 IMPLIED FREEDOM OF POLITICAL COMMUNICATION

12.1 Overview

This chapter examines an implied restriction on power: the implied freedom of political communication. The *Australian Constitution* establishes a system of representative and responsible government. The High Court has explained that because freedom of political communication is necessary for such a system to function it follows that laws that impermissibly burden communication about political matters must be invalid.

The High Court has developed a three-stage framework of analysis for assessing the validity of laws challenged for breach of the implied freedom. That framework requires examining whether the law has the effect of burdening political communication, whether the purpose of the law is legitimate, and whether the operation of the law is proportionate. The High Court has been clear that the implied freedom is a restriction on power, rather than an individual right, and that it protects only communication about governmental and political matters rather than freedom of speech more broadly.

Key concepts considered in this chapter include:

- political communication
- burdens on political communication
- legitimate purposes
- compatibility with representative and responsible government
- reasonably appropriate and adapted
- structured proportionality.

12.2 Source of the implied freedom of political communication

The *Australian Constitution* does not protect political communication expressly. However, a number of provisions mandate a system of representative and responsible government in which members of Parliament are freely chosen by the people and the Executive Government is accountable to Parliament.

Australian Constitution

Section 7 The Senate

The Senate shall be composed of senators for each State, directly chosen by the people of the State ...

Section 24 Constitution of House of Representatives

The House of Representatives shall be composed of members directly chosen by the people of the Commonwealth ...

Section 64 Ministers of State

...

After the first general election no Minister of State shall hold office for a longer period than three months unless he is or becomes a senator or a member of the House of Representatives.

Section 128 also vests power to alter the *Constitution* in the people of the Commonwealth: the Constitution cannot be altered except with the approval of the people voting in a referendum.

The High Court first accepted the existence of a constitutional protection of political communication in two cases handed down on the same day: ***Nationwide News v Wills*** and ***Australian Capital Television v Commonwealth***. Those cases explain that an implied freedom of political communication exists because it is necessary for the functioning of the system of representative and responsible government mandated by the *Constitution*. A law that impairs the functioning of the *Constitution* cannot be valid.

Nationwide News Pty Ltd v Wills (1992) 177 CLR 1

Legislation made it an offence to publish material bringing the Industrial Relations Commission into disrepute. The publisher of a newspaper was prosecuted for printing an article that was highly critical of the Industrial Relations Commission. The High Court held that the offence was invalid.

Deane and Toohey JJ

In implementing the doctrine of representative government, the Constitution reserves to the people of the Commonwealth the ultimate power of governmental control. It provides for the exercise of that ultimate power by two electoral processes. The first is the election of the members of the Parliament in which is vested the legislative power of the Commonwealth and which, under the Cabinet system of government which the Constitution assumes ... The second is ... the amendment of the Constitution itself. Under the Constitution, those ultimate powers which the Constitution reserves to the people of the Commonwealth are exercisable by direct vote ...

The people of the Commonwealth would be unable responsibly to discharge and exercise the powers of governmental control which the Constitution reserves to them if each person was an island, unable to communicate with any other person ...

It follows from what has been said above that there is to be discerned in the doctrine of representative government which the Constitution incorporates an implication of freedom of communication of information and opinions about matters relating to the government of the Commonwealth. In so far as the people of the Commonwealth are concerned, that implication of freedom of communication operates at two levels. The first is the level of communication and discussion between the represented and their representatives, that is to say, the level of communication and discussion between the people of the Commonwealth on the one hand and the Parliament and its members and other Commonwealth instrumentalities and institutions on the other ...

The second level at which the implication of freedom of communication and discussion operates is the level of communication between the people of the Commonwealth. Inherent in the Constitution's doctrine of representative government is an implication of the freedom of the people of the Commonwealth to communicate information, opinions and ideas about all aspects of the government of the Commonwealth, including the qualifications, conduct and performance of those entrusted (or who seek to be entrusted) with the exercise of any part of the legislative, executive or judicial powers of government which are ultimately derived from the people themselves ...

Australian Capital Television Pty Ltd v Commonwealth (1992) 177 CLR 106

Legislation prohibited the broadcast of political advertising on television and radio during election campaign periods and required television and radio stations to broadcast political advertising free of charge at certain times. The High Court held that the relevant provisions were invalid.

Mason CJ

Freedom of communication in the sense just discussed is so indispensable to the efficacy of the system of representative government for which the Constitution makes provision that it is necessarily implied in the making of that provision ...

Lange, which has become the leading case on the implied freedom, emphasises that the implication arises from the text and structure of the *Constitution* itself and not from general political or philosophical notions of representative and responsible government. *Lange* also emphasises that the implied freedom is not a personal right.

Lange v Australian Broadcasting Corporation (1997) 189 CLR 520

An episode of the Australian Broadcasting Corporation's* Four Corners *investigative journalism program covered allegations that the Prime Minister of New Zealand, David Lange, was corrupt and had allowed his government to be influenced improperly by big business donors. Lange sued for defamation. The High Court held that the common law, including the common law of defamation, cannot operate counter to constitutional imperatives.

Brennan CJ, Dawson, Toohey, Gaudron, McHugh, Gummow and Kirby JJ

[T]he Constitution gives effect to the institution of "representative government" only to the extent that the text and structure of the Constitution establish it. In other words, to say that the Constitution gives effect to representative government is a shorthand way of saying that the Constitution provides for that form of representative government which is to be found in the relevant sections. Under the Constitution, the relevant question is not, "What is required by representative and responsible government?" It is, "What do the terms and structure of the Constitution prohibit, authorise or require?"

Moreover, although it is true that the requirement of freedom of communication is a consequence of the Constitution's system of representative and responsible government, it is the requirement and not a right of communication that is to be found in the Constitution. Unlike the First Amendment to the United States Constitution, which has been interpreted to confer private rights, our Constitution contains no express right of freedom of communication or expression. Within our legal system, communications are free only to the extent that they are left unburdened by laws that comply with the Constitution.

To the extent that the requirement of freedom of communication is an implication drawn from ss 7, 24, 64, 128 and related sections of the Constitution, the implication can validly extend only so far as is necessary to give effect to these sections. Although some statements in the earlier cases might be thought to suggest otherwise, when they are properly understood, they should be seen as purporting to give effect only to what is inherent in the text and structure of the Constitution ...

The ***Lange*** analysis of the basis for the implied freedom of political communication is settled law as seen, for example, in the joint judgment in ***Unions NSW (No 1)***.

Unions NSW v New South Wales (No 1) (2013) 252 CLR 530

French CJ, Hayne, Crennan, Kiefel and Bell JJ

Lange v Australian Broadcasting Corporation confirmed that the implied freedom of political communication is an indispensable incident of that system of representative government for which the Constitution provides. The Constitution does so by directing that the members of the two Houses of Parliament shall be directly chosen by the people of the Commonwealth and States. Sections 7 and 24 and related sections of the Constitution are therefore to be seen as protecting the freedom of political communication in order that people are able to exercise a free and informed choice as electors ...

12.3 Framework for assessing whether a law infringes the implied freedom

The analytical framework, or test, for assessing whether a law fringes the implied freedom involves three questions. Those questions are:

1. Does the law effectively burden freedom of political communication?
2. Is the purpose of the law legitimate, in the sense that it is compatible with the maintenance of the constitutionally prescribed system of government?
3. Is the law reasonably appropriate and adapted to advance that purpose in a manner compatible with the maintenance of the constitutionally prescribed system of government?

Question 1 is a threshold question, directed to whether a law engages the implied freedom. If the answer to question 1 is 'no', in the sense that the law does not burden freedom of political communication, then the law obviously does not infringe the implied freedom. Questions 2 and 3 are about whether any burden is justified.

Question 2 concerns the purpose of the law and involves what is called 'compatibility testing'. Question 2 is directed to whether the burden has a proper purpose.

Question 3 concerns the operation of the law and involves what is called 'proportionality testing'. Question 3 is directed to whether the operation of the law is reasonable. If the answer to either or both of questions 2 and 3 is 'no', then the law in question infringes the implied freedom of political communication and is invalid.

Where a plaintiff establishes that a law burdens freedom of political communication, the practical onus shifts: the onus is on the relevant government to establish that the burden is justified in the sense of persuading the court that the answer is Yes to both Questions 2 and 3. The answer will not be Yes where the answer is No or where there is insufficient material on which to reach a conclusion either way.

Unions NSW v New South Wales (No 3) [2023] HCA 4

The High Court held that a law imposing a spending limit of $20,000 on third-party campaigners (that is, actors other than candidates and political parties) in State by-elections was invalid. The State chose to offer up no justification for the burden on political communication (because it intended to significantly increase the spending limit), with the result that the High Court held the burden had not been justified and was therefore invalid.

Kiefel CJ, Gageler, Gordon, Gleeson and Jagot JJ

It was also accepted that the polity imposing the burden on political communication bears the persuasive onus of establishing that justification. That is, at least in a practical sense, it is for the State defending the validity of the impugned provisions to justify the burden. The Court must be satisfied of the existence of facts on which the State's justification for the burden depends.

The three-question analytical framework took some years to evolve into its current form. The leading case of ***Lange*** established a two-question framework. That framework was modified in subsequent cases.

Lange v Australian Broadcasting Corporation (1997) 189 CLR 520

Brennan CJ, Dawson, Toohey, Gaudron, McHugh, Gummow and Kirby JJ

When a law of a State or federal Parliament or a Territory legislature is alleged to infringe the requirement of freedom of communication imposed by ss 7, 24, 64 or 128 of the Constitution, two questions must be answered before the validity of the law can be determined. First, does the law effectively burden freedom of communication about government or political matters either in its terms, operation or effect? Second, if the law effectively burdens that freedom, is the law reasonably appropriate and adapted to serve a legitimate end the fulfilment of which is compatible with the maintenance of the constitutionally prescribed system of representative and responsible government and the procedure prescribed by s 128 for submitting a proposed amendment of the Constitution to the informed decision of the people (hereafter collectively "the system of government prescribed by the Constitution"). If the first question is answered "yes" and the second is answered "no", the law is invalid ...

Coleman v Power modified the second ***Lange*** question to emphasise that both the purpose of a law and the manner in which a law operates must be compatible with the constitutionally prescribed system of government.

Coleman v Power (2004) 220 CLR 1

McHugh J

In the two-limb test formulated in *Lange*, the adjectival phrase "compatible with the maintenance of the constitutionally prescribed system of representative and responsible government" does not merely qualify the expression "legitimate end". It qualifies the compound conception of the fulfilment of such an end, and the emphasis of the qualification is on the term "fulfilment" rather than "end". That is to say, it is the manner of achieving the end as much as the end itself that must be compatible with the maintenance of the constitutionally prescribed system of representative and responsible government. Of course, the end itself may be incompatible with the system of representative and responsible government. It will be incompatible, for example, if it is designed to undermine that system.

No doubt the Court would have made the meaning of the second limb in *Lange* clearer if it had used the phrase "in a manner" instead of the phrase "the fulfilment of" in that limb. The second limb would then have read "is the law reasonably appropriate and adapted to serve a legitimate end [in a manner] which is compatible with the maintenance of the constitutionally prescribed system of representative and responsible government?". However, it is clear that the Court did intend the second limb to be read in a way that requires that both the end and the manner of its achievement be compatible with the system of representative and responsible government ...

In ***McCloy***, the High Court split the second modified ***Lange*** question in two, in recognition that it really involves two separate inquiries. This was not intended to change the substance of the legal test. It was merely intended to re-express the required analytical steps in a more methodical way.

McCloy v New South Wales (2015) 257 CLR 178

French CJ, Kiefel, Bell and Keane JJ

As explained in the reasons that follow, the question whether an impugned law infringes the freedom requires application of the following propositions derived from previous decisions of this Court and particularly *Lange v Australian Broadcasting Corporation* and *Coleman v Power*.

A. The freedom under the Australian Constitution is a qualified limitation on legislative power implied in order to ensure that the people of the Commonwealth may "exercise a free and informed choice as electors." It is not an absolute freedom. It may be subject to legislative restrictions serving a legitimate purpose compatible with the system of representative government for which the Constitution provides, where the extent of the burden can be justified as suitable, necessary and adequate, having regard to the purpose of those restrictions.

B. The question whether a law exceeds the implied limitation depends upon the answers to the following questions, reflecting those propounded in *Lange* as modified in *Coleman v Power*.

1. Does the law effectively burden the freedom in its terms, operation or effect?

   If "no", then the law does not exceed the implied limitation and the enquiry as to validity ends.

2. If "yes" to question 1, are the purpose of the law and the means adopted to achieve that purpose legitimate, in the sense that they are compatible with the maintenance of the constitutionally prescribed system of representative government? This question reflects what is referred to in these reasons as "compatibility testing".

   The answer to that question will be in the affirmative if the purpose of the law and the means adopted are identified and are compatible with the constitutionally prescribed system in the sense that they do not adversely impinge upon the functioning of the system of representative government.

   If the answer to question 2 is "no", then the law exceeds the implied limitation and the enquiry as to validity ends.

3. If "yes" to question 2, is the law reasonably appropriate and adapted to advance that legitimate object? This question involves what is referred to in these reasons as "proportionality testing" to determine whether the restriction which the provision imposes on the freedom is justified ...

   If the measure does not meet these criteria of proportionality testing, then the answer to question 3 will be "no" and the measure will exceed the implied limitation on legislative power ...

McCloy expressed questions 2 and 3 in a way that might be taken as suggesting that the second ***Lange*** question, as modified in ***Coleman v Power***, was being modified further rather than being merely re-expressed. There was no such intention. ***Brown*** reformulated questions 2 and 3 to make clear that splitting the second *Lange* question, as modified by *Coleman v Power*, into two questions does not modify the required analysis.

Brown v Tasmania (2017) 261 CLR 328

Kiefel CJ, Bell and Keane JJ

In *Coleman v Power* it was said that the adjectival phrase referred to above does not merely qualify the "legitimate end". It qualifies the compound conception of the fulfilment of such an end. That is to say, the manner of achieving the statute's purpose, as well as the purpose itself, must be compatible with the maintenance of the constitutionally prescribed system of representative and responsible government.

In its submissions in this matter the Commonwealth, intervening, drew attention to the summary version of this requirement of the Lange test which appears at the outset of the joint reasons in *McCloy*. The Commonwealth said that it may be understood to suggest that a conclusion as to whether the means adopted to achieve the statutory object are "reasonably appropriate and adapted" or proportionate to a legitimate end is to be reached at a point before proportionality testing is undertaken. Clearly the statute's purpose must be assessed for compatibility with the constitutionally prescribed system of government at this stage, but in practical terms the means adopted could not be. The point is well made. The commencing words of Questions 2 and 3 stated in *McCloy* should read:

2. If "yes" to question 1, is the purpose of the law legitimate, in the sense that it is compatible with the maintenance of the constitutionally prescribed system of representative and responsible government?
3. If "yes" to question 2, is the law reasonably appropriate and adapted to advance that legitimate object in a manner that is compatible with the maintenance of the constitutionally prescribed system of representative and responsible government? ...

The three-question analytical framework set out in ***Brown*** is a more logical and methodical expression of the two ***Lange*** questions as modified in ***Coleman v Power***. *Brown* does not overrule that earlier reasoning. *Brown* merely expresses the earlier reasoning more clearly.

12.4 Question 1: Burdens on political communication

The first question in the analytical framework concerns whether an impugned law burdens political communication. This question requires an understanding of what is meant by 'political communication' and an understanding of how burdens on political communication are identified.

The concept of political communication

The concept of political communication is broad. The implied freedom protects communications about all matters of public affairs. The implied freedom is not limited only to matters concerning federal politics.

Australian Capital Television Pty Ltd v Commonwealth (1992) 177 CLR 106

Mason CJ

The concept of freedom to communicate with respect to public affairs and political discussion does not lend itself to subdivision. Public affairs and political discussion are indivisible and cannot be subdivided into compartments that correspond with, or relate to, the various tiers of government in Australia. Unlike the legislative powers of the Commonwealth Parliament, there are no limits to the range of matters that may be relevant to debate in the Commonwealth Parliament or to its workings. The consequence is that the implied freedom of communication extends to all matters of public affairs and political discussion, notwithstanding that a particular matter at a given time might appear to have a primary or immediate connection with the affairs of a State, a local authority or a Territory and little or no connection with Commonwealth affairs ...

The implied freedom protects only political communication. It is not a general protection of free speech. The implied freedom does not apply to communications about non-political matters. ***APLA v Legal Services Commissioner*** provides an example. The New South Wales law considered in this case prohibited lawyers advertising their services for personal injury matters. The High Court held that the burden the law imposed on communication was a burden on non-political communication, specifically the marketing of professional services. The result was that the implied freedom of political communication was not engaged.

APLA Ltd v Legal Services Commissioner (NSW) (2005) 224 CLR 322

Gleeson CJ and Heydon J

Restrictions on the advertising of goods and services limit freedom of communication ...

The possibility that an advertisement of the kind prohibited by the regulations might mention some political or governmental issue, or might name some politician, does not mean that the regulations infringe the constitutional requirement. The regulations do not, in their terms, prohibit communications about government or political matters. They prohibit communication between lawyers and people who, by hypothesis, are not their clients, aimed at encouraging the recipients of the communications to engage the services of lawyers. Such communications are an essentially commercial activity. The regulations are not aimed at preventing discussion of, say, "tort law reform", or some other such issue of public policy. They restrict the marketing of professional services ...

How burdens on political communication are identified

The implied freedom of political communication is not a personal right. It is wrong to ask whether a law limits a person's ability to communicate on political matters. The correct inquiry is whether a law limits communication on political matters generally.

Unions NSW (No 1) and ***Brown v Tasmania*** both explain that identifying when a law burdens political communication involves comparing the practical ability of people to engage in political communication *without* the law and the practical ability of people to engage in political communication *with* the law.

Unions NSW v New South Wales (No 1) (2013) 252 CLR 530

French CJ, Hayne, Crennan, Kiefel and Bell JJ

The first question posed by *Lange* is whether s 96D effectively burdens the freedom of political communication either in its terms, operation or effect. It requires consideration as to how the section affects the freedom generally.

In addressing this question, it is important to bear in mind that what the Constitution protects is not a personal right. A legislative prohibition or restriction on the freedom is not to be understood as affecting a person's right or freedom to engage in political communication, but as affecting communication on those subjects more generally. The freedom is to be understood as addressed to legislative power, not rights, and as effecting a restriction on that power. Thus the question is not whether a person is limited in the way that he or she can express himself or herself, although identification of that limiting effect may be necessary to an understanding of the operation of a statutory provision upon the freedom more generally. The central question is: how does the impugned law affect the freedom? ...

Brown v Tasmania (2017) 261 CLR 328

Kiefel CJ, Bell and Keane JJ

Where a statute is said to impermissibly burden the freedom, the first enquiry is whether the statute in fact burdens the freedom. The extent of the burden is a matter which falls to be considered in relation to the assessments required by the second limb of *Lange*. The first enquiry requires consideration as to how the statute affects the freedom generally. It is not answered by reference to the operation of the statute in individual cases, although such evidence may provide useful examples of the statute's practical effect, and therefore of the burden the statute may have on the freedom. This Court has said more than once that the freedom spoken of is not a personal right or freedom. The freedom is better understood as affecting communication on the subjects of politics and government more generally and as effecting a restriction on legislative power which burdens communications on those subjects ...

Gageler J

Whether, and if so how and how intensely, a law effectively burdens freedom of political communication is a qualitative question to be answered by reference to the legal operation and practical effect of the law. The expression "effectively burden[s]" has been recognised to mean "nothing more complicated than that the effect of the law is to prohibit, or put some limitation on, the making or the content of political communications".

The effect of a law on the making or content of political communications is in turn gauged by nothing more complicated than comparing: the practical ability of a person or persons to engage in political communication with the law; and the practical ability of that same person or those same persons to engage in political communication without the law ...

Nettle J

A law is taken to impose an effective burden on the implied freedom of political communication if it at all prohibits or limits political communication, unless perhaps the prohibition or limitation is so slight as to have no real effect. Whether the terms, operation or effect of the Protesters Act so burden the implied freedom is to be assessed by reference to the freedom of political communication generally as opposed to any notion of an individual's right to communicate. Questions of the extent of the burden assume principal significance in relation to the assessment, to be undertaken later in these reasons, of whether the law is appropriate and adapted to its purpose. As Gageler J observed in *McCloy*, however, the first stage of analysis is not perfunctory: the careful identification of the burden upon the implied freedom is the foundation for any posterior analysis of its justification ...

Farm Transparency explains that in practice the burden imposed by a law is best understood as being *incremental* because the challenged law operates in the context of other laws that affect what is possible.

Farm Transparency International Ltd v New South Wales [2022] HCA 23

This case concerned a challenge by animal rights activists, who had filmed an abattoir's operations in an effort to show that existing regulations permitted animal cruelty, to statutory provisions making it unlawful to surreptitiously make a video recording on private premises or to publish such a video.

Kiefel CJ and Keane J

The extent of the burden effected by ss 11 and 12 is not to be assessed by reference to the operation and effect of those provisions alone. The burden effected by the prohibitions in ss 11 and 12 must be assessed by reference to the restraints which the law – understood as the common law, equity, and statute law – already imposes upon a person's ability to publish records of activities obtained surreptitiously and by conduct which amounts to trespass. The relevant burden is the incremental effect of the impugned law on the ability of a person to engage in a communication which the law may already validly restrict. It is that burden which is to be justified.

If a law does burden political communication it is necessary to explain the nature and extent of the burden. It is impossible to answer the third question in the analytical framework without having first identified the nature and extent of the burden.

Example of no burden on political communication

Not every law that might be said to be *about* political communication in some way has the effect of burdening political communication.

Ruddick provides an example of a law that did not impose a burden on political communication. The High Court found that the effect of the law under challenge was to enhance rather than restrict political communication.

Ruddick v Commonwealth [2022] HCA 9

Amendments enacted in 2021 had the effect that a political party must be deregistered or refused registration if its name contains a word (with the exception of words like 'the', 'of' and 'Australian') that is in the name of an earlier registered political party. The principal effect of deregistration or non-registration is that the name of the party cannot appear on ballot papers; the party's candidates may still contest elections; and the party still may engage in political activity. The amendments were a response to voter confusion at a federal election arising from the similarity of the names of the Liberal Party (a major party) and the Liberal Democratic Party (a minor party).

Gordon, Edelman and Gleeson JJ

Mr Ruddick effectively asks this Court to infer that the quality of electoral choice, or the freedom of communication on government or political matters, will be impaired due to the inability of a candidate to have, accompanying their name on the ballot paper, the name and logo of a party which includes a word used in another party's name. That conclusion is not self-evident. Rather, on the material before the Court, the expected conclusion would be the opposite. The likely effect of the narrow restrictions imposed by the 2021 Amendments is, overall, to improve the clarity, and hence the quality, of electoral choice or communication on government or political matters.

...

Apart from the content of the ballot paper, deregistration of the Liberal Democratic Party would not preclude any communication with the public, including communication using the name "Liberal Democratic Party". The only potential restraint on the quality of electoral choice by the public, or on communication on government or political matters to the public, is that, by s 169 of the *Commonwealth Electoral Act*, a candidate for election endorsed by the Liberal Democratic Party, such as Mr Ruddick, would be unable to have that party name printed adjacent to their name on the ballot paper. Yet, as the 2013 election demonstrated, that would have the effect of reducing confusion and thus enhancing the quality of electoral choice by the public.

Even if it were accepted that there was some small constraint upon political communication and the quality of electoral choice by the inability of a candidate endorsed by the Liberal Democratic Party to use the word "liberal" on the ballot paper, the net effect would still be an enhancement of electoral choice and the quality of communication on government or political matters to the public. Contrary to Mr Ruddick's submissions, the Liberal Democratic Party would not be precluded, or impaired in any real way, from using its name to communicate any message of political philosophy.

Examples of burdens on political communication

Laws can burden political communication in many different ways.

Restrictions on the manner or medium of political communication constitute burdens on the implied freedom. The federal law considered in ***ACTV v Commonwealth*** prohibited the broadcast of party political advertising on television and radio during federal election campaigns. The burden on political communication was the practical effect of preventing people from using radio and television as the medium for political communication.

Australian Capital Television Pty Ltd v Commonwealth (1992) 177 CLR 106

Mason CJ

The effect of Pt IIID, especially ss 95B, 95C and 95D, is, as the plaintiffs submit, to exclude the use of radio and television during election periods as a medium of political campaigning and even as a medium for the dissemination of political information, comment and argument and as a forum of discussion except in so far as (a) s 95A permits the broadcasting of news and current affairs items and talkback radio programmes ...

The consequence is that Pt IIID severely impairs the freedoms previously enjoyed by citizens to discuss public and political affairs and to criticize federal institutions. Part IIID impairs those freedoms by restricting the broadcasters' freedom to broadcast and by restricting the access of political parties, groups, candidates and persons generally to express views with respect to public and political affairs on radio and television.

Deane and Toohey JJ

The ban on political communication through the medium of advertising on television or radio must be assessed in the context in which it operates, namely, a context where advertising in general is permitted on commercial radio and television stations. It is in that context that the ban must be seen as a legislative prohibition not of advertising as such but of political communication to and by the people of the Commonwealth through two of the methods by which such communications could otherwise be lawfully made ...

Restrictions on the content of political communications constitute burdens on the implied freedom. In ***Nationwide News***, a federal law made it unlawful to 'use words calculated ... to bring a member of the [Industrial Relations] Commission or the [Industrial Relations] Commission into disrepute'. The law burdened political communication by suppressing criticism of a governmental instrumentality.

Nationwide News Pty Ltd v Wills (1992) 177 CLR 1

Brennan J

By prohibiting justifiable revelations of any corruption or other vice affecting the workings of the Commission and by prohibiting criticisms made fairly and reasonably, para (d)(ii) purports impermissibly to prevent public discussion about an important agency of social regulation. It purports to stifle that free discussion which is essential to expose defects in, and to maintain the integrity of, any institution vested with power to affect the lives of the people living in a representative democracy.

Deane and Toohey J

As has been seen, however, s 299(1)(d)(ii) goes far beyond protecting the Commission and its members from unfounded and illegitimate attack. It purports to forbid, under the sanction of fine and/or imprisonment, the use of words calculated to bring the Commission or a member of the Commission into disrepute regardless of whether what is written or said is well founded and relevant. A prohibition of the communication of well-founded and relevant criticism of a governmental instrumentality or tribunal, such as the Commission or a Commonwealth court, cannot be justified as being, on balance, in the public interest merely because it is calculated to bring the instrumentality or tribunal or its members into disrepute. To the contrary, if criticism of a governmental instrumentality or tribunal or its members is well founded and relevant, its publication is an incident of the ordinary working of representative government and the fact that it will, if published, bring the relevant instrumentality or tribunal into deserved disrepute is, from the point of view of the overall public interest, a factor supporting publication rather than suppression ...

The Queensland law at issue in ***Coleman v Power*** made it an offence to use 'insulting words' in a public place. The law burdened political communication by preventing the use of insults in political communications occurring in public places.

Coleman v Power (2004) 220 CLR 1

Gleeson CJ

It was accepted by the Attorney-General of Queensland that s 7(1)(d) is capable of having a practical operation that, in some circumstances, may burden communication about governmental or political matters, whatever the precise ambit of the concept of governmental or political matters may be. That is true in the sense that threatening, abusive, or insulting words might be used in the course of communicating about any subject, including governmental or political matters ...

McHugh J

Under the Constitution, a law that, without qualification, makes it an offence to utter insulting words in or near a public place cannot validly apply to insulting words that are uttered in the course of making statements concerning political or governmental matters ...

Insults are as much a part of communications concerning political and government matters as is irony, humour or acerbic criticism. Many of the most biting and offensive political insults are as witty as they are insulting ...

Gummow and Hayne JJ

Insult and invective have been employed in political communication at least since the time of Demosthenes ...

Laws that restrict or limit the extent or amount of political communication burden political communication. Two New South Wales laws were considered in ***Unions NSW (No 1)***: one law prohibited the making of donations to political parties or candidates in New South Wales elections unless the donor was an individual entitled to vote; the second law combined electoral spending by political parties and affiliated organisations for the purposes of a statutory limit on the amount of money political parties may spend on election advertising. The first law burdened political communication by reducing the ability of political parties to engage in political advertising by reducing parties' ability to pay for political advertising. The second law burdened political communication by limiting the amount of political advertising in which a political party may engage.

Unions NSW v New South Wales (No 1) (2013) 252 CLR 530

French CJ, Hayne, Crennan, Kiefel and Bell JJ

[T]he question whether s 96D limits the freedom is simply resolved. That section effects a restriction upon the funds available to political parties and candidates to meet the costs of political communication by restricting the source of those funds. The public funding provided by the [Electoral Funding, Expenditure and Disclosures] Act is not equivalent to the amount which may be paid by way of electoral communication expenditure under the Act. It is not suggested that a party or candidate is likely to spend less than the maximum allowed. The party or the candidate will therefore need to fund the gap. It follows that the freedom is effectively burdened. The concession made by the defendant, that there is an indirect burden which is more than inconsequential, is inevitable ...

Section 95G(6) also effects a burden on freedom of political communication in restricting the amount that a political party may incur by way of electoral communication expenditure in a relevant period. It does this by deeming the amount of electoral communication expenditure made by industrial organisations (and other organisations) with which it is affiliated as having been made by that party for the purposes of the applicable cap. The party affected by the provision is the Australian Labor Party (NSW Branch), with which industrial organisations, including the second, third and sixth plaintiffs, are affiliated ...

The two New South Wales laws considered in ***McCloy*** burdened political communication in the same way as the laws considered in ***Unions NSW (No 1)*** – by reducing the ability to pay for, and therefore to engage in, political communication. The first law provided for a cap of $5000 on the value of political donations that a person could make to or for the benefit of a particular political party, elected member, group, candidate, or third-party campaigner. The second law prohibited the making or acceptance, directly or indirectly, of a political donation by property developers. The High Court also held that making a political donation is not itself a form of political communication.

McCloy v New South Wales (2015) 257 CLR 178

French CJ, Kiefel, Bell and Keane JJ

In *Unions NSW*, it was accepted by the parties, and by the Court, that the provisions of the EFED Act effect a burden on the freedom. A restriction on the funds available to political parties and candidates to meet the costs of political communication, which operates by restricting the source of those funds, effectively burdens the freedom because, even with the public funding which is provided for, a party or candidate will have to fund any shortfall. The restrictions imposed by the general capping provisions of Div 2A, and the prohibitions upon political donations from property developers in Div 4A and upon indirect campaign contributions in s 96E, burden the freedom in this sense ...

The plaintiffs contend that the provisions in question have a further effect on the freedom, namely upon the ability of donors to make substantial political donations in order to gain access and make representations to politicians and political parties. They accept, as they must, that the act of donation is not itself a political communication, but they submit that donors are entitled to "build and assert political power" and that this is an aspect of the freedom which has been recognised by this Court. Political influence may be acquired by many means, they say, and paying money to a political party or an elected member is but one ...

[W]hat the plaintiffs identify is something in the nature of a personal right ... The EFED Act is not to be approached by viewing the restrictions it imposes upon the plaintiffs' ability to access politicians as a burden on the freedom. The relevant burden is that identified in *Unions NSW* ...

Laws that restrict or limit the time, manner and place in which political communication may take place burden political communication. ***Brown v Tasmania*** involved a Tasmanian law that prohibited protestors, but not others, from entering onto business premises (defined to include forestry land) and blocking access to business premises. The law also permitted police to remove protestors who police suspected were intending to engage in such activities. The law burdened political communication by effectively preventing on-site protests against forestry activity.

Brown v Tasmania (2017) 261 CLR 328

Kiefel CJ, Bell and Keane JJ

The implied freedom protects the free expression of political opinion, including peaceful protest, which is indispensable to the exercise of political sovereignty by the people of the Commonwealth ...

The first enquiry requires consideration as to how the statute affects the freedom generally. It is not answered by reference to the operation of the statute in individual cases, although such evidence may provide useful examples of the statute's practical effect, and therefore of the burden the statute may have on the freedom. This Court has said more than once that the freedom spoken of is not a personal right or freedom. The freedom is better understood as affecting communication on the subjects of politics and government more generally and as effecting a restriction on legislative power which burdens communications on those subjects.

In any event, Tasmania's argument that, with respect to the facts of the present case, it is not shown that the freedom is effectively burdened should not be accepted. The circumstances relating to the plaintiffs show clearly how the freedom is burdened. Even if the plaintiffs were not on business premises or in a business access area the police officers who arrested and removed them were unable to correctly determine whether they were on those premises or in that area. As a result of their error the plaintiffs' protests and their communications to others about the forest operations were silenced ...

Gageler J

The nature and intensity of the burden imposed on political communication by the impugned provisions of the Protesters Act fall therefore to be considered against a background of historical and continuing public access to permanent timber production zone land, of limited statutory regulation of that public access, and of historical and likely continuing on-site political protests directed to bringing about legislative or regulatory change on environmental issues on Crown land in Tasmania.

The nature of the burden imposed on political communication by the impugned provisions is that the burden can be expected to fall in practice almost exclusively on on-site political protests of that description. Not only are the provisions targeted by the definition of protester to political communication, but they are targeted by the same definition to political communication occurring at particular geographical locations. Given those geographical locations, and given the history of on-site protests in Tasmania, it would be fanciful to think that the impugned provisions are not likely to impact on the chosen method of political communication of those whose advocacy is directed to bringing about legislative or regulatory change on environmental issues and would have little or no impact on political communication by those whose advocacy is directed to other political ends ...

The Queensland law considered in ***Wotton*** prohibited prisoners on parole giving media interviews without permission, which might be granted subject to conditions. The law burdened political communication by restricting the occasions and manner in which a person on parole might engage in political communication.

Wotton v Queensland (2012) 246 CLR 1

French CJ, Gummow, Hayne, Crennan and Bell JJ

The relevant burden imposed by par (a) of s 132(1) is the obligation to seek and obtain under par (d) of s 132(2) the written approval of the chief executive to interview a parolee, such as the plaintiff, outside a corrective services facility. The relevant burden imposed by s 200(2) is the observance of conditions the Parole Board reasonably considers necessary to ensure good conduct of the parolee and to stop the parolee committing an offence ...

12.5 Question 2: Compatibility testing

The second question in the analytical framework concerns whether the purpose of an impugned law is *legitimate*. The second question is directed to whether the law is justified. As the text of the second question indicates, a purpose is legitimate if it is *compatible* with the constitutionally prescribed system of representative and responsible government.

McCloy explains that a purpose is compatible with the constitutionally prescribed system of government if it does not adversely impinge upon the functioning of that system. *McCloy* also holds that the purpose of a law is identified through the process of statutory construction: why was the law enacted and at what mischief is it directed?

The purpose of the particular statutory provision under challenge might not be the same as the purpose of the statute as a whole as expressed in the statute's general objects clause. A particular provision might have a more specific purpose, additional consistent purposes, an unrelated purpose or no purpose at all.

McCloy v New South Wales (2015) 257 CLR 178

French CJ, Kiefel, Bell and Keane JJ

[L]egitimate, in the sense that they are compatible with the maintenance of the constitutionally prescribed system of representative government? This question reflects what is referred to in these reasons as "compatibility testing".

The answer to that question will be in the affirmative if the purpose of the law ... [is] compatible with the constitutionally prescribed system in the sense that [it does] not adversely impinge upon the functioning of the system of representative government ... The process of justification called for by *Lange* commences with the requirement that the purpose of the provisions in question, which is to be identified by a process of construction, must be compatible with the system of representative government for which the Constitution provides. Other legal systems which employ proportionality testing to determine the limits of legislative power to restrict a right or freedom also require, before that testing commences, that there be a legitimate purpose, because only a legitimate purpose can justify a restriction. But what is there spoken of as legitimate is that the purpose is one permitted by the relevant constitution. The test in Lange requires more, both as to what qualifies as legitimate, and as to what must meet this qualification. It requires, at the outset, that consideration be given to the purpose of the legislative provisions and the means adopted to achieve that purpose in order to determine whether the provisions are directed to, or operate to, impinge upon the functionality of the system of representative government. If this is so, no further enquiry is necessary. The result will be constitutional invalidity ...

Justice Hayne's separate judgment agreed with the joint judgment on this definition and gave a series of examples of compatible purposes identified in the decided cases.

McCloy v New South Wales (2015) 257 CLR 178

Hayne J

In *Lange*, the Court said that the object or end to which the impugned law is directed must be "compatible with the maintenance of the constitutionally prescribed system of representative and responsible government or the procedure for submitting a proposed amendment to the Constitution to the informed decision of the people". It follows that to be a "legitimate" object or end, that object or end must be compatible with the constitutional system of representative and responsible government. But what it means to be "legitimate" in this context can and should be identified more precisely. Because freedom of political communication is an indispensable incident of the constitutionally prescribed system of government, an object or end can be compatible with the system only if it is compatible with the freedom. And that is why, in *Lange*, the Court said that the purpose of the law of defamation was not "incompatible with the requirement of freedom of communication imposed by the Constitution".

The object or end pursued by the impugned law need not itself be the maintenance or enhancement of the system of representative and responsible government or of the freedom of political communication. But it must be compatible with them. The Constitution provides only limited guidance on the requirements of the system of government which it establishes. Legitimate ends are not expressly listed in the Constitution as they sometimes are in other jurisdictions. In many cases it will be profitable to examine how the general law operates and has developed over time, not because the general law in any way limits or restrains the exercise of legislative power but because the implied freedom of political communication must be understood and applied having regard to what may be learned from consideration of the general law. In most cases it will be much less useful to examine what is considered legitimate in other jurisdictions with their own constitutional contexts, especially where those legitimate ends are expressly identified.

The decided cases show that the protection of reputation (*Lange v ABC*), the prevention of physical injury (*Levy v Victoria* (1997) 189 CLR 579), the prevention of violence in public places (*Coleman v Power*), the maintenance of a system for the continuing supervision of some sexual offenders who have served their sentences (*Hogan v Hinch* (2011) 243 CLR 506), "community safety and crime prevention through humane containment, supervision and rehabilitation of offenders" (*Wotton v Queensland*), and "the imposition of conditions [a parole board] considers reasonably necessary to ensure good conduct and to stop [a] parolee committing an offence" (*Wotton v Queensland*) are legitimate objects or ends compatible with the maintenance of the constitutionally prescribed system of government. These are no more than examples of legitimate objects or ends that have so far been identified in the cases. The list is not closed ...

The laws at issue in ***McCloy*** had the purposes of preventing corruption and undue influence in government, and preventing the perception of corruption and undue influence in government, both generally and in respect of particular categories of donors. Both purposes were held to be legitimate.

McCloy v New South Wales (2015) 257 CLR 178

French CJ, Kiefel, Bell and Keane JJ

The provisions of Div 2A are most clearly directed to the object stated in s 4A(c), the prevention of "corruption and undue influence in the government of the State". The capping provisions of Div 2A are intended to reduce the risk of corruption by preventing payments of large sums of money by way of political donation. It may be accepted, as the plaintiffs submit, that the EFED Act targets money which may be used for political communication, but this is not inconsistent with a purpose to prevent corruption ...

They are also directed to overcoming perceptions of corruption and undue influence, which may undermine public confidence in government and in the electoral system itself ...

The plaintiffs' submission, that the relevant provisions of the EFED Act have as their true purpose the removal of the ability of persons to make large donations in the pursuit of political influence, would appear to confuse the effect of Div 2A, and other measures employed, with the overall purpose of these provisions ...

Capping of political donations is a measure which has been adopted by many countries with systems of representative government. It is a means that does not impede the system of representative government for which our Constitution provides.

The purpose of Div 2A and the means employed to achieve that purpose are not only compatible with the system of representative government; they preserve and enhance it ...

New South Wales submits that the degree of dependence of property developers on decisions of government about matters such as the zoning of land and development approvals distinguishes them from actors in other sectors of the economy. Property developers are sufficiently distinct to warrant specific regulation in light of the nature of their business activities and the nature of the public powers which they might seek to influence in their self-interest, as history in New South Wales shows ...

The Independent Commission Against Corruption ("ICAC") and other bodies have published eight adverse reports since 1990 concerning land development applications. Given the difficulties associated with uncovering and prosecuting corruption of this kind, the production of eight adverse reports in this time brings to light the reality of the risk of corruption and the loss of public confidence which accompanies the exposure of acts of corruption ...

The purpose of Div 4A is to reduce the risk of undue or corrupt influence in an area relating to planning decisions, where such risk may be greater than in other areas of official decision-making. This purpose furthers the general purpose of Pt 6 of the EFED Act and is "legitimate" within the meaning given to that term in *Lange* ...

Brown v Tasmania explains that protecting businesses and their operations from damage and disruption from protestors is a legitimate purpose.

Brown v Tasmania (2017) 261 CLR 328

Kiefel CJ, Bell and Keane JJ

It is important, however, to be clear about the purpose of the Protesters Act. It is not correctly stated simply as the protection of the interests of business just as it is not the prevention of protests. It is the protection of businesses and their operations, here forest operations, from damage and disruption from protesters who are engaged in particular kinds of protests. This is the mischief to which the statute is directed.

Compatibility

In *McCloy* it was said that the process for the justification of the burden the statute places on the freedom commences with the requirement, stated in *Lange*, that the purpose of the provisions in question be "compatible with the maintenance of the constitutionally prescribed system of representative and responsible government". Clearly enough, the purpose of the Protesters Act, understood in the way described above, could not be said to be incompatible with the freedom ...

Coleman v Power explains that preventing the use of insults in political discourse is not a legitimate purpose.

Coleman v Power (2004) 220 CLR 1

McHugh J

[I]nsults are a legitimate part of the political discussion protected by the Constitution. An unqualified prohibition on their use cannot be justified as compatible with the constitutional freedom. Such a prohibition goes beyond anything that could be regarded as reasonably appropriate and adapted to maintaining the system of representative government.

The second justification for upholding the conviction of the appellant under s 7(1)(d) must also be rejected ...

It is not always easy to identify the purpose of a law. In ***Monis v The Queen***, the High Court was evenly divided as to what purpose was served by a law making it an offence to use the postal service in a manner that reasonable persons would regard as menacing, harassing or offensive. Three judges – French CJ, Hayne and Heydon JJ – held that the purpose of the law was merely to prevent offensiveness and that this purpose was not compatible with the constitutionally prescribed system of representative government. Three judges – Crennan, Kiefel and Bell JJ – held that the purpose of the law was the prevention of intrusions into a person's private life causing serious offence of a kind causing significant emotional reactions or psychological responses and that this purpose was compatible.

Monis v The Queen (2013) 249 CLR 92

The appeal in this case was dismissed pursuant to section 23(2)(a) of the* Judiciary Act 1903 *(Cth) governing cases where the High Court is evenly divided.

French CJ

Section 471.12 having been found to impose an effective burden upon the implied freedom of political communication, the question arises what if any legitimate end it serves. The legitimate ends enunciated in the Court of Criminal Appeal and by the respondents and interveners were various. They included the protection of persons from being subjected to offensive material, the promotion and protection of postal and similar services that bring material into homes and offices, the regulation of postal services, the protection of the integrity of such services and the protection of those who participate in the constitutionally mandated system of government.

Having regard to the scope of the term "offensive" as properly construed and the range of the "postal or similar services" to which s 471.12 applies, it is not possible to define its purpose by reference to common characteristics of such services. In practical terms it is difficult, if not impossible, to distinguish the purpose of s 471.12 from that of a law which makes it an offence to send or deliver offensive communications to anyone by any means. References to the promotion or protection of postal and similar services, the integrity of the post and public confidence in the post do not define in any meaningful way a legitimate end served by s 471.12. Its purpose is properly described as the prevention of the conduct which it prohibits. That is the prevention of uses of postal or similar services which reasonable persons would regard as being, in all the circumstances, offensive. That should not be regarded as a legitimate end not least because, as explained below, its very breadth is incompatible with its implementation in a way that is consistent with the maintenance of that freedom of communication which is a necessary incident of the system of representative government prescribed by the Constitution.

The second question going to the validity of s 471.12 has two limbs. The first is whether the section serves a legitimate end. The second is whether, if so, it serves that end in a manner which is compatible with the maintenance of the constitutionally prescribed system of representative government and the procedure prescribed by s 128 of the Constitution for submitting a proposed amendment to the Constitution to the informed decision of the people. In this case those two limbs collapse into one. The purpose of the prohibition imposed by s 471.12 is as broad as its application. On its proper construction it cannot be applied in such a way as to meet the compatibility requirement. As explained above, the reasonable persons test, even when applied to a high threshold definition of what is "offensive", does not prevent the application of the prohibition to communications on government or political matters in a range of circumstances the limits of which are not able to be defined with any precision and which cannot be limited to the outer fringes of political discussion. Section 471.12, in its application to the offensive content of communications made using postal or similar services, is invalid.

Crennan, Kiefel and Bell JJ

No conclusion can be reached regarding the construction of that part of s 471.12 which concerns offensive communications without identifying its purpose. The identification of that purpose is essential for the application of the Lange test. In the context of offence provisions, the question of purpose is rarely answered by reference only to the words of the provision, which commonly provide the elements of the offence and no more. It may be necessary to consider the context of the provision including other provisions in the statute and the historical background to the provision. Further, in the case of many crimes, the social objective of the legislation can be self-evident, and, in these appeals, may readily be inferred in respect of s 471.12 ...

The protective purpose of s 471.12 is directed to the misuse of postal services to effect an intrusion of seriously offensive material into a person's home or workplace ...

A purpose of protecting citizens from such intrusion is not incompatible with the maintenance of the constitutionally prescribed system of government or the implied freedom which supports it ...

Some laws may serve no particular purpose. ***Unions NSW (No 1)*** provides an example of laws that serve no particular purpose at all, and which therefore necessarily fail the second question in the framework of analysis. The impugned provisions considered in this case were held to not to contribute to the legitimate overall anti-corruption purposes served by the legislation in which they were located. The High Court held that the provisions served no purpose and were therefore invalid.

Unions NSW v New South Wales (No 1) (2013) 252 CLR 530

French CJ, Hayne, Crennan, Kiefel and Bell JJ

The plaintiffs accept that it is the legitimate aim of the EFED Act to regulate the acceptance and use of political donations in order to address the possibility of undue or corrupt influence being exerted. However, it is the plaintiffs' submission that s 96D does nothing calculated to promote the achievement of those legitimate purposes. There is no purpose to the prohibition, other than its achievement. It is therefore simply a burden on the freedom without a justifying purpose. These submissions should be accepted.

The terms of s 96D do not reveal any purpose other than that political donations may not be accepted from persons who are not enrolled as electors, or from corporations or other entities. The context of the other provisions of Pt 6 does not illuminate the purpose of s 96D, rather they point up its absence of evident purpose and lack of connection to the scheme of Pt 6.

In contrast to the general, practical provisions for capping of political donations and electoral communication expenditure, s 96D is selective in its prohibition. Yet the basis for the selection was not identified and is not apparent. By contrast, the connection of the other provisions of Pt 6 to the general purposes of the EFED Act is evident. They seek to remove the need for, and the ability to make, large-scale donations to a party or candidate. It is large-scale donations which are most likely to effect influence, or be used to bring pressure to bear, upon a recipient. These provisions, together with the requirements of public scrutiny, are obviously directed to the mischief of possible corruption. The same cannot be said of s 96D, in its wide-ranging prohibition on the sources of donations ...

It is not evident, even by a process approaching speculation, what s 96D seeks to achieve by effectively preventing all persons not enrolled as electors, and all corporations and other entities, from making political donations. It might be assumed that many of them will have a legitimate interest in political matters, as discussed earlier in these reasons. Why then was it considered necessary to prohibit donations from these sources, but not from electors? More importantly, how does it further the anti-corruption purposes of the EFED Act? ...

The result is that the purpose of its wide, but incomplete, prohibition is inexplicable. In the result, further consideration of the application of the second limb of the Lange test to s 96D is forestalled. It cannot be undertaken because it is not possible to attribute a purpose to s 96D that is connected to, and in furtherance of, the anti-corruption purposes of the EFED Act. The second limb of the Lange test cannot be satisfied. The burden imposed by s 96D on the freedom cannot be justified. Section 96D is invalid ...

It may be inferred that it is the purpose of s 95G(6) to reduce the amount which a political party affiliated with industrial organisations may incur by way of electoral communication expenditure and likewise to limit the amount which may be spent by an affiliated industrial organisation. What cannot be deduced is how this purpose is connected to the wider anti-corruption purposes of the EFED Act, or how those legitimate purposes are furthered by the operation and effect of s 95G(6). Industrial organisations are identified in the EFED Act as potential donors to political parties or candidates, and as likely to themselves expend monies on political communication. They are not identified as prohibited donors and the defendant did not seek to justify s 95G(6) and the targeting of industrial organisations and the parties with whom they are affiliated by analogy with the provisions of Div 4A. There is therefore nothing in the provision to connect it to the general anti-corruption purposes of the EFED Act.

Absent a legislative purpose for s 95G(6) which is conformable with those of the EFED Act, no further consideration can be given as to whether the provision is justified. The provision is invalid ...

12.6 Question 3: Proportionality testing

The third question in the analytical framework asks whether the law is reasonably appropriate and adapted to advance its purpose in a manner compatible with the maintenance of the constitutionally prescribed system of government. The focus is on the operation of the law and involves what is called 'proportionality testing'. The basic idea is that it is not permissible to use a sledgehammer to crack a nut.

The reasonably appropriate and adapted test

In ***Monis***, Crennan, Kiefel and Bell JJ criticised the reasonably appropriate and adapted test as being vague and expressed the view that it should be renamed the proportionality test. Their reasoning was not that the test was wrong but that renaming it would lead to clearer statements of reasoning when judges apply the test.

Monis v The Queen (2013) 249 CLR 92

Crennan, Kiefel and Bell JJ

It has been observed that the phrase "reasonably appropriate and adapted" was imported into Australian constitutional proportionality case law from a judgment of Marshall CJ given in 1819. It is cumbersome and lacks clarity of meaning and application as a test. The only real affinity the phrase bears to a test involving proportionality analysis is the employment of the word "reasonably", but even then it does not describe how, and by reference to what factors, it is intended to operate. The phrase provides no guidance as to its intended application and tends to obscure the process undertaken by the court. Its use may encourage statements of conclusion absent reasoning. It cannot be denied that *Lange* involves a level of proportionality analysis, albeit one which is to be applied in the setting of the Australian Constitution. So much was said in *Lange* ...

[I]t is an analysis based in reasonable proportionality and it would be preferable, to avoid confusion and for clarity, to identify the process by its name and explain how it is applied.

The second limb of *Lange* looks, in the first place, to whether the law is proportionate to the end it seeks to serve. In *Lange*, it will be recalled, once the common law of defamation was adapted it was regarded as going no further than was necessary having regard to the legitimate purpose of protection of reputation. Where there are other, less drastic, means of achieving a legitimate object, the relationship with the legislative purpose may not be said to be proportionate, at least where those means are equally practicable and available. Given the proper role of the courts in assessing legislation for validity, such a conclusion would only be reached where the alternative means were obvious and compelling ...

The High Court acted on this criticism in ***McCloy***. *McCloy* established a three-step structured proportionality test as a tool for applying the reasonably appropriate and adapted test.

McCloy v New South Wales (2015) 257 CLR 178

French CJ, Kiefel, Bell and Keane JJ

The proportionality test involves consideration of the extent of the burden effected by the impugned provision on the freedom. There are three stages to the test – these are the enquiries as to whether the law is justified as suitable, necessary and adequate in its balance in the following senses: *suitable* – as having a rational connection to the purpose of the provision; *necessary* – in the sense that there is no obvious and compelling alternative, reasonably practicable means of achieving the same purpose which has a less restrictive effect on the freedom; *adequate in its balance* – a criterion requiring a value judgment, consistently with the limits of the judicial function, describing the balance between the importance of the purpose served by the restrictive measure and the extent of the restriction it imposes on the freedom.

If the measure does not meet these criteria of proportionality testing, then the answer to question 3 will be "no" and the measure will exceed the implied limitation on legislative power ...

Acceptance of the utility of such criteria as tools to assist in the determination of the limits of legislative powers which burden the freedom does not involve a general acceptance of the applicability to the Australian constitutional context of similar criteria as applied in the courts of other jurisdictions. It does not involve acceptance of the application of proportionality analysis by other courts as methodologically correct. The utility of the criteria is in answering the questions defining the limits of legislative power relevant to the freedom which are derived from *Lange* ...

McCloy explained that structured proportionality is simply one way to apply the reasonably appropriate and adapted test and that it is superior to the approach in some earlier cases which involved impressionistic reasoning or merely statements of conclusion without reasons.

McCloy v New South Wales (2015) 257 CLR 178

French CJ, Kiefel, Bell and Keane JJ

Proportionality provides a uniform analytical framework for evaluating legislation which effects a restriction on a right or freedom. It is not suggested that it is the only criterion by which legislation that restricts a freedom can be tested. It has the advantage of transparency. Its structured nature assists members of the legislature, those advising the legislature, and those drafting legislative materials, to understand how the sufficiency of the justification for a legislative restriction on a freedom will be tested ...

So far as concerns the courts, the question whether a legislative measure which restricts the freedom can be said to be justified is not to be approached as a matter of impression. It should not be pronounced as a conclusion, absent reasoning. It is not to be inferred that, in stating the test in *Lange*, it was intended that the test was to be answered by reference to a value judgment as to what is reasonable, made without reference to any generally applicable criteria ...

Suitability is also referred to as "appropriateness" or "fit". Despite this language, it does not involve a value judgment about whether the legislature could have approached the matter in a different way. If the measure cannot contribute to the realisation of the statute's legitimate purpose, its use cannot be said to be reasonable. This stage of the test requires that there be a rational connection between the provision in question and the statute's legitimate purpose, such that the statute's purpose can be furthered. This was the approach followed in *Unions NSW*. It is an enquiry which logic requires.

The second stage of the test – necessity – generally accords with the enquiry identified in *Unions NSW* as to the availability of other, equally effective, means of achieving the legislative object which have a less restrictive effect on the freedom and which are obvious and compelling. If such measures are available, the use of more restrictive measures is not reasonable and cannot be justified.

It is important to recognise that the question of necessity does not deny that it is the role of the legislature to select the means by which a legitimate statutory purpose may be achieved. It is the role of the Court to ensure that the freedom is not burdened when it need not be. Once within the domain of selections which fulfil the legislative purpose with the least harm to the freedom, the decision to select the preferred means is the legislature's ...

The purpose of and benefit sought to be achieved by legislative provisions assume relevance in the third stage of the test for proportionality. This stage, that of strict proportionality or balancing, is regarded by the courts of some legal systems as most important. It compares the positive effect of realising the law's proper purpose with the negative effect of the limits on constitutional rights or freedoms. It requires an "adequate congruence between the benefits gained by the law's policy and the harm it may cause", which is to say, a balance. Balancing is required because it is rare that the exercise of a right or freedom will be prohibited altogether. Only aspects of it will be restricted, so what is needed, to determine whether the extent of this restriction is reasonable, is a consideration of the importance of the purpose and the benefit sought to be achieved.

Logically, the greater the restriction on the freedom, the more important the public interest purpose of the legislation must be for the law to be proportionate ...

Justice Gageler agreed with the joint judgment that the laws under challenge were invalid but expressed reservations about the structured proportionality test.

McCloy v New South Wales (2015) 257 CLR 178

Gageler J

The content and consequences of the approach now propounded by a majority of this Court must await consideration in future cases ... Without the benefit of full argument in this case, I limit myself to recording two principal reservations.

First, I am not convinced that one size fits all. In particular, I am not convinced that standardised criteria, expressed in unqualified terms of "suitability" and "necessity", are appropriate to be applied to every law which imposes a legal or practical restriction on political communication irrespective of the subject-matter of the law and no matter how large or small, focussed or incidental, that restriction on political communication might be ...

Second, I am not convinced that to require a law which burdens political communication to be "adequate in its balance" is to adopt a criterion of validity which is sufficiently focussed adequately to reflect the reasons for the implication of the constitutional freedom and adequately to capture considerations relevant to the making of a judicial determination as to whether or not the implied freedom has been infringed ...

In my view, it is imperative that the entirety of the *Lange* analysis is undertaken in a manner which cleaves to the reasons for the implication of the constitutional freedom which it is the sole function of the *Lange* analysis to protect. Whatever other analytical tools might usefully be employed, fidelity to the reasons for the implication is in my view best achieved by ensuring that the standard of justification, and the concomitant level or intensity of judicial scrutiny, not only is articulated at the outset but is calibrated to the degree of risk to the system of representative and responsible government established by the Constitution that arises from the nature and extent of the restriction on political communication that is identified at the first step in the analysis ...

In ***Brown v Tasmania***, a majority of the Court applied structured proportionality in answering the third question. The majority judges emphasised that structured proportionality is merely one tool for applying the reasonably appropriate and adapted test. The majority judges also suggested that structured proportionality will be applied unless the party seeking to uphold an impugned law proposes an alternative tool and persuades the Court of its usefulness.

Brown v Tasmania (2017) 261 CLR 328

Kiefel CJ, Bell and Keane JJ

In the course of argument it was pointed out that in *McCloy* it was said that the methods of proportionality analysis there referred to might not be the only criteria by which legislation can be tested in accordance with *Lange*. Tasmania did not suggest any alternative method. Queensland proposes that the question whether a statute could be said to be reasonably appropriate and adapted could be answered, for example, by simply determining if it went "too far". Such an approach would invite little more from the Court than an impression. It does not address the need for transparency in reasoning which was regarded as necessary by a majority of Justices in *McCloy* ...

The point presently to be made is that whilst the Court may propose methods of analysis, of what is proportionate or reasonably appropriate and adapted, it is for those supporting the impugned legislation to justify any of its measures which burden the freedom ...

Nettle J

[T]he stages of analysis posited in *McCloy* are not constituent parts of the second question posed in *Lange* but rather are tools for the assessment of whether a law is reasonably appropriate and adapted to serving a legitimate end as required by *Lange* ...

Justice Gageler agreed that the impugned laws were invalid but repeated his concerns about structured proportionality, labelling it a 'pre-determined all-encompassing algorithm'.

Brown v Tasmania (2017) 261 CLR 328

Gageler J

Three-staged proportionality testing was not sought to be characterised in *McCloy* as anything more than a tool of analysis, not to be confused with the constitutional principle it served. The plurality did not suggest that its adoption is compelled by the reasoning which supports the implication of the freedom of political communication as authoritatively expounded in *Lange*. The plurality also disavowed any suggestion that "it is the only criterion by which legislation that restricts a freedom can be tested".

The point is therefore not one of reopening and overruling *McCloy*: nobody has suggested that *McCloy* was wrongly decided; *McCloy* does not elevate three-staged proportionality testing to the level of constitutional principle; and *McCloy* does not endow it with precedential status. The point is one of emphasising that the tool is, at best, a tool. For my own part, I have never considered it to be a particularly useful tool ...

Constitutional adjudication within our tradition occurs through the elaboration of considerations seen in the light of history, of precedent and of contemporary circumstances to bear on the resolution of matters in issue. Constitutional analysis within that tradition cannot be reduced to the application of some pre-determined all-encompassing algorithm, and the inappropriateness of attempting to construct such an algorithm cannot be overcome by increasing its complexity ...

Where a law effectively burdens freedom of political communication, and does so in pursuit of a legitimate purpose, the degree of fit between means (the manner in which the law pursues its purpose) and ends (the purpose it pursues) needed to conclude that the law is reasonably appropriate and adapted to advance its purpose in a manner that is compatible with the maintenance of the constitutionally prescribed system of government needs to be calibrated to the degree of risk which the burden imposed by the means chosen poses to the maintenance of representative and responsible government ...

Justice Gageler proposed a tool of calibration for applying the reasonably appropriate and adapted test. Laws that impose direct and substantial burdens on political communication would require a compelling justification, and laws that impose indirect or insubstantial burdens on political communication would require only a rational connection to the pursuit of the law's purpose.

Brown v Tasmania (2017) 261 CLR 328

Gageler J

In *Australian Capital Television*, Deane and Toohey JJ presciently observed that "a law whose character is that of a law with respect to the prohibition or restriction of [political] communications ... will be much more difficult to justify ... than will a law whose character is that of a law with respect to some other subject and whose effect on such communications is unrelated to their nature as political communications".

Noting that their Honours' observation had been accepted and applied in a number of subsequent cases, before and after *Lange*, I sought to expand on that observation in *Tajjour v New South Wales* when I referred to the level of scrutiny appropriate to be brought to bear on a law which imposes a burden on political communication as lying within a spectrum. Using language drawn from the analyses of Gaudron J in *Levy* and of Gleeson CJ in *Mulholland*, I said:

> At one end of the spectrum, establishment of a sufficient justification may require 'close scrutiny, congruent with a search for "compelling justification"', constituted by establishing that the law pursues an end identified in terms of the protection of a public interest which is itself so pressing and substantial as properly to be labelled compelling and that the law does so by means which restrict communication on governmental or political matter no more than is reasonably necessary to achieve that protection. At the other end of the spectrum, establishment of a sufficient justification may require nothing more than demonstration that the means adopted by the law are rationally related to the pursuit of the end of the law, which has already been identified as legitimate. ...

For a legitimate purpose to be compelling, it must be seen to be protective of a public interest of sufficient importance reasonably to warrant that label ...

The structured proportionality approach has since become in practice the only approach (as opposed to merely a tool) adopted by those judges who endorse it.

Farm Transparency International Ltd v New South Wales [2022] HCA 23

Edelman J

The legal exercise of assessing whether a burden on the freedom of political communication is justified should be transparent, principled, and structured. Otherwise, it could become, or could be seen to become, an exercise of weighing the burdening effect of a law against little more than a judge's idiosyncratic policy preferences. A structured proportionality approach, repeatedly employed by a majority of this Court, aims to avoid such problems by assessing whether the law is justified by asking (i) whether its anticipated effects are suitable or rationally connected to its legitimate purpose; (ii) whether there were alternative, "reasonably necessary", means of achieving the same object but with a less restrictive effect upon the freedom of political communication; and (iii) if the anticipated effects are suitable and reasonably necessary, whether they are adequate in the balance between the purpose to be achieved by the law and the extent of the burden imposed on the freedom.

It has never been satisfactorily explained why, without any room for extra-judicial policy preferences, a law that fails one of these three criteria for structured proportionality, when they are properly applied, would be consistent with the implied freedom of political communication. Nor has it ever been explained why the implied freedom should invalidate a law that is suitable, reasonably necessary to achieve its legitimate purpose and adequate in the balance. The lack of any acceptable answer to that challenge demonstrates the utility of an analysis based on structured proportionality.

In practice, the key area of debate in answering Question 3 is ordinarily at the point of reasonable necessity.

LibertyWorks Inc v Commonwealth [2021] HCA 18

The High Court held that the* Foreign Influence Transparency Scheme Act 2018 (Cth)*, which requires individuals and entities that communicate political material to the Australian public on behalf of foreign principals (including foreign corporations and individuals) to record their details on a public register, did not contravene the implied freedom of political communication.

Edelman J

As to the first stage, "suitability", a provision will rarely fail for lacking rational connection with the legitimate purpose of Parliament for the obvious reason that Parliament's purpose is itself ascertained and derived in part from the expected operation of the provision. Unless the provision is truly arbitrary, serving no purpose at all, a conclusion that a provision has no rational connection with its legitimate purpose - ie that the means employed are incapable of realising its ostensible purpose - will usually mean that Parliament has misstated its purpose. And the third stage, "adequacy in the balance", is only reached once it has been concluded that the provision is a reasonably necessary means of achieving the legitimate purpose. Hence, a conclusion that a provision is inadequate in the balance will often mean that Parliament is entirely precluded from achieving its legitimate policy objective. For an implication founded upon representative democracy, this would be a remarkable outcome. As I have explained previously, invalidation of a law at this third stage should only occur in extreme cases where the purpose is trivial when compared with the great burden that the law places upon political communication.

In most cases, the heartland of the dispute in the application of structured proportionality will be at the second stage of that analysis, reasonable necessity.

Examples of laws that adopt reasonably appropriate and adapted means

Comcare v Banerji concerned the dismissal of a public servant who was discovered to have made a series of anonymous social media posts criticising the policies implemented by the agency for which she worked. Statutory provisions require public servants to uphold certain values, including by behaving in an apolitical way at all times. Other provisions permitted the imposition of a range of sanctions for contraventions including dismissal in the most serious cases. The High Court held that the provisions had the legitimate purpose of maintaining and protecting an apolitical and professional public service. The High Court rejected an argument that the provisions were disproportionate in extending to allowing disciplinary action for anonymous criticism.

Comcare v Banerji (2019) 267 CLR 373

Kiefel CJ, Bell, Keane and Nettle JJ

The requirement imposed on employees of the APS by ss 10(1) and 13(11) of the *Public Service Act* at all times to behave in a way that upholds the APS Values and the integrity and good reputation of the APS represents a rational means of realising those objectives and thus of maintaining and protecting an apolitical and professional public service. The impugned provisions are suitable in the necessary sense.

... Here, the respondent's argument that the impugned provisions impose an unjustified burden on the implied freedom of political communication by proscribing "anonymous" communications thus reduces in effect to a submission that an obvious and compelling alternative to the impugned provisions would be to exclude "anonymous" communications from their scope of application.

The argument must be rejected. For the reasons earlier given, "anonymous" communications are at risk of ceasing to be anonymous, and thereby damaging the integrity and good reputation of the APS as an apolitical and professional public service. Further, as has been explained, depending on the circumstances and content of an "anonymous" communication, the communication may damage the good reputation of the APS even while it remains anonymous. Consequently, if the impugned provisions were restricted in their operation to communications other than "anonymous" communications, the impugned provisions would cease to operate as a deterrent against a significant potential source of damage to the integrity and good reputation of the APS. Restricting their operation to communications other than "anonymous" communications is for that reason not an obvious and compelling alternative to their present form.

...

Given the impugned provisions have a significant purpose consistent with the system of representative and responsible government mandated by the Constitution, and are necessary in the sense that there is no obvious and compelling alternative, there is nothing about the procedures for the assessment of the nature and gravity of contravention of s 13(11) or the imposition of the appropriate penalty in accordance with the procedures for which s 15 provides that at all supports the idea that the benefit sought to be achieved by the impugned provisions is manifestly outweighed by their effect on the implied freedom. To the contrary, the impugned provisions, including their prescription of the range of penalties and the procedures for the assessment of breach and the imposition of penalty and review, present as a plainly reasoned and focussed response to the need to ensure that the requirement of upholding the APS Values and the integrity and good reputation of the APS trespasses no further upon the implied freedom than is reasonably justified.

In ***Farm Transparency***, the High Court held that a New South Wales law making it unlawful to surreptitiously make a video recording on private premises or to publish such a video did not impermissibly burden the implied freedom of political communication. The law pursued the legitimate purpose of the protection of privacy. Significantly, while other States had legislative schemes dealing with the same issue that might be seen as imposing a lighter burden on political communication, those were not obvious and compelling alternatives because they had slightly different purposes. The case highlights how easy it can be for a government to distinguish the laws of other jurisdictions in order to satisfy the necessity test.

Farm Transparency International Ltd v New South Wales [2022] HCA 23

Kiefel CJ and Keane J

It may be accepted that, generally speaking, the other statutory schemes pursue the purpose of protection of privacy. But the privacy interest to which they refer differs from the SD Act [*Surveillance Devices Act 2007* (NSW)]. The Victorian and other statutes are based upon a conception of privacy viewed from the perspective of the parties to a private activity and their personal interests. The SD Act seeks to protect privacy interests in activities conducted on premises as an aspect of a person's possessory rights over their property. It may therefore be concluded that the Victorian and other statutes do not pursue the same purpose when regard is had to the interests that they seek to protect.

Edelman J

The plaintiffs pointed to "alternative models" in laws of Victoria, the Northern Territory, South Australia, Western Australia, and Queensland. None of those laws are obvious and compelling alternatives to ss 8, 11 and 12 of the *Surveillance Devices Act* which could be clearly expected to achieve the same purposes, to at least the same extent, and to do so with a significantly lesser burden.

In some respects, although not in others, the alternative models impose a burden on political communication that is deeper than that imposed by ss 8, 11 and 12 of the *Surveillance Devices Act*. For instance, the alternative models that are concerned with optical surveillance of activities all prohibit obtaining or publishing a record or report of a "private activity" from an optical surveillance device even in circumstances where the record or report was obtained lawfully.

More fundamentally, the alternative models might not be expected to achieve the purposes of the protection of privacy and dignity and the protection of property rights to the same degree as the *Surveillance Devices Act*. The alternative models, to different degrees, permit exceptions to the offence including, in broad terms, where the communication or publication is: (i) to a media organisation, or by a media organisation and in the public interest, and the device was used in the public interest; (ii) no more than is reasonably necessary in the public interest; or (iii) authorised by a court order based on public interest grounds and no more than is reasonably necessary in the public interest, where the installation or use of the device was not unlawful.

In each case, the exceptions in the alternative models might be expected to detract from the achievement of the legislative purposes of the protection of privacy and dignity and the protection of property rights ...

Perhaps most fundamentally, the purposes of the alternative models are not the same as those of the *Surveillance Devices Act*. For instance, there is no mention of privacy in the general objects clause in the Victorian or Northern Territory legislation and the Queensland legislation is concerned with the recording of conversations by listening devices and not with the recording of activities by optical surveillance devices.

Ultimately, the alternative models do little more than illustrate the existence of a range of different legislative choices available in a representative democracy to implement different, although perhaps related, policy goals.

Examples of laws that do not adopt reasonably appropriate and adapted means

The impugned law considered in ***Coleman v Power*** failed the third question because, assuming the purpose of the law was the prevention of breaches of the peace, there were other means available of achieving that purpose that imposed a lighter burden on political communication.

Coleman v Power (2004) 220 CLR 1

McHugh J

In so far as insulting words are used in the course of political discussion, an unqualified prohibition on their use cannot be justified as compatible with the constitutional freedom. An unqualified prohibition goes beyond anything that could be regarded as reasonably appropriate and adapted for preventing breaches of the peace in a manner compatible with the prescribed system. Without seeking to state exhaustively the qualifications needed to prevent an infringement of the freedom of communication, the law would have to make proof of a breach of the peace and the intention to commit the breach elements of the offence. It may well be the case that, in the context of political communications, further qualifications would be required before a law making it an offence to utter insulting words would be valid. In the present case, it is enough to say that s 7(1)(d) infringed the constitutional freedom by simply making it an offence to utter insulting words in or near a public place whether or not a person hears those words even when they were used in the discussion of political and governmental matters ...

In ***McCloy*** the impugned laws were found to be suitable even though they may not have been capable of fully achieving the purpose of the law. The laws were found to be necessary because the suggested alternative measures were not equally capable of achieving the law's purpose. The laws were found to be adequate in balance because the law imposed an indirect burden on political communication in pursuit of a purpose that enhances the system of representative government.

McCloy v New South Wales (2015) 257 CLR 178

French CJ, Kiefel, Bell and Keane JJ

The plaintiffs submit that Div 2A and Div 4A have no rational connection to the purpose of targeting corruption. In the language of proportionality analysis, discussed later in these reasons, that is a submission that the impugned provisions are not "suitable". By analogy with the reasons of the joint judgment in *Unions NSW*, the plaintiffs submit that it is not explained why Div 4A targets only corporations and their close associates who are property developers and not individuals or firms ...

If there is a deficiency of the kind contended for by the plaintiffs, it is not one which severs the connection to the anti-corruption purpose of the EFED Act ...

An equally practicable alternative? – necessity

In *Monis v The Queen* it was said that any alternative means must be "obvious and compelling", a qualification which, as French CJ pointed out in *Tajjour v New South Wales*, ensures that the consideration of alternative means is merely a tool of analysis in applying this criterion of proportionality. Courts must not exceed their constitutional competence by substituting their own legislative judgments for those of parliaments.

The plaintiffs put forward two alternatives to the measures in Div 2A. They say that it would be less restrictive of the freedom if the prohibition on receiving political donations in excess of the applicable caps were confined to those donations which are intended as corrupting; which is to say to limit it to occasions of bribery. They also say that the best method of targeting corruption is transparency and that the requirements in the EFED Act for disclosure of donations could be strengthened ...

Whilst provisions requiring disclosure of donations are no doubt important, they could not be said to be as effective as capping donations in achieving the anti-corruption purpose of the EFED Act.

Limiting restrictions on political donations to acts of bribery would undoubtedly reduce the efficacy of the statutory scheme. The difficulties inherent in detecting and proving bribery in the context of political donations do not suggest that it can be considered a reasonable alternative to capping. Further, it is not the subjective intention of the donor so much as the objective tendency of large payments of money to corrupt both government and the electoral system which is the justification for the restriction ...

In this case, the third stage of the test presents no difficulty for the validity of the impugned provisions. The provisions do not affect the ability of any person to communicate with another about matters of politics and government nor to seek access to or to influence politicians in ways other than those involving the payment of substantial sums of money. The effect on the freedom is indirect. By reducing the funds available to election campaigns there may be some restriction on communication by political parties and candidates to the public. On the other hand, the public interest in removing the risk and perception of corruption is evident. These are provisions which support and enhance equality of access to government, and the system of representative government which the freedom protects. The restriction on the freedom is more than balanced by the benefits sought to be achieved ...

In ***Brown***, the majority held that certain provisions were not rational because they could not be seen as directed to the purposes of the Act in which they were found and appeared to be directed only at preventing protests. The majority also held that the provisions were not reasonably necessary because the provisions they had replaced had the same purpose but imposed a lighter burden on political communication.

Brown v Tasmania (2017) 261 CLR 328

Kiefel CJ, Bell and Keane JJ

Connection to purpose

Given that the purpose of the Protesters Act is to prevent damage and disruption to forest operations from the conduct of protesters, the question arises whether the provisions referred to above can be said to pursue that purpose. In *McCloy*, the enquiry was said to be whether the statutory provisions in question have a rational connection to their purpose. If they do not, it would follow that they are simply a burden on the freedom without a justifying purpose ...

The prohibitions in s 6 clearly enough reflect the purpose of the Protesters Act. The fact that protesters are targeted is explained by the history of protests which provided a catalyst for the Act ...

Section 8(1)(b) cannot be said to share the purpose of the Protesters Act. It deters a person being in any business access area on pain of arrest or penalty, even though they may not present any threat of damage or disruption and may not reasonably be considered to contravene s 6(1), (2) or (3). The inference to be drawn is that it is directed solely to the purpose of deterring protesters. Accordingly, it fails the test of suitability.

The same conclusion may be reached with respect to s 11(7) and (8), which effect a blanket exclusion of a whole group of persons from an area by a single direction of a police officer, even when the police officer could not conceivably have formed any view about whether each person is about to contravene the Protesters Act. So understood, the only purpose of these provisions must be to bring a protest to an end and deter further protests, regardless of whether damage or disruption is foreseeable ...

Are the measures reasonably necessary?

The FMA does not burden the freedom to the same extent as does the Protesters Act. It seeks to ensure that only those persons, protesters included, whose presence or activities are likely to interfere with forest operations will be excluded from forestry land. The Protesters Act operates more widely than its purpose requires. It is principally directed to preventing protesters being present within ill-defined areas in the vicinity of forest operations or access points to those areas, whereas its purpose is similar to that of the FMA ...

In ***Unions NSW (No 2)***, the High Court held that a law will be held to be invalid whenever there is no proof that a law burdening political communication is necessary in the

McCloy sense. In this case, there was no evidence to allow the High Court to say one way or the other if the law was necessary. For that reason, the High Court could not say that the law's burden on political communication was actually justified, with the result that the law was held to be invalid.

The challenged New South Wales law in this case had the effect of reducing the amount of money a 'third-party campaigner' (that is, entities and persons other than candidates and political parties) could lawfully spend on political advertising for a State election from $1 050 000 to $500 000. There was no evidence that the law lowering the cap was reasonably necessary to achieve what was assumed to be the law's legitimate purpose of preventing the drowning out of voices in the political process by the distorting influence of money. Without proof of necessity, the law was unjustified and therefore invalid.

Unions NSW v New South Wales (No 2) [2019] HCA 1

Kiefel CJ, Bell and Keane JJ

In May 2014 the New South Wales Government appointed an independent expert panel to consider and report on options for long-term reform of the State's electoral funding laws. The panel delivered a report to government in December 2014 ("the Expert Panel Report")

...

The Expert Panel Report accepted that there is widespread support for third-party participation in elections "within limits". It supported an approach which caps their expenditure in the same way as for parties and candidates, but was of the view that the current cap is "too high" and suggested it be halved to $500,000 "to guard against third parties coming to dominate election campaigns" ...

Following the release of the Expert Panel Report, the New South Wales Government indicated its in-principle support for all but one of the Expert Panel Report's 50 final recommendations. It referred the report and the Government's response to it to the Joint Standing Committee on Electoral Matters ("the JSCEM") ...

The JSCEM Report noted that three unions had spent considerably more than the proposed cap in the period 1 July 2014 to 30 June 2015. The JSCEM Report endorsed the Expert Panel Report's conclusion that third parties should not be able to run campaigns to the same extent as candidates and parties. However, noting submissions from constitutional lawyers that the cap must not be set so low that a third-party campaigner cannot reasonably present its case, the JSCEM recommended that before decreasing the cap to $500,000, the New South Wales Government consider whether there was sufficient evidence that a third-party campaigner could reasonably present its case within that expenditure limit. No material has been placed before the Court which suggests that such an analysis was undertaken ... It is well understood that an enquiry as to the necessity of a provision which effectively burdens the implied freedom is one of the tests of structured proportionality analysis. If the provision fails the necessity test, then, on that approach, it will be held invalid ...

As the plaintiffs point out, no basis was given in the Expert Panel Report for a halving of the figure previously allowed for third-party campaigning expenses. It may have been thought to be a reasonable allowance given the level of expenditure by third-party campaigners at the 2011 election. The report recommended that the figure be checked against expenditure for the 2015 election. If that enquiry had been undertaken, a different conclusion might have been reached. And despite the recommendation of the JSCEM, no enquiry as to what in fact is necessary to enable third-party campaigners reasonably to communicate their messages appears to have been undertaken. The defendant has not justified the burden on the implied freedom of halving the cap in s 29(10) as necessary to prevent the drowning out of voices other than those of third-party campaigners. The plaintiffs' submissions in this regard should be accepted. Section 29(10) is invalid.

Nettle J

The plaintiffs contended that, in this case, there is not any, let alone clear and convincing, demonstration of why a cut in the third-party campaigner expenditure cap to half of that which applied under the Previous Act is necessary, and thus that it should be concluded that the reduction, or at least the amount of it, is an unjustified burden on the implied freedom ...

[A]lthough it is apparent from the expert panel's report that the panel considered it to be desirable for the achievement of a level playing field to limit the expenditure of third-party campaigners relative to parties and candidates, it is also clear that the expert panel considered it was necessary to gather evidence to establish the appropriate relativity before the change was enacted. Yet, for reasons which do not appear, that recommendation went unheeded. It is as if Parliament simply went ahead and enacted the Electoral Funding Act without pausing to consider whether a cut of as much as 50 per cent was required.

In the result, it is impossible to say whether or not the differential remains within the bounds of what might reasonably be required and, for that reason, impossible for the Court to be persuaded that the extent of the cut in the third-party campaigner expenditure cap is necessary. Therefore, it has not been demonstrated that the extent of the cut is appropriate and adapted to the achievement of the legitimate purpose of maintaining a level playing field.

For these reasons, I agree in the answers proposed by the plurality to the questions set out in the special case.

Gordon J

[E]ven if the [Third Party Campaigner] Expenditure Cap is rationally connected to the legitimate purposes it seeks to serve, the Court is unable to assess whether the burden is justified and is not "undue". That is, the Court cannot answer, one way or another, the final aspect of the *Lange* questions: it cannot be satisfied that the level of the expenditure cap is reasonably appropriate and adapted to achieve the asserted constitutionally permissible end ...

[T]he Court cannot be satisfied that the burden of the [Third Party Campaigner] Expenditure Cap on the implied freedom is justified. The burden is therefore impermissible, and the [Third Party Campaigner] Expenditure Cap invalid.

12.7 DISCUSSION QUESTIONS

1. What is the constitutional basis for the implied freedom of political communication?
2. What sorts of communication does the implied freedom protect?
3. Explain how the second question in the framework for assessing the validity of a law challenged for breaching the implied freedom operates.
4. Explain how the third question in the framework for assessing the validity of a law challenged for breaching the implied freedom operates.
5. Problem question: Consider the following hypothetical legislation.

Control of Parolees Act 2023 (Qld)

1. This Act may be cited as the *Control of Parolees Act 2023*.
2. The object of this Act is to ensure community safety and promote rehabilitation of criminals by regulating the activities in which a prisoner released on parole may engage.
3. A prisoner released on parole must not attend or in any other way participate in any of the following events:
   a. a meeting of a political party;
   b. a meeting of a car enthusiasts' club or association;
4. A prisoner released on parole must not create or cause to be created any profile on any dating website or application.
5. A prisoner released on parole who contravenes sections 3 or 4 of this Act may have their parole revoked by the Parole Board if the Parole Board considers it appropriate in all of the circumstances.

Does the *Control of Parolees Act 2023* (Qld) impermissibly burden the implied freedom of political communication?

13 FREEDOM OF INTER-STATE TRADE, COMMERCE AND INTERCOURSE

13.1 Overview

This chapter examines the guarantee section 92 provides for freedom of inter-State trade, commerce and intercourse. While the High Court previously interpreted section 92 as providing for two separate guarantees (one guaranteeing freedom of inter-State trade and commerce, and one guaranteeing freedom of inter-State intercourse) with different analytical frameworks, section 92 is now understood as being a composite provision having two limbs – the inter-State trade and commerce limb and the inter-State intercourse limb – with a common analytical framework for determining whether a law contravenes the provision.

Australian Constitution

Section 92 Trade within the Commonwealth to be free

On the imposition of uniform duties of customs, trade, commerce, and intercourse among the States, whether by means of internal carriage or ocean navigation, shall be absolutely free.

The guarantee of freedom of inter-State trade and commerce ensures free trade within Australia. It operates to invalidate discriminatory burdens of a protectionist kind imposed on inter-State trade and commerce. The guarantee of freedom of inter-State intercourse ensures freedom of movement from one State to another. It operates to invalidate all discriminatory burdens on inter-State intercourse. It also operates to invalidate disproportionate incidental burdens on inter-State intercourse.

Key concepts considered in this chapter include:

- trade and commerce
- discriminatory burdens
- of a protectionist kind
- reasonable necessity
- intercourse
- proportionality.

13.2 The purpose underlying section 92

Section 92's purpose is to ensure free trade and freedom of movement between the States. ***Cole v Whitfield*** is the starting point for modern section 92 jurisprudence. The High Court identified section 92's purpose by looking to the drafting history of the provision.

Cole v Whitfield (1988) 165 CLR 360

Mason CJ, Wilson, Brennan, Deane, Dawson, Toohey and Gaudron JJ

The purpose of the section is clear enough: to create a free trade area throughout the Commonwealth and to deny to Commonwealth and States alike a power to prevent or obstruct the free movement of people, goods and communications across State boundaries. Free trade was understood to give "equality of trade", which Mr McMillan (of the New South Wales delegation) asserted to be "one grand principle involved in the whole of our federation". (Convention Debates (Melbourne 1898), vol II, at p 2345.) The enemies of free trade were border taxes, discrimination, especially in railway freight rates, and preferences. Higgins pointed out: "what will be the use of talking about free-trade between the states, and diminishing the friction upon the borders, if we do not provide against a war of railway rates?" (Ibid, at p 1268.) To complement the s 92 prohibition against discriminatory laws which prevented the free flow of trade, ss 99 and 102 were introduced to prohibit preferences ...

Attention to the history which we have outlined may help to reduce the confusion that has surrounded the interpretation of s 92. That history demonstrates that the principal goals of the movement towards the federation of the Australian colonies included the elimination of intercolonial border duties and discriminatory burdens and preferences in intercolonial trade and the achievement of intercolonial free trade. As we have seen, apart from ss 99 and 102, that goal was enshrined in the various draft clauses which preceded s 92 and ultimately in the section itself ...

The expression "free trade" commonly signified in the nineteenth century, as it does today, an absence of protectionism, that is, the protection of domestic industries against foreign competition. Such protection may be achieved by a variety of different measures – eg, tariffs that increase the price of foreign goods, non-tariff barriers such as quotas on imports, differential railway rates, subsidies on goods produced and discriminatory burdens on dealings with imports – which, alone or in combination, make importing and dealings with imports difficult or impossible. Sections 92, 99 and 102 were apt to eliminate these measures and thereby to ensure that the Australian States should be a free trade area in which legislative or executive discrimination against inter-State trade and commerce should be prohibited. Section 92 precluded the imposition of protectionist burdens: not only inter-State border customs duties but also burdens, whether fiscal or non-fiscal, which discriminated against inter-State trade and commerce. That was the historical object of s 92 and the emphasis of the text of s 92 ensured that it was appropriate to attain it ...

[T]he failure of the section to define expressly what inter-State trade and commerce was to be immune from is to be explained by reference to the dictates of political expediency, not by reference to a purpose of prohibiting all legal burdens, restrictions, controls or standards. In that context, to construe s 92 as requiring that inter-State trade and commerce be immune only from discriminatory burdens of a protectionist kind does not involve inconsistency with the words "absolutely free": it is simply to identify the kinds or classes of burdens, restrictions, controls and standards from which the section guarantees absolute freedom ... The history of s 92 points to the elimination of protection as the object of s 92 in its application to trade and commerce. The means by which that object is achieved is the prohibition of measures which burden inter-State trade and commerce and which also have the effect of conferring protection on intra-State trade and commerce of the same kind. The general hallmark of measures which contravene s 92 in this way is their effect as discriminatory against inter-State trade and commerce in that protectionist sense. There can be no doubt that s 92 guarantees absolute freedom of inter-State trade and commerce from all inter-State border duties and other discriminatory fiscal charges levied on transactions of inter-State trade and commerce.

13.3 Freedom of inter-State trade and commerce and freedom of inter-State intercourse are two limbs of a composite expression

Palmer v Western Australia (No 1) holds that section 92 is a composite provision having two limbs – the inter-State trade and commerce limb and the inter-State intercourse limb – with a common analytical framework for determining whether a law contravenes the provision. ***Cole v Whitfield*** had previously held that section 92 provided for two separate guarantees of freedom – freedom of inter-State trade and commerce and freedom of inter-State intercourse – with different tests applicable for each limb.

Cole v Whitfield (1988) 165 CLR 360

Mason CJ, Wilson, Brennan, Deane, Dawson, Toohey and Gaudron JJ

Below, we trace the transition of this clause into s 92 of the Constitution. At this stage, we note that "intercourse" appeared in the words of the provision as a distinct and independent concept the freedom of which was guaranteed from the very beginning.

It was not, as has sometimes been suggested (see, eg, per Dixon J, *Bank of NSW v Commonwealth* ("*Banking Case*") (1948) 76 CLR 1, at p 381), added as some kind of afterthought to "trade" and "commerce". As will be seen, it was the word "commerce" which was last added to complete the phrase "trade, commerce and intercourse" in the section. The relevance of that for present purposes is that it precludes the approach that the content of the guarantee of freedom of inter-State intercourse must be governed by the pre-existing content of a guarantee of freedom of inter-State trade and commerce into which it was introduced.

The notions of absolutely free trade and commerce and absolutely free intercourse are quite distinct and neither the history of the clause nor the ordinary meaning of its words require that the content of the guarantee of freedom of trade and commerce be seen as governing or governed by the content of the guarantee of freedom of intercourse. We shall return to the topic of intercourse and the question of its relationship with trade and commerce later in these reasons ...

Palmer v Western Australia (No 1) (2021) 246 CLR 182

A government official issued Directions under State public health legislation during the COVID-19 pandemic which had the effect of preventing entry into Western Australia of persons from other parts of Australia except in very limited circumstances. Palmer, a Queensland resident, argued that the Directions contravened section 92's guarantee of freedom of inter-State intercourse. The High Court unanimously rejected that argument. It held that the correct level of analysis is to argue either (1) that the primary legislation contravenes the constitutional limitation or (2) that the primary legislation when interpreted so as not to contravene the constitutional limitation does not authorise the subordinate legislation or action taken under the primary legislation. Here, the legislation did not contravene section 92 and the High Court was not asked to decide whether the Directions were not authorised by the primary legislation.

Kiefel CJ and Keane J

Although it is sometimes convenient to refer to s 92 as having two limbs – the trade and commerce limb and the intercourse limb – the words "trade, commerce, and intercourse" are stated in the section as a composite expression. The observation that until *Cole v Whitfield* decisions of this Court did not treat the two limbs as substantially different is clearly correct. Section 92 has been regarded as concerned with all kinds of movement across State borders ...

...

The distinction drawn in *Cole v Whitfield* has the obvious consequence that guarantees of freedoms appearing in the one provision of the Constitution are to be treated differently. This might suggest incoherence, which is not regarded as a desirable outcome for constitutional interpretation. More importantly, the distinction drawn in *Cole v Whitfield* is not consistent with a modern approach to constitutional interpretation. The distinction does not derive any support from the text of s 92. The text does not provide a basis for treating one of three elements of the composite expression "trade, commerce, and intercourse among the States" as connoting or requiring that some different test be applied to them ...

Gageler J

By way of summation, the constitutional purpose of s 92 identified in *Cole v Whitfield* is best served by "re-integrating" its two limbs: by continuing to accept the trade and commerce limb as a guarantee that interstate trade and commerce is to be absolutely free from discriminatory burdens of a protectionist kind, and by recognising the intercourse limb as a guarantee that interstate intercourse is to be absolutely free from discriminatory burdens of any kind. Re-integration is supported by the reasoning of Brennan J in *Nationwide News* and by the reasoning of Brennan and Toohey JJ in *Cunliffe*, is consistent with the reasoning of Gleeson CJ, McHugh and Gummow JJ in *AMS* and is not prevented by the approach taken in the absence of contrary argument in *APLA*.

Gordon J

The first step is to ask whether the impugned law, in its legal or practical operation, imposes a differential burden on interstate trade, commerce or intercourse in favour of intrastate trade, commerce or intercourse. If there is no such differential burden, that is the end of the inquiry and the law does not infringe the constitutional guarantee in s 92.

Where, however, the law does impose a differential burden of that kind on interstate trade, commerce or intercourse, it is necessary to identify the law's object or objects ... If the only object of the law is to erect State borders as barriers against freedom of trade, commerce or intercourse, that will be the end of the inquiry. Without more, the law is discriminatory; it will infringe the constitutional guarantee in s 92 and be invalid.

But where the law has a legitimate object, the question then is whether the differential burden imposed by that law is justified.

The effect of ***Palmer v WA (No 1)*** is that the analytical framework for assessing whether a law is consistent with the guarantees in section 92 requires asking:

1. Does the law impose a discriminatory burden on inter-State trade, commerce or intercourse?
2. Does the law have a legitimate purpose?
3. Is the law reasonably necessary to achieve its legitimate purpose?

Question 1 is a threshold question, directed to whether the law engages any of the protected freedoms. If the answer to question 1 is 'no', in the sense that the law does not burden inter-State trade, commerce or intercourse in the relevant sense, then the law does not contravene section 92. If the answer to question 1 is 'yes', then it is necessary to continue applying the analytical framework.

Question 2 concerns the purpose of the law imposing the burden. If the law is aimed at inter-State trade, commerce or intercourse in the sense of directly burdening inter-State trade, commerce or intercourse then the law will be invalid. However, if the law serves some other purpose and burdens inter-State trade, commerce or intercourse only indirectly or incidentally then it is necessary to consider question 3. Question 3 concerns the manner in which the law indirectly or incidentally burdens inter-State trade, commerce or intercourse in furtherance of some other purpose. A law that indirectly or incidentally burdens inter-State trade, commerce or intercourse in a manner that goes further than what is reasonably necessary to achieve its purpose will be invalid.

13.4 Discriminatory burdens on inter-State trade, commerce and intercourse

The nature of the discriminatory burden prohibited by section 92 is different in respect of inter-State trade and commerce and inter-State intercourse. As the passages from ***Cole v Whitfield*** and ***Palmer v Western Australia (No 1)*** above explain, in respect of inter-State trade and commerce, the discriminatory burden must be of a protectionist kind. In this context, 'protectionist' is used in the economic sense of anti-free trade; it does not refer to things like protection of the environment or protection of public health. In respect of inter-State intercourse, the discriminatory burden may be of any kind.

Palmer v Western Australia (No 1) (2021) 246 CLR 182

Gageler J

[T]he guarantee of absolute freedom of interstate intercourse mirrors the guarantee of absolute freedom of interstate trade and commerce to the extent that: each invokes the same essential notion of discrimination as lying in "the unequal treatment of equals, and, conversely, in the equal treatment of unequals"; each posits the same essential comparison between that which is interstate and that which is intrastate; each demands "an acceptable explanation or justification for [any] differential treatment"...

The guarantee of absolute freedom of interstate intercourse differs from the guarantee of absolute freedom of interstate trade and commerce only to the extent that absolute freedom of interstate intercourse extends to freedom from discriminatory burdens of any kind. That is to say, the guarantee of absolute freedom of interstate intercourse is infringed by any differential burden on interstate intercourse that cannot be justified. An unjustified differential burden on interstate intercourse need not operate to the competitive advantage of intrastate trade or commerce.

However, in *obiter* comments Edelman J suggested that the discriminatory burden on inter-State trade and commerce need not be of a protectionist kind. The other judgments do not support this suggestion.

Palmer v Western Australia (No 1) (2021) 246 CLR 182

Edelman J

The second strand is the assumption of the Court that the discrimination with which the trade and commerce aspect is concerned is limited to protectionism, the most prolific form of discrimination among States in trade and commerce. Although it is not necessary to decide this point finally in this case, the proscribed discrimination should not have been so limited ...

[P]rotectionism is only one form of discrimination in trade and commerce that imposes burdens on persons in one State compared with another. Although protectionism is by far the most common form of discrimination relevant to the trade and commerce aspect of s 92, and the form with which the Court was concerned in *Cole v Whitfield*, there are other forms of discrimination that could be just as damaging to the purpose of s 92. For instance, State legislation might have the unintended effect of conferring a competitive disadvantage upon local trade and commerce when compared with another State. Or the Commonwealth might confer a competitive advantage on one State to the disadvantage of another. Or a State might confer a competitive advantage on one foreign State over another in an industry in which there is no competition in the local State. For instance, suppose that Western Australian legislation imposed an unjustified prohibition upon the sale in Western Australia of a type of good insofar as it was manufactured in New South Wales but not insofar as that type of good was manufactured in Queensland. Even if no manufacturer in Western Australia competed in the market for that type of good, so that the discrimination was only between products from New South Wales and Queensland, it is difficult to see why that discrimination, if unjustified, would be consistent with the freedom of trade rationale underlying s 92.

The High Court accepts that discrimination may be of two types. Direct or legal discrimination exists where the law on its face subjects inter-State trade or commerce to a disability. Indirect or factual discrimination exists where the law has the effect of subjecting inter-State trade or commerce to a disability.

Cole v Whitfield (1988) 165 CLR 360

Mason CJ, Wilson, Brennan, Deane, Dawson, Toohey and Gaudron JJ

The concept of discrimination in its application to inter-State trade and commerce necessarily embraces factual discrimination as well as legal operation. A law will discriminate against inter-State trade or commerce if the law on its face subjects that trade or commerce to a disability or disadvantage or if the factual operation of the law produces such a result ...

Cole v Whitfield provides a clear example of the multiple steps of analysis required in a freedom of inter-State trade and commerce limb case.

The challenged law prohibited catching or selling undersized crayfish in Tasmania. The purpose of the law was to protect crayfish stocks. The prohibition on selling undersized crayfish applied to all crayfish whether sourced in Tasmania or elsewhere. Due to water temperatures, crayfish grow to a smaller size in South Australia such that a mature crayfish from South Australia is the same size as a juvenile crayfish from Tasmania.

Whitfield imported crayfish into Tasmania from South Australia that were below the Tasmanian minimum size but above the South Australian minimum size. Whitfield was convicted under the Tasmanian law. The High Court held that the Tasmanian law did not contravene section 92.

The law imposed an indirect burden on inter-State trade and commerce. However, that burden was not economically protectionist in nature because it gave no competitive advantage to intra-State trade over inter-State trade. That is, whether a discriminatory burden is protectionist is determined by whether the burden gives competitive advantage to intra-State trade over inter-State trade. Furthermore, even if the indirect burden did advantage intra-State trade, the law's purpose concerned the environmental protection and conservation of crayfish stocks rather than being aimed at inter-State trade and commerce and the law implemented a necessary means of pursuing that non-protectionist purpose since there was no practical means of distinguishing between Tasmanian and other crayfish.

Cole v Whitfield (1988) 165 CLR 360

Mason CJ, Wilson, Brennan, Deane, Dawson, Toohey and Gaudron JJ

The question which we must now determine is whether reg 31(1)(d) of the *Sea Fisheries Regulations* which reveals no discriminatory purpose on its face is impermissibly discriminatory in effect. In other words, whether the burden which the regulation imposes on inter-State trade in crayfish goes beyond the prescription of a reasonable standard to be observed in all crayfish trading and, if so, whether the substantial effect of that regulation is to impose a burden which so disadvantages inter-State trade in crayfish as to raise a protective barrier around Tasmanian trade in crayfish. The latter questions are questions of fact and degree on which minds might legitimately differ.

The regulation neither operates at the border or frontier nor distinguishes between local and inter-State trade or produce. However, the limitation on the size of crayfish that may be sold or possessed in Tasmania is unquestionably a burden on the inter-State trade and commerce in crayfish caught in South Australian waters and sold in Tasmania. But does it bear the character of being discriminatory against that inter-State trade and commerce? The prohibitions against the sale and possession of undersized crayfish apply alike to crayfish caught in Tasmanian waters and to those that are imported. In that respect no discriminatory protectionist purpose appears on the face of the law. Furthermore, the object of the prohibitions, in conjunction with the prohibition against catching undersized crayfish, is to assist in the protection and conservation of an important and valuable natural resource, the stock of Tasmanian crayfish. Although the legislation operates in this way to protect the Tasmanian crayfish industry, it is not a form of protection that gives Tasmanian crayfish production or intra-State trade and commerce a competitive or market advantage over imported crayfish or the trade in such crayfish.

And, even if the legislation were to give an advantage to the local trade by improving the competitive qualities of mature Tasmanian crayfish by eliminating undersized imported crayfish from the local market, the agreed facts make it clear that the extension of the prohibitions against sale and possession to imported crayfish is a necessary means of enforcing the prohibition against the catching of undersized crayfish in Tasmanian waters. The State cannot undertake inspections other than random inspections and the local crayfish are indistinguishable from those imported from South Australia. On the materials before the Court, the legislation and the burden which it imposes on inter-State trade and commerce are not properly to be described as relevantly discriminatory and protectionist.

The multiple steps of analysis are considered in detail below.

13.5 Identifying burdens on inter-State trade and commerce

Discriminatory burdens

Discrimination involves a comparison. The comparison required by section 92 is between intra-State trade and commerce and inter-State trade and commerce of the same kind.

Bath v Alston Holdings provides an example of direct discrimination. Victorian legislation required tobacco retailers to pay a licence fee calculated by reference to the value of tobacco products purchased from non-Victorian tobacco wholesalers. The High Court held that this method of calculating the fee imposed a discriminatory burden on the retail trade in non-Victorian tobacco. The law did not treat the retail trade in Victorian and non-Victorian tobacco products equally because it differentiated between tobacco products by reference to the State in which the relevant wholesaler operated.

Bath v Alston Holdings Pty Ltd (1988) 165 CLR 411

The case was a challenge to Business Franchise (Tobacco) Act 1974 (Vic) *section 10(1)(c) and (d) which provided that a retail tobacconist's licence fee would consist of a flat fee plus an amount equal to 25 per centum of the value of tobacco sold by the applicant in the course of tobacco retailing in the relevant period (other than tobacco purchased in Victoria from the holder of a wholesale tobacco merchant's licence or a group wholesale tobacco merchant's licence).*

Mason CJ, Brennan, Deane and Gaudron JJ

[T]he essential question is whether the statutory imposition upon a retailer of the obligation to pay a licence fee calculated in the manner provided by the Act is, in the circumstances, properly to be characterized as discriminatory against inter-State trade and commerce in a protectionist sense ...

If the Act imposed the ad valorem licence fee by reference to the value of all tobacco products sold by a retailer in the relevant period, the imposition of the fee would not contravene s 92 since it would not differentiate between tobacco purchased in Victoria and tobacco purchased outside Victoria; a fortiori it would not discriminate in a protectionist sense against the purchase of tobacco outside Victoria. The exclusion of tobacco purchased in Victoria from a licensed wholesaler from the total sale value of tobacco used as the basis of the calculation of the ad valorem licence fee does, however, involve an element of differentiation and at least prima facie discrimination. Since the effect of the Act is to require all Victorian wholesalers selling tobacco products in Victoria to be licensed, the tobacco products purchased by the ordinary Victorian retailer from a local wholesaler will, for practical purposes, be all purchased from the holder of a wholesaler's licence under the Act. That being so, the exclusion of tobacco purchased in Victoria from the holder of a wholesaler's licence from the value of tobacco sold in the relevant preceding period has the effect that, for practical purposes, the licence fee paid by a Victorian retailer will ordinarily consist of the flat fee ... together with an amount equal to 25 per centum of the value of any tobacco purchased from an inter-State wholesaler. In other words, the retailer who sells only tobacco products purchased by him from a Victorian wholesaler will pay the appropriate flat fee for his licence, while a retailer who sells only tobacco products purchased from an inter-State wholesaler will pay that flat fee plus 25 per centum of the value of tobacco sold in the preceding relevant period.

It follows that, if they be viewed in isolation, the provisions of the Act imposing the obligation to pay a retail tobacconist's licence fee ... plus an amount calculated by reference to the value of tobacco sold which has not been purchased in Victoria from a licensed wholesaler, discriminate against inter-State purchases of tobacco in favour of purchases in Victoria ...

For practical purposes, their operation is to impose on Victorian retailers who, during the relevant earlier period, purchased tobacco products both locally and in the markets of another State, an obligation to pay to Victorian consolidated revenue an ad valorem tax calculated by reference to the sale value of so much of those products as came from inter-State ... [T]he effect of s 10(1)(c) and (d) is to discriminate against tobacco products sold by wholesalers in the markets of another State and to protect both Victorian wholesalers and the products which they sell from the competition of out of State wholesalers and their products. The wholesaler's licence fee, imposed on local wholesalers by reference to all their local sales, does not infringe s 92 in that it does not discriminate against goods coming from another State. The ad valorem content of the retailer's licence fee does infringe s 92 in that it discriminates against inter-State trade and commerce in a protectionist sense by taxing a retailer only because of, and by reference to the value of, his actual or imputed purchases of products in any State other than Victoria ...

A tax upon retailers in respect of their trading in goods may burden their trade in inter-State goods consistently with the guarantee of s 92 only if it applies equally to the inter-State and local goods which the retailers sell; it cannot lawfully discriminate between them so as to protect the local goods.

Castlemaine Tooheys v South Australia provides an example of indirect discrimination. South Australian regulations imposed different costs on the use of refillable bottles compared with the use of non-refillable bottles. This made the sale of beer in non-refillable bottles commercially disadvantageous. Breweries operating in South Australia sold their beer mainly in refillable bottles. Breweries operating outside South Australia sold their beer mainly in non-refillable bottles. The High Court held that the effect of the regulations was to impose a discriminatory burden on inter-State trade and commerce in bottled beer.

Castlemaine Tooheys Ltd v South Australia (1990) 169 CLR 436

Mason CJ, Brennan, Deane, Dawson and Toohey JJ

It is common ground between the parties that the object and effect of the 1986 Act was to make the sale of beer in non-refillable bottles commercially disadvantageous. The plaintiffs go further and assert that the effect of the 1986 Act, the regulations and the notice under s 5b was to discriminate against the sale in South Australia of packaged beer brewed interstate and to protect the beer brewed in South Australia from interstate competition.

On the other hand the defendant claims that the 1986 Act and regulations promoted litter control and conserved energy and resources. According to the defendant, this effect was achieved by the imposition of a deposit on non-refillable containers in an amount judged sufficient to ensure their return and discourage their use and by providing a refund point – in practice any place of sale – to encourage return and to discourage manufacturers from using such containers ...

Cole v Whitfield established that a law which imposes a burden on interstate trade and commerce but does not give the domestic product or the intrastate trade in that product a competitive or market advantage over the imported product or the inter-State trade in that product, is not a law which discriminates against inter-State trade and commerce on protectionist grounds. The present case stands on a different footing because the facts recited in the special case show that the Bond brewing companies were disadvantaged in the two respects already mentioned which gave the South Australian brewers a competitive or market advantage ...

The particular question in the present case is: how should the Court approach the determination of the validity of State legislation which attempts on its face to solve pressing social problems by imposing a solution which disadvantages the trade in beer brewed outside the State as against the trade in beer brewed within the State? The central problems addressed by the legislation are the litter problem and the need to conserve energy resources. If the South Australian legislation were not attempting to provide a solution to these problems, the burden on interstate trade would be discriminatory in a protectionist sense because its operation would be discriminatory and protectionist in effect, even though the legislation on its face would treat interstate and intrastate trade evenhandedly.

As explained below, the High Court went on to hold that this indirect discrimination was of a protectionist kind.

Barley Marketing Board v Norman provides an example of treatment that is not discriminatory at all. New South Wales legislation vested all barley grown in New South Wales in the Barley Marketing Board. The purpose of this scheme was that all New South Wales barley would be sold by the Board at the same minimum price. This would prevent large purchasers pressuring smaller barley growers to accept unreasonably low prices. The High Court held that this scheme did not discriminate against inter-state trade in barley. All purchasers of barley grown in New South Wales had to pay the same purchase price whether the purchaser was located in New South Wales or elsewhere. There was no discrimination because everyone was treated equally.

Barley Marketing Board (NSW) v Norman (1990) 171 CLR 182

Mason CJ, Brennan, Deane, Dawson, Toohey, Gaudron and McHugh JJ

The principal argument presented by the first and second defendants in support of their case of discrimination is that legislation creating a marketing scheme which seeks to ensure a minimum price for producers is necessarily protectionist. This is because it protects small producers by giving them the benefit of the marketing authority's increased bargaining power against large purchasers, especially interstate maltsters, the purchase of malting grade barley across State borders being one of the reasons why barley prices were kept low, according to the plaintiff's notice stating its reasons for divesting malting grade barley. But this element of "protection" in favour of growers, especially small growers, is not accompanied by any element of discrimination against the interstate trade in barley or interstate traders in that commodity. The scheme may terminate an advantage formerly enjoyed by New South Wales border growers but that is not to the point ...

In so far as the marketing scheme terminates an advantage in the form of lower prices obtainable by Victorian maltsters from New South Wales border growers – this being an avowed object of the divesting of malting grade barley – those maltsters may now pay more than they did when they purchased from border growers in that State, but they are treated equally with maltsters in that State. In-State and out-of-State maltsters must buy from the plaintiff if they wish to make purchases of barley produced in New South Wales. Accordingly, there is no discrimination against the out-of-State maltster.

Another variation of this argument is that, apart from the factors already mentioned, the New South Wales maltsters are free to buy malting grade barley from border growers in Victoria whereas Victorian maltsters are no longer able to buy from border growers in New South Wales. But, for reasons already explained, this involves no discrimination in any relevant sense. The purchasing entitlements of the maltsters in each of the two States are identical. Both Victorian and New South Wales maltsters have equal access to the barley sold by Victorian growers and that sold by the plaintiff. The maltsters in both States are denied direct access to the growers in New South Wales. The Act does not result in the exclusion of one group but not the other from any market; nor does the Act lead to any difference in price of product to maltsters in the two

States. Consequently the New South Wales maltster is given no competitive advantage over his Victorian counterpart. So the operation of the Act does not result in "a departure from equality of treatment" of interstate and intrastate trade and commerce, that being the object of the constitutional injunction in s 92.

Of a protectionist kind

As ***Cole v Whitfield*** makes clear, and ***Palmer v Western Australia (No 1)*** affirms, discriminatory burdens on inter-state trade and commerce are prohibited only if the burden is of a protectionist kind.

Bath v Alston Holdings demonstrates that a discriminatory burden will be of a protectionist kind if the effect of the discrimination is to give a competitive advantage to in-State trade and commerce. In this case, the competitive advantage consisted of the removal of a competitive advantage otherwise enjoyed by out-of-State goods.

Bath v Alston Holdings Pty Ltd (1988) 165 CLR 411

Victoria required tobacco wholesalers to pay a licence fee calculated by reference to the value of product sold. Inevitably, the cost of the fee would be passed onto retailers who would in turn pass the cost onto consumers. To ensure that all tobacco products sold in Victoria were impacted by equivalent costs and thus to level the playing field, Victoria also required tobacco retailers to pay a licence fee calculated by reference to the value of tobacco products sourced from non-Victorian wholesalers. In the passages extracted above, the High Court held that this retailer's licence fee involved a discriminatory burden on inter-state goods. In the following passages, the High Court holds that the discriminatory burden is of a protectionist kind.

Mason CJ, Brennan, Deane and Gaudron JJ

If it be viewed in isolation, that discrimination is undeniably protectionist both in form and substance. In form, the provisions of s 10(1)(c) and (d) select the fact that tobacco was "purchased in Victoria" from a licensed wholesaler as the qualifying condition for exemption from inclusion in the products by reference to which liability to ad valorem tax is calculated. In substance, those provisions protect local wholesalers and the tobacco products they sell from the competition of an out of State wholesaler whose products might be cheaper in some other Australian market place for a variety of possible reasons, for example, that the laws of the State in which he carries on his business as a wholesaler either do not require that he hold a licence at all or exact a licence fee comparatively lower than the fee exacted from a Victorian wholesaler ...

Seen as a licence fee, the taxes imposed upon wholesalers are part of the costs of a Victorian wholesaler in carrying on his business. He will enjoy a competitive advantage or disadvantage in relation to an out of State wholesaler according to the comparative level of taxes and other costs which he must bear in carrying on his business. The fact that taxes paid by a wholesaler in one State are higher than the taxes paid by a wholesaler in a second State may provide an inducement for the first State to protect local goods and local wholesalers by the imposition of an "equalizing" tax upon its retailers in respect of their purchases of products from that other State. The most that such notions of economic equalization can do, however, is to provide some local justification for the imposition of a protectionist tax in respect of inter-State goods at the later retail stage of distribution. They do not alter the character of the tax as such or remove it from the ambit of s 92.

Indeed, to hold that a law which protects local goods by imposing a discriminatory tax on inter-State goods at the retail level is consistent with s 92 because the law equalizes in favour of the local goods an advantage which the inter-State goods enjoy in their State of origin in the course of manufacture or distribution would be to disregard the critical constitutional purpose which the section is designed to serve ...

If the tax is imposed, whether directly or indirectly, on a transaction in the chain of distribution of goods, the relevant inquiry is whether the tax is imposed only on transactions where the goods involved have come from or are going to another State or whether the tax is imposed on all transactions of the relevant kind without differentiation based on the source or destination of the goods involved. If the tax is imposed on transactions in a particular market – in this case, the Victorian retail tobacco market – it is the effect of the tax on transactions in that market which is material. In this case, the effect is on the supply of goods to that market. The effect of an equivalent tax on transactions at another stage in the chain of distribution of the same goods or goods of the same kind is immaterial. That must be so unless s 92 permits the protection of an entire chain of distribution of goods within a State against competition from goods which might otherwise enter the chain from inter-State. That proposition has only to be stated to be rejected. If that proposition were accepted, s 92 would present no impediment to the imposition of border duties – at all events if they did not exceed the amount necessary to place on inter-State goods a tax burden equivalent to the tax burden earlier placed on similar goods already in the local chain of distribution.

Bath v Alston Holdings would be decided differently today due to another provision of the *Constitution*. The High Court now accepts that a licence fee calculated by reference to the value of products sold is in substance a tax on goods and therefore an excise duty. Section 90 of the *Constitution* prohibits the States imposing excise duties. This does not negate the principles concerning section 92 that the case articulates.

On inter-State trade and commerce

The comparison required by section 92 is between intra-State and inter-State trade and commerce *of the same kind*. A necessary first step in that comparison is identifying the relevant market or field of trade or commerce. The basic proposition is that goods or services exist in the same market if they satisfy the same consumer desire and are therefore in competition with each other.

In ***Sportsbet***, the High Court referred to ***Bath v Alston Holdings*** to explain that how the relevant market is identified and defined can change the result of a case.

Sportsbet Pty Ltd v New South Wales (2012) 249 CLR 298

This case arose under a provision of the Northern Territory (Self-Government) Act 1978 *(Cth) which guarantees that trade, commerce and intercourse between the Northern Territory and the States shall be absolutely free. It is accepted that this provision is equivalent to section 92 of the* Constitution.

French CJ, Gummow, Hayne, Crennan, Kiefel and Bell JJ

The term "practical operation", in its present use as a criterion of constitutional validity, is not "virtually devoid of content". However, its imprecision in meaning and application is apt to generate significant differences of opinion when the term is applied in particular disputes. ...

The point is further illustrated by the division between Mason CJ, Brennan, Deane and Gaudron JJ, and Wilson, Dawson and Toohey JJ, in *Bath v Alston Holdings Pty Ltd.* The case was argued immediately after *Cole v Whitfield* and judgment was given a month after that in the latter case.

The minority in *Bath* emphasised that if regard were had to the practical operation of the *Business Franchise (Tobacco) Act 1974* (Vic), it would be seen that the object of the legislation was not to favour Victorian trade at the expense of the interstate trade in tobacco. All trade in tobacco in Victoria was subjected to the franchise fee at one point or another, whether wholesale or retail, and the economic effect of the tax was the same, whether the retailer acquired the tobacco from a local wholesaler who was liable to pay the tax, or an out of State wholesaler who was not liable to pay it. On the other hand, the majority directed attention to a particular market – "the Victorian retail tobacco market" – and to the effect of the tax on the supply of goods to that market. Their Honours added that:

> [t]he effect of an equivalent tax on transactions at another stage in the chain of distribution of the same goods ... is immaterial.

It may perhaps be said, and it is unnecessary to pursue the matter here, that, by the focus upon a "market" solely at the retail level, the majority in *Bath* favoured the legal operation of the tax at the expense of the practical operation of the statute as a whole ...

Barley Marketing Board v Norman explains that the field of trade and commerce burdened by a law is not necessarily trade and commerce in the commodity or service directly affected by the law. The High Court gave the example of a State law prohibiting the export of a raw material for the purpose of ensuring that in-State manufacturers of a product made using that raw material have preferential access to that raw material. Such a law imposes a discriminatory burden in the field of trade and commerce for the manufacture and sale of products made from the raw material rather than in the field of the sale of the raw material itself.

Barley Marketing Board (NSW) v Norman (1990) 171 CLR 182

Mason CJ, Brennan, Deane, Dawson, Toohey, Gaudron and McHugh JJ

If a State having a scarce resource or the most inexpensive supplies of a raw material needed for a manufacturing operation prohibited the export of material from that resource or those supplies in order to confer a benefit on its domestic manufacturers as against their out-of-state competitors, that prohibition would discriminate against interstate trade and commerce in a protectionist sense. However, in the present case, there is no evidence to suggest that the marketing scheme operates in such a way as to restrict the supply of barley to interstate maltsters. They are able to compete on an even footing with domestic maltsters in purchasing malting grade barley from the plaintiff.

Plainly enough, mischief at which the section is directed embraces discrimination against out-of-State producers and traders achieved by restrictions upon commodities or services upon which those producers and traders rely in competing with in-State producers and traders in trade or commerce of the same kind.

But the passage cited should not be understood as holding that such discrimination cannot occur where the commodities or services upon which a restriction is imposed are not the particular commodities or services which are affected by discrimination. In such a case, the relevant discrimination is to be found by comparison between in-State trade or commerce and out-of-State trade or commerce of the same kind, the restrictions imposed on commodities or services which result in differential treatment of in-State and out-of-State trade or commerce being the means by which that discrimination is created. So much was recognized in *Castlemaine Tooheys Ltd v South Australia* where a law which imposed restrictions on the use of non-refillable bottles was held to discriminate against the out-of-State trade in bottled beer and to confer protection on the domestic brewers of bottled beer. It happened to be the case in *Cole v Whitfield* that the commodity upon which restrictions were imposed, namely, crayfish, was the same as the commodity, the out-of-State trade and commerce in which was said to have been discriminated against in a protectionist sense. And that was also the case in *Bath v Alston Holdings Pty Ltd* where restrictions were imposed on tobacco and tobacco products. It was the in-State trade or commerce in these commodities which was held by the majority to benefit from discrimination in a protectionist sense against out-of-State trade or commerce in commodities of the same kind, contrary to s 92.

Identification of the relevant field of trade and commerce said to be burdened by a law directs attention to the fact that section 92 protects trade and commerce rather than individual traders. In other words, section 92 is not about individual rights. ***Sportsbet*** and ***Betfair No 2***, which were argued together and handed down on the same day, both emphasise that section 92 protects inter-State trade and commerce and not individual participants in inter-State trade and commerce. The relevant inquiry is about the effect of a law on inter-State trade and commerce. A law that has the effect of imposing a competitive disadvantage on an inter-State *trader* does not necessarily have the effect of imposing a competitive disadvantage on inter-State *trade*.

Betfair Pty Ltd v Racing New South Wales (No 2) (2012) 249 CLR 217

Betfair operated an online betting exchange in Hobart to conduct wagering on horse racing, including racing in New South Wales. New South Wales law required that a fee be paid by any wagering operator for the use of New South Wales horse racing field information. Betfair argued that the fees had the effect of protecting New South Wales wagering operators, particularly TAB Ltd, from competition from wagering operators in other States. Betfair said this effect arose because the fees were calculated as a percentage of the amounts wagered on back bets, which would have a higher financial impact on Betfair due to its business model than on other wagering operators, such as TAB Ltd. The High Court held that this argument did not demonstrate any discrimination against inter-state trade and commerce as opposed to possible detriment to Betfair itself.

French CJ, Gummow, Hayne, Crennan and Bell JJ

Not every measure which has an adverse effect between competitors will attract the operation of s 92. The "confined area" in which s 92 operates was emphasised in *Cole v Whitfield*. Betfair must establish that the fee conditions imposed upon it by RNSW and HRNSW were unauthorised because their practical effect is to discriminate against interstate trade and thereby protect intrastate trade of the same kind. What is posited here is an essentially objective inquiry. It is the concept of protectionism which supplies the criterion by which discriminatory laws may be classified as rendering less than absolutely free trade and commerce among the States. At various stages in its submissions, Betfair appeared, by emphasising notions of discrimination, to seek to diminish the requirement of protectionism ...

In the present case, the Full Court [of the Federal Court, which heard the case below,] pointed as follows to what it held was a fatal defect in Betfair's case:

> The relevant inquiry as to whether a law or other governmental measure operates in fact to impose a protectionist burden on interstate trade contrary to s 92 of the Constitution is not concerned to vindicate a right in individual traders to carry on their business as they wish. The inquiry is whether the individual trader, as a participant in interstate trade, is subject to a differential burden by reason of the operation of the law or measure in the common circumstances of the trade. The differential burden must be imposed by the law or executive measure in the common circumstances of the milieu in which the trade occurs: the inquiry is as to whether there is a denial by the law or measure of a competitive advantage in trade, not whether an individual trader's particular circumstances are such that its trade may be adversely affected by a law of general application to all traders.

In the course of argument in this Court, the emphasis by Betfair upon its particular circumstances attracted further submissions, particularly by Victoria, which should be accepted. First, emphasis upon the circumstances of particular traders, and upon features which may be accidental to those circumstances and to the interstate transactions in which the traders may engage, risks characterisation of the law in question not by its effect upon interstate trade, the constitutional issue, but by its effect upon particular traders ...

[T]he subject of s 92 is interstate trade, not traders, whose transactions may or may not consist wholly of interstate transactions or of intrastate transactions ...

The questions presented in the present appeal thus become: (i) whether the practical operation of the fee structure shows an objective intention to treat interstate and intrastate trade in wagering transactions alike, notwithstanding a relevant difference between them; and, if so, (ii) whether the fee structure burdens interstate trade to its competitive disadvantage; and, if so, (iii) whether that burden nonetheless is reasonably necessary for New South Wales to achieve a legitimate non-protectionist purpose. If an affirmative answer were given to (i) and (ii) then, unless (iii) be answered in the negative, the conclusion would be that the fee structure gives to intrastate wagering transactions which utilise NSW race field information such a competitive or market advantage over those interstate wagering transactions which also do so, as to raise a protective barrier around those intrastate transactions. For the reasons which follow the case presented by Betfair fails at step (i), and, in any event, at step (ii), so step (iii) is not presented for decision ...

In the present case, the circumstance that the fee structure adopted by Betfair for its wagering operations differed from that adopted by other wagering operators did not constitute a relevant difference which, consistently with s 92, could not be disregarded by treating alike interstate and intrastate wagering transactions utilising NSW race field information. All that Betfair established was that by maintaining its current pricing structures, and given its low margin, the fees imposed by RNSW and HRNSW absorbed a higher proportion of its turnover on interstate transactions than that of the turnover of TAB, the principal intrastate wagering operator.

Nor did Betfair demonstrate that the likely practical effect of the imposition of the fees will be loss to it of market share or profit or an impediment to increasing that share or profit ...

Sportsbet Pty Ltd v New South Wales (2012) 249 CLR 298

Sportsbet, a bookmaker operating in the Northern Territory, argued that the same New South Wales laws under challenge in Betfair *were inconsistent with the guarantee of freedom of trade and commerce between the Territory and the States found in the* Northern Territory (Self-Government) Act 1978 *(Cth).*

French CJ, Gummow, Hayne, Crennan, Kiefel and Bell JJ

Both in this case and *Betfair* the appellant fixes upon the practical operation of the fee structure in the State licensing systems upon its business operations as an interstate (or extra-Territorial) trader and contrasts this with the position of what it categorises as one or more competitors who are intrastate traders. But the minute analysis of business models, as applied from time to time, which this approach invites distracts attention from the concern of s 92 with effect upon trade, not prejudice to particular traders.

Betfair (No 1) shows that the effect of a law on a particular inter-State trader may indeed demonstrate the effect of a law on inter-State trade if that particular inter-State trader is representative of inter-State trade and commerce as a whole. ***Betfair (No 1)*** also demonstrates that the relevant market or field of trade and commerce is not necessarily co-extensive with the scope of a particular trader's operations.

In this case, Betfair operated an online betting exchange. Online betting exchanges provide one method of placing fixed odds wagers. The other method is bookmakers. Another method of placing wagers is the non-fixed odds wagering offered by totaliser agencies. The High Court held that the relevant field of trade and commerce should be seen as the general market for wagering on racing events rather than simply the market for online betting exchange fixed odds wagering. The reason for this identification of the relevant field of trade and commerce was 'cross-elasticity' of demand and substitutability: all three forms of wagering satisfy the same consumer desire, are interchangeable and are in competition with each other. Similarly, in ***Castlemaine Tooheys***, the breweries selling beer in refillable bottles were in competition with the breweries selling beer in non-refillable bottles in the same field of trade and commerce, namely, the market for bottled beer. In other words, if goods or services satisfy the same consumer desire and are in competition with each other then they exist in the same market.

Betfair Pty Ltd v Western Australia (No 1) (2008) 234 CLR 418

Betfair operated an online betting exchange in Hobart to conduct wagering on sporting events taking place around Australia. Western Australia enacted legislation making it a criminal offence for a person in Western Australia to place a bet through an online betting exchange or for a wagering operator to accept such a bet from a person in Western Australia. Wagering operators located in Western Australia did not use online betting exchanges. The High Court held that the law breached section 92.

Gleeson CJ, Gummow, Kirby, Hayne, Crennan and Kiefel JJ

The plaintiffs (with the support of Tasmania, one of the interveners) challenge the validity of the relevant provisions of the law of Western Australia, principally by reliance upon s 92 of the Constitution. They put their case for the application of s 92 upon two bases. The first is that the legislation of Western Australia impermissibly precludes, with respect to internet transactions having a geographical connection with that State, that increase in competition, on the supply side, within the national market for betting services which would be provided, on the demand side, by the presence within Western Australia at any one time of such persons as Mr Erceg. The second is that the legislation also applies to deny to the out-of-State operator in the position of Betfair access for the purposes of its Australia-wide operations to information respecting race fields which is generated by racing operators in Western Australia, whilst in-State wagering operators do not suffer that disadvantage. As will appear in these reasons, the case formulated by the plaintiffs in these terms should be accepted ...

Section 27D(1)

This provision applies to the conduct of Betfair in publishing or otherwise making available a WA race field. This burdens interstate trade and commerce, both directly and indirectly. It does so directly because it denies to Betfair use of an element in Betfair's trading operations. It does so indirectly by denying to Betfair's registered players receipt and consideration of the information respecting the latest WA race fields by access to Betfair's website or by communication with its telephone operators. These effects of s 27D(1) operate to the competitive disadvantage of Betfair and to the advantage of RWWA and the other in-State wagering operators. The law in its application to Betfair answers the description of a discriminatory burden on interstate trade of a protectionist kind ...

Section 24(1aa)

The relevant effect of this provision is to prohibit a person in Western Australia from placing a particular form of fixed odds bet by means of a cross-border electronic communication, and to render the out-of-State wagering operator liable for aiding, counselling or procuring an offence by Betfair's registered players even if all its acts occurred outside Western Australia.

It is true that this particular form of fixed odds betting also is denied to in-State wagering operators and their customers. But that does not deny to s 24(1aa) its character of a discriminatory burden on interstate trade of a protectionist kind. The sub-section operates to protect the established wagering operators in Western Australia, including RWWA, from the competition Betfair otherwise would present. What has been said above respecting cross-elasticity of demand is relevant here. The intrastate trade and interstate trade are of "the same kind" whether the subject matter be different species of fixed odds betting or the general field of wagering upon racing and sporting events.

That view of the matter proceeds from the evidence indicating cross-elasticity of demand. Some analogy is provided by the situation in *Castlemaine Tooheys*. There the discrimination was between bottles having different characteristics; here it is between different but competing forms of wagering on racing and sporting events. The effect of s 24(1aa) is to prohibit Betfair, an out-of-State wagering operator, from providing a betting exchange for registered players in Western Australia, leaving the in-State operators able to supply customers with their services without the competition to their revenue which Betfair would present. This is another discriminatory burden of a protectionist kind.

13.6 Identifying burdens on inter-State intercourse

Inter-State intercourse is about movement from one State to another State.

Palmer v Western Australia (No 1) (2021) 246 CLR 182

Kiefel CJ and Keane J

The guarantee of freedom of interstate intercourse may be taken to refer to both physical movement and communication across State borders, and to be directed to the circumstance where borders are used as barriers to freedom of movement between States.

In ***Gratwick v Johnson***, the High Court struck down federal regulations prohibiting rail travel from one State to another State without a permit. The regulations on their face imposed a differential burden on inter-State rail travel compared with intra-State rail travel.

Gratwick v Johnson (1945) 70 CLR 1

The Restriction of Interstate Passenger Transport Order, made under the National Security (Land Transport) Regulations *authorised by* National Security Act 1939–1943 *(Cth), provided that, subject to some exceptions, no person should without a permit travel by rail from any State to any other State. The High Court held that the Order breached section 92.*

Starke J

It is provided by s 92 of the Constitution that trade, commerce and intercourse among the States, whether by means of internal carriage or ocean navigation, shall be absolutely free. The people of Australia are thus free to pass to and fro among the States without burden, hindrance or restriction ...

And it follows that legislation pointed directly at the passing of people to and fro among the States also contravenes the provisions of s 92. It is immaterial, as I understand the cases, that the object or purpose of the legislation, gathered from its provisions, is for the public safety or defence of the Commonwealth or any other legislative purpose if it be pointed directly at the right guaranteed and protected by the provisions of s 92 of the Constitution. It does not follow that legislation which is not so pointed or that acts done pursuant to such legislation will not contravene the constitutional provision, but it is enough in this case to say that the Order attacked is so pointed, and consequently is, to that extent, bad.

Gratwick v Johnson concerned the movement of people from one State to another State. The three judges in ***Nationwide News v Wills*** who considered section 92 held that the concept of intercourse among the States extends beyond the movement of people from one State to another State. Inter-State intercourse includes the movement of goods and people as well as inter-State communications.

Nationwide News Pty Ltd v Wills (1992) 177 CLR 1

The case concerned an article published in The Australian *newspaper. The article was said to contravene a law making it an offence to publish words calculated to bring the Australian Industrial Relations Commission into disrepute. The newspaper was printed in Sydney and distributed throughout Australia.*

Brennan J

Submitting that the communication of any form of information or any expression of ideas across a State border is a species of "intercourse among the States", the defendant contended that s 92 precluded any restrictions on the content of the communication "save those which are necessary for the reasonable regulation and adjustment of the competing interests of people in the community at large" ...

The characteristic of every phenomenon falling within the section, however, is geographical movement. Each of the terms "trade, commerce and intercourse" in s 92 is qualified by the phrase "among the States" and that qualification is essential to attract the operation of the section. There must be some border crossing involved before any phenomenon of trade, commerce or intercourse comes within the reach of the section

The protection of s 92 is given to the movement of people, the transport of goods, the transmission of communications, the passage of signals of any kind and any other means by which "interchange, converse and dealings between States in the affairs of life" are carried on across State boundaries. The protection is given to the movement of persons and things across the border or, in the case of intangibles, to the means by which their movement is effected. The means of movement will vary with what is moved; it is not essential that the means of movement be physically perceptible. But it is essential that something (or some person) be moved. Ideas cannot be moved. They have no geographical location. The expression of ideas, whether in literary or other form, can be moved and a movement of that kind across State borders is capable of attracting the operation of s 92.

Deane and Toohey JJ

Clearly enough, the guarantee of freedom of inter-State intercourse is not confined to the physical movement or carriage of goods or things among the States. It encompasses all of the modern forms of inter-State communication.

13.7 Justifying indirect burdens on inter-State trade, commerce and intercourse

Indirect burdens on inter-State trade, commerce or intercourse will be valid if they are reasonably necessary to achieve a legitimate purpose. A legitimate purpose is any purpose that is not the purpose of erecting State borders as barriers against freedom of trade, commerce or intercourse. A burden will be reasonably necessary to achieve such a purpose where it satisfies the structured proportionality analysis of being suitable, necessary and adequate in balance.

The development of this analytical position took more than three decades starting with *Cole v Whitfield* in 1988 and culminating in *Palmer v Western Australia (No 1)* in 2021.

Castlemaine Tooheys, a case about inter-State trade and commerce, put forward a test of proportionality. A law which burdens inter-State trade and commerce is not protectionist if it is appropriate and adapted to the achievement of a non-protectionist purpose and any burden imposed on inter-State trade and commerce is incidental and proportionate to the achievement of that purpose. In this case, the burden on inter-State trade was held to be disproportionate to the achievement of the non-protectionist purposes of energy conservation and reduction of litter.

Castlemaine Tooheys Ltd v South Australia (1990) 169 CLR 436

Mason CJ, Brennan, Deane, Dawson and Toohey JJ

The particular question in the present case is: how should the Court approach the determination of the validity of State legislation which attempts on its face to solve pressing social problems by imposing a solution which disadvantages the trade in beer brewed outside the State as against the trade in beer brewed within the State? The central problems addressed by the legislation are the litter problem and the need to conserve energy resources. If the South Australian legislation were not attempting to provide a solution to these problems, the burden on interstate trade would be discriminatory in a protectionist sense because its operation would be discriminatory and protectionist in effect, even though the legislation on its face would treat interstate and intrastate trade evenhandedly. What difference then does it make that the burden is imposed by legislation which on its face appears to be directed to the solution of social and economic problems, not being the uncompetitive quality or character of domestic trade or industry? Is the burden non-discriminatory in the relevant sense on that account? If so, how is that conclusion to be justified? ...

An analogous field is the legislative implementation of treaty obligations under s 51(xxix) of the Constitution. The true object of the law in such a case is critical to its validity. The Court has upheld the validity of legislative provisions if they are appropriate and adapted to the implementation of the provisions of the treaty ... But if the means which the law adopts are disproportionate to the object to be achieved, the law has not been considered to be appropriate to the achievement of the object ... There is a compelling case for taking a similar approach to the problem now under consideration ...

If we accept, as we must, that the legislature had rational and legitimate grounds for apprehending that the sale of beer in non-refillable bottles generates or contributes to the litter problem and decreases the State's finite energy resources, legislative measures which are appropriate and adapted to the resolution of those problems would be consistent with s 92 so long as any burden imposed on interstate trade was incidental and not disproportionate to their achievement. Accordingly, the validity of the 1986 legislation rests on the proposition that the legislative regime is appropriate and adapted to the protection of the environment in South Australia from the litter problem and to the conservation of the State's finite energy resources and that its impact on interstate trade is incidental and not disproportionate to the achievement of those objects ...

If, in the light of these facts, the legislature reasonably apprehended that the sale of beer in non-refillable bottles manufactured in South Australia constituted a threat to the State's reserves of natural gas, one might have expected the legislature to introduce legislation prohibiting the sale in the State of beer in non-refillable bottles produced in the State. Alternatively, and more directly, the legislature might have legislated to prohibit the manufacture in South Australia of such bottles with the use of natural gas, or at all. But none of these means was adopted. Instead a regime was introduced which subjected the Bond brewing companies' interstate trade to serious competitive disadvantages by reason of their selling beer in non-refillable bottles, even though those bottles are manufactured outside the State and do not, as far as we know, involve the use of South Australian natural gas. It may be that the result is that local trade and commerce may need to be harmed if State gas reserves are to be protected. But if that is the case, it should not be surprising, because local businesses are likely to be significant users of those reserves.

It follows that neither the need to protect the environment from the litter problem nor the need to conserve energy resources offers an acceptable explanation or justification for the differential treatment given to the products of the Bond brewing companies. Accordingly, in our view, that treatment amounted to discrimination in a protectionist sense in relation to their interstate trade.

In ***Nationwide News***, a case about freedom of inter-State intercourse, Brennan J also set out a test of proportionality. He held that a law will not breach section 92 if the law is enacted for a purpose other than preventing or impeding a crossing of a State border, and the imposition of the burden is appropriate and adapted to the fulfilment of the other purpose.

Nationwide News Pty Ltd v Wills (1992) 177 CLR 1

Brennan J

The freedom guaranteed to interstate intercourse by s 92 denies the validity of any law the purpose or effect of which is simply the prohibition or impeding of movement between States in any of the ways in which intercourse is carried on ...

The problem is to determine what restriction or regulation is compatible with the freedom guaranteed to interstate intercourse by s 92 ...

Cole v Whitfield was concerned to identify the character of the burdens imposed by laws which impair the freedom of interstate trade and commerce. In doing so, the judgment left open the character of the burdens imposed by laws which impair the freedom of interstate intercourse ...

While the freedom of interstate trade and commerce predicates an absence of discrimination between interstate and intrastate trade and commerce, discrimination is not an essential feature of an impermissible burden imposed on interstate intercourse.

Of course, the appearance of discrimination against interstate intercourse of a particular kind and in favour of intrastate intercourse of a like kind would be a badge of invalidity. But discrimination in that sense is not an indicium of invalidity of a law burdening interstate intercourse. The general criterion of invalidity of a law which places a burden on interstate intercourse is that the law is enacted for the purpose of burdening interstate intercourse.

If the law is enacted for some other purpose then, provided the law is appropriate and adapted to the fulfilment of that other purpose, an incidental burdening of interstate intercourse may not be held to invalidate the law. A law may be found to be enacted for the prohibited purpose by reference to its meaning or by reference to its effect. If a law imposes a burden by reason of the crossing of the border ... the law offends s 92 unless it falls into one of the exceptional categories presently to be mentioned. Similarly, a law which has the effect of preventing or impeding the crossing of the border will be held invalid if the circumstances are such as to show that that is its only or chief purpose. There are exceptions to these propositions ...

Where the true character of a law, ascertained by reference to the "grounds and design of the legislation, and the primary matter dealt with, (and) its object and scope", is to protect the State or its residents from injury, a law which expressly prohibits or impedes movement of the apprehended source of injury across the border into the State may yet be valid.

Although State borders are not to be regarded "as in themselves possible barriers to intercourse between Australians", they do mark the territorial end of one area of legislative competence and the territorial beginning of another. Since State legislative competence is maintained by ss 106 and 107 of the Constitution, s 92 cannot transform a mere change in legal regime applicable to a person, thing or intangible that is moved across a State boundary into an impermissible burden on that movement. The change in the legal regime on one side of the border may impose a burden that is not imposed on the other, but that is not enough in itself to amount to an impermissible burden. Nor does s 92 purport to place interstate intercourse in a position where it is immune from the operation of laws of general application which are not aimed at interstate intercourse. The object of s 92 is to preclude the crossing of the border from attracting a burden which the transaction would not otherwise have to bear; its object is not to remove a burden which the transaction would otherwise have to bear if there were no border crossing. Section 92 does not invalidate laws that do not select a movement across a State border as a criterion of the imposition of the burden but do have the effect of burdening interstate intercourse provided (1) the law is enacted chiefly for a purpose other than preventing or impeding a crossing of a State border, (2) the imposition of the burden is appropriate and adapted to the fulfilment of the other purpose ...

The movement of the article (or the movement of the expression of the article) was not burdened in any way by s 299(1)(d)(ii) of the Act. If that provision were held to prohibit its publication in any State to which the article had been disseminated other than New South Wales, the prohibition would be wholly unrelated to the fact that the article had been moved from one State to another. The purpose of s 299(1)(d)(ii) is wholly unrelated to the placing of any burden on any movement across State boundaries. Section 92 thus has no application to s 299(1)(d)(ii) of the Act and is therefore immaterial to the effect of that provision on the dissemination of the article or the lawfulness of its publication.

In ***Cunliffe v Commonwealth***, a case about freedom of inter-State intercourse, McHugh J proposed a stricter test: the law must be proportionate to a purpose that is a necessary purpose. It is not enough that the purpose is merely any purpose that does not directly target inter-state intercourse.

Cunliffe v Commonwealth (1994) 182 CLR 272

Federal legislation prohibited the giving of immigration assistance unless a person was registered as a migration agent. The law effected an incidental burden on inter-state intercourse since immigration assistance could be provided by a person in one State to a person in another State by means of inter-state communications.

McHugh J

But given that emphatic injunction that the freedom of intercourse is absolute, it is a natural, if not necessary, conclusion that the freedom of intercourse guaranteed by s 92 should be impaired only by laws that are necessary for the government of the nation or its constituent parts. A law is necessary in the relevant sense only if there is a real social need for it and the restriction or burden on interstate intercourse is "no more than is proportionate to the legitimate aim pursued". Unless the impact of legislation on the freedom of interstate intercourse is so restricted, the freedom of intercourse that s 92 guarantees would be a freedom that was subject to enacted laws. Such a construction would make s 92 superfluous and fail to give effect to the injunction that the freedom is to be absolute. The words "intercourse among the States ... shall be absolutely free" in s 92 should, therefore, be given their ordinary and natural meaning, limited only by the need to accommodate laws that are reasonably necessary for the government of a free society regulated by the rule of law.

Obviously, a law that incidentally restricts or burdens interstate intercourse as the consequence of regulating another subject matter will be easier to justify as being consistent with the freedom guaranteed by s 92 than a law that directly restricts or burdens a characteristic of interstate intercourse. But whether the restriction or burden is direct or indirect, it is inconsistent with the freedom guaranteed by s 92 unless the restriction or burden is reasonably necessary for the government of a free society regulated by the rule of law.

In ***AMS v AIF***, a majority of the High Court, including McHugh J, held that where a law imposes an incidental burden on inter-State intercourse the law will be valid if the burden or restriction imposed is not greater than reasonably required to achieve the law's objects. The purpose of the law need only be any purpose that does not directly target inter-State intercourse.

AMS v AIF (1999) 199 CLR 160

Section 49 of the Northern Territory (Self-Government) Act 1978 *(Cth) provides: 'Trade, commerce and intercourse between the Territory and the States, whether by means of internal carriage or ocean navigation, shall be absolutely free.' It was accepted that this provision has the same meaning as section 92 of the* Constitution. *The Family Court of Western Australia made an order under a State law that the principal place of residence of a child be in the Perth metropolitan area with the mother. The mother argued that this burdened intercourse between Western Australia and the Northern Territory to where she wished to relocate. The order was found to be invalid on other grounds but the High Court nevertheless offered comments on the intercourse argument.*

Gleeson CJ, McHugh and Gummow JJ

In the working out of the measure of freedom from legislative, executive or curial interference which s 92 now is to be taken to provide in respect of interstate intercourse, each case should be decided "so far as may be, on the specific considerations or features which it presents" ...

The 1975 WA Act did not in terms apply to impose a burden or restriction upon movement across the borders of Western Australia. Rather, subject to the operation of s 109 of the Constitution, the 1975 WA Act empowered the State Family Court to impose a burden or restriction upon movement by orders made in exercise of its discretionary powers with respect to the custody and guardianship of children. In the present case, the order of which the mother complains does not enjoin movement as such from the State to the Northern Territory. However, its practical operation is to hinder or restrict such movement by the mother by reason of the requirement that she not change the principal place of residence of the child. This, of itself, would not be fatal to validity. The question becomes whether the impediment so imposed is greater than that reasonably required to achieve the objects of the 1975 WA Act. If the order in question does answer that description, it would, as indicated above, be liable to appellate correction as having been made in an exercise of discretion which was tainted by an error of law ...

When the matter is heard again, it will be for the State Family Court to take into account, upon the evidence then before it and in framing any orders it may make, the need not to impose upon the freedom of intercourse of either party between Western Australia and the Northern Territory, or between that State and any other State, an impediment greater than that reasonably required to achieve the objects of the applicable legislation

Hayne J

For the reasons given by Gleeson CJ, McHugh and Gummow JJ, I agree that in this appeal (brought by the father) the application to revoke the grant of special leave should be refused, the appeal should be allowed and orders made in the terms their Honours propose ...

[F]or the reasons given by Gleeson CJ, McHugh and Gummow JJ, s 49 is to be given an ambulatory meaning and the question presented by s 49 (and s 92) in a case such as the present is whether an impediment imposed under the 1975 State Act is greater than that reasonably required to achieve the objects of that Act. I agree that custody and guardianship legislation may present a question whether the statute empowers the making of orders that have a practical effect of imposing upon freedom of intercourse an impediment greater than reasonably required to achieve the object of the legislation. But construing the legislation applied in this case in the way I have, I do not consider that any separate question would then arise under s 49 or s 92. A proper exercise of the discretion would not impose an impediment upon freedom of intercourse greater than reasonably required to achieve the object of providing for the guardianship and custody of and access to children.

APLA Ltd v Legal Services Commissioner approved the test set out in ***AMS v AIF***. Justice Hayne explained that requiring a court to assess the merits of the purpose of a law is not an appropriate judicial function.

APLA Ltd v Legal Services Commissioner (NSW) (2005) 224 CLR 322

New South Wales regulations prohibited lawyers in New South Wales from advertising legal services in relation to personal injury claims. The High Court held that the regulation's burden on inter-State communication was reasonably required to achieve the regulation's objective of prohibiting New South Wales lawyers from advertising personal injury legal services.

Gleeson CJ and Heydon J

The regulations should be understood as dealing with advertising in relation to the providing of legal services in New South Wales. They are not aimed at interstate communications, and they certainly do not discriminate against them. Even so, their effect would extend to advertising by way of interstate communications. Indeed, if it were not so, evasion of the regulations, especially by means of electronic communications, would be simple …

The regulations would also prohibit advertising of legal services which may not be part of trade and commerce. Communication is intercourse, and covers advertising which is not part of trade and commerce. Let it be assumed that at least some of the advertising covered by the regulations is in that category. The object of the regulations is not to impede interstate intercourse. The test to be applied therefore is whether the impediment to such intercourse imposed by the regulations is greater than is reasonably required to achieve the object of the regulations. The object of the regulations is to restrict the advertising of legal services to be provided in New South Wales. That object can only be achieved by a general restriction on the advertising of such services. The impediment to interstate intercourse is no greater than is reasonably required to achieve the object of the regulations.

Gummow J

[I]t is convenient to consider the bearing of the "intercourse" limb of s 92 upon interstate communications advertising or promoting the provision without charge of legal services in New South Wales by non-profit bodies. This is on the assumption, which it is unnecessary to test, that such communications are not in trade or commerce …

More recently, in *AMS v AIF*, Gleeson CJ, McHugh and Gummow JJ said that, in working out the measure of freedom from interference which s 92 now is to be taken to provide in respect of interstate intercourse, the question becomes one whether the impediment imposed on that intercourse is greater than that reasonably required to achieve the objects of the legislation in question. Their Honours pointed out that the circumstance that the order made by the State Family Court in exercise of jurisdiction conferred by State legislation had a practical operation of hindering or restricting movement by the mother (by reason of the requirement that she not change the principal place of residence of the child) was not necessarily fatal to validity. Hayne J said in the same case:

> I agree that custody and guardianship legislation may present a question whether the statute empowers the making of orders that have a practical effect of imposing upon freedom of intercourse an impediment greater than reasonably required to achieve the object of the legislation.

This approach should be accepted as the doctrine of the Court ...

In the present case, on the assumption that the prohibition imposed by Pt 14 may apply to interstate communication which answers the description of "intercourse" in s 92, nevertheless, in that operation, Pt 14 is not invalid. This is because the effect of the prohibition on interstate communications is no greater than is reasonably required to achieve the object of Pt 14. That object could not be fully achieved if legal practitioners were permitted to direct from outside New South Wales to persons in New South Wales advertisements promoting the provision in New South Wales of the particular legal services with which the legislation is concerned.

Hayne J

The proposition that the application of the interstate intercourse limb of s 92 requires reference to a standard external to the law in question (the needs of an "ordered society") was not taken up by any member of the Court in *AMS v AIF* ... Upon what bases would the Court form a judgment about the needs of such an ordered society if the judgment of the legislature were to be treated as either irrelevant or not determinative?

It is difficulties of this kind which are to be seen as underpinning the rejection of reference to a standard external to the law in question and the adoption by the majority in *Cunliffe* and in *AMS v AIF* of a test that looks to the objects of that law.

In *AMS v AIF*, Gleeson CJ, McHugh and Gummow JJ said that where a law, by its practical operation rather than by its terms, imposes a burden or restriction on interstate intercourse, the law will be valid if the burden or restriction imposed is not greater than that reasonably required to achieve the *law's* objects. Leaving aside, then, laws which are specifically aimed at interstate intercourse, the test stated in the joint reasons in *AMS v AIF* invites attention to consideration of the objects of the law in question. And as Gummow J concludes in his reasons in the present matter, the principles stated in *AMS v AIF* should now be accepted as the applicable doctrine. Appeal to a standard external to the law in question (the needs of an ordered society) should be rejected. It is not a view that commands assent in the decided cases. It is a view which presents questions that find no ready answer ...

In so far as they would inhibit certain interstate communications by persons or bodies, like the amici curiae, who do not pursue commercial ends and whose communications do not form a part of interstate trade and commerce, the impugned regulations do not infringe the freedom of interstate intercourse. First, the impugned regulations are not aimed at impeding interstate intercourse. Secondly, the inhibition which the impugned regulations work on interstate intercourse is no greater than is necessary to achieve their purpose of preventing the advertisement, in New South Wales, of the legal services with which they deal.

Betfair (No 1), a case about inter-State trade and commerce, rejected the proportionality test adopted in ***Castlemaine Tooheys*** for being too deferential to legislative judgement and giving insufficient weight to the constitutional imperative for an Australia-wide free trade area. The case holds that the test is reasonable necessity. A law burdening inter-State trade and commerce is not of a protectionist kind if the burden is reasonably necessary to achieve a non-protectionist purpose. In this case, the High Court held that the test of reasonable necessity was not satisfied because other means of achieving the non-protectionist purpose that imposed a lighter burden on inter-State trade and commerce existed. The law was therefore invalid for breaching section 92.

Betfair Pty Ltd v Western Australia (2008) 234 CLR 418

Western Australia legislated to ban the placing of bets through online betting exchanges or offering to accept bets through online betting exchanges in relation to sporting events taking place in Western Australia. Western Australia argued this was necessary to maintain the integrity of racing since online betting exchanges allow bets to be placed on losers as well as winners. Tasmania had legislation allowing online betting exchanges with safeguards to guard against integrity issues. The High Court held the Western Australian law was not necessary to pursue the integrity purpose because the Tasmanian law demonstrated that the maintaining integrity purpose could be achieved by less drastic means.

Gleeson CJ, Gummow, Kirby, Hayne, Crennan and Kiefel JJ

However, with respect to the "appropriate and adapted" criterion expressed in *Castlemaine Tooheys*, counsel for the plaintiffs and for Tasmania submitted that necessarily it involves the existence of a "proportionality" between, on the one hand, the differential burden imposed on an out-of-State producer, when compared with the position of in-State producers, and, on the other hand, such competitively "neutral" objective as it is claimed the law is designed to achieve.

That "proportionality" must give significant weight to the considerations referred to earlier in these reasons ... These involve the constraint upon market forces operating within the national economy by legal barriers protecting the domestic producer or trader against the out-of-State producer or trader, with consequent prejudice to domestic customers of that out-of-State producer or trader. They suggest the application here, as elsewhere in constitutional, public and private law, of a criterion of "reasonable necessity". For example, in *North Eastern Dairy Co Ltd v Dairy Industry Authority of NSW*, Mason J said:

> As the defendant has failed to show that the discriminatory mode of regulation selected is necessary for the protection of public health, it is in my judgment not a reasonable regulation of the interstate trade in pasteurized milk.

His Honour also referred to remarks in a similar vein by the Privy Council in *Commonwealth v Bank of NSW*.

That view of the matter should be accepted as the doctrine of the Court. It is consistent with the explanation given in *Cole v Whitfield* of the justification of the total prohibition in the Tasmanian legislation on the sale of all undersized crayfish, irrespective of origin, as supplied by its objective of the conservation of the stock of Tasmanian crayfish. The Court held that the prohibition was a "necessary means of enforcing the prohibition against the catching of undersized crayfish in Tasmanian waters" because that State "cannot undertake inspections other than random inspections and the local crayfish are indistinguishable from those imported from South Australia".

Further reference also should be made here to the resolution in *Castlemaine Tooheys* by Mason CJ, Brennan, Deane, Dawson and Toohey JJ of the question of the validity of the South Australian legislation at stake there. They concluded from the facts, that the legislature of that State had "reasonably apprehended" that the sale of beer in non-refillable bottles manufactured in South Australia constituted a threat to the reserves of that State of natural gas. Their Honours then said that it might have been expected that State legislation would have prohibited the sale in South Australia of beer in non-refillable bottles produced in that State. They went on to note that an alternative measure might have been the prohibition of the manufacture in South Australia of such bottles, either at all, or with the use of natural gas. However, neither of these measures was adopted ...

[T]here was a lack of evidence of any increase in Australia of dishonest practices attributable to the operation of the betting exchange by Betfair. It will be recalled that Betfair's exchange remains accessible under the laws of the other States.

In that setting, it cannot be found in this case that prohibition was necessary in the stated sense for the protection or preservation of the integrity of the racing industry.

Both the plaintiffs and Tasmania put the case initially at the level that the protection of integrity was not a "substantial purpose" or "the real object" of the legislation. It is unnecessary to decide the case by ruling on that submission. This is because these parties also submitted that even if that object be seen as legitimate, the means adopted, prohibition, was not appropriate and adapted to achieve it given the avenue of regulation in a non-discriminatory manner ...

Finally, in ***Palmer v Western Australia (No 1)***, the High Court held that the reasonable necessity test applies consistently to section 92. The High Court said that the 'reasonably required' formulation in the earlier intercourse cases was simply a linguistic variation on 'reasonable necessity' but means the same thing. However, the judges were divided on how the reasonable necessity test should be applied.

A majority of the High Court (Kiefel CJ, Keane and Edelman JJ) held that the test of reasonable necessity should be applied using the structured proportionality approach of asking whether the means adopted by the law to achieve its purpose are suitable, necessary and adequate in balance. The details of structured proportionality are examined in detail in Chapter 12 in respect of the implied freedom of political communication.

Palmer v Western Australia (No 1) (2021) 246 CLR 182

Kiefel CJ and Keane J

Section 92 may be understood to preclude a law which burdens any of the freedoms there stated, as subjects of constitutional protection, where the law discriminates against interstate trade, commerce or intercourse and the burden cannot be justified as proportionate to the non-discriminatory, legitimate purpose of the law which is sought to be achieved. Whether it is proportionate is to be determined by the tests of structured proportionality as explained by this Court.

Edelman J

Structured proportionality makes explicit and transparent the only three independent grounds upon which a law might be held invalid as contrary to s 92. First, a law will be invalid if its very purpose is to undermine the freedom guaranteed by s 92. Secondly, a law will be invalid if its means of achieving its legitimate purpose are not "reasonably necessary", in the sense that those means burden the freedom guaranteed by s 92 substantially more than obvious and compelling alternatives which could achieve the purpose of the law to the same extent. Thirdly, and in absolutely exceptional cases, a law will be invalid if its legitimate, but trivial, purpose is inadequate to support the extent of the burden placed upon the high constitutional purpose of s 92.

The "structure" in structured proportionality is rigid in its refusal to countenance fictions or hidden grounds for invalidating legislation. As a matter of logic, each stage of the enquiry also follows the preceding stage. The first requires the identification of a legitimate purpose. The second requires assessment of the extent to which the means of achieving that legitimate purpose, not some other – hypothetical or fictional – purpose, is necessary. The third assesses whether, despite the reasonable necessity of the means adopted to achieve the legitimate purpose, the purpose nevertheless cannot justify the burden upon the constitutional freedom.

The High Court was clear that the holding that structured proportionality should be used to apply the reasonable necessity test should not be taken to cast doubt on the outcome of any of the earlier decisions considered in this chapter.

Palmer v Western Australia (No 1) (2021) 246 CLR 182

Kiefel CJ and Keane J

An acceptance of the tests of structured proportionality does not affect what was said in *Cole v Whitfield*. It simply explicates the tests for justification.

Consistently with their views in respect of the analytical framework for the implied freedom of political communication considered in Chapter 12, a minority of the High Court (Gageler and Gordon JJ) rejected structured proportionality, instead holding that the test of reasonable necessity should be applied by an evaluative judgement unconstrained by predetermined considerations.

13.8 When conduct is both 'trade and commerce' and 'intercourse'

There will be situations where conduct answers the description of both trade and commerce among the States *and* intercourse among the States. When section 92 was understood to be two distinct guarantees there was some uncertainty about how to assess law said to burden both inter-State trade and commerce and inter-State intercourse. The 're-integration' of the two limbs of section 92 by ***Palmer v Western Australia (No 1)*** has resolved that past uncertainty.

Palmer v Western Australia (No 1) (2021) 246 CLR 182

Gageler J

Re-integration brings complementarity. Recognising that each limb of s 92 of the Constitution guarantees freedom from discriminatory burdens, and that each limb demands the same standard of justification for a law imposing a differential burden, harmonises the operation of the two limbs in a manner that meets concerns expressed in *Nationwide News* and in *APLA* that each limb might have the potential to subsume the other. Each limb has a separate operation. In respect of intercourse occurring in trade or commerce, the two limbs overlap. To the extent they overlap, the guarantee of each must be observed.

13.9 DISCUSSION QUESTIONS

1. What do the words 'absolutely free' in section 92 mean?
2. What factors are relevant in determining the relevant field of trade and commerce? Answer with reference to the facts of ***Betfair (No 1)*** and ***Castlemaine Tooheys***.
3. When is a discriminatory burden on inter-state trade and commerce not of a protectionist kind?
4. What sorts of movements are included in the concept of 'intercourse'?
5. Problem question: Consider the following hypothetical scenario. There is a busy road between a town in the north of New South Wales and a town in the south of Queensland. There is no other convenient route between the two towns. Residents of the Queensland town often travel to a shopping centre in the New South Wales town. The New South Wales Government is concerned that the Queenslanders travelling on the road are a nuisance for New South Wales drivers at certain times of the day. The New South Wales Government constructs a gate across the road a few metres from the New South Wales–Queensland border that it keeps closed between the hours of 6 am and 10 am, but otherwise leaves open.

   Sally lives in the Queensland town and operates a business delivering milk to cafes in the surrounding regions, including in the New South Wales town. Her husband, Samuel, often does the family grocery shopping in the New South Wales town.

   Can Sally and Samuel challenge the New South Wales policy of closing the gate across the road on section 92 grounds?

PART

4

THE FEDERAL PARLIAMENT

THE FEDERAL PARLIAMENT

14

14.1 Overview

This chapter examines the Federal Parliament as an institution, focusing on its composition. The *Australian Constitution* prescribes that the Federal Parliament consists of the monarch, a Senate and a House of Representatives.

The *Constitution* provides that senators are chosen from each State but also provides that laws may be enacted granting parliamentary representation to the Territories. The High Court has read these provisions together to permit senators to be chosen from the Territories. The *Constitution* also sets out various grounds which disqualify a person from being chosen or serving as a parliamentarian.

Key concepts considered in this chapter include:

- representation
- citizen of a foreign power
- entitled to the rights and privileges of a citizen of a foreign power
- constitutional imperative
- under sentence or subject to be sentenced
- office of profit under the Crown
- indirect pecuniary interest
- agreement with the Public Service.

14.2 Composition of the Federal Parliament

Section 1 of the *Constitution* provides that the Federal Parliament consists of three elements: the monarch, a Senate and a House of Representatives.

Australian Constitution

Section 1

The legislative power of the Commonwealth shall be vested in a Federal Parliament, which shall consist of the Queen, a Senate, and a House of Representatives, and which is hereinafter called The Parliament, or The Parliament of the Commonwealth.

The monarch

Australia's Federal Parliament is usually described as being bicameral, in the sense of consisting of two Houses (rather than unicameral, consisting of one House). Section 1 of the *Constitution* is plain that the monarch is a third constituent element of the Federal Parliament. The *Constitution* was drafted during the reign of Queen Victoria with the result that various provisions refer to 'the Queen'. Covering clause 2 states that 'The provisions of this Act referring to the Queen shall extend Her Majesty's heirs and successors'.

John Quick and Robert Garran, *The Annotated Constitution of the Commonwealth of Australia* (Angus & Robertson, 1901)

The Federal Parliament consists of the Queen, the Senate, and the House of Representatives. This is a statutory recognition of the Queen as a constituent part of Parliament. In the British Constitution, and in most of the colonial constitutions, the King or Queen for the time being has up to the present been recognized in form and in theory, at least, as the principal legislator, if not the sole legislator, acting by and with the consent of the parliamentary bodies. For over three hundred years every Act of Parliament passed in England has begun with the well-known formula "Be it enacted by the King's (Queen's) most excellent Majesty by and with the advice and consent," &c. In the Australian Constitutional Acts, 5 and 6 Vic. c. 76, and 13 and 14 Vic. c. 59, the legislative power was vested in the Governor by and with the advice and consent of the Legislative Council, &c. In the subsequent constitutions of the self-governing Australian colonies (1855) the power of legislation was conferred upon the Queen "by and with the advice and consent of the said Council and Assembly."

In the Constitution of the Commonwealth the old fiction that the occupant of the throne was the principal legislator, as expressed in the above formula, has been disregarded; and the ancient enacting words will hereafter be replaced by words more in harmony with the practice and reality of constitutional government. The Queen, instead of being represented as the principal or sole legislator, is now plainly stated to be one of the co-ordinate constituents of the Parliament. Consequently, federal legislation will begin with such mandatory words as "Be it enacted by the Queen, the Senate, and the House of Representatives," or, "Be it enacted by the Parliament of the Commonwealth of Australia."

Various provisions of Chapter 1, The Parliament, provide for the monarch's powers in respect of legislation.

Australian Constitution

Section 58 Royal Assent to Bills

When a proposed law passed by both Houses of the Parliament is presented to the Governor-General for the Queen's assent, he shall declare, according to his discretion, but subject to this Constitution, that he assents in the Queen's name, or that he withholds assent, or that he reserves the law for the Queen's pleasure.

Recommendations by Governor-General

The Governor-General may return to the house in which it originated any proposed law so presented to him, and may transmit therewith any amendments which he may recommend, and the Houses may deal with the recommendation.

Section 59 Disallowance by the Queen

The Queen may disallow any law within one year from the Governor-General's assent, and such disallowance on being made known by the Governor-General by speech or message to each of the Houses of the Parliament, or by Proclamation, shall annul the law from the day when the disallowance is so made known.

Section 60 Signification of Queen's pleasure on Bills reserved

A proposed law reserved for the Queen's pleasure shall not have any force unless and until within two years from the day on which it was presented to the Governor-General for the Queen's assent the Governor-General makes known, by speech or message to each of the Houses of the Parliament, or by Proclamation, that it has received the Queen's assent.

In practice, Royal Assent is granted to the Bills duly passed by the House of Representatives and the Senate by the Governor-General acting on the advice of Ministers.

The Senate

The Senate is the upper house of the Federal Parliament. Section 7 of the *Constitution* is the key provision describing the composition of the Senate. Section 7 provides that:

- senators represent States
- senators for each State are chosen by the people of each State
- each original State is guaranteed an equal number of Senators, and
- senators serve fixed terms of six years.

Australian Constitution

Section 7 The Senate

The Senate shall be composed of senators for each State, directly chosen by the people of the State, voting, until the Parliament otherwise provides, as one electorate.

But until the Parliament of the Commonwealth otherwise provides, the Parliament of the State of Queensland, if that State be an Original State, may make laws dividing the State into divisions and determining the number of senators to be chosen for each division, and in the absence of such provision the State shall be one electorate.

Until the Parliament otherwise provides there shall be six senators for each Original State. The Parliament may make laws increasing or diminishing the number of senators for each State, but so that equal representation of the several Original States shall be maintained and that no Original State shall have less than six senators.

The senators shall be chosen for a term of six years, and the names of the senators chosen for each State shall be certified by the Governor to the Governor-General.

Section 51(xxxvi) of the *Constitution* gives the Federal Parliament power to make laws concerning 'matters in respect of which this Constitution makes provision until the Parliament otherwise provides'. Parliament has used this power in respect of section 7 to increase the size of the Senate over time. With effect from 1984, each State now has 12 senators.

Representation Act 1983 (Cth)

Section 3 Representation of each State in the Senate

The number of senators for each State shall be 12.

The *Senate (Representation of Territories) Act 1973* (Cth) amended the *Commonwealth Electoral Act 1918* (Cth) to provide for two senators each from the Australian Capital Territory and the Northern Territory.

Commonwealth Electoral Act 1918 (Cth)

Section 40 Representation of the Territories in the Senate

(1) Subject to subsection (2), the Australian Capital Territory and the Northern Territory shall each be represented in the Senate by 2 senators for the Territory directly chosen by the people of the Territory voting as one electorate.

(2) Where the number of members of the House of Representatives to be chosen in the Australian Capital Territory or the Northern Territory at a general election is 6 or more, that Territory shall, on and from the day of the general election, be represented in the Senate by one senator for every 2 members of the House of Representatives to be chosen in that Territory.

The validity of senators for the Territories is considered below.

The House of Representatives

The House of Representatives is the lower house of the Federal Parliament. Section 24 of the *Constitution* is the key provision describing the composition of the House of Representatives. Section 24 provides that:

- there must be, as nearly as practicable, twice the number of members of the House of Representative as senators
- the number of members of the House of Representatives chosen from each State must be in proportion to the size of the population of each State, and
- there must be at least five members of the House of Representatives chosen from each original State.

Australian Constitution

Section 24 Constitution of House of Representatives

The House of Representatives shall be composed of members directly chosen by the people of the Commonwealth, and the number of such members shall be, as nearly as practicable, twice the number of the senators.

The number of members chosen in the several States shall be in proportion to the respective numbers of their people, and shall, until the Parliament otherwise provides, be determined, whenever necessary, in the following manner:

(i) a quota shall be ascertained by dividing the number of the people of the Commonwealth, as shown by the latest statistics of the Commonwealth, by twice the number of the senators;

(ii) the number of members to be chosen in each State shall be determined by dividing the number of the people of the State, as shown by the latest statistics of the Commonwealth, by the quota; and if on such division there is a remainder greater than one-half of the quota, one more member shall be chosen in the State.

But notwithstanding anything in this section, five members at least shall be chosen in each Original State.

The *Commonwealth Electoral Act 1918* (Cth) now provides for the representation of the Territories in the House of Representatives. Territories are entitled to representation in the House of Representatives subject to meeting a minimum population threshold. The exceptions to this are the Australian Capital Territory and the Northern Territory, which are each entitled to at least one member in the House of Representatives regardless of population.

Commonwealth Electoral Act 1918 (Cth)

48 Determination of number of members of House of Representatives to be chosen in States and Territories

...

(2A) The Electoral Commissioner shall divide the number of people of each Territory, as ascertained in accordance with section 46, by the quota ascertained under paragraph (2)(a) and, subject to subsections (2B), (2BA), (2C) and (2F), shall determine:

- (a) if the result of the division is less than or equal to 0.5–that no member of the House of Representatives be chosen in the Territory at a general election;
- (b) if the result of the division is greater than 0.5 and less than or equal to 1.5–that one member of the House of Representatives be chosen in the Territory at a general election; or
- (c) in any other case–that the number of members of the House of Representatives to be chosen in the Territory at a general election is the number ascertained by the division or, if there is a remainder greater than one-half of the quota, that number increased by one.

(2B) At least one member of the House of Representatives shall be chosen in the Australian Capital Territory and in the Northern Territory at a general election.

14.3 Parliamentary representatives for the Territories

Section 7 refers expressly to the Senate being composed of senators for the States. Section 24 refers to choosing members of the House of Representatives from each State. While neither of these provisions refers to the Territories, section 122 indicates that the Territories may be granted parliamentary representation.

Australian Constitution

122 Government of territories

The Parliament may make laws for the government of any territory surrendered by any State to and accepted by the Commonwealth, or of any territory placed by the Queen under the authority of and accepted by the Commonwealth, or otherwise acquired by the Commonwealth, and may allow the representation of such territory in either House of the Parliament to the extent and on the terms which it thinks fit.

The High Court has confirmed that the type of 'representation' section 122 permits includes senators for the Territories with full membership of the Senate and for members of the House of Representatives chosen from the Territories with full membership of the House of Representatives.

In the ***First Territory Senators Case***, the States argued that legislation providing for senators for the Northern Territory was invalid. The argument was that the words 'The Senate shall be composed of senators for each State' in section 7 of the *Constitution* precluded the possibility of Territory senators. A majority of the High Court disagreed.

The majority judges – McTiernan, Mason, Jacobs and Murphy JJ – held that section 7 should be understood as prescribing the situation until the Parliament acts under section 122 to provide for Territory representation in the Senate. The majority held that the concept 'representation' used in section 122 was wide enough to include full senators with the same rights as other senators.

Western Australia v Commonwealth ('First Territory Senators Case') (1975) 134 CLR 201

Mason J

With respect to representation of a Territory in either House of the Commonwealth Parliament the Parliament has, by virtue of s 122, power to determine (a) the extent of the representation and (b) the terms of that representation. By way of contrast, upon the admission or establishment of a new State pursuant to s 121, the Parliament only has power to determine the extent of the representation to be accorded the new State. The inclusion in s 122 of a specific power to allow representation upon any terms which the Parliament thinks fit makes it plain that the Parliament may confer on representatives of a Territory rights and privileges identical or inferior to those enjoyed by a member of either House. But in the case of a new State, Parliament has power to determine only the number of representatives a new State may have; the representatives of a new State necessarily enjoy the rights and privileges of the representatives of the original States – Parliament cannot diminish their rights and privileges ...

Just as s 122 requires to be read with Ch I so also account must be taken of s 122 in the interpretation of ss 7 and 24. If they are to be read as limiting the composition of each House for all time to representatives of the States, it follows that the power given to Parliament by s 122 to "allow the representation of such Territory in either House of the Parliament to the extent and on the terms which it thinks fit" must be confined to a power to provide for the appointment of representatives of the Territories who are voteless, if not voiceless. To so construe the power is to deprive it of significant content, notwithstanding the wide and general words by which it is conferred. The section would then admit only of representation by a person who was not a member of the House and who did not enjoy the rights of a member to vote. The attribution of such a restricted concept of "representation" to s 122 would stand in stark contrast with the concept of "representation" in the complete sense of membership which is evident in s 121.

The apparent opposition which arises from the reference to representation of the territories in s 122 and the absence of any such reference in ss 7 and 24 is irreconcilable only if it be assumed that Ch I in making provision for the composition of the Senate and the House is necessarily speaking for all time. To my mind this assumption is misconceived. Sections 7 and 24 should be regarded as making provision for the composition of each House which nevertheless, in the shape of s 122, takes account of the prospective possibility that Parliament might deem it expedient, having regard to the stage which a Territory might reach in the course of its future development, to give it representation in either House by allowing it to elect members of that House. To the framers of the Constitution in 1900 the existing condition of the Territories was not such as to suggest the immediate likelihood of their securing representation in either House, but the possibility of such a development occurring in the future was undeniable. The prospect of its occurrence was foreseen and in my view it found expression in s 122.

Understood in this light, ss 7 and 24 make exhaustive provision for the composition of each House until such time as Parliament might see fit to allow representation to a territory under s 122 ...

Murphy J

The critical word in s 122 is "representation". Its ordinary dictionary meaning is "the fact of representing or being represented in a legislative or deliberative assembly, especially in Parliament" (The Oxford English Dictionary). The word "representation" appears in other sections of the Constitution, and the presumption is that when identical words are used in different parts of a statute their meaning is the same ... Thus, using the Constitution as a dictionary, the word "representation" in s 122 plainly means "membership" which accords with its ordinary meaning ...

The Constitution is designed for a democratic society. Except for the role of the Queen, which by convention has become largely formal, the Constitution is based on the concept of democracy. It was written against the background of the struggle, substantially fought out over the previous hundred and fifty years, for the representative form of popular democratic government ...

There is little doubt that s 122 was inserted to ensure that the privilege of membership in each House should not be denied forever to the people of the territories ...

The permanent deprivation of representation by membership in the Senate or the House of Representatives is a serious exclusion from the democratic process. These houses are our most important political institutions, the principal organs of our democracy; their decisions are vital to every Australian. Their importance to the people of the territories is not less than their importance to the people of the States. It is contrary to the democratic theme of the Constitution that Parliament should not be able to allow representation by membership in either House to territories at the time and on the terms which the Parliament considers appropriate ...

The key difference between the majority and dissenting judgments is that the majority judges emphasise the democratic character of the *Constitution* and the dissenting judges emphasise the federal character of the *Constitution*. The dissenting judges – Barwick CJ, Gibbs and Stephen JJ – held that sections 7 and 122 could be read together as permitting

Territory representation in the Senate by means other than the creation of senators for the Territories such as by non-voting delegates with only a right to speak. They considered that this approach would preserve the federal character of the *Constitution* and the role of the Senate as the States' House.

Western Australia v Commonwealth ('First Territory Senators Case') (1975) 134 CLR 201

Barwick CJ (dissenting)

There is no form of representation which the language of s 122 compels. It could not be said that if representation is provided it must, in relation to the Senate, be by a senator with full rights and privileges of a senator for a State. Nor could it be said, in my opinion, that to make provision for a non-voting delegate would not be to allow representation.

On the other hand, the federal nature of the Constitution and the sections to which I have referred, point against such a form of representation as would alter or affect such an essential part of the federation as to the relationship of the States to the Commonwealth and to one another provided by the establishment of the Senate as a "States House". It must be representation of a kind which does not qualify or impinge upon the unqualified specification of s 7 – "The Senate shall be composed of Senators for each State, directly chosen by the people of the State, voting, until the Parliament otherwise provides, as one electorate". I have already emphasized that by no proper method of construction could the words "until the Parliament otherwise provides" be implied as a controlling preface to ss 7 and 24: nor can s 122 be read as if ss 7 and 24 were so controlled ...

In the United States, whose Constitution provided in large part a model for the Constitution of Australia, the District of Columbia, a territory of the United States, was not regarded in 1900 as entitled to representation in the Congress. In effect, it was allowed delegates to the Congress who were not members of the Congress, nor entitled to vote on any matter, including matters which might exclusively relate to the District of Columbia. Even as of this time, dependent territories of the United States, deriving from the federal government such governmental authority as they exercise, having no senators or representatives in the Congress other than delegates with limited functions. The absence from the American Constitution of a counterpart of s 122 does not in my opinion weaken the significance of the American experience. There is thus, in my opinion, no incongruity in confining the power to allow representation of a dependent territory of a federation to a power to provide for a non-voting delegate or delegates ...

The outcome of the ***First Territory Senators Case*** was affirmed in the ***Second Territory Senators Case.*** The *First Territory Senators Case* was a challenge only to the constitutional validity of Territory Senators. The *Second Territory Senators Case* was a challenge to the constitutional validity of both Territory senators and Territory members of the House of Representatives.

Queensland v Commonwealth ('Second Territory Senators Case') (1977) 139 CLR 585

Stephen J

Some two years ago a full bench of this Court heard and, by a majority of four to three, determined in favour of the Commonwealth actions instituted by the States of Western Australia, Queensland and New South Wales challenging the validity of (inter alia) the *Senate (Representation of Territories) Act 1973*. One ground of such challenge was that the Act was beyond the legislative power of the Commonwealth. A majority of the Court concluded that the power conferred upon Parliament by s 122 of the Constitution, to "allow the representation of such territory in either House of the Parliament to the extent and on the terms which it thinks fit", extended to authorize the Act.

The State of Queensland now again comes to this Court seeking a declaration that this same Act is beyond the legislative power of the Commonwealth; the State of Western Australia, in two separate writs, seeks declarations that the *Northern Territory Representation Act 1922* and the *Australian Capital Territory Representation (House of Representatives) Act 1973* are similarly beyond power ...

In these proceedings opposing counsel have each marshalled sets of divergent considerations which are said to support their competing submissions. Despite the powerful submissions which have been urged justifying a reconsideration of *Western Australia v Commonwealth* submissions the attraction of which has not been diminished by the fact that I formed one of the minority in that case, I have concluded that it should not be reviewed but should be regarded as an authority determinative of this appeal ...

I will not set out all the rival considerations which have been urged but will confine myself to those matters which, together, have, for me, proved conclusive.

The first concerns the nature of the precedent authority in question. It is a very recent decision in which all members of the Court participated and in which, after full argument, a majority, in elaborately reasoned judgments, dealt in specific terms and as the principal point for decision with the very matter now in question, the effect of the concluding words of s 122 of the Constitution. The second relates to the nature of the subject-matter for decision; what was in issue was the interpretation of the words of the section in their context. There existed no precedent cases nor any settled principles of the law which provided clear guidance. The case was very much one upon which different minds might reach different conclusions, no one view being inherently entitled to any pre-eminence as conforming better than others to principle or to precedent ...

Mason J

Whether the representation of a Territory by a voting member in a House of the Parliament is consistent with the Federal compact depends upon the terms of the Federal compact as it is expressed in the Constitution. But in so far as the plaintiffs' case may be thought to draw independent support from considerations deriving from the Federal compact, it is to be noted that since *Western Australia v Commonwealth* was decided the Constitution was amended in 1977 so as to accord to the people in the Territories a vote in referenda for amending the Constitution.

The power of Parliament to provide for representation of the Territories in the Senate is coextensive with its power to provide for their representation in the House of Representatives. As I said *Western Australia v Commonwealth*, in terms of Territory representation no distinction can be drawn between the House and Senate. The apparent conflict between s 7 and s 122 is reflected in the relationship which exists between s 24 and s 122. It was not suggested in argument in this case that any relevant distinction could be drawn between representation in the Senate and representation in the House. The result is that if the Court were to depart from its earlier decision the departure would necessarily entail the invalidity of the legislation providing for Territory representation in the House of Representatives as well as in the invalidity of the legislation providing for Territory representation in the Senate.

However, as it is my view that *Western Australia v Commonwealth* was correctly decided, I would uphold the demurrers in the three actions.

14.4 Disqualification from the Federal Parliament

The *Constitution* prescribes various grounds of disqualification for membership of the Senate and House of Representatives.

Australian Constitution

Section 44 Disqualification

Any person who:

(i) is under any acknowledgment of allegiance, obedience, or adherence to a foreign power, or is a subject or a citizen or entitled to the rights or privileges of a subject or a citizen of a foreign power; or

(ii) is attainted of treason, or has been convicted and is under sentence, or subject to be sentenced, for any offence punishable under the law of the Commonwealth or of a State by imprisonment for one year or longer; or

(iii) is an undischarged bankrupt or insolvent; or

(iv) holds any office of profit under the Crown, or any pension payable during the pleasure of the Crown out of any of the revenues of the Commonwealth; or

(v) has any direct or indirect pecuniary interest in any agreement with the Public Service of the Commonwealth otherwise than as a member and in common with the other members of an incorporated company consisting of more than twenty-five persons;

shall be incapable of being chosen or of sitting as a senator or a member of the House of Representatives.

But subsection (iv) does not apply to the office of any of the Queen's Ministers of State for the Commonwealth, or of any of the Queen's Ministers for a State, or to the receipt of pay, half pay, or a pension, by any person as an officer or member of the Queen's navy or army, or to the receipt of pay as an officer or member of the naval or military forces of the Commonwealth by any person whose services are not wholly employed by the Commonwealth.

Section 45 Vacancy on happening of disqualification

If a senator or member of the House of Representatives:

(i) becomes subject to any of the disabilities mentioned in the last preceding section; or

(ii) takes the benefit, whether by assignment, composition, or otherwise, of any law relating to bankrupt or insolvent debtors; or

(iii) directly or indirectly takes or agrees to take any fee or honorarium for services rendered to the Commonwealth, or for services rendered in the Parliament to any person or State; his place shall thereupon become vacant.

The temporal element of disqualification

The grounds of disqualification in section 44 are expressed to operate to render a person incapable of *being chosen* or of *sitting* as a senator or a member of the House of Representatives. ***Sykes v Cleary*** explains that the process of being chosen referred to in section 44 commences when a person nominates for election to Federal Parliament. A person who at the time of their nomination or at any time thereafter falls within any of the grounds provided for in section 44 is disqualified.

Sykes v Cleary (1992) 176 CLR 77

A person fell within the terms of section 44(iv) at the time of his nomination for election to the House of Representatives but altered his circumstances such that he did not fall within the terms of section 44(iv) at the time the result of the election was declared. The High Court held that the person was disqualified.

Mason CJ, Toohey and McHugh JJ

As a matter of language, the disqualifying characteristics set out in s 44 are related to "being chosen". Whether those words refer to the act of choice or the process of being chosen is a question to be determined. Even on the narrower of the alternatives, namely, that the words refer to the act of choice, the outcome would be unfavourable to the first respondent. The people exercise their choice by voting ... so that it is the polling day rather than the day on which the poll is declared that marks the time when a candidate is chosen by the people. Of course, an absentee or postal vote may be cast before the polling day and, in situations of emergency, arrangements may be made for the casting of votes after the polling day (The Electoral Act, s 241). But these characteristics of the polling do not justify the conclusion that the declaration of the poll, which is the formal announcement of the result of the poll, amounts to, or even coincides with, the choosing by the electors of the member for the relevant electoral division. The declaration of the poll is the announcement of the choice made; it is not the making of the choice.

The interpretation just rejected would, if it were upheld, enable a public servant who falls within par (iv) in s 44 to avoid disqualification by resigning from the relevant office of profit after the polling day but before the declaration of the poll. The public servant could be nominated and stand for election and, if he or she secured a majority of votes, have an option to resign and be declared elected or not to resign and be disqualified. The adverse consequences this would have for the electoral process are an additional reason for rejecting the suggested interpretation. The inclusion in the list of candidates on polling day of a candidate who may opt for disqualification may well constitute an additional and unnecessary complication in the making by the electors of their choice. Furthermore, it is hardly conducive to certainty and speed in the ascertainment of the result of the election that it should depend upon a decision to be made by a candidate on or after polling day. Speed and certainty in the ascertainment of the result of the first election to the Parliament of the Commonwealth were enhanced by the fact that in 1901, in all the Australian colonies other than Queensland and parts of Tasmania, the "first past the post" system of electoral voting prevailed in lower House elections (See Constitution, s 1, which provided for the application of State laws in relation to the election of members of the House of Representatives.).

Reflection on these considerations persuades us that the words "shall be incapable of being chosen" refer to the process of being chosen, of which nomination is an essential part ...

Re Canavan affirmed the decision in ***Sykes v Cleary*** as to the temporal dimension indicated by the words 'incapable of being chosen'.

Re Canavan (2017) 349 ALR 534

Kiefel CJ, Bell, Gageler, Keane, Nettle, Gordon and Edelman JJ

It is settled by authority, and not disputed by any party, that in s 44 the words "shall be incapable of being chosen" refer to the process of being chosen, of which nomination is an essential part. Accordingly, the temporal focus for the purposes of s 44(i) is upon the date of nomination as the date on and after which s 44(i) applies until the completion of the electoral process ...

Section 45(i) makes clear that a parliamentarian who, although not disqualified at the time they nominate for election or at any other time during the process of being chosen, later falls within any of the circumstances listed in section 44 becomes disqualified and that parliamentarian's seat becomes vacant.

There is a difference between a person having been incapable of being chosen in accordance with section 44 and a seat becoming vacant because a parliamentarian becomes disqualified during their term in office in accordance with section 45(i). A person incapable of being chosen by reason of section 44 was never validly a parliamentarian. In the case of the House of Representatives, a by-election is held to fill the seat. In the case of the Senate, a special count of the votes is held to determine who should fill the seat. ***Re Nash (No 2)*** explains that the vacancy in the seat is a result of the electoral process – the process of choosing parliamentarians – not yet being complete.

Re Nash (No 2) (2017) 350 ALR 204

Senator Nash was found to have been incapable of being chosen as a senator. A special count of the votes to determine who should fill the seat would have returned Ms Hughes. However, believing Senator Nash to have been properly elected and therefore that she had not won a seat, Ms Hughes accepted appointment to an office of profit under the Crown. Because Senator Nash was incapable of being chosen, the process of choosing senators had not yet been completed even though it was 13 months since polling day. The result was Ms Hughes fell within one of the grounds of disqualification during the period of choosing senators and was therefore incapable of being chosen.

Kiefel CJ, Bell, Gageler, Keane and Edelman JJ

The question of the temporal end-point of what in *Sykes v Cleary* was identified as "the process of being chosen", during which a disqualification under s 44 takes effect, must therefore be accepted to be one which has been left unanswered by binding authority. The question now falls to be resolved at the level of principle by reference to the text and structure of the Constitution having due regard to the course of its interpretation ...

Whatever the end-point of the process of being chosen to which s 44 refers, a person has become a senator or member of the House of Representatives within the meaning of s 45 once that end-point is reached. If the person thereafter becomes subject to a disability mentioned in s 44, not only does s 44 operate to prevent the person from sitting but s 45(i) operates to vacate his or her place. Section 45(i) has that operation even if the person has not yet taken his or her seat for the place for which he or she was chosen and, by reason of becoming subject to the disability, is prevented by s 44 from ever doing so ...

The processes of choice which the Parliament has prescribed in the Act for the purposes of ss 7 and 24 of the Constitution continue until a candidate is determined in accordance with those processes to have been chosen. They are brought to an end only with the declaration of the result of the election and of the names of the candidates elected, after which certification of those names and return of the writ is a formality ...

Ms Hughes was disqualified by operation of s 44(iv) of the Constitution from being elected as a senator for the State of New South Wales for the place for which Ms Nash was returned because Ms Hughes held an office of profit under the Crown during a period in which the disqualification of Ms Nash from being validly returned as elected meant that the process of choice prescribed by the Parliament for the purpose of s 7 of the Constitution remained incomplete. By reason of Ms Hughes' disqualification, the Attorney-General's summons seeking an order that she be declared duly elected as a senator was dismissed.

Lest it might seem harsh or unduly technical, this result needs to be understood in context. The issue of whether Ms Hughes was ineligible to be chosen arose only as an incident of the ultimate determination of questions concerning the existence of a vacancy in the representation of New South Wales in the Senate for the place for which Ms Nash was returned which the Senate resolved to refer to the Court of Disputed Returns some 13 months after Ms Nash was in fact returned. Ms Hughes' acceptance in the meantime of appointment to the Administrative Appeals Tribunal, with the entitlement to remuneration which that appointment brought, was understandable. But it was a voluntary step which she took in circumstances where reference by the Senate to the Court of

Disputed Returns of a question concerning whether a vacancy existed in the representation of New South Wales in the Senate by reason of the disqualification or lack of qualification of a senator who had been returned as elected was always a possibility. By choosing to accept the appointment for the future, Ms Hughes forfeited the opportunity to benefit in the future from any special count of the ballot papers that might be directed as a result of such a vacancy being found ...

A person disqualified by section 45(i) was initially validly a parliamentarian but only later became disqualified. The vacancy in the seat is a casual vacancy. Casual vacancies also occur when a parliamentarian resigns their position. In the case of the House of Representatives, a by-election is held to fill the seat. In the case of the senate, a new senator is chosen to fill the vacancy by the Parliament of the State for which the senator was chosen in accordance with section 15 of the *Constitution*, which governs casual vacancies in the Senate.

Legislation empowers the Court of Disputed Returns to determine issues concerning the qualification of parliamentarians. The *Commonwealth Electoral Act 1918* (Cth) provides for the validity of any election (including a challenge to the qualifications of a person elected) to be disputed in the Court of the Disputed Returns by petition filed within 40 days of the election. That statute also empowers the relevant House at any time to refer questions in respect of the qualifications of a parliamentarian to the Court of Disputed Returns for determination.

14.5 Section 44(i) – disqualification of dual citizens

Section 44(i) provides for multiple grounds of disqualification. There are competing views as to whether section 44(i) consists of two or three limbs. The most recent authority holds that section 44(i) consists of two limbs and disqualifies:

- any person who is under any acknowledgment of allegiance, obedience or adherence to a foreign power, and
- any person who is a subject or a citizen or entitled to the rights or privileges of a subject or a citizen of a foreign power.

The three-limb understanding of section 44(i) splits the second limb into two limbs: one dealing with any person who is a subject or citizen of a foreign power and the other dealing with any person who is entitled to the rights or privileges of a subject or citizen of a foreign power. There does not appear to be any practical difference between the two-limb and three-limb view of section 44(i).

Re Canavan (2017) 349 ALR 534

Kiefel CJ, Bell, Gageler, Keane, Nettle, Gordon and Edelman JJ

As to the text and structure of s 44(i), in *Sykes v Cleary* Brennan J said that "[p]utting acknowledgment of adherence to a foreign power to one side", s 44(i) consists of three categories of disqualification, each of which describes a source of a duty on the part of a candidate for parliamentary office ...

The amicus submitted that s 44(i) has two limbs, not three as was suggested by Brennan J ...

There is evident force in the submission of the amicus that s 44(i) consists of only two limbs: the verb "is" is used in s 44(i) only twice, and there is a comma followed by the disjunctive "or" at the end of the first limb but not within the second limb.

For present purposes, however, little turns upon this difference between the analysis of Brennan J in *Sykes v Cleary* and that of the amicus; indeed, Brennan J dealt with his "second and third categories" together. Each approach highlights the distinction expressly drawn in s 44(i) between a voluntary act of allegiance on the part of the person concerned on the one hand, and a state of affairs existing under foreign law, being the status of subjecthood or citizenship or the existence of the rights or privileges of subjecthood or citizenship, on the other. For the sake of clarity, these reasons will use the two-limb classification adopted by the amicus ...

There have been no cases decided by a full bench of the High Court on the ground that a person is under any acknowledgment of allegiance, obedience or adherence to a foreign power.

When is a person a citizen or subject of a foreign power?

Re Canavan explains that citizenship of a foreign power is a question of legal status determined by the operation of foreign law. The case concerned the situation of seven parliamentarians, each of whom was alleged to have been a dual citizen: that is, both an Australian citizen and a citizen of another country. The High Court held that five of the parliamentarians were citizens of foreign powers because they each held the status of citizen under the law of the foreign powers in question. It was irrelevant that the parliamentarians may not have known they held that legal status.

Re Canavan (2017) 349 ALR 534

Kiefel CJ, Bell, Gageler, Keane, Nettle, Gordon and Edelman JJ

In *Sykes v Cleary*, the plurality, comprising Mason CJ, Toohey and McHugh JJ, said that s 44(i) was adopted to ensure "that members of Parliament did not have a split allegiance".

Brennan J explained that the purpose of s 44(i) "is to ensure that no candidate, senator or member of the House of Representatives owes allegiance or obedience to a foreign power or adheres to a foreign power." Deane J said that the "whole purpose" of s 44(i) is to "prevent persons with foreign loyalties or obligations from being members of the Australian Parliament."

It is evident that the first limb of s 44(i) pursues this purpose by looking to the conduct of the person concerned. The second limb of s 44(i) does not look to conduct manifesting an actual split in the allegiance of the person concerned or the person's subjective feelings of allegiance. On the contrary, it operates to disqualify the candidate whether or not the candidate is, in fact, minded to act upon his or her duty of allegiance.

In the course of arguing that a candidate cannot be disqualified by the second limb of s 44(i) if he or she does not know that he or she has the status of a foreign citizen, Senior Counsel for Mr Joyce MP and Senator Nash made the rhetorical point that "[y]ou cannot heed a call that you cannot hear and you will not hear the call of another citizenship if you do not know you are a citizen of that other country." The answer to that point is that, as a matter of the ordinary meaning of the second limb of s 44(i), proof of actual allegiance as a state of mind is not required. Rather, as Brennan J explained in *Sykes v Cleary*, the second limb is concerned with the existence of a duty to a foreign power as an aspect of the status of citizenship ...

Whether a person has the status of a subject or a citizen of a foreign power necessarily depends upon the law of the foreign power. That is so because it is only the law of the foreign power that can be the source of the status of citizenship or of the rights and duties involved in that status ...

Section 44(i) does not say that it operates only if the candidate knows of the disqualifying circumstance ...

[W]hile it may be said that it is harsh to apply s 44(i) to disqualify a candidate born in Australia who has never had occasion to consider himself or herself as other than an Australian citizen and exclusively an Australian citizen, nomination for election is manifestly an occasion for serious reflection on this question; the nomination form for candidates for both the Senate and the House of Representatives requires candidates to declare that they are not rendered ineligible by s 44 ...

Section 44(i) operates to render "incapable of being chosen or of sitting" persons who have the status of subject or citizen of a foreign power. Whether a person has the status of foreign subject or citizen is determined by the law of the foreign power in question. Proof of a candidate's knowledge of his or her foreign citizenship status (or of facts that might put a candidate on inquiry as to the possibility that he or she is a foreign citizen) is not necessary to bring about the disqualifying operation of s 44(i) ...

Of the remaining two parliamentarians considered in ***Re Canavan***, one (Senator Xenophon) was held to hold a legal status that did not amount to citizenship in the sense that concept is used in section 44 (see below) and there was insufficient proof that the other (Senator Canavan) held the status of citizen under Italian law as was alleged.

When is a person entitled to the rights and privileges of a foreign citizen?

Re Canavan explains that a person is entitled to the rights and privileges of a citizen of a foreign power if the person has a right of abode in the territory of the foreign power or owes a duty of loyalty to the foreign power. On the facts of this case, Senator Xenophon held the status of 'British overseas citizen' under United Kingdom law but that status did not come with a right of abode in the United Kingdom or an obligation of loyalty to the United Kingdom. For that reason, the High Court held that Senator Xenophon was neither a citizen of the United Kingdom nor entitled to the rights and privileges of a United Kingdom citizen.

Re Canavan (2017) 349 ALR 534

Kiefel CJ, Bell, Gageler, Keane, Nettle, Gordon and Edelman JJ

As will appear, Senator Xenophon was a "British overseas citizen" ("BOC") at the date of his nomination for election as a senator for South Australia. On 25 August 2017, Senator Xenophon signed an application to renounce his British overseas citizenship. On 31 August 2017, the United Kingdom Home Office informed Senator Xenophon that he ceased to be a BOC on 30 August 2017.

The issue is whether as a BOC Senator Xenophon was incapable of being chosen as a senator because he was "a subject or a citizen of a foreign power" or a person "entitled to the rights or privileges of a subject or a citizen of a foreign power" for the purposes of s 44(i) of the Constitution. The answer is that Senator Xenophon was not disqualified under s 44(i). To explain why that is so it is necessary to describe the incidents of British overseas citizenship ...

There is no question that Senator Xenophon was a BOC at the date he nominated for election as a senator for South Australia. While under domestic law British overseas citizenship is treated as a form of British nationality, Mr Fransman explains that it is a residuary form of nationality that differs from British citizenship in important respects: importantly, a BOC does not have the right of abode in the United Kingdom. The right of abode includes the right to enter and to reside in the country of nationality. As Mr Fransman observes, the right of abode is one of the main characteristics of a national under international law.

In this regard, unlike a British citizen, a BOC may only enter the United Kingdom by satisfying the requirements of immigration control ...

A further respect in which Mr Fransman states that the incidents, privileges and obligations of a BOC differ from those of a British citizen is in the nature of the duty of loyalty: a person who is registered as a BOC is not required to pledge loyalty to the United Kingdom ...

The status of BOC distinctly does not confer the rights or privileges of a citizen as that term is generally understood: a BOC does not have the right to enter or reside in the United Kingdom. Critically, taking into account the purpose of s 44(i), which is to ensure that members of the Parliament do not have split allegiance, it does not appear that Senator Xenophon's status as a BOC entailed any reciprocal obligation of allegiance to the United Kingdom per se or to Her Majesty the Queen in right of the United Kingdom.

For the purposes of s 44(i), Senator Xenophon was not a subject or a citizen of the United Kingdom at the date of his nomination and election as a senator. Nor was he entitled to the rights and privileges of a subject or citizen of the United Kingdom. Accordingly, there is no vacancy in the representation of South Australia in the Senate for the place for which Senator Xenophon was returned ...

Limitation as to the operation of foreign law

There is an important limitation to the proposition that whether a person is a citizen or entitled to the rights or privileges of a foreign power is a question of legal status in accordance with the law of foreign countries. The High Court describes that limitation as 'the constitutional imperative that an Australian citizen not be irremediably prevented by foreign law from participation in representative government'.

The constitutional imperative was first discussed in ***Sykes v Cleary***. The constitutional imperative is premised on the proposition that the *Constitution* does not intend to permit foreign law to prevent for all time an Australian citizen seeking election to the Federal Parliament.

Sykes v Cleary (1992) 176 CLR 77

Two candidates who held Swiss and Greek citizenship respectively were held to be disqualified. Neither had taken reasonable steps to renounce their foreign citizenship.

Mason CJ, Toohey and McHugh JJ

To do so might well result in the disqualification of Australian citizens on whom there was imposed involuntarily by operation of foreign law a continuing foreign nationality, notwithstanding that they had taken reasonable steps to renounce that foreign nationality. It would be wrong to interpret the constitutional provision in such a way as to disbar an Australian citizen who had taken all reasonable steps to divest himself or herself of any conflicting allegiance ...

What is more, s 44(i) finds its place in a Constitution which was enacted at a time, like the present, when a high proportion of Australians, though born overseas, had adopted this country as their home. In that setting, it could scarcely have been intended to disqualify an Australian citizen for election to Parliament on account of his or her continuing to possess a foreign nationality, notwithstanding that he or she had taken reasonable steps to renounce that nationality. In this respect it is significant that s 42 of the Constitution requires a member of Parliament to take an oath or affirmation of allegiance in the form set out in the schedule to the Constitution.

What amounts to the taking of reasonable steps to renounce foreign nationality must depend upon the circumstances of the particular case. What is reasonable will turn on the situation of the individual, the requirements of the foreign law and the extent of the connection between the individual and the foreign State of which he or she is alleged to be a subject or citizen. And it is relevant to bear in mind that a person who has participated in an Australian naturalization ceremony in which he or she has expressly renounced his or her foreign allegiance may well believe that, by becoming an Australian citizen, he or she has effectively renounced any foreign nationality ...

The second respondent omitted to make a demand for release from Swiss citizenship which would have been granted automatically as he has no residence in Switzerland and has been an Australian citizen for thirty-two years. Because he has failed to make such a demand, it cannot be said that he has taken reasonable steps to divest himself of Swiss citizenship and the rights and privileges of such a citizen.

The third respondent has omitted to seek the approval of the appropriate Greek Minister for the discharge of his Greek nationality. Whether the grant of that approval is a matter of discretion or is automatic is not altogether clear. Presumably it is the former. But, in the absence of an application for the exercise of the discretion in favour of releasing the third respondent from his Greek citizenship, it cannot be said that he has taken reasonable steps to divest himself of Greek citizenship and the rights and privileges of such a citizen ...

Re Canavan explains that section 44(i) does *not* have a reasonable steps requirement. Reasonable steps is an element in determining whether the constitutional imperative is engaged.

Re Canavan; Re Ludlam; Re Waters; Re Roberts (No 2); Re Joyce; Re Nash; Re Xenophon (2017) 349 ALR 534

Kiefel CJ, Bell, Gageler, Keane, Nettle, Gordon and Edelman JJ

Section 44(i) is not concerned with whether the candidate has been negligent in failing to comply with its requirements. Section 44(i) does not disqualify only those who have not made reasonable efforts to conform to its requirements. Section 44(i) is cast in peremptory terms. Where the personal circumstances of a would-be candidate give rise to disqualification under s 44(i), the reasonableness of steps taken by way of inquiry to ascertain whether those circumstances exist is immaterial to the operation of s 44(i).

The reasons of the majority in *Sykes v Cleary* do not support the proposition that a person who is a foreign citizen contravenes the second limb of s 44(i) only if that person actually knows that he or she is a foreign citizen and fails to take reasonable steps available to him or her to divest himself or herself of that status under the foreign law. Nor do the reasons of the majority in *Sykes v Cleary* support the view that a person who is a foreign citizen is not disqualified if, not knowing of that status, he or she fails to take steps to divest himself or herself of that status ...

The plurality in *Sykes v Cleary* said that the steps reasonably available to a candidate to free himself or herself from the ties of foreign citizenship depend on "the situation of the individual, the requirements of the foreign law and the extent of the connexion between the individual and the foreign State". The circumstance that Mr Kardamitsis had participated in a naturalisation ceremony in which he had expressly renounced his foreign allegiance was not sufficient to justify the conclusion that he had taken reasonable steps to divest himself of his foreign citizenship because under the foreign law he could have applied for the favourable exercise of a discretion by the appropriate Minister of the Greek government to release him from his citizenship. The application for the favourable exercise of the discretion was a step reasonably open to him.

Such a step may be contrasted, for example, with a requirement of foreign law that the citizens of the foreign country may renounce their citizenship only by acts of renunciation carried out in the territory of the foreign power. Such a requirement could be ignored by an Australian citizen if his or her presence within that territory could involve risks to person or property. It is not necessary to multiply examples of requirements of foreign law that will not impede the effective choice by an Australian citizen to seek election to the Commonwealth Parliament. It is sufficient to say that in none of the references with which the Court is concerned were candidates confronted by such obstacles to freeing themselves of their foreign ties ...

A person who, at the time that he or she nominates for election, retains the status of subject or citizen of a foreign power will be disqualified by reason of s 44(i), except where the operation of the foreign law is contrary to the constitutional imperative that an Australian citizen not be irremediably prevented by foreign law from participation in representative government. Where it can be demonstrated that the person has taken all steps that are reasonably required by the foreign law to renounce his or her citizenship and within his or her power, the constitutional imperative is engaged ...

Re Gallagher confronted the scope of the constitutional imperative directly. The High Court held that the constitutional imperative is engaged only where both of two circumstances exist:

1. The foreign law must operate irremediably to prevent an Australian citizen from participation in Australian electoral democracy.
2. The person must have taken all steps reasonably required by the foreign law which are within his or her power to free himself or herself of the foreign nationality.

Where the constitutional imperative is engaged a person is not disqualified by reason of section 44(i).

Re Gallagher (2018) 355 ALR 1

Kiefel CJ, Bell, Keane, Nettle and Gordon JJ

The particular constitutional context for the imperative is s 44(i) and the disqualification it effects by reference to a person's status as a foreign citizen. Its concern, properly understood, is that an Australian citizen might forever be unable to participate in elections because a foreign law prevents that person from freeing himself or herself of the foreign citizenship which, if s 44(i) were to apply in its terms, would disqualify that person from nomination ...

[F]or s 44(i) to be read as subject to the exception two circumstances must be present. The first arises from the terms of the constitutional imperative. It is that a foreign law operates irremediably to prevent an Australian citizen from participation. The second is that that person has taken all steps reasonably required by the foreign law which are within his or her power to free himself or herself of the foreign nationality.

A foreign law will not "irremediably prevent" an Australian citizen from renouncing his or her citizenship simply by requiring that particular steps be taken to achieve it. For a foreign law to meet the description in *Re Canavan* and *Sykes v Cleary* it must present something of an insurmountable obstacle, such as a requirement with which compliance is not possible. Consistently with the approach taken in *Re Canavan*, the operation of the foreign law and its effect are viewed objectively.

In *Re Canavan* an example was given of a foreign law which operated in a way that would engage the constitutional imperative. The example was a foreign law which permitted renunciation of foreign citizenship but required foreign citizens to carry out the necessary acts of renunciation in the territory of the foreign power. Compliance with this requirement was not possible because it put the person at risk. So understood, the foreign law would irremediably disqualify the person.

The operation of such a law was contrasted with one which required a foreign citizen to apply for the favourable exercise of a discretion to permit renunciation of that foreign citizenship. That is a step required by foreign law which is reasonably open to the person and must be taken. It was for this reason that it could not be concluded that in *Sykes v Cleary* Mr Kardamitsis had taken reasonable steps to divest himself of his foreign citizenship ... It may be added, for completeness, that all steps must be taken even though the foreign law will in any event operate to prevent renunciation being effected. The reason for such a requirement lies in the concerns of s 44(i) about a person's duty or allegiance to the foreign power. In *Sykes v Cleary*, in a passage quoted in *Re Canavan*, Brennan J explained that so long as the duty remained under foreign law it may be seen as an impediment to unqualified allegiance to Australia. It is therefore only after all reasonable steps have been taken under foreign law to renounce the status, and with it the duty, of foreign citizenship that it is possible to say that the purpose of s 44(i) would not be fulfilled by recognition of the foreign law. To this may be added, consistently with the objective approach applied in *Re Canavan*, that it is not until it is manifest that a person has done all he or she can towards renunciation that the exception should apply ...

In this case, the fact that Senator Gallagher had taken all steps required of her under United Kingdom law to renounce her United Kingdom citizenship before nominating for election was not sufficient to engage the constitutional imperative. Senator Gallagher applied to renounce her United Kingdom citizenship shortly before nominating for election, but that application was not processed and did not take effect until after she had nominated. Although the processing delay had the effect of preventing Gallagher from validly contesting one election, nothing in United Kingdom law operated to *irremediably* prevent renunciation of citizenship and thus participation in Australian representative democracy. It followed that the constitutional imperative was not engaged.

Re Gallagher (2018) 355 ALR 1

Kiefel CJ, Bell, Keane, Nettle and Gordon JJ

It is Senator Gallagher's contention that by 20 April 2016, when she submitted her declaration of renunciation, or at the latest 6 May 2016, when her credit card was debited with the required fee, she had taken every step required by s 12(1) of the British Nationality Act 1981 that was within her power to secure a release of her British citizenship. The reason why she did not cease to be a British citizen before the date of her nomination lay in matters outside her control, namely the time and manner in which the Secretary of State chose to perform the duty under s 12(1) [to process the renunciation]. It is submitted that the ability of the Secretary of State to choose the time and manner in which the duty was to be performed was an irremediable impediment to her participation in the 2016 election. The constitutional imperative referred to in *Re Canavan* was therefore engaged, entitling her to participate in the election ...

Senator Gallagher does not identify any aspect of the relevant British law which operates to prevent her irremediably from nominating for an election. No requirement of the relevant provisions could be described as onerous. The procedure is simple. There was never any doubt that a decision to register would be made. The issue for Senator Gallagher was only ever to be the timing of the registration.

Senator Gallagher's contention is that because she had done all that was required of her by British law and which was within her power to do, everything that occurred thereafter under British law which prevented her nomination is to be regarded as an irremediable impediment. Such a submission finds no support from what was said in *Re Canavan*. It is not sufficient for the exception to s 44(i) to apply for a person to have made reasonable efforts to renounce. In *Re Canavan* it was explicitly said that the majority in *Sykes v Cleary* did not suggest that a candidate who made a reasonable effort to comply with s 44(i) was thereby exempt from compliance with it.

The questions in this reference turn upon one issue: whether British law operated to irremediably prevent an Australian citizen applying for renunciation of his or her British citizenship from ever achieving it. An affirmative answer cannot be given merely because a decision might not be provided in time for a person's nomination. The exception is not engaged by a foreign law which presents an obstacle to a particular individual being able to nominate for a particular election ...

14.6 Section 44(ii) – disqualification of convicted criminals

Section 44(ii) disqualifies any person who has been convicted of an offence punishable by imprisonment for one year or longer *and* is either currently serving the sentence or awaiting sentencing.

The mere fact of a conviction does not disqualify a person. ***Nile v Wood*** explains that a person convicted of the requisite type of offence is disqualified only while awaiting sentencing or while serving the sentence.

Nile v Wood (1987) 76 ALR 91

This case was an application to declare a senator incapable of being chosen by reason of section 44(ii). The High Court struck out the matter on the ground that the petition was defective but offered comments on the substantive matter.

Brennan, Deane and Toohey JJ

It is not conviction of an offence per se of which s 44(ii) of the Constitution speaks. The disqualification operates on a person who has been convicted of an offence punishable by imprisonment for one year or more and is under sentence or subject to be sentenced for that offence. The references to conviction and sentence are clearly conjunctive, although counsel for the petitioner argued otherwise. This is so as a matter of construction of the language used in s 44(ii). And it is apparent that it was the intention of the framers of the Constitution that the disqualification under this paragraph should operate only while the person was under sentence ...

Re Culleton (No 2) considered how section 44(ii) applies when a conviction has been annulled. Before nominating for Parliament, Senator Culleton was convicted in his absence of an offence punishable by imprisonment for two years. After the election, that conviction was annulled. The High Court held that on its proper interpretation the legislation governing annulments had the effect that annulments operated only prospectively and not retrospectively. It followed that at the relevant times Senator Culleton fell within section 44(ii).

Re Culleton (No 2) (2017) 341 ALR 1

Kiefel, Bell, Gageler and Keane JJ

On 2 March 2016, prior to his nomination for election and before polling day for the election, Senator Culleton was convicted, in his absence, in the Local Court of New South Wales, of the offence of larceny. He was then liable to be sentenced to imprisonment for a maximum term of two years when he was brought before that Court. The Local Court subsequently granted an annulment of the conviction, proceeded to deal with the matter afresh, found Senator Culleton guilty of the offence, on his own plea, but dismissed the charge without proceeding to conviction ...

Senator Culleton was a person who had been convicted and was subject to be sentenced for an offence punishable by imprisonment for one year or longer at the date of the 2016 election. That was so, both as a matter of fact and as a matter of law. The subsequent annulment of the conviction had no effect on that state of affairs. It follows from s 44(ii) that Senator Culleton was "incapable of being chosen" as a Senator ...

Senator Culleton submitted that the effect of the annulment on 8 August 2016 was to render the conviction void ab initio, and restore the status quo ante ...

Whether an annulment operates retrospectively or prospectively inevitably depends upon the statutory context in which the term is used. The argument for Senator Culleton ignores the terms of the Appeal and Review Act as they inform the meaning of annulment in s 10(1) of that Act ...

Section 10(1) of the Appeal and Review Act provides that "[o]n being annulled, a conviction ... ceases to have effect and any enforcement action previously taken is to be reversed." This provision states the extent to which the annulment may affect the legal position established by the conviction. The annulment of the conviction was not apt to expunge the legal rights and obligations arising from it, save in relation to the future and in the reversal of things done under it. The provisions of the Appeal and Review Act to which reference has been made indicate that a conviction is annulled only for the future: these provisions do not purport to operate retroactively to deny legal effect to a conviction from the time that it was recorded ...

Justice Nettle was the only judge to consider what the result would have been had the annulment operated retrospectively. Justice Nettle held that the mere fact of a conviction of the relevant kind, even if later annulled with retrospective effect, was enough to engage section 44(ii).

Re Culleton (No 2) (2017) 341 ALR 1

Nettle J

[T]he need for certainty in the electoral process makes it highly desirable that, if a person is convicted of a relevant offence, he or she should forthwith cease to be eligible for election, or, if already elected, should cease to be capable of sitting, until and unless the conviction is quashed or annulled or the sentence is spent. If it were otherwise, there could be long periods following conviction of a relevant offence until an appeal or application for annulment is finally heard and determined in which it would be impossible to say whether the person so convicted is or is not eligible to be elected, or is or is not eligible to continue to sit as a senator or member of the House of Representatives ...

Up to the point of its annulment, Mr Culleton's conviction was voidable, not void. Consequently, until it was annulled, it remained a valid conviction determinative of his convict status for the purposes of s 44(ii). It follows that, at the time of his nomination, he was not capable of being chosen as a senator, notwithstanding the later annulment of his conviction ...

14.7 Section 44(iv) – disqualification of holders of public offices

Section 44(iv) disqualifies any person who holds an office of profit under the Crown. Consistently with the requirement in section 64 of the *Constitution* for Ministers to hold seats in Parliament, section 44 expressly excepts Ministers from the scope of section 44(iv).

Sykes v Cleary and ***Re Lambie*** explain that the purpose of section 44(iv) is to avoid the possibility of financial influence by the Executive Government over parliamentarians.

Sykes v Cleary (1992) 176 CLR 77

Mason CJ, Toohey and McHugh JJ

The disqualification of a person who holds an office of profit under the Crown has its origins in the law which developed in England in relation to disqualification of the members of the House of Commons. Section 44(iv) is modelled on a provision of the Act of Settlement 1701, which was repealed and replaced by provisions of the Succession to the Crown Act 1707. It has been said that the English provisions give effect to three main considerations or policies. They are:

(1) the incompatibility of certain non-ministerial offices under the Crown with membership in the House of Commons (here, membership must be taken to cover questions of a member's relations with, and duties to, his or her constituents);

(2) the need to limit the control or influence of the executive government over the House by means of an undue proportion of office-holders being members of the House; and

(3) the essential condition of a certain number of Ministers being members of the House for the purpose of ensuring control of the executive by Parliament ...

The exclusion of permanent officers of the executive government from the House was a recognition of the incompatibility of a person at the one time holding such an office and being a member of the House. There are three factors that give rise to that incompatibility. First, performance by a public servant of his or her public service duties would impair his or her capacity to attend to the duties of a member of the House. Secondly, there is a very considerable risk that a public servant would share the political opinions of the Minister of his or her department and would not bring to bear as a member of the House a free and independent judgment. Thirdly, membership of the House would detract from the performance of the relevant public service duty ...

Re Lambie (2018) 351 ALR 559

Kiefel CJ, Bell, Gageler, Keane, Nettle and Gordon JJ

[H]owever, s 44(iv) is not designed to eliminate a conflict merely between the duty which a person might have as the holder of an office and the duty which that person would assume as a senator or member of the House of Representatives. Were that its design, the confining of its relevant operation to an office of profit and the carving out from its operation of State Ministers would make no sense. To the extent s 44(iv) has the effect of eliminating such a conflict between duties, the operation of the provision has been consequential but serendipitous.

Rather, s 44(iv) can be seen to be quite narrowly tailored to eliminate a particular form of conflict of duty and interest. The targeted conflict is between the parliamentary duty of a senator or member and a pecuniary interest of a kind which, if permitted, would give rise to a real capacity for executive influence over the performance of that duty. The particular form of conflict to which the first clause of the provision is addressed is that which would arise from a senator or member being able to hold at the will of an executive government an office in respect of which he or she receives a financial gain.

Concern to eliminate a similar conflict between parliamentary duty and pecuniary interest is evident in the disqualification by the second clause of s 44(iv) of a person who holds a pension payable during the pleasure of the Crown out of any of the revenues of the Commonwealth. Commenting on an early draft of that second clause in the course of debate at the National Australasian Convention in 1891, in language that can fairly be treated as applicable to what was to become s 44(iv) in its entirety, Sir Samuel Griffith summed up its object as being "to prevent persons who are dependent for their livelihood upon the government, and who are amenable to its influence, from being members of the legislature".

Within that relatively narrow yet important compass, s 44(iv) in combination with s 45(i) has a prophylactic quality. Not only does s 44(iv) operate to prevent a person who holds at the will of executive government an office in respect of which he or she receives a financial gain from being chosen as a senator or member, but s 44(iv) and s 45(i) operate together to limit the capacity for a person who has been chosen as a senator or member to be influenced by the prospect of obtaining any present or future financial gain at the will of the executive during the period in which the person serves as a senator or member ...

Sykes v Cleary holds that 'the Crown' includes the Crown in right of the Commonwealth and the Crown in right of each of the States. In other words, section 44(iv) applies to both federal and State offices of profit.

The case also holds that whether a person is currently in receipt of remuneration is not relevant to the question of whether an office is 'of profit'. What matters is whether remuneration is attached to the office held and that the office is under the Crown. In this case, a Victorian public school teacher on leave without pay was held to hold an office of profit under the Crown.

Sykes v Cleary (1992) 176 CLR 77

Mason CJ, Toohey and McHugh JJ

Although a teacher is not an instance of the archetypical public servant at whom the disqualification was primarily aimed, a permanent public servant who is a teacher falls within the categories of public servants whose public service duties are incompatible, on the three grounds mentioned previously, with the duties of a member of the House of Representatives or of a senator ...

The taking of leave without pay by a person who holds an office of profit under the Crown does not alter the character of the office which he or she holds. The person remains the holder of an office, notwithstanding that he or she is not in receipt of pay during the period of leave ...

The reference in s 44(iv) to "any office of profit under the Crown" is apt to include an office of profit under the Crown in right of a State. Not only are the words wide enough to achieve this result but also the last paragraph of the section proceeds on the footing that, but for that paragraph, a State Minister would hold an office of profit under the Crown in right of a State and be disqualified. If such an office of profit in a State stood outside s 44(iv), there would have been no need to exclude State Ministers from the disqualification. The Convention Debates reveal that the exclusion of State Ministers from the disqualification was put forward because it was believed that State Ministers otherwise would be disqualified because each of them was relevantly the holder of an office of profit under the Crown (*Official Report of the National Australasian Convention Debates*, Adelaide, 22 April 1897, p 1198; Melbourne, 7 March 1898, pp 1941–1942). The exclusion of State Ministers from the disqualification was designed to ensure their availability for election at the inception of the Commonwealth Parliament ...

It follows that the first respondent, as the holder of an office of profit under the Crown, fell within s 44(iv) until he resigned that office on 16 April 1992 ...

Re Lambie explains that an office of profit is *under* the Crown in two circumstances:

1. if the office-holder is appointed at the will of the Executive Government of the Commonwealth or a State, or
2. if the office-holder's continued holding of that office or continued profiting from holding that office is dependent on the will of the Executive Government of the Commonwealth or of a State.

Re Lambie (2018) 351 ALR 559

Kiefel CJ, Bell, Gageler, Keane, Nettle and Gordon JJ

The disqualification set out in the first clause of s 44(iv) is given the greatest certainty of operation that is consistent with its language and with its purpose of eliminating or reducing the executive influence over a senator or member which would arise from a relationship of financial dependency by adopting an interpretation of the word "under" which substantially accords with that proposed by the Attorney-General of the Commonwealth. An office of profit is "under" the Crown within the meaning of the provision if the holding or continued holding of that office, or the receipt of profit from it, depends on the will or continuing will of the executive government of the Commonwealth or of a State.

The disqualification effected by the provision as so interpreted can be seen to have two distinct aspects.

First, the provision operates to disqualify any person who holds any office of profit to which that person has been appointed at the will of the executive government of the Commonwealth or of a State. The security of the person's tenure in such an office and the mechanism by which the person might be removed from such an office are irrelevant to that aspect of the provision's operation: a sinecure to which a person might be appointed at the will of an executive government as an inducement is no less attractive because it is secure. Mere appointment to an office of profit at the will of an executive government of itself gives rise to the capacity for the executive government to influence the performance of the parliamentary duty of a senator or member, which influence it is the constitutional design to eliminate.

Second, the provision operates to disqualify a person who holds an office of profit to which that person has not been appointed at the will of the executive government of the Commonwealth or of a State if the continued holding of that office or continued profiting from holding that office is dependent on the will of the executive government of the Commonwealth or of a State. To this aspect of the operation of the provision, the security of the person's tenure and remuneration in such an office, the means by which the person might be removed or suspended from it, and any means by which emoluments of the office might be withheld, are all of critical importance. Executive control over the performance of the functions of the office is relevant only in so far as it might bear on the nature and degree of any executive capacity to achieve such removal or suspension or withholding. The second aspect of the provision's operation will be engaged if, but only if, the executive government has such power over the continued holding of the office or profiting from holding the office as to amount to effective control over holding or profiting from holding the office.

The first aspect of the operation of the provision is sufficient to explain the disqualification of Mr Cleary in *Sykes v Cleary* and of Ms Hughes in *Re Nash (No 2)*. Each held an office of profit to which officeholders were appointed by executive government. On the issues relevantly joined in argument in *Sykes v Cleary*, it was held not to matter that Mr Cleary's office had become "unattached" and that he had taken leave without pay. The security of Mr Cleary's and Ms Hughes' tenure was irrelevant and, notably, was not explored in the reasoning in either case ...

In this case, a person who had been elected as a local councillor and mayor was not the holder of an office of profit under the Crown.

Re Lambie (2018) 351 ALR 559

Kiefel CJ, Bell, Gageler, Keane, Nettle and Gordon JJ

Mr Martin, in contrast, does not hold an office of profit to which officeholders are appointed by executive government. The offices of mayor and of councillor are offices to which officeholders are elected. Mr Martin's position therefore turns on the second aspect of the operation of s 44(iv), namely, whether the continued holding of those offices, or the receipt of profit from them, turns on the will or continuing will of the executive government of the Commonwealth or of a State.

Application of s 44(iv) of the Constitution

The incidents of the offices of mayor and of councillor of Devonport City Council, including those which bear on the relationship between those offices and the executive government of Tasmania, are to be found entirely within the provisions of the Local Government Act and subordinate legislation ...

With the exception of interim suspension by the Minister pending the outcome of a Board of Inquiry established under Pt 13, suspension or removal or dismissal pursuant to the second, third and fourth sets of provisions is in each case the culmination of an administrative process which involves an administrative finding of non-compliance with a statutory norm involving a measure of misconduct or dereliction of duty. The interim suspension that can occur pending the outcome of a Board of Inquiry established under Pt 13 is in the context of an administrative process having been commenced which may lead to an administrative finding of that nature. The suspension or removal or dismissal is in each case capable of being imposed only in the exercise of a statutory discretion the permissible exercise of which is bounded by the subject matter, scope and purposes of the Local Government Act. Ensuring the lawful exercise of that discretion within those bounds is in each case within the supervisory jurisdiction of the Supreme Court of Tasmania.

When regard is had to those additional features, the power which the provisions individually and cumulatively confer on the executive government of Tasmania to suspend or remove or dismiss a councillor from office cannot be characterised as rising to the level of control ...

14.8 Section 44(v) – disqualification of persons with a pecuniary interest in agreements with the Commonwealth

Section 44(v) disqualifies any person who has any direct or indirect pecuniary interest in any agreement with the Public Service of the Commonwealth otherwise than as a member and in common with the other members of an incorporated company consisting of more than 25 persons.

In ***Re Webster***, Barwick CJ sitting alone gave the provision a very narrow interpretation.

Re Webster (1975) 132 CLR 270

Senator Webster was a shareholder in, and for a time managing director of, a company with fewer than 25 shareholders. Part of the company's business was to sell timber. From time to time, the Commonwealth Public Service would purchase timber from the company. Chief Justice Barwick held that: (1) there was no agreement of the kind necessary to engage section 44(v); and (2) Senator Webster had no interest of the kind necessary to engage section 44(v).

Barwick CJ

It is fundamental to the decision of the questions posed by the Senate to bear in mind the purposes which s 44(v) of the Constitution is designed to achieve. The paragraph derives ultimately from the provisions of the statute 7 & 8 Wm III c 25 passed in the year 1696 to secure the freedom and independence of the Parliament from the Crown and its influence ...

Because of the evident purpose of the disqualification provision, it applies only to executory contracts, that is to say, to contracts under which at the relevant time something remains to be done by the contractor in performance of the contract: ...

It seems to me that, upon the proper construction of the paragraph, bearing in mind the purpose of its presence in the Constitution, the agreement to fall within the scope of s 44(v) must have a currency for a substantial period of time, and must be one under which the Crown could conceivably influence the contractor in relation to parliamentary affairs by the very existence of the agreement, or by something done or refrained from being done in relation to the contract or to its subject matter, whether or not that act or omission is within the terms of the contract ... Further, it seems to me that the interest in the agreement of the person said to be disqualified must be pecuniary in the sense that through the possibility of financial gain by the existence or the performance of the agreement, that person could conceivably be influenced by the Crown in relation to Parliamentary affairs ...

In considering whether there is a relevant agreement, it must be remembered that there being no standing agreement, each order creates a separate and distinct agreement. Thus, the possibility of influence by the Crown must be considered in relation to the single instance of a specific order for specific and described goods, a single instance uncontrolled and unregulated by any overall standing agreement. For that reason, I have referred to "isolated orders".

After a good deal of consideration, I have come to the conclusion that the agreement so formed does not come within the operation of s 44(v). The agreement really has no term. It is not continuing: it is really casual and transient. I cannot conceive that, in these days, the Crown could exert any influence in Parliamentary affairs by anything it could do, properly or improperly, in relation to such an agreement.

Re Day (No 2) overruled ***Re Webster***. *Re Day (No 2)* explains that section 44(v) serves multiple purposes such as:

- to ensure that the Public Service of the Commonwealth is not in a position to exercise undue influence over members of Parliament through the medium of agreements, and
- to ensure that members of Parliament will not seek to benefit by such agreements or to put themselves in a position where their duty to the people they represent and their own personal interests may conflict.

Re Day (No 2) (2017) 343 ALR 181

Kiefel CJ, Bell and Edelman JJ

[At] the Convention Debates in Adelaide and Sydney[:] The discussions were not just about the influence which the Crown, or the Executive Government, could exert over contractors who were members of Parliament. On the topic of whether the disqualification should extend to professional men, including barristers, as well as contractors, there was certainly discussion about the possibility of corruption by the Executive Government giving contracts or briefs to such persons. But, in the course of the debate, reference was made more generally to the need to separate the personal interests of a parliamentarian from the exercise of his public duties. The freedom spoken of was not just from the executive, but from a person's own business interests, so that that person could more effectively represent others ...

When regard is had to the terms of s 44(v), it is obvious that it is also concerned with the interest that a parliamentarian might have in agreements with the Commonwealth. A conclusion that s 44(v) has some purpose wider than the protection of the freedom and independence of parliamentarians from the influence of the Crown is inescapable. That wider purpose can only be the prevention of financial gain which may give rise to a conflict of duty and interest. The Convention Debates identify that as the subject to which the clause which became s 44(v) was addressed ...

It follows from what has already been said in these reasons that s 44(v) has a wider purpose than that given to it by Barwick CJ in *Webster*. Its object is to ensure not only that the Public Service of the Commonwealth is not in a position to exercise undue influence over members of Parliament through the medium of agreements; but also that members of Parliament will not seek to benefit by such agreements or to put themselves in a position where their duty to the people they represent and their own personal interests may conflict. Recalling that s 44(v) should be construed in the context of the Constitution as a whole, it may also be observed that this wider purpose is consistent with s 44(iv) of the Constitution. That provision provides that a person who "holds any office of profit under the Crown" or "any pension payable during the pleasure of the Crown" is incapable of being chosen as a member of Parliament.

A construction of s 44(v) which proceeds from an understanding that parliamentarians have a duty as a representative of others to act in the public interest is consistent with the place of that provision in its wider constitutional context. The representative parliamentary democracy, for which the Constitution provides, informs an understanding of specific provisions such as s 44(v) and assists in determining the content of that duty, which includes an obligation to act according to good conscience, uninfluenced by other considerations, especially personal financial considerations.

It follows that the narrow definitions of 'agreement' and 'indirect pecuniary interest' given in ***Re Webster*** are not correct.

Agreement with the Public Service of the Commonwealth

Re Day (No 2) gives a broad understanding to the concept of 'an agreement with the Public Service of the Commonwealth'. In this case, the relevant agreement with the

Public Service was a lease to which the Commonwealth Department of Finance was a party. *Re Day (No 2)* also notes that a right to receive government payments, benefits or subsidies in common with other citizens does not involve an agreement with the Public Service of the Commonwealth because either there is no agreement at all (but rather a statutory entitlement) or any agreement is not with the Public Service.

Re Day (No 2) (2017) 343 ALR 181

Kiefel CJ, Bell and Edelman JJ

[I]t is necessary to resolve the issue which arises by reason of s 44(v), that is, whether Mr Day at any relevant time had a "direct or indirect pecuniary interest" in an agreement, namely, the lease. There is no dispute that the lease was an agreement with the Public Service of the Commonwealth. Mr Day was not a party to the lease and therefore did not have a direct interest in it as such, but he was the owner of the bank account nominated as the recipient of the rental monies ...

There can be no relevant interest if the agreement in question is one ordinarily made between government and a citizen. Were this otherwise, every day-to-day dealing which a citizen has with government could result in the disqualification of a citizen who happens to be a parliamentarian ...

Keane J

[I]n the context in which s 44(v) appears, the circumstance that the Commonwealth is the source of the benefit is not sufficient to engage the incapacitating effect of s 44(v). That effect will be engaged only if the agreement is made with "the Public Service of the Commonwealth". An agreement with the Commonwealth (for the creation of which the Constitution provides) or with the Crown in right of the Commonwealth (to which s 44(iv) expressly refers) made under a law of the Commonwealth of general application is not within the letter of s 44(v).

The disqualifying interest contemplated by s 44(v) is a pecuniary interest generated by an agreement made with the Public Service of the Commonwealth. Of course, while the Commonwealth will inevitably be the ultimate source of the benefit under such an agreement, it is the circumstance that the source of the benefit is in an agreement made with the Public Service of the Commonwealth which engages the disqualifying effect of the provision. It is only a pecuniary interest in such an agreement that is within the purview of s 44(v). Pecuniary benefits available generally to members of the Australian community are not within the mischief at which s 44(v) is directed merely because the Commonwealth is the ultimate source of the benefit. Given the purpose that informs s 44(v), there is no reason to expand its disqualifying effect to any person who might obtain a pecuniary benefit conferred by the Commonwealth which is available generally to the community. Such a benefit does not fall within the spirit of s 44(v) ...

Pecuniary interest

Re Day (No 2) explains that an indirect pecuniary interest in an agreement exists where a person has an expectation that carrying out the agreement will result, either by reason of a legally-enforceable right or simply by practical effect, in the person receiving money or money's worth. The facts of this case provide an example. A company, controlled by an associate of Senator Day's wife and a trust, owned office space that was leased to the Department of Finance (for the purpose of serving as Senator Day's office). The lessors directed that the rent payments be paid into a bank account owned by Senator Day personally. The High Court held that under this arrangement Senator Day had an indirect pecuniary interest in the lease.

Re Day (No 2) (2017) 343 ALR 181

Kiefel CJ, Bell and Edelman JJ

Mr Day was not a party to the lease and therefore did not have a direct interest in it as such, but he was the owner of the bank account nominated as the recipient of the rental monies.

It is quite difficult to comprehend that this does not amount to an interest in the lease agreement of a monetary kind. It is not difficult to infer from other facts that Mr Day brought the nomination about and that it was his purpose to apply the monies to the loan facility with respect to the Fullarton Road property. These matters may be put to one side. It is sufficient for the resolution of the questions referred to the Court to focus upon the fact that he was to receive the rental monies payable under the lease ...

Whilst a person does not need to be a party to an agreement to have an interest in it, the requirement that the interest be "in" an agreement implies some personal connection to it, albeit indirect. The mischief to which the provision is addressed has this connotation. It looks to the personal financial circumstances of a parliamentarian and the possibility of a conflict of duty and interest ...

Keane J

Mr Day also argued that the interest must be "in the agreement"; and that having such an interest is narrower than having a pecuniary interest "as a result of an agreement", or "flowing from an agreement", or "arising out of" an agreement. Mr Day argued that the mere possibility that Fullarton Investments might receive moneys under the Lease and then exercise its discretion as trustee to pay amounts to B & B Day, which might, in turn, exercise its discretion as trustee to pay amounts to Mr Day, could not establish that Mr Day had even an indirect interest in the Lease ...

[I]t is not necessary in this case to resolve any question as to whether the corporate and trust structures established by Mr Day were apt to avoid the disqualifying effect of s 44(v). An expectation of a gain or loss of money generated by a promise may exist without a legally enforceable entitlement to payment of money. Given the constitutional context, it is enough that the person's pockets were or might be affected.

The term "indirect" indicates that, here, regard may be had "to practical as well as legal effect", so that a person has at least an "indirect" interest of a pecuniary nature in an agreement if the agreement is such that it can give rise to an expectation of a monetary gain or loss if it is performed. A person who has an expectation of a benefit dependent on the performance of an agreement is naturally said to be indirectly interested in the agreement ...

That Mr Day hoped for a pecuniary benefit from the Lease is undeniable, given the directions that the rent be paid into the bank account of Fullarton Nominees, which was owned by him. The direction of 26 February 2016 meant that the Lease would, in fact, put money into Mr Day's pocket. From that date he had an expectation of a benefit dependent on the performance of the Lease by the Commonwealth ...

14.9 DISCUSSION QUESTIONS

1. How does the High Court reconcile the words of section 7 of the *Constitution* with the words of section 122 to permit Territory senators?
2. Which provisions of the qualification disqualifies a person: (1) who ceases to hold an office of profit under the Crown on the day before polling day; and (2) who takes up an office of profit under the Crown on the day after she takes her seat in Parliament?
3. When is an office of profit 'under' the Crown?
4. When does a person have an indirect pecuniary interest in an agreement with the Public Service of the Commonwealth?
5. Problem question: Consider the following hypothetical scenario. Ms Mutton is a member of the House of Representatives. During her term in office, she is convicted in the Local Court of New South Wales of an offence carrying a maximum penalty of two years' imprisonment. Two months later, on appeal to the District Court of New South Wales, Ms Mutton is acquitted of the offence (that is, she is found not guilty).

   Ms Mutton is also a beneficiary of a discretionary trust that owns childcare centres. The trust enters into a contract with the Department of Finance to operate a childcare centre in one of the Department's buildings to provide childcare for Departmental officials' children.

   Is Ms Mutton disqualified from Parliament?

CHOOSING MEMBERS OF FEDERAL PARLIAMENT

15

15.1 Overview

This chapter examines the constitutional parameters concerning the scope and operation of the federal franchise.

The *Australian Constitution* contains a provision expressly guaranteeing a right to vote, which has been interpreted in such a way that it has no ongoing operation. However, the *Constitution* also demands that parliamentarians be 'chosen by the people'. The High Court has interpreted this requirement to ensure a minimum level of democracy, in that the result of any method of choosing parliamentarians must meet the description 'chosen by the people'. The High Court has also interpreted the requirement that parliamentarians be 'chosen by the people' to impose a restriction on the ability of Parliament to take away an existing right to vote or to take away an existing opportunity to exercise a right to vote.

The *Constitution* also prescribes minimum standards governing the method of voting.

Key concepts considered in this chapter include:

- adult person
- acquires a right to vote
- directly chosen
- chosen by the people
- method of voting.

15.2 Power to make laws about the franchise

The *Australian Constitution* does not (at least anymore) prescribe the scope of the franchise (that is, who is entitled to vote) and the way in which federal elections are to be conducted. (Sections 10 and 31 provide, as transitional provisions, that State electoral laws apply in respect of federal elections until the Federal Parliament enacts federal electoral laws.) The Federal Parliament's power to make laws prescribing the scope of the franchise and the way in which federal elections are conducted arises principally from the combined effect of sections 8, 10, 30 and 51(xxxvi).

Australian Constitution

Section 8 Qualification of electors

The qualification of electors of senators shall be in each State that which is prescribed by this Constitution, or by the Parliament, as the qualification for electors of members of the House of Representatives; but in the choosing of senators each elector shall vote only once.

Section 10 Application of State laws

Until the Parliament otherwise provides, but subject to this Constitution, the laws in force in each State, for the time being, relating to elections for the more numerous House of the Parliament of the State shall, as nearly as practicable, apply to elections of senators for the State.

Section 30 Qualification of electors

Until the Parliament otherwise provides, the qualification of electors of members of the House of Representatives shall be in each State that which is prescribed by the law of the State as the qualification of electors of the more numerous House of Parliament of the State; but in the choosing of members each elector shall vote only once.

Section 51 Legislative powers of the Parliament

The Parliament shall, subject to this Constitution, have power to make laws for the peace, order, and good government of the Commonwealth with respect to:

...

(xxxvi) matters in respect of which this Constitution makes provision until the Parliament otherwise provides;

...

The exercise of this power is subject to limitations on power found elsewhere in the *Constitution*.

The *Commonwealth Electoral Act 1918* (Cth) is the current legislation governing the conduct of elections, including setting out the qualifications of those entitled to vote. Section 93 of that statute provides that the basic qualifications for voting are being an

Australian citizen aged 18 years or over. The same section sets out the principal categories of disqualification from voting, which are: by reason of 'unsound mind', being incapable of understanding the nature and significance of enrolment and voting; having been convicted of treason or treachery; or currently serving a sentence of imprisonment of three years or longer.

15.3 Express right to vote

Section 41 is the one provision in the *Constitution* guaranteeing a right to vote for certain people. However, on the interpretation given to it by the High Court, the provision is now spent and has no operation because no one alive today falls within its scope.

Australian Constitution

Section 41 Right of electors of States

No adult person who has or acquires a right to vote at elections for the more numerous House of the Parliament of a State shall, while the right continues, be prevented by any law of the Commonwealth from voting at elections for either House of the Parliament of the Commonwealth.

'Adult person'

King v Jones holds that the term 'adult person' means a person who has attained the age of 21 years.

King v Jones (1972) 128 CLR 221

In 1971, South Australia lowered the voting age for State elections from 21 years to 18 years. At the 1972 federal election, the federal voting age was 21 years. King was an 18-year-old South Australian and thus entitled to vote in South Australian State elections. The High Court held that she was not an adult person for the purposes of section 41.

Barwick CJ

[T]he words "no adult person" means no person of or above the age of twenty-one. In my opinion, they meant that in 1900: and they mean it now. Because that is their connotation, there is no room for any change in their denotation, for that connotation is referable to the attainment of age specified by a number of years. A person was adult in the law in 1900, in my opinion, when he or she was of full age. Until that point of time he or she was in law an infant in contrast to being an adult. An instance of the grant of legislative power to the Parliament by reference to the contrasting concept of infancy may be seen in s 51(xxii). Further, the requirement that to be an adult a person should have become of full age, attained his or her majority, or the age of twenty-one years, is in conformity with the common law and also, in my opinion, with general usage of language, both as in 1900 and as at the present time ...

In ***Ex parte Sipka***, Murphy J expressed the view that ***King v Jones*** should be overruled and the term 'adult person' understood as meaning a person who has attained the age of 18 years. None of the other judges in that case needed to consider the meaning of 'adult person'.

R v Pearson; Ex parte Sipka (1983) 152 CLR 254

Murphy J

But now in all States and Territories males and females of eighteen years can vote, make a will, marry without parental consent and enter enforceable contracts. In 1973 the *Commonwealth Electoral Act 1918* was amended to give eighteen years olds the right to vote. Leaving aside s 41, it was not disputed that for all relevant legal purposes eighteen years in the age of adulthood. In so far as *King v Jones* held that the words "adult person" in s 41 should be forever construed as meaning a person who has attained twenty-one years of age, the decision should, in my opinion, be overruled; that approach is inconsistent with general principles of constitutional interpretation which would give such words an ambulatory operation ...

Who acquires a right to vote

The judgments in ***King v Jones*** contain dicta to the effect that section 41 is not a transitional provision. In other words, section 41 does not protect only those people who had a right to vote in 1901 but has the effect that a person who at any time acquires a right to vote in State elections automatically has a right to vote in federal elections.

King v Jones (1972) 128 CLR 221

Menzies J

The character of s 41 is that of a permanent constitutional provision. It is not a provision to make temporary arrangements for the period between the establishment of the Constitution and the making of Commonwealth laws. It applies to a person, who, in 1901, had or who, in the future, acquires particular voting rights by the laws of a State ...

That dicta was not followed in ***Ex parte Sipka***, which holds that section 41 protects only those individuals who personally had or acquired a right to vote in State elections before the first federal franchise laws were enacted. In other words, there are no people alive today who are protected by section 41. Section 41 is entirely spent.

R v Pearson; Ex parte Sipka (1983) 152 CLR 254

Federal electoral law required potential voters to enrol by 6 pm on the day writs for an election were issued. A person not on the roll of electors was unable to cast a vote. People entitled to vote in New South Wales elections failed to enrol federally by the deadline but argued that section 41 guaranteed their right to vote in the federal election.

Gibbs CJ, Mason and Wilson JJ

The section prevents the Commonwealth Parliament from taking away a right to vote; it does not create an entitlement which does not otherwise exist. Under the Constitution, persons qualified as electors for the more numerous House of the Parliament of a State were qualified to vote for the election of members of the House of Representatives, but only until the Parliament otherwise provided ...

[O]nce a Commonwealth law had been passed completely establishing the franchise, no person, not already qualified to vote at Commonwealth elections, could become so qualified by virtue of the Constitution alone. No future law could be said to prevent such persons from voting, since there was nothing in the Constitution or in the law that gave them a right to vote. This construction, which requires that the right to vote to which s 41 refers must have been acquired by the persons concerned before the federal franchise was established, gives a narrow effect to s 41. However, this construction of the section is supported not only by obvious considerations of policy, but also by the history of the section.

If the section gave a right to vote at Commonwealth elections to any person who, after the Commonwealth franchise was established, became entitled to vote by virtue of amendments to the State laws, the result would be that the uniform franchise established under ss 30 and 51 (xxxvi) of the Constitution would be subject to amendment by the laws of the various States. The Commonwealth law could in effect be amended by any State law which conferred a more liberal franchise. In other words, any State could, unilaterally, alter the Commonwealth franchise in a way which discriminated in favour of its own citizens. It is impossible to suppose that results of this kind were intended ...

As a matter of historical fact, the object intended by the framers of the Constitution to be achieved by s 41 is quite clear ... the apprehended mischief which s 41 was designed to prevent was that the women of South Australia might be deprived of the federal franchise by the Commonwealth Parliament. At the time of the debates women were entitled to vote only in South Australia; in the other colonies the suffrage was restricted to males, although by the time the Constitution came into operation the women of Western Australia were also enfranchised ...

Brennan, Deane and Dawson JJ

It is impermissible to construe a provision relating to the prevention of the exercise of a right to vote as the source of the right itself. The right to vote to which s 41 relates is the constitutional franchise conferred by ss 30 and 8. The purpose of s 41 is clear from its constitutional context: it was to ensure that those who enjoyed the constitutional franchise should not lose it when the statutory franchise was enacted. The statute was to govern the subsequent acquisition of the right to vote at federal elections. The persons to whom s 41 applies are the persons who acquired the right to vote pursuant to ss 30 and 8. After the Parliament enacted the *Commonwealth Franchise Act 1902*, which was entitled "An act to provide for an Uniform Federal Franchise", no person could acquire the right to vote at federal elections save in accordance with its terms ...

It follows, of course, that the practical effect of s 41 is spent. Most of the electors who acquired a right to vote at federal elections under ss 30 and 8 of the Constitution would have died. Since 12 June 1902, when the Commonwealth Franchise Act came into force, no person has acquired a right to vote the exercise of which is protected by s 41. None of the present applicants is a person to whom s 41 applies.

Justice Murphy dissented and held that section 41 should be understood as having an ongoing operation. Justice Murphy disputed each of the reasons given by the majority for their narrow interpretation.

R v Pearson; Ex parte Sipka (1983) 152 CLR 254

Murphy J

Guarantees of personal rights should not be read narrowly. A right to vote is so precious that it should not read out of the Constitution by implication. Rather every reasonable presumption and interpretation should be adopted which favours the right of people to participate in the elections of those who represent them.

Plain meaning. The purpose conveyed by its plain words is a constitutional guarantee that every adult person who has a right to vote at State elections shall not be prevented by any Commonwealth law from voting at federal elections. The only sensible meaning is that the persons described are entitled to vote in federal elections. The respondents contend that s 41 does not confer any right to vote at federal elections; it merely says that no Commonwealth laws shall prevent the persons described from voting in federal elections and that the right to vote must be found elsewhere. This ridicules the constitutional guarantee. Such a pedantic interpretation should not be adopted to nullify this important personal right ...

The context. Section 41 is the first section in Pt IV of the Constitution which is headed "Both Houses of Parliament". The sections which follow immediately deal with oaths or affirmations of senators and members (s 42); ineligibility of members of one House to be chosen or sitting as a member in the other (s 43); disqualifications (s 44); vacancies (s 45), are not of limited duration. They are all prospective, ambulatory and constantly speaking. This context strongly suggests a similar interpretation of s 41.

Contrast with transitional provisions. Where it was intended in Pt IV that a constitutional provision was to be transitional the section is introduced by the words "Until the Parliament otherwise provides" (see ss 46, 47, 48). The same clause is expressed in other parts of the Constitution (see ss 3, 7, 10, 20, 29, 30, 31, 34, 39, 65, 66, 67, 73, 87, 93, 96 and 97). There is no warrant for reading it into s 41. When the framers intended such a limitation they expressed it. Its omission was intended to ensure that the Parliament could not prevent adult persons with a right to vote in State elections from voting in federal elections. If it were included, expressly or impliedly, s 41 would be nonsensical. A section which read, until Parliament otherwise provides, no adult person etcetera ... shall be prevented by any law of the Commonwealth etcetera, would be internally contradictory. It would say that no law of the Commonwealth shall prevent voting until the law of the Commonwealth did prevent it.

Policy considerations. One of the arguments against giving the s 41 guarantee the full scope of its plain meaning is that this would be undesirable, in particular that it would at least from the viewpoint of 1901 and subsequent history have made ineffective the desirable goal of a uniform federal franchise which was achieved by the Commonwealth Franchise Act 1902. This does not bear examination ... The Commonwealth Franchise Act 1902 purported to be "An Act to provide for an Uniform Federal Franchise". Policy arguments by the respondents are based on it being such an Act. It was not. Its s 4 provided:

> No aboriginal native of Australia, Asia, Africa or the Islands of the Pacific except New Zealand shall be entitled to have his name placed on an Electoral Roll unless so entitled under section forty-one of the Constitution.

Although the Act extended the franchise to women in general, by disqualifying aboriginals who were not entitled to vote in State elections (and thus entitled by s 41) it deliberately abstained from introducing uniform federal franchise ...

15.4 Implied right to vote

Although there is no express constitutional right to vote, given the interpretation given to section 41 and that Parliament has express power to prescribe the qualifications of who may vote in federal elections, there are limitations on the ability of Parliament to prevent people voting.

Section 7 requires Senators to be 'directly chosen by the people' and section 24 requires members of the House of Representatives to be 'directly chosen by the people'.

Australian Constitution

Section 7 The Senate

The Senate shall be composed of senators for each State, directly chosen by the people of the State, voting, until the Parliament otherwise provides, as one electorate ...

Section 24 Constitution of House of Representatives

The House of Representatives shall be composed of members directly chosen by the people of the Commonwealth, ...

These provisions require that parliamentarians be 'chosen' by 'the people'. Parliament cannot exercise its power to prescribe the franchise in a way that results in parliamentarians not being chosen by the people. One consequence of this requirement is that there is a limit on excluding people from voting – either by taking away the right to vote or by preventing people from exercising the right to vote – in federal elections. This limitation is sometimes, albeit inexactly, referred to as an 'implied right to vote'.

Taking away the right to vote

Roach holds that a law taking away the right to vote from a class of electors will not be valid merely because the franchise it prescribes is still consistent with the description of Parliament being 'chosen by the people'. Rather, a law taking away the right to vote from a class of electors will breach sections 7 and 24 unless the law is justified.

The case considered the validity of laws disqualifying a particular class of people not previously disqualified from voting. Amendments introduced in 2006 disqualified any person serving any sentence of imprisonment from voting in a federal election. The law had previously disqualified only persons serving sentences of three years or more. The High Court held that the amendments were invalid for contradicting the constitutional requirement that parliamentarians be chosen by the people. The disqualification effected by the amendments was not justified.

Chief Justice Gleeson held that 'to be valid' a law taking away a right to vote in a federal election must have a rational connection between the ground of disqualification and either identification of community membership or the capacity to exercise a free choice.

Roach v Electoral Commissioner (2007) 233 CLR 162

Gleeson CJ

[Sections] 7 and 24 of the Constitution, which require that the senators and members of the House of Representatives be "directly chosen by the people" of the State or the Commonwealth respectively ...

[U]niversal adult suffrage was a long established fact, and that anything less could not now be described as a choice by the people. I respectfully agree. As Gummow J said in *McGinty v Western Australia*, we have reached a stage in the evolution of representative government which produces that consequence. I see no reason to deny that, in this respect, and to this extent, the words of ss 7 and 24, because of changed historical circumstances including legislative history, have come to be a constitutional protection of the right to vote. That, however, leaves open for debate the nature and extent of the exceptions. The Constitution leaves it to Parliament to define those exceptions, but its power to do so is not unconstrained. Because the franchise is critical to representative government, and lies at the centre of our concept of participation in the life of the community, and of citizenship, disenfranchisement of any group of adult citizens on a basis that does not constitute a substantial reason for exclusion from such participation would not be consistent with choice by the people. To say that, of course, raises questions as to what constitutes a substantial reason, and what, if any, limits there are to Parliament's capacity to decide that matter ...

There would need to be some rationale for the exception; the definition of the excluded class or group would need to have a rational connection with the identification of community membership or with the capacity to exercise free choice. Citizenship, itself, could be a basis for discriminating between those who will and those who will not be permitted to vote. Citizens, being people who have been recognised as formal members of the community, would, if deprived temporarily of the right to vote, be excluded from the right to participate in the political life of the community in a most basic way. The rational connection between such exclusion and the identification of community membership for the purpose of the franchise might be found in conduct which manifests such a rejection of civic responsibility as to warrant temporary withdrawal of a civic right ...

The rationale for excluding persons of unsound mind is obvious, although the application of the criterion of exclusion may be imprecise, and could be contentious in some cases. The rationale is related to the capacity to exercise choice ...

The rationale for the exclusion from the franchise of some prisoners, that is, those who have been convicted and are serving sentences, either of a certain duration or of no particular minimum duration, must lie in the significance of the combined facts of offending and imprisonment, as related to the right to participate in political membership of the community ...

Since what is involved is not an additional form of punishment, and since deprivation of the franchise takes away a right associated with citizenship, that is, with full membership of the community, the rationale for the exclusion must be that serious offending represents such a form of civic irresponsibility that it is appropriate for Parliament to mark such behaviour as anti-social and to direct that physical separation from the community will be accompanied by symbolic separation in the form of loss of a fundamental political right ...

It is consistent with our constitutional concept of choice by the people for Parliament to treat those who have been imprisoned for serious criminal offences as having suffered a temporary suspension of their connection with the community, reflected at the physical level in incarceration, and reflected also in temporary deprivation of the right to participate by voting in the political life of the community. It is also for Parliament, consistently with the rationale for exclusion, to decide the basis upon which to identify incarcerated offenders whose serious criminal wrongdoing warrants temporary suspension of a right of citizenship. I have no doubt that the disenfranchisement of prisoners serving three-year sentences was valid, and I do not suggest that disenfranchisement of prisoners serving sentences of some specified lesser term would necessarily be invalid. The specification of a term reflects a judgment by Parliament which marks off serious criminal offending ...

Justices Gummow, Kirby and Crennan held that, to be valid, the disqualification must be for a substantial reason, in the sense that the disqualification is 'reasonably appropriate and adapted to serve an end which is consistent or compatible with the maintenance of the constitutionally prescribed system of representative government'.

Roach v Electoral Commissioner (2007) 233 CLR 162

Gummow, Kirby and Crennan JJ

In *McGinty* Brennan CJ considered the phrase "chosen by the people" as admitting of a requirement "of a franchise that is held generally by all adults or all adult citizens unless there be substantial reasons for excluding them". This proposition reflects the understanding that representative government as that notion is understood in the Australian constitutional context comprehends not only the bringing of concerns and grievances to the attention of legislators but also the presence of a voice in the selection of those legislators ...

The question with respect to legislative disqualification from what otherwise is adult suffrage (where 18 is now the age of legal majority throughout Australia) thus becomes a not unfamiliar one. Is the disqualification for a "substantial" reason? A reason will answer that description if it be reasonably appropriate and adapted to serve an end which is consistent or compatible with the maintenance of the constitutionally prescribed system of representative government. When used here the phrase "reasonably appropriate and adapted" does not mean "essential" or "unavoidable". Rather, as remarked in *Lange*, in this context there is little difference between what is conveyed by that phrase and the notion of "proportionality" ...

Section 93(8AA) operates without regard to the nature of the offence committed, the length of the term of imprisonment imposed, or the personal circumstances of the offender ...

The legislative pursuit of an end which stigmatises offenders by imposing a civil disability during any term of imprisonment takes s 93(8AA) beyond what is reasonably appropriate and adapted (or "proportionate") to the maintenance of representative government. The net of disqualification is cast too wide by s 93(8AA). The result is that ss 93(8AA) and 208(2)(c) are invalid.

Taking away an opportunity to vote

Rowe considered the validity of laws that did not remove the right to vote but that had the practical effect of reducing an existing opportunity for people to enrol to vote. *Rowe* struck down a law removing an existing opportunity to enrol up to seven days after the issue of the writs for an election because the law could not be justified in the way ***Roach*** requires.

Rowe confirms that the question is not whether the electoral system implemented by a law is merely consistent with the description of Parliament being chosen by the people. *Rowe* explains that any unjustified reduction in the scope of the franchise or of opportunities to exercise voting rights is unconstitutional.

Rowe v Electoral Commissioner (2010) 243 CLR 1

French CJ

The Constitution requires that members of Parliament be "directly chosen by the people" ...

An electoral law which denies enrolment and therefore the right to vote to any of the people who are qualified to be enrolled can only be justified if it serves the purpose of the constitutional mandate. If the law's adverse legal or practical effect upon the exercise of the entitlement to vote is disproportionate to its advancement of the constitutional mandate, then it may be antagonistic to that mandate. If that be so, it will be invalid ...

The content of the constitutional concept of "chosen by the people" has evolved since 1901 and is now informed by the universal adult-citizen franchise which is prescribed by Commonwealth law. The development of the franchise was authorised by ss 8 and 30 of the Constitution, read with s 51(xxxvi). Implicit in that authority was the possibility that the constitutional concept would acquire, as it did, a more democratic content than existed at Federation. That content, being constitutional in character, although it may be subject to adjustment from time to time, cannot now be diminished ...

The validity of a provision of the [*Commonwealth Electoral Act*] disqualifying as voters persons serving any sentence of imprisonment for an offence against a Commonwealth or State law was in issue in *Roach*. The section, which was held invalid, operated by way of an exception to universal adult-citizen franchise. The decision in *Roach* is not therefore directly applicable to this case. The general approach of the majority in *Roach* is, however, instructive. It informs, by close analogy, the approach which should be taken in this case to the challenged law in light of the constitutional mandate ...

The present case concerns an electoral law of a procedural or machinery character. It does not in terms carve out an exception to the franchise. It does, however, have a substantive effect upon entitlements to vote and so affects the exercise of the franchise ...

"[T]he people" is not a term the content of which is shaped by laws creating procedures for enrolment and for the conduct of elections. If such a law denies the right to vote to any class of person entitled to be an elector, it denies it to that class of "the people". Such a law may be valid. But the logic of the constitutional scheme for a representative democracy requires that the validity of such a law be tested by reference to the constitutional mandate of direct choice by "the people". Where, as in the present case, the law removes a legally sanctioned opportunity for enrolment, it is the change effected by the law that must be considered. It is not necessary first to determine some baseline of validity. Within the normative framework of a representative democracy based on direct choice by the people, a law effecting such a change causes a detriment. Its justification must be that it is nevertheless, on balance, beneficial because it contributes to the fulfilment of the mandate. If the detriment, in legal effect or practical operation, is disproportionate to that benefit, then the law will be invalid as inconsistent with that mandate, for its net effect will be antagonistic to it. Applying the terminology adopted in *Roach*, such a law would lack a substantial reason for the detriment it inflicts upon the exercise of the franchise. It is therefore not sufficient for the validity of such a law that an election conducted under its provisions nevertheless results in members of Parliament being "directly chosen by the people" ...

The legal effect of the impugned provisions is clear. They diminish the opportunities for enrolment and transfer of enrolment that existed prior to their enactment. These were opportunities that had been in place as a matter of law for eight federal elections since 1983. They were consistent with an established executive practice which provided an effective period of grace for nearly 50 years before 1983. The practical effect of the Amendment Act was that a significant number of persons claiming enrolment or transfer of enrolment after the calling of an election could not have their claims considered until after the election. That practical effect cannot be put to one side with the observation, which is undoubtedly correct, that those persons were so affected because of their own failures to claim enrolment or transfer of enrolment in accordance with their statutory obligations. The reality remains that the barring of consideration of the claims of those persons to enrolment or transfer of enrolment in time to enable them to vote at the election is a significant detriment in terms of the constitutional mandate. That detriment must be considered against the legitimate purposes of the Parliament reflected in the [Joint Standing Committee on Electoral Matters] Report. Those purposes addressed no compelling practical problem or difficulty in the operation of the electoral system. Rather they were directed to its enhancement and improvement. In my opinion, the heavy price imposed by the Amendment Act in terms of its immediate practical impact upon the fulfilment of the constitutional mandate was disproportionate to the benefits of a smoother and more efficient electoral system to which the amendments were directed ...

Crennan J

[T]he impugned provisions have not been shown to be necessary or appropriate for the protection of the integrity of the Rolls, as that object was advanced by the Commonwealth. First, this is because the Australian Electoral Commission had no difficulty in processing the volume of late enrolments which occurred with the previous seven day cut-off period. Secondly, to seek to discourage a surge of late claims for enrolment by disentitling or excluding those making them constitutes a failure to recognise the centrality of the franchise to a citizen's participation in the political life of the community. Thirdly, the main reason put forward by the Commonwealth as the justification for the impugned provisions – namely, that they will operate to protect the Rolls from the risk of, or potential for, systematic electoral fraud – is to protect the Rolls from a risk or potential which has not been substantiated to date.

Accordingly, the justification put forward to support the impugned provisions does not constitute a substantial reason, that is, a reason of real significance, for disentitling a significant number of electors from exercising their right to vote for parliamentary representatives in the State and Subdivision in which they reside. The impugned provisions cannot be reconciled with the constitutional imperative of choice by the people of those representatives ...

No requirement to maximise electoral participation

Murphy holds that sections 7 and 24 do not mandate that Parliament legislate to maximise participation in choosing parliamentarians. The *Constitution*: (1) requires that electoral laws yield a Parliament directly chosen by the people; and (2) grants Parliament legislative power to design and enact electoral laws that bring about that result.

Provided that electoral laws do result in a Parliament directly chosen by the people, there is no breach of the *Constitution* simply because a different electoral system might result in greater voter participation. The principles articulated in ***Roach*** and ***Rowe*** concern only *removing* opportunities to participate in choosing parliamentarians.

Murphy v Electoral Commissioner (2016) 261 CLR 28

Legislation had long provided that the opportunity to enrol to vote ended seven days after the issue of the writs for an election. The plaintiffs argued that because it was possible to extend that seven-day period, which would increase voter participation, the provisions prescribing the seven-day period were invalid. The High Court held that this argument misunderstood the requirements of sections 7 and 24.

French CJ and Bell J

The plaintiffs' case did not involve a challenge, as in *Roach v Electoral Commissioner*, to a disqualifying provision targeting a particular class of persons such as sentenced prisoners. Nor was it, as in *Rowe v Electoral Commissioner*, a challenge to a law removing an existing opportunity to enrol up to seven days after the issue of the writs for an election. In this case the plaintiffs said, in effect, that Parliament had not gone far enough when it left in place long-standing time limits, essentially dating back to the 1930s, on the processing of new and transferred enrolments, objections and amendments to the Rolls ...

The impugned laws in this case were similar to the impugned laws in *Rowe* only to the extent that they both provided for suspension periods during which claims for enrolment, transfers of enrolment, objections and corrections to the Roll could not be considered. The significant difference was that, unlike the present case, *Rowe* concerned laws which reduced existing opportunities for enrolment or transfer of enrolment prior to an election. The plaintiffs' case depended upon a generalisation of *Roach* and *Rowe* and a characterisation of the impugned provisions as imposing a burden upon the realisation of the constitutional mandate of choice by the people ...

The impugned provisions do not become invalid because it is possible to identify alternative measures that may extend opportunities for enrolment. That would allow a court to pull the constitutional rug from under a valid legislative scheme upon the court's judgment of the feasibility of alternative arrangements. The plaintiffs' premise that the suspension period reflects a burden on the constitutional mandate of popular choice was not made out. The failure of that premise was fatal to the plaintiffs' attempts to generalise *Roach* and *Rowe* in support of their argument ...

Kiefel J

A further observation may also be made about *Roach* and *Rowe*, as relevant to the plaintiffs' argument. Neither of those decisions is authority for the proposition that it is a constitutional imperative that the maximum number of persons entitled to be enrolled and vote have the opportunity to be enrolled and vote ...

Gageler J

A substantial reason, equating to a substantial justification, for an exclusion from the franchise was seen by the majority in each of *Roach* and *Rowe* to require the provisions effecting the exclusion to be judged "reasonably appropriate and adapted to serve an end which is consistent or compatible with the maintenance of the constitutionally prescribed system of representative government"...

The impugned provisions do no more than give contemporary expression to a standard incident of the traditional legislative scheme for the orderly conduct of national elections. That is the reason for them, and that reason is substantial. Whether or not cutting off enrolment at a fixed time seven days after the issue of a writ might be regarded as outmoded, that cut-off is not so unfit for the purpose for which it was long ago designed that it can no longer be said to be reasonably appropriate and adapted to serve that purpose.

Stricter scrutiny is not warranted, and greater justification is not required. Unlike *Roach* and *Rowe*, this is not a case in which provisions impugned have expanded an exclusion from the franchise ...

Through the application of an abstracted top-down analysis, they would have had the Court compel the Parliament to maximise the franchise by redesigning the legislative scheme to adopt what the plaintiffs put forward currently to be best electoral practice ... The plaintiffs' efforts to expand the franchise would be better directed to the Parliament than to the Court.

Keane J

In *Langer v Commonwealth*, Toohey and Gaudron JJ explained that the phrase "chosen by the people", understood in its context, "prohibits any feature [of legislation] that prevents it being said that the Senate or the House of Representatives is ... composed of persons 'chosen by the people'." These observations do not, however, support the notion that a failure to maximise voting opportunity has the prohibited effect. Only in the reasons of Gummow and Bell JJ in *Rowe* is there arguable support for the view that the constitutional role of the Parliament in relation to the electoral system is constrained by a mandatory requirement of maximum participation in voting. And, as will be said, to ascribe that view to their Honours' observations is to misstate their effect ...

[T]heir case was no more than a complaint that better arrangements might be made to fulfil the mandate ...

Nettle J

Rowe ... is not authority for the proposition that "chosen by the people" in ss 7 and 24 of the Constitution mandates making elections as expressive of the popular choice as practical considerations properly permit ...

Gordon J

[A] fundamental flaw in the plaintiffs' argument[:] The plaintiffs assumed that the Constitution requires the Parliament to enact legislation to provide for "elections as expressive of the popular choice as practical considerations properly permit". That assumption cannot be sustained. It finds no support or foundation in the text or structure of the Constitution, or elsewhere ...

It follows from ***Roach, Rowe*** and ***Murphy*** that Parliament has some flexibility in designing laws prescribing the operation of federal elections and who is qualified to vote in federal elections.

No requirement to maximise information available to voters

Ruddick holds that Parliament can legislate for a voting scheme that prevents the names of certain political parties appearing on ballot papers alongside the candidates contesting an election for those parties.

Ruddick v Commonwealth [2022] HCA 9

Amendments enacted in 2021 had the effect that a political party must be deregistered or refused registration if its name contains a word (with the exception of words like 'the', 'of' and 'Australian') that is in the name of an earlier registered political party. The principal effect of deregistration or non-registration is that the name of the party cannot appear on ballot papers; the party's candidates may still contest elections and the party still may engage in political activity. The Liberal Democratic Party was impacted by the amendments, since the word 'liberal' appears also in the name of the Liberal Party, and challenged this provision. One of its politicians claimed that the party had received many votes from voters who mistook the Liberal Democratic Party for the Liberal Party. A majority of the High Court (Gordon, Edelman and Gleeson JJ, and Steward J) held that the 2021 amendments imposed no burden on the free choice of electors required by sections 7 and 24.

Gordon, Edelman and Gleeson JJ

None of the material in the special case demonstrates that the 2021 Amendments impair or burden the quality of any electoral choice by the people or the freedom of political communication. The *Constitution* does not confer upon political parties a licence to obtain votes by confusion ...

The decisions of this Court in *Roach v Electoral Commissioner*, *Rowe v Electoral Commissioner*, and *Murphy v Electoral Commissioner* recognised that one requirement of direct choice by the people in ss 7 and 24 is that the reference to "the people" restricts the extent to which Parliament can burden or reduce the universal adult franchise. Provided that the threshold issue of a burden upon the franchise is established, Parliament will only be justified in imposing that burden if it does so for a substantial reason, being a reason which is "reasonably appropriate and adapted to serve an end which is consistent or compatible with the maintenance of the constitutionally prescribed system of representative government". What a court will accept as a substantial reason will vary over time, including with changing social conditions. For instance, whether or not they could ever have been justified, there could not be any justification for the laws that existed in all States except South Australia and Western Australia that denied the vote at the first Commonwealth election to women, or the laws in Queensland and Western Australia that banned Aboriginal people from the electoral roll.

In the assessment of whether a substantial reason exists to justify imposing a burden on the franchise, it must be borne in mind that the requirement of "direct choice by the people" was intended only as a basic structural requirement, or the "bare foundations of the electoral law". This deliberate design of the Constitution included leaving Parliament with a wide leeway of choice, even concerning the fundamental features of the operation of elections ...

Like the restriction implied by the notion of "the people", the restriction implied by the requirement of "choice" in ss 7 and 24 must not be applied in an over broad manner which would fail to respect the constitutional design of leaving to Parliament the choice of how to legislate for every aspect, except the bare foundations, of the electoral system. It can be accepted that the implied constitutional mandate that the choice be informed takes the meaning of ss 7 and 24 further than the "common parlance" of "to choose", which "means no more than to make a selection between different things or alternatives submitted, to take by preference out of all that are available".

An example where care was taken not to apply the constraints of ss 7 and 24 in an overly broad manner is the decision in *Langer v Commonwealth*. In that case, five members of this Court upheld the validity of an amendment to the *Commonwealth Electoral Act* which prohibited the printing, publication, or distribution of material that encouraged people to vote at an election in a way that would be informal. The provision was valid, even though it deprived electors of information that would assist them to vote, in a lawful manner, so as to deny their preferences going to a candidate for whom they did not want to vote ...

Mr Ruddick effectively asks this Court to infer that the quality of electoral choice ... will be impaired due to the inability of a candidate to have, accompanying their name on the ballot paper, the name and logo of a party which includes a word used in another party's name. That conclusion is not self evident. Rather, on the material before the Court, the expected conclusion would be the opposite. The likely effect of the narrow restrictions imposed by the 2021 Amendments is, overall, to improve the clarity, and hence the quality, of electoral choice and communication on government or political matters.

Apart from the content of the ballot paper, deregistration of the Liberal Democratic Party would not preclude any communication with the public, including communication using the name "Liberal Democratic Party". The only potential restraint on the quality of electoral choice by the public ... is that, by s 169 of the *Commonwealth Electoral Act*, a candidate for election endorsed by the Liberal Democratic Party, such as Mr Ruddick, would be unable to have that party name printed adjacent to their name on the ballot paper.

Even if it were accepted that there was some small constraint upon ... the quality of electoral choice by the inability of a candidate endorsed by the Liberal Democratic Party to use the word "liberal" on the ballot paper, the net effect would still be an enhancement of electoral choice ...

For the minority judges (Kiefel CJ and Keane J, and Gageler J), the 2021 amendments had the effect of taking away an existing ability of electors to see on the ballot paper the party affiliation of some candidates. The minority judges did not accept that there was evidence establishing voter confusion was a problem. Accordingly, the 2021 amendments had the effect of diminishing the informed choice of electors for no substantial reason.

Ruddick v Commonwealth [2022] HCA 9

Gageler J

Denial of registration of a political party prevents information about the party affiliation of candidates affiliated with that party from appearing on ballot papers for elections to the Senate and to the House of Representatives. The impugned items accordingly create a legal impediment to the receipt by electors of information which bears on the making of an informed choice between candidates in the casting of their ballots ...

What the material in the special case fails to demonstrate is that the mere fact that one political party contains in its registered name a word contained in the registered name of another, earlier registered political party is alone enough to support the conclusion that there exists a meaningful risk of confusion on the part of electors as to the party affiliation of candidates for election to the Senate or to the House of Representatives. No necessity for the impugned items has therefore been demonstrated to exist, much less a necessity which can be characterised as rising to the level of a compelling justification.

15.5 Electorate sizes: Voter equality

There is nothing in section 24 of the *Constitution* requiring voter equality in the sense of the principle of 'one vote, one value'. It is open to Parliament to enact electoral laws establishing electoral divisions (commonly called 'electorates' or 'seats') for the House of Representatives with unequal numbers of voters. If one electorate has a smaller voter population than another electorate, a voter in the smaller electorate has a more powerful vote than a voter in the larger electorate.

McKinlay rejected an argument that the requirement in section 24 that members of the House of Representatives be 'directly chosen by the people' entailed a requirement for electoral divisions to have approximately an equal number of voters. However, the High Court noted that grossly disproportionate electorate voter population sizes might fail to answer the description 'directly chosen by the people'.

Attorney-General (Cth) ex rel McKinlay v Commonwealth (1975) 135 CLR 1

McTiernan and Jacobs JJ

The primary submission on behalf of the plaintiffs has been that members are not directly chosen by the people of the Commonwealth unless any law passed pursuant to s 29 and by virtue of s 51(xxxvi) ensures that every division in a State for which a member or members may be chosen is as nearly as practicable equal in number of people to every other division in the State. It is said that that is the meaning of the words "chosen by the people" in s 24. We do not think that any such exact content can by definition be given to these words. The words express a distinct concept or notion capable of application as a constitutional requirement but they are not words which can be re-written or paraphrased in such an exact manner.

The words embrace the notion of equality of numbers in so far as the choice of members must be by the people of the Commonwealth. Inequality of distribution of numbers between districts or divisions in respect of which members are chosen is one factor which may lead to a choice on the basis of such an unequal distribution being unable to be described as a choice by the people of the Commonwealth ...

But there is nothing in our history and our development as a nation which would require that before a member be described as chosen by the people of the Commonwealth absolute or as nearly as practicable absolute equality of numbers of the people exist in every constituted electoral district in a State ...

Gibbs J

It is said that the members must be chosen by, or perhaps more precisely by electors representing, all the people, and that it must be implied or inferred that all people are to be placed on the same footing, so that each member will represent the same number of people or at least of electors. Further, it is said that the section is intended to ensure that the House of Representatives is elected on democratic principles, and that such principles require that electoral divisions should contain equal numbers of people or of electors. We have to decide whether s 24, properly interpreted, does have this effect. If it does not, we are not justified in importing new requirements into it simply because, as a matter of policy, they may seem to be desirable ...

The section says nothing in terms as to the weight to be given to the votes of those people who cast them. It does not mention equality. Moreover, the concluding words of s 24, by providing a minimum number of members for each original State, create an exception to the rule that the number of members chosen in the several States shall be in proportion to the respective numbers of their people, and have the result that so long as the population of any State is so small that its representation, if fixed proportionately, would be less than five, it will be impossible to achieve equality in the number of people or of electors in electoral divisions throughout Australia ...

Mason J

All that the paragraph in s 24 requires is that there should be a direct choice of the members by the people – a prescription which does not cease to be satisfied because there is some, or even a marked, variation in the number of persons or electors in the electoral divisions within a State. The existence of such variations does not detract from the accuracy of the description of our existing electoral system as one in which the members of the House are directly chosen by the people of the Commonwealth ...

It is perhaps conceivable that variations in the numbers of electors or people in single member electorates could become so grossly disproportionate as to raise a question whether an election held on boundaries so drawn would produce a House of Representatives composed of members directly chosen by the people of the Commonwealth, but this is a matter quite removed from the proposition that s 24 insists upon a practical equality of people or electors in single member electorates ...

McGinty concerned an argument that the *Constitution* contains a requirement that each vote should, as far as practicable, be equal in value and that this requirement extended to State elections. The whole Court held that even if the *Constitution* gave rise to such a requirement for the federal electoral system it did not do so for State electoral systems.

The majority also affirmed ***McKinlay*** and rejected the idea that section 24 of the *Constitution* contains a requirement that each vote should, as far as practicable, be equal in value for the federal electoral system. The judges identified features of the *Constitution* pointing to an acceptance of this sort of voter inequality

McGinty v Western Australia (1996) 186 CLR 140

Dawson J

There can be no implication that a particular electoral system, of the many available, is required by the Constitution. There is, of course, the express requirement that whatever system is employed it must result in a direct choice by the people. That must mean direct choice by the people through those eligible to vote at elections, but beyond that the matter of electoral systems, including the size of electoral divisions, and indeed whether to have divisional representation at all, is left to the parliament ... It is true that in *McKinlay*, McTiernan and Jacobs JJ suggested that the notion of equality is to some extent present in the words "chosen by the people" so that at some point electoral inequality might be inconsistent with a choice by the people. They rejected, however, any requirement of absolute equality or nearly as practicable equality ... In my view, both McTiernan and Jacobs JJ and Mason J had in mind extreme situations ...

McHugh J

Equality of voting power is not a fundamental feature of the Constitution. On the contrary, inequality of individual voting power is one of its striking features. Thus, under s 128 of the Constitution, an amendment cannot be made to the Constitution unless a majority of electors in a majority of States approve the proposed law to amend the Constitution. Accordingly, the votes of the persons living in one of the less populous States are equivalent to the votes of the persons living in one of the more populous States. If the majority of New South Wales voters approve a constitutional amendment but a majority of Tasmanians reject it, their votes cancel each other out, notwithstanding the enormous population difference between the two States. Thus, the share in the right to amend the Constitution of each Tasmanian voter can be more than 12 times as great as the share of each New South Wales voter ...

Part II of Ch 1 of the Constitution, which deals with the Senate, is also a powerful indicator that equality of individual voting power is not a feature, let alone a fundamental feature, of the Constitution. Section 7 provides for the equal representation of the States and declares "that equal representation of the several Original States shall be maintained and that no Original State shall have less than six senators". Thus the Senate vote of an elector in Tasmania is 10 times more valuable than the Senate vote of an elector in Victoria ...

Section 121 of the Constitution is another strong indication that equality of individual voting power is not a general requirement of the Constitution or s 24. It provides that the Parliament may admit new States to the Commonwealth upon "such terms and conditions, including the extent of representation in either House of the Parliament, as it thinks fit". The words of s 24 must give way to this express provision in s 121 ... Thus under s 121 as under s 122, in the case of the Territories, the Parliament may prescribe a number of representatives for a new State without reference to the population of the new State or the population of the rest of Australia. The House of Representatives may therefore be composed of members from States and Territories whose share of representation is not proportional to their population. In the face of ss 121 and 122, it is difficult to imply in s 24 a requirement that electoral divisions for elections to the House of Representatives must be equal in numbers ...

Gummow J

McKinlay necessarily still stands for the ... proposition, also negative in nature, that s 24 does not require equality in electoral divisions.

To reject this branch of the plaintiffs' case is not necessarily to reject their broader submission that malapportionment, if sufficiently serious, may deny the system of representative government established for the Commonwealth by the Constitution, taken as a whole ...

It does not follow from the prescription by the Constitution of a system of representative government that a voting system with a particular characteristic or operation is required by the Constitution. What is necessary is the broadly identified requirement of ultimate control by the people, exercised by representatives who are elected periodically. Elements of the system of government which were consistent with, albeit not essential for, representative government might have been constitutionally entrenched or left by the Constitution itself to the legislature to provide and modify from time to time. This is what was done.

15.6 Methods of voting

The *Constitution* requires voting but does not require any particular method of voting beyond the requirement that parliamentarians be directly, as opposed to indirectly, chosen by the people.

Voting generally

Langer holds that Parliament may enact whatever voting system it pleases provided the result of that system is a Parliament consisting of representatives freely chosen by the people. In this case, the High Court held that a system of preferential voting requiring voters to number each candidate in order of preference is one way of freely choosing parliamentarians and therefore open to the Parliament to adopt. There is no contravention of the constitutional requirement just because other methods for expressing a voter's choice might better reflect a voter's choice or political preferences.

Langer v Commonwealth (1996) 186 CLR 302

This case considered the validity of law making it unlawful to encourage people to cast their vote other than in accordance with the prescribed method. The validity of the prescribed method of voting therefore needed to be decided.

Brennan CJ

The method of voting prescribed by this section can be described as full preferential voting. To cast an effective vote, a voter must indicate an order of preference as among all the candidates whose names appear on the ballot paper ...

The plaintiff contends that he is constitutionally entitled to publish material encouraging persons to fill in their ballot papers otherwise than in accordance with s 240 so that, if the encouragement is taken, their ballot papers would be informal or would be saved from informality by the saving provisions. This entitlement is said to be conferred by the requirement expressed in s 24 of the Constitution that the members of the House of Representatives be "chosen by the people". A voter, so the argument goes, must be free to indicate the candidates which the voter does not choose as well as the candidate or candidates which the voter does choose and, in some circumstances, that can be done only by the filling in of a ballot paper otherwise than in accordance with s 240. If I apprehend correctly the next step in the argument, it is said that s 329A cannot validly prohibit the encouragement of voters to exercise that right of choice which the Constitution allows ...

What the Constitution requires is that the law prescribe a method of voting which leaves the voter free to make a choice, not that the law leave the voter free to choose the method of voting by which a voter's choice is to be made. A method which requires full preferential voting satisfies the constitutional requirement ...

Provided the prescribed method of voting permits a free choice among the candidates for election, it is within the legislative power of the Parliament. Section 24 of the Constitution does not limit the Parliament's selection of the method of voting by which a voter's choice is made known so long as the method allows a free choice. Section 240 permits a voter to make a discriminating choice among the candidates for election to the House of Representatives. An election in which members of the House of Representatives are elected pursuant to such a method of voting achieves what s 24 requires, namely, a House of Representatives composed of members directly chosen by the people.

It follows that the Parliament is empowered to prescribe a method of voting in an election for the House of Representatives that requires a voter to fill in a ballot paper in accordance with s 240, although that method requires a voter to choose by allocating preferences among candidates for whom the voter does not wish to vote. It is not to the point that, if a ballot paper were filled in otherwise than in accordance with s 240, the vote would better express the voter's political opinion ...

Day v Electoral Officer holds that 'above the line' voting in Senate elections is a valid method for *directly* choosing senators. The plaintiffs argued that 'above the line' voting was an *indirect* method of choosing senators. The High Court disagreed, explaining that 'above the line' voting expresses the voter's personal choice as to who should be elected and is therefore a *direct* choice. Indirect methods of choosing parliamentarians involve mechanisms involving intermediaries such as electing delegates to an electoral college which then chooses parliamentarians.

Day also holds that permitting voters to record their choice of candidates either 'above the line' or 'below the line' does not constitute more than one method of voting in breach of section 9's requirement that a single method of choosing senators be adopted. Each of 'above the line' and 'below the voting' is simply a way of expressing the voter's preference list of candidates. The single method of voting is listing candidates in preference order.

Day v Australian Electoral Officer for the State of South Australia (2016) 261 CLR 1

French CJ, Kiefel, Bell, Gageler, Keane, Nettle and Gordon JJ

Two applications have been brought in the original jurisdiction of the Court challenging the validity of provisions of the *Commonwealth Electoral Act 1918* (Cth) ("the Act") as amended by the *Commonwealth Electoral Amendment Act 2016* (Cth) ("the Amendment Act"). The challenged provisions concern the new form of the Senate ballot paper and the process for marking it. The new process requires an elector to number sequentially at least six squares above the dividing line on the ballot paper. A group of candidates may be granted a square above the line on request. Where a group of candidates has so requested, the name of the political party that endorsed them and the party logo will appear adjacent to the square above the line. The numbering of squares above the line indicates the elector's preference for the candidates in the first numbered group or party in the order in which they appear below the dividing line, followed by the candidates of the second numbered group or party and so on up to the number of the elector's choices. The new process also requires electors who wish to vote below the dividing line to number at least 12 candidates in the order of their preference ...

[The plaintiffs] separately contend that by allowing electors to indicate a vote for a party or group designated above the line on the ballot paper, the Act departs from the requirement in s 7 that Senators will be "directly chosen by the people". The basis for that argument is that a vote above the line is a vote for the relevant group or party as an intermediary and not a direct choice of named candidates ...

The plaintiffs' arguments may be summarised as follows:

A. The option of "optional first past the post/preferential" voting for parties above the line and "compulsory preferential" voting for candidates below the line, for which the Act now provides, constitutes more than one method of choosing Senators and is contrary to the requirement in s 9 of the Constitution that there be only one method.

B. The option of above the line voting for one or more registered parties or groups contravenes the requirement in s 7 of the Constitution that Senators for each State be "directly chosen by the people" ...

Argument A: The method of choosing Senators

Each of the above the line and below the line voting options is a way of casting votes for a number of candidates named on the ballot paper. A formal vote can be cast above the line by marking a square against the name of just one political party whose candidates appear below the line. Such a vote adopts as the elector's order of preference the order in which candidates appear below the line. In the case of a party with only two candidates, an example offered by the plaintiffs, an elector who numbers only that party's square above the line votes for its two candidates in the order in which they appear below the line. An elector casting a vote below the line may number as few as six named candidates and still cast a formal vote.

The common effect of the different ways of completing a formal Senate ballot paper is to require the elector to choose between named candidates, but to leave the number of candidates chosen to the discretion of the elector, within the limits described. The availability of that discretion does not involve the creation of more than one method of choosing Senators. The plaintiffs' submissions should be rejected ...

Argument B: Senators "directly chosen"

The plaintiffs submitted that the requirement in s 7 of the Constitution that the Senators for each State be "directly chosen by the people of the State" refers to candidates elected without the intervention of any intermediary or third party. Above the line voting by marking squares designated by reference to political parties was said to offend against that requirement ...

The plaintiffs submitted that above the line voting was not a vote for an individual "except derivatively through the operation of the Act". The vote cast was for an intermediary, being the named political party. That characterisation was said to be made clear because it was not possible to preference individual candidates in above the line voting but only parties or groups registered for that purpose.

The plaintiffs' characterisation should not be accepted. A vote marked above the line is as much a direct vote for individual candidates as a vote below the line. To number a square above the line identifies the candidates appearing beneath that square below the line. That much was made plain by the plaintiffs' own examples of ballot papers completed above the line. An elector is provided with a direct choice. An elector who does not wish to use the above the line facility is able to vote by allocating preferences below the line.

The term "directly chosen by the people" appearing in s 7 also appears in s 24 of the Constitution, which requires that the House of Representatives "shall be composed of members directly chosen by the people". The requirement of direct choice excludes indirect choice by an electoral college or some other intermediary. That is not the case here.

The argument that above the line voting amounts to something other than a direct choice of individuals is untenable. The plaintiffs' submission must be rejected.

Compulsory voting

Voting in federal elections has been compulsory in Australia since 1924. ***Judd v McKeon*** explains that compulsory voting is not inconsistent with the idea of freely choosing parliamentarians.

Judd v McKeon (1926) 38 CLR 380

Knox CJ, Gavan Duffy and Starke JJ

The appellant was convicted on a charge of failing to vote at an election of Senators for New South Wales without a valid and sufficient reason for such failure, contrary to the provisions of s 128A of the *Commonwealth Electoral Act 1918–1925*. That section provides, by sub-s 1, that it shall be the duty of every elector to record his vote at each election, and, by sub-s 12, that every elector who fails to vote at an election without a valid and sufficient reason for such failure shall be guilty of an offence. On appeal to Quarter Sessions the conviction was affirmed; and this appeal is brought by special leave from that decision.

The appellant contends that the provisions of s 128A above quoted are beyond the powers of the Commonwealth Parliament ...

By s 9 of the Constitution Parliament is empowered to make laws prescribing the method of choosing Senators, subject to one condition or qualification only, namely, that the method shall be uniform for all the States. This power, subject only to the condition mentioned, is plenary and unrestricted; and the only reason advanced for denying to Parliament the right to prescribe that every qualified elector shall record his vote was founded on the use of the word "choosing." It was said that the choosing of a candidate implied a desire on the part of the elector that that candidate should be elected, and that consequently the power of Parliament was limited to prescribing the method by which electors desiring that a candidate should be elected should signify that desire.

We do not think the meaning of the expression "choosing Senators" in s 9 of the Constitution can be so restricted. In common parlance "to choose" means no more than to make a selection between different things or alternatives submitted, to take by preference out of all that are available. As an illustration of the meaning of the corresponding noun "choice" the Oxford Dictionary quotes the phrase "I have given thee thy choice of the manner in which thou wilt die," and this use of the word seems to exclude the idea that a right of choice can only be said to be given when one or other of the alternatives submitted is desired by the person who is to exercise the right, or, in other words, to choose between them ...

Isaacs J

A method of choosing which involves compulsory voting, so long as it preserves freedom of choice of possible candidates, does not offend against the freedom of elections ...

The compulsory performance of a public duty is entirely consistent with freedom of action in the course of performing it. A tribunal may, for instance, be required, by mandamus, to determine a controversy, but its determination is to be freely arrived at. It is the failure to observe this distinction that lies at the root of the first objection, which must fail ...

In ***Holmdahl***, the Full Court of the Supreme Court of South Australia rejected another challenge to compulsory voting. The Full Court's reasoning is expressed in language reflecting the development of the case law subsequent to ***Judd v McKeon***.

Holmdahl v Australian Electoral Commission (No 2) (2012) 277 FLR 101

Gray J (Kourakis CJ and Sulan J concurring)

The defendant and appellant, Nils Anders Holmdahl, both at trial and on appeal, raised a challenge to section 245(15) of the *Commonwealth Electoral Act 1918* (Cth). Together sections 245(1) and 245(15) provide for compulsory voting at Commonwealth elections ...

[T]he phrase "directly chosen by the people" is a broad expression used to identify the requirement of a popular vote. The phrase should not be dissected in a way that would give the expression an operation distinct from sections 7 and 24 read as a whole. It does not require a particular electoral system or that it have some particular feature. The expression admits a considerable measure of legislative freedom as to the method of choice of members of Parliament. As much is plain from the decisions of the High Court in *Ex rel McKinlay v Commonwealth, McGinty v Western Australia, Langer v The Commonwealth* and *Mulholland v Australian Electoral Commission* ...

It must also be borne in mind that the method of choice adopted by the Commonwealth Parliament is not an end in itself but a means to an end, namely, the election of senators and members of the House of Representatives "directly chosen by the people", of the respective States, in the case of the Senate, and of the Commonwealth, in the case of the House of Representatives ...

The starting point for determining whether a law as to the method of choice of senators and members of the House of Representatives is a valid law of the Commonwealth Parliament is to ask whether the law is one with respect to the head of power contained in sections 10, 31 and 51(xxxvi). If it is, subject to the constitutional mandate of sections 7 and 24, the law is valid. Whether or not the law offends the constitutional mandate contained in sections 7 and 24 is determined by asking two questions. First, does the law operate so as to detract from the constitutional mandate: *Rowe v Electoral Commissioner*. Second, if the answer to the first question is in the affirmative, is the law nevertheless reasonably appropriate and adapted to serve an end consistent with the maintenance of the constitutionally prescribed system of representative government: *Rowe v Electoral Commissioner; Roach v Electoral Commissioner*.

The mandate is flexible with the consequence that whether or not a law with respect to the subject matter is inconsistent with it imports questions of fact and degree having regard to contemporary circumstances. The High Court has not as yet settled upon any one test for determining the outcome of what is an evaluative exercise.

Section 245(15) of the Commonwealth Electoral Act is a law with respect to elections. It is, therefore, supported by sections 10, 31 and 51(xxxvi) of the Commonwealth Constitution. It is also a law which operates to promote full, equal and effective participation in the electoral process and is clearly capable of being viewed as operating to further the constitutional mandate. No need arises to consider whether or not section 245(15) of the Commonwealth Electoral Act is reasonably appropriate and adapted to serve an end consistent with the constitutional mandate ...

15.7 DISCUSSION QUESTIONS

1. What is the reasoning underlying the conclusion that section 41 is spent and has no going operation? Is that reasoning persuasive?
2. How do sections 7 and 24 operate to restrict the power to enact laws taking away the right to vote or preventing the exercise of the right to vote?
3. What is the distinction between direct and indirect methods of choosing parliamentarians?
4. Why is it not unconstitutional for electoral districts for the House of Representatives to have uneven voter populations?
5. Problem question: Consider the following hypothetical scenario. The Commonwealth Special Minister of State, whose portfolio responsibilities include electoral laws, seeks your advice as to whether the Commonwealth Parliament has power to enact a law providing that henceforth applications to enrol to vote or to update enrolment details may only be submitted using online forms. The current law allows the use of either paper forms or online forms. The Minister's motivation is to reduce printing and postage costs, to be environmentally friendly by reducing paper usage, and to reduce administrative costs associated with transcribing information from paper forms into the Australian Electoral Commission's databases.

   Advise the Minister.

PART

5

THE COURTS AND JUDICIAL POWER

THE SCOPE OF FEDERAL JUDICIAL POWER

16

16.1 Overview

This chapter examines the scope of federal judicial power. Chapter III of the *Australian Constitution* sets out a comprehensive regime for the exercise of federal judicial power. This means that federal judicial power can be exercised only in the way prescribed by Chapter III.

There is no comprehensive definition of 'judicial power', although there are some functions that are always judicial in nature and some functions that are never judicial in nature. Federal jurisdiction – that is, the exercise of federal judicial power – is limited to the subject-matters set out in sections 75 and 76 of the *Constitution* and also limited to 'matters' respecting those subject-matters.

Key concepts addressed in this chapter include:

- judicial power
- federal judicial power
- jurisdiction
- federal jurisdiction
- matter.

16.2 The characteristics of judicial power

The *Constitution* refers to the 'judicial power of the Commonwealth' but it does not define 'judicial power'.

Australian Constitution

Section 71 Judicial Power and Courts

The judicial power of the Commonwealth shall be vested in a Federal Supreme Court, to be called the High Court of Australia, and in such other federal courts as the Parliament creates, and in such other courts as it invests with federal jurisdiction. The High Court shall consist of a Chief Justice, and so many other Justices, not less than two, as the Parliament prescribes.

In ***Huddart, Parker & Co v Moorehead***, Griffith CJ gave what has come to be accepted as a classic definition of 'judicial power'.

Huddart, Parker & Co Pty Ltd v Moorehead (1909) 8 CLR 330

Griffith CJ

I am of the opinion that the words "judicial power" as used in s 71 of the Constitution mean the power which every sovereign authority must of necessity have to decide controversies between its subjects, or between itself and its subjects, whether the rights relate to life, liberty or property. The exercise of this power does not begin until some tribunal which has power to give a binding and authoritative decision (whether subject to appeal or not) is called upon to take action.

The concept of 'judicial power' is impossible to define exhaustively. Instead, the case law has been concerned mainly with identifying indicia or characteristics of judicial power. Chief Justice Griffith notes three key characteristics:

1. Judicial power involves deciding controversies.
2. A judicial decision is binding and authoritative.
3. Judicial power must be called upon and is not self-initiating, in the sense that some interested party must bring the controversy to the court.

Nevertheless, there are some functions that are always judicial in character and some that are never judicial in character. ***Brandy v Human Rights and Equal Opportunity Commission*** is authority for the proposition that making a non-consensual, enforceable decision about legal rights in issue between private parties is always judicial in character. The judgment in ***Brandy's Case*** also commented on another characteristic of judicial power: that judicial power involves resolving controversies by the application of some pre-existing standard rather than by the formulation of a new policy.

Brandy v Human Rights and Equal Opportunity Commission ('Brandy's Case') (1995) 183 CLR 245

The **Racial Discrimination Act 1975 (Cth)** *empowered the Human Rights and Equal Opportunity Commission ('HREOC') to receive complaints and make findings that a person had engaged in unlawful conduct, to declare that the person should perform some act of redress, and to declare that the person should pay compensation. The legislation also provided that such determinations were to be lodged in a Registry of the Federal Court at which point they would have effect as if they were orders made by the Federal Court. Brandy was subject to HREOC findings and argued that the registration of declarations and their taking effect as if orders of the Federal Court meant that the HREOC was exercising judicial power. The High Court agreed.*

Deane, Dawson, Gaudron and McHugh JJ

Difficulty arises in attempting to formulate a comprehensive definition of judicial power not so much because it consists of a number of factors as because the combination is not always the same. It is hard to point to any essential or constant characteristic. Moreover, there are functions which, when performed by a court, constitute the exercise of judicial power but, when performed by some other body, do not ...

One is tempted to say that, in the end, judicial power is the power exercised by courts and can only be defined by reference to what courts do and the way in which they do it, rather than by recourse to any other classification of functions. But that would be to place reliance upon the elements of history and policy which, whilst they are legitimate considerations, cannot be conclusive ...

[I]t is not every binding and authoritative decision made in the determination of a dispute which constitutes the exercise of judicial power. A legislative or administrative decision may answer that description. Another important element which distinguishes a judicial decision is that it determines existing rights and duties and does so according to law. That is to say, it does so by the application of a pre-existing standard rather than by the formulation of policy or the exercise of an administrative discretion ...

However, there is one aspect of judicial power which may serve to characterize a function as judicial when it is otherwise equivocal. That is the enforceability of decisions given in the exercise of judicial power. ... Turning to the present case, it is apparent that the Commission's functions point in many respects to the exercise of judicial power. It decides controversies between parties and does so by the determination of rights and duties based upon existing facts and the law as set out in Pt II of the Racial Discrimination Act. Indeed, the relevant function of the Commission is essentially to determine whether the provisions of ss 9 and 15, which prohibit certain kinds of racial discrimination, have been contravened. That is clearly indicative of the exercise of judicial power ...

Moreover, the remedies which the Commission may award (see s 25Z) include damages as well as declaratory or injunctive relief and, according to whether they may be viewed as punitive or otherwise, make its functions closely analogous to those of a court in deciding criminal or civil cases.

However, if it were not for the provisions providing for the registration and enforcement of the Commission's determinations, it would be plain that the Commission does not exercise judicial power. That is because, under s 25Z(2), its determination would not be binding or conclusive between any of the parties and would be unenforceable. That situation is, we think, reversed by the registration provisions ...

Nothing that the Federal Court does gives a determination the effect of an order. That is done by the legislation operating upon registration. The result is that a determination of the Commission is enforceable by execution under s 53 of the Federal Court Act. It is the determination of the Commission which is enforceable ...

For these reasons, ss 25ZAA, 25ZAB and 25ZAC, which combine to make a determination of the Commission binding, authoritative and enforceable, invalidly purport to invest judicial power in the Commission.

Brandy's Case can be contrasted with ***TCL Air Conditioner (Zhongshan) Co Ltd v The Judges of the Federal Court of Australia.*** In *TCL Air Conditioner,* the High Court held that an arbitral tribunal does not exercise judicial power. Arbitration involves deciding controversies about legal rights and obligations in dispute between private parties by the application of pre-existing legal standards. Arbitral decisions or awards are binding on the parties and will be enforced by the courts.

However, unlike judicial proceedings and unlike the situation considered in ***Brandy's Case,*** arbitration proceedings require the consent of all parties in order to be commenced. Arbitral awards are binding by reason ultimately of that consent. A court will enforce an arbitral award just as a court will enforce obligations arising out of any other contractual agreement. By contrast, judicial power is non-consensual and coercive.

TCL Air Conditioner (Zhongshan) Co Ltd v The Judges of the Federal Court of Australia (2013) 251 CLR 533

Section 16(1) of the **International Arbitration Act 1974** *(Cth) provided that the* **UNCITRAL Model Law on International Commercial Arbitration** *has 'the force of law in Australia'. Article 35 of the Model Law provided that an arbitral award shall be enforced upon application to a 'competent court', which included the Federal Court. One argument in this case was that by making arbitral awards enforceable by courts, the Act impermissibly delegated judicial power to a non-judicial body. The High Court held that arbitral tribunals do not exercise judicial power.*

French CJ and Gageler J

The judicial power of the Commonwealth has defied precise definition. One dimension concerns the nature of the function conferred: involving the determination of a question of legal right or legal obligation by the application of law as ascertained to facts as found "so that an exercise of the power creates a new charter by reference to which that question is in future to be decided as between those persons or classes of persons". Another dimension concerns the process by which the function is exercised: involving an open and public enquiry (unless the subject-matter necessitates an exception), and observance of the rules of procedural fairness. Yet another dimension concerns the overriding necessity for the function always to be compatible with the essential character of a court as an institution that is, and is seen to be, both impartial between the parties and independent of the parties and of other branches of government in the exercise of the decision-making functions conferred on it.

Underlying each of those dimensions of the judicial power of the Commonwealth is its fundamental character as a sovereign or governmental power exercisable, on application, independently of the consent of those whose legal rights or legal obligations are determined by its exercise. That fundamental character of the judicial power of the Commonwealth is implicit in the frequently cited description of judicial power as "the power which every sovereign authority must of necessity have to decide controversies between its subjects, or between itself and its subjects", the exercise of which "does not begin until some tribunal which has power to give a binding and authoritative decision (whether subject to appeal or not) is called upon to take action". Judicial power "is conferred and exercised by law and coercively", "its decisions are made against the will of at least one side, and are enforced upon that side *in invitum*", and it "is not invoked by mutual agreement, but exists to be resorted to by any party considering himself aggrieved".

Therein is the essential distinction between the judicial power of the Commonwealth and arbitral authority, of the kind governed by the Model Law, based on the voluntary agreement of the parties. The distinction has been articulated in the following terms:

"Where parties agree to submit their differences for decision by a third party, the decision maker does not exercise judicial power, but a power of private arbitration. Of its nature, judicial power is a power that is exercised independently of the consent of the person against whom the proceedings are brought and results in a judgment or order that is binding of its own force. In the case of private arbitration, however, the arbitrator's powers depend on the agreement of the parties, usually embodied in a contract, and the arbitrator's award is not binding of its own force. Rather, its effect, if any, depends on the law which operates with respect to it."

The making of an arbitral award, which is recognised as binding on the parties from the time it is made by force of Art 35 of the Model Law, is not an exercise of the judicial power of the Commonwealth. That is because the existence and scope of the authority to make the arbitral award is founded on the agreement of the parties in an arbitration agreement. The exercise of that authority by an arbitral tribunal to determine the dispute submitted to arbitration for that reason lacks the essential foundation for the existence of judicial power ...

Enforcement of an arbitral award is enforcement of the binding result of the agreement of the parties to submit their dispute to arbitration, not enforcement of any disputed right submitted to arbitration.

Adjudging and punishing criminal guilt is always judicial in character. However, not every decision that involves a determination that criminal conduct has occurred amounts to adjudging criminal guilt. ***Australian Communications and Media Authority v Today FM (Sydney) Pty Ltd*** provides an example. In that case, an administrative determination that conduct amounting to a criminal offence had taken place was a step in an administrative process and was not a *binding determination* of criminal guilt.

Australian Communications and Media Authority v Today FM (Sydney) Pty Ltd (2015) 255 CLR 352

Today FM held a radio broadcasting licence under federal legislation. One condition of that licence was that the licensee not use the broadcasting service in the commission of an offence. The Australian Communications and Media Authority ('ACMA') had power to take administrative enforcement action against a licensee that breached a licence condition. Today FM presenters rang a London hospital where the Duchess of Cambridge was being treated and pretended to be the Queen and the Prince of Wales. The phone prank was recorded and broadcast. Broadcasting a conversation recorded without a person's consent was an offence under New South Wales law, but no criminal proceedings were brought in relation to the matter. ACMA conducted an investigation and took action against Today FM's licence. Today FM argued that ACMA was adjudging criminal guilt. The High Court disagreed.

French CJ, Hayne, Kiefel, Bell and Keane JJ

More generally ... it is not offensive to principle that an administrative body is empowered to determine whether a person has engaged in conduct that constitutes a criminal offence as a step in the decision to take disciplinary or other action ...

The finding that Today FM's broadcasting service was used in the commission of an offence does not resolve a controversy respecting pre-existing rights or obligations. It is a step in the determination of breach of the cl 8(1)(g) licence condition and is the foundation for the Authority to institute civil penalty proceedings in the Federal Court of Australia or to take administrative enforcement measures ...

It is well settled that functions may be judicial or administrative depending upon the manner of their exercise. Edmonds J rightly concluded that none of the features of the power conferred on the Authority to investigate and report on breach of the cl 8(1)(g) licence condition and to take consequential administrative enforcement action support the conclusion that it is engaged in the exercise of judicial power.

Gageler J

The function of judging and punishing criminal guilt, which is exclusively judicial in character and no part of which can be conferred by Commonwealth legislation on a body that is not a Ch III court, is the function of conclusively determining a controversy about criminal liability and the punitive consequences of that criminal liability. An administrative body does not perform any part of that exclusively judicial function merely by making its own inquiry and determining for itself that a person has committed a criminal offence.

This Court has repeatedly held that a power of inquiry and determination takes its legal character from the purpose for which it is undertaken, and that a power of inquiry and determination undertaken for a non-curial purpose (be it arbitral, administrative, executive or legislative) can encompass formation and expression of an opinion about an existing legal right or obligation. No distinction has been drawn in that respect between an opinion about an existing legal obligation sounding only in civil liability and an opinion about an existing legal obligation sounding only, or also, in criminal liability ...

As narrowed in the course of oral argument before this Court, the question came down to whether the Authority would exercise judicial power were it to act on its own view that conduct constitutes the commission of an offence in going on to exercise the power conferred on it by s 143(1) to suspend or cancel a commercial radio broadcasting licence on the basis of breach of the condition of that licence in cl 8(1)(g).

The short answer is that there is no basis on which the Authority, in so acting, could be said to exercise judicial power. None of the indicia of exclusively judicial power would be present. The Authority's cancellation or suspension of the licence would not be, in form or in substance, the imposition of punishment for the commission of an offence against a Commonwealth, State or Territory law. The Authority would not be declaring or enforcing any existing criminal liability or civil liability of the licensee or of anyone else. The Authority would not be resolving, conclusively or at all, any controversy between parties.

The Authority would need to satisfy itself that there was or had been conduct constituting the commission of an offence within the scope of cl 8(1)(g) as an element of satisfying itself that it had power to cancel or suspend the licence by reference to s 143(1). That is because the fact of breach of a licence condition is, for the purpose of s 143(1), a "jurisdictional fact" in the sense that it is a fact which must exist as a precondition to the valid exercise of the discretion of the Authority to cancel or suspend a licence. But the Authority's own view that there was or had been conduct constituting the commission of an offence within the scope of cl 8(1)(g) would have no operative legal effect.

Duncan v New South Wales provides another example of a non-judicial body forming the view that conduct amounting to a criminal offence has occurred and taking consequential steps without that action amounting to adjudging or punishing criminal guilt. Both in this case and in ***ACMA v Today FM*** there was no *binding determination* that criminal conduct had occurred.

Duncan v New South Wales (2015) 255 CLR 388

The New South Wales Parliament enacted legislation to cancel mining licences that the Independent Commission Against Corruption had found were issued corruptly. Owners of mining licences that were cancelled argued that the legislation involved an exercise of judicial power by the New South Wales Parliament because it punished them by depriving them of property (namely, the mining licences) as a consequence of criminal conduct. The licence-holders argued that the legislation was invalid because, they said, the New South Wales Parliament cannot exercise judicial power. The High Court avoided deciding whether a State Parliament can exercise judicial power because it found that the legislation did not involve an exercise of judicial power.

French CJ, Hayne, Kiefel, Bell, Galeger, Keane and Nettle JJ

Some functions of their nature pertain exclusively to judicial power. The determination and punishment of criminal guilt is one of them: *Chu Kheng Lim v Minister for Immigration, Local Government and Ethnic Affairs*. The non-consensual ascertainment and enforcement of rights in issue between private parties is another: *Brandy v Human Rights and Equal Opportunity Commission*. The termination of a right conferred by statute is not of that nature. That is so even where the basis for termination is satisfaction of the occurrence of conduct which, if proved on admissible evidence to the criminal standard, would constitute a criminal offence: *Australian Communications and Media Authority v Today FM (Sydney) Pty Ltd*.

In terminating exploration licences issued under the Mining Act and in making consequential provision, the Amendment Act exhibits none of the typical features of an exercise of judicial power. It quells no controversy between parties. It precludes no future determination by a court of past criminal or civil liability. It does not determine the existence of any right that has accrued or any liability that has been incurred. Save for the limited immunity it confers on the State and its current or former employees, it does not otherwise affect any accrued right or existing liability ...

The Amendment Act does not adopt, and does not fasten upon, any of the numerous specific findings made by ICAC in the Operation Acacia report and in the Operation Jasper report as to the corrupt conduct of individuals. Nor does it impose any legal burden on any of those individuals. They remain subject to the ordinary processes of the criminal law.

What the New South Wales Parliament has done in the Amendment Act is of a different nature. Having informed itself by reference to the Operation Acacia report, the Operation Jasper report and the December report, but without having limited its consideration or linked its conclusions to any one or more specific findings in those reports, the Parliament has formed and expressed its own satisfaction that the administrative processes by which the three specified exploration licences were issued were tainted by corruption. The Parliament has gone on to express, and to give effect to, its own determination that it was in the public interest that the products of those tainted processes - the licences themselves - be cancelled, that the State be restored so far as possible to the position the State would have been in had those licences not been issued, and that those who had held the licences not obtain any advantage from having done so ...

That NuCoal, Mt Penny and Glendon Brook were deprived by those provisions of valuable assets, for which they were not compensated by the State, does not mean that they were thereby punished in the sense in which that term is used when describing an exercise of judicial power consequent on a finding of criminal guilt. Legislative detriment cannot be equated with legislative punishment.

Alexander provides a contrasting example in which there was an exercise of judicial power. An executive officer formed the view that conduct amounting to a criminal offence had occurred and as a consequence made a decision under a statute to impose a detriment on the person that was punitive in character. In accordance with the separation of federal judicial power doctrine (considered in Chapter 17), the law empowering the executive officer's decision was held to be invalid because it vested an exclusively judicial power in an executive officer. *Alexander* differs from *ACMA v Today FM* in an important respect: in *Alexander* the Executive Government's decision imposed a *punishment* for criminal wrongdoing whereas in *ACMA v Today FM* the Executive Government's decision imposed a *non-punitive detriment* as part of a regulatory regime.

Alexander v Minister for Home Affairs [2022] HCA 19

Section 36B of the* Australian Citizenship Act 2007 (Cth) *provided that the Minister for Home Affairs may make a determination that a person ceases to be an Australian citizen if satisfied that the person engaged in specified conduct demonstrating repudiation of allegiance to Australia. Alexander travelled to al-Raqqa Province in Syria (a declared area under the* Criminal Code (Cth)*) and fought with ISIS (a proscribed terrorist group under the* Criminal Code (Cth)*). Entering and remaining in a declared area and fighting with a proscribed terrorist group are offences against the* Criminal Code (Cth)*. The Minister exercised the section 39B citizenship-stripping power. The High Court held section 39B was invalid in its operation in respect of Alexander because it reposed in the Minister the exclusively judicial function of punishing criminal guilt.

Kiefel CJ, Keane and Gleeson JJ

Mr Alexander argued that s 36B of the Citizenship Act reposes in the Minister the power to adjudge and punish criminal conduct by involuntary denaturalisation ...

The consequences of a determination under s 36B for the citizen, the legislative policy which informs the operation of s 36B, and a comparison of the operation of s 36B with the provisions of s 36D (which authorise the same consequences for the citizen only upon conviction after a trial), all point to the conclusion that the power reposed in the Minister by s 36B(1) is a power which Ch III of the Constitution requires to be exercised by a court that is part of the federal judicature ...

[T]he principal purpose of s 36B is retribution for conduct deemed to be so reprehensible as to be "incompatible with the shared values of the Australian community". That characterisation of the principal purpose of s 36D as punitive accords with the long-held understanding of exile as a form of punishment ...

Visnic v Australian Securities and Investments Commission and *Australian Communications and Media Authority v Today FM (Sydney) Pty Ltd* were cited by the defendants' counsel in support of the argument that a determination under s 36B is neither an adjudgment of guilt nor an imposition of punishment. Crucially, these cases dealt with the revocation of licences or other statutory privileges, rather than citizenship. These cases are examples of the point that the hardship or detriment involved in the revocation of a statutory licence or other privilege, where the holder of the licence or privilege is shown to be not a fit and proper person to enjoy the privilege or the licence, is not "punishment", which is an exclusively judicial function. But the punishment of an individual involving the deprivation of citizenship by reason of that person's misconduct is punishment of a different order from the loss of a statutory privilege or a licence under a regulatory regime. The consequence for a person who voluntarily does the acts described in s 36B(5)(h) is no different in substance from the punishment meted out pursuant to s 36D. Such a consequence cannot be equated with the cancellation of a licence or other privilege conferred by a statute which regulates business or other activities.

There are some functions that are never judicial in character. One example is the function of issuing warrants such as search warrants or telephone intercept warrants under powers conferred by legislation. Warrants such as these authorise action such as trespass that would otherwise be tortious or criminal.

Love v Attorney-General (NSW) (1990) 169 CLR 307

State legislation authorised judges to issue warrants permitting the installation and use of listening devices. One of the issues for the High Court was whether issuing the warrant was judicial or administrative in character.

Mason CJ, Brennan, Dawson, Toohey and Gaudron JJ

[T]he exercise of the power is essentially administrative in nature. The warrant is the outcome of a complaint upon which the judge must bring his or her judicial mind to bear and decide on the material before him or her whether the warrant should issue. The judge is under a duty to act judicially and to that extent the issue of the warrant is a judicial act but it is not a "judicial act in the same sense as is an adjudication to determine the rights of parties" ... It is not an order *inter partes* from which a party whose conversations may be overheard has a right of appeal. To adapt the language used in *Hilton v Wells*, under s 16 a judge makes no order and nothing that he or she does is enforced as an order of the court. Therefore, if a warrant is granted, its effect depends entirely upon the State Act.

... the issue of the warrant under s 16 is a step in the administrative process and is thus an administrative function. Granted that a judge considering an application for a warrant under s 16 is bound to act judicially, that is, in a just and fair manner, with judicial detachment, this circumstance is not conclusive, for the same is true of many administrative powers.

There are some functions that may or may not be judicial in character depending on the cumulative effect of the features of a particular function and the context in which the function is to be performed. ***Thomas v Mowbray*** highlights some of the difficulties in determining whether a power is judicial in character. The case notes that there are some functions that might be regarded as judicial or non-judicial depending on the character of the institution to which the function is entrusted.

Thomas v Mowbray (2007) 233 CLR 307

Gleeson CJ

Deciding whether a governmental power or function is best exercised administratively or judicially is a regular legislative exercise. If, as in the present case, Parliament decides to confer a power on the judicial branch of government, this reflects a parliamentary intention that the power should be exercised judicially, and with the independence and impartiality which should characterise the judicial branch of government ...

This is sometimes referred to as the 'chameleon doctrine', because the character of the function can change according to context.

In ***Brandy's Case***, one of the ways the High Court approached working out whether judicial power was involved was by making a comparison with functions that courts traditionally perform and that are accepted as being judicial in character. That approach was also adopted in ***Thomas v Mowbray***. That case held that the power to issue a control order against a person, restricting where the person may reside and what activities the person may undertake, was judicial in character. The High Court held that a particular function was judicial in character because it was analogous to other functions that were generally accepted to be judicial in character and which had a long historical pedigree of being performed by courts. The case also demonstrates that judicial power does not always involve resolving controversies about existing rights and obligations.

Thomas v Mowbray (2007) 233 CLR 307

Thomas had trained with Al-Qa'ida and later returned to Australia. He was later the subject of an Interim Control Order issued by the Federal Magistrates Court. The power to make a control order was given by the* Commonwealth Criminal Code *section 104.4, which was in these terms:

(1) The issuing court may make an order under this section in relation to the person, but only if:

- *(a) the senior AFP member has requested it in accordance with section 104.3; and*
- *(b) the court has received and considered such further information (if any) as the court requires; and*
- *(c) the court is satisfied on the balance of probabilities:*
  - *(i) that making the order would substantially assist in preventing a terrorist act; or*
  - *(ii) that the person has provided training to, or received training from, a listed terrorist organisation;*

... and

- *(d) the court is satisfied on the balance of probabilities that each of the obligations, prohibitions and restrictions to be imposed on the person by the order is reasonably necessary, and reasonably appropriate and adapted, for the purpose of protecting the public from a terrorist act.*

Thomas argued that issuing a control order was not an exercise of judicial power because it does not resolve a dispute about existing rights and duties but creates new legal obligations. The High Court disagreed.

Gleeson CJ

The plaintiff's written submissions contend that Div 104 confers non-judicial power on a federal court in that it confers upon the court the power to determine what legal rights and obligations should be created, rather than the power to resolve a dispute about existing rights and obligations by determining what those rights and obligations are, and the power to deprive a person of liberty on the basis of what that person might do in the future, rather than on the basis of a judicial determination of what that person has done. It is said that, by reason of those characteristics of a control order, the governmental power that is exercised when such an order is made is peculiarly or distinctively legislative or executive, and therefore not a power that may be conferred upon the judiciary.

The power to restrict or interfere with a person's liberty on the basis of what that person might do in the future, rather than on the basis of a judicial determination of what the person has done, which involves interfering with legal rights, and creating new legal obligations, rather than resolving a dispute about existing rights and obligations, is in truth a power that has been, and is, exercised by courts in a variety of circumstances. It is not intrinsically a power that may be exercised only legislatively, or only administratively. If it were otherwise, the federal Parliament would lack the capacity to confide an exercise of such power to the judicial branch of government ...

Two familiar examples of the judicial exercise of power to create new rights and obligations which may restrict a person's liberty are bail, and apprehended violence orders. The restraints imposed on the plaintiff by the order made against him are similar to conditions commonly found in a bail order. Of course, there are differences between bail and a control order, but the example of bail shows that imposition of restrictions of the kind imposed on the plaintiff is not foreign to judicial power. Apprehended violence orders have many of the characteristics of control orders, including the fact they may restrain conduct that is not in itself unlawful. For example, an apprehended violence order may forbid a person to approach another person, or to attend a certain place. As a matter of history, apprehended violence orders have their origin in the ancient power of justices and judges to bind persons over to keep the peace ...

A function that is capable of being judicial in character (such as issuing a control order) may turn out to be non-judicial in character in a particular context if the function: (1) is incapable of being exercised in a judicial manner; or (2) is required to be exercised in a non-judicial manner. In ***Thomas v Mowbray***, the High Court accepted this proposition but held that the impugned standards were in fact capable of application in a judicial manner.

The High Court concluded that the particular standards were not incapable of judicial application by showing that those standards had long been used in other judicial contexts.

Thomas v Mowbray (2007) 233 CLR 307

Thomas also argued that even if issuing a control order could be judicial in character, the legislation in question conferred a non-judicial function because the standards of 'reasonable necessity' and 'reasonably appropriate and adapted' were too vague to be capable of judicial application and involved predictive considerations incapable of judicial assessment. The High Court disagreed.

Gleeson CJ

A narrower argument for the plaintiff turns upon the Criminal Code's criteria for the making of a control order. This argument looks at the legal incidents of the power as expressed in the

Criminal Code, and asserts that such power is antithetical to the judicial function and cannot be conferred on the federal judiciary consistently with Ch III. In particular, the argument points to the stipulation that a control order may be made only if the court is satisfied on the balance of probabilities that each of the obligations, prohibitions and restrictions to be imposed by the order is reasonably necessary, and reasonably appropriate and adapted, for the purpose of protecting the public from a terrorist act ...

It is not difficult to see where Parliament found the language of s 104.4(1)(d) of the Criminal Code. The language is taken from a long line of decisions of this Court, and of English courts, and from local and foreign statutes. Against this background of judicial and legislative usage it cannot plausibly be suggested that the standard of reasonably necessary and reasonably appropriate and adapted for the purpose of protecting the public is inherently too vague for use in judicial decision-making ...

Reference was earlier made to apprehended violence orders, and to the restraints on liberty which they may involve. I am unable to accept that there is a qualitative difference between deciding whether an angry person poses an unacceptable risk to his or her family, or to the community or some section of the community, or whether a sexually dysfunctional man poses an unacceptable risk to women, and deciding whether someone who has been trained by terrorists poses an unacceptable risk to the public. The possibility that the person will do what he or she has been trained to do, or will be used as a "resource" by others who have been so trained, is capable of judicial evaluation. I do not accept that these issues are insusceptible of strictly judicial decision-making.

The discussion above focuses on understanding the concept of 'judicial power'. However, Chapter III of the *Constitution* deals with the 'judicial power of the Commonwealth'. The next two sections look at what makes judicial power *federal* judicial power.

16.3 Federal judicial power is limited as to subject-matter

An important characteristic of federal judicial power is that it is limited as to subject-matter.

In ***R v Kirby; Ex parte Boilermakers' Society of Australia*** (1956) 94 CLR 254, the High Court said that Chapter III provides 'an exhaustive statement of the manner in which the judicial power of the Commonwealth is or may be vested ... No part of the judicial power can be conferred in virtue of any other authority or otherwise than in accordance with the provisions of Ch III.'

It follows that federal judicial power is exercised only when adjudicating the matters set out in sections 75 and 76 of the *Constitution*. If the subject-matter of an exercise of judicial power is not one of the subject-matters set out in sections 75 and 76 then, by definition, *federal* judicial power is not involved. Section 77 empowers Parliament to make laws governing which courts apart from the High Court may exercise federal jurisdiction.

Australian Constitution

Section 75 Original jurisdiction of High Court

In all matters:

(i) arising under any treaty;
(ii) affecting consuls or other representatives of other countries;
(iii) in which the Commonwealth, or a person suing or being sued on behalf of the Commonwealth, is a party;
(iv) between States, or between residents of different States, or between a State and a resident of another State;
(v) in which a writ of Mandamus or prohibition or an injunction is sought against an officer of the Commonwealth; the High Court shall have original jurisdiction.

Section 76 Additional original jurisdiction

The Parliament may make laws conferring original jurisdiction on the High Court in any matter:

(i) arising under this Constitution, or involving its interpretation;
(ii) arising under any laws made by the Parliament;
(iii) of Admiralty and maritime jurisdiction;
(iv) relating to the same subject-matter claimed under the laws of different States.

Section 77 Power to define jurisdiction

With respect to any of the matters mentioned in the last two sections the Parliament may make laws:

(i) defining the jurisdiction of any federal court other than the High Court;
(ii) defining the extent to which the jurisdiction of any federal court shall be exclusive of that which belongs to or is invested in the courts of the States;
(iii) investing any court of a State with federal jurisdiction.

The High Court explained in ***Rizeq v Western Australia*** that jurisdiction is the authority to decide and that federal jurisdiction is the authority to decide matters listed in sections 75 and 76. Federal judicial power is the judicial power exercised when deciding matters within federal jurisdiction (that is, deciding any of the matters listed in sections 75 and 76).

Rizeq v Western Australia (2017) 344 ALR 421

Bell, Gageler, Keane, Nettle and Gordon JJ

Federal jurisdiction ... is authority to adjudicate on a matter within any of the five enumerated categories of matter in respect of which the High Court is given entrenched original jurisdiction by s 75, or within any of the four additional enumerated categories of matter in respect of which the Parliament is empowered to confer original jurisdiction on the High Court under s 76. The Parliament of the Commonwealth has additional specific power under s 77(ii) to define the extent to which the jurisdiction of any federal court, including the High Court, is to be exclusive of State jurisdiction.

The authority to adjudicate comprised in the conferral of federal jurisdiction is authority to exercise, within the limits permitted by or under s 75, s 76 or s 77, the judicial power of the Commonwealth, which s 71 provides is to be vested in the High Court, in such other federal courts as the Parliament creates and in such other courts as it invests with federal jurisdiction. The essential character of judicial power, as has repeatedly been emphasised, stems from the unique and essential function that judicial power performs by quelling controversies about legal rights and legal obligations through ascertainment of facts, application of law and exercise, where appropriate, of judicial discretion.

The character of judicial power, as distinct from the source of the authority of a particular court to adjudicate a particular justiciable controversy, is unaffected by the source of the law that is to be applied to determine the legal rights and legal obligations in controversy.

The proposition that federal jurisdiction is limited to those subject-matters listed in sections 75 and 76 says nothing about the source of law to be applied in the exercise of federal judicial power to resolve a case. ***Re Wakim*** explained that State law may be applied when adjudicating matters within federal jurisdiction.

Re Wakim; Ex parte McNally (1999) 198 CLR 511

In this case, the High Court held that legislation attempting to authorise federal courts to exercise State jurisdiction was invalid because Chapter III permits federal courts to exercise only federal jurisdiction (see Chapter 17). The High Court explained that State law may be applied in deciding cases within federal jurisdiction.

McHugh J

[T]he settled doctrine of this Court is that Ch III exhaustively defines the "matters" that may be the subject of the judicial power of the Commonwealth and exhaustively defines the "matters" that the Parliament of the Commonwealth may invest in the federal courts which it creates. The irresistible conclusion from the terms of Ch III is that it authorises the Parliament of the Commonwealth to create federal courts but only for the purpose of exercising jurisdiction with respect to the matters specified in ss 75 and 76 of the Constitution. As Dixon CJ, McTiernan, Fullagar and Kitto JJ pointed out in *R v Kirby; Ex parte Boilermakers' Society of Australia*:

> The fact that affirmative words appointing or limiting an order or form of things may have also a negative force and forbid the doing of the thing otherwise was noted very early in the development of the principles of interpretation. In Chap III we have a notable but very evident example.

If the terms of ss 71, 75 and 76 of the Constitution impliedly forbid the Parliament of the Commonwealth from adding to the ss 75 and 76 jurisdiction of the federal courts, as everyone accepts that they do, those sections must also logically forbid the States from doing so ... What prevents a State conferring jurisdiction on a federal court in respect of a matter specified in ss 75 or 76 is not s 109, but the negative implications arising from Ch III of the Constitution. By granting power to the Parliament of the Commonwealth to create federal courts and by expressly stating the matters in respect of which the Parliament may confer jurisdiction on those courts, Ch III impliedly forbids the conferring of any other jurisdiction on those courts by the Commonwealth or the States ...

State judicial power has nothing to do with federal jurisdiction. If the substratum of fact which gives rise to a matter in federal jurisdiction cannot be effectively disposed of without the application of State law, the issues of State law are determined in the exercise of federal jurisdiction. As Mason, Brennan and Deane JJ pointed out in *Stack v Coast Securities (No 9) Pty Ltd*, federal jurisdiction is "not restricted to the determination of the federal claim or cause of action in the proceeding, but extend[s] beyond that to the litigious or justiciable controversy between parties of which the federal claim or cause of action forms part." The determination of State law issues in such circumstances is part of the "accrued jurisdiction" of the federal court. Federal courts do not need the States, with or without the consent of the Parliament of the Commonwealth, to confer jurisdiction upon them before they can determine issues arising under their accrued jurisdiction. But the jurisdiction which the legislation in the present proceedings purports to confer upon the federal courts is not accrued federal jurisdiction. It is an attempt to confer State jurisdiction in respect of controversies that fall outside the realm of federal jurisdiction.

Momcilovic provides a mundane example of applying State law to decide a matter within federal jurisdiction. Victorian police discovered that Momcilovic was involved in drug crimes in Victoria some years before she moved to Queensland. Momcilovic was charged by Victorian authorities with an offence under a Victorian statute, and prosecuted in the County Court of Victoria. Even though the case was heard by a State court and even though a State law was being applied, the criminal trial was a matter arising within federal jurisdiction because it was one of the types of matter listed in sections 75 and 76. ***Momcilovic*** involved a matter between a State and a resident of another State (section 75(iv)) – the State of Victoria's prosecution of Momcilovic, a Queensland resident. As Chapter 17 explains, Chapter III provides that the judicial power of the Commonwealth can be exercised by State courts. When State courts do so, they are exercising federal jurisdiction.

Momcilovic v The Queen (2011) 245 CLR 1

Gummow J

The presentment was filed ... some years after the date of the offence alleged. At trial the appellant gave unchallenged evidence that she ... had moved to Queensland, where she now resided at Main Beach and pursued her occupation of a registered trademarks attorney. That meant that ... she was a resident of Queensland within the meaning of s 75(iv) of the Constitution ...

Section 75(iv) relevantly provides that this Court shall have original jurisdiction in "all matters ... between a State and a resident of another State" ...

The significance of the scope of s 75(iv) ... lies ... in the avenue of appeal to this Court which s 73(ii) of the Constitution provides in respect of any court of a State exercising federal jurisdiction.

Because the prosecution of the appellant was a "matter" which was "between a State and a resident of another State", the County Court was invested with federal jurisdiction ... and the judicial power of the Commonwealth was engaged. This is so whether or not that was apparent at the time to the County Court ...

16.4 Federal jurisdiction is limited to 'matters'

Federal jurisdiction is not only limited as to subject-matter. Federal jurisdiction is also limited to 'matters' concerning any of the subject-matters listed in sections 75 and 76. A 'matter' is not simply a legal proceeding.

In ***Re Judiciary and Navigation Acts***, the High Court held a 'matter' involves the administration or application of a law. In this case, the High Court held that legislation purporting to give the High Court jurisdiction to give advisory opinions on the constitutional validity of legislation at the request of the Governor-General was invalid. Giving advisory opinions on questions of law does not involve applying or administering a law and therefore does not involve a 'matter'.

Re Judiciary and Navigation Acts (1921) 29 CLR 257

Knox CJ, Gavan Duffy, Powers, Rich and Starke JJ

It is true that the answer to the question submitted for our determination does involve the interpretation of the Constitution, but is there a matter within the meaning of s 76? We think not. It was suggested in argument that "matter" meant no more than legal proceeding, and that Parliament might at its discretion create or invent a legal proceeding in which this Court might be called on to interpret the Constitution by a declaration at large. We do not accept this contention; we do not think that the word "matter" in s 76 means a legal proceeding, but rather the subject matter for determination in a legal proceeding.

In our opinion there can be no matter within the meaning of the section unless there is some immediate right, duty or liability to be established by the determination of the Court. If the matter exists, the Legislature may no doubt prescribe the means by which the determination of the Court is to be obtained, and for that purpose may, we think, adopt any existing method of legal procedure or invent a new one. But it cannot authorize this Court to make a declaration of the law divorced from any attempt to administer that law. The word "matter" is used several times in Chapter III of the *Constitution* (ss 73, 74, 75, 76, 77), and always, we think, with the same meaning.

... [a] matter under the judicature provisions of the Constitution must involve some right or privilege or protection given by law, or the prevention, redress or punishment of some act inhibited by law. The adjudication of the Court may be sought in proceedings *inter partes* or *ex parte*, or, if Courts had the requisite jurisdiction, even in those administrative proceedings with reference to the custody, residence and management of the affairs of infants or lunatics. But we can find nothing in Chapter III. of the *Constitution* to lend colour to the view that Parliament can confer power or jurisdiction upon the High Court to determine abstract questions of law without the right or duty of any body or person being involved.

A decision on a question of law that does not immediately decide a controversy between parties is not necessarily an advisory opinion. ***Mellifont v Attorney-General (Qld)*** demonstrates two important points. First, a 'matter' may have parts. The High Court held that the determination by a full court of a question of law referred to it by a trial court is not an advisory opinion divorced from an attempt to administer the law. The High Court explained that such determinations are an integral part of the process of determining the rights of the parties to the litigation.

Mellifont v Attorney-General (Qld) (1991) 173 CLR 289

Queensland legislation allowed for referring a question of law that arises during a criminal trial to an appellate court for determination. The legislation provided that where an accused person is acquitted, an unfavourable ruling on a question of law would not affect the acquittal. In this case, the trial judge made a ruling on a point of law unfavourable to the prosecution, which led to the prosecution dropping the charges. Mellifont was therefore not acquitted. The Attorney-General then referred the question of law to the Court of Appeal, which overturned the trial judge's ruling. The prosecution commenced a new prosecution against Mellifont. Mellifont wanted to appeal the Court of Appeal's decision to the High Court, arguing that the trial judge was correct. The High Court's appellate jurisdiction under section 73 of the Constitution *extends to appeals from all 'judgments, decrees, orders and sentences' of State Supreme Courts. The immediate question for the High Court was whether the Court of Appeal's determination fell within those concepts.*

Mason CJ, Deane, Dawson, Gaudron and McHugh JJ

The Solicitor-General for Queensland argues that this Court lacks jurisdiction to hear an appeal in this case because the decision of the Court of Criminal Appeal was not a judgment, decree, order or sentence within the meaning of s 73 of the Constitution. The Solicitor-General submits that, in order to constitute a judgment, decree or order from which an appeal lies to this Court under s 73, the decision must be a judicial decision in the sense that it was made in the exercise of judicial power. So much is established by decisions of this Court ...

In conformity with the general principle that an appeal does not lie from a decision made otherwise than in the exercise of judicial power, it has been held that, interlocutory orders aside, an appeal will not lie under s 73 from a decision which does not finally determine the parties' rights and obligations in controversy ...

In *In re Judiciary and Navigation Acts* ... [t]he Court ... stated that the legislature: cannot authorize this Court to make a declaration of the law divorced from any attempt to administer that law. ... we can find nothing in Chapter III of the Constitution to lend colour to the view that Parliament can confer power or jurisdiction upon the High Court to determine abstract questions of law without the right or duty of any body or person being involved.

The passage contains two critical concepts. One is the notion of an abstract question of law not involving the right or duty of any body or person; the second is the making of a declaration of law divorced or dissociated from any attempt to administer it.

... [A]nswers given by the full court of a court to questions reserved for its consideration in the course of proceedings in a "matter" pending in that court do not constitute an advisory opinion or abstract declaration of the kind dealt with in *In re Judiciary and Navigation Acts* whether or not those answers, of themselves, determine the rights of the parties. Such answers are not given in circumstances divorced from an attempt to administer the law as stated by the answers; they are given as an integral part of the process of determining the rights and obligations of the parties which are at stake in the proceedings in which the questions are reserved. Once this is accepted, as indeed it must be, it follows inevitably that the giving of the answers is an exercise of judicial power because the seeking and the giving of the answers constitutes an important and influential, if not decisive, step in the judicial determination of the rights and liabilities in issue in the litigation ...

The consequence is that the answers fall within the description "judgments, decrees, orders" in s 73 of the Constitution ...

The second point that ***Mellifont*** demonstrates is that questions arising out of a 'matter' are an extension of that matter. The High Court held that a decision on a question of law on an appeal following an acquittal, which is unable to affect the rights of any party or impact the acquittal, arises out of and is an extension of the underlying criminal matter. For that reason, those types of decisions are not divorced from an attempt to administer the law.

Mellifont v Attorney-General (Qld) (1991) 173 CLR 289

Mason CJ, Deane, Dawson, Gaudron and McHugh JJ

However, this conclusion does not dispose of the objection to jurisdiction in the present case. The Attorney-General's power under the Code to refer a point of law to the Court of Criminal Appeal for its consideration arises only if the accused has been acquitted of the charge in the indictment or if the accused has been discharged in respect of that charge after counsel for the Crown, as a result of a ruling by the trial judge on that point of law, has informed the court that the Crown will not proceed further upon the indictment in respect of that charge. In other words, in the case of discharge, the exercise of the power to refer and the exercise of jurisdiction by the Court pursuant to the reference both proceed on the footing that no further proceedings on the indictment in respect of the relevant charge will be taken. Consequently, the ruling on the point of law pursuant to the reference will not play any part in the subsequent determination of the charge on the indictment. Likewise, in the case of acquittal, the ruling on the reference has no impact on the acquittal. In this respect, the decision on the point of law referred stands in a different position from answers given by a full court to questions reserved in a stated case in the situation previously discussed.

Although the indictment itself cannot serve as a vehicle for the further determination of the charge in consequence of the statement by counsel for the Crown and the subsequent filing of the *nolle prosequi*, the reference and the decision on the reference arise out of the proceedings on the indictment and are a statutory extension of those proceedings ...

In this situation, the decision on the reference was made with respect to a "matter" which was the subject-matter of the legal proceedings at first instance and was not divorced from the ordinary administration of the law. The decision is therefore to be distinguished from the abstract declaration sought by the Executive Government in *Re Judiciary and Navigation Acts*. That opinion was academic, in response to an abstract question, and hypothetical in the sense that it was unrelated to any actual controversy between parties.

The cases considered above emphasise that a matter involves an attempt to administer the law. The law to be administered may be legislation or common law or it may be the *Constitution* itself. ***Croome v Tasmania*** provides an example. A declaration by a court that legislation is constitutionally invalid involves administering the *Constitution* and therefore involves a matter.

Croome v Tasmania (1997) 191 CLR 119

Tasmanian legislation made sexual activity between consenting adult men a criminal offence. Federal legislation declared that sexual conduct involving only consenting adults acting in private could not be subject to arbitrary interference by a State law. Croome filed a statement of claim admitting to engaging in sexual activity with men and seeking a declaration that the Tasmanian legislation was invalid under section 109 of the Constitution *by reason of its being inconsistent with the federal legislation. Tasmania argued that Croome's application for a declaration did not involve a matter. Tasmania argued that because Croome had not been charged under the Tasmanian law there was no attempt to administer the law and that Croome's application did not involve the rights or obligations of any person.*

Brennan CJ, Dawson and Toohey JJ

The Solicitor-General for Tasmania ... submits that, as no proceedings have been brought or are threatened against the plaintiffs in respect of the conduct pleaded in par 7 of the statement of claim, there is no "matter" within the meaning of that term in s 76 of the Constitution ... which can be judicially determined in proceedings between the plaintiffs and the defendant State. If that submission be well founded, there can be no federal jurisdiction to entertain the action commenced by the plaintiffs.

A "matter" must be distinguished from the action or judicial proceeding which is commenced in order to obtain a determination of a controversy between the parties. The "matter" is not the proceeding but the subject of the controversy which is amenable to judicial determination in the proceeding ...

The Solicitor-General for Tasmania submits that the plaintiffs' action does not seek to establish any immediate right, duty or liability nor is the Court called upon to administer the relevant law. However, the question of law that the plaintiffs seek to raise is not whether they or either of them has engaged in conduct proscribed by s 122(a) or (c) or by s 123 of the Code; nor whether the plaintiffs should be prosecuted, convicted or punished for their conduct. The question is whether those provisions operate and, since the enactment of s 4 of the *Human Rights (Sexual Conduct) Act*, have operated in Tasmania. The Solicitor-General's submission that no prosecution under the Code is pending or threatened does not touch that question.

It is a long-standing doctrine that a "matter" may consist of a controversy between a person who has a sufficient interest in the subject and who asserts that a purported law is invalid and the polity whose law it purports to be ... It is a misconception of the principle in *In re Judiciary and Navigation Act* to suggest that, in proceedings for a declaration of invalidity of an impugned law, no law is administered unless the executive government has acted to enforce the impugned law. The law that is being administered in such proceedings is not the impugned law but the constitutional or administrative law which determines the validity or invalidity of the impugned law ...

However, such a justiciable controversy does not arise unless the person who seeks to challenge the validity of the law has a sufficient interest to do so ...

A person with a sufficient interest to raise a justiciable controversy as to the validity of a law is regarded as having or claiming a right to a declaration and that right satisfies the requirement of some "right, duty or liability to be established by the determination of the Court" ...

The plaintiffs plead that they have engaged in conduct which, if the impugned provisions of the Code were and are operative, renders them liable to prosecution, conviction and punishment. The fact that the Director of Public Prosecutions does not propose to prosecute does not remove that liability. Liability to prosecution under the impugned provisions of the Code will be established if the Court were to determine the action against the plaintiffs even if liability to conviction and punishment under those provisions cannot be determined by civil process. Controversy as to the operative effect of the impugned provisions of the Code will be settled and binding on the parties. The plaintiffs have a sufficient interest to support an action for a declaration of s 109 invalidity.

Gaudron, McHugh and Gummow JJ

Their Honours in *In re Judiciary and Navigation Acts* are not to be taken as lending support to the notion that, where the law of a State imposes a duty upon the citizen attended by liability to prosecution and punishment under the criminal law, and the citizen asserts that, by operation of s 109 of the Constitution, the law of the State is invalid, there can be no immediate right, duty or liability to be established by determination of this Court, in an action for declaratory relief by the citizen against the State, unless the Executive Government of the State has, at least, invoked legal process against the particular citizen to enforce the criminal law.

Abebe v Commonwealth demonstrates that a single set of facts can give rise to multiple matters. The case holds that there is no constitutional problem with legislation conferring jurisdiction on a federal court to decide only some of the matters arising from a particular set of facts. The High Court emphasised that the subject-matter of a controversy between parties is not the same thing as a 'matter'.

Abebe v Commonwealth (1999) 197 CLR 510

Legislation gave the Federal Court a judicial review jurisdiction in respect of some types of decisions made under the* Migration Act. *The grounds on which those decisions could be reviewed were limited by the legislation. It was argued that the legislation was invalid, because by limiting the grounds of review the legislation purported to confer jurisdiction on a court with respect to only parts of a matter rather than an entire matter.

Gleeson CJ and McHugh J

According to the plaintiff's argument, a grant of jurisdiction with respect to a justiciable controversy arising under a law of the Parliament necessarily involves conferring power to quell the entire controversy ...

When s 77(i) of the Constitution empowers the Parliament to make laws "defining the jurisdiction of any federal court other than the High Court" with respect to any of the "matters" mentioned in ss 75 and 76 of the Constitution, it means that the Parliament may make laws giving federal courts authority to decide subject matters that answer any of the descriptions in pars (i)-(v) of s 75 or pars (i)-(iv) of s 76 of the Constitution. Jurisdiction is the authority to decide. The jurisprudence of this Court makes it clear that federal jurisdiction is limited to deciding "matters". Central to the notion of a "matter" is the determination of rights, duties, liabilities and obligations in a legal proceeding ...

Nothing in the terms of s 77 or Ch III of the Constitution requires the Parliament to give a federal court authority to decide every legal right, duty, liability or obligation inherent in a controversy between subjects or between a subject and the Crown merely because it has jurisdiction over some aspect of the controversy. Nor does anything in s 77 or Ch III of the Constitution require a federal court dealing with a legal controversy to have authority to deal with every legal ground that a party wishes to put forward ...

The power of the Parliament to make laws defining the jurisdiction of a federal court "[w]ith respect to any of the matters" mentioned in ss 75 and 76 is a power to make laws with respect to a class of things which answer a certain description. A law concerning that description brings within its scope each concrete factual situation which constitutes a "matter". But s 77(i) is not concerned with any particular case. It is concerned with the general, not the particular. It is necessarily pitched at a level of generality that covers an infinite variety of factual situations, each of which itself is a "matter" which answers the relevant constitutional description ...

[A] law defines the jurisdiction of a federal court with respect to any of the "matters" mentioned in ss 75 and 76 when it defines the authority of that court to decide what are the rights of parties in a proceeding that may be brought in that court with respect to any of those "matters". Thus, a law authorised by s 77 may confer or invest jurisdiction in a federal or State court over the whole range of rights, powers, privileges and liabilities arising from the operation of a law or the existence of a state of affairs answering any of the descriptions in ss 75 and 76 of the Constitution. On the other hand, a s 77 law may validly confer or invest jurisdiction in respect of some only of those rights, powers, privileges and liabilities and may even limit the remedies which are available to a person affected by a breach of those rights ...

A "matter" cannot exist in the abstract. If there is no legal remedy for a "wrong", there can be no "matter". A legally enforceable remedy is as essential to the existence of a "matter" as the right, duty or liability which gives rise to the remedy. Without the right to bring a curial proceeding, there can be no "matter" ...

The existence of a "matter", therefore, cannot be separated from the existence of a remedy to enforce the substantive right, duty or liability. That does not mean that there can be no "matter" unless the existence of a right, duty or liability is established. It is sufficient that the moving party claims that he or she has a legal remedy in the court where the proceedings have been commenced to enforce the right, duty or liability in question. It does mean, however, that there must be a remedy enforceable in a court of justice, that it must be enforceable in the court in which the proceedings are commenced and that the person claiming the remedy must have sufficient interest in enforcing the right, duty or liability to make the controversy justiciable. Questions of standing cannot be divorced from the notion of a "matter" ...

Once it is accepted that a "matter" cannot be identified without regard to the remedies available in the court where it is litigated, it necessarily follows that the same legal controversy can give rise to separate matters because different courts may provide different remedies. Until the "fusion" of law and equity, for example, a person might obtain an injunction to restrain a continuing breach of contract in the Court of Chancery and damages for the breach in action at law ... the "matter" determined in one court is separate and independent from the "matter" determined in the other court even though each "matter" arises out of the same factual substratum.

It also follows from these premises that, when Parliament enacts a law under s 77 and gives a court authority to grant some legal remedy in aid of a right or the enforcement of a duty or liability falling within any of the classes in the numbered paragraphs in ss 75 and 76, it defines the jurisdiction of that court with respect to a "matter". The fact that Parliament has elected not to give the court all the remedies that might be available to resolve the controversy or has conferred jurisdiction to deal with only part of the subject matter of the controversy cannot alter the fact that Parliament has defined the jurisdiction of the court with respect to a "matter".

A matter involves some immediate right, duty or liability to be established by the determination of the court. ***Re McBain*** demonstrates that an *immediate* right, duty or liability is one directly affecting the parties in question, such that questions of standing are subsumed into the inquiry as to the existence of a matter.

Re McBain; Ex parte Australian Catholic Bishops Conference (2002) 209 CLR 372

Victorian legislation provided that only women who were married or in a de facto relationship could access IVF treatment. Dr McBain ran an IVF practice and intended to treat single women. McBain won a case in the Federal Court against the State of Victoria having the Victorian legislation declared invalid for being inconsistent with the federal Sex Discrimination Act. *The Australian Catholic Bishops Conference appeared as* amicus curiae *in the Federal Court arguing for the validity of the Victorian legislation because the State of Victoria did not disagree with McBain's argument. Because the Bishops Conference was not a party, its representatives could not appeal the Federal Court decision. Instead, they attempted to seek* certiorari *in the High Court to quash the Federal Court's decision. The High Court held that the application for* certiorari *did not involve a matter because the Bishops Conference had no immediate right, duty or liability at stake.*

Gaudron and Gummow JJ

[T]he task of identification of the "matter" said to be the subject of the present litigation is to be approached as a tripartite inquiry: first, the identification of the subject-matter for determination in [the proceedings]; secondly, the identification of the right, duty or liability to be established in each proceeding; thirdly, the identification of the controversy between the parties to [the proceedings] for the quelling of which the judicial power of the Commonwealth is invoked. Whilst each of these inquiries may be pursued separately, all are related aspects of the basal question, "is there a 'matter' in the sense required by Ch III of the Constitution?" In our view, there is no such "matter" ...

There is no controversy apparent between the applicants and the respondents, Sundberg J and Dr McBain ...

The subject-matter for determination in each proceeding is whether there is an error of law on the face of the record of the Federal Court, represented by the outcome of the proceeding before Sundberg J, and the purging of that record by administration of a remedy in the nature of certiorari. None of the applicants presents a claim for declaratory relief to reflect a particular view of the construction of the Commonwealth Act and the State Act and the operation of s 109 of the *Constitution*. Rather, the whole of the relief the applicants seek is directed to the outcome of the particular proceeding which was disposed of in the Federal Court ...

[T]here is no general proposition respecting Ch III that the "immediate right, duty or liability to be established by the determination of the Court", spoken of in *In re Judiciary and Navigation Acts*, must be a right, duty or liability in which the opposing parties have correlative interests. Thus, the prosecutor of an offence against a law of the Commonwealth and the defendant do not have correlative interests. Nevertheless, the proceeding seeks to vindicate and enforce the duty or liability of the defendant to observe the criminal law of the Commonwealth.

It is here that the present applications founder. Where is the right, title, privilege or immunity under the Constitution which is asserted by the applicants?

... The concern of the Bishops and the Episcopal Conference is that the decision of Sundberg J provides a precedent which would influence the outcome of future litigation in which they or others seek relief upholding the validity of s 8 and allied provisions of the State Act. Hence the subject-matter of this litigation is the purging, by order of this Court, of the record of the Federal Court.

However, those concerns and objectives of the ecclesiastical authorities do not represent a claim by them in this present litigation of a right, title, privilege or immunity under the Constitution; nor do they present, necessarily and directly rather than incidentally, an issue upon the interpretation of the Constitution. In short, the controversy between these parties and the respondents to these applications is not one which comprises a "matter" described in s 76(i) of the *Constitution.*

Palmer v Ayres holds that an *immediate* right, duty or liability is a *claimed* right, duty or liability and that a matter exists even if ultimately the moving party is unsuccessful at trial in proving their case. A pre-trial procedure such as discovery or examination that may assist in identifying and proving a substantive right, duty or liability involves a matter for two reasons. First, the pre-trial procedure itself involves rights and obligations concerning information and evidence. Secondly, the pre-trial procedure is connected with a future substantive claim and therefore arises out of the same matter.

Palmer v Ayres (2017) 259 CLR 478

Section 596A of the* Corporations Act 2001 *(Cth) permits the liquidators of an insolvent corporation to apply to a court for orders requiring persons to attend before the court to provide information about the affairs of the corporation. The former director of an insolvent corporation argued that an order under section 596A did not involve a matter and that therefore section 596A was invalid. The High Court disagreed.

Kiefel, Keane, Nettle and Gordon JJ

A "matter", as a justiciable controversy, is not co-extensive with a legal proceeding, but rather means the subject matter for determination in a legal proceeding – "controversies which *might* come before a Court of Justice" (emphasis added). It is identifiable independently of proceedings brought for its determination and encompasses all claims made within the scope of the controversy ...

The requirement that, for there to be a "matter", there must be an "immediate right, duty or liability to be established by the determination of the Court" reinforces that the controversy that the court is being asked to determine is genuine, and not an advisory opinion divorced from a controversy, and, further, that only a *claim* is necessary. A matter can exist even though a right, duty or liability has not been, and may never be, established.

"Matter" before the Federal Court

The Special Purpose Liquidators of QN applied to the Federal Court under s 596A for an order that defined persons, former directors of QN, be summoned to attend before that Court to provide information about the examinable affairs of QN.

The application under s 596A was made by the Special Purpose Liquidators to aid the performance of their statutory functions and powers: first, to establish what are the assets of the corporation, including whether there are rights and obligations that could be realised, secured or litigated for the benefit of the unsecured creditors generally; and, second, to get in all of those assets.

The s 596A power looks forward, using the concept of "examinable affairs" of the corporation, to the possibility that information gathered in the course of an examination under s 597 will support a claim for relief against the examinee or some other person. Section 596A looks forward to such a claim as a "matter": a controversy relating to the pecuniary rights or liabilities or wrongdoing of the corporation and the examinee or some other person ...

Put another way, the s 596A power is a procedure that gives a liquidator the right to seek to examine certain persons involved in the corporation about the affairs of that corporation and thereby seek to establish, and then enforce, a potential right to relief against those with liabilities to the corporation, including alleged wrongdoers. Although the application arose out of events that had already occurred, the claim – one of potential rights, liabilities or wrongdoing – was a controversy where rights and liabilities could be established by a determination of the court made in due course in possible further litigation by reference to legal rules, principles or standards. In that context, the Summons Order made by the Federal Court under s 596A was made in the exercise of judicial power.

Indeed, an order made under s 596A, and the other provisions in Div 1 of Pt 5.9, determine whether, and the extent to which, the examinee may not remain silent but rather is obliged to be examined about the examinable affairs of a corporation. Such an order also determines whether, and the extent to which, there is an intrusion on the examinee's privilege to keep confidential books and papers in their possession or control.

That the application under s 596A for a summons is made ex parte, and that the criteria for the making of an order may in some cases clearly be satisfied, does not deny that the court must be satisfied, by evidence, that the criteria are met. The resolution of the "matter" yields, as its immediate result, an order for examination with direct loss of privileges for the examinee the subject of the order. Rights and liabilities are determined by that judicial determination – they are not merely affected. That alone, independent of the role of the liquidator as one class of "eligible applicants", suffices to create the necessary "matter".

But the making of a summons order by a court not only decides and declares the right of the eligible applicant (here, the Special Purpose Liquidators) to apply for and be granted the order, it determines the rights, status or obligations of the applicant and the examinee (here, each former director), who were, and remain, subject to the jurisdiction of the court. Here, a right to examine was granted to the applicant (the Special Purpose Liquidators) and, as a result, the examinee (each former director) was obliged to attend the court, to produce specified books not otherwise compellable to be produced and to answer questions without the benefit of the privilege against self-incrimination. The examinee was obliged to do those things on the basis that the evidence given by the examinee could be used in certain subsequent legal proceedings against the examinee.

16.5 Chapter III provides an exhaustive regime for the exercise of federal jurisdiction

The provisions of Chapter III exhaustively identify the possibilities for the authoritative adjudication of the matters listed in sections 75 and 76. If a legal proceeding answers the description of any of the nine subject-matters listed in sections 75 and 76, then the legal proceeding must involve a 'matter' even if the matter is being decided in State courts and involves State laws.

The ***Queen of Queensland Case*** considered the validity of Queensland legislation that purported to authorise the Queensland Government to seek advisory opinions from the Judicial Committee of the Privy Council in relation to questions of law arising under or concerning any law in force in Queensland. The High Court held that the legislation was invalid because it purported to authorise the giving of advisory opinions in respect of legal issues identified in sections 75 and 76.

Commonwealth v Queensland ('Queen of Queensland Case') (1975) 134 CLR 298

Jacobs J

But it was also held in *In re the Judiciary Act 1903–1920* and *In re the Navigation Act 1912–1920* that Ch III was an exhaustive statement of the judicial power which may be conferred under the chapter ...

In my opinion the judicial power delineated in Ch III is exhaustive of the manner in and the extent to which judicial power may be conferred on or exercised by any court in respect of the subject matters set forth in ss 75 and 76, "matters" in those sections meaning "subject matters". This is so not only in respect of federal courts but also in respect of State courts whether or not they are exercising federal jurisdiction conferred on them under s 77(iii).

In respect of the subject matters set out in ss 75 and 76 judicial power may only be exercised within the limits of the kind of judicial power envisaged in Ch III and if in respect of those matters an investing with federal jurisdiction of a State court does not enable it to perform the particular judicial function, then in respect of those matters the State court cannot under any law exercise that judicial function. Therefore, if in respect of those matters a State court exercising federal jurisdiction cannot give "advisory opinions" it cannot in respect of the same matters give such opinions in exercise of some State jurisdiction.

Chapter III of the Constitution is so constructed that the limits of the Commonwealth power to invest State courts with federal jurisdiction with respect to the matters mentioned in ss 75 and 76 mark out the limits of the judicial power or function which in any case State courts can exercise in respect of those matters. A State thus could not empower one of its courts to give advisory opinions on those subject matters. The court would be exercising judicial power but not a judicial power envisaged by Ch III and able to be conferred on it by the Commonwealth. It is then no answer to say that the State is conferring a judicial power which the Commonwealth is unable to confer. There is here no residuary State power, because Ch III is an exhaustive enunciation ...

I therefore summarize my conclusions as follows:

(a) The giving of an advisory opinion on a question of law by a court is an exercise of judicial power.

(b) The giving of such an opinion is not a judicial power which can be conferred by the Commonwealth on federal or State courts in respect of the subject matters of judicial power set out in ss 75 and 76.

(c) It is not a judicial power which can be conferred by a State on any of its courts in respect of those subject matters.

(d) It is not a judicial power which can be exercised in respect of those subject matters by the Judicial Committee on a referral of a matter to it by the Sovereign under the 1833 Act because the prerogative right to refer matters to the Judicial Committee for the exercise of the judicial power, including the power of giving an "advisory opinion", is extinguished at least in respect of those subject matters by the enactment by the Imperial Parliament of the *Commonwealth of Australia Constitution Act*.

Because there is no strict separation of State judicial power (see Chapter 17), a State Parliament may authorise bodies such as tribunals that are not courts to exercise State judicial power and decide controversies arising under State laws. ***Burns v Corbett*** demonstrates that a State cannot authorise a non-court to decide a controversy arising under State laws if that controversy involves one of the subject-matters identified in sections 75 or 76 of the *Constitution*. If a controversy involves one of the subject-matters identified in sections 75 or 76 then, by definition, it arises in federal jurisdiction, even if it involves State laws. Chapter III requires that federal jurisdiction be exercised only by courts.

Burns v Corbett (2018) 265 CLR 304

The New South Wales Civil and Administrative Tribunal ('NCAT') has jurisdiction to decide cases arising under the Anti-Discrimination Act 1977 *(NSW). Burns made a complaint under the Act against Corbett in relation to conduct that occurred in New South Wales. Burns was a resident of New South Wales. Corbett was a resident of Victoria. The case therefore involved a 'matter' 'between residents of different States' as described in section 75(iv) of the* Constitution. *All parties assumed that NCAT was not a 'court' for the purposes of this case.*

Kiefel CJ, Bell and Keane JJ

The first issue in these appeals is whether the *Commonwealth Constitution* precludes the Parliament of a State from conferring jurisdiction in respect of a matter between residents of different States within s 75(iv) of the Constitution on a tribunal which is not one of the "courts of the States" referred to in s 77 ("the Implication Issue") ...

The Implication Issue should be resolved in the affirmative. Considerations of constitutional text, structure and purpose compel the conclusion that a State law that purports to confer jurisdiction with respect to any of the matters listed in ss 75 and 76 of the Constitution on a tribunal that is not one of the courts of the States is inconsistent with Ch III of the Constitution, and is, therefore, invalid.

Chapter III of the *Constitution* provides for the authoritative adjudication of matters listed in ss 75 and 76 by federal courts and by State courts co-opted for that purpose as components of the federal Judicature. The provisions of Ch III exhaustively identify the possibilities for the authoritative adjudication of matters listed in ss 75 and 76. Adjudication by an organ of State government other than the courts of the States is not included within those possibilities and is therefore excluded from them. While s 77(ii) contemplates the possibility that, unless and until the Commonwealth Parliament legislates under s 77(iii), the courts of the States may continue to exercise their existing adjudicative authority, if any, finally to resolve such matters, it does not contemplate that this authority – the authority characteristically exercised by courts – will be exercised by agencies of the executive government of the States ...

[A]djudicative authority in respect of the matters listed in ss 75 and 76 of the Constitution may be exercised only as Ch III contemplates and not otherwise. Chapter III contemplates the exercise of adjudicative power only by this Court, by other federal courts created by the Commonwealth Parliament, by State courts invested with such power by the Commonwealth Parliament or by State courts to which such adjudicative authority belongs or in which it is invested. Accordingly, even if the Commonwealth Parliament had made no law under s 77(ii) or (iii), a State law purporting to authorise an agency of the government of a State other than a court to determine, for example, a dispute between residents of different States would be invalid because Ch III left no room for such an adjudication ...

Gageler J

The High Court has in the past made plain that, except with respect to the subject matters identified in ss 75 and 76 of the Constitution, a State Parliament can confer State judicial power on a State tribunal that is not a court of that State. The ultimate question now for determination is whether the exception is warranted.

My opinion is that the exception is warranted as a structural implication from Ch III of the Constitution. The implication is needed because State legislative power to confer State judicial power on a State tribunal that is not a court of a State must be denied in order to ensure the effective exercise of the legislative powers conferred on the Commonwealth Parliament by s 77(ii) and (iii) to produce by legislation the constitutionally permissible result that an exercise of judicial power with respect to a subject matter identified in s 75 or s 76 occur only under the authority of Commonwealth law, in a forum which meets the minimum characteristics of a Ch III court, so as to give rise to a judgment or order that is appealable directly to the High Court subject only to such exceptions or regulations as the Commonwealth Parliament may prescribe under s 73(ii).

In the result, I agree with the conclusion and substantially with the reasoning of Kiefel CJ, Bell and Keane JJ on the Implication Issue ...

Consistently with the reasoning of both Gibbs J and Jacobs J [in the *Queen of Queensland case*], the constitutional implication applicable to the resolution of this case is that judicial power with respect to the subject matters identified in ss 75 and 76 of the Constitution is confined to judicial power of a kind that is: (1) exercisable in respect of justiciable controversies answering the constitutional description of "matters"; and (2) conferred on or invested in institutions answering the constitutional description of "courts". With respect to the subject matters identified in ss 75 and 76, the Commonwealth Parliament and State Parliaments each lack legislative power to confer or invest judicial power of any other kind.

In ***Attorney-General (NSW) v Gatsby*** (2018) 361 ALR 570, a five-judge bench of the New South Wales Court of Appeal held that the assumption in ***Burns v Corbett*** that NCAT was not a 'court' within the meaning of Chapter III of the *Constitution* was correct. The Court of Appeal held that NCAT did not possess the minimum defining characteristics of a 'court' (see Chapter 19).

Cawthorn provides another example of a case involving the application of State law that would ordinarily be decided by a State tribunal arising within federal jurisdiction such that the case falls outside the jurisdiction of the State tribunal. *Cawthorn* explains that where a federal argument (that is, an argument relying on a federal statute or the *Constitution*) is genuinely raised and is not incapable on its face of legal argument, even if it ultimately fails and turns out to be wrong, the effect is that the matter arises within federal jurisdiction. This is because the matter answers the description of a matter 'arising under this Constitution' (section 76(i)) or 'arising under any laws made by the [Federal] Parliament' (section 76(ii)).

Citta Hobart Pty Ltd v Cawthorn [2022] HCA 16

Cawthorn alleged that Citta Hobart Pty Ltd had discriminated against him contrary to the **Anti-Discrimination Act 1998** ***(Tas) and commenced proceedings in the Tasmanian Anti-Discrimination Tribunal. In its defence, Citta Hobart argued that the relevant provisions of the Tasmanian statute were inconsistent with the*** **Disability Discrimination Act 1992** ***(Cth) and the*** **Disability (Access to Premises – Buildings) Standards 2010** ***(Cth). The Tribunal held that the defendant raising that argument meant that the matter arose in federal jurisdiction and that therefore it could not decide the case. The High Court held that the Tribunal was correct to hold that it lacked jurisdiction to decide the case.***

Kiefel CJ, Gageler, Keane, Gordon, Steward and Gleeson JJ

Following *Burns*, this appeal concerns the exclusion from State jurisdiction conferred on a State tribunal of matters, referred to in s 76(i) or s 76(ii) of the Constitution, arising under the Constitution or arising under laws made by the Commonwealth Parliament. How is a justiciable controversy to be identified as a matter answering one or other of those descriptions?

... And amongst the circumstances in which a justiciable controversy answers the description in s 76(i) of a matter "arising under" the *Constitution* is where the invalidity or inoperability of a Commonwealth or State law is asserted in the course of the controversy in reliance on the *Constitution*. In each case, the assertion operates to characterise the totality of the justiciable controversy and continues to characterise the totality of the justiciable controversy even where the assertion is later resolved in the exercise of judicial power or even withdrawn ...

[T]he subject-matter of the complaint referred to the Tribunal was a justiciable controversy about the entitlement of the respondent to an order under the State Act on the basis that the appellants discriminated on the ground of disability in the provision of a facility by failing to provide adequate wheelchair access in the construction of Parliament Square in Hobart. The assertion by the appellants by way of defence to the complaint that the State Act is in relevant part inoperative by force of s 109 of the *Constitution* by reason of inconsistency with the Commonwealth Act and the Commonwealth Standards formed part of the one justiciable controversy for the reason that the determination of the constitutional defence was essential to the determination of the claim. That was so notwithstanding the incapacity of the Tribunal judicially to determine the constitutional defence in the exercise of the limited jurisdiction conferred by the State Act. The totality of that single justiciable controversy was therefore one matter meeting the descriptions in both s 76(i) and s 76(ii) of the *Constitution*. Having attracted that character by the raising of the constitutional defence, the single justiciable controversy encompassing both the statutory claim and the constitutional defence would retain that character even if the constitutional defence were later to be considered and rejected by the Supreme Court.

... [F]or a claim or defence in reliance on a Commonwealth law or in reliance on the *Constitution* to give rise to a matter of a description in s 76(i) or s 76(ii) of the *Constitution*, it is enough that the claim or defence be genuinely in controversy and that it give rise to an issue capable of judicial determination. That is to say, it is enough that the claim or defence be genuinely raised and not incapable on its face of legal argument ...

Thus, the State jurisdiction of a State tribunal that is not a court of the State within the meaning of s 77(ii) and s 77(iii) of the *Constitution* is not denied, just as the federal jurisdiction of this Court under s 76(i) or s 76 (ii) or of another court under s 77(i) or s 77(iii) of the *Constitution* is not engaged, by the assertion of a claim or defence that amounts to "constitutional nonsense" or any other form of legal nonsense. But examination of what the prospects of success of a legally coherent claim or defence might be, were that claim or defence to be judicially determined on its merits, forms no part of the requisite assessment.

16.6 DISCUSSION QUESTIONS

1. Make a list of the characteristics of judicial power noted in the cases considered in this chapter.
2. What characteristics of the decisions in question meant that there was no adjudging of criminal guilt in ***ACMA v Today FM*** and ***Duncan v NSW***? What makes these cases different from ***Alexander***?
3. What are the defining characteristics of a 'matter'?
4. Why can a State court decide a case involving a matter identified in sections 75 and 76 of the *Constitution* but a State tribunal that is not a court cannot?
5. Problem question: Consider the following hypothetical scenario. James is a resident of South Australia, but travels to Tasmania every three months for a couple of days to visit family. During a visit to Tasmania, James is caught drink driving. James is charged with an offence under Tasmanian criminal law. The trial takes place in the Magistrates Court of Tasmania. Is the Magistrates Court exercising federal jurisdiction? Explain your answer.

   James' sister, Jennifer, is a resident of Tasmania. The day after James was caught drink driving, Jennifer is caught drink driving at the same location. Jennifer is charged with an offence under Tasmanian criminal law. The trial takes place in the Magistrates Court of Tasmania. Is the Magistrates Court exercising federal jurisdiction? Explain your answer.

17 SEPARATION OF FEDERAL JUDICIAL POWER

17.1 Overview

This chapter examines the idea of separation of judicial power. There is a strict separation of federal judicial power arising from Chapter III of the *Australian Constitution*. There is no strict separation of State judicial power.

Chapter III has the effect that: (1) federal judicial power can be exercised only by courts; and (2) federal courts can exercise only federal judicial power. However, judges of federal courts acting in their capacity as private individuals may be granted non-judicial functions in limited circumstances. By contrast, nothing in Chapter III or in State Constitutions requires that State judicial power be exercised only by courts.

Key concepts addressed in this chapter include:

- Chapter III courts
- delegation of judicial power
- *persona designata*
- incompatibility.

17.2 Separation of judicial power in theory

Philosophical discussions about the separation of powers often start with the reflections of the French political philosopher Baron de Montesquieu in *The Spirit of the Laws*. Montesquieu argued that separating the three branches of government is essential for ensuring liberty and preventing arbitrary government.

Baron de Montesquieu, *The Spirit of the Laws* (Cambridge University Press, 1989, first published 1793)

In every government there are three sorts of power: the legislative; the executive in respect to things dependent on the law of nations; and the executive in regard to matters that depend on the civil law.

By virtue of the first, the prince or magistrate enacts temporary or perpetual laws, and amends or abrogates those that have been already enacted. By the second, he makes peace or war, sends or receives embassies, establishes the public security, and provides against invasions. By the third, he punishes criminals, or determines the disputes that arise between individuals. The latter we shall call the judiciary power, and the other, simply, the executive power of the state.

The political liberty of the subject is a tranquillity of mind arising from the opinion each person has of his safety. In order to have this liberty, it is requisite the government be so constituted as one man need not be afraid of another.

When the legislative and executive powers are united in the same person, or in the same body of magistrates, there can be no liberty; because apprehensions may arise, lest the same monarch or senate should enact tyrannical laws, to execute them in a tyrannical manner.

Again, there is no liberty if the judiciary power be not separated from the legislative and executive. Were it joined with the legislative, the life and liberty of the subject would be exposed to arbitrary control; for the judge would be then the legislator. Were it joined to the executive power, the judge might behave with violence and oppression.

Montesquieu wrongly believed that the United Kingdom operated a system of government with a separation of powers. The British system of responsible government (which Australia adopted) is inconsistent with a strict separation between the legislative and executive arms of government. Although judicial independence has long been an important constitutional value in the United Kingdom, there has never been a strict separation of judicial power in the United Kingdom. Until 2009, when the Supreme Court of the United Kingdom was established, the highest court in the United Kingdom was a parliamentary committee; namely, the Appellate Committee of the House of Lords. The idea of a strict separation of judicial power is also incompatible with parliamentary sovereignty with its consequence that the United Kingdom Parliament can make and unmake any law it wants, including laws inconsistent with ideas about the separation of judicial power.

Montesquieu's ideas were influential with the framers of the *United States Constitution* and are reflected in the *United States Constitution's* separation of each of the three branches of government. The Australian situation is different. The historical record suggests that the framers of the *Australian Constitution* were concerned to ensure judicial independence but gave no real thought to the concept of the separation of judicial power.

Fiona Wheeler, 'Original intent and the doctrine of the separation of powers in Australia' (1996) 7 *Public Law Review* 96

But whereas the concepts of federalism, responsible government and equality of trade pervade the Convention Debates, the doctrine of separation of powers, even the doctrine of the separation of federal judicial power, was accorded scant attention by the founding fathers. To the extent that one can glean the collective intent of several dozen men from the bare record of their debate one hundred years after the event, the introduction of an Antipodean version of the doctrine of separation of powers appears to have been, at best, a somewhat hazy consideration in the establishment of the Commonwealth. For the most part, delegates appear not to have turned their minds to the issue, or, if their attention was so directed, not to have apprehended its significance ...

But despite the framers' failure to cast the debate concerning the drafting of s 71 in terms of the language of separation of powers, their much expressed desire to ensure the absolute independence of the federal judiciary as the "bulwark of the Constitution" coupled with the positive steps taken in s 72 to secure that independence, is hardly consistent with an intention on their part that the federal judicial power be generally capable of assumption by bodies standing outside the framework of Ch III ...

In light of the High Court's interpretation of the judiciary provisions of the Constitution since federation (and particularly in recent times), it is tempting to seize on the few fragments of debate from last century which support the strict separation of the federal judicial power in an attempt to sanctify modern doctrine as blessed by the framers. But to do so ignores the fact that, overall, the doctrine of separation of powers was barely mentioned in the Conventions of the 1890s, and, that on the one occasion when the doctrine was discussed at length, it was in defence of a clause ultimately omitted from the Constitution. The primary historical material simply does not support the conclusion that the framers expressly intended to adopt, as a principle of their Constitution, a doctrine of separation of powers – be that doctrine narrowly or broadly conceived.

But to say this of the framers' express intent is not to exclude the possibility that, for example, had these men been confronted with the question whether a body external to Ch III could validly be entrusted with the exercise of federal judicial power, they would have responded in the negative.

Despite not being the express intention, the effect of what the framers did has been taken by the High Court to give rise to a strict separation of federal judicial power.

17.3 The *Boilermakers'* doctrine: Separation of federal judicial power

The text of section 71 makes clear that only 'courts' may exercise federal judicial power. What makes an entity a 'court' is considered in Chapter 19. For present purposes, the key point is that entities that are not courts, such as institutions of the Executive Government or the Federal Parliament, cannot exercise federal judicial power.

Australian Constitution

Section 71 Judicial Power and Courts

The judicial power of the Commonwealth shall be vested in a Federal Supreme Court, to be called the High Court of Australia, and in such other federal courts as the Parliament creates, and in such other courts as it invests with federal jurisdiction. The High Court shall consist of a Chief Justice, and so many other Justices, not less than two, as the Parliament prescribes.

A number of cases decided in the High Court in the first half of the 1900s held that a separation of federal judicial power arose from the *Australian Constitution*. In ***R v Kirby; Ex parte Boilermakers' Society of Australia ('Boilermakers' Case')***, those principles crystallised into a clear doctrine with two limbs:

1. The judicial power of the Commonwealth can be exercised only by those courts identified in Chapter III of the *Constitution*.
2. Federal courts cannot exercise non-judicial power.

Boilermakers' Case (1956) 94 CLR 254

The Boilermakers' Society was an industrial union that had arranged for its members to engage in industrial action contrary to the relevant industrial award. The Commonwealth Court of Conciliation and Arbitration ordered the union to comply with the award. The Boilermakers' Society did not comply with that order and was fined for contempt of court. The Boilermakers' Society argued in the High Court that the Commonwealth Court of Conciliation and Arbitration was not really a 'court' and so could not exercise federal judicial power. The High Court agreed.

Dixon CJ, McTiernan, Fullagar and Kitto JJ

The attack upon the jurisdiction to make these orders is based upon the ground that they could be made only in the exercise of the judicial power of the Commonwealth and that the Constitution does not authorize the legislature to establish a tribunal which at once performs the function of industrial arbitration and exercises part of the judicial power of the Commonwealth ...

In a federal form of government a part is necessarily assigned to the judicature which places it in a position unknown in a unitary system or under a flexible constitution where Parliament is supreme ... The conception of independent governments existing in the one area and exercising powers in different fields of action carefully defined by law could not be carried into practical effect unless the ultimate responsibility of deciding upon the limits of the respective powers of the governments were placed in the federal judicature ... The powers of the federal judicature must therefore be at once paramount and limited. The organs to which federal judicial power may be entrusted must be defined, the manner in which they may be constituted must be prescribed and the content of their jurisdiction ascertained. These very general considerations explain the provisions of Chap III of the Constitution which is entitled "The Judicature" and consists of ten sections ...

But the existence in the Constitution of Chap III and the nature of the provisions it contains make it clear that no resort can be made to judicial power except under or in conformity with ss 71–80 ...

Section 51(xxxix) extends to furnishing courts with authorities incidental to the performance of the functions derived under or from Chap. III and no doubt to dealing in other ways with matters incidental to the execution of the powers given by the Constitution to the federal judicature. But, except for this, when an exercise of legislative powers is directed to the judicial power of the Commonwealth it must operate through or in conformity with Chap. III. For that reason it is beyond the competence of the Parliament to invest with any part of the judicial power any body or person except a court created pursuant to s 71 and constituted in accordance with s 72 or a court brought into existence by a State. It is a proposition which has been repeatedly affirmed and acted upon by this Court ...

Indeed to study Chap III is to see at once that it is an exhaustive statement of the manner in which the judicial power of the Commonwealth is or may be vested ...

A number of considerations exist which point very definitely to the conclusion that the Constitution does not allow the use of courts established by or under Chap III for the discharge of functions which are not in themselves part of the judicial power and are not auxiliary or incidental thereto. First among them stands the very text of the Constitution. If attention is confined to Chap III it would be difficult to believe that the careful provisions for the creation of a federal judicature as the institution of government to exercise judicial power and the precise specification of the content or subject matter of that power were compatible with the exercise by that institution of other powers ...

With reference to the federal judicature, the true contrast in federal powers is not between judicial power lying within Chap III and judicial power lying outside Chap III. That is tenuous and unreal. It is between judicial power within Chap III and other powers. To turn to the provisions of the Constitution dealing with those other powers surely must be to find confirmation for the view that no functions but judicial may be reposed in the judicature. If you knew nothing of the history of the separation of powers, if you made no comparison of the American instrument of government with ours, if you were unaware of the interpretation it had received before our Constitution was framed according to the same plan, you would still feel the strength of the logical inferences from Chaps I, II and III and the form and contents of ss 1, 61 and 71. It would be difficult to treat it as a mere draftsman's arrangement. Section 1 positively vests the legislative power of the Commonwealth in the Parliament of the Commonwealth. Then s 61, in exactly the same form, vests the executive power of the Commonwealth in the Crown. They are the counterparts of s 71 which in the same way vests the judicial power of the Commonwealth in this Court, the federal courts the Parliament may create and the State courts it may invest with federal jurisdiction. This cannot all be treated as meaningless and of no legal consequence ... it is hardly consistent with the form and contents of Chaps I, II and III to assign no legal consequence to the division.

The High Court relied upon both the text and structure of the *Constitution* to reach its conclusion. As to text, the High Court pointed out that section 71 states explicitly which entities the judicial power of the Commonwealth is or may be vested in: all of those entities are 'courts'. The High Court read section 71 as an exhaustive statement of which entities are capable of exercising federal judicial power. As to structure, the High Court pointed to the fact that the provisions of the *Constitution* dealing with federal judicial power are all to be found in a single chapter of the *Constitution*, separate from other provisions of the *Constitution* dealing with other matters.

The High Court's decision was appealed to Privy Council, which came to the same conclusion.

Attorney-General (Cth) v The Queen (1957) 95 CLR 529

Viscount Simonds delivered the judgment of the Judicial Committee of the Privy Council comprising Viscount Kilmuir LC, Viscount Simonds and Lords Morton of Henryton, Tucker, Cohen, Keith of Avonholm and Somervell of Harrow.

Section 1 which vests legislative power in a Federal Parliament at the same time negatives such power being vested in any other body. In the same way s 71 and the succeeding sections while affirmatively prescribing in what courts the judicial power of the Commonwealth may be vested and the limits of their jurisdiction negatives the possibility of vesting such power in other courts or extending their jurisdiction beyond these limits. It is to Chap III alone that the Parliament must have recourse if it wishes to legislate in regard to the judicial power. That Chapter is in its terms detailed and exhaustive, and their Lordships dissent from the contention sometimes explicitly, sometimes implicitly, advanced that, inasmuch as there is no express prohibition of other legislation in this field, it is open to the Parliament to turn from Chap III to some other source of power ...

Yet this general proposition is subject to a qualification and it is a qualification which powerfully supports the proposition. For in s 51, the final matters in respect of which the Parliament is empowered to make laws are found in placitum (xxxix) "Matters incidental to the execution of any power vested by this Constitution in the Parliament or in either House thereof or in the Government of the Commonwealth or in the Federal Judicature or in any Department or officer of the Commonwealth". This placitum looks forward to the vesting of power in the Federal Judicature which is found in Chap III: it assumes such vesting and empowers the Parliament to make laws in respect of matters incidental to the execution of such power. The conferment of such a limited power of legislation in s 51 makes it very clear that it is in Chap III alone that a larger power is contained.

The argument so far appears to lead irresistibly to the conclusion that it is only in Chap III that legislative authority is to be found to vest the judicial power of the Commonwealth. If so, it is to the provisions of that Chapter that one must look to find authority for the vesting in a court powers and functions which are not judicial or to vest in a body of persons exercising non-judicial functions part of the judicial power of the Commonwealth ... The question in whatever form it is stated is whether and how far judicial and non-judicial power can be united in the same body. Their Lordships do not doubt that the decision of the High Court is right and that there is nothing in Chap III, to which alone recourse can be had, which justifies such a union. It may be repeated that this is subject to such qualification as is imposed by s 51 (xxxix) ...

There may be a theoretical conundrum inherent in the Privy Council deciding the ***Boilermakers' Case***. Both the High Court and the Privy Council said that it is only the three categories of 'court' identified in section 71 that may exercise the judicial power of the Commonwealth. Yet, section 74 of the *Constitution* permits appeals to the Queen-in-Council in limited circumstances. It was pursuant to section 74 that the Privy Council heard the case. The conundrum arises because the monarch is obviously not a court and is also part of the legislative and executive branches of government, and because the Privy Council is not a court. The Privy Council serves as an advisory body to the monarch and comprises a very large number of members, including every member of the British Cabinet. The Privy Council has a Judicial Committee, consisting of senior judges, which hears judicial matters. The conundrum may be resolved by holding that the rule is that, except as expressly provided by the *Constitution* (such as by section 74), only the three categories of 'court' identified in section 71 may exercise the judicial power of the Commonwealth. As Chapter 1 explained, the Privy Council can no longer hear appeals from Australian courts.

17.4 The first limb of *Boilermakers'* and its exceptions

The first limb of the ***Boilermakers'*** doctrine states that the judicial power of the Commonwealth may be exercised only by Chapter III courts. Chapter III courts are those 'courts' identified in section 71, which states that the judicial power of the Commonwealth shall be vested:

1. in 'a Federal Supreme Court, to be called the High Court of Australia'
2. in 'such other federal courts as the Parliament creates', and
3. in 'such other courts as it invests with federal jurisdiction'.

There are thus three categories of Chapter III court. The first category is the High Court and needs no explanation. The second category of courts is those courts created by the Federal Parliament. Currently, these courts include the Federal Court of Australia, and the Federal Circuit and Family Court of Australia. The third category of courts – 'such other courts' – refers to the State and Territory courts.

The ability to vest federal judicial power in the State courts is sometimes called the 'autochthonous expedient'. The framers of the *Australian Constitution* considered that it would be convenient or expedient if the State courts were able to resolve cases involving federal law. This would avoid the need for the Federal Parliament to establish an elaborate system of federal courts, at least for a considerable period of time. The word 'autochthonous' means native and refers to the fact that this feature of the *Australian Constitution* was not copied from the United States, where State courts cannot exercise federal judicial power.

There are three key 'exceptions' to the first limb of the ***Boilermakers'*** doctrine:

1. the power of each House of Parliament to punish for contempt
2. the power of military command to punish military personnel for a service offence following a court-martial
3. the ability of courts to delegate some exercises of judicial power to officers of courts.

The word 'exceptions' is put in quotation marks since at least some of the exceptions do not actually, despite initial appearances, involve the exercise of federal judicial power.

Power of the Houses of Parliament to punish for contempt

Section 49 of the *Constitution* has the effect that each House of Parliament has power to punish a person for contempt.

Australian Constitution

Section 49 Privileges etc of Houses

The powers, privileges, and immunities of the Senate and of the House of Representatives, and of the members and the committees of each House, shall be such as are declared by the Parliament, and until declared shall be those of the Commons House of Parliament of the United Kingdom, and of its members and committees, at the establishment of the Commonwealth.

R v Richards; Ex parte Fitzpatrick and Browne confirmed that this power includes a power to punish, including by imprisonment, a person for contempt of Parliament. The High Court explained that this power to punish for contempt is not a breach of the *Constitution* because: (1) due to historical considerations, the power may not be considered 'judicial' in character; and (2) section 49 expressly grants this power to each House of Parliament.

R v Richards; Ex parte Fitzpatrick and Browne (1955) 92 CLR 157

The House of Representatives resolved that Fitzpatrick and Browne were guilty of contempt of the House and should be imprisoned. The Speaker issued warrants for the detention of Fitzpatrick and Browne. After being taken into custody, Fitzpatrick and Browne each sought* habeus corpus *in the High Court challenging the validity of their detention. One of their arguments was a House of Parliament has no power to punish a person for contempt because that would involve the House exercising federal judicial power contrary to Chapter III. The High Court disagreed.

Dixon CJ for the Court

It is said that the power exercised by resolving upon the imprisonment of two men and issuing a warrant to carry it into effect belonged to the judicial power and ought therefore not to be conceded under the words of s 49 to either House of the Parliament. It is correct that the Constitution is based in its structure upon the separation of powers. It is true that the judicial power of the Commonwealth is reposed exclusively in the courts contemplated by Chap III. It is further correct that it is a general principle of construction that the legislative powers should not be interpreted as allowing of the creation of judicial powers or authorities in any body except the courts which are described by Chap. III of the Constitution. Accordingly, it is argued that a strong presumption exists against construing s 49 in a sense which would enable the particular power we have before us to be exercised by the Senate or the House of Representatives ...

The consideration we have already mentioned is of necessity an answer to this contention, namely, that in unequivocal terms the powers of the House of Commons [which includes power to punish for contempt] have been bestowed upon the House of Representatives. It should be added to that very simple statement that throughout the course of English history there has been a tendency to regard those powers as not strictly judicial but as belonging to the legislature, rather as something essential or, at any rate, proper for its protection. This is not the occasion to discuss the historical grounds upon which these powers and privileges attached to the House of Commons. It is sufficient to say that they were regarded by many authorities as proper incidents of the legislative function, notwithstanding the fact that considered more theoretically – perhaps one might even say, scientifically – they belong to the judicial sphere. But our decision is based upon the ground that a general view of the Constitution and the separation of powers is not a sufficient reason for giving to these words, which appear to us to be so clear, a restrictive or secondary meaning which they do not properly bear.

Power of military command to punish military personnel for a service offence following a court-martial

The High Court has made clear in a number of cases that there is no exercise of federal judicial power where a member of the Australian Defence Force is punished for a service offence following a court-martial.

The High Court has explained that courts-martial operate within the military chain of command and make no authoritative or binding decisions about criminal guilt, and that any punishment imposed is imposed within the chain of command. However, if Parliament wishes to have service offences dealt with as criminal matters then the ordinary requirements of Chapter III apply. ***Lane v Morrison, Haskins v Commonwealth*** and ***Private R v Cowen*** articulate all these propositions.

Lane v Morrison (2009) 239 CLR 230

Legislation established the Australian Military Court ('AMC') as a court of record to try charges of service offences to replace the system of military courts-martial. The AMC was constituted by Military Judges appointed for 10-year terms. Lane was convicted and sentenced for a service offence. Lane argued that the AMC was not a 'federal court' within the meaning of Chapter III because section 72 of the Constitution *provides that judges of courts created by Parliament have security of tenure until age 70. Lane further argued that there was a breach of the* Boilermakers' *doctrine because the AMC was exercising federal judicial power. The High Court agreed.*

Hayne, Heydon, Crennan, Kiefel and Bell JJ

[T]he question which is presented by Ch III of the Constitution is whether the body under consideration exercises the judicial power *of the Commonwealth*. To speak of a court-martial exercising a species of judicial power is unhelpful if it distracts attention from the relevant constitutional question.

That constitutional question was resolved in respect of courts-martial, as it was in *R v Bevan*, *R v Cox* and later *Re Tracey*, at a time when courts-martial were not independent of the chain of command of the forces. Courts-martial were convened only by order from within the chain of command; conclusions of guilt and determinations of punishment were subject to review or confirmation within that chain of command. A court-martial did not make a binding and authoritative decision of guilt or determination of punishment. A court-martial did not enforce its decisions. Enforcement of any decision, other than acquittal of the accused, depended upon the outcome of review of the decision within the chain of command. But a central purpose of the creation of the AMC was to have the new body make binding and authoritative decisions of guilt and determinations about punishment which, without further intervention from within the chain of command, would be enforced.

That the AMC is to make binding and authoritative decisions on the issues identified without further intervention from within the chain of command is reason enough to conclude that it is to exercise the judicial power of the Commonwealth.

... For the AMC to make a binding and authoritative determination of such issues pursuant to the [*Defence Force Discipline Act*] is to exercise the judicial power of the Commonwealth. There is no dispute that the AMC is not constituted in accordance with Ch III.

In ***Haskins v Commonwealth***, the High Court reaffirmed that punishment for a service offence imposed within the chain of command involves an exercise of the power of military command which is a defining feature of a defence force. It does not involve an exercise of the judicial power of the Commonwealth.

Haskins v Commonwealth (2011) 244 CLR 22

Following Lane v Morrison*, Parliament enacted legislation providing that 'the rights and liabilities of all persons ... to be, and always to have been, the same as if' a court-martial had taken place instead of a trial in the AMC. The legislation also provided for 'punishment reviews' to take place within the chain of command and that no punishment was to be carried out unless the punishment was confirmed within the chain of command. Lane argued that the legislation meant that Parliament had made a legislative determination of criminal guilt and imposed a punishment. The High Court disagreed.*

French CJ, Gummow, Hayne, Crennan, Kiefel and Bell JJ

First, it is inapposite to describe the impugned provisions as having imposed a punishment on those with whom the AMC had dealt. Second, the impugned provisions made no legislative determination of guilt and did not make crimes of any acts after they had been done.

As explained earlier, the *Interim Measures No 2 Act* provided that the declaration of rights and liabilities was "subject to the outcome of any review" provided for by Pt 7 of Sched 1. Because the plaintiff was sentenced to detention there was an automatic review of the punishment imposed on him. On 29 March 2010, the reviewing authority upheld the punishment imposed on the plaintiff. The final decision about his punishment was therefore made within the chain of command; the punishment to which he was declared liable by the *Interim Measures No 2 Act* was not finally fixed by the Act. And because those who had been sentenced to some lesser form of punishment could seek a punishment review, this punishment, too, was not necessarily fixed finally by the Act ...

In cases where the punishment that was imposed by the AMC had been fully satisfied by the time the impugned provisions came into force (as, for example, by the service of the whole of a period of detention and the expiration of any period for which an order of detention was suspended) it would not be right to describe the effect of the provisions as being a legislative *imposition* of punishment. The better description of the provisions would be that they were in the nature of an act of indemnity intended to preclude liability for past acts ...

Nor was there any legislative finding of contravention of a norm of conduct. The impugned provisions said nothing about the contraventions of the *Discipline Act* that lay behind the punishments with which the *Interim Measures No 2 Act* dealt. The sole focus of the latter Act, and more particularly the impugned provisions, was punishments that had been imposed, not what had prompted those punishments. Thus, contrary to the plaintiff's submissions, the impugned provisions did not determine any question of guilt, or make crimes of any acts, let alone crimes of acts after they had been committed ...

The proper ambit of what is described as an "exception" or "qualification" to Ch III cannot be identified without close attention to both the reasons for, and the content of, the principle or principles that yield the exception.

Two kinds of consideration lead to the conclusion that disciplinary measures can be applied in the defence force without exercise of the judicial power of the Commonwealth. First, there is not the exercise of the judicial power of the Commonwealth in such a case because the punishment is imposed by the (legislatively regulated) exercise of the power of command that is a necessary and defining characteristic of the defence force: a power of command that is essential to the creation and maintenance of a disciplined and effective fighting force. Second, there is not the exercise of the judicial power of the Commonwealth in such a case because there is not the binding and authoritative decision of guilt or determination of punishment for a service offence that stands apart from the chain of command of the defence force.

Once it is observed, as has already been explained, that the impugned provisions focus only upon punishments that have been imposed and are subject to review within the chain of command of the defence force, it is then apparent that no new or larger exception must be made to the application of Ch III to conclude that the impugned provisions are valid.

Private R v Cowen was principally about whether a law creating a particular service offence was within the scope of Federal Parliament's power to make laws with respect to defence under section 51(vi) of the *Constitution*. In the course of holding that the law was supported by that head of federal legislative power, the High Court reaffirmed unanimously that the power to impose discipline on defence personnel within the chain of military command does not contravene Chapter III. However, the High Court was divided on the rationale for this proposition.

For Kiefel CJ, Bell and Keane JJ the power to punish defence personnel for service offences within the chain of military command does not contravene Chapter III because the power involved is not judicial power.

Private R v Cowen (2020) 271 CLR 316

Kiefel CJ, Bell and Keane JJ

[T]he system of military justice pursues the specific purpose of securing and maintaining discipline within the armed forces rather than the general purpose of punishing those guilty of criminal conduct.

Given that "[a] function may take its character from that of the tribunal in which it is reposed", and given further the long history of the exercise of disciplinary jurisdiction by service tribunals within the chain of command established under s 68 of the Constitution, it may be more accurate to say that the power so exercised is executive or administrative in character.

For Nettle, Gordon and Edelman JJ in separate judgments the power involved in punishing defence personnel for service offences within the chain of military command is judicial power but the long history of military justice operating apart from the ordinary courts from the seventeenth century in England through to the pre-Federation colonial period requires an exception to Chapter III. Justice Gageler did not directly address whether the power was judicial but agreed that the exception is explained and limited by history.

Private R v Cowen (2020) 271 CLR 316

Edelman J

A purist approach to s 51(vi) would preclude Parliament from conferring most judicial power upon service tribunals under s 51(vi) due to conflict with the principle that the judicial power of the Commonwealth can only be exercised by the courts designated by Ch III. The purist conception treats the pre-Federation history of service tribunals as a matter that carries no interpretative weight in the application of s 51(vi). The purist view is effectively that everything adjusted on Federation so that legislation is invalid, no matter how long established its historical antecedents, if it cannot be accommodated to implications derived, independently from that history, from the text and structure of the Constitution. No matter how strong the expressed expectations at Federation or how long established the jurisdiction of the service tribunals before Federation, they could not qualify the implication of the exclusivity of the vesting of the "judicial power of the Commonwealth" in courts designated by Ch III with regard to the application of s 51(vi), a provision that is expressly "subject to" the Constitution.

The purist approach inverts the proper process of reasoning by which the scope of a constitutional implication is shaped by historical considerations, not superimposed upon them. It denies the usual role of history and associated public expressions of expectations at Federation as a baseline from which the application of essential constitutional meaning develops. ...

Provided that a service tribunal is constituted in a manner that is broadly consistent with its core historical antecedents it will not infringe the constitutional implication that the judicial power of the Commonwealth can only be exercised in accordance with Ch III of the Constitution. However, where the Commonwealth Parliament confers judicial power that extends beyond those historical roots, that can only be done consistently with the requirements of Ch III. Hence, the purported creation by the Commonwealth Parliament of an Australian Military Court could not be supported by s 51(vi), and independently of Ch III, because it was 'established to make binding and authoritative decisions of guilt or innocence independently from the chain of command of the defence forces'.

Federal judicial power may, in limited circumstances, be exercised by officers of a Chapter III court who are not judges

Federal judicial power can be exercised only by Chapter III courts but this does not mean that federal judicial power must be exercised only by judges of those courts. ***Harris v Caladine*** explains that, in limited circumstances, federal judicial power may be delegated to and then exercised by officers of a Chapter III court, such as registrars.

Harris v Caladine (1991) 172 CLR 84

The **Family Law Rules** *provided that certain powers of the Family Court of Australia could be exercised by registrars and that any such exercise of power by a registrar was subject to review by a judge of the Family Court who would make a fresh decision about the exercise of the power in question. The High Court rejected an argument that section 79, which provides that 'The federal jurisdiction of any court may be exercised by such number of judges as the Parliament prescribes', implied that only judges could exercise federal judicial power.*

Mason CJ and Deane J

It would not be correct to read into s 79 an implication that the entire federal jurisdiction of a Ch III court must be exercised by a judge ... All that the section does is to enable the Parliament to prescribe the number of judges who shall exercise the federal jurisdiction of a court, whether generally or in the particular class of case ... The section enables Parliament to preclude a delegation of federal jurisdiction to persons who are not judges. To that extent it is inconsistent with the notion that s 71 itself impliedly prohibits such a delegation ...

The legislative power of Parliament to authorize the exercise by officers of the Family Court of part of its jurisdiction, powers and functions is subject to some limitation, as is the power of the Court to delegate some part of its jurisdiction, powers and functions ...

It seems to us that, so long as two conditions are observed, the delegation of some part of the jurisdiction, powers and functions of the Family Court as a federal court to its officers is permissible and consistent with the control and supervision of the Family Court's jurisdiction by its judges. The first condition is that the delegation must not be to an extent where it can no longer properly be said that, as a practical as well as a theoretical matter, the judges constitute the court. This means that the judges must continue to bear the major responsibility for the exercise of judicial power at least in relation to the more important aspects of contested matters. The second condition is that the delegation must not be inconsistent with the obligation of a court to act judicially and that the decisions of the officers of the court in the exercise of their delegated jurisdiction, powers and functions must be subject to review or appeal by a judge or judges of the court. For present purposes it is sufficient for us to say that, if the exercise of delegated jurisdiction, powers and functions by a court officer is subject to review or appeal by a judge or judges of the court on questions of both fact and law, we consider that the delegation will be valid. Certainly, if the review is by way of hearing de novo, the delegation will be valid. The importance of insisting on the existence of review by a judge or an appeal to a judge is that this procedure guarantees that a litigant may have recourse to a hearing and a determination by a judge. In other words, a litigant can avail him or herself of the judicial independence which is the hallmark of the class of court presently under consideration.

17.5 The second limb of *Boilermakers'* and its exceptions

The second limb of the ***Boilermakers'*** doctrine states that federal courts can exercise only judicial power. This says nothing about whether State courts can exercise non-judicial power.

The ***Boilermakers' Case*** holds that federal courts can exercise only judicial power. In ***Re Wakim, Ex parte McNally,*** the second limb of the *Boilermakers'* doctrine was refined to the proposition that federal courts can exercise only *federal* judicial power. In *Re Wakim*, the High Court struck down legislation that purported to vest State jurisdiction in federal courts.

Re Wakim; Ex parte McNally (1999) 198 CLR 511

At the time, regulation of corporations occurred partly under federal legislation and partly under State legislation. A 'co-operative federalism' agreement was reached between the Commonwealth and the States, where the States agreed to vest State jurisdiction in respect of certain matters in the federal courts and the Commonwealth agreed to vest federal jurisdiction in respect of certain matters in the State courts. This was called a cross-vesting scheme. The High Court held that federal courts can only exercise federal jurisdiction and struck down the legislation vesting State jurisdiction in federal courts.

McHugh J

My reasons for reaching the conclusion that the *Corporations Act 1989* and the *Corporations (New South Wales) Act 1990* are invalid in so far as they purport to give the Federal Court of Australia jurisdiction to exercise State judicial power can be stated fairly shortly ...

Section 71, which is in Ch III of the Constitution, gives the Parliament of the Commonwealth the power to create federal courts to exercise the judicial power of the Commonwealth. But as Dixon CJ, McTiernan and Kitto JJ pointed out in *Cockle v Isaksen*, "the jurisdiction which a federal court so created may exercise cannot come from s 71 alone. It must be conferred and defined by the exercise of further legislative power." Sections 75, 76 and 77 of Ch III of the Constitution give the Parliament that legislative power by empowering it to confer jurisdiction on federal courts in respect of the "matters" specified in ss 75 and 76. State jurisdiction or State judicial power is not one of those "matters" ...

Leaving aside the appellate jurisdiction of this Court conferred by s 73 of the Constitution, the exercise of the judicial power of the Commonwealth is confined to the matters specified in ss 75 and 76 of the Constitution. For nearly 80 years, the accepted doctrine of this Court has been that the "express statement of the matters in respect of which and the Courts by which the judicial power of the Commonwealth may be exercised is, we think, clearly intended as a delimitation of the whole of the original jurisdiction which may be exercised under the judicial power of the Commonwealth, and as a necessary exclusion of any other exercise of original jurisdiction." It follows, and it is also established doctrine, that the power conferred by s 51(xxxix) to make laws with respect to "matters incidental to the execution of any power vested by this Constitution ... in the Federal Judicature" does not authorise the vesting of jurisdiction in federal courts. Consequently, the Parliament of the Commonwealth can only invest federal courts with jurisdiction to decide the "matters" specified in ss 75 and 76 of Ch III of the Constitution ...

How then can a State Parliament invest a federal court with a jurisdiction which the Parliament of the Commonwealth, which has created the court, cannot invest in that court? Co-operative federalism is the chief answer given by the parties and the interveners supporting the validity of the legislation. But co-operative federalism is not a constitutional term. It is a political slogan, not a criterion of constitutional validity or power ...

There is not a word in Ch III which indicates expressly or by implication that it authorises the Parliament of the Commonwealth to create federal courts to exercise State jurisdiction or State judicial power. Nor is there a word in Ch III which indicates that the States can invest such jurisdiction or power in the federal courts ...

But in addition, the settled doctrine of this Court is that Ch III exhaustively defines the "matters" that may be the subject of the judicial power of the Commonwealth and exhaustively defines the "matters" that the Parliament of the Commonwealth may invest in the federal courts which it creates. The irresistible conclusion from the terms of Ch III is that it authorises the Parliament of the Commonwealth to create federal courts but only for the purpose of exercising jurisdiction with respect to the matters specified in ss 75 and 76 of the Constitution ...

By granting power to the Parliament of the Commonwealth to create federal courts and by expressly stating the matters in respect of which the Parliament may confer jurisdiction on those courts, Ch III impliedly forbids the conferring of any other jurisdiction on those courts by the Commonwealth or the States. The express statement of those "matters" would be pointless if the Parliament or the States could disregard them.

There are two key exceptions to the second limb of the ***Boilermakers'*** doctrine:

1. federal courts may exercise non-judicial powers that are incidental to the exercise of federal judicial power, and
2. the *persona designata* doctrine, which says judges of federal courts acting in their personal capacity may perform non-judicial functions in limited circumstances.

Federal courts may exercise powers that are incidental to the exercise of federal judicial power

Section 51(xxxix) gives Parliament power to make laws with respect to 'matters incidental to the execution of any power vested by this Constitution ... in the Federal Judicature'. The High Court acknowledged this exception in the ***Boilermakers' Case.***

One example is the power to make rules of court that prescribe procedures for how a court and its registry operate. That power might be understood as legislative in character since it is a rule-making power. However, making rules of court is necessary to enable a court to do its judicial work of deciding cases.

R v Davison (1954) 90 CLR 353

Dixon CJ and McTiernan J

An extreme example of a function that may be given to courts as an incident of judicial power or dealt with directly as an exercise of legislative power is that of making procedural rules of court.

Nicholas v The Queen (1998) 193 CLR 173

Brennan CJ

The conferral of jurisdiction prima facie carries the power to do whatever is necessary or convenient to effect its exercise. The practice and procedure of a court may be prescribed by the court in exercise of its implied power to do what is necessary for the exercise of its jurisdiction but subject to overriding legislative provision governing that practice or procedure.

Judges of federal courts may exercise non-judicial power *persona designata*

Because courts are made up of judges, it would be a breach of the second limb of the ***Boilermakers'*** doctrine to grant a non-judicial power to a judge of a federal court in their capacity as a judge. However, a person who is a federal judge acting not in their capacity as judge but in their private capacity as a designated person (that is, acting *persona designata*) may be granted non-judicial powers and functions. The *persona designata* doctrine is subject to an 'incompatibility' limitation.

The *persona designata* doctrine was accepted by the High Court for the first time in ***Hilton v Wells***.

Hilton v Wells (1985) 157 CLR 57

The case involved a challenge to the admissibility of evidence obtained as a result of telephone tapping that had been authorised by warrant. The Telecommunications (Interception) Act 1979 *authorised 'a judge' to issue telephone tapping warrants. If the legislation granted the power to issue warrants to 'a judge' in their capacity as a judge then the legislation would be invalid because issuing warrants is not an exercise of judicial power. It would follow that the evidence was obtained illegally and was therefore inadmissible. If the legislation granted the power to issue warrants to 'a judge' in their capacity as a designated individual then the legislation would not be in breach of Chapter III.*

Gibbs CJ, Wilson and Dawson JJ

Although the Parliament cannot confer non-judicial powers on a federal court, or invest a State court with a non-judicial power, there is no necessary constitutional impediment which prevents it from conferring non-judicial power on a particular individual who happens to be a member of a court ...

The question for decision in the present case then is whether s 20 confers powers on (inter alia) the Federal Court, or on the judges individually as designated persons. It is a question which involves fine distinctions, which some may regard as unsatisfactory ...

It clearly appears from these authorities that where a power, judicial or non-judicial, is conferred by statute upon a court or a judge, it is not necessarily conferred on the court or the judge as such – the question is one of construction. Where the power is conferred on a court, there will ordinarily be a strong presumption that the court as such is intended. Where the power is conferred on a judge, rather than on a court, it will be a question whether the distinction was deliberate, and whether the reference to "judge" rather than to "court" indicates that the power was intended to be invested in the judge as an individual who, because he is a judge, possesses the necessary qualifications to exercise it ...

[T]he nature of the power conferred is of importance in deciding whether the judge on whom it is conferred is intended to exercise it in his capacity as a judge or as a designated person. If the power is judicial, it is likely that it is intended to be exercisable by the judge by virtue of that character; if it is purely administrative, and not incidental to the exercise of judicial power, it is likely that it is intended to be exercised by the judge as a designated person ...

We conclude that s 20 confers no power on the Federal Court and does not infringe the rule laid down in the *Boilermakers' Case*. It was submitted by Mr Ellicott that the separation of judicial and administrative power is not merely a matter of verbal formulae and that is of course correct. If the nature or extent of the functions cast upon judges were such as to prejudice their independence or to conflict with the proper performance of their judicial functions, the principle underlying the *Boilermakers' Case* would doubtless render the legislation invalid. But the exercise of the functions conferred by s 20 would not have that result. The section designates the judges as individuals particularly well qualified to fulfil the sensitive role that the section envisages, and confers on them a function which is not incompatible with their status and independence or inconsistent with the exercise of their judicial powers.

For these reasons we hold that s 20 of the *Telecommunications (Interception) Act* is a valid enactment of the Commonwealth Parliament.

Grollo v Palmer gave a fuller explanation of the limitations on when non-judicial functions may be conferred on judges *persona designata*. The High Court held that non-judicial functions may be conferred on a judge *persona designata* only with the consent of the judge. The High Court also held that a non-judicial function cannot be conferred on a judge *persona designata* if the function is incompatible with the judge's performance of judicial functions or with the exercise by the judiciary of its functions as an institution exercising judicial power. *Grollo v Palmer* therefore holds that incompatibility may be: (1) personal incompatibility; or (2) institutional incompatibility. The case shows that any non-judicial function must be performed independently in order to avoid incompatibility.

Grollo v Palmer (1995) 184 CLR 348

The* Telecommunications (Interception) Act 1979 *was amended to authorise an 'eligible judge' to issue telecommunications interception warrants. 'Eligible judge' was defined to mean 'a person who is' a judge of a federal court who had consented to being nominated as a person empowered to issue warrants. The legislation also provided that in the exercise of the function of issuing warrants an eligible judge had the same protection and immunity as a justice of the High Court has in relation to proceedings in the High Court. The legislation set out the matters that must be considered in deciding whether to issue a warrant and provided that an eligible judge was to exercise an independent discretion in deciding whether to issue a warrant. The High Court held that the function was conferred on judges* persona designata *and did not breach any incompatibility condition.

Brennan CJ, Deane, Dawson and Toohey JJ

The applicant's counsel based their submissions on alternative propositions as to the nature of the power to issue interception warrants and as to the repository of the power to do so. If the power be regarded as administrative in nature and eligible Judges be regarded as *personae designatae*, the provisions of the Act purporting to confer the power on those Judges are said to be invalid because the power is such that its exercise is incompatible with judicial functions. Alternatively, the provisions which permit the appointment of all Federal Court Judges and which have in fact permitted the appointment of a substantial majority of the Judges of that Court to be "eligible Judges" are said to be merely a device which, in substance, vests non-judicial power in the Judges of that Court. That is said to be contrary to the *Boilermakers* exposition of the constitutional imperative of the separation of powers.

... Those powers are now expressed to be conferred not on all Judges of the Federal Court but only on "a person who is" a Judge of a court created by the Parliament and who has consented to be nominated as an eligible Judge and who has been declared by the Minister to be an eligible Judge. The Act as it now stands, in comparison with the Act as it stood when considered in *Hilton v Wells*, contains even clearer indicia showing that the power to issue interception warrants is conferred on Judges as designated persons and not on the courts of which eligible Judges are members ...

The conditions thus expressed on the power to confer non-judicial functions on Judges as designated persons are twofold: first, no non-judicial function that is not incidental to a judicial function can be conferred without the Judge's consent; and, second, no function can be conferred that is incompatible either with the Judge's performance of his or her judicial functions or with the proper discharge by the judiciary of its responsibilities as an institution exercising judicial power ("the incompatibility condition") ...

The incompatibility condition may arise in a number of different ways. Incompatibility might consist in so permanent and complete a commitment to the performance of non-judicial functions by a Judge that the further performance of substantial judicial functions by that Judge is not practicable. It might consist in the performance of non-judicial functions of such a nature that the capacity of the Judge to perform his or her judicial functions with integrity is compromised or impaired. Or it might consist in the performance of non-judicial functions of such a nature that public confidence in the integrity of the judiciary as an institution or in the capacity of the individual Judge to perform his or her judicial functions with integrity is diminished. Judges appointed to exercise the judicial power of the Commonwealth cannot be authorised to engage in the performance of non-judicial functions so as to prejudice the capacity either of the individual Judge or of the judiciary as an institution to discharge effectively the responsibilities of exercising the judicial power of the Commonwealth. So much is implied from the separation of powers mandated by Chs I, II and III of the Constitution and from the conditions necessary for the valid and effective exercise of judicial power.

... It is an eligible Judge's function of deciding independently of the applicant agency whether an interception warrant should issue that separates the eligible Judge from the executive function of law enforcement. It is the recognition of that independent role that preserves public confidence in the judiciary as an institution.

Wilson v Minister for Aboriginal and Torres Strait Islander Affairs shows that not only must a non-judicial function be performed independently in fact but also that a non-judicial function must be immunised from the mere potential for interference in order to avoid incompatibility. Judges acting *persona designata* must be and appear to be independent. The case also explains in more detail how the existence of incompatibility is determined.

Wilson v Minister for Aboriginal and Torres Strait Islander Affairs (1996) 189 CLR 1

Under the Aboriginal and Torres Strait Islander Heritage Protection Act 1984 *(Cth), the Minister could declare a particular site to be protected. The Act required that before making a declaration the Minister must receive a report prepared by a person appointed by the Minister describing various matters including the significance of the area to Aboriginal*

peoples, the extent of any threat of injury to the area, the extent of the area that should be protected, and what restrictions should be made in respect of the area. Justice Jane Matthews accepted appointment to conduct inquiries and provide a report to the Minister. The High Court held that the appointment of Justice Matthews was unlawful.

Brennan CJ, Dawson, Toohey, McHugh and Gummow JJ

[I]f the function of reporting is constitutionally incompatible with the holding of office as a Ch III judge, s 10(1)(c) must be read down so as to preclude the Minister's nomination of a person who holds office as a Ch III judge. So construed, s 10(1)(c) would afford no authority to the Minister to nominate Justice Mathews and consequently would deny to Justice Mathews the capacity to accept any purported nomination ... The constitutional condition on the vesting of non-judicial power in (or the conferring of a non-judicial function on) a Ch III judge is that the exercise of the power (or the performance of the function) be compatible with performance of judicial functions as stated in *Grollo*. When that condition is satisfied, judges not only are, but are seen to be, independent of the other branches of government. The appearance of independence preserves public confidence in the judicial branch.

... [The incompatibility doctrine's] purpose is to protect effectively the independence of Ch III judges from the political branches of government as a guarantee of liberty and as a buttress to public confidence in the administration of justice by Ch III courts ...

In the present case, the category of incompatibility that arises for consideration is "the performance of non-judicial functions of such a nature that public confidence in the integrity of the judiciary as an institution or in the capacity of the individual judge to perform his or her judicial functions with integrity is diminished".

[I]ncompatibility ... is discovered on the face of the statute, or on the face of those measures taken pursuant to a statute, that purports or purport to confer a non-judicial function on a Ch III judge. That is not to say that constitutional incompatibility is a matter of mere form. The operation of the statute or of the measures taken pursuant to it is ascertained by looking to the circumstances in which the purported function might be performed. Where a non-judicial power is purportedly conferred, constitutional incompatibility is ascertained by reference to the function that has to be performed to exercise the power.

The statute or the measures taken pursuant to the statute must be examined in order to determine, first, whether the function is an integral part of, or is closely connected with, the functions of the Legislature or the Executive Government. If the function is not closely connected with the Legislature or the Executive Government, no constitutional incompatibility appears.

Next, an answer must be given to the question whether the function is required to be performed independently of any instruction, advice or wish of the Legislature or the Executive Government, other than a law or an instrument made under a law (hereafter "any non-judicial instruction, advice or wish"). If an affirmative answer does not appear, it is clear that the separation has been breached. The breach is not capable of repair by the Ch III judge on whom the function is purportedly conferred, for the breach invalidates the conferral of the function.

If the function is one which must be performed independently of any non-judicial instruction, advice or wish, a further question arises: Is any discretion purportedly possessed by the Ch III judge to be exercised on political grounds – that is, on grounds that are not confined by factors expressly or impliedly prescribed by law?

In considering these questions, it will often be relevant to note whether the function to be performed must be performed judicially, that is, without bias and by a procedure that gives each interested person an opportunity to be heard and to deal with any case presented by those with opposing interests. An obligation to observe the requirements of procedural fairness is not necessarily indicative of compatibility with the holding of judicial office under Ch III, for many persons at various levels in the executive branch of government are obliged to observe those requirements. But, conversely, if a judicial manner of performance is not required, it is unlikely that the performance of the function will be performed free of political influence or without the prospect of exercising a political discretion ...

In ***Wilson***, the judge acting *persona designata* could be removed from her non-judicial function by a Minister and was subject to direction by a Minister. Although the judge was not in fact removed or in fact subject to direction, the potential for removal and direction gave rise to a breach of the incompatibility condition. In addition, the nature of the non-judicial function itself gave rise to a breach of the incompatibility condition. The High Court held that it is improper for a judge acting *persona designata* to give legal advice to government.

Wilson v Minister for Aboriginal and Torres Strait Islander Affairs (1996) 189 CLR 1

Brennan CJ, Dawson, Toohey, McHugh and Gummow JJ

The only power conferred by s 10 of the Act is the power conferred on the Minister to make a declaration. A report is no more than a condition precedent to the exercise of the Minister's power to make a declaration. The function of a reporter under s 10 is not performed by way of an independent review of an exercise of the Minister's power. It is performed as an integral part of the process of the Minister's exercise of power. The performance of such a function by a judge places the judge firmly in the echelons of administration, liable to removal by the Minister before the report is made and shorn of the usual judicial protections, in a position equivalent to that of a ministerial adviser ...

Significantly, the competing interests of Aboriginal applicants and of others whose proprietary or pecuniary interests are liable to be affected by the making of a declaration have to be determined. Such a determination is essentially a political function. A reporter may choose to act independently of the Minister in determining the interests to be preferred, but the Act does not require the reporter to disregard ministerial instruction, advice or wish in preparing the report. The report may be prepared so as to accord with ministerial policy. If the Minister has no policy instruction or intimation to give to the reporter, the reporter himself or herself must make political decisions: "the extent of the area that should be protected", "the prohibitions and restrictions to be made" and "the duration of any declaration". These decisions are not necessarily made by finding the nature and extent of an Aboriginal connection with the land or by an assessment of the extent to which Aboriginal beliefs or lifestyles are under threat. The decisions to be made by a reporter are political in character. In addition, the reporter is required by s 10(4)(g) to furnish advice to the Minister upon a question of law, namely, the extent to which the area in question is or may be protected by or under a law of a State or Territory. Yet the giving to the executive of advisory opinions on questions of law is quite alien to the exercise of the judicial power of the Commonwealth. The separation of the Ch III judge acting as reporter from the Minister has been breached. The function of reporting is therefore incompatible with the holding of office as a Ch III judge.

17.6 Non-separation of State judicial power

There has never been a case holding that ***Boilermakers'***-style separation of *State* judicial power exists, and the weight of authority and principle is against the idea.

The case law is clear that no ***Boilermakers'***-style separation of State judicial power arises from the State Constitution Acts. In ***Clyne v East***, the New South Wales Court of Appeal explained that the idea of a separation of State judicial power doctrine arising from State Constitutions would be inconsistent with the possession by State Parliaments of plenary legislative power.

Clyne v East (1967) 68 SR (NSW) 385

Sugerman JA

The Constitution of New South Wales is now embodied in the *Constitution Act, 1902*, as amended. The structure and provisions of that Act provide no ground for importing into it a similar principle of separation of power. Moreover, except in respects not here relevant, the Constitution is a flexible or uncontrolled Constitution. Section 5 of the Act provides: "5. The Legislature shall, subject to the provisions of the Commonwealth of Australia Constitution Act, have power to make laws for the peace, welfare and good government of New South Wales in all cases whatsoever ..." ...

Furthermore, *McCawley v The King* was itself a case of an ordinary Act of the legislature which was inconsistent with a provision of the Queensland *Constitution Act* as to the tenure of judges; the *Constitution Act* was held to possess no such special quality as to preclude its amendment by the methods which are appropriate in the case of any other statute.

In ***Kable v DPP (NSW)***, the High Court pointed out that, in the case of New South Wales, there is nothing in the text or structure of the *Constitution Act 1902* (NSW) comparable to the text and structure of Chapter III of the *Australian Constitution* that could give rise to a ***Boilermakers'***-type doctrine concerning State judicial power.

Kable v Director of Public Prosecutions (NSW) (1996) 189 CLR 51

Dawson J

The appellant contended that the [NSW] *Constitution Act 1902* embodies a separation of powers whereby the judicial power of the State is separated from its legislative and executive powers. As a consequence, he said, judicial power is exercisable only by the judiciary, which is incapable of exercising functions which are not judicial or ancillary thereto. However, there is nothing in the structure of the *Constitution Act 1902* to support this contention.

That Act vests legislative power in the legislature and leaves unaffected the exercise of executive power through the Governor otherwise than on the advice of the Executive Council. There is provision for the continuance of an Executive Council and the Premier and other Ministers of the Crown are to be appointed from its members. Whilst Pt 9 of that Act is headed "The Judiciary" nowhere does it provide that the judicial power of the State is vested in the judiciary. Section 53, which is contained in Pt 9, provides that no holder of judicial office may be removed from office save on an address of both Houses of Parliament seeking removal on the ground of proved misbehaviour or incapacity. There are additional provisions relating to the suspension of judicial office and the fixing or changing of retirement age. Section 56 provides that Pt 9 does not prevent abolition by legislation of a judicial office whether that be done directly or indirectly by the abolition of a court or part of a court.

Whilst these provisions are concerned with the preservation of judicial independence, they cannot be seen as reposing the exercise of judicial power exclusively in the holders of judicial office. Nor can they be seen as precluding the exercise of non-judicial power by persons in their capacity as holders of judicial office. They clearly do not constitute an exhaustive statement of the manner in which the judicial power of the State is or may be vested. Had Pt 9 attempted such an exercise it would have cut across a long history of the exercise of non-judicial power by the courts and the exercise of judicial power by bodies exercising non-judicial functions.

Even if a State Constitution Act had text or a structure similar to Chapter III of the *Australian Constitution,* the reasoning in ***Clyne v East*** (and the discussion in Chapter 2) makes clear that any inconsistent legislation would be taken to impliedly repeal that text or structure.

There are observations in High Court judgments to the effect that there is definitely not any ***Boilermakers'***-style separation of State judicial power arising from any source.

K-Generation Pty Ltd v Liquor Licensing Court (2009) 237 CLR 501

Gummow, Hayne, Heydon, Crennan and Kiefel JJ

There is no doubt that ... the State legislatures may confer judicial powers on a body that is not a "court of a State" and that in respect of a body that is a "court of a State", they may confer non-judicial powers.

In ***Duncan v New South Wales***, the High Court avoided deciding whether Chapter III of the *Australian Constitution* requires a separation of State judicial power.

Duncan v New South Wales (2015) 255 CLR 388

French CJ, Hayne, Kiefel, Bell, Gageler, Keane and Nettle JJ

Second, it is contended that the Amendment Act is a legislative exercise of judicial power by that Parliament, contrary to what is argued to be an implied limitation, which derives either from an historical limitation on colonial legislative power unaffected by the *Australia Act 1986* (Cth) or from Ch III of the *Constitution* ...

The Amendment Act is not an exercise of judicial power by that Parliament. The existence and scope of any implied limitation on the ability of a State Parliament to exercise judicial power therefore does not arise for consideration and is not explored in these reasons for judgment ...

The Amendment Act cannot be characterised as an exercise of judicial power. The argument that the Amendment Act contravenes an implied limitation on State legislative power therefore fails on its minor premise without the need to examine its major premise.

The idea that a ***Boilermakers'***-style separation of State judicial power arises from the *Australian Constitution* is inconsistent with the reasoning in ***Clyne v East***. That case reflects the settled understanding that the States possess plenary legislative power, which, as Chapter 2 explained, is a close approximation of the British idea of parliamentary sovereignty.

While there is no ***Boilermakers'***-style separation of State judicial power, there are two key limitations on what States can do in respect of judicial power and courts arising from Chapter III of the *Australian Constitution*. Chapter 16 considers the first limitation: States cannot authorise entities that are not 'courts' to exercise federal jurisdiction or authorise 'courts' to exercise federal judicial power in a manner inconsistent with Chapter III. Chapter 19 considers the second limitation: States cannot impair the institutional integrity of any entity that is a 'court'.

17.7 DISCUSSION QUESTIONS

1. What is the reasoning underlying the ***Boilermakers'*** doctrine?
2. Could Parliament vest federal judicial power in a New Zealand court on the basis that a New Zealand court answers the description of 'such other courts as it invests with federal jurisdiction'?
3. Is the distinction between judges acting as judges and judges acting *persona designata* a distinction without difference?
4. Make (1) a list of the inquiries relevant to determining incompatibility for the purposes of the *persona designata* doctrine and (2) a list of practical examples of incompatibility.

5. Problem question: Consider the following hypothetical legislation and scenario. The Commonwealth Parliament enacts the *Terrorist Control Orders Tribunal Act 2023.* The statute provides:

    1. The Control Orders Tribunal is hereby established.
    2. The Control Orders Tribunal is comprised of a person appointed by the Governor-General who is:
        a. a judge of the Federal Circuit Court of Australia, and
        b. consents to his or her appointment to the Tribunal.
    3. An appointment to the Control Orders Tribunal is for a period of five years.
    4. The Control Orders Tribunal must issue a control order against a person confining that person to their place of usual residence between the hours of 10 pm and 6 am if:
        a. the Commissioner of the Australian Federal police makes an application for a control in respect of the person, and
        b. the Control Orders Tribunal is satisfied that the person has been convicted of a criminal offence.

    You are the lawyer for a person who is subject to a control order. Your client wants to know whether there are any constitutional arguments available to him to challenge the statute. Advise.

NON-JUDICIAL DETENTION

18

18.1 Overview

This chapter examines the extent to which detention otherwise than as punishment for a crime is constitutionally permissible. Chapter 17 explained that only Chapter III courts may exercise federal judicial power, and Chapter 16 explained that punishment is an exclusively judicial function. There is a general presumption that detention serves punitive purposes. It follows that a federal law may not authorise the Federal Executive Government to detain a person for punitive purposes otherwise than as a judicially-imposed punishment.

A body of case law has developed explaining the extent to which detention otherwise than as punishment for a crime is constitutionally permissible. The basic proposition is that detention for non-punitive purposes is not judicial in character, and that this remains so even if the conditions of detention are prison-like or harsh. Detention must be limited to what is reasonably necessary for non-punitive purposes, otherwise the presumption that detention is punitive in character will apply and render the detention unconstitutional.

Most of the case law concerns immigration detention, but the general principles are not limited to that context.

Key concepts considered in this chapter include:

- detention
- non-judicial detention
- non-punitive purpose
- reasonably necessary.

18.2 Detention is presumed to serve punitive purposes

It is settled law that the adjudication and punishment of criminal guilt is exclusively judicial in character. It follows that any federal law authorising a non-Chapter III court to inflict punishment is invalid because it will breach Chapter III's separation of federal judicial power (see Chapter 17).

What has become known as the ***Lim*** principle holds that a law requiring or authorising detention by the Federal Executive Government otherwise than as punishment imposed by a court for criminal offending is *presumed* to serve punitive purposes; where that presumption is not rebutted, such a law contravenes the separation of federal judicial power mandated by Chapter III. However, detention will be non-judicial in character, and therefore not part of federal judicial power, where:

1. the detention has a non-punitive purpose, and
2. the detention goes no further than what is reasonably necessary to achieve that non-punitive purpose.

Chu Kheng Lim v Minister for Immigration, Local Government and Ethnic Affairs (1992) 176 CLR 1

Brennan, Deane and Dawson JJ

In exclusively entrusting to the courts designated by Ch III the function of the adjudgment and punishment of criminal guilt under a law of the Commonwealth, the Constitution's concern is with substance and not mere form. It would, for example, be beyond the legislative power of the Parliament to invest the Executive with an arbitrary power to detain citizens in custody notwithstanding that the power was conferred in terms which sought to divorce such detention in custody from both punishment and criminal guilt. The reason why that is so is that, putting to one side the exceptional cases to which reference is made below, the involuntary detention of a citizen in custody by the State is penal or punitive in character and, under our system of government, exists only as an incident of the exclusively judicial function of adjudging and punishing criminal guilt ...

There are some qualifications which must be made to the general proposition that the power to order that a citizen be involuntarily confined in custody is, under the doctrine of the separation of judicial from executive and legislative powers enshrined in our Constitution, part of the judicial power of the Commonwealth entrusted exclusively to Ch III courts. The most important is that ... the arrest and detention in custody, pursuant to executive warrant, of a person accused of crime to ensure that he or she is available to be dealt with by the courts. Such committal to custody awaiting trial is not seen by the law as punitive or as appertaining exclusively to judicial power. Even where exercisable by the Executive, however, the power to detain a person in custody pending trial is ordinarily subject to the supervisory jurisdiction of the courts ... to order that a person committed to prison while awaiting trial be admitted to bail. Involuntary detention in cases of mental illness or infectious disease can also legitimately be seen as non-punitive in character and as not necessarily involving the exercise of judicial power ...

In this Court, it has been consistently recognized that the power of the Parliament to make laws with respect to aliens includes not only the power to make laws providing for the expulsion or deportation of aliens by the Executive but extends to authorizing the Executive to restrain an alien in custody to the extent necessary to make the deportation effective ...

It can therefore be said that the legislative power conferred by s 51(xix) of the Constitution encompasses the conferral upon the Executive of authority to detain (or to direct the detention of) an alien in custody for the purposes of expulsion or deportation. Such authority to detain an alien in custody, when conferred upon the Executive in the context and for the purposes of an executive power of deportation or expulsion, constitutes an incident of that executive power. By analogy, authority to detain an alien in custody, when conferred in the context and for the purposes of executive powers to receive, investigate and determine an application by that alien for an entry permit and (after determination) to admit or deport, constitutes an incident of those executive powers. Such limited authority to detain an alien in custody can be conferred on the Executive without infringement of Ch III's exclusive vesting of the judicial power of the Commonwealth in the courts which it designates. The reason why that is so is that, to that limited extent, authority to detain in custody is neither punitive in nature (See, generally, *Ex parte Walsh and Johnson; In re Yates* (1925) 37 CLR, at pp 60–61, 96; *O'Keefe v Calwell* (1949) 77 CLR, at p 278; *Koon Wing Lau v Calwell* (1949) 80 CLR, at p 555; *Chu Shao Hung v The Queen* (1953) 87 CLR, at p 589) nor part of the judicial power of the Commonwealth. When conferred upon the Executive, it takes its character from the executive powers to exclude, admit and deport of which it is an incident ...

In ***Lim***, a law enacted under section 51(xix) (the 'aliens power': see Chapter 7) included provisions requiring the detention in custody of a certain sub-class of aliens for the purpose of either facilitating their deportation or processing any application for an individual's lawful admission to Australia. The High Court held that the provisions served non-punitive purposes and limited detention to what was reasonably necessary to achieve those purposes. It followed that the detention was not judicial in character and did not breach Chapter III.

Chu Kheng Lim v Minister for Immigration, Local Government and Ethnic Affairs (1992) 176 CLR 1

Brennan, Deane and Dawson JJ

In the light of what has been said above, the two sections will be valid laws if the detention which they require and authorize is limited to what is reasonably capable of being seen as necessary for the purposes of deportation or necessary to enable an application for an entry permit to be made and considered. On the other hand, if the detention which those sections require and authorize is not so limited, the authority which they purportedly confer upon the Executive cannot properly be seen as an incident of the executive powers to exclude, admit and deport an alien. In that event, they will be of a punitive nature and contravene Ch III's insistence that the judicial power of the Commonwealth be vested exclusively in the courts which it designates ...

Section 54P(1) sets the context in which the other provisions of Div 4B operate. It provides that an officer must remove a designated person from Australia as soon as practicable if the designated person asks the Minister, in writing, to be removed. It follows that, under Div 4B, it always lies within the power of a designated person to bring his or her detention in custody to an end by requesting to be removed from Australia. Once such a request has been made, further detention in custody is authorized by Div 4B only for the limited period involved, in the circumstances of a particular case, in complying with the statutory requirement of removal "as soon as practicable". It is only if an alien who is a designated person elects, by failing to make a request under s 54P(1), to remain in the country as an applicant for an entry permit that detention under Div 4B can continue. In the context of that power of a designated person to bring his or her detention in custody under Div 4B to an end at any time, the time limitations imposed by other provisions of the Division suffice, in our view, to preclude a conclusion that the powers of detention which are conferred upon the Executive exceed what is reasonably capable of being seen as necessary for the purposes of deportation or for the making and consideration of an entry application.

It follows that the powers of detention in custody conferred by ss 54L and 54N are an incident of the executive powers of exclusion, admission and deportation of aliens and are not, of their nature, part of the judicial power of the Commonwealth.

M68 holds that the ***Lim*** principle applies only in cases where detention is by the Commonwealth. *M68* concerned the participation by the Federal Executive Government in the detention of a person by a foreign country. A majority of the High Court – French CJ, Kiefel, Nettle and Keane JJ – held that the *Lim* principle is engaged only where detention is either in the custody of the Commonwealth or is controlled by the Commonwealth. *Lim* has nothing to say about the validity of the Federal Executive Government assisting a foreign government to detain a person under foreign law. In such a situation, the Federal Executive Government is not detaining anyone and therefore is not exercising federal judicial power.

M68 involved a challenge to the then regime of mandatory detention of asylum seekers in Nauru. Australia entered into an agreement with the Government of Nauru under which the Nauruan Government would detain asylum seekers on Nauruan territory in return for Australia providing the funds necessary to operate the detention regime. In the High Court, it was argued that the Australian law authorising the Australian Government to enter into the agreement with Nauru and to make the necessary payments to Nauru breached the principle in ***Lim***. The High Court held that the Commonwealth was not detaining anyone.

Plaintiff M68/2015 v Minister for Immigration and Border Protection (2016) 257 CLR 42

French CJ, Kiefel and Nettle JJ

The central question identified by the plaintiff is whether the Commonwealth's involvement in her detention was authorised by a valid Commonwealth statute.

It is necessary at the outset to be clear about who detained the plaintiff on Nauru. "Detention" in this context is detention in the custody of the State and involves the exercise of governmental power ...

Contrary to the plaintiff's submissions, it is very much to the point that the restrictions applied to the plaintiff are to be regarded as the independent exercise of sovereign legislative and executive power by Nauru. The recognition that it was Nauru that detained the plaintiff is important, for it is central to the plaintiff's case that the legislative authority which the Commonwealth required, and which it is argued was not provided, is an authority to detain the plaintiff, with the concomitant power to authorise others to effect that detention ...

The plaintiff contends that her detention on Nauru was "funded, authorised, caused, procured and effectively controlled by, and was at the will of, the Commonwealth". She relies upon the statement in *Lim* that an officer of the Commonwealth Executive who "purports to authorize or enforce the detention in custody of ... an alien" without judicial mandate will be acting lawfully only to the extent that their conduct is justified by a valid statutory provision.

Clearly the Commonwealth sought the assistance of Nauru with respect to the processing of claims by persons such as the plaintiff. It may be accepted that the Commonwealth was aware that Nauru required the plaintiff to be detained. In order to obtain Nauru's agreement to receive the plaintiff, the Commonwealth funded the Centre and the services provided there in accordance with the Administrative Arrangements. The Commonwealth concedes the causal connection between its conduct and the plaintiff's detention. It may be accepted that its involvement was materially supportive, if not a necessary condition, of Nauru's physical capacity to detain the plaintiff. But, for the reasons given above, it cannot be said that the Commonwealth thereby authorised or controlled the plaintiff's detention in the sense discussed in *Lim*. That is sufficient to remove the basis for the plaintiff's reliance upon what was said in that case ...

Contrary to the plaintiff's submissions, *Lim* does not refer more generally to a "concept of 'authorise or enforce' detention" which extends to a situation in which the detention is "not actually implemented" by the Commonwealth and its officers. Lim has nothing to say about the validity of actions of the Commonwealth and its officers in participating in the detention of an alien by another State ...

Keane J

It is important to appreciate that the statement of constitutional principle from *Lim* on which the plaintiff's argument rests is concerned with "detention in custody" by the Commonwealth. That statement elaborates one consequence of the separation of judicial power from the other governmental powers of the Commonwealth effected by Ch III of the Constitution. This principle is engaged by the statutory conferral upon the Commonwealth Executive of the power to detain a person in custody for the purpose of punishment, that power being essentially judicial in character. It may be noted at this point that the actual decision in *Lim* recognised that laws for the detention by the Executive of aliens necessary to enable their deportation are not punitive in character; but the point of central importance is that the relevant limitation on Commonwealth legislative power is concerned with detention of an alien in the custody of the Commonwealth; that is, with the legal authority of the Commonwealth to hold an alien in detention.

The plaintiff's detention in Nauru was not detention in the custody of the Commonwealth ... The plaintiff's detention in Nauru was in the custody of the Republic of Nauru. That is because the legal authority by which she was held in custody in Nauru, an independent sovereign nation, was that of Nauru and not that of the Commonwealth. While it might be said that the Commonwealth's arrangements with Nauru procured or funded or caused restraints over the plaintiff's liberty, the plaintiff's detention in custody was a consequence of the exercise of governmental power, being that of Nauru, an independent sovereign State.

There was no suggestion in the Special Case that the Commonwealth requested or required that the Nauruan regime of detention in custody be put in place. Indeed, to the contrary, the parties agreed that it was the fact that, if Nauru had not sought to impose these restrictions on the plaintiff, none of the Commonwealth, the Minister, Transfield or its subcontractors would have sought to impose such restraints over the plaintiff's liberty in Nauru or asserted any right to impose such restraints.

Accordingly, the limitation on Commonwealth executive power discussed in *Lim* is not engaged in the circumstances of this case ...

Two judges – Bell and Gageler JJ – held that the ***Lim*** principle applies to cases where the Federal Executive Government *participates in* a person's detention by a foreign country. The logic underlying this position was recognition that the federal law authorising that participation might serve punitive purposes and therefore involve judicial power. However, on the facts of this case, these judges found that the *Lim* principle had not been breached.

Plaintiff M68/2015 v Minister for Immigration and Border Protection (2016) 257 CLR 42

Bell J

The constitutional holding in *Lim* is that a law, authorising or requiring the detention in custody of an alien without judicial warrant, will not contravene Ch III of the Constitution provided the detention that the law authorises or requires is limited to that which is reasonably capable of being seen as necessary for the purposes of deportation or for the purposes of enabling an application by the alien to enter and remain in Australia to be investigated and determined. So limited, the detention is an incident of executive power. If not so limited, the detention is punitive in character and ceases to be lawful.

There is no principled reason why the Parliament may confer a power on the Commonwealth to cause and effectively control the detention of an alien taken from Australia, to a country which has been designated by Australia as a regional processing country, without being subject to the same constitutional limitations as apply to the detention of aliens for the purposes of processing their protection claims in Australia.

In my opinion, the plaintiff's invocation of the *Lim* principle fails, not because that principle has no application but because her detention in Nauru did not infringe the principle ...

Gageler J

The plaintiff's argument that s 198AHA is inconsistent with Ch III of the Constitution warrants closer consideration. The plaintiff does not argue that executive detention of a non-citizen outside Australia pending assessment of a claim by that non-citizen to refugee status is detention for a purpose that is inherently incompatible with Ch III. The plaintiff accepts the application of the holding in *Chu Kheng Lim* to the purpose of regional processing: that authority to detain an alien in custody can constitute a valid incident of executive power. What the plaintiff argues is that a legislative mandate for executive detention must be for no longer than is reasonably necessary for the administrative processes required to carry that purpose into effect. Section 198AHA, the plaintiff argues, does not have that requisite characteristic.

I accept the major premise of the plaintiff's Ch III argument. I have recently explained my understanding that no law conferring a power of executive detention could escape characterisation as punitive (and therefore as transgressing on the inherently judicial) unless the duration of that detention meets at least two conditions. The duration of the detention must be reasonably necessary to effectuate a purpose which is identified in the statute conferring the power to detain and which is capable of fulfilment. The duration of the detention must also be capable of objective determination by a court at any time and from time to time. In that regard, I see no principled reason to distinguish between a law which confers a power of executive detention and a law which confers a capacity for executive detention so as to allow for the exercise of power from another legislative source.

On its proper construction, however, I am satisfied that s 198AHA meets those conditions ...

The High Court has consistently affirmed the ***Lim*** principle. In ***Plaintiff M96A***, the High Court summarised the principle.

Plaintiff M96A/2016 v Commonwealth (2017) 261 CLR 582

Kiefel CJ, Bell, Keane, Nettle, Gordon and Edelman JJ

As has been reiterated on a number of occasions in this Court, the majority in *Chu Kheng Lim v Minister for Immigration* said that laws with respect to aliens within s 51(xix) of the Constitution, which authorise or require the Executive to detain non-citizens in custody, will not contravene Ch III of the Constitution if, and only if, "the detention which they require and authorize is limited to what is reasonably capable of being seen as necessary for the purposes of deportation or necessary to enable an application for an entry permit to be made and considered". This requires two matters to be considered. First, it requires the purpose of the detention to be identified. Secondly, it requires consideration of the time necessarily involved in the particular case to deport the non-citizen or to receive, investigate, consider, and determine an application for permission to remain in Australia ...

In ***Falzon***, the High Court emphasised that the ***Lim*** principle is not about a constitutionally guaranteed freedom from executive detention. The *Lim* principle is about enforcing the constitutionally-mandated separation of federal judicial power.

Falzon v Minister for Immigration and Border Protection (2018) 351 ALR 61

Kiefel CJ, Bell, Keane and Edelman JJ

In *Lim*, this Court confirmed that the power to adjudge and to punish guilt for an offence against a law of the Commonwealth is exclusive to the Ch III judiciary under the Commonwealth Constitution. Chapter III therefore prevents the enactment of any law purporting to vest any part of that function in the Commonwealth Executive Government. The plaintiff seeks to clarify the statement of principle in *Lim* in one respect. He submits that the exclusive power is to "adjudge guilt of, *or* determine punishment for, breach of the law". On this view, it is sufficient for invalidity, by reference to Ch III, if the statutory provision punishes a person for an offence. This does not appear to be disputed by the defendant.

One form of punishment is involuntary detention. In *Lim* it was said that it would be beyond the legislative power of the Parliament to invest the Executive with arbitrary power to detain citizens in custody notwithstanding that the power was conferred in terms which sought to divorce such detention in custody from both punishment and criminal guilt. That is because the involuntary detention of a citizen in custody by the State is penal or punitive in character and under our system of government exists only as an incident of the exclusively judicial function of adjudging or punishing criminal guilt.

The plaintiff accepts that not all laws authorising or requiring detention will infringe Ch III. In *Lim* it was held that the legislative power conferred by s 51(xix) of the Constitution encompasses the conferral on the Executive of authority to detain an alien for the purposes of expulsion or deportation. Such an authority constitutes an incident of the executive power of deportation or expulsion. This limited authority to detain an alien in custody can be conferred upon the Executive without infringing Ch III because the authority to detain is neither punitive in nature nor part of the judicial power of the Commonwealth. When conferred on the Executive it takes its character from the executive power to exclude or deport ...

Contrary to the plaintiff's submissions, these decisions do not establish that there is a constitutionally guaranteed freedom from executive detention ...

In the joint judgment in *Lim* the issue was raised whether two of the statutory provisions there in question, which required a designated person to be detained and kept in custody, were valid by reference to Ch III. The issue was stated to be whether the detention so authorised and required is "reasonably capable of being seen as necessary for the purposes of deportation or necessary to enable an application for an entry permit to be made and considered". If the detention is not limited to those purposes, their Honours said, the authority conferred on the Executive "cannot properly be seen as an incident of the executive powers to exclude, admit and deport an alien. In that event, they will be of a punitive nature and contravene Ch III's insistence that the judicial power of the Commonwealth be vested exclusively in the courts which it designates." ...

The starting point for the enquiry referred to in *Lim* is that the power to remove or deport aliens from a country is executive in nature and it is non-punitive. The question which then arises with respect to a statutory power given to the Executive to detain an alien in custody is whether it is given in order to facilitate or effect the removal of that person, which is the subject of executive power. The enquiry is as to whether it is "necessary" to that purpose. If it is, it may be considered to be an incident of the executive power and will not be an exercise of judicial power. If the power goes further than to achieve that limited purpose it may be otherwise. In such circumstance, it may be inferred that the law has a purpose of its own, a purpose to effect punishment ...

It may nevertheless be accepted that a legislative power to detain must be justified, in the sense that it must be shown to be directed to a purpose other than to punish ...

Falzon also emphasises that the principle in ***Lim*** applies only to laws requiring or authorising detention. The challenge in *Falzon* was to a statutory provision requiring the cancellation of the visa of persons convicted of serious criminal offences. A person without a valid visa was liable to detention pursuant to other statutory provisions (which had previously been upheld as valid by the High Court) for the purposes of facilitating the person's deportation. The High Court held that a *Lim* challenge to the provision requiring visa cancellations was misconceived because that provision did not require or authorise detention.

Falzon v Minister for Immigration and Border Protection (2018) 351 ALR 61

Kiefel CJ, Bell, Keane and Edelman JJ

A cancellation decision has the immediate effect that the person's status is changed from that of a lawful non-citizen to an unlawful non-citizen. Section 501(3A) merely provides the basis for the change in status. It does not authorise detention. It is that new status that exposes the person to detention under s 189 ...

Gageler and Gordon JJ

In short, the principle in *Lim* is engaged only by laws that require or authorise detention. Section 501(3A) does not take on that character, and does not engage the principle in *Lim*, simply because a person whose visa is cancelled under that provision becomes liable to be detained under different provisions (none of which were themselves suggested to be invalid) ...

18.3 Non-punitive purposes

The first condition necessary for a federal law requiring or authorising detention to escape characterisation as a purported exercise of judicial power is that the law have non-punitive purposes. The case law has identified a variety of non-punitive purposes.

In ***Lim*** (extracted above), the High Court identified several examples where detention serves non-punitive purposes, including:

- arrest and detention in custody, pursuant to executive warrant, of a person accused of a crime to ensure that he or she is available to be dealt with by the courts
- involuntary detention of a person in cases of mental illness or infectious disease for the protection of the individual and community
- detention of aliens to facilitate their expulsion or deportation, and
- detention of aliens to enable their applications for an entry permit to be made and considered.

The High Court has emphasised the purpose of detention is to be assessed objectively taking into account all of the circumstances.

Plaintiff M96A/2016 v Commonwealth (2017) 261 CLR 582

Kiefel CJ, Bell, Keane, Nettle, Gordon and Edelman JJ

[T]he purpose of … detention is assessed objectively by reference to all of the circumstances.

In ***Kruger***, the High Court held that the detention of Indigenous children at 'Aboriginal reserves' by the Chief Protector of Aborigines (who was the children's legal guardian) during the early part of the twentieth century in the Northern Territory served non-punitive welfare purposes.

Kruger v Commonwealth ('Stolen Generations Case') (1997) 190 CLR 1

Dawson J

The plaintiffs contend that the actions of which they complain amounted to the exercise of judicial power otherwise than by courts constituted in accordance with Ch III of the Constitution and hence could not be validly authorised by the 1918 Ordinance. That contention is dependent upon acceptance of the view that the removal and detention of Aboriginal children pursuant to the powers conferred by the 1918 Ordinance were of a penal character and hence constituted judicial rather than executive functions. It is by no means apparent that this view can be sustained. However much one may with hindsight debate the appropriateness of the actions authorised by the 1918 Ordinance, those actions may legitimately be seen as non-punitive. The

Chief Protector (and then the Director) was the legal guardian of Aboriginals and that position, although its precise scope was uncertain, clearly imposed an obligation to act in the interests of the Aboriginal community but did not involve the performance of judicial functions. No relevant decision could legitimately be taken under the 1918 Ordinance without regard to the interests of Aboriginals involved and those of the wider Aboriginal population. No doubt it may be said with justification that the events in question did not promote the welfare of Aboriginals, but that does not mean that the decisions made and the actions taken were of a judicial rather than an executive character ...

Toohey J

Judged by current standards, the involuntary detention of an Aboriginal pursuant to such a provision as s 16 of the Ordinance could hardly be brought within any of the recognised exceptions to the general proposition. Conscious of this, the Commonwealth submitted that the welfare and protection object of the legislation must be judged by the values and standards prevailing at the time. The plaintiffs' reply was that, even by the standards prevailing in 1918, the Ordinance was one which expressly contemplated permanent institutionalisation and carried an unqualified power of indefinite detention, unlimited by the objects or circumstances of necessity said to justify that power.

A welfare purpose is evident in the legislation, emphasised by the legislative history to which reference has been made. The Chief Protector (and later the Director) was the legal guardian of Aboriginals. His duties, identified in s 5(1), included the distribution of forms of "relief or assistance to the aboriginals", the supply of food and shelter, medicine, provision for custody, maintenance and education and

> (f) to exercise a general supervision and care over all matters affecting the welfare of the aboriginals, and to protect them against immorality, injustice, imposition and fraud.

Section 6(1) empowered the Chief Protector

> to undertake the care, custody, or control of any aboriginal or half-caste, if, in his opinion it is necessary or desirable in the interests of the aboriginal or half-caste for him to do so.

The responsibility for welfare cast upon the Chief Protector is at odds with the notion that the powers conferred by the Ordinance are of themselves punitive and necessarily involve the exercise of judicial power[166]. And this is the argument with which we are presently concerned. While this does not necessarily provide an answer to other bases of the plaintiffs' claim, the argument based on judicial power cannot succeed ...

Gummow J

The powers of the Chief Protector to take persons into custody and care under the 1918 Ordinance were, whilst that law was in force, and are now, reasonably capable of being seen as necessary for a legitimate non-punitive purpose (namely the welfare and protection of those persons) rather than the attainment of any punitive objective.

This is apparent from various matters. There is the creation of legal guardianship in the Chief Protector by s 7, the specification in s 5(1) of the duties of the Chief Protector, the conditioning of the power under s 6 by an opinion as to exercise of the power being necessary or desirable in the interests of the persons in question for the Chief Protector to take them into care and custody, the exclusion from the operation of s 16 of those persons for whom, in the opinion of the Chief Protector, "satisfactory provision is otherwise made", and the existence before 1918 of long-established statutory regimes in the colonies and States which were directed to the welfare and protection of other indigenous persons ...

In ***Al-Kateb***, a majority of the High Court held that a law does not lose its non-punitive purpose simply because that purpose is impossible to achieve, or is unlikely to be achieved, in the foreseeable future in a particular case. In this case, Mr Al-Kateb, a stateless asylum seeker of Palestinian origin, was detained for the purpose of facilitating his deportation as soon as reasonably practicable. Deportation was practically impossible in the foreseeable future because no country would agree to receive Al-Kateb. A majority of the High Court held that the purpose of Al-Kateb's detention was to facilitate his deportation as soon as reasonably practicable. The reality that Al-Kateb might be detained indefinitely did not change the purpose for which he was detained.

Al-Kateb v Godwin (2004) 219 CLR 562

McHugh J

[T]he continued detention of a person who cannot be deported immediately infringe Ch III of the Constitution. Chapter III is always infringed where the detention of a person other than by a curial order – whatever the purpose of the detention – is authorised by a law of the Commonwealth and imposes punishment ...

A law requiring the detention of the alien takes its character from the purpose of the detention. As long as the purpose of the detention is to make the alien available for deportation or to prevent the alien from entering Australia or the Australian community, the detention is non-punitive. The Parliament of the Commonwealth is entitled, in accordance with the power conferred by s 51(xix) and without infringing Ch III of the Constitution, to take such steps as are likely to ensure that unlawful non-citizens do not enter Australia or become part of the Australian community and that they are available for deportation when that becomes practicable ...

Nor is it possible to hold that detention of unlawful non-citizens – even where their deportation is not achievable – cannot be reasonably regarded as effectuating the purpose of preventing them from entering Australia or entering or remaining in the Australian community. Indeed, detention is the surest way of achieving that object. If the Parliament of the Commonwealth enacts laws that direct the executive government to detain unlawful non-citizens in circumstances that prevent them from having contact with members of or removing them from the Australian community, nothing in the Constitution – including Ch III – prevents the Parliament doing so. For such laws, the Parliament and those who introduce them must answer to the electors, to the international bodies who supervise human rights treaties to which Australia is a party and to history. Whatever criticism some – maybe a great many – Australians make of such laws, their constitutionality is not open to doubt.

Hayne J

It is essential to confront the contention that, because the time at which detention will end cannot be predicted, its indefinite duration (even, so it is said, for the life of the detainee) is or will become punitive. The answer to that is simple but must be made. If that is the result, it comes about because the non-citizen came to or remained in this country without permission. The removal of an unlawful non-citizen from Australia then depends upon the willingness of some other country to receive that person. If the unlawful non-citizen is stateless, as is Mr Al-Kateb, there is no nation state which Australia may ask to receive its citizen. And if Australia is unwilling to extend refuge to those who have no country of nationality to which they may look both for protection and a home, the continued exclusion of such persons from the Australian community in accordance with the regime established by the Migration Act does not impinge upon the separation of powers required by the Constitution ...

Callinan J

The fact that deportation may not be imminent, or even that no current prediction as to a date and place of it can be made, does not mean that the purpose of the detention, deportation, has been or should be regarded as abandoned ...

Behrooz holds that detention for a non-punitive purpose does not become punitive in character simply because the conditions of detention are harsh. The High Court explained that the lawfulness of detention and the lawfulness of the conditions of detention are separate issues. ***Lim*** is concerned only with the lawfulness of detention. Harsh conditions of detention may be remedied by the application of criminal law, tort law and administrative law.

Behrooz v Secretary, Department of Immigration and Multicultural and Indigenous Affairs (2004) 219 CLR 486

Gleeson CJ

In the case of a citizen, what is punitive in nature about involuntary detention (subject to a number of exceptions) is the deprivation of liberty involved. But an alien does not have a right without permission to enter Australia or to become part of the community. The alien's vulnerability to exclusion and deportation alters the nature of the detention when it is for the purpose described above. It is an incident of the executive power to exclude people who have no right to enter Australia, to process their applications for permission to enter, and to deport them if their applications fail.

That being the nature of the power of detention, there is no warrant for concluding that, if the conditions of detention are sufficiently harsh, there will come a point where the detention itself can be regarded as punitive, and an invalid exercise of judicial power. Whatever the conditions of detention, the detention itself involves involuntary deprivation of liberty. For a citizen, that alone would ordinarily constitute punishment. But for an alien, the detention is an incident of the exclusion and deportation to which an alien is vulnerable. Harsh conditions of detention may violate the civil rights of an alien. An alien does not stand outside the protection of the civil and criminal law. If an officer in a detention centre assaults a detainee, the officer will be liable to prosecution, or damages. If those who manage a detention centre fail to comply with their duty of care, they may be liable in tort. But the assault, or the negligence, does not alter the nature of the detention. It remains detention for the statutory purpose identified above. The detention is not for a punitive purpose. The detainee is deprived of his or her liberty, but not as a form of punishment ...

Callinan J

It is the appellant's principal submission that if the conditions of his detention can be shown to be inhumane in fact, the detention is in substance punitive no matter how it is described, and indeed, regardless of any expressed purpose. As to this, the respondents' argument should be accepted: that the appellant's submission conflates two separate issues, of the unlawful authority to detain, on the one hand, and of the conditions within detention on the other. The constitutional requirement of the exercise of judicial power by the judiciary is only infringed if the conferral of authority to detain does not fall within an exceptional class not of a punitive character. The question whether the law authorizing detention (and saying nothing about the conditions of it) is reasonably capable of being seen as necessary for a legitimate purpose within the aliens power, cannot be concerned with a qualitative assessment of the conditions of detention. It is concerned with the purpose of the law authorizing detention.

The appellant accepts that the Act and the detention under it do not deprive him of his right to sue in tort or to pursue other causes of action generally available to citizens and others in the community. Similarly, it may be that remedies would be available for infringement of, or failure to comply with, regulations or guidelines (if any) governing or affecting immigration detention ...

Re Woolley holds that detention for a non-punitive purpose does not become punitive in character simply because the conditions of detention might be more severe for a particular or more vulnerable sub-class of detainees. This case considered an argument that a law requiring the detention of asylum seekers for the purpose of facilitating their deportation or processing applications for entry permits was punitive in its application to child asylum seekers because they felt the conditions of detention more severely than did adult asylum seekers.

Re Woolley (2004) 225 CLR 1

Gleeson CJ

Nowhere was it suggested, in the reasoning of Brennan, Deane and Dawson JJ, or Mason CJ, or any member of the Court, that the power of detention conferred by the legislation in that case would take on a different character if, in its application to some particular detainees, or some class of detainees, it was capable of causing particular hardship. One of the most obvious features of the system of mandatory detention considered in *Chu Kheng Lim*, as of the system with which this case is concerned, is that it does not address the particular circumstances of individual detainees. That is the difference between mandatory and discretionary detention. If the possibility of the severity of the operation of mandatory detention in a particular case or class of case altered the character of the power of detention from an incident of executive power to extra-judicial and unconstitutional punishment, then the system of mandatory detention would have been found unconstitutional. Furthermore, it is impossible to identify the criterion by which severity of application would be measured. There is no reason why it would be limited to children, or to some children. Children might constitute a class whose members would include specially vulnerable people, but so would the elderly, the infirm, and perhaps others ...

Gummow J

Once it is accepted that administrative detention of alien children is reasonably capable of being seen as necessary for a permitted purpose, the circumstance that such detention may have serious or injurious effects on those children does not necessarily constrain the scope of the aliens power. The effects of detention will be relevant only to the extent that they are indicative of the purpose for which detention is authorised ...

Hayne J

For present purposes, it is important to recognise that *Chu Kheng Lim v Minister for Immigration* decided that mandatory detention of unlawful non-citizens can validly be provided without contravention of Ch III. It follows that unlawful non-citizens have no unqualified immunity from detention and attention must then be focused upon the purpose of the detention. Once it is accepted, as I do, that the aliens and immigration powers support a law directed to excluding a non-citizen from the Australian community (by segregating that person from the community) the effluxion of time, whether judged alone or in the light of the vulnerability of those who are detained, will not itself demonstrate that the purpose of detention has passed from exclusion by segregation to punishment ...

Callinan J

Does it make a relevant legal difference that the applicants are children? The answer, as I have foreshadowed, is "no". The purpose of the detention remains the deciding factor. Arguments to the contrary dissolve ultimately into questions about the wisdom of the policy behind the detention of children, or perhaps the nature of it. These are difficult questions involving matters of social, humanitarian and migration policy and are ones to which the courts cannot provide the answers ...

Alien children have legal rights just as do alien adults. But those rights, so far as removal from this country and detention for that purpose is concerned, are no different from the rights of adults which are governed by those sections of the Act to which I have referred ...

18.4 Detention limited to what is reasonably necessary for non-punitive purposes

The second condition necessary for a federal law requiring or authorising detention to escape characterisation as a purported exercise of judicial power is that the detention is limited to what is reasonably necessary for the non-punitive purpose.

A statutory power to detain a person that goes further than is reasonably necessary to achieve a non-punitive purpose will breach the principle in ***Lim***. Where a law goes further than is reasonably necessary to achieve a non-punitive purpose, the presumption that detention is punitive in character applies and renders the detention unconstitutional.

Falzon v Minister for Immigration and Border Protection (2018) 351 ALR 61

Kiefel CJ, Bell, Keane and Edelman JJ

The starting point for the enquiry referred to in *Lim* is that the power to remove or deport aliens from a country is executive in nature and it is non-punitive. The question which then arises with respect to a statutory power given to the Executive to detain an alien in custody is whether it is given in order to facilitate or effect the removal of that person, which is the subject of executive power. The enquiry is as to whether it is "necessary" to that purpose. If it is, it may be considered to be an incident of the executive power and will not be an exercise of judicial power. If the power goes further than to achieve that limited purpose it may be otherwise. In such circumstance, it may be inferred that the law has a purpose of its own, a purpose to effect punishment ...

Plaintiff S4 explains that the rule that detention must be limited to what is reasonably necessary for the non-punitive purpose gives rise to a requirement that the duration of any form of detention must be capable of being determined at any time and from time to time. In other words, the law requiring or authorising detention for a non-punitive purpose must set objective criteria against which the lawfulness of detention is to be judged.

Plaintiff S4/2014 v Minister for Immigration and Border Protection (2014) 253 CLR 219

French CJ, Hayne, Crennan, Kiefel and Keane JJ

Importantly, the Court [in *Lim*] further held that the provisions of the Act which then authorised mandatory detention of certain aliens were valid laws if the detention which those laws required and authorised was limited to what was reasonably capable of being seen as necessary for the purposes of deportation or to enable an application for permission to enter and remain in Australia to be made and considered ...

> The duration of any form of detention, and thus its lawfulness, must be capable of being determined at any time and from time to time. Otherwise, the lawfulness of the detention could not be determined and enforced by the courts, and, ultimately, by this Court ...

These criteria, against which the lawfulness of detention is to be judged, are set at the start of the detention. No doubt, the facts to which these criteria are to be applied may, and often will, vary according to the course of inquiries and decisions that are made along the way. In cases like the present, where inquiries were made about whether to permit the plaintiff to apply for a protection visa, application of the criteria which fix the duration of detention varies according to such matters as whether the detainee is found to be a refugee within the meaning of Art 1 of the Refugees Convention. But the criteria to be applied at any time during the currency of the detention in determining its lawfulness do not, and may not, vary ...

Plaintiff M96A explains that the requirement that the period of detention be capable of objective determination by a court at any time, and from time to time, is not a requirement that a precise deadline on the duration of detention be capable of determination. In this case, asylum seekers were detained in Australia for the purpose of deportation once they no longer required medical treatment. Just because it was not possible to know in advance when medical treatment may no longer be required did not mean there was no objective criteria governing the duration of detention. The High Court explained that the duration of detention was governed by objective criteria, albeit relying on factors (in this case, the medical needs of the asylum seekers) beyond the control of the Federal Executive Government. At all times, it was possible for a court, relying on expert evidence, to determine whether there was a need for medical treatment.

Plaintiff M96A/2016 v Commonwealth (2017) 261 CLR 582

Kiefel CJ, Bell, Keane, Nettle, Gordon and Edelman JJ

The second basis upon which the plaintiffs submitted that ss 189 and 196 of the Act were invalid exercises by the Executive of the judicial power of the Commonwealth was that the sections permitted the detention of transitory persons for a time which was incapable of being objectively determined. The plaintiffs relied upon various passages from decisions in this Court in support of their submission, including *Plaintiff S4/2014 v Minister for Immigration and Border Protection*, where this Court said:

> The duration of any form of detention, and thus its lawfulness, must be capable of being determined at any time and from time to time. Otherwise, the lawfulness of the detention could not be determined and enforced by the courts, and, ultimately, by this Court.

The plaintiffs submitted that the period of detention of transitory persons brought to Australia under s 198B is governed only by the question whether and when the person "no longer needs to be in Australia" for the relevant purpose and that this invalidated the detention. This was said to be for two reasons: first, because the period of time for detention is not readily capable of objective determination by a court at any time, and from time to time; and secondly, because the temporal limits are not connected with the limited permissible purposes of administrative detention such that the power to detain is not unconstrained.

The first of these two alleged reasons for invalidity misunderstands the requirement that the duration of any form of detention must be capable of being determined at any time, and from time to time. The requirement ... is that there must be objectively determinable criteria for detention. In other words, Parliament cannot avoid judicial scrutiny of the legality of detention by criteria which are too vague to be capable of objective determination. This would include an attempt to make the length of detention at any time dependent upon the unconstrained, and unascertainable, opinion of the Executive.

The duration of the detention of transitory persons who are detained under s 189 of the Act is able to be objectively determined at any time, and from time to time. At any time it can be concluded that detention in Australia will conclude if any of the various preconditions explained above are met. One precondition is that detention in Australia will come to an end under s 198(1) as soon as reasonably practicable after the transitory person asks the Minister, in writing, to be removed from Australia. Another precondition is that the person no longer needs to be in Australia for the temporary purpose. This precondition arises from the operation of either s 198(1A), or s 198AD(2) read with s 198AH(1A)(c) ...

The second reason why the plaintiffs alleged that the duration of detention led to invalidity was also based upon a misconception. The plaintiffs' submission that the temporal limits of detention are not connected with the limited permissible purposes of administrative detention assumed that the purpose of administrative detention in Australia was for medical treatment. Alternatively, the submission assumed that if the purpose of administrative detention was for removal it would be unlawful for the duration of detention to be predicated not on the effectuation of removal itself, but on an apparently unrelated factum: the need to be in Australia for the medical treatment. As we have explained above, the detention was for the purpose of removal from Australia when preconditions are met, including where there is no longer a need for the transitory person to be in Australia for the temporary purpose. The detention does not become an exercise of judicial power merely because the precondition, and hence the period of detention, is determined by matters beyond the control of the Executive. This will frequently be the case where, for instance, questions arise as to whether it is reasonably practicable to remove a person from Australia ...

In ***ALJ20***, a majority of the High Court held that a law requiring the detention of a person for a non-punitive purpose does not lose its non-punitive purpose simply because the Executive fails to comply with the statutory requirements that ensure the law goes no further than is necessary to achieve its non-punitive purpose. The Executive's failure does not affect the characterisation of the law's purpose and can be addressed by administrative law remedies compelling compliance with the statute.

Commonwealth v ALJ20 (2021) 273 CLR 43

ALJ20 was an unlawful non-citizen and detained under the mandatory detention provisions of the* Migration Act 1958 (Cth)*. The Commonwealth admitted that it had failed to execute its statutory obligation to take steps to facilitate ALJ20's removal from Australia or grant him a visa. The High Court held that the Executive's failure did not render the relevant statutory provisions unconstitutional.

Kiefel CJ, Gageler, Keane and Steward JJ

When the Executive executes a statute of the Commonwealth ... the constitutional question is whether the statutory authority conferred on the Executive is within the competence of the Parliament; the statutory question is whether the executive action in question is authorised by the statute. If the statute, properly construed, can be seen to conform to constitutional limitations upon legislative competence without any need to read it down to save its validity, then it is valid in all its applications, and no further constitutional issue arises. The question then is whether the executive action in question was authorised by the statute, with that question to be resolved by reference to the statute as a matter of administrative law ...

Nor can one discern in, or attribute to, the plurality's statement in *Plaintiff M96A* or the reasoning in *Lim* (or the passages in *Plaintiff S4* to which reference has been and will be made) any adherence to the heresy that, where a law is within the Parliament's competence because of the imposition of duties on officers of the Executive, delay in performance of those duties by those officers can take the law outside Parliament's competence. A failure by the Executive diligently to perform the duties that give effect to the legitimate non-punitive purposes for which detention is authorised and required by the Act erases neither those duties nor the statutory purposes which those duties support. Were it otherwise, the supremacy of the Parliament over the Executive would be reversed and the rule of law subverted ...

The conclusion that officers of the Executive have not discharged their statutory duty to remove the respondent from Australia as soon as reasonably practicable affords a basis for orders requiring that they do their duty. Orders to that effect are appropriate to enforce the scheme of the Act. In contrast, to order that the respondent be released into the Australian community because officers of the Executive have not performed their statutory duty to remove him from Australia is to subvert that scheme.

18.5 The *Lim* principle does not prohibit courts from imposing non-punitive detention

Benbrika is a case both about the scope of federal judicial power and the scope of the *Lim* principle. The case demonstrates that: (1) ordering non-punitive detention can be an exercise of judicial power (and an exercise of federal judicial power when done under federal legislation); and (2) *Lim* does not mean that non-punitive detention under federal legislation can never be imposed by courts. The case also demonstrates that detaining a person because that person poses an unacceptable risk of engaging in terrorist activity is non-punitive in character because it is aimed at protecting the community from serious harm.

Benbrika was detained under Division 105A of the *Criminal Code* (Cth) following the expiration of his sentence because a judge found that he posed an unacceptable risk of engaging in terrorist activity and no less restrictive means of protecting the community from that unacceptable risk were available. Benbrika argued that Division 105A was unconstitutional. His argument had two starting premises. First, punishment under federal law may be imposed only by a court for a contravention of law. Secondly, detention is, subject to the *Lim* exceptions, always punitive in character. It followed, Benbrika argued, that his continuing detention was invalid because it was the imposition of a punishment by a court but not for any contravention of law. The High Court held that the detention was non-punitive in nature and a valid exercise of federal judicial power.

Minister for Home Affairs v Benbrika (2021) 272 CLR 68

Division 105A of the* Criminal Code *(Cth) has as its statutory object 'to ensure the safety and protection of the community by providing for the continuing detention of terrorist offenders who pose an unacceptable risk of committing serious Part 5.3 offences [i.e. terrorism-related offences] if released into the community'.

Kiefel CJ, Bell, Keane and Steward JJ

Division 105A of the *Criminal Code* (Cth) (the Code) empowers the Supreme Court of a State or Territory, on the application of the Minister for Home Affairs (the Minister), to order that a person who has been convicted of a terrorist offence be detained in prison for a further period after the expiration of his or her sentence of imprisonment ... The question in this proceeding is whether the Supreme Court of a State or Territory may commit a person to prison in the exercise of federal judicial power after determining, by orthodox judicial process, that the person presents an unacceptable risk of committing a terrorist offence if released from custody. For the reasons to be given, the answer is that it may ...

It is the separation of powers that is said to explain why an order for continuing detention may be made in the exercise of State judicial power but not in the exercise of federal judicial power. Mr Benbrika points to judicial statements that have acknowledged that the separation of powers in the Australian constitutional setting ensures that Ch III courts serve as a bulwark of liberty. They do so, he submits, because, as the principle was explained in the joint reasons of Brennan, Deane and Dawson JJ in *Chu Kheng Lim v Minister for Immigration*, exceptional cases aside, the involuntary detention of a citizen in custody by the State is penal or punitive in character and exists only as an incident of the exclusively judicial function of adjudging and punishing criminal guilt (the "*Lim* principle") ...

The Commonwealth contests that *Lim* is authority for the proposition that power to order the detention of a person in the custody of the State can only be within the judicial power of the Commonwealth if it is an incident of adjudging and punishing criminal guilt. In the Commonwealth's submission, correctly understood *Lim* is authority for the principle that the power to detain for a punitive purpose is exclusively judicial. Detention for any non-punitive purpose, in the Commonwealth's submission, may be conferred on the executive or on a Ch III court ...

The answer to the question reserved does not require consideration of the scope of exceptions to the *Lim* general proposition that the power to order that a person be involuntarily detained in the custody of the State is entrusted exclusively to Ch III courts. Division 105A confers power on a Ch III court. The question reserved is concerned with the allied *Lim* principle that involuntary detention in the custody of the State under our system of government exists only as an incident of the adjudgment and punishment of criminal guilt.

As the joint reasons in *Lim* acknowledged, there are exceptions to the characterisation of detention by the State as penal or punitive in character ...

There is no principled reason for distinguishing the power of a Ch III court to order that a mentally ill person be detained in custody for the protection of the community from harm and the power to order that a terrorist offender be detained in custody for the same purpose. It is the protective purpose that qualifies a power as an exception to a principle that is recognised under our system of government as a safeguard on liberty. Demonstration that Div 105A is non-punitive is essential to a conclusion that the regime that it establishes can validly be conferred on a Ch III court, but that conclusion does not suffice. As a matter of substance, the power must have as its object the protection of the community from harm ...

The object of Div 105A, set out earlier in these reasons, is plainly directed to the protection of the community from harm ... Div 105A is rightly characterised as directed to ensuring the safety and protection of the community from the risk of harm posed by the threat of terrorism.

Division 105A validly confers the judicial power of the Commonwealth on the Supreme Court of a State or Territory.

18.6 DISCUSSION QUESTIONS

1. What are the two conditions necessary for a federal law requiring or authorising detention to escape characterisation as a purported exercise of judicial power? Why are they the relevant conditions?
2. What reason did the High Court give for holding that a law authorising the Federal Executive Government to participate in the detention of a person by another country does not engage the ***Lim*** principle?
3. What reason did the High Court give in ***Al-Kateb*** for holding that indefinite detention is not necessarily unconstitutional?
4. Is the result in ***Al-Kateb*** consistent with the requirement that the duration of detention be capable of objective determination by the courts at any time and from time to time?
5. Problem question: Consider the following hypothetical legislation. The Federal Parliament enacts the *Expulsion of New Zealander Wrong-doers Act 2023* (Cth). Section 5 of the Act provides:

Section 5 Expulsion

1. This section applies to any person who is:
   a. a citizen of New Zealand or entitled to reside in New Zealand, and
   b. is in Australia, and
   c. not entitled to be in Australia.
2. The Minister must cause any person to whom this section applies to be detained in an immigration detention facility for a period of not less than 28 days and, after the expiration of that 28 days of detention, cause the person to be removed from Australia.

Is section 5 unconstitutional by reason of Chapter III? (You may assume that section 5 is supported by section 51(xix) (the aliens power).)

19

INSTITUTIONAL INTEGRITY OF COURTS

19.1 Overview

This chapter examines how Chapter III of the *Australian Constitution* protects the institutional integrity of Chapter III courts. This doctrine is often called the ***Kable*** doctrine after the name of the case in which it was first established. The doctrine holds that it is beyond power for any Parliament to impair the institutional integrity of a Chapter III court by depriving it of any of the defining characteristics of a court.

Key concepts addressed in this chapter include:

- institutional integrity
- courts
- defining characteristics
- independent and impartial tribunal
- decisional independence
- federal courts
- supervisory jurisdiction.

19.2 Institutional integrity of Chapter III courts

It is beyond power for any Parliament to impair the institutional integrity of any court by depriving a court of any of the defining characteristics of a 'court'. This is known as the ***Kable*** doctrine, after the name of the case in which the doctrine was first established.

The rationale for the ***Kable*** doctrine arises from the text of Chapter III. Section 71 vests the judicial power of the Commonwealth in the High Court, 'such other federal courts as the Parliament creates', and 'such other courts as it invests with federal jurisdiction'. The point to note here is that, by its express terms, section 71 provides that federal judicial power can be exercised only by 'courts'. The *Constitution* requires that courts remain courts in substance – that is, possess all of the characteristics that make a court a court – and not just in name.

All of the three categories of court identified in section 71 are, by the terms of that section, potential repositories of federal judicial power. Chapter III courts must therefore remain fit repositories – that is, remain courts without impairment of their institutional integrity as courts – for the exercise of federal judicial power.

The rationale for and scope of the ***Kable*** doctrine was not articulated clearly in ***Kable's Case.*** In subsequent cases, the rationale was explained more clearly and as outlined above. In *Kable,* some judges appeared to limit the doctrine's application to situations only where State courts were in fact exercising federal judicial power. Some judges appeared to justify the doctrine on the basis of notions of public confidence.

Kable v Director of Public Prosecutions (NSW) (1996) 189 CLR 51

Section 5 of the Community Protection Act 1994 *(NSW) provided that the Supreme Court could order that a person be detained in prison if satisfied that the person is more likely than not to commit a serious act of violence and that detention in custody was appropriate for the protection of the community. Notwithstanding the generality of section 5, section 3(3) provided: 'This Act authorises the making of a detention order against Gregory Wayne Kable and does not authorise the making of a detention order against any other person.' Kable argued that the legislation was unconstitutional because the function the Act conferred on the Supreme Court was incompatible with the exercise by State courts of Commonwealth judicial power. The function conferred on the Court had the effect of undermining the independence of the Court by requiring the Court to act as an instrument of the Executive Government. The High Court agreed.*

Toohey J

To the extent that they are invested with federal jurisdiction, the federal courts and the courts of the States exercise a common jurisdiction. It follows that in the exercise of its federal jurisdiction a State court may not act in a manner which is incompatible with Ch III of the *Commonwealth Constitution*. ...

The argument is not one which relies upon the alleged separation of legislative and judicial functions under the Constitution of New South Wales. Rather it is that the jurisdiction exercised under the Act is inconsistent with Ch III of the *Commonwealth Constitution* because the very nature of the jurisdiction is incompatible with the exercise of judicial power.

By reason of the issues raised in the case, the Supreme Court exercised federal jurisdiction. It is not the investing of the Supreme Court with federal jurisdiction that is in issue; it is the exercise of federal jurisdiction by the Supreme Court in the circumstances arising under the Act that is challenged ...

In *Grollo v Palmer* the Court held that the vesting in designated judges of the Federal Court of the power to issue interception warrants was not incompatible either with the judge's performance of his or her judicial functions or with the proper discharge by the judiciary of its responsibilities as an institution exercising judicial power. Nevertheless the Court emphasised that "no function can be conferred that is incompatible ... with the proper discharge by the judiciary of its responsibilities as an institution exercising judicial power". It is true that the proposition was enunciated in the context of the power to confer non-judicial functions on judges as designated persons but in my view it holds good whenever Ch III of the Constitution is operative ...

The Act answers that aspect of incompatibility which was identified in *Grollo v Palmer* as "the performance of non-judicial functions of such a nature that public confidence in the integrity of the judiciary as an institution ... is diminished".

Gaudron J

Several arguments were advanced in favour of the appellant's contention. I need deal with one only, namely, that Ch III of the *Constitution* impliedly prevents the Parliament of a State from conferring powers on the Supreme Court of a State which are repugnant to or inconsistent with the exercise by it of the judicial power of the Commonwealth ...

The question whether the Constitution requires that State Courts not have particular powers conferred upon them depends, in my view, on a proper understanding of the integrated judicial system for which Ch III provides – the "autochthonous expedient", as it has been called. One thing which clearly emerges is that, although it is for the States to determine the organisation and structure of their court systems, they must each maintain courts, or, at least, a court for the exercise of the judicial power of the Commonwealth. Were they free to abolish their courts, the autochthonous expedient, more precisely, the provisions of Ch III which postulate an integrated judicial system would be frustrated in their entirety. To this extent, at least, the States are not free to legislate as they please.

Two other matters of significance emerge from a consideration of the provisions of Ch III. The first is that ... there is nothing anywhere in the Constitution to suggest that it permits of different grades or qualities of justice, depending on whether judicial power is exercised by State courts or federal courts created by the Parliament.

The second and, perhaps, the more significant matter which emerges from a consideration of the provisions of Ch III is ... that State courts, when exercising federal jurisdiction "are part of the Australian judicial system created by Ch III of the Constitution and, in that sense and on that account, they have a role and existence which transcends their status as courts of the States". Once the notion that the Constitution permits of different grades or qualities of justice is rejected, the consideration that State courts have a role and existence transcending their status as State courts directs the conclusion that Ch III requires that the Parliaments of the States not legislate to confer powers on State courts which are repugnant to or incompatible with their exercise of the judicial power of the Commonwealth ...

The integrity of the courts depends on their acting in accordance with the judicial process and, in no small measure, on the maintenance of public confidence in that process.

McHugh J

Because the State courts are an integral and equal part of the judicial system set up by Ch III, it also follows that no State or federal parliament can legislate in a way that might undermine the role of those courts as repositories of federal judicial power. Thus, neither the Parliament of New South Wales nor the Parliament of the Commonwealth can invest functions in the Supreme Court of New South Wales that are incompatible with the exercise of federal judicial power ...

One of the basic principles which underlie Ch III and to which it gives effect is that the judges of the federal courts must be, and must be perceived to be, independent of the legislature and the executive government. Given the central role and the status that Ch III gives to State courts invested with federal jurisdiction, it necessarily follows that those courts must also be, and be perceived to be, independent of the legislature and executive government in the exercise of federal jurisdiction. Public confidence in the impartial exercise of federal judicial power would soon be lost if federal or State courts exercising federal jurisdiction were not, or were not perceived to be, independent of the legislature or the executive government.

In the case of State courts, this means they must be independent and appear to be independent of their own State's legislature and executive government as well as the federal legislature and government ...

While nothing in Ch III prevents a State from conferring non-judicial functions on a State Supreme Court in respect of non-federal matters, those non-judicial functions cannot be of a nature that might lead an ordinary reasonable member of the public to conclude that the Court was not independent of the executive government of the State ... The law would fail not because it breached any entrenched doctrine of separation powers in the State Constitution but because it gave the appearance that a court invested with federal jurisdiction was not independent of its State government ...

[I]t is a necessary implication of the Constitution's plan of an Australian judicial system with State courts invested with federal jurisdiction that no government can act in a way that might undermine public confidence in the impartial administration of the judicial functions of State courts. If it could, it would inevitably result in a lack of public confidence in the administration of invested federal jurisdiction in those courts. State governments therefore do not have unrestricted power to legislate for State courts or judges. ... But under the Constitution the boundary of State legislative power is crossed when the vesting of those functions or duties might lead ordinary reasonable members of the public to conclude that the State court as an institution was not free of government influence in administering the judicial functions invested in the court.

More succinct statements of the ***Kable*** doctrine and its rationale were given in subsequent cases such as ***Forge*** and ***Wainohu***.

Forge v Australian Securities and Investments Commission (2006) 228 CLR 45

Gummow, Hayne and Crennan JJ

One operation of that limitation on State legislative power was identified in *Kable*. The legislation under consideration in *Kable* was found to be repugnant to, or incompatible with, "that institutional integrity of the State courts which bespeaks their constitutionally mandated position in the Australian legal system". The legislation in *Kable* was held to be repugnant to, or incompatible with, the institutional integrity of the Supreme Court of New South Wales because of the nature of the task the relevant legislation required the Court to perform. At the risk of undue abbreviation, and consequent inaccuracy, the task given to the Supreme Court was identified as a task where the Court acted as an instrument of the Executive. The consequence was that the Court, if required to perform the task, would not be an appropriate recipient of invested federal jurisdiction. But as is recognised in *Kable*, *Fardon v Attorney-General (Qld)* and *North Australian Aboriginal Legal Aid Service Inc v Bradley*, the relevant principle is one which hinges upon maintenance of the defining characteristics of a "court", or in cases concerning a Supreme Court, the defining characteristics of a State Supreme Court. It is to those characteristics that the reference to "institutional integrity" alludes. That is, if the institutional integrity of a court is distorted, it is because the body no longer exhibits in some relevant respect those defining characteristics which mark a court apart from other decision-making bodies.

Wainohu v New South Wales (2011) 243 CLR 181

French CJ and Kiefel J

Decisions of this Court, commencing with *Kable*, establish the principle that a State legislature cannot confer upon a State court a function which substantially impairs its institutional integrity, and which is therefore incompatible with its role, under Ch III of the *Constitution*, as a repository of federal jurisdiction and as a part of the integrated Australian court system. The term "institutional integrity", applied to a court, refers to its possession of the defining or essential characteristics of a court.

Although the ***Kable*** doctrine was first articulated in a case concerning a State court, and although most of the cases considering and applying the *Kable* doctrine concern State courts, the constitutional requirement of institutional integrity applies to all the categories of court identified by Chapter III, that is, all federal, State and Territory courts.

The application of ***Kable*** to Territory courts is settled law.

Ebner v Official Trustee in Bankruptcy (2000) 205 CLR 337

Gaudron J

Because State courts are part of the Australian judicial system created by Ch III of the Constitution and may be invested with the judicial power of the Commonwealth, the Constitution also requires, in accordance with *Kable v Director of Public Prosecutions (NSW)*, that, for the maintenance of public confidence, they be constituted by persons who are impartial and who appear to be impartial even when exercising non-federal jurisdiction. And as courts created pursuant to s 122 of the Constitution may also be invested with the judicial power of the Commonwealth, it should now be recognised, consistently with the decision in *Kable*, that the Constitution also requires that those courts be constituted by persons who are impartial and who appear to be impartial.

Justice Gaudron's recognition that ***Kable*** applies to Territory courts was later approved in ***North Australian Aboriginal Legal Aid Service Inc v Bradley***.

North Australian Aboriginal Legal Aid Service Inc v Bradley (2004) 218 CLR 146

McHugh, Gummow, Kirby, Hayne, Callinan and Heydon JJ

Counsel for the Legal Aid Service put an argument in three steps. The first is that a court of the Territory may exercise the judicial power of the Commonwealth pursuant to investment by laws made by the Parliament. That proposition, to which there was no demurrer by the Territory or by the Attorney-General of the Commonwealth who intervened in this Court, is supported by the citations of authority by Gaudron J in the above passage from *Ebner*. It should be accepted.

The second step in the Legal Aid Service's argument is that it is implicit in the terms of Ch III of the *Constitution*, and necessary for the preservation of that structure, that a court *capable* of exercising the judicial power of the Commonwealth be and appear to be an independent and impartial tribunal. That proposition, which again appears in the passage from *Ebner*, also should be accepted ...

In ***North Australian Aboriginal Justice Agency Ltd v Northern Territory***, the High Court gave a pithy explanation of why ***Kable*** applies to Territory courts.

North Australian Aboriginal Justice Agency Ltd v Northern Territory (2015) 256 CLR 569

French CJ, Kiefel and Bell JJ

Courts of the Northern Territory may exercise the judicial power of the Commonwealth in the exercise of jurisdiction conferred upon them by laws made by the Commonwealth Parliament.

It follows that *Kable* applies to the Supreme Court of the Territory and to Territory courts as Ch III courts.

The rationale underlying the ***Kable*** doctrine being concerned with the institutional integrity of Chapter III courts means that the doctrine applies also to federal courts. In ***TCL Air Conditioner (Zhongshan) Co Ltd v The Judges of the Federal Court of Australia***, the High Court rejected an argument that particular legislation impaired the institutional integrity of the Federal Court.

TCL Air Conditioner (Zhongshan) Co Ltd v The Judges of the Federal Court of Australia (2013) 251 CLR 533

French CJ and Gageler J

The plaintiff's argument, as refined in oral submissions, reduces to the proposition that the inability of the Federal Court under Arts 35 and 36 of the Model Law to refuse to enforce an arbitral award on the ground of error of law appearing on the face of the award either: undermines the institutional integrity of the Federal Court as a court exercising the judicial power of the Commonwealth, by requiring the Federal Court knowingly to perpetrate legal error; or impermissibly confers the judicial power of the Commonwealth on the arbitral tribunal that made the award, by giving the arbitral tribunal the last word on the law applied in deciding the dispute submitted to arbitration ...

The inability of the Federal Court, as a competent court under Arts 35 and 36 of the Model Law, to refuse to enforce an arbitral award on the ground of error of law appearing on the face of the award does nothing to undermine the institutional integrity of the Federal Court. Enforcement of an arbitral award is enforcement of the binding result of the agreement of the parties to submit their dispute to arbitration, not enforcement of any disputed right submitted to arbitration.

Hayne, Crennan, Kiefel and Bell JJ

The first objection of TCL, concerning the institutional integrity of the Federal Court, invoked the constitutional principle enunciated in *Kable v Director of Public Prosecutions* (NSW) ("*Kable*") in connection with the Supreme Court of a State. The legislation considered in *Kable* was found to be repugnant to, or incompatible with, the institutional integrity of the Supreme Court of New South Wales because of the nature of the task that the legislation required the Court to perform. The plurality in *Forge v Australian Securities and Investments Commission* explained that the principle recognised in "is one which hinges upon maintenance of the defining characteristics of a 'court'". The plurality continued:

> [I]f the institutional integrity of a court is distorted, it is because the body no longer exhibits in some relevant respect those defining characteristics which mark a court apart from other decision-making bodies.

The defining characteristic of a court upon which TCL fastened was judicial independence, which was said to be "distorted" by the absence of scope for substantive review of an award for error of law when the Federal Court determines the enforceability of an award under the IA Act. The submission fails to take into account the consensual foundation of private arbitration. This failure underpinned TCL's misunderstanding of the relationship between private arbitration and courts.

If it is right to apply directly to a court created by the federal Parliament the doctrines enunciated in *Kable* with respect to State courts, there is no distortion of the institutional integrity of the Federal Court.

19.3 Defining characteristics of 'courts'

This section looks at a series of cases to identify some of the defining characteristics of 'courts'. The cases considered in this section also explore the ways in which those defining characteristics might be impaired.

Methodology for identifying defining characteristics

A preliminary issue is the methodology for identifying defining characteristics of 'courts'. In ***Assistant Commissioner Condon v Pompano Pty Ltd***, French CJ explained that the defining characteristics of courts derive from the text and structure of the *Constitution* informed by the common law and history.

Assistant Commissioner Condon v Pompano Pty Ltd (2013) 252 CLR 38

French CJ

The respondents invoke the general principle, established in decisions of this Court, that a State legislature cannot confer upon a court of a State a function which impairs its institutional integrity and which is therefore incompatible with the role of that court as a repository of federal jurisdiction. The "institutional integrity" of a court is said to be distorted if it no longer exhibits in some relevant aspect the defining characteristics which mark a court apart from other decision-making bodies. The defining characteristics of courts include:

- the reality and appearance of decisional independence and impartiality;
- the application of procedural fairness;
- adherence as a general rule to the open court principle;
- the provision of reasons for the courts' decisions.

Those characteristics are not exhaustive. As Gummow, Hayne and Crennan JJ said in *Forge v Australian Securities and Investments Commission*:

> It is neither possible nor profitable to attempt to make some single all-embracing statement of the defining characteristics of a court. The cases concerning identification of judicial power reveal why that is so.

The defining or essential characteristics of courts are not attributes plucked from a platonic universe of ideal forms. They are used to describe limits, deriving from Ch III of the Constitution, upon the functions which legislatures may confer upon State courts and the commands to which they may subject them. Those limits are rooted in the text and structure of the Constitution informed by the common law, which carries with it historically developed concepts of courts and the judicial function. Historically evolved as they are and requiring application in the real world, the defining characteristics of courts are not and cannot be absolutes. Decisional independence operates within the framework of the rule of law and not outside it. Procedural fairness, manifested in the requirements that the court be and appear to be impartial and that parties be heard by the court, is defined by practical judgments about its content and application which may vary according to the circumstances. Both the open court principle and the hearing rule may be qualified by public interest considerations such as the protection of sensitive information and the identities of vulnerable witnesses, including informants in criminal matters.

To understand a case invoking the institutional integrity doctrine it is necessary to identify: (1) the defining characteristic of a court that is said to be impaired by the impugned legislation; and (2) the way in which the impugned legislation impairs or does not impair that defining characteristic.

The cases considering the defining characteristics of courts can be grouped into the themes of institutional independence, procedural independence and decisional independence. This thematic grouping of cases is a convenient way of understanding the existing case law and is not a rigid or formal taxonomy.

Institutional independence as a defining characteristic

A key defining characteristic of courts is their institutional independence. In ***Baker v The Queen***, the defining characteristic in issue was the appearance and reality of independence from the other branches of government. The High Court rejected an argument that legislation providing that a court could not set a non-parole period for certain prisoners unless 'special reasons' existed had the effect of giving the appearance of judicial process to what was a legislative decree that certain individuals should not be released from prison. The case also highlights the importance of statutory interpretation in assessing the constitutional validity of legislation.

Baker v The Queen (2004) 223 CLR 513

Sentencing legislation in New South Wales permitted prisoners who had been sentenced to life imprisonment to apply to the Supreme Court for a determination of a minimum sentence. The prisoner was then able to apply for parole after serving the minimum sentence. Amending legislation later introduced a new qualification to the minimum sentence determination regime:

> *A person who is the subject of a non-release recommendation is not eligible for the determination of a minimum term and an additional term under this section, unless the*

> *Supreme Court, when considering the person's application under this section, is satisfied that special reasons exist that justify making the determination.*

A 'non-release recommendation' was defined to mean comments or expressions of opinion by a sentencing judge that the prisoner should never be released. Baker argued that the amending legislation breached the Kable doctrine. He argued the 'special reasons' criterion lacked meaning and was a charade by the New South Wales Parliament designed to bring about the result that no member of the class of prisoners would ever be released. The High Court disagreed, holding that the meaning of 'special reasons' was simply a question of statutory interpretation.

Gleeson CJ

The ground of appeal to this Court is that the 1997 legislation which amended s 13A to introduce special provisions about people who were the subject of non-release recommendations was invalid ...

Senior counsel for the appellant acknowledged in the course of argument that, if Parliament had simply named the persons in question and excluded them from the operation of s 13A, then his *Kable* argument would not have arisen ...

The weight of the appellant's *Kable* argument was put upon the requirement of "special reasons" in s 13A(3A). In the context of s 13A, that requirement was said to be devoid of content, and illusory. On that premise, in its application to people the subject of non-release recommendations, s 13A involved the Supreme Court in a charade. The legislature was using the forms of judicial procedure to mask the reality of the legislative decree, which was that these people were never to be released. On that premise, as a matter of principle, the case would be very close to *Kable*. It is the premise that is in contest ...

There is nothing unusual about legislation that requires courts to find "special reasons" or "special circumstances" as a condition of the exercise of a power. This is a verbal formula that is commonly used where it is intended that judicial discretion should not be confined by precise definition, or where the circumstances of potential relevance are so various as to defy precise definition. That which makes reasons or circumstances special in a particular case might flow from their weight as well as their quality, and from a combination of factors.

It is the duty of a court to give meaning to the requirement of "special reasons" in sub-s (3A) unless that is impossible. That elementary principle of statutory interpretation cannot be ignored ...

We are not dealing with an argument that it is difficult to satisfy the requirements of sub-s (3A). We are dealing with an argument that it is impossible to satisfy the requirements because the statutory phrase "special reasons" is, in this context, devoid of content ...

The appellant's submission, that it will always be impossible to establish "special reasons" under sub-s (3A), was not simply a rhetorical overstatement of a complaint about unfairness. It was the basis for the contention that, in its application to persons the subject of non-release recommendations, the legislative scheme was a charade, and the Supreme Court's judicial process was being used merely to implement a legislative intention that such persons would never be released. In order to make that argument good, it is not sufficient to show that it is difficult to establish special reasons, or that successful applications are likely to be rare. It is necessary to show that it is impossible to establish special reasons, and that no application could succeed. That has not been shown.

Institutional independence is also affected by remuneration arrangements for judicial officers. In ***North Australian Aboriginal Legal Aid Service v Bradley***, the High Court accepted that remuneration arrangements for judicial officers that made judicial officers wholly dependent on the discretion of the Executive Government for their remuneration would impair the appearance and reality of the independence of the court of which the judicial officer was a member. In this case, the High Court rejected a claim that setting judicial remuneration for two years impaired judicial independence, because the remuneration legislation required that remuneration be set again after the two-year period at the same or higher rate.

North Australian Aboriginal Legal Aid Service Inc v Bradley (2004) 218 CLR 146

McHugh, Gummow, Kirby, Hayne, Callinan and Heydon JJ

The appellant ("the Legal Aid Service") renews in this Court its unsuccessful challenge to the validity of the appointment with effect from 9 March 1998 of the first respondent ("Mr Bradley") as Chief Magistrate under the *Magistrates Act* (NT) ("the Magistrates Act") ...

In the course of argument, the case for the Legal Aid Service was developed and refined. The contention is that a declaration should be made that Mr Bradley was not validly appointed to the office of Chief Magistrate. That invalidity would be the consequence of a holding which should be made by this Court that the Magistrates Act is invalid in so far as it authorised the appointment of a Chief Magistrate to age 65 but with remuneration fixed only for the first two years of the term.

The invalidity of the Magistrates Act and, as a consequence, the invalidity of the appointment of Mr Bradley, is said to follow from the application to the statute of the principles derived from *Kable v Director of Public Prosecutions (NSW)*. In particular, the Legal Aid Service submits that the provisions in the Magistrates Act respecting appointment and remuneration deprive the courts of the Territory in which the appointees serve of the character of independent and impartial tribunals ...

[I]t is implicit in the terms of Ch III of the *Constitution* ... that a court capable of exercising the judicial power of the Commonwealth be and appear to be an independent and impartial tribunal ...

This requires discernment of the relevant minimum characteristic of an independent and impartial tribunal exercising the jurisdiction of the courts over which the Chief Magistrate presides ...

Section 6 confers upon a magistrate appointed under s 4(3) the right to receive certain remuneration and allowances and attaches terms and conditions to the office held by the magistrate. The content of the right to receive payment is supplied by the determination by the Administrator ...

Section 6 is to be construed by preferring "a construction that promotes the purpose or object underlying the [Magistrates] Act (whether the purpose or object is expressly stated in the Act or not) ... to a construction that does not promote the purpose or object". The text is that of s 62A of the *Interpretation Act* (NT). It is with that precept in mind that the phrase in s 6, "from time to time", is to be determined.

The purpose or object of the Magistrates Act included the advancement of the standing of the magistracy in the Territory by supporting what in the Second Reading Speech had been identified as "the principle of judicial independence". Provisions securing remuneration serve that end and enhance the appearance of impartial decision-making. A construction of s 6 which requires a determination to be made by the Administrator with initial or continued effect at the commencement of an appointment by the Administrator under s 4(3) advances the purpose or object of the legislation ...

But the phrase "from time to time" is not to be read as permitting the Administrator to fail to exercise the power under s 6 where that failure would produce a hiatus where no determination was in operation. A construction which permitted such a state of affairs would place the officeholder wholly at the favour of the executive government respecting a basic attribute of the judicial independence the legislation was designed to promote ...

To the contrary, where a determination has been made under s 6 of the Magistrates Act for a limited period, as in this case, the Administrator is required to make a subsequent determination in the manner described above. The purpose or object of the exercise of that power, consistently with that of the statute, cannot be to diminish that which has been provided already; it must be to continue or to enhance that provision ...

The position thus is reached that the premise upon which the Legal Aid Service based its argument, namely that Mr Bradley took up his office with no rights secured under s 6 beyond 8 March 2000, is not made good ...

A court's institutional independence is affected by its composition. ***Forge v ASIC*** considered an argument that the appointment of acting judges to the Supreme Court of New South Wales deprived that Court of independence because acting judges lacked long-term security of tenure. The High Court held that the appointment of acting judges does not of itself impair the independence of a court. The High Court held that it is not a defining characteristic of a court that it be composed of only permanent full-time judges.

Forge v Australian Securities and Investments Commission (2006) 228 CLR 45

The Supreme Court of New South Wales heard corporate law proceedings involving Mr Forge and ASIC. Acting Justice Foster decided the case. Section 37 of the Supreme Court Act 1970 *(NSW) permitted the appointment of acting judges. Forge argued that Foster AJ's decision was invalid because, whether or not it was the correct decision, the appointment of acting judges to a court breached the* Kable *doctrine. The High Court disagreed.*

Gummow, Hayne and Crennan JJ

An important element, however, in the institutional characteristics of courts in Australia is their capacity to administer the common law system of adversarial trial. Essential to that system is the conduct of trial by an independent and impartial tribunal.

It by no means follows, however, that the only means of securing an independent and impartial Supreme Court is to require that the court is made up of none other than full-time permanent judges with security of tenure ...

No matter whether the conclusion, that s 37 does not give unlimited power to make acting appointments, is seen as following from the words of the Act, or as reinforced or required by constitutional considerations, it is a conclusion that proceeds from an unstated premise about what constitutes a "court". Thus, the conclusion may proceed from a premise that a court, or at least the Supreme Court, of a State must *principally* be constituted by permanent judges (who have tenure of the kind for which the *Act of Settlement* provided: appointment during good behaviour for life, or, now, until a set retirement age, with no diminution of remuneration during tenure). Or the conclusion may proceed from a premise that is stated at a higher level of abstraction: that the courts, and in particular the Supreme Court, of a State must be institutionally independent and impartial.

The first statement of the premise may be seen as focusing upon quantitative considerations. On what terms are *most* of the judges appointed? The second statement of the premise may be seen as pointing to qualitative rather than quantitative considerations. But both statements of the relevant premise rest ultimately upon considerations of the fact and appearance of institutional independence and impartiality ...

The institutional integrity of State Supreme Courts is not inevitably compromised by the appointment of an acting judge. But the institutional integrity of the body may be distorted by such appointments if the informed observer may reasonably conclude that the institution no longer is, and no longer appears to be, independent and impartial as, for example, would be the case if a significant element of its membership stood to gain or lose from the way in which the duties of office were executed ...

Section 37 of the *Supreme Court Act* is not invalid. It is not demonstrated that s 37 was not validly engaged to appoint Foster AJ as an acting judge of the Supreme Court of New South Wales.

The High Court explained that in some circumstances the appointment of acting judges would impair the institutional integrity of a court, and identified various factors relevant to determining when such a circumstance exists.

Forge v Australian Securities and Investments Commission (2006) 228 CLR 45

Gummow, Hayne and Crennan JJ

Whether, or when, the institutional integrity of the court is affected depends, then, upon consideration of much more than the bare question: how many acting judges have been appointed?

Regard must be paid to who has been appointed, for how long, to do what, and, no less importantly, why it has been thought necessary to make the acting appointments that have been made. Those alleging invalidity in the present matter did not seek to make a case founded in any examination of the circumstances that led either to the successive appointments of Foster AJ, or any of the other appointments made at or about the time of his appointments. To the extent that those alleging invalidity sought to make any case separate from and additional to their basic proposition that s 37 is wholly invalid, they did no more than point to the numbers of appointees. For the reasons that have been given, s 37 is not to be read down by reference to some numerical criterion.

A court's institutional independence is also affected by the tasks given to its judges outside of their official judicial roles. ***Wainohu v New South Wales*** shows that it is a defining characteristic of courts that they give reasons for their decisions. The case also demonstrates how the institutional integrity doctrine operates to limit the type and nature of functions that might be granted to a State judge *persona designata*.

The High Court held that the institutional integrity of a court will be impaired if a function conferred on one of its judges *persona designata* is incompatible with the judge's performance of judicial functions or with the exercise by the judiciary of its functions as an institution exercising judicial power. ***Wainohu*** shows that the incompatibility condition of the *persona designata* exception to the federal ***Boilermakers'*** doctrine applies also to the institutional integrity doctrine. In both cases, the incompatibility doctrine is directed at preserving the institutional integrity of courts.

In this case, New South Wales legislation empowered a Supreme Court judge acting *persona designata* to issue a declaration that an organisation is a criminal organisation, and provided that reasons need not be given for making such a declaration. The legislation also empowered the Supreme Court, acting in its capacity as a court, to issue a control order against any person proven to be a member of a declared organisation. The High Court held that the legislation impaired the institutional integrity of the Supreme Court for a number of related reasons. First, the function conferred on the judge *persona designata* impaired the fact and appearance of the Supreme Court's independence and impartiality because the function was incompatible with the holding of judicial office due to the absence of a requirement to give reasons. Secondly, the appearance of the Supreme Court's independence and impartiality was impaired because the Supreme Court's judicial function was closely connected to the administrative function undertaken by one of its judges *persona designata* in a manner incompatible with judicial office. Thirdly, the appearance of the Supreme Court's independence and impartiality was impaired because the legislation created the impression that the judge acting *persona designata* in a manner incompatible with judicial office was acting in their capacity as a member of the Supreme Court.

Wainohu v New South Wales (2011) 243 CLR 181

Part 2 of the Crimes (Criminal Organisations Control) Act 2009 *(NSW) allowed the Commissioner of Police to apply to a judge who had been designated by the Attorney-General as an 'eligible judge' for a declaration in relation to an organisation. If the eligible judge makes the declaration which is sought, then Part 3 of the Act empowered the Supreme Court, on the application of the Commissioner of Police, to make control orders against individual members of the Club. Wainohu was a member of the Hells Angels Motorcycle Club, which was a declared organisation. Pre-empting an application for a control order made against him, Wainohu challenged the constitutional validity of the Act.*

French CJ and Kiefel J

The plaintiff, Derek Wainohu, is a member of the Club and ... challenges the Act's validity on the basis that it confers functions upon eligible judges and upon the Supreme Court which undermine the institutional integrity of that Court ...

An eligible judge may make a determination under Pt 2 upon information and submissions, without regard to the rules of evidence, partly based on information and submissions not able to be disclosed to the organisation or its members, and with no obligation to provide reasons for the determination which is made. The Act thus provides for the enlistment of judges of the Supreme Court to determine applications for declarations using processes which, if adopted by the Court itself, would be repugnant to the judicial function.

The making of a declaration by an eligible judge is a necessary condition for the exercise by the Court of its jurisdiction to make a control order ...

[A State] cannot confer administrative functions on a court which are incompatible with the court's essential and defining characteristics as a court and thereby with its place in the national integrated judicial system for which Ch III of the Constitution provides. Nor, as is explained in these reasons, can a State legislature confer upon judges of a State court administrative functions which substantially impair its essential and defining characteristics as a court.

The Act effects such an impairment. It does so because it provides, in effect, that the jurisdiction of the Supreme Court to make control orders against members of an organisation will be enlivened by a decision of a judge of the Court, after an adversarial proceeding, on complex and important matters of fact, for which the Act provides that no reasons need be given. The Act also creates an impression of a connection between the performance of a non-judicial function and the following exercise of judicial power, such that the performance of that function may affect perceptions of the judge, and of the court of which he or she is a member, to the detriment of that court. The plaintiff's challenge to the validity of the Act should succeed ...

[I]t is also a defining characteristic of a court that it generally gives reasons for its decisions ...

The principle in *Kable* also leads to the conclusion that a State legislature cannot enact a law conferring upon a judge of a State court a non-judicial function which is substantially incompatible with the functions of the court of which the judge is a member. Although the function may be conferred upon the judge in his or her capacity as an individual, the statute may create a close connection and therefore an association with the person's role as a judge ... The question which then arises is whether the performance of that function would impair the defining characteristics of that court ...

The jurisdiction of the Supreme Court that can be invoked after a declaration has been made can lead to the imposition of significant restrictions on the freedoms of individuals, including individuals who have not engaged in any criminal activity, and are not likely to do so. The statutory exclusion of a duty on the part of the eligible judge to provide reasons for his or her decisions under Pt 2 contrasts sharply with the general duty of judges of the Supreme Court to give reasons for their judicial decisions. It also means that the basis of the eligible judge's satisfaction as to a necessary condition for the exercise by the Supreme Court of its jurisdiction to make a control order or interim control order may be unexplained to that Court or to anybody else ...

The centrality, to the judicial function, of a public explanation of reasons for final decisions and important interlocutory rulings has long been recognised ...

Whether or not an eligible judge acts persona designata under Pt 2 or as a member of the Supreme Court, requirements of compatibility direct attention to the functions conferred upon the judge, the extent to which they are connected to or integrated with the exercise of the Court's jurisdiction, and the degree of decisional independence enjoyed by the judge in the exercise of those functions ...

In this case, however, the non-judicial function conferred by the Act on the eligible judge is closely connected to the exercise of the jurisdiction conferred by the Act on the Supreme Court. A declaration under Pt 2 is a condition precedent to the exercise of the Court's jurisdiction to make control orders and interim control orders under Pt 3 ...

Under the scheme of the Act, a judge of the Supreme Court of New South Wales, appearing to all the world as a judge of the Court sitting as such, hears and determines a substantial, contested application on "information" and "submissions" the nature and provenance of which is not limited by any statutory definition ...

To the extent that the statute effectively immunises the eligible judge from any obligation to provide such reasons, it marks the function which that judge carries out as lacking an essential incident of the judicial function. At the same time, however, the Act creates a connection between the non-judicial function conferred upon an eligible judge by Pt 2 of the Act and the exercise of jurisdiction by the Supreme Court under Pt 3 of the Act.

This has the consequence that a judge of the Court performs a function integral to the exercise of jurisdiction by the Court, by making the declaration, but lacks the duty to provide reasons for that decision. The appearance of a judge making a declaration is thereby created whilst the giving of reasons, a hallmark of that office, is denied. These features cannot but affect perceptions of the role of a judge of the Court, to the detriment of the Court.

Procedural independence as a defining characteristic

Another group of cases considering the defining characteristics of courts share the theme of procedural independence. These cases are about courts being free from improper direction or control as to the exercise of their jurisdiction and courts affording parties procedural fairness.

Gypsy Jokers Motorcycle Club v Commissioner of Police involved a claim that legislation deprived a court of the overarching characteristic of independence by subjecting the court to external direction or control over the exercise of its jurisdiction. The High Court held that, on its proper construction, the impugned legislation did not subject the court to external control or direction. In this case, legislation prohibited the disclosure of information to one party if the court was satisfied that the information met certain criteria. However, the legislation did not control the way in which the court itself could use that information in making its decision or direct the court to make a particular decision.

Gypsy Jokers Motorcycle Club Inc v Commissioner of Police (2008) 234 CLR 532

It was believed that 'bikie gangs' fortified their clubhouses to frustrate police operations. The* Corruption and Crime Commission Act 2003 *was enacted in Western Australia to empower the Commissioner of Police to order the removal of fortifications if the Commissioner believed that premises were heavily fortified and habitually used as a place of resort by people who may reasonably be suspected of being involved in organised crime. The legislation permitted the owner of premises to apply to the Supreme Court for a review of whether the Commissioner could reasonably have held the belief required to issue a removal order. Section 76 governed reviews. Sub section (2) provided:

> *The Commissioner of Police may identify any information provided to the court for the purposes of the review as confidential if its disclosure might prejudice the operations of the Commissioner of Police, and information so identified is for the court's use only and is not to be disclosed to any other person, whether or not a party to the proceedings, or publicly disclosed in any way.*

The Gypsy Jokers Motorcycle Club argued this provision impaired the institutional integrity of the Supreme Court because it rendered the Commissioner's decision unexaminable by the Supreme Court.

Gummow, Hayne, Heydon and Kiefel JJ

[I]t may be said that the conditions which must exist for courts in this country to administer justice according to law are inconsistent with some forms of external control of those courts appropriate to the exercise of authority by public officials and administrators. The appellant contends that the legislation under challenge does purport to exercise an impermissible form of control over the exercise by the Supreme Court of its jurisdiction.

The first step in the making of that assessment of the validity of any given law is one of statutory construction. So far as different constructions appear to be available, a construction is to be selected which would avoid rather than lead to a conclusion of constitutional invalidity ...

Counsel for the respondent put at the forefront of his oral submissions to this Court the proposition that s 76(2) does not render unexaminable by the Supreme Court the decision of the

Commissioner of Police. That submission should be accepted and the contrary submission by the appellant rejected ...

Any exercise by the Commissioner of Police of the power conferred by s 76(2) is conditioned upon the requirement introduced by the phrase "if its disclosure might prejudice the operations of the Commissioner of Police". The power is not conditioned upon the existence of the opinion of the Commissioner to that effect. Rather, the condition operates in circumstances where information is provided by the Commissioner to the Supreme Court and it is for the Supreme Court to determine upon evidence provided to it whether the disclosure of the information might have the prejudicial effect spoken of in the sub-section ...

The dissenting judgment of Wheeler JA in the Court of Appeal largely was premised upon a construction of s 76 which gave to the Commissioner the power to determine "unilaterally" that materials were not to be disclosed, with the result that the Supreme Court was constrained by the Commissioner of Police, an officer of the Executive Branch of government, in the independent performance of its review function under s 76. However, for the reasons given above, that premise should not be accepted and as a result the stated consequence of Executive Branch constraint does not follow.

What then of the second part of s 76(2)? This states that the information is for "the use" only of the Supreme Court. However, that "use" entails all that is necessary or appropriate for the exercise by the Supreme Court of its jurisdiction to conduct the "review" identified in s 76(1) ...

The preferable construction of the words "and is not to be disclosed to any other person, whether or not a party to the proceedings" is that they deny what otherwise would be any standing or entitlement of parties and non-parties under the usual processes of the Supreme Court in civil litigation to obtain any order or relief whether by way of discovery, subpoena or otherwise, which would entail disclosure of the information. However, two points should be made here. The first is that the operation of this legislative regime has an outcome comparable with that of the common law respecting public interest immunity, but with the difference that the Court itself may make use of the information in question. The second is related to the first, and is that the operation of this provision, like the balance of s 76(2), is conditioned upon the Supreme Court first having determined that disclosure of the information, identified by the Commissioner from that provided to the Court, might prejudice the operations of the Commissioner. Accordingly, there is here no legislative mandate for dictation to the Supreme Court by the Commissioner of the performance of its review function ...

As a general proposition, it may be accepted that legislation which purported to direct the courts as to the manner and outcome of the exercise of their jurisdiction would be apt impermissibly to impair the character of the courts as independent and impartial tribunals ...

In their application to the Supreme Court itself, the words "[nor] publicly disclosed in any way" should not be read as an attempted legislative direction as to the manner of the outcome of any review application made under s 76. The words are no more than an attempt at exhortation and an effort to focus attention by the Court to the prejudicial effect disclosure may have. That is, however, something the Supreme Court necessarily will have in mind throughout, given the framework provided by s 76(2).

In ***K-Generation Pty Ltd v Liquor Licensing Court***, the High Court again accepted that the defining characteristic of independence would be impaired if a court was subject to direction or control as to the manner of the exercise of its jurisdiction. The impugned legislation in this case required a court, on the application of an Executive Government official, to 'take steps to maintain confidentiality of information classified by the Commissioner of Police as criminal intelligence'. The High Court held that the legislation did not impair the institutional integrity of the court because it was for the court to determine what particular steps should be taken and for the court to determine what weight should be given to the classified information.

K-Generation Pty Ltd v Liquor Licensing Court (2009) 237 CLR 501

A new section 28A(5) was inserted into the Liquor Licensing Act 1997 *(SA), which provided:*

> *In any proceedings under this Act, the [Liquor] Commissioner, the Court or the Supreme Court –*
>
> *(a) must, on the application of the Commissioner of Police, take steps to maintain the confidentiality of information classified by the Commissioner of Police as criminal intelligence, including steps to receive evidence and hear argument about the information in private in the absence of the parties to the proceedings and their representatives; and*
>
> *(b) may take evidence consisting of or relating to information classified by the Commissioner of Police as criminal intelligence by way of affidavit of a police officer of or above the rank of superintendent.*

K-Generation argued that the provision had the effect of authorising the Executive Government to direct the court in the exercise of its jurisdiction. The High Court held that, properly interpreted, the provision did not require a court to act at the direction of the Executive Government.

French CJ

Section 28A infringes upon the open justice principle that is an essential part of the functioning of courts in Australia. It also infringes upon procedural fairness to the extent that it authorises and effectively requires the Licensing Court and the Supreme Court to consider, without disclosure to the party to whom it relates, criminal intelligence information submitted to the Court by the Commissioner of Police.

However, it cannot be said that the section confers upon the Licensing Court or the Supreme Court functions which are incompatible with their institutional integrity as courts of the States or with their constitutional roles as repositories of federal jurisdiction. Properly construed the section leaves it to the courts to determine whether information classified as criminal intelligence answers that description. It also leaves it to the courts to decide what steps may be necessary to preserve the confidentiality of such material. The courts may, consistently with the section, disclose the material to legal representatives of the party affected on conditions of confidentiality enforced by undertaking or order. It leaves it open to the courts to decide whether to accept or reject such material and to decide what if any weight shall be placed upon it.

Gummow, Hayne, Heydon, Crennan and Kiefel JJ

The sole ground on which special leave was given is that the Full Court erred in law in finding s 28A of the Act to be valid notwithstanding that it required the Licensing Court to hear and determine the review without disclosing to K-Generation information classified as "criminal intelligence" which had been relied upon by the Liquor Commissioner in refusing the application for an entertainment venue licence ...

[The appellants] contend that the effect of s 28A of the Act is to deprive the Licensing Court of the reality or appearance of independence or impartiality ...

[T]he definition of "criminal intelligence" in s 4, is so drawn that had a challenge been presented by the appellants it would have been for the Licensing Court to be satisfied that facts existed sufficient to found the expectation of the prejudicial consequences spelt out in the definition; or, that the classification was "objectively correct" ... In this way, the decision of the Commissioner of Police to classify material involved in this litigation as "criminal intelligence" would have been open to "collateral attack" by the appellants in the Licensing Court. Accordingly, it is not correct, as the appellants would have it, that the Licensing Court had been obliged to accept the information classified by the Commissioner as "criminal intelligence".

Thereafter, and upon application by the Commissioner of Police, the Licensing Court is required to take steps towards a particular outcome. That outcome is the maintenance of the confidentiality of the information. The Licensing Court is not directed as to which particular steps may be taken, nor is it denied the assistance of submissions by the legal representatives of parties other than the Police Commissioner as to what those steps should be. The steps taken may be provisional in the sense that they may be varied, added to or subtracted from, as the exigencies of the litigation in the Licensing Court progressively appear and as submissions are made to the Licensing Court.

The steps which are taken may go so far as to involve the reception of evidence and the hearing of argument by the Licensing Court in private and in the absence of the parties and their representatives. However, the phrase "including steps" in par (a) of s 28A(5) does not mandate the taking of such steps. Rather, the phrase appears in s 28A(5) to mark out the limits of the range within which the Licensing Court may act in particular cases when determining how to maintain the confidentiality of the information.

Further, the Licensing Court is not bound to accept in its terms the "criminal intelligence" upon which the Police Commissioner relies. The Court itself may question the evidence in closed session ...

The result is that s 28A(5) did not operate to deny to the Licensing Court the constitutional character of an independent and impartial tribunal ...

In ***International Finance Trust Co Ltd v New South Wales Crime Commission***, the High Court held that legislation directing a court to exercise its jurisdiction in a way that denies procedural fairness to a party deprives the court of the characteristic of being an independent and impartial tribunal.

International Finance Trust Co Ltd v New South Wales Crime Commission (2009) 240 CLR 319

French CJ

The *Criminal Assets Recovery Act 1990* (NSW) ("the CAR Act") empowers the New South Wales Crime Commission ("the Commission") to apply to the Supreme Court of New South Wales for a restraining order in respect of some or all of the property of a person suspected of having committed a serious offence. The provisions relating to restraining orders are in aid of the Commission's power to apply to the Court for forfeiture of the relevant property.

The Commission may apply to the Court for a restraining order without notice to the person affected. If the application is supported by an affidavit stating that the person affected is suspected of having engaged in "serious crime related activities", and setting out the grounds for that suspicion, and if the Court considers, having regard to the affidavit, that there are reasonable grounds for the suspicion, then the Court must make the order sought ...

The basis of the challenge is that the CAR Act imposes upon the Supreme Court functions which so distort its institutional integrity as to be inconsistent with its status as a repository of federal jurisdiction, conferred pursuant to Ch III of the Commonwealth Constitution. The challenge relies upon the decision of this Court in *Kable v Director of Public Prosecutions (NSW).*

On its proper construction, s 10 of the CAR Act requires the Supreme Court to hear and determine, without notice to the persons affected, applications for restraining orders made ex parte by the Commission. For that reason the section impermissibly directs the Court as to the manner of the exercise of its jurisdiction and restricts the application of procedural fairness in the judicial process and conditions its full application upon a discretion exercised by the Executive branch of the government of New South Wales. It is not to the point that the restriction is temporary, nor that the scope of the order may subsequently be varied by an exclusion order, which can only be made if the party affected shows, on the balance of probabilities, that the affected property was not illegally acquired. In my opinion the section is invalid ...

Procedural fairness or natural justice lies at the heart of the judicial function. In the federal constitutional context, it is an incident of the judicial power exercised pursuant to Ch III of the Constitution. It requires that a court be and appear to be impartial, and provide each party to proceedings before it with an opportunity to be heard, to advance its own case and to answer, by evidence and argument, the case put against it.

According to the circumstances, the content of the requirements of procedural fairness may vary. When an ex parte application for interlocutory relief is made the court, in the ordinary course, has a discretion whether or not to hear the application without notice to the party to be affected. In exercising that discretion it will have regard to the legitimate interests of the moving party which have to be protected, whether there is likely to be irrevocable damage to the interests of the affected party if the order is made, and what provision can be made for the affected party to be heard to have the order discharged or varied after it has been made. In so saying, it is not intended to suggest that an official cannot validly be authorised by statute to bring an application ex parte to a federal court or to a State or Territory court capable of exercising federal jurisdiction. The CAR Act takes the further step of requiring the Supreme Court to hear and determine such an application ex parte.

To require a court, as s 10 does, not only to receive an ex parte application, but also to hear and determine it ex parte, if the Executive so desires, is to direct the court as to the manner in which it exercises its jurisdiction and in so doing to deprive the court of an important characteristic of judicial power. That is the power to ensure, so far as practicable, fairness between the parties ...

In my opinion the power conferred on the Commission to choose, in effect, whether to require the Supreme Court of New South Wales to hear and determine an application for a restraining order without notice to the party affected is incompatible with the judicial function of that Court. It deprives the Court of the power to determine whether procedural fairness, judged by reference to practical considerations of the kind usually relevant to applications for interlocutory freezing orders, requires that notice be given to the party affected before an order is made. It deprives the Court of an essential incident of the judicial function. In that way, directing the Court as to the manner of the exercise of its jurisdiction, it distorts the institutional integrity of the Court and affects its capacity as a repository of federal jurisdiction.

Three dissenting judges held that the impugned legislation did not in fact require a denial of procedural fairness. However, these judges accepted the general proposition that legislation that requires a court to deny procedural fairness to a party would impair the court's institutional integrity.

International Finance Trust Co Ltd v New South Wales Crime Commission (2009) 240 CLR 319

Hayne, Crennan and Kiefel JJ (dissenting)

Do the statute's requirements that the Supreme Court freeze dealings in any property of a person on ex parte application by the executive, and proof of mere suspicion that the person has committed a crime (based on articulated grounds and found by the Court to be reasonable), require the Supreme Court to engage in activity repugnant to the judicial process to such a degree that the statute is beyond the legislative power of the State? These reasons will demonstrate that this question should be answered "no" ...

What is presently important is that, because the CAR Act gives the Supreme Court the jurisdiction to make a restraining order, the Act takes the Court and its processes as it finds them, except to the extent the Act modifies or qualifies those processes. Any modification of, or qualification to, that rule would require the clearest language. There is no provision of the CAR Act that expressly modifies that "elementary rule of justice" that a party affected by a judicial order obtained ex parte may apply for its discharge. No implied modification or qualification of the rule can be spelled out from the terms of the CAR Act, whether by reference to the Act's provisions about ancillary orders or otherwise.

Assistant Commissioner Condon v Pompano Pty Ltd involved Queensland control order legislation permitting the Queensland Supreme Court to receive and use classified information that could not be made available to the respondent in a contested hearing. The argument was that the legislation impaired the institutional integrity of the Supreme Court by requiring it to conduct a proceeding in a way that denied procedural fairness to the respondent. The High Court held that the legislation did not deny procedural fairness to the respondent. The legislation denied the respondent knowledge of how the applicant sought to prove an allegation made against the respondent but did not deny the respondent knowledge of the allegation itself.

Assistant Commissioner Condon v Pompano Pty Ltd (2013) 252 CLR 38

French CJ

Understandably the respondents placed great emphasis on the provision for special closed hearings and the secrecy attaching to criminal intelligence tendered to the Supreme Court. Those provisions undoubtedly represent incursions upon the open court principle and procedural fairness. The Supreme Court, however, retains its decisional independence and the powers necessary to mitigate the extent of the unfairness to the respondent in the circumstances of the particular case. It retains the responsibility to determine what weight, if any, to give to criminal intelligence and, in particular, hearsay evidence relating to information provided by informants. The power of the Supreme Court to control its own proceedings in order to avoid unfairness also suggests that it would have a discretion to refuse to act upon criminal intelligence where to do so would give rise to a degree of unfairness in the circumstances of the particular case which could not have been contemplated at the time that the criminal intelligence declaration was made.

Despite the incursions on the open court principle and the normal protections of procedural fairness effected by the impugned provisions of the COA, they do not so impair the essential or defining characteristics of the Supreme Court as a court as to be beyond the legislative power of the Queensland Parliament. The impugned provisions are valid.

Hayne, Crennan, Kiefel and Bell JJ

The procedural unfairness which it was said was worked by the criminal intelligence provisions of the CO Act was identified as being the denial to the respondent of any opportunity to test the criminal intelligence ...

[T]he criminal intelligence provisions deny a respondent knowledge of *how* the Commissioner seeks to prove an allegation; they do not deny the respondent knowledge of *what* is the allegation that is made against it ...

In deciding any application for declaration of an organisation as a criminal organisation, the Supreme Court would know that evidence of those assertions and allegations that constituted criminal intelligence had not been and could not be challenged directly. The Court would know that the respondent and its members could go no further than make general denials of any wrongdoing of the kind alleged. What weight to give to that evidence would be a matter for the Court to judge.

Contrary to a proposition which ran throughout the respondents' submissions in this case, noticing that the Supreme Court must take account of the fact that a respondent cannot controvert criminal intelligence does not seek to deny the allegation of legislative invalidity by asserting that the Supreme Court can be "relied on" to remedy any constitutional infirmity or deficiency in the legislative scheme. Rather, it points to the fact that under the impugned provisions the Supreme Court retains its capacity to act fairly and impartially. Retention of the Court's capacity to act fairly and impartially is critical to its continued institutional integrity ...

Consideration of the continued institutional integrity of the State courts directs attention to questions of independence, impartiality and fairness. In cases where it is said that the courts have been conscripted to do the Executive's bidding, the principal focus will likely fall upon questions of independence and impartiality. But that is not and was not said to be this case. Where, as here, a novel procedure is said to deny procedural fairness, attention must be directed to questions of fairness and impartiality. Observing that the Supreme Court can and will be expected to act fairly and impartially points firmly against invalidity.

Gageler J

My view, in short, is that Ch III of the Constitution mandates the observance of procedural fairness as an immutable characteristic of a Supreme Court and of every other court in Australia. Procedural fairness has a variable content but admits of no exceptions. A court cannot be required by statute to adopt a procedure that is unfair. A procedure is unfair if it has the capacity to result in the court making an order that finally alters or determines a right or legally protected interest of a person without affording that person a fair opportunity to respond to evidence on which that order might be made ...

The criminal intelligence provisions are saved from incompatibility with Ch III of the Constitution only by the capacity for the Supreme Court of Queensland to stay a substantive application in the exercise of inherent jurisdiction in a case where practical unfairness becomes manifest ...

Chapter III of the Constitution admits of legislative choice as to how, not whether, procedural fairness is provided in the exercise of a jurisdiction invested in, or power conferred on, a court. Procedural fairness can be provided by different means in different contexts and may well be provided by different means in a single context. The legislative choice as to how procedural fairness is provided extends to how procedural fairness is accommodated, in a particular context, to competing interests ...

In ***SDC v Director-General of Security***, the High Court again affirmed that affording procedural fairness is a defining characteristic of courts. A majority of the Court held that procedural fairness is about avoiding practical injustice rather than fixed rules about a 'minimum requirement' of procedural applying in every case. In the situation considered in this case, the fact that a party was denied access to materials available for the Court to consider in its decision-making did not cause practical injustice.

SDC v Director-General of Security [2022] HCA 32

SDC unsuccessfully sought merits review in the Administrative Appeals Tribunal of an adverse security assessment made against him by the Australian Security Intelligence Organisation ('ASIO'). Secrecy provisions in the legislation enabled the Tribunal to have access to the contents of the security assessment but prohibited SDC and his lawyers from having access to those contents or to a summary of those contents. The secrecy provisions had the same operation when SDC challenged the Tribunal's decision via a statutory appeal mechanism in the Federal Court. SDC could also have challenged the Tribunal's decision by launching an ordinary judicial review action in the Federal Court, but the rules of public interest immunity would have prevented both the Court and SDC and his lawyers from having access to the contents of the security assessment. In the High Court, SDC argued that the secrecy provisions were unconstitutional because they required the Federal Court to deny him procedural fairness. A majority of the High Court rejected that argument, emphasising that any disadvantage experienced by SDC was a consequence of his decision to use the statutory appeal mechanism rather the ordinary judicial review mechanism.

Kiefel CJ, Keane and Gleeson JJ

The appeal to this Court is concerned only with the appellant's challenge to the validity of s 46(2) of the AAT Act. The appellant's contention is that Ch III of the *Constitution* precludes the making of a law that denies a party to proceedings in a court of the federal judicature a fair opportunity to respond to the evidence on which an order of the court which finally alters or determines a right or legally protected interest of that party might be based, and that s 46(2) is such a law ...

It was common ground in this Court, as it was in the Federal Court, that Parliament cannot require a court within Ch III of the *Constitution* to exercise the judicial power of the Commonwealth in a manner inconsistent with the character of a court or the nature of judicial power. It was also common ground that procedural fairness is an essential feature of a Ch III court and that, as was said by the plurality in *Condon v Pompano Pty Ltd*, the ultimate question is "whether, taken as a whole, the court's procedures for resolving the dispute accord both parties procedural fairness and avoid 'practical injustice'".

The critical divergence between the appellant and the respondents is that the respondents argued that the "minimum requirement" of an opportunity to know and respond to adverse material before the Federal Court, insisted upon by the appellant, is not invariably required to prevent practical injustice in an appeal under s 44 of the AAT Act from the Tribunal to the Federal Court.

The question whether practical injustice may be caused to a litigant is not to be resolved by reference to fixed rules as to the "minimum requirement" of procedural fairness that apply in every case in which the judicial power of the Commonwealth is engaged. Whether practical injustice may be occasioned to a litigant depends upon the nature of the proceedings and the rights and interests at stake ...

An appeal under s 44 of the AAT Act, to which s 46 applies, is additional to the available remedies under s 75(v) of the *Constitution* or s 39B of the *Judiciary Act*. As a practical matter, any "disadvantage" to the appellant occasioned by s 46(2) would have been avoided by the choice of proceedings under these other remedies. But such a choice would have denied the appellant the forensic advantage offered by s 46(1) in having the certificated matter provided to the Court. Section 46(2) operated inseparably from s 46(1) to provide the appellant with forensic advantages different from those otherwise provided by law. The appellant, having chosen to pursue the remedy that afforded those advantages, suffered no practical injustice.

The separate dissenting judgments of Gageler and Gordon JJ made two key points. The first was that, unlike the legislation considered in other cases, the Federal Court had no residual discretion to modify its processes to alleviate any unfairness that might arise from the non-disclosure. The second was to emphasise that the existence of an alternative judicial review jurisdiction for challenging a decision was not relevant to the issue of whether the statutory appeal jurisdiction actually exercised was procedurally fair.

SDC v Director-General of Security [2022] HCA 32

Gordon J

By forbidding the Court in any and every case from making any certified matter available to the applicant or any representative of the applicant, s 46(2) binds the Federal Court to a procedure that has the potential to result in unfairness. Viewed as a whole, s 46 renders the Federal Court unable to respond to potential "practical injustice". Put differently, s 46(2) deprives the Federal Court of "the power to ensure, so far as practicable [having regard to the particular context of the case], fairness between the parties". Insofar as s 46(2) operates in respect of a certificate issued under s 39B(2)(a), it imposes a blanket and inflexible non-disclosure requirement, operating as a strait-jacket on the Court's ability to minimise or alleviate practical injustice and requiring the Court to act "unjudicially" ...

The point of present importance is that the Court is deprived of any capacity to consider and mould its procedures to avoid practical injustice to the parties in a particular proceeding. That deprives the Court of an essential incident of the judicial function and thus an essential characteristic of a court ...

The jurisdiction of the Federal Court to hear and determine appeals under s 44(1) of the AAT Act from decisions of the Tribunal reviewing a security assessment "is necessarily conditioned by the requirement that it observe procedural fairness in the exercise of that jurisdiction". Having established a mechanism for seeking merits review of a security assessment (which Parliament did not have to do) and having established an avenue of appeal on a question of law to the Federal Court (which Parliament also did not have to do), the question is whether that regime impairs an essential characteristic of the Court or an essential incident of the exercise of judicial power. The availability and possible forensic advantages or disadvantages of a separate avenue of review (judicial review under s 75(v) of the *Constitution* or s 39B of the *Judiciary Act*) ... have no bearing on that question; they are irrelevant to the validity of s 46(2).

Decisional independence as a defining characteristic

Decisional independence is the theme shared by another group of cases considering the defining characteristics of courts. This characteristic is concerned with courts undertaking a genuine adjudicative process to reach decisions.

In ***South Australia v Totani***, the High Court held that decisional independence is part of what makes a court an independent and impartial body. Chief Justice French's judgment summarised much of the existing case law and doctrine.

South Australia v Totani (2010) 242 CLR 1

Section 14(1) of the Serious and Organised Crime (Control) Act 2008 *(SA) provided that the Magistrates Court 'must, on the application of the Commissioner, make a control order against a person (the defendant) if the Court is satisfied that the defendant is a member of a declared organisation'. Section 10 gave the Attorney-General power to make a declaration in respect of an organisation if satisfied that its members are involved in 'serious criminal activity' and that the organisation represents a risk to public safety and order in South Australia.*

Totani was a member of the Finks Motorcycle Club. The Club was a declared organisation under the Act. The Magistrates Court made a control order against Totani. Totani argued that section 14(1) impaired the institutional integrity of the Magistrates Court. The High Court agreed.

French CJ

At the heart of judicial independence, although not exhaustive of the concept, is decisional independence from influences external to proceedings in the court, including, but not limited to, the influence of the executive government and its authorities. Decisional independence is a necessary condition of impartiality. Procedural fairness effected by impartiality and the natural justice hearing rule lies at the heart of the judicial process. The open-court principle, which provides, among other things, a visible assurance of independence and impartiality, is also an "essential aspect" of the characteristics of all courts, including the courts of the States

The text and structure of Ch III of the Constitution postulate an integrated Australian court system for the exercise of the judicial power of the Commonwealth with this Court at its apex. There is no distinction, so far as concerns the judicial power of the Commonwealth, between State courts and federal courts created by the Parliament. The consequences of the constitutional placement of State courts in the integrated system include the following:

1. A State legislature cannot confer upon a court of a State a function which substantially impairs its institutional integrity and which is therefore incompatible with its role as a repository of federal jurisdiction: *Kable; Fardon v Attorney-General (Qld).*
2. State legislation impairs the institutional integrity of a court if it confers upon it a function which is repugnant to or incompatible with the exercise of the judicial power of the Commonwealth: *Kable; Fardon v Attorney-General (Qld).*
3. The institutional integrity of a court requires both the reality and appearance of independence and impartiality: *Forge* citing *Ebner v Official Trustee in Bankruptcy.*

4. The principles underlying the majority judgments in *Kable* and further expounded in the decisions of this Court which have followed after *Kable* do not constitute a codification of the limits of State legislative power with respect to State courts. Each case in which the *Kable* doctrine is invoked will require consideration of the impugned legislation because [*Fardon v Attorney-General (Qld)*]

   > the critical notions of repugnancy and incompatibility are insusceptible of further definition in terms which necessarily dictate future outcomes.

   For legislators this may require a prudential approach to the enactment of laws directing courts on how judicial power is to be exercised, particularly in areas central to the judicial function such as the provision of procedural fairness (*International Finance Trust Co Ltd*) and the conduct of proceedings in open court. It may also require a prudential approach to the enactment of laws authorising the executive government or its authorities effectively to dictate the process or outcome of judicial proceedings.
5. The risk of a finding that a law is inconsistent with the limitations imposed by Ch III, protective of the institutional integrity of the courts, is particularly significant where the law impairs the reality or appearance of the decisional independence of the court.

... The question indicated by the use of the term "integrity" is whether the court is required or empowered by the impugned legislation to do something which is substantially inconsistent or incompatible with the continuing subsistence, in every aspect of its judicial role, of its defining characteristics as a court ...

[O]ne of the characteristics required of all courts capable of exercising the judicial power of the Commonwealth (including the courts of the Territories) is that they be, and appear to be, independent and impartial tribunals. Forms of external control of courts "appropriate to the exercise of authority by public officials and administrators" are inconsistent with that requirement. The requirement is not a judicially generated imposition. It derives from historically based assumptions about courts which were extant at the time of Federation ...

In ***Totani***, the High Court struck down legislation that required a court to issue a control order against a person if the court was satisfied that the person was a member of an organisation declared to be a prohibited organisation by a Minister. The High Court explained that the legislation required the court to implement what was in reality an Executive Government decision rather than reach its own genuinely independent decision. Decisional independence involves a court undertaking a genuinely adjudicative process to reach its own decision. Legislation that has the effect of compelling a court to make pre-determined decisions impairs the court's institutional integrity.

South Australia v Totani (2010) 242 CLR 1

French CJ

The question in the present case is whether s 14(1) of the SOCC Act requires the Magistrates Court of South Australia to do something which is not consistent with the assumption of independence and impartiality of courts underlying Ch III of the Constitution ...

Section 14(1) represents a substantial recruitment of the judicial function of the Magistrates Court to an essentially executive process. It gives the neutral colour of a judicial decision to what will be, for the most part in most cases, the result of executive action. That executive action involves findings about a number of factual matters including the commission of criminal offences. None of those matters is required by the SOCC Act to be disclosed to the Court, nor is the evidence upon which such findings were based. In some cases the evidence, if properly classified as "criminal intelligence", would not be disclosable. Section 14(1) impairs the decisional independence of the Magistrates Court from the executive in substance and in appearance in areas going to personal liberty and the liability to criminal sanctions which lie at the heart of the judicial function.

I agree with the conclusion of Gummow J, Crennan and Bell JJ and Kiefel J that s 14(1) authorises the executive to enlist the Magistrates Court to implement decisions of the executive in a manner incompatible with that Court's institutional integrity. I agree also with the conclusion reached by Hayne J about the operation of s 14(1) in permitting the executive to enlist the Magistrates Court for the purpose of applying special restraints to particular individuals identified by the executive as meriting application for a control order and the repugnancy of that function to the institutional integrity of the Court.

In the exercise of the function conferred on it by s 14(1), the Magistrates Court loses one of its essential characteristics as a court, namely, the appearance of independence and impartiality. In my opinion, s 14(1) is invalid.

Crennan and Bell JJ

These considerations show that, in conferring a power on the court to make control orders under s 14(1), the State requires the court to exercise judicial power to make a control order after undertaking an adjudicative process that is so confined, and so dependent on the Executive's determination in the declaration, that it departs impermissibly from the ordinary judicial processes of an independent and impartial tribunal. Specifically, s 14(1) operates to draw the court into the implementation of the legislative policy expressed in the objects of the Act. The conditions upon which the court must make a control order require the court to give effect to the determination of the Executive in the declaration (which implements the legislative policy), without undertaking any independent curial determination, or adjudication, of the claim or premise of an application for a control order by the Commissioner of Police, that a particular defendant poses risks in terms of the objects of the Act.

This has the effect of rendering the court an instrument of the Executive, which undermines its independence. Section 14(1) requires the Magistrates Court of South Australia to act in a way which is incompatible with its constitutional position and the proper discharge of federal judicial responsibilities, and with its institutional integrity.

Magaming v The Queen demonstrates that mandatory minimum sentences for criminal offences do not impair the institutional integrity of courts by denying decisional independence. The High Court explained that a legislatively-prescribed minimum sentence is a yardstick to guide sentencing discretion just as a legislatively-prescribed maximum sentence is yardstick to guide sentencing discretion: each sets one end of the range within which a sentence may be set.

Magaming v The Queen (2013) 252 CLR 381

French CJ, Hayne, Crennan, Kiefel and Bell JJ

The *Migration Act* 1958 (Cth) ("the Act") created two offences prohibiting a person organising or facilitating the bringing or coming to Australia of persons who are not citizens and have no lawful right to come to Australia. (Non-citizens with no lawful right to come to Australia were referred to in argument as "unlawful non-citizens" and it is convenient to adopt that usage.) One offence (called "people smuggling") was to organise or facilitate the bringing or coming to Australia of another person who was an unlawful non-citizen. The other (described as an "[a] ggravated offence of people smuggling (at least 5 people)") was to organise or facilitate the bringing or coming to Australia of a group of at least five persons, at least five of whom were unlawful non-citizens.

The first, simple, form of offence (created by s 233A(1)) carried no mandatory minimum sentence; the second, aggravated, offence (created by s 233C(1)) carried a mandatory minimum term of imprisonment of five years with a minimum non-parole period of three years. A person who smuggled a group of five or more unlawful non-citizens could be charged with either offence ...

[T]he appellant submitted that the relevant provisions of the Act were invalid as "incompatible with the separation of judicial and prosecutorial functions", as "incompatible with the institutional integrity of the courts" or as requiring "the court to impose sentences that are arbitrary and non-judicial" ...

If, as in this case, one available charge is of an offence for which a mandatory minimum penalty is provided and there is another available charge of a different offence for which no minimum penalty is prescribed, the prescription of a mandatory minimum penalty for one of the offences does not lead to any different conclusion. Prosecutorial choice between the two charges is not an exercise of judicial power ...

It is enough to conclude that the availability or exercise of a choice between charging an accused with the aggravated offence created by s 233C, rather than one or more counts of the simple offence created by s 233A, is neither incompatible with the separation of judicial and prosecutorial functions nor incompatible with the institutional integrity of the courts. Legislative prescription of a mandatory minimum penalty for the offence under s 233C neither permits nor requires any different answer ...

As the appellant rightly submitted, adjudging and punishing criminal guilt is an exclusively judicial function. In very many cases, sentencing an offender will require the exercise of a discretion about what form of punishment is to be imposed and how heavy a penalty should be imposed. But that discretion is not unbounded. Its exercise is always hedged about by both statutory requirements and applicable judge-made principles. Sentencing an offender must always be undertaken according to law.

In *Markarian v The Queen*, the plurality observed that "[l]egislatures do not enact maximum available sentences as mere formalities. Judges need sentencing yardsticks." The prescription of a mandatory minimum penalty may now be uncommon but, if prescribed, a mandatory minimum penalty fixes one end of the relevant yardstick.

The appellant may be right to have submitted, as he did, that, even at 1901, mandatory minimum custodial sentences were "rare and exceptional". But as the appellant's submission implicitly recognised, mandatory sentences (including, at 1901, sentence of death and, since, sentence of life imprisonment) were then, and are now, known forms of legislative prescription of penalty for crime. Legislative prescription of a mandatory minimum term of imprisonment for an offence was not, and is not, on that account alone inconsistent with Ch III.

In ***Kuczborski v Queensland***, the High Court explained that legislation requiring a court to conduct a criminal trial in the ordinary manner in respect of new criminal offences that might be considered draconian or unreasonable does not deprive the court of any of its defining characteristics.

Kuczborski v Queensland (2014) 254 CLR 51

Queensland legislation established a suite of new criminal offences aimed at disrupting the activities of 'bikie gangs'. It was an offence for a participant in a 'criminal organisation' to attend the premises of the organisation, to attend social events with other participants in the organisation, to wear the logo or insignia of the organisation on licensed premises, and to encourage other persons to join the organisation. A 'criminal organisation' was an organisation declared by the Minister under regulations in accordance with various criteria. The Hells Angels Motorcycle Club was declared to be a criminal organisation. Kuczborski, a member of that association, argued that the new offences enlisted the courts in implementing a legislative and executive decision similarly to the legislation in* Totani. *The High Court disagreed.

Crennan, Kiefel, Gageler and Keane JJ

In truth, these laws do not declare membership of any organisation a criminal offence. Rather, they make membership of a designated association one ingredient of an offence. The commission of the offence must be proved in order to establish criminal guilt and liability to criminal punishment. Notwithstanding the colour lent to the plaintiff's argument by the tendentious language in which these provisions are expressed, their effect is not to enlist the courts to implement the policies of the executive or legislative branches of government.

These laws do not require a court to give effect, by judicial order, to a legislative or executive decision which establishes new norms of conduct for the plaintiff or other members of any association. Nor do they require a court to proceed otherwise than in accordance with the processes which are understood to characterise the exercise of judicial power. In these respects, the present case stands in contrast to the decision in *South Australia v Totani* ...

The judgments of the members of the majority in *Totani* identified the vice of s 14 of the SOCC Act, in terms of the *Kable* principle, as the requirement that the Magistrates Court create new norms of conduct the content of which was determined by the executive and legislature, and which restricted the liberty of the subject (over and above the norms binding the public under the general law), without any inquiry by the Court into past or threatened contraventions by the individual of any existing legal norm. The Court was called upon to implement, under the forms of judicial process, an executive judgment to restrict the liberty of any person who was a member of a declared organisation. It was this combination of features which warranted the description of s 14 of the SOCC Act as a provision which sought to enlist the Court to implement the policy of the executive and legislature under the guise of judicial determination.

Sections 60A, 60B and 60C of the *Criminal Code* do not require a court to lay down new norms of conduct. The new norms of conduct are created by the legislature anterior to the performance of the judicial function. Sections 60A, 60B and 60C do not require a court to perform any function other than a characteristically judicial function. They do not require a court to give effect to an executive or legislative decision to subject a given individual to new norms of conduct, much less that it should do so independently of the contravention of existing norms. They require the court to find facts and impose punishment as a result of the contravention of norms of conduct laid down by the legislature. That is not unorthodox: it is at "the heart of judicial power" to determine whether a person has engaged in conduct which is forbidden by law and, if so, to make an order as to the consequences which the law imposes by reason of that conduct ...

The only judicial activity which attends the enforcement of these laws is the characteristically judicial process of a criminal trial, upon which these laws do not trench.

Garlett is a similar case in that the law at issue might be considered draconian. The institutional integrity doctrine does not invalidate bad, harsh or unjust laws unless they deprive a court of one or more of its defining characteristics. The *High Risk Serious Offenders Act 2020* (WA) requires the Supreme Court of Western Australia to make a restriction order in relation to a serious offender if the Court is satisfied that such an order is necessary to ensure the adequate protection of the community against an unacceptable risk that the offender will commit a serious offence. Restriction orders can be either supervision orders (imposing bail-like conditions on a person) or detention orders (resulting in a person's detention in custody for so long as they pose an unacceptable risk to the community of committing a serious offence). The High Court rejected an argument that including robbery within the definition of serious offence within this legislative scheme contravened the institutional integrity doctrine.

Garlett v Western Australia [2022] HCA 30

Garlett, an Aboriginal man, had a long history of substance abuse and a criminal record for offences including robbery and assault. A detention order was made against him under the High Risk Serious Offenders Act 2020 *(WA).*

Kiefel CJ, Keane and Steward JJ

Section 48 of the HRSO Act contemplates that the Supreme Court "must" make a restriction order if it is satisfied that the offender is a "high risk serious offender" ...

The circumstance that the Court is not invested with a residual discretion to decline to make a restriction order does not establish that it is acting upon the dictation of the executive government as to the manner of deciding the case or its outcome. While s 48(1) is couched in mandatory terms, the terms of s 48(2) and the definition of "high risk serious offender" in s 7(1) mean that the judicial evaluation upon which the Court's determination depends is essential to the making of a restriction order. The decisive nature of the Court's evaluation is distinctly inconsistent with the suggestion that it must act upon the dictation of the legislature or the executive as to whether a restriction order should be made in any particular case.

Whether or not a risk that an offender will commit a "serious offence" is "unacceptable" is a question which requires the Court's judgment as to the nature and extent of the harm said to be in prospect. Further, whether a restriction order is "necessary" to protect against that risk requires recognition of what would otherwise be the offender's entitlement to be at liberty, an entitlement not lightly to be denied. The Court must consider whether a restriction order is necessary to ensure adequate protection of the community. The Court is required to perform this evaluative exercise and come to its own determination as to whether to make a restriction order; it does not automatically follow from the inclusion of an offence in Sch 1 that a restriction order must be made ...

The inclusion of an offence, such as robbery, in Sch 1 to the HRSO Act reflects a legislative judgment as to the kinds of offences which may be such as to cause harm of a kind from which the community needs protection different from that provided by the criminal law. It is not inimical to the institutional integrity of the Court to act upon a legislative judgment that robbery should be included in the serious offences listed in Sch 1. That is especially so where an element of the offence is violence to person or property, or the threat of such violence ...

[T]he Court, in making a restriction order, is required to act upon its own evaluative judgment, by reference to prescribed criteria, in order to determine whether such an order is necessary for the purpose of protecting the community from harm. The performance by the Court of this function proceeds by processes which are familiar aspects of the exercise of judicial power.

In dissent, Gordon J took a broader view of the legislative scheme. The legislative scheme had the effect of involving the courts in the executive function of crime prevention in respect of ordinary and unexceptional offences, thereby blurring the institutional separation of the courts from the other branches of government.

Garlett v Western Australia [2022] HCA 30

Gordon J

The HRSO Act goes beyond the exceptional. It can be engaged in respect of any of numerous so-called "serious offences". Not only that, but the future conduct to be considered is equally broad and, in the case of robbery, is not so exceptional as to warrant such a scheme. The judiciary is left to perform the executive function of preventing a wide range of crimes one offender at a time. And it is required to do that without identifying any underlying justification of the kind that might be identified with respect to sexual offending or terrorism ...

Indeed, the Solicitor-General for Western Australia frankly acknowledged during oral argument that, on the submissions of the Attorney-General for Western Australia, "as a matter of principle", there was "probably not" any offence in the *Criminal Code* (WA) that could not be the subject of the preventive detention regime under the HRSO Act ...

The normalisation of judicial preventive detention orders means that "the distinctive character of the judiciary as the constitutional arbiter of disputes about rights between the citizen and the State will become increasingly less distinct. Incrementally but inexorably the judiciary will be drawn ever more deeply into a process in which institutional boundaries are blurred and by which its institutional independence is diminished".

That cannot be permitted because it is corrosive to - it erodes - the core constitutional values underpinning and protected by Ch III of the *Constitution*: the judicial protection of liberty and the protection of the independence and impartiality of the judiciary ...

The fact that, in a particular case, the Supreme Court might decide that a particular offender does not present an "unacceptable" risk of committing a serious offence or that it is not "necessary", in a particular case, to make a restriction order to adequately protect the community from an unacceptable risk, does not address or overcome the issues of principle identified above.

19.4 Additional defining characteristics of 'federal courts'

The second category of courts identified in section 71 of the *Constitution* as repositories of federal judicial power are 'such other federal courts as the Parliament creates'. A federal court must possess all of the minimum characteristics of a court. This section looks at what additional defining characteristics makes a court a 'federal court'.

The key additional defining characteristic of *federal* courts concerns the appointment, tenure and remuneration of the judges of those courts. Section 72 sets out the rules.

Australian Constitution

Section 72 Judges' appointment, tenure, and remuneration

The Justices of the High Court and of the other courts created by the Parliament:

(i) shall be appointed by the Governor-General in Council;

(ii) shall not be removed except by the Governor-General in Council, on an address from both Houses of the Parliament in the same session, praying for such removal on the ground of proved misbehaviour or incapacity;

(iii) shall receive such remuneration as the Parliament may fix; but the remuneration shall not be diminished during their continuance in office.

The appointment of a Justice of the High Court shall be for a term expiring upon his attaining the age of seventy years, and a person shall not be appointed as a Justice of the High Court if he has attained that age.

The appointment of a Justice of a court created by the Parliament shall be for a term expiring upon his attaining the age that is, at the time of his appointment, the maximum age for Justices of that court and a person shall not be appointed as a Justice of such a court if he has attained the age that is for the time being the maximum age for Justices of that court.

Subject to this section, the maximum age for Justices of any court created by the Parliament is seventy years.

The Parliament may make a law fixing an age that is less than seventy years as the maximum age for Justices of a court created by the Parliament and may at any time repeal or amend such a law, but any such repeal or amendment does not affect the term of office of a Justice under an appointment made before the repeal or amendment.

A Justice of the High Court or of a court created by the Parliament may resign his office by writing under his hand delivered to the Governor General.

Lane v Morrison provides an example of the Commonwealth attempting to create a 'federal court' that does not comply with the requirements of section 72. The High Court held that the body designated the Australian Military Court was not a 'federal court' because it was composed of judges without the tenure provided for in section 72.

Lane v Morrison (2009) 239 CLR 230

Legislation established the Australian Military Court as a court of record to try charges of service offences to replace the system of military courts-martial. The Australian Military Court was constituted by Military Judges appointed for 10-year terms. Lane was convicted and sentenced for a service offence. Lane argued that the AMC was not a 'federal court' within the meaning of Chapter III because section 72 of the* Constitution *provides that judges of courts created by Parliament have security of tenure until age 70. The High Court agreed.

French CJ and Gummow J

The powers of the Parliament to create courts are found only in ss 71, 72 and 122 of the Constitution. The creation of the AMC is not supported by s 122 as a law with respect to the government of any territory. Nor is the AMC comprised of Justices who are appointed by the Governor-General in Council and with the tenure provided by s 72 of the Constitution ...

The "creation" or "erection" of a "court" provides for the formation and constitution of a body which answers that description ...

Section 71 speaks of "such other federal courts as the Parliament creates". The Justices of those federal courts are appointed in accordance with, and have the tenure and remuneration provided in, s 72. Whilst in office they cannot be removed otherwise than as provided by s 72(ii) ...

The upshot is that while the Parliament has given to the AMC some of the attributes of a court which may be created by the Parliament for the exercise of the judicial power of the Commonwealth, it has not created such a body.

19.5 Additional defining characteristics of a 'Supreme Court of a State'

Section 73(ii) gives the High Court jurisdiction to hear appeals from the 'Supreme Court of any State'. It is a constitutional requirement that each State have a Supreme Court. A State Supreme Court must possess all of the minimum characteristics of a court. This section looks at what additional defining characteristics makes a court a 'Supreme Court'.

The High Court has explained that it is a defining characteristic of a State Supreme Court that it possesses a supervisory jurisdiction to enforce the limits on the exercise of State executive and judicial power. This proposition was established in ***Kirk v Industrial Court of NSW***. It follows that privative clauses that purport to oust the jurisdiction of a State Supreme Court to review exercises of State executive and judicial power for jurisdictional error are invalid.

Kirk v Industrial Court of New South Wales (2010) 239 CLR 531

The principal issue in this case was the validity of a privative clause purporting to immunise decisions of the Industrial Court from judicial review by the Supreme Court for jurisdictional error.

French CJ, Gummow, Hayne, Crennan, Kiefel and Bell JJ

A privative provision in State legislation, which purports to strip the Supreme Court of the State of its authority to confine inferior courts within the limits of their jurisdiction by granting relief on the ground of jurisdictional error, is beyond the powers of the State legislature. It is beyond power because it purports to remove a defining characteristic of the Supreme Court of the State ...

In considering State legislation, it is necessary to take account of the requirement of Ch III of the Constitution that there be a body fitting the description "the Supreme Court of a State", and the constitutional corollary that "it is beyond the legislative power of a State so to alter the constitution or character of its Supreme Court that it ceases to meet the constitutional description".

At Federation, each of the Supreme Courts referred to in s 73 of the *Constitution* had jurisdiction that included such jurisdiction as the Court of Queen's Bench had in England. It followed that each had "a general power to issue the writ [of certiorari] to any inferior Court" in the State ... That is, accepted doctrine at the time of federation was that the jurisdiction of the colonial Supreme Courts to grant certiorari for jurisdictional error was not denied by a statutory privative provision.

The supervisory jurisdiction of the Supreme Courts was at federation, and remains, the mechanism for the determination and the enforcement of the limits on the exercise of State executive and judicial power by persons and bodies other than the Supreme Court. That supervisory role of the Supreme Courts exercised through the grant of prohibition, certiorari and mandamus (and habeas corpus) was, and is, a defining characteristic of those courts ...

To deprive a State Supreme Court of its supervisory jurisdiction enforcing the limits on the exercise of State executive and judicial power by persons and bodies other than that Court would be to create islands of power immune from supervision and restraint ... And as already demonstrated, it would remove from the relevant State Supreme Court one of its defining characteristics.

19.6 DISCUSSION QUESTIONS

1. What is the rationale underlying the ***Kable*** doctrine?
2. Make a list of the defining characteristics of 'courts' identified in the case law.
3. Does the use of the word 'must' in legislation always mean that a court is subject to direction and control?
4. What makes a court a 'federal' court?
5. Problem question: Consider the following hypothetical legislation and scenario. The New South Wales Parliament enacts the *Gambling Control Orders Act 2023*. The Act establishes a regime of control orders to be issued against problem gamblers. The Act has three key features:
   - The Act permits the Commissioner of the New South Wales Police Force to apply to the New South Wales District Court for a control order to be issued against any person who has ever contacted the Gambling Help Line (a telephone counselling service for problem gamblers).
   - The Act provides in section 7 that the District Court 'must issue a control order against a person if that person has ever contacted the Gambling Help Line, confining that person to their place of usual residence between the hours of 10 pm and 6 am, if satisfied that the person has committed a criminal offence within a period of three years before a control order application is made'.
   - The Act provides in section 8 that 'A decision or purported decision to issue a control order under this Act is not amenable to review in any court on the ground of jurisdictional error'.

   You are the lawyer for a person who is subject to a control order. Your client wants to know whether there are any constitutional arguments available to her to challenge the statute. Advise.

PART 6

THE FEDERAL EXECUTIVE

FEDERAL EXECUTIVE POWER

20

20.1 Overview

This chapter examines the executive power of the Commonwealth. The provisions of the *Constitution* concerning the structure of the Federal Executive Government and the exercise of federal executive power do not fully describe how the Federal Executive Government operates in practice. Those provisions need to be understood in light of the conventions of responsible government governing the actual operation of the Federal Executive Government and the exercise of its powers.

The Federal Executive Government cannot be treated as if it was an ordinary legal person with capacity to act as it pleases subject only to the general law. The Federal Executive Government can only exercise powers which it lawfully possesses. Federal executive power includes powers derived from the royal prerogative, powers derived from Australia's status as a nation, and powers conferred on the Federal Executive Government by statute.

Key concepts addressed in this chapter include:

- executive power
- responsible government

- depth of power
- breadth of power
- Royal Prerogative
- nationhood power.

20.2 The structure of the Federal Executive Government

Chapter II of the *Constitution* is titled 'The Executive Government'. The key provisions relating to the structure of the Executive Government are sections 61–65.

Australian Constitution

Chapter II – The Executive Government

Section 61 Executive power

The executive power of the Commonwealth is vested in the Queen and is exercisable by the Governor-General as the Queen's representative, and extends to the execution and maintenance of this Constitution, and of the laws of the Commonwealth.

Section 62 Federal Executive Council

There shall be a Federal Executive Council to advise the Governor-General in the government of the Commonwealth, and the members of the Council shall be chosen and summoned by the Governor-General and sworn as Executive Councillors, and shall hold office during his pleasure.

Section 63 Provisions referring to Governor-General

The provisions of this Constitution referring to the Governor-General in Council shall be construed as referring to the Governor-General acting with the advice of the Federal Executive Council.

Section 64 Ministers of State

The Governor-General may appoint officers to administer such departments of State of the Commonwealth as the Governor-General in Council may establish.

Such officers shall hold office during the pleasure of the Governor-General. They shall be members of the Federal Executive Council, and shall be the Queen's Ministers of State for the Commonwealth.

Ministers to sit in Parliament

After the first general election no Minister of State shall hold office for a longer period than three months unless he is or becomes a senator or a member of the House of Representatives.

Section 65 Number of Ministers

Until the Parliament otherwise provides, the Ministers of State shall not exceed seven in number, and shall hold such offices as the Parliament prescribes, or, in the absence of provision, as the Governor-General directs.

In summary, Chapter II provides that:

- The monarch is the repository of federal executive power, which is exercisable by the Governor-General on her behalf.
- The Governor-General has power to establish government departments.
- The Governor-General appoints Ministers to administer government departments. The only qualification for appointment as a Minister is that a person must hold a seat in Parliament.
- A Federal Executive Council exists to advise the Governor-General in the exercise of his or her powers, and its members are appointed by the Governor-General.

However, the structure of the Federal Executive Government cannot be understood by looking only to the provisions of the *Constitution*. It was always intended that the conventions of responsible government would help structure the Federal Executive Government and govern the exercise of its powers. Responsible government and constitutional conventions were examined in Chapter 1.

In practice, the conventions of responsible government have the effect that:

- The leader of the party or coalition of parties that holds a majority of seats in the House of Representatives, or the person who otherwise has the confidence of the House of Representatives, is entitled to be appointed Prime Minister. The Prime Minister determines who the other Ministers will be and the structure of government departments. The Governor-General will appoint those people and establish those departments.
- The monarch and Governor-General, except in the rare case of an exercise of reserve powers, exercise their powers only on the advice of Ministers.
- A Cabinet exists as the central executive coordinating body.
- The Federal Executive Council is not a deliberative body and meets, constituted only by Ministers of the Government currently in power, for the sole purpose of giving effect to Government decisions.

The *Ministers of State Act 1952* (Cth) sets a limit on the total number of Ministers of State. The current limit is 42 (including those designated as Parliamentary Secretaries or Assistant Ministers). The allocation of responsibilities between the various ministers and departments is determined by Administrative Arrangements Orders.

Legislation Handbook (Department of the Prime Minister and Cabinet, 2017)

Who has responsibility for which legislation?

The Governor-General, on the advice of the Prime Minister, makes an Administrative Arrangements Order (AAO) under section 61 of the *Constitution* to assign responsibilities to ministers (references to ministers throughout the handbook could include assistant ministers and parliamentary secretaries) and departments.

The AAO sets out the legislation administered by ministers who are appointed to administer a department, and the matters to be dealt with by each department. Where a portfolio has more than one minister, each of those ministers administer the department with the effect that all ministers are formally able to administer the legislation associated with the department (see *Acts Interpretation Act 1901*, sections 19 and 19A).

In practice, each minister in a portfolio will have discrete areas of policy and legislative responsibility.

20.3 Federal executive power

The *Constitution* does not define 'executive power'. Section 61 gives only a partial definition of the 'executive power of the Commonwealth' by providing that it 'extends to the execution and maintenance of this Constitution, and of the laws of the Commonwealth'.

It is common to divide components of federal executive power into the categories of *statutory executive powers* and *non-statutory executive powers*. Statutory executive powers are those powers conferred on the Federal Executive Government by legislation enacted by Parliament. Non-statutory executive powers are those powers arising directly from section 61, the exercise of which requires no statutory authorisation.

The text of section 61 indicates that federal executive power includes powers and capacities for the execution and maintenance of the *Constitution*. The *Constitution* has a number of provisions granting particular powers to the Federal Executive Government. These might be seen as powers falling within the concept 'execution ... of this Constitution'. These powers include:

- section 64: power to administer government departments
- section 67: power to appoint civil servants
- section 68: power to exercise command of the naval and military forces of the Commonwealth
- section 72(i): power to appoint federal judges
- section 86: power to collect customs duties.

Other non-statutory executive powers are commonly divided into the categories of *prerogative power* and *nationhood power*. Dividing that power into these categories is often convenient but must not be allowed to distract attention from the fact that in all cases what is being considered is 'the executive power of the Commonwealth'. Indeed, there may be overlap between the categories of 'prerogative power' and 'nationhood power'. For example, the power to declare and wage war is traditionally understood as a prerogative power, but that power also satisfies the description of a nationhood power.

In ***Plaintiff M68/2015 v Minister for Immigration and Border Protection***, Gageler J explained that section 61 is the source of all non-statutory federal executive power. That is, except for powers granted by statutes passed by Parliament, all other executive powers of the Federal Executive Government come from section 61.

Justice Gageler also explained that federal executive power can be understood with respect to both its breadth and depth:

- The breadth of federal executive power concerns the *subject-matters* with respect to which the Federal Executive Government may act.
- The depth of federal executive power concerns the *types of actions* the Federal Executive Government may take.

As a question, it may be asked: does section 61 empower the Federal Executive Government to undertake this type of action (depth) in respect of this particular subject-matter (breadth)?

The depth of federal executive power includes:

- *powers,* which are capable of interfering with the legal rights of others (for example, detaining a person), and
- *capacities,* which the Federal Executive Government may exercise but subject to the general law (for example, entering into a contract for the purchase of land).

Plaintiff M68/2015 v Minister for Immigration and Border Protection (2016) 257 CLR 42

Gageler J

The nature of Commonwealth executive power ... is described - not defined - in s 61 of the Constitution, in that it is extended - not confined - by that section to the "execution and maintenance" of the Constitution and of laws of the Commonwealth. It is therefore "barren ground for any analytical approach". Alfred Deakin said of it in a profound opinion which he gave as Attorney-General in 1902 that "it would be dangerous, if not impossible, to define", emphasising that it "is administrative, as well as in the strict sense executive; that is to say, it must obviously include the power not only to execute laws, but also to effectively administer the whole Government".

Without attempting to define Commonwealth executive power, Professor Winterton usefully drew attention to its dimensions when he distinguished its "breadth" from its "depth": "breadth" referring to the subject-matters with respect to which the Executive Government of the Commonwealth is empowered to act having regard to the constraints of the federal system; "depth" referring to the precise actions which the Executive Government is empowered to undertake in relation to those subject-matters.

Put in terms of the nomenclature of Professor Winterton, Mason J referred to the breadth of Commonwealth executive power when, in a frequently cited passage, he said that it "enables the Crown to undertake all executive action which is appropriate to the position of the Commonwealth under the Constitution and to the spheres of responsibility vested in it by the Constitution". He referred to its depth when he immediately added that it "includes the prerogative powers of the Crown, that is, the powers accorded to the Crown by the common law".

Put in terms of the same nomenclature, Brennan J referred exclusively to the depth of Commonwealth executive power when he noted that "an act done in execution of an executive power of the Commonwealth is done in execution of one of three categories of powers or capacities: a statutory (non-prerogative) power or capacity, a prerogative (non-statutory) power or capacity, or a capacity which is neither a statutory nor a prerogative capacity".

In framing those categories of actions which the Executive Government is empowered to undertake in relation to subject-matters with respect to which the Executive Government is empowered to act, Brennan J used the term "prerogative" in the strict and narrow sense in which it had been used by Sir William Blackstone in the middle of the eighteenth century: to refer only to "those rights and capacities which the King enjoys alone, in contradistinction to others, and not to those which he enjoys in common with any of his subjects". He framed the second and third categories of permissible acts so as together to cover the wider sense in which Professor Dicey had used the same term in the late nineteenth century, after the emergence of responsible government in the United Kingdom: to refer to "the residue of discretionary or arbitrary authority, which at any given time is legally left in the hands of the Crown" and thereby to encompass "[e]very act which the executive government can lawfully do without the authority of [an] Act of Parliament".

The tripartite categorisation posited by Brennan J has utility in highlighting, in relation to acts done in the exercise of a non-statutory power or capacity, the essential difference between an act done in the execution of a prerogative executive power and an act done in the execution of a non-prerogative executive capacity.

An act done in the execution of a prerogative executive power is an act which is capable of interfering with legal rights of others. An act done in the execution of a non-prerogative executive capacity, in contrast, involves nothing more than the utilisation of a bare capacity or permission, which can also be described as ability to act or as a "faculty". Such effects as the act might have on legal rights or juridical relations result not from the act being uniquely that of the Executive Government but from the application to the act of the same substantive law as would be applicable in respect of the act had it been done by any other actor. In this respect, the Executive Government "is affected by the condition of the general law". Subject to statute, and to the limited extent to which the operation of the common law accommodates to the continued existence of "those rights and capacities which the King enjoys alone" and which are therefore properly to be categorised as prerogative, the Executive Government must take the civil and criminal law as the Executive Government finds it, and must suffer the civil and criminal consequences of any breach ...

The tripartite categorisation posited by Brennan J also has utility in highlighting, in relation to acts done by the Executive Government in the exercise of non-statutory power or capacity, the essential similarity between an act done in the execution of a prerogative executive power or capacity and an act done in the execution of a non-prerogative executive capacity. The essential similarity lies in the identity of their provenance.

Non-prerogative executive capacities, no less than prerogative executive powers and capacities, are within the non-statutory executive power of the Commonwealth which is constitutionally conferred by s 61 of the Constitution and which is accordingly constitutionally limited by s 61 of the Constitution. Its constitutional limits are to be understood (as distinct from merely interpreted) in light of the purpose of Ch II being to establish the Executive Government as a national responsible government and in light of constitutional history and the tradition of the common law ...

20.4 Executive power derived from the Royal Prerogative and attributable to the Commonwealth

Section 61 executive power includes content derived from the Royal Prerogative. In ***Barton v Commonwealth*** (1974) 131 CLR 477, 498, Mason J defined prerogative powers as 'the powers accorded to the Crown by the common law'. In other words, prerogative powers and capacities are those powers and capacities that the common law historically treated as necessary for an executive government to possess. Those powers and capacities are referred to collectively as the 'Royal Prerogative'. The name reflects English history when the monarch personally led the Executive Government. Examples of prerogative powers include the power to declare and wage war, the power to enter into treaties, and the power to confer honours such as knighthoods.

Because Australia is a federation with independent federal and State governments, not every component of the Royal Prerogative as it existed in the United Kingdom forms part of section 61 federal executive power. Only those powers and capacities appropriate to the Commonwealth form part of section 61 federal executive power.

In the ***Tampa Case***, the Full Court of the Federal Court explained that determining whether a prerogative power forms part of section 61 federal executive power involves two steps: first, determining whether an asserted power was part of the royal prerogative; and, if so, secondly, determining whether that power is appropriate to the Commonwealth. A power or capacity forming part of the royal prerogative at common law will not be attributable to the Commonwealth if: (1) it is inconsistent with the *Constitution* and therefore has no existence in Australian law; or (2) it is a power that is attributable only to the States rather than to the Commonwealth.

Ruddock v Vardalis ('Tampa Case') (2001) 110 FCR 491

A Norwegian container ship, the MV Tampa, *rescued 433 people from a sinking boat near Christmas Island but outside Australian waters. The captain was told by Australian authorities not to enter Australian waters but he nevertheless did. Australian soldiers were deployed to board the vessel, detain the rescuees, and transfer them to Nauru and New Zealand where their status as refugees would be assessed. A single judge of the Federal Court granted* habeas corpus *ordering the release of the rescuees. On appeal, the Commonwealth argued that its actions were an exercise of federal executive power conferred on it by section 61. A majority of the Full Court of the Federal Court found that section 61 included a power derived from the prerogative to do things necessary to prevent the entry of non-citizens into Australia. A minority of the Court held that if any such power ever existed it had been abrogated by statute. Justice French gave the leading judgment for the majority.*

French J

Section 61 is the primary source of executive power. Its content extends to the execution and maintenance of the Constitution and the laws of the Commonwealth. It is also limited by those terms in so far as it will not authorise the Commonwealth to act inconsistently with the distribution of powers and the limits on power for which the Constitution provides. Nor will it authorise the Commonwealth to act otherwise than according to the laws of the Commonwealth. Other provisions of the Constitution vesting powers in the Governor-General may be seen as distinct sources of executive power on their specific topics and as giving content to the power conferred by s 61 ...

The modern relationship of the power to the prerogatives of the Crown was stated by Mason J in *Barton v Commonwealth* (1974) 131 CLR 477 at 498:

> The Constitution established the Commonwealth of Australia as a political entity and brought it into existence as a member of the community of nations ... By s 61 the executive power of the Commonwealth was vested in the Crown. It extends to the execution and maintenance of the Constitution and of the laws of the Commonwealth. It enables the Crown to undertake all executive action which is appropriate to the position of the Commonwealth under the Constitution and to the spheres of responsibility vested in it by the Constitution. It includes the prerogative powers of the Crown, that is, the powers accorded to the Crown by the common law.

The use of the "prerogative" to describe such a power may properly acknowledge its historical antecedents but not adequately illuminate its origins in s 61 of the Constitution. For it is s 61 that "... confers on the Commonwealth all the prerogative powers of the Crown except those that are necessarily exercisable by the States under the allocation of responsibilities made by the Constitution and those denied by the Constitution itself." – *Davis v Commonwealth* (1988) 166 CLR 79 at 93 (Mason CJ, Deane and Gaudron JJ) citing *Commonwealth v Colonial Combing, Spinning and Weaving Co Ltd* ("the Wooltops case") (1922) 31 CLR 421 at 437–439 ...

The executive power of the Commonwealth under s 61 cannot be treated as a species of the royal prerogative, "The residue of discretionary or arbitrary authority which at any given time is legally left in the hands of the Crown." – *De Keyser* at 526. While the executive power may derive some of its content by reference to the royal prerogative, it is a power conferred as part of a negotiated federal compact expressed in a written Constitution distributing powers between the three arms of government reflected in Chapters I, II and III of the Constitution and, as to legislative powers, between the polities that comprise the federation ...

It is not necessary for present purposes to consider the full content of executive power and the extent to which it may operate upon the subject matter of the heads of Commonwealth legislative power. Given that the legislative powers conferred by s 51 are concurrent with those of the States, subject to the paramountcy of Commonwealth statutes, (covering cl 5 and s 109) it could not be said that, absent statutory authority, executive power may be exercised in relation to all those matters. There are legislative powers however which may be seen as central to the expression of Australia's status and sovereignty as a nation. They include the powers to make laws with respect to naturalisation and aliens (s 51(xix)), immigration and emigration (s 51(xxvii)) and the influx of criminals (s 51(xxviii)). Australia's status as a sovereign nation is reflected in its power to determine who may come into its territory and who may not and who shall be admitted into the Australian community and who shall not. That power may also be linked to the foundation of the Constitution in popular sovereignty implied in the agreement of the "people" of the pre-federation colonies "to unite in one indissoluble federal Commonwealth". It may be said that the people, through the structures of representative democracy for which the

Constitution provides, including an Executive responsible to the Parliament, may determine who will or will not enter Australia. These powers may be exercised for good reasons or bad. That debate, however, is not one for this Court to enter.

In my opinion, the executive power of the Commonwealth, absent statutory extinguishment or abridgement, would extend to a power to prevent the entry of non-citizens and to do such things as are necessary to effect such exclusion. This does not involve any conclusion about whether the Executive would, in the absence of statutory authority, have a power to expel non-citizens other than as an incident of the power to exclude. The power to determine who may come into Australia is so central to its sovereignty that it is not to be supposed that the Government of the nation would lack under the power conferred upon it directly by the Constitution, the ability to prevent people not part of the Australia community, from entering.

In ***Cadia Holdings v New South Wales***, the High Court explained that only those royal prerogative powers at common law in the United Kingdom *in the form they existed at the time the common law was received into Australia* are potential components of section 61 federal executive power. The case concerned an ancient prerogative power that had been modified by English statutes in the 1600s. It was the modified version of the prerogative power that was received into Australia.

The High Court also commented on the methodology for determining whether a prerogative power is attributable to the Commonwealth or to the States. The methodology involves identifying the purpose and operation of the power as understood and exercised in Australia in the period before Federation (as opposed to the original understanding in England, which might be different) and determining how those purposes align with the *Constitution's* distribution of functions between the Commonwealth and States. In ***Cadia Holdings***, the prerogative right in issue – ownership of gold and silver – was understood originally in England to be associated with the ability to wage war and coin money, both of which functions the *Constitution* allocates to the Commonwealth. However, the prerogative right in issue was understood in pre-Federation Australia to be associated with the ability to grant title to land. That function is a function which the *Constitution* does not mention, let alone allocate to the Commonwealth. The result was that the prerogative right in issue was attributable to the States only and not to the Commonwealth.

Cadia Holdings Pty Ltd v New South Wales (2010) 242 CLR 195

The Mining Act 1992 *(NSW) required miners to pay royalties to the State in respect of 'publicly owned' minerals they extracted by mining. Cadia operated a mine in which copper was extracted, intermingled with gold. Ownership of gold and silver is a Royal Prerogative. That prerogative originally extended to ownership of other metals with which gold or silver was mixed but was modified by statute in the 1600s to exclude mines of copper. New South Wales argued that the minerals extracted by Cadia were publicly owned and therefore Cadia*

was required to pay royalties. The issues for the High Court were whether ownership of gold and silver admixtures is a Royal Prerogative and, if so, whether that Royal Prerogative was attributable to the State or the Commonwealth.

French CJ

In 1568, an English court held that the Crown had the prerogative right to mines of gold and silver and other metals, such as copper, with which gold or silver in those mines was mixed. In a context of constitutional upheaval, that right was modified, in favour of the owners of base-metal mines, by an Act of the English Parliament in 1688. It was modified again in 1693. Those events, which occurred more than three centuries ago, determine today the amount of royalties payable to the New South Wales Minister for Mineral Resources ("the Minister") in respect of copper mined by Cadia Holdings Pty Ltd ("Cadia") from land near Orange which is owned by it and Newcrest Operations Ltd ("NOL").

When the Crown's prerogative right to mines of gold and silver was judicially recognised in 1568 it was as an aspect of the Crown's fiscal prerogatives. It was justified by the Crown's need to obtain precious metal for the making of coins, a monopoly which was another aspect of the royal prerogative, and by the need to pay military defence forces ...

The Constitutions of the former colonies, the powers of the former colonial Parliaments and the laws in force in the former colonies relating to matters within the powers of the Commonwealth Parliament were continued after Federation subject to the Constitution of the Commonwealth. No distribution of prerogative powers and rights between the Commonwealth and the States is spelt out in the Constitution. Indeed the word "distribution" may mislead. Prerogative powers and rights enjoyed by the Crown in the colonies before Federation may be seen as informing, or forming part of, the content of the executive powers of the Commonwealth and the States according to their proper functions. In some cases, the location of particular prerogative powers and rights in, or as an incident of, the executive power of the Commonwealth or of the States is straightforward. As Professor Zines has observed, there is no difficulty in determining the repository of the prerogative power relating to a subject matter within the exclusive legislative competence of the Commonwealth or a State:

> Clearly only the Commonwealth can declare war, or enter into treaties. Similarly where a prerogative power, or a particular exercise of it, is concerned with a subject that is not within Commonwealth legislative power, it is exercisable only by the Governor of a State, such as the incorporation by royal charter of a school or the dissolution of State Parliament.

A prerogative power or right concerned with a subject within the area of concurrent legislative power of the Commonwealth and the States may become an element of concurrent power or rights in both polities. This was the case with the Crown's priority in respect of debts, held in *Federal Commissioner of Taxation v Official Liquidator of E O Farley Ltd* to be enjoyed concurrently by the Commonwealth and the States ...

The original justification for the prerogative in mines of gold and silver as ancillary to prerogative powers with respect to coinage and the raising of military forces might suggest, having regard to the exclusive nature of Commonwealth powers in these two areas, that it could logically have found its place as an element or incident of Commonwealth executive power. On the other hand, the prerogative right appears to have subsisted at Federation independently of the original justifications proffered in argument in the *Case of Mines*. Moreover, the constitutional powers of the States to dispose of waste lands of the Crown and the proprietary character of the prerogative weigh in favour of the view that it remained with the States after Federation ...

Gummow, Hayne, Heydon and Crennan JJ

On the establishment of federation in Australia, while s 91 of the Constitution permitted States to grant aid to and bounty on mining for gold, silver and other metals, s 115 forbad the States to coin money. Further, insofar as the reasoning in the *Case of Mines* supported the prerogative of ownership as necessary to provide for national defence, s 114 of the Constitution forbids a State, without the consent of the federal Parliament, to raise or maintain any naval or military force.

The executive power of the Commonwealth of which s 61 of the Constitution speaks enables the Commonwealth to undertake executive action appropriate to its position under the Constitution and to that end includes the prerogative powers accorded the Crown by the common law ...

However, the creation of the federation presented issues still not fully resolved of the allocation between the Commonwealth and States of prerogatives which pre-federation had been divided between the Imperial and colonial governments, and of their adaptation to the division of executive authority in the federal system established by the Constitution ...

Evatt J said that "as a general rule" prerogatives which partook of the nature of proprietary rights and which before federation had been exercisable by the executive governments of the colonies were exercisable by the executives of the various States: *Federal Commissioner of Taxation v Official Liquidator of E O Farley Ltd* (1940) 63 CLR 278 at 322.

The present litigation was conducted on the same assumption, identifying the State as the repository of the relevant prerogative; the dispute was as to the scope of the prerogative with respect to the copper mined by Cadia. Accordingly, it is inappropriate to consider the matter further here.

The area of dispute in submissions to this Court centred upon what the appellants contended ... was the removal in England of the prerogative with respect to gold and copper admixture by statute in the immediate wake of the Revolution of 1688, namely by s 3 of the *Royal Mines Act* 1688 ...

The significant consequence of the enactment of s 3 of the Royal Mines Act, as the appellants submit, is that by the time the common law was received in the colony of New South Wales, and well before any of the grants from which stem the titles of the appellants, that part of the common law of England represented by the prerogative identified in the *Case of Mines* had been abridged. What later was received in New South Wales was the common law in its condition at the time of reception. Section 3 of the Royal Mines Act had done its work long before and forthwith, as the Convention Parliament plainly intended, and as an element in the constitutional rearrangements made at that time.

It is to that abridged form of the prerogative in respect of gold mines and silver mines that s 379 of the 1992 Act speaks.

The judgments in ***Cadia Holdings*** observe that some prerogative powers and capacities may exist as components of both federal and State executive power. One example is the prerogative of mercy, which allows the Executive Government to pardon criminal offenders or remit criminal penalties. Criminal offences exist under both federal and State laws. The breadth of the federal prerogative of mercy is limited to federal criminal convictions. The breadth of the State prerogative of mercy is limited to State criminal convictions.

20.5 Executive power derived from Australia's status as a nation ('nationhood power')

Federal executive power includes powers and capacities appropriate to Australia's status and character as an independent nation. This is often spoken of as the 'nationhood power' component of section 61. The words 'maintenance of this *Constitution*' provide a textual basis for this component of federal executive power. Maintaining the *Constitution* encompasses maintaining the nation created by the *Constitution*.

Davis v Commonwealth explained the nationhood power. Mason CJ, Deane and Gaudron JJ held that section 61 authorises the Federal Executive Government to engage in lawful activities in connection with matters falling within the peculiar province of the Commonwealth in its capacity as the national and federal government. Brennan J held that section 61 authorises the Federal Executive Government to engage in enterprises and activities peculiarly adapted to the government of a nation and which cannot otherwise be carried on for the benefit of the nation.

In ***Davis***, conducting national celebrations to commemorate the bicentenary of the arrival of the First Fleet was held to be a matter within the peculiar province of the Commonwealth as the national government. Section 61 therefore authorised the Federal Executive Government to set up a company under companies legislation with the object of facilitating national celebrations.

Davis v Commonwealth (1988) 166 CLR 79

Mason CJ, Deane and Gaudron JJ

The Commonwealth submits that its executive power under s 61 of the Constitution extends to the incorporation of a company in the Australian Capital Territory having as its object the commemoration of the Bicentenary throughout Australia ...

If we ask the question whether the commemoration of the Bicentenary is a matter falling within the peculiar province of the Commonwealth in its capacity as the national and federal government, the answer must be in the affirmative. That is not to say that the States have no interest or no part to play in the commemoration. Clearly they have such an interest and such a part to play, whether as part of an exercise in co-operative federalism or otherwise. But the interest of the States in the commemoration of the Bicentenary is of a more limited character. It cannot be allowed to obscure the plain fact that the commemoration of the Bicentenary is pre-eminently the business and the concern of the Commonwealth as the national government and as such falls fairly and squarely within the federal executive power.

Implicit in what we have just said is a rejection of any notion that the character and status of the Commonwealth as the government of the nation is relevant only in the ascertainment of the scope of the executive power in the area of Australia's external relations ...

From the conclusion that the commemoration of the Bicentenary falls squarely within Commonwealth executive power other consequences follow. The first is that the executive power extends to the incorporation of a company as a means for carrying out and implementing a plan or programme for the commemoration. There is no constitutional bar to the setting up of a corporate authority to achieve this object or purpose in preference to executive action through a Ministry of the Crown. Certainly there is no such bar to the incorporation of a company in the Australian Capital Territory, though we very much doubt that this procedure would enable the Commonwealth to circumvent limitations or restrictions which would otherwise attach to the federal executive power in so far as it extends to the commemoration of the Bicentenary ...

Wilson and Dawson JJ

Indeed, the execution and maintenance of the Constitution and of the laws of the Commonwealth are concepts which seem to us to comprehend all that is to be implied "from the existence and nature of the Constitution as the foundation of a body politic."

... [T]he character and status of the Commonwealth as a national government is an element to be considered in the construction of s 61 of the Constitution ...

The truth is that the character and status of the Commonwealth as a national government are qualities which are themselves to be found within the confines of the Constitution ...

Brennan J

Section 61 refers not only to the execution and maintenance of the laws of the Commonwealth (a function characteristically to be performed by execution of statutory powers); it refers also to "the execution and maintenance of this Constitution" (a function to be performed by execution of powers which are not necessarily statutory) ... [T]he phrase "maintenance of this Constitution" imports the idea of Australia as a nation. I would briefly state my reasons for holding that the function which that phrase assigns to the Executive Government relates not only to the institutions of government but more generally to the protection and advancement of the Australian nation ...

This Court has not settled the questions whether and to what extent it is within the executive power of the Commonwealth for the Executive Government of the Commonwealth to exercise its prerogative powers or to engage in lawful activities or enterprises calculated to advance the national interest. Though the Constitution gives no express answer to these questions, the answer may be derived from what the Constitution was intended to do and has done. With great respect to those who hold an opposing view, the Constitution did not create a mere aggregation of colonies, redistributing powers between the government of the Commonwealth and the governments of the States. The Constitution summoned the Australian nation into existence, thereby conferring a new identity on the people who agreed to unite "in one indissoluble Federal Commonwealth", melding their history, embracing their cultures, synthesizing their aspirations and their destinies. The reality of the Australian nation is manifest, though the manifestations of its existence cannot be limited by definition. The end and purpose of the Constitution is to sustain the nation.

If the executive power of the Commonwealth extends to the protection of the nation against forces which would weaken it, it extends to the advancement of the nation whereby its strength is fostered. There is no reason to restrict the executive power of the Commonwealth to matters within the heads of legislative power. So cramped a construction of the power would deny to the Australian people many of the symbols of nationhood – a flag or anthem, for example – or the benefit of many national initiatives in science, literature and the arts.

It does not follow that the Executive Government of the Commonwealth is the arbiter of its own power or that the executive power of the Commonwealth extends to whatever activity or enterprise the Executive Government deems to be in the national interest. But s 61 does confer on the Executive Government power "to engage in enterprises and activities peculiarly adapted to the government of a nation and which cannot otherwise be carried on for the benefit of the nation", to repeat what Mason J said in the *AAP Case*. In my respectful opinion, that is an appropriate formulation of a criterion to determine whether an enterprise or activity lies within the executive power of the Commonwealth. It invites consideration of the sufficiency of the powers of the States to engage effectively in the enterprise or activity in question and of the need for national action (whether unilateral or in co-operation with the States) to secure the contemplated benefit. The variety of enterprises or activities which might fall for consideration preclude the a priori development of detailed criteria but, as cases are decided, perhaps more precise tests will be developed ...

Pape v Commissioner of Taxation holds that spending public money for the purpose of responding to adverse economic conditions affecting the nation as a whole on a crisis scale is an exercise of the nationhood component of federal executive power. (Chapter 21 considers the full requirements for the expenditure of public money.)

Pape v Commissioner of Taxation (2009) 238 CLR 1

This case concerned the Commonwealth Government's response to the Global Financial Crisis of 2007–08. One of the issues in the case was whether the Tax Bonus for Working Australians Act 2009 *was valid under section 51(xxxix), which authorises legislation incidental to an exercise of executive power. The claimed executive power was a power said to form part of the nationhood component of section 61 to spend money to respond to economic crises. A majority of the High Court agreed that such an executive power existed as part of the nationhood component of section 61.*

French CJ

The executive power of the Commonwealth conferred by s 61 of the Constitution extends to the power to expend public moneys for the purpose of avoiding or mitigating the large scale adverse effects of the circumstances affecting the national economy disclosed on the facts of this case, and which expenditure is on a scale and within a time-frame peculiarly within the capacity of the national government ...

It is not necessary for present purposes to consider the full extent of the powers and capacities of the Executive Government of the Commonwealth. Such powers as may be conferred upon the Executive by statutes made under the Constitution are plainly included. So too are those powers which are called the prerogatives of the Crown, for example the power to enter into treaties and to declare war. In addition, whatever the source, the Executive possesses what have been described as the "capacities" which may be possessed by persons other than the Crown.

The collection of statutory and prerogative powers and non-prerogative capacities form part of, but do not complete, the executive power. They lie within the scope of s 61, which is informed by history and the common law relevant to the relationship between the Crown and the Parliament. That history and common law emerged from what might be called an organic evolution. Section 61 is an important element of a written constitution for the government of an independent nation. While history and the common law inform its content, it is not a locked display cabinet in a constitutional museum. It is not limited to statutory powers and the prerogative. It has to be capable of serving the proper purposes of a national government.

On the other hand, the exigencies of "national government" cannot be invoked to set aside the distribution of powers between Commonwealth and States and between the three branches of government for which this Constitution provides, nor to abrogate constitutional prohibitions. As for this case, it is difficult to see how the payment of moneys to taxpayers, as a short-term measure to meet an urgent national economic problem, is in any way an interference with the constitutional distribution of powers ...

The executive power extends, in my opinion, to short-term fiscal measures to meet adverse economic conditions affecting the nation as a whole, where such measures are on their face peculiarly within the capacity and resources of the Commonwealth Government. This is consistent with the executive power as broadly explained by Mason CJ, Brennan, Deane and Gaudron JJ in *Davis* ... To say that the executive power extends to the short-term fiscal measures in question in this case does not equate it to a general power to manage the national economy. In this case the Commonwealth had the resources and the capacity to implement within a short time-frame measures which, on the undisputed facts, were rationally adjudged as adapted to avoiding or mitigating the adverse effects of global financial circumstances affecting Australia as a whole, along with other countries ...

Gummow, Crennan and Bell JJ

[T]he executive power of the Commonwealth enables the undertaking of action appropriate to the position of the Commonwealth as a polity created by the Constitution and having regard to the spheres of responsibility vested in it.

With that understanding, the phrase "maintenance of this Constitution" in s 61 imports more than a species of what is identified as "the prerogative" in constitutional theory. It conveys the idea of the protection of the body politic or nation of Australia ...

But what are the respective spheres of exercise of executive power by the Commonwealth and State governments? We have posed the question in that way because it is only by some constraint having its source in the position of the Executive Governments of the States that the government of the Commonwealth is denied the power, after appropriation by the Parliament, of expenditure of moneys raised by taxation imposed by the Parliament ...

After denying the proposition that the Constitution created no more than an aggregation of colonies, with a redistribution of powers between the federal and State governments, Brennan J went on in *Davis v The Commonwealth* to say:

> It does not follow that the Executive Government of the Commonwealth is the arbiter of its own power or that the executive power of the Commonwealth extends to whatever activity or enterprise the Executive Government deems to be in the national interest. But s 61 does confer on the Executive Government power 'to engage in enterprises and activities peculiarly adapted to the government of a nation and which cannot otherwise be carried on for the benefit of the nation', to repeat what Mason J said in the AAP Case. In my respectful opinion, that is an appropriate formulation of a criterion to determine whether an enterprise or activity lies within the executive power of the Commonwealth.

That formulation should be accepted, subject to qualifications which it will be necessary to develop later in these reasons ...

In determining whether the Bonus Act is supported by s 61 and s 51(xxxix) of the Constitution, it is necessary to ask whether determining that there is the need for an immediate fiscal stimulus to the national economy, in the circumstances set out above, falls within executive power and then to ascertain whether s 51(xxxix) of the Constitution supports the impugned legislation as a law which is incidental to that exercise of executive power ...

As already mentioned, that there is a global financial and economic crisis is not contested in this proceeding. It can hardly be doubted that the current financial and economic crisis concerns Australia as a nation. Determining that there is the need for an immediate fiscal stimulus to the national economy in the circumstances set out above is somewhat analogous to determining a state of emergency in circumstances of a natural disaster. The Executive Government is the arm of government capable of and empowered to respond to a crisis be it war, natural disaster or a financial crisis on the scale here. This power has its roots in the executive power exercised in the United Kingdom up to the time of the adoption of the Constitution but in form today in Australia it is a power to act on behalf of the federal polity ...

The intervening States do not seriously dispute that only the Commonwealth has the resources available to respond promptly to the present financial crisis on the scale exemplified by the Bonus Act. The submissions of the interveners appear to have been moved more by apprehension of a wide reading of the scope of s 61. But in considering what enterprises and activities are peculiarly adapted to the government of the country and which cannot otherwise be carried on for its benefit, this case may be resolved without going beyond the notions of national emergency and the fiscal means of promptly responding to that situation ...

The present is an example of the engagement by the Executive Government in activities peculiarly adapted to the government of the country and which otherwise could not be carried on for the public benefit.

Justices Hayne and Kiefel dissented on the nationhood power issue. They complained that the majority conflated means and ends. Identifying the existence of a large-scale national crisis provides a vague and uncertain criterion for identifying the breadth of federal executive power; that is, the subject-matters with respect to which the Federal Executive Government may act. They also complained that identifying the existence of a large-scale national crisis provides no criteria at all for identifying the depth of federal executive power; that is, the types of action the Federal Executive Government may take.

Pape v Commissioner of Taxation (2009) 238 CLR 1

Hayne and Kiefel JJ

It is not shown that so much of the expenditure as is not supported by a head of legislative power is to be supported as an exercise of executive power identified as derived from the character and status of the Commonwealth as a national polity or as deduced from the existence and character of the Commonwealth as a national government. That proposed expenditure is not shown to fall within this area by demonstrating only that the expenditure in question is directed to an end that is described as a national economic emergency. It is necessary to say something in amplification of this last point.

It is said that, because there is a national economic crisis or emergency to which a *national* response must be made, the executive power under s 61, to spend money that has been lawfully appropriated, extends to spending money to meet that crisis in whatever way the Executive chooses ...

Words like "crisis" or "emergency" do not readily yield criteria of constitutional validity. It may be accepted, for the purposes of argument, both that there is shown to be a national crisis to which a national response is required and that only the Commonwealth has the administrative and financial resources to respond. It does not follow, however, that the Commonwealth's executive power to respond to such circumstances by spending money is a power that is unbounded ...

Though variously expressed, the argument by reference to national "crisis" or "emergency" can be summed up as being: "There is a crisis; if the Commonwealth cannot do this, who can?"

What that and similar forms of rhetorical question obscure is a conflation of distinct questions about ends and means ... But if that is the *end* to which the exercise of power is to be directed, it by no means follows that any and every *means* of achieving that end must be within power. To argue from the existence of an emergency to either a general proposition that the Executive may respond to the crisis in any way it sees fit, or to some more limited proposition that the Executive has power to make this particular response, is circular ....

Describing the expenditure in issue in this matter as a "short term fiscal [measure] to meet adverse economic conditions affecting the nation as a whole" engages no constitutional criterion of a kind hitherto enunciated by this Court. It is a description that conflates the distinction between ends and means that this Court must maintain. It is for the political branches of government, not this Court, to fix upon the ends to be sought by legislative or executive action. It is for the Court, not the political branches of government, to decide whether the means chosen to achieve particular political ends are constitutionally valid and it is for the Court to identify the criteria that are to be applied to determine whether those particular means are constitutionally valid ...

Reference to notions as protean and imprecise as "crisis" and "emergency" (or "adverse effects of circumstances affecting the national economy") to indicate the boundary of an aspect of executive power carries with it difficulties and dangers that raise fundamental questions about the relationship between the judicial and other branches of government ...

20.6 Executive power conferred by statute

The text of section 61 indicates that federal executive power also includes powers and capacities to execute and maintain 'the laws of the Commonwealth'. This is predominantly the domain of administrative law rather than constitutional law. Constitutional law is concerned with what powers and capacities statutes may validly confer on the Federal Executive Government. Administrative law is concerned with whether powers and capacities conferred on the Federal Executive Government by statute have been exercised lawfully.

A key constitutional issue is the extent to which Parliament may delegate law-making power to the Federal Executive Government. Delegated legislation, or subordinate legislation, is legislation made by a non-parliamentary body in accordance with power granted by a statute. Delegated legislation often takes the form of regulations.

Dignan's Case explains that there is no constitutional separation of powers doctrine prohibiting Parliament from delegating power to make laws. The *Constitution* does not vest legislative power exclusively in the Parliament. It is in the nature of legislative power in a system of responsible government that it can be delegated to the Executive Government.

The High Court explained that a law delegating law-making power over a particular subject-matter within the scope of a head of power is a law with respect to that head of power, and valid for that reason. The High Court also explained that the power of delegating law-making power stops short of abdicating law-making power with respect to the entirety of a head of power. A law purporting to abdicate legislative power is not law with respect to a head of power and is therefore beyond federal legislative power.

Victorian Stevedoring and General Contracting Co Pty Ltd v Dignan ('Dignan's Case') (1931) 46 CLR 73

Dixon J

[Section] 3 of the *Transport Workers Act* assumes to commit to the Executive Government an extensive power to make regulations which ... shall have the force of law. The validity of this provision is now attacked upon the ground that it is an attempt to grant to the Executive a portion of the legislative power vested by the Constitution in the Parliament, which is inconsistent with the distribution made by the Constitution of legislative, executive and judicial powers ...

[B]ecause of the distribution of the functions of government and of the manner in which the Constitution describes the tribunals to be invested with the judicial power of the Commonwealth, and defines the judicial power to be invested in them, the Parliament is restrained both from reposing any power essentially judicial in any other organ or body, and from reposing any other than that judicial power in such tribunals. The same or analogous considerations apply to the provisions which vest the legislative power of the Commonwealth in the Parliament, describe the constitution of the Legislature and define the legislative power. Does it follow that in the exercise of that power the Parliament is restrained from reposing any power essentially legislative in another organ or body? ...

[A] statute conferring upon the Executive a power to legislate upon some matter contained within one of the subjects of the legislative power of the Parliament is a law with respect to that subject, and that the distribution of legislative, executive and judicial powers in the Constitution does not operate to restrain the power of the Parliament to make such a law. This does not mean that a law confiding authority to the Executive will be valid, however extensive or vague the subject matter may be, if it does not fall outside the boundaries of Federal power. There may be such a width or such an uncertainty of the subject matter to be handed over that the enactment attempting it is not a law with respect to any particular head or heads of legislative power. Nor does it mean that the distribution of powers can supply no considerations of weight affecting the validity of an Act creating a legislative authority ...

The existence in Parliament of power to authorize subordinate legislation may be ascribed to a conception of that legislative power which depends less upon juristic analysis and perhaps more upon the history and usages of British legislation and the theories of English law. In English law much weight has been given to the dependence of subordinate legislation for its efficacy, not only on the enactment, but upon the continuing operation of the statute by which it is so authorized.

Evatt J

The argument is put in a slightly different form by saying that the legislative power of the Commonwealth Parliament to authorize the making of rules and regulations by the Executive Government does not extend to such a delegation as is authorized by s 3, ... because the *Australian Constitution* requires that all legislative power shall be exercised exclusively by Parliament ...

In dealing with the doctrine of "separation" of legislative and executive powers, it must be remembered that, underlying the Commonwealth frame of government, there is the notion of the British system of an Executive which is responsible to Parliament. That system is not in operation under the *United States Constitution.* Nor, indeed, had it been fully developed in England itself at the time when Montesquieu first elaborated the doctrine or theory of separation of governmental powers. But, prior to the establishment of the Commonwealth of Australia in 1901, responsible government had become one of the central characteristics of our polity. Over and over again, its existence in the constitutional scheme of the Commonwealth has been recognized by this Court.

It is very difficult to maintain the view that the Commonwealth Parliament has no power, in the exercise of its legislative power, to vest executive or other authorities with some power to pass regulations, statutory rules, and by-laws which, when passed, shall have full force and effect. Unless the legislative power of the Parliament extends this far, effective government would be impossible.

The statesmen and lawyers concerned in the framing of the *Australian Constitution*, when they treated of "legislative power" in relation to the self-governing colonies, had in view an authority which, over a limited area or subject matter, resembled that of the British Parliament. Such authority always extended beyond the issue by Parliament itself of binding commands. Parliament could also authorize the issue of such commands by any person or authority it chose to select or create. "Legislative power" connoted the power to deposit or delegate legislative power because this was implied in the idea of parliamentary sovereignty itself. It was, of course, always understood that the power of the delegate or depositary could be withdrawn by the Parliament that had created it, and in this sense Parliament had to preserve "its own capacity intact" ...

The true nature and quality of the legislative power of the Commonwealth Parliament involves, as part of its content, power to confer law-making powers upon authorities other than Parliament itself ... The matter may be illustrated by an example. Assume that the Commonwealth Parliament passes an enactment to the following effect: "The Executive Government may make regulations having the force of law upon the subject of trade and commerce with other countries or among the States." ...

I think that in ordinary circumstances a law in the terms described would be held to be beyond the competence of the Commonwealth Parliament. The nature of the legislative power of the Commonwealth authority is plenary, but it must be possible to predicate of every law passed by the Parliament that it is a law with respect to one or other of the specific subject matters mentioned in ss 51 and 52 of the *Constitution*. The only ground upon which the validity of such a law as I have stated could be affirmed, is that it is a law with respect to trade and commerce with other countries or among the States. But it is, in substance and operation, not such a law, but a law with respect to the legislative power to deal with the subject of trade and commerce with other countries or among the States ...

On final analysis therefore, the Parliament of the Commonwealth is not competent to "abdicate" its powers of legislation. This is not because Parliament is bound to perform any or all of its legislative powers or functions, for it may elect not to do so; and not because the doctrine of separation of powers prevents Parliament from granting authority to other bodies to make laws or by-laws and thereby exercise legislative power, for it does so in almost every statute; but because each and every one of the laws passed by Parliament must answer the description of a law upon one or more of the subject matters stated in the Constitution. A law by which Parliament gave all its law-making authority to another body would be bad merely because it would fail to pass the test last mentioned.

The ***WorkChoices Case*** involved an argument, relying on comments in ***Dignan's Case***, that a statutory provision delegating law-making power to the Federal Executive Government was too broad to be a 'law' at all or to be a law with respect to any head of federal legislative power. The legislation in question provided that employment contracts must not include 'prohibited content', but did not define that concept. The legislation also empowered the Federal Executive Government to specify by regulation matters that are prohibited content. The High Court held that it was possible by the process of statutory interpretation to work out the limits of the Federal Executive Government's power to prescribe prohibited content. The High Court held that because there was a limit to the delegated legislative power and the power had a sufficient connection to a head of power, the delegation of law-making power was valid.

WorkChoices demonstrates that a delegation of law-making power to the Federal Executive Government can be very broad and will be valid provided that the delegation of law-making power is subject to some statutory limit. If the delegation of law-making power was not subject to some statutory limit as to its scope, it would be an abdication of law-making power.

New South Wales v Commonwealth ('WorkChoices Case') (2006) 229 CLR 1

Gleeson CJ, Gummow, Hayne, Heydon and Crennan JJ

The AWU alleged that the provisions of subdiv B of Div 7 of Pt 8 and s 436 were invalid because they turned on the expression "prohibited content", and that expression was not defined in the new Act: its content was left for specification by regulation without stipulation of any relevant criteria. In consequence, the expression of Parliament's intention with respect to subdiv B of Div 7 of Pt 8 had been completely delegated to the Executive ...

Section 321 provides that "prohibited content" has "the meaning given by section 356".

Section 356 provides:

> The regulations may specify matters that are *prohibited content* for the purposes of this Act.

Section 846(1) provides:

> The Governor-General may make regulations, not inconsistent with this Act, prescribing all matters:
>
> (a) required or permitted by this Act to be prescribed; or
>
> (b) necessary or convenient to be prescribed for carrying out or giving effect to this Act.

... It should be said that the technique employed in s 356 is an undesirable one which ought to be discouraged. For one thing it requires the lawyers (and the many non-lawyers) who have to work with the new Act to look outside it in order to apply it: identifying what regulations are in force is a task which many inquirers have found difficult. And it creates difficulty in assessing whether particular regulations made under the legislation are intra vires. However, to make these criticisms is one thing; to conclude that there is constitutional invalidity is another ...

The AWU submitted that to confer on the Governor-General a power to make regulations as broadly expressed as ss 356 and 846(1) without also stipulating matters stated in the new Act, or to be implied from it, as indicating the parameters within which those regulations could extend, was invalid for two distinct reasons. The first was that no "law" had been enacted, because ... there had been no indication of "a rule of conduct", and no "declaration as to power, right or duty". The AWU went so far as to submit that the legislation said no more than that "[p]rohibited content is whatever the Executive Government says should not be contained in a workplace agreement". The second reason advanced by the AWU was that even if a "law" had been enacted, there was, in the words of Dixon J [in *Dignan's case*], "such a width or such an uncertainty of the subject matter ... handed over" by the Parliament to the Executive that it was not a law with respect to any identifiable head of Commonwealth legislative power ...

It is convenient first to deal with the AWU's submission that there was no stipulated ambit of the regulation-making power because the legislation said no more than that "[p]rohibited content is whatever the Executive Government says should not be contained in a workplace agreement". That submission must be rejected because ... it is erroneous.

The first error is that it would not be open to the Executive to say that a workplace agreement should not contain any of the matters which are required content [as set out in the Act]. That is because s 846(1) requires that the regulations not be inconsistent with the new Act; it might be so even without that provision ...

[E]ven if the AWU had modified its submission to accommodate the points just made by conceding that some things were prohibited and contending that no ambit was defined beyond the limit of those prohibitions, the submission would fail. Section 356 provides that the regulations *may* specify matters that are prohibited content. Regulations of that kind would be regulations "prescribing ... matters ... permitted by this Act to be prescribed", and hence would fall within s 846(1)(a). In the absence of express language precisely defining the ambit of the permitted prescription beyond the ... matters just mentioned, that ambit would be identical with the ambit of the prescription contemplated by s 846(1)(b), namely that the regulations prescribe all matters "necessary or *convenient* to be prescribed for carrying out or giving effect to this Act" (emphasis added). It would be absurd if regulations could be made under s 846(1)(b) by reference to wider criteria than those applying to s 846(1)(a).

[The Act] provides for some things workplace agreements must contain, but, apart from the matters already mentioned, it does not state what they may not contain save through the use of regulations made under s 356. The new Act has laid down the main outlines of policy in relation to workplace agreements but has indicated an intention of leaving it to the Executive to work out that policy in relation to what workplace agreements may not contain by specific regulation. Section 356 thus has a wide ambit. Its ambit must be construed conformably with the scope and purposes of the new Act as a whole, and with the provisions of Pt 8 in relation to workplace agreements in particular. The extent of the power is marked out by inquiring whether any particular regulation about the prohibited content of workplace agreements can be said to have a rational connection with the regime established by the new Act for workplace agreements.

It follows that although the ambit of the regulation-making power so stated is imprecise, with the result that assessing whether particular regulations are ultra vires may not be easy, s 356, read with s 846(1), is a "law".

In *Dignan*, Evatt J said that a provision in a statute conferring the power to make regulations "ordinarily ... will ... retain the character of a law with respect to the subject matter dealt with in the statute". The AWU pointed out that Evatt J's statement was predicated on the existence of "a scheme contained in the statute itself" which the regulations were to carry out. That is true, but the AWU's first challenge failed on the ground that there is a scheme here of the kind just discussed, and there is no reason not to conclude that the regulation-making power is a law with respect to the same heads of legislative power as supported the other provisions of the new Act ...

20.7 Executive power to enter into contracts

The Federal Executive Government has the capacity to enter into contracts. The case law has been concerned principally with the breadth of that capacity.

The decided cases do not give a comprehensive answer as to when and why section 61 authorises the Federal Executive Government to enter into contracts under section 61. The case law is mostly concerned with outlining some of the circumstances where section 61 does *not* authorise the Federal Executive Government to enter into contracts.

In ***Williams v Commonwealth (No 1)***, the High Court made two important points about the capacity of the Federal Executive Government to enter into contracts:

1. The Federal Executive Government does not possess an unlimited capacity under section 61 to make contracts in respect of any subject-matter whatsoever.
2. The Federal Executive Government does not possess capacity under section 61 to make contracts in respect of any of the subject-matters in respect of which the Federal Parliament can legislate without statutory authorisation.

Williams (No 1) notes that section 61 does authorise the Federal Executive Government to make contracts without statutory authorisation in limited circumstances. In this case, section 61 did not authorise the Federal Executive Government to enter into a contract with a private organisation under which the Commonwealth agreed to pay funds to the organisation in return for the organisation employing a person to provide pastoral care services at a specified Queensland public school.

Williams v Commonwealth (No 1) (2012) 248 CLR 156

French CJ

The Commonwealth ... contended that the executive power supports executive action dealing at least with matters within the enumerated heads of Commonwealth legislative power.

The broad proposition in each of its manifestations should not be accepted. The exercise of legislative power must yield a law able to be characterised as a law with respect to a subject matter within the constitutional grant of legislative authority to the Parliament. The subject matters of legislative power are specified for that purpose, not to give content to the executive power. Executive action, except in the exercise of delegated legislative authority, is qualitatively different from legislative action ...

There are undoubtedly significant fields of executive action which do not require express statutory authority ... [T]he executive power of the Commonwealth extends to the doing of all things which are necessary or reasonably incidental to the execution and maintenance of a valid law of the Commonwealth once that law has taken effect ... The necessary power can be found in the words "execution and maintenance ... of the laws of the Commonwealth" appearing in s 61 of the Constitution. The field of non-statutory executive action also extends to the administration of departments of State under s 64 of the Constitution and those activities which may properly be characterised as deriving from the character and status of the Commonwealth as a national government. To accept those propositions is not to accept the broad proposition for which the Commonwealth contended, nor does such a proposition have the authority of a decision of this Court ...

The metes and bounds of aspects of executive power, however, are not to be measured by undiscriminating reference to the subject matters of legislative power. Those subject matters are diverse in character. Some relate to activities, others to classes of persons or legal entities, some to intangible property rights and some to status. Some are purposive. The submission invites the Court to determine whether there is a hypothetical law which could validly support an impugned executive contract and expenditure under such a contract. There might be a variety of laws which could validly authorise or require contractual or spending activity by the Commonwealth. The location of the contractual capacity of the Commonwealth in a universe of hypothetical laws which would, if enacted, support its exercise, is not a means by which to judge its scope ...

There are consequences for the Federation which flow from attributing to the Commonwealth a wide executive power to expend moneys, whether or not referable to a head of Commonwealth legislative power, and subject only to the requirement of a parliamentary appropriation. Those consequences are not to be minimised by the absence of any legal effect upon the laws of the States. Expenditure by the Executive Government of the Commonwealth, administered and controlled by the Commonwealth, in fields within the competence of the executive governments of the States has, and always has had, the potential, in a practical way of which the Court can take notice, to diminish the authority of the States in their fields of operation. That is not a criterion of invalidity. It is, however, a reason not to accept the broad contention that such activities can be undertaken at the discretion of the Executive, subject only to the requirement of appropriation ... The Commonwealth is not just another legal person like a private corporation or a natural person with contractual capacity ...

There is no clear evidence of a common understanding, held by the framers of the Constitution, that the executive power would support acts of the Executive Government of the Commonwealth done without statutory authority provided they dealt with matters within the enumerated legislative powers of the Commonwealth Parliament. A Commonwealth Executive with a general power to deal with matters of Commonwealth legislative competence is in tension with the federal conception which informed the function of the Senate as a necessary organ of Commonwealth legislative power. It would undermine parliamentary control of the executive branch and weaken the role of the Senate ...

Neither the DHF Agreement nor the expenditure made under it was done in the administration of a department of State in the sense used in s 64 of the Constitution. Neither constituted an exercise of the prerogative aspect of the executive power. Neither involved the exercise of a statutory power, nor executive action to give effect to a statute enacted for the purpose of providing chaplaincy or like services to State schools. Whatever the scope of that aspect of the executive power which derives from the character and status of the Commonwealth as a national government, it did not authorise the contract and the expenditure under it in this case. The field of activity in which the DHF Agreement and the expenditure was said, by the Commonwealth, to lie within areas of legislative competency of the Commonwealth Parliament under either s 51(xxiiiA) or s 51(xx) of the Constitution. Assuming it to be the case that the DHF Agreement and expenditure under it could be referred to one or other of those fields of legislative power, they are fields in which the Commonwealth and the States have concurrent competencies subject to the paramountcy of Commonwealth laws effected by s 109 of the Constitution. The character of the Commonwealth Government as a national government does not entitle it, as a general proposition, to enter into any such field of activity by executive action alone. Such an extension of Commonwealth executive powers would, in a practical sense, as Deakin predicted, correspondingly reduce those of the States and compromise what Inglis Clark described as the essential and distinctive feature of "a truly federal government".

Gummow and Bell JJ

The Commonwealth parties make the general submission that the executive power extends to entry into contracts and the spending of money without any legislative authority beyond an appropriation. The determinative question on this Special Case thus becomes whether the executive power is of sufficient scope to support the entry into and making of payments by the Commonwealth to SUQ under the Funding Agreement. For the reasons which follow this question should be answered in the negative ...

The plaintiff submitted that the relevant aspect of the executive power was that concerned with the ordinary course of administering a recognised part of the Government of the Commonwealth or with the incidents of the ordinary and well-recognised functions of that Government. These functions would vary from time to time, but would include the operation of the Parliament, and the servicing of the departments of State of the Commonwealth, the administration of which is referred to in s 64 of the Constitution, including the funding of activities in which the departments engage or consider engagement. The plaintiff accepted that this aspect of the executive power encompassed expenditure without legislative backing beyond an appropriation and the Commonwealth parties appeared to accept that concession.

However, the plaintiff contended that expenditure upon the NSCP does not fall within any ordinary and well-recognised functions of the Government of the Commonwealth ...

[F]uller attention to *Pape* nevertheless yields support to the conclusion sought by the plaintiff: that the executive power does not go so far as to support the entry by the Commonwealth into the Funding Agreement, and the making of payments by the Commonwealth to SUQ ...

Further, as noted above, the NSCP contracts, such as the Funding Agreement, present an example where within the Commonwealth itself there is a limited engagement of the institutions of representative government. The Parliament is engaged only in the appropriation of revenue, where the role of the Senate is limited. It is not engaged in the formulation, amendment or termination of any programme for the spending of those moneys.

The present case, unlike *Pape*, does not involve a natural disaster or national economic or other emergency in which only the Commonwealth has the means to provide a prompt response. In *Pape*, the short-term, extensive and urgent nature of the payments to be made to taxpayers necessitated the use of the federal taxation administration system to implement the proposal, rather than the adoption of a mechanism supported by s 96. However, the States have the legal and practical capacity to provide for a scheme such as the NSCP. The conduct of the public school system in Queensland, where the Darling Heights State Primary School is situated, is the responsibility of that State. Indeed, Queensland maintains its own programme for school chaplains ...

[T]he Commonwealth parties presented their ultimate submission. This was that because the capacities to contract and to spend moneys lawfully available for expenditure do not "involve interference with what would otherwise be the legal rights and duties of others" which exist under the ordinary law, the Executive Government in this respect possesses these capacities in common with other legal persons. The capacity to contract and to spend then was said to take its legal effect from the general law ...

[T]he Commonwealth parties' ultimate submission appears to proceed from the assumption that the executive branch has a legal personality distinct from the legislative branch, with the result that the Executive is endowed with the capacities of an individual. The legal personality, however, is that of the Commonwealth of Australia, which is the body politic established under the *Commonwealth of Australia Constitution Act* 1900 (Imp) ...

Crennan J

[T]he Commonwealth's capacities to contract and to spend are not precisely analogous to those of a natural person or any non-governmental juristic person.

First, the Consolidated Revenue Fund is distinguishable from funds available to non-governmental juristic persons, consisting as it does of revenues and moneys raised from the public, Parliament holding exclusive powers to raise taxes and grant supply.

Secondly, the Commonwealth's capacities to contract and to spend are circumscribed by s 81, in the sense that moneys appropriated must be for some governmental purpose, a circumstance which is distinct from the rights and duties created by contracts entered into by the voluntary acts of private parties.

Thirdly, unlike the capacities of a non-governmental juristic entity to contract and to spend, the Commonwealth's capacities to do so are capable of being utilised to regulate activity in the community in the course of implementing government policy. This consideration highlights the importance of the mechanisms for responsible government designed to protect the community from arbitrary government action ...

Fourthly, as the plaintiff, supported by Western Australia, contended, if the Commonwealth's capacities to contract and to spend generally permitted the Commonwealth Executive to intrude into areas of responsibility within the legislative and executive competence of the States in the absence of statutory authority other than appropriation Acts, access to s 109 of the Constitution may be impeded ...

These considerations support the rejection of the submission that an exercise of the Commonwealth's capacities to contract and to spend would never require statutory authority, or would always, in the absence of statutory authority, fall within the scope of s 61 ...

The abovementioned limits on the Commonwealth Executive's capacities to contract and to spend demonstrate that, despite recognised exceptions, expenditure by the Commonwealth Executive will often require statutory authority beyond appropriation Acts. The Commonwealth Executive's entry into the Funding Agreement and the making of payments to SUQ could not be characterised as falling within any of the recognised exceptions and did not fall within the scope of s 61. For these reasons, the Commonwealth defendants' wider submission must be rejected ...

The Commonwealth defendants' first alternative contention (the narrower submission) was that the NSCP (and the Executive's entry into the Funding Agreement and associated spending) could have been authorised by Parliament under either s 51(xxiiiA) or s 51(xx) of the Constitution, and that this was sufficient authorisation for the Executive's entry into the Funding Agreement and spending on NSCP activities ...

If the fact that the Parliament *could* pass valid Commonwealth legislation were sufficient authorisation for any expenditure by the Commonwealth Executive, and, in this case, if the possibility of enabling legislation permitted the Commonwealth Executive to enter the Funding Agreement and make payments to SUQ, the Commonwealth's capacities to contract and to spend would operate, in practice, indistinguishably from the Commonwealth Executive's exercise of a prerogative power. Such a view ignores the restrained approach to the prerogative adopted by Brennan J in *Davis* ... and disregards the constitutional relationship between the Executive and Parliament affecting spending. For these reasons, the Commonwealth defendants' narrower submission must also be rejected.

The judgments in ***Williams (No 1)*** refer to some of the circumstances where section 61 authorises the Federal Executive Government to enter into contracts. These include contracts made for the purpose of administering government departments established under section 64 of the *Constitution*. Such a contract might be a contract for office supplies for a government agency.

The conclusions about the scope of federal executive power in ***Williams (No 1)*** were reaffirmed in ***Williams (No 2)***. In *Williams (No 2)*, the High Court acknowledged that *Williams (No 1)* does not set out any comprehensive criteria for determining when section 61 does and does not authorise the Federal Executive Government to enter into contracts or spend money pursuant to contractual obligations. In *Williams (No 2)*, the High Court also explained that it is wrong to assume the Federal Executive Government has the same powers and capacities as the United Kingdom's Executive Government. Unlike the United Kingdom, Australia has a written Constitution distributing powers and functions between two levels of government.

Williams v Commonwealth (No 2) (2014) 252 CLR 416

French, Hayne, Kiefel, Bell and Keane JJ

In 2012, this Court held that an agreement the Commonwealth had made to pay money for provision of chaplaincy services in schools, and the payments the Commonwealth had made under that agreement, were not supported by the executive power of the Commonwealth under s 61 of the Constitution. Soon after the Court published its decision, the Parliament enacted legislation evidently intended to provide legislative authority to make not only the agreement and payments which had been held to have been invalidly made, but also many other agreements and arrangements for the outlay of public money and the payments made or to be made under those agreements or arrangements ...

[T]he Commonwealth parties in *Williams (No 1)* did not submit that making the funding agreement in issue, or the payments for which it provided, was supported by those aspects of executive power which might be referred to loosely as the Executive's power to deal with or respond to a national emergency (considered in *Pape*) or other matters of the kind commonly grouped under the heading "nationhood".

Six members of the Court held that the agreement providing for payments to SUQ was invalid, because it was beyond the executive power of the Commonwealth under s 61 of the Constitution, and that the making of the relevant payments by the Commonwealth to SUQ under that agreement was not supported by the executive power of the Commonwealth under s 61 ...

[In this case, the] conclusion that the impugned provisions are not laws supported by either s 51(xxiiiA) or s 51(xx) determines the outcome of the litigation unless one or more of the several arguments advanced by the Commonwealth parties about the ambit of the Executive's power to spend is made out. The Commonwealth parties advanced their arguments under the cloak of an application to reopen the decision in *Williams (No 1)*.

The argument that *Williams (No 1)* should be reopened because it did not give a single and comprehensive answer to when and why Commonwealth spending needs statutory authorisation and did not decide what powers the Executive Governments of the States have to spend or contract should also be rejected. *Williams (No 1)* decided the issues which were tendered for decision in the case ...

The Commonwealth parties submitted that determining the content of executive power (but not the limitations on its exercise) should proceed from only two premises. First, "a polity must possess all the powers that it needs in order to function as a polity". Second, "the executive power is all that power of a polity that is not legislative or judicial power". Both of those premises may be accepted. But the conclusion the Commonwealth parties sought to draw from those premises about the content of Commonwealth executive power does not follow unless there is a third premise for the argument: that the executive power of the Commonwealth should be assumed to be no less than the executive power of the British Executive. This third premise is false ...

But why the executive power of the new federal entity created by the Constitution should be assumed to have the same ambit, or be exercised in the same way and same circumstances, as the power exercised by the Executive of a unitary state having no written constitution was not demonstrated. To make an assumption of that kind, as the arguments of the Commonwealth parties did, begs the question for decision ... Consideration of the executive power of the Commonwealth will be assisted by reference to British constitutional history. But the determination of the ambit of the executive power of the Commonwealth cannot begin from a premise that the ambit of that executive power must be the same as the ambit of British executive power ...

This assumption, which underpinned the arguments advanced by the Commonwealth parties about executive power, denies the "basal consideration" that the Constitution effects a distribution of powers and functions between the Commonwealth and the States. The polity which, as the Commonwealth parties rightly submitted, must "possess all the powers that it needs in order to function as a polity" is the central polity of a federation in which independent governments exist in the one area and exercise powers in different fields of action carefully defined by law. It is not a polity organised and operating under a unitary system or under a flexible constitution where the Parliament is supreme. The assumption underpinning the Commonwealth parties' submissions about executive power is not right and should be rejected.

20.8 Parliament's power to make laws incidental to exercises of federal executive power

Section 51(xxxix) of the *Constitution* gives the Federal Parliament power to make laws with respect to matters incidental to particular exercises of federal executive power. It is *not* a power to make laws with respect to matters incidental to the subject-matter of federal executive power generally.

Australian Constitution

Section 51

The Parliament shall, subject to this Constitution, have power to make laws for the peace, order, and good government of the Commonwealth with respect to:

...

(xxxix) matters incidental to the execution of any power vested by this Constitution in the Parliament or in either House thereof, or in the Government of the Commonwealth, or in the Federal Judicature, or in any department or officer of the Commonwealth.

In ***Plaintiff M68/2015 v Minister for Immigration and Border Protection***, Gageler J explained that the incidental power can be used to enact legislation that facilitates the exercise of a federal executive power and to enact legislation that controls or restricts the exercise of a federal executive power.

Plaintiff M68/2015 v Minister for Immigration and Border Protection (2016) 257 CLR 42

Gageler J

"[I]t is of the very nature of executive power in a system of responsible government that it is susceptible to control by the exercise of legislative power by Parliament". That critical aspect of the relationship between the Executive Government of the Commonwealth and the Parliament of the Commonwealth was not left to chance in the design of the Constitution. In addition to giving the Parliament power to legislate for the appointment and removal of all officers of the Executive Government other than the Governor-General and Ministers, and in addition to enumerating other subject-matters of legislative power under which the Parliament might confer statutory authority on an officer of the Executive Government of the Commonwealth, Ch I of the Constitution conferred on the Parliament by s 51(xxxix) specific power to make laws with respect to matters "incidental to the execution" of power vested by the Constitution "in the Government of the Commonwealth" as well as "in any department or officer of the Commonwealth".

Subject to constitutional limitations, including limitations imposed by Ch III of the Constitution, the incidental power conferred by s 51(xxxix) extends not only to legislative facilitation of the execution of the executive power of the Commonwealth, but also to legislative regulation of the manner and circumstances of the execution of the executive power of the Commonwealth. The result is that:

> Whatever the scope of the executive power of the Commonwealth might otherwise be, it is susceptible of control by statute. A valid law of the Commonwealth may so limit or impose conditions on the exercise of the executive power that acts which would otherwise be supported by the executive power fall outside its scope.

...

[The exercise of federal executive power] by the Executive Government and by officers and agents of the Executive Government is and was always to be susceptible of control by Commonwealth statute.

Using the incidental power to facilitate the exercise of federal executive power

Davis v Commonwealth explains that section 51(xxxix) gives power to make laws with respect to matters incidental to *particular exercises* of federal executive power and not matters incidental to the subject-matter of federal executive power. The High Court held that whether a law is incidental to an exercise of federal executive power involves: (1) identifying the particular exercise of federal executive power in question; and (2) asking whether the law is proportionate, or reasonably appropriate and adapted, to achieving the purpose of an exercise of federal executive power.

In ***Davis***, the High Court held that the incidental power would support a law authorising the expenditure of appropriated funds to pay for an exercise of federal executive power that involves expenditure. The High Court also held that the incidental power would support a law creating criminal offences to protect an exercise of federal executive power from interference.

Davis v Commonwealth (1988) 166 CLR 79

In the passages extracted above, the High Court held that the nationhood component of federal executive power extended to conducting celebrations to commemorate the Bicentenary of the arrival of the First Fleet and to setting up a corporation to organise those celebrations. In the passages extracted below, the High Court holds that section 51(xxxix) supports laws authorising the expenditure of appropriated funds to cover the corporation's expenses and laws prohibiting the use of the corporation's symbols and logos. The High Court held that section 51(xxxix) did not support laws prohibiting the use of expressions like '1988' because that went beyond what was incidental: such a law was not necessary to protect the exercise of federal executive power from interference.

Mason CJ, Deane and Gaudron JJ

Section 51(xxxix) of the Constitution enables the Parliament to legislate in aid of an exercise of the executive power. So, once it is accepted that the executive power extends to the incorporation of the Authority with the object set out in cl 3 of its memorandum of association, s 51(xxxix) authorizes legislation regulating the administration and procedures of the Authority and conferring on it such powers and protection as may be appropriate to such an authority ...

We turn now to the challenge to the validity of ss 22 and 23. The defendants submit that the validity of these sections is sustained by the incidental or implied legislative powers ...

[T]he federal executive power authorizes the commemoration of the Bicentenary and what is incidental to it. Likewise, in the manner already discussed, federal legislative power extends to the same extent. In exercising that power the Parliament may protect the name of the Authority, authorize the prescription of appropriate official symbols for use by the Authority and prohibit unauthorized use by others of the Authority's name or of those symbols, or likenesses of them, for the purpose of protecting their integrity. The ... incidental power (s 51(xxxix)), enables Parliament to enact coercive laws ... Consequently, if the provisions of ss 22 and 23 relating to the use of the Authority's name and prescribed symbols stood on their own we would uphold their validity ...

If we look to s 22(1)(a) as it applies to prescribed expressions, the first six expressions prescribed by s 22(6)(d)(i) are expressions which may be used in conjunction with "1788", "1988" or "88", in connection with a business, trade, profession or occupation, in a great variety of circumstances, without prejudicing in any way the commemoration of the Bicentenary or the attainment of the objects of the Authority. The expressions are commonly used by all sections of the community, particularly in this the Bicentennial year. There is every reason for thinking that a wide range of persons, companies and organizations have occasion to use them otherwise than for purposes of advertising and publicity, if only to record what they are doing in the Bicentennial year. And there is no reason for thinking that the protection of the integrity of the commemoration of the Bicentenary and the attainment by the Authority of its objects require the prohibition of such a use of the six prescribed expressions in the circumstances mentioned in s 22(1), subject only to the written consent of the Authority.

The difficulties do not stop at this point. Take the prescription of "Melbourne" and "Sydney" in par (d)(i). The use of "Family Law Conference Melbourne 1988", without the prior written consent of the Authority, in connection with a conference of the legal profession in that city this year would infringe s 22(1)(a). Yet it is impossible to perceive how the prohibition of such a use contributes to the protection of the integrity of the commemoration of the Bicentenary or the attainment of the objects of the Authority. Many similar illustrations (e.g., clothing or emblems displaying support for sporting teams) might be given of the use of a combination of "Melbourne" and "1988" or "Sydney" and "1988".

The illustrations given in the two preceding paragraphs indicate that the effect of the provisions is to give the Authority an extraordinary power to regulate the use of expressions in everyday use in this country, though the circumstances of that use in countless situations could not conceivably prejudice the commemoration of the Bicentenary or the attainment by the Authority of its objects. In arming the Authority with this extraordinary power the Act provides for a regime of protection which is grossly disproportionate to the need to protect the commemoration and the Authority ...

Although the statutory regime may be related to a constitutionally legitimate end, the provisions in question reach too far. This extraordinary intrusion into freedom of expression is not reasonably and appropriately adapted to achieve the ends that lie within the limits of constitutional power.

Brennan J

The scope of the legislative power conferred by s 51(xxxix) in conjunction with s 61 depends on what the Executive Government has done or intends to do in execution of its power. Section 51 (xxxix) confers a power to make a law not with respect to the subject matter of an executive power of the Commonwealth, nor even with respect to a matter incidental to that subject matter; it confers a power to make a law only with respect to a matter "incidental to the execution" of an executive power of the Commonwealth ...

In the present context, the legislative power extends only to a matter attending or arising in the execution of the executive power. It fastens on and is limited by what the Executive Government does or intends to do in exercise of its executive power ...

By reason of the confined scope of the power conferred by s 51(xxxix), the area within which a law enacted under that paragraph may create offences is necessarily confined ... What offences can be created by a law with respect to a matter incidental to the execution of an executive power? ... In my opinion, the legislative power with respect to matters incidental to the execution of the executive power does not extend to the creation of offences except insofar as is necessary to protect the efficacy of the execution by the Executive Government of its powers and capacities ...

If the executive power of the Commonwealth includes a power to organize the commemoration through the agency of the Authority, the Act which governs the relationship of the Executive Government with the agent and which provides for the funding of the organization and the distribution of any surplus on winding up is clearly a law with respect to matters incidental to that activity ...

As the Bicentenary can properly be seen as a matter for commemoration by the Commonwealth, the executive power of the Commonwealth extends to the organization of the commemoration of the Bicentenary, and the agency of the Authority is merely the administrative means by which that activity is to be carried into effect. Section 51(xxxix) empowered the Parliament to make a law in aid of that activity. Putting aside ss 22 and 23 for the moment, the Act is supported by s 51(xxxix) of the Constitution.

That conclusion disposes of any challenge to the validity of the appropriation of moneys for expenditure under the Act ...

Freedom of speech may sometimes be a casualty of a law of the Commonwealth made under a specific head of legislative power – for example, wartime censorship – or of a law designed to protect the nation – for example, a law against seditious utterances – but freedom of speech can hardly be an incidental casualty of an activity undertaken by the Executive Government to advance a nation which boasts of its freedom. If a special provision were necessary to suppress fraud, deceit or the misapplication of Commonwealth funds in the commemoration of the Bicentenary, an appropriate offence-creating provision may have been supportable as a protection of the organization which the Executive Government had set up.

But a prohibition on the use of symbols and expressions of communication relating to the Bicentenary in the several ways specified in s 22(1) is not a law with respect to a matter incidental to the execution of a power to organize the commemoration; it is not a law which protects the efficacy of what the Executive Government has done or may do in organizing the commemoration. It is a law with respect to the subject matter of the executive power: the commemoration itself. Such a law purports to control the commemoration in a manner which is beyond the executive power of the Commonwealth and which is not incidental to the execution of that power ...

But it cannot be incidental to the organization of the commemoration of the Bicentenary to prohibit, under criminal sanctions, the peaceful expression of opinions about the significance of the events of 1788. By prohibiting the use of the symbols and expressions apt to express such opinions, ss 22 and 23 forfeit any support which s 51(xxxix) might otherwise afford.

Pape held that the nationhood component of section 61 federal executive power authorised the Federal Executive Government to spend money to stimulate the economy as a response to the Global Financial Crisis of 2007–08. The case also held that section 51(xxxix) supported legislation providing the necessary funds to the Federal Executive Government and regulating the details of the spending authorised by section 61.

Pape v Commissioner of Taxation (2009) 238 CLR 1

Gummow, Crennan and Bell JJ

In determining whether the Bonus Act is supported by s 61 and s 51(xxxix) of the Constitution, it is necessary to ask whether determining that there is the need for an immediate fiscal stimulus to the national economy, in the circumstances set out above, falls within executive power and then to ascertain whether s 51(xxxix) of the Constitution supports the impugned legislation as a law which is incidental to that exercise of executive power ...

[O]nly the Commonwealth has the resources to meet the emergency which is presented to it as a nation state by responding on the scale of the Bonus Act. That Australia is a federal state does not produce the consequence that the policy determined upon by the Executive Government cannot be put into effect by measures such as the Bonus Act. The present is an example of the engagement by the Executive Government in activities peculiarly adapted to the government of the country and which otherwise could not be carried on for the public benefit.

To the extent that the implementation of this policy involves the creation by s 7 of the Bonus Act of a right to receive the tax bonus and the imposition by s 8 of an obligation to restore overpayments, legislation is necessary and the authority to enact it is supplied by s 51(xxxix) of the Constitution ...

The entitlement to payment which is conferred by the Bonus Act ... is incidental to the effectuation of the fiscal stimulus policy.

Using the incidental power to control and regulate federal executive power

Justice Gageler explained in ***Plaintiff M68*** that section 51(xxxix) can be used to enact legislation to control and regulate exercises of section 61 federal executive power. Parliament can also enact legislation to control and regulate exercises of section 61 federal executive power under its other heads of legislative power. Whether legislation has such an effect is a question of statutory interpretation.

In the ***Tampa Case***, the Full Court of the Federal Court had to consider whether legislation enacted under a particular head of power abrogated a component of federal executive power. The principles of statutory interpretation outlined in that case apply to legislation enacted under all heads of power including section 51(xxxix).

In the ***Tampa Case***, there was a difference between the majority and minority judges as to whether the prerogative power in question – namely, the power to prevent the entry of aliens into the country – had been abrogated by statute. The judges all agreed that a statute could abrogate a prerogative power. The minority held that a prerogative power is displaced where legislation merely covers the same area of operation as the prerogative power. The majority judges held that the test was one of legislative intent. The majority reasoned that although the legislation in question provided for a comprehensive regime in the same area of operation as the prerogative power there was no legislative intention to displace the prerogative power. The legislative provisions were facultative (empowering the Federal Executive Government to do things) rather than prohibitive (restricting or limiting the Federal Executive Government's ability to do things), and therefore did not manifest a legislative intention to deprive power.

Ruddock v Vardalis ('Tampa Case') (2001) 110 FCR 491

French J

The executive power can be abrogated, modified or regulated by laws of the Commonwealth. Its common law ancestor, the Royal Prerogative, was similarly subject to abrogation, modification or regulation by statute ...

The conceptual bases upon which it is said that statute law may abrogate or regulate the prerogative were variously proposed in *Attorney-General v De Keyser's Royal Hotel, Limited* [1920] AC 50. Implied assent by the Crown, the futility of concurrent powers, one regulated and the other not, a presumption that the Crown resorts to statute rather than its unqualified power and simple parliamentary sovereignty encapsulate the approaches taken by the Law Lords in that case. In the end, however, there was nothing in their approaches which permitted avoidance of the need to construe the relevant statute to determine whether, by express words or necessary implication, it has any, and if so what, operation upon the prerogative power ...

The executive power of the Commonwealth under s 61 cannot be treated as a species of the royal prerogative, "The residue of discretionary or arbitrary authority which at any given time is legally left in the hands of the Crown." – *De Keyser* at 526. While the executive power may derive some of its content by reference to the royal prerogative, it is a power conferred as part of a negotiated federal compact expressed in a written Constitution distributing powers between the three arms of government reflected in Chapters I, II and III of the Constitution and, as to legislative powers, between the polities that comprise the federation.

The power is subject, not only to the limitations as to subject matter that flow directly from the Constitution but also to the laws of the Commonwealth made under it. There is no place then for any doctrine that a law made on a particular subject matter is presumed to displace or regulate the operation of the executive power in respect of that subject matter. The operation of the law upon the power is a matter of construction.

That construction, while governed ultimately by the terms of the statute under consideration, is informed by a requirement for a clear intention to displace the power ...

The greater the significance of a particular executive power to national sovereignty, the less likely it is that, absent clear words or inescapable implication, the parliament would have intended to extinguish the power. In such a case close scrutiny will be required of any contention that a statute, without express words to that effect, has displaced the operation of the executive power by virtue of "covering the field" of the subject matter ...

It was submitted for VCCL and Vadarlis that the Act covers the field of unlawful entry into Australia in a way that manifests an intention to displace any executive power in relation to the same subject matter ...

The question is whether the Act operates to abrogate the executive power under s 61 to prevent aliens from entering into Australia. There are no express words to that effect. It is necessary then to look to whether by implication it has that effect. It is not necessary for this purpose either to determine the full extent of the executive power or the full effect of the Act upon it. It is sufficient to ask whether the Act evinces a clear and unambiguous intention to deprive the Executive of the power to prevent entry into Australian territorial waters of a vessel carrying non-citizens apparently intending to land on Australian territory and the power to prevent such a vessel from proceeding further towards Australian territory and to prevent non-citizens on it from landing upon Australian territory.

In considering what is the implied intention of the Act and in particular the provisions referred to earlier, it is necessary to have regard not only to the general approach, supported by authority, to the question whether executive power is taken to be abrogated by statute, but also the importance to national sovereignty of the particular power in question. In my opinion the Act, by its creation of facultative provisions, which may yield a like result to the exercise of executive power, in this particular application of it cannot be taken as intending to deprive the Executive of the power necessary to do what it has done in this case. The Act confers power. It does not in the specific area evidence an intention to take it away. The term "intention" of course is a fiction.

What must be asked is whether the Act operates in a way that is necessarily inconsistent with the subsistence of the executive power described. It is facultative. Its object is control of entry. Subject to certain specific provisions, such as those relating to the grant of protection visas, its object is not to confer rights upon non-citizens seeking to enter Australia. ...

In ***Cadia Holdings***, the High Court adopted the same reasoning as French J in the ***Tampa Case***.

Cadia Holdings Pty Ltd v New South Wales (2010) 242 CLR 195

Gummow, Hayne, Heydon and Crennan JJ

[I]t remains an orthodox approach by the courts to statutory construction to say that the prerogative of the Crown is not displaced except by express words or by necessary implication.

20.9 DISCUSSION QUESTIONS

1. For each of the following cases identify the breadth and depth of non-statutory federal executive power under consideration: ***Davis v Commonwealth*, *Tampa Case*, *Williams (No 1)*, *Pape*.**
2. Why did Hayne and Kiefel JJ dissent in ***Pape*** on the nationhood power issue? Are their concerns valid?
3. What was the argument in the ***WorkChoices Case*** concerning delegation of legislative power? Why did the High Court reject that argument?
4. How is it determined whether a statute has modified or abrogated a non-statutory executive power?
5. Problem question: Consider the following hypothetical legislation and scenario. The Commonwealth Government has formed the opinion, based on advice from the Department of Education, the Treasury and other experts, that there is a vocational training crisis in Australia. The Government believes that the Australian economy requires approximately 10 per cent more tradespeople to be trained each year than are currently being trained. Without the extra tradespeople, the Treasury expects the Australian economy to experience a 0.5 per cent contraction in growth each year for three years. This will result in a serious increase in unemployment.

   The Commonwealth Parliament enacts the *Vocational Training Assistance Act 2023* (Cth). The key features of the Act are:

   - Section 1 provides that the object of the Act is to encourage the establishment of more vocational training providers and to increase the number of Australians with vocational training qualifications to address Australia's economic problems.
   - Part 2 of the Act makes it an offence for a person to cause physical damage to a vocational training provider's property and provides that a person convicted of such an offence must not go within 100 metres of a vocational training provider's premises except in cases of necessity (such as to go past en route to hospital).
   - Part 3 of the Act authorises the Commonwealth to enter into contracts with vocational training providers under which the Commonwealth will pay providers to provide vocational training to such individuals as a Federal Minister decides should receive free training following applications to the Minister by interested individuals. (The Commonwealth will not employ those individuals following their training).

   You are a government legal advisor and have been asked to advise whether the legislation is constitutionally valid.

POWER TO SPEND MONEY

21

21.1 Overview

This chapter examines the capacity of the Federal Executive Government to spend money. The ability to spend is important to the functioning of government because of the need to pay public service salaries and to the implementation of government policies because many policy areas require large amounts of spending.

Consistent with principles of responsible government, public funds are subject to parliamentary control through two constitutional requirements. First, all government revenue must be held in a single Consolidated Revenue Fund. Secondly, funds in the Consolidated Revenue Fund can be accessed only if appropriated by law.

Funds that have been lawfully appropriated from the Consolidated Revenue Fund may be expended by the Federal Executive Government only if some law authorises that expenditure. Parliament also has power to grant funds to States on such terms and conditions as Parliament thinks fit. This power is regularly used to pay the States to implement policies that the Commonwealth lacks constitutional power to implement itself.

Key concepts addressed in this chapter include:

- consolidated revenue fund
- appropriations
- purposes of the Commonwealth
- grants
- terms and conditions.

21.2 Parliamentary control of public funds: The Consolidated Revenue Fund and appropriations

The idea that Parliament, and not the Executive Government, has control of public funds originates in seventeenth-century English political turmoil and constitutional debates. In what became known as the Glorious Revolution, James II fled England and the English Parliament enacted the *Bill of Rights 1688* declaring William and Mary of Orange to be King and Queen of England and subordinating royal power to parliamentary control. Among other things, the *Bill of Rights 1688* also asserted parliamentary control over public money.

Bill of Rights 1688, 1 Will & Mar Sess 2, c2

Article 4

That levying money for or to the use of the Crown by pretence of prerogative, without grant of Parliament, for longer time, or in other manner than the same is or shall be granted, is illegal.

The constitutional debates also led to the principle that only the House of Commons, as the House representing the people, could initiate Bills imposing taxes or appropriating public funds.

Victoria v Commonwealth (1975) 134 CLR 338

Stephen J

In 1661 the Commons reiterated its objection to the initiation of money bills by the Lords, a complaint initially expressed early in the 15th century; in 1665 the principle of appropriation of supply for specific purposes was re-established by the Commons after its initial emergence in the 14th century and its subsequent demise; in 1671 the Commons resolved that money bills should not be amended by the Lords and in 1678 it resolved that it alone might originate such bills. All this occurred between Rebellion and Revolution; after the Revolution the Lords were left only with a power to withhold assent to money bills.

The *Australian Constitution* follows this tradition.

The Consolidated Revenue Fund

Section 81 of the *Constitution* requires all federal public revenue to be located in a single fund called the Consolidated Revenue Fund. Section 83 provides that money can be drawn from the Consolidated Revenue Fund only by an appropriation made by law. In this way, Parliament has control over public money because the Federal Executive Government requires parliamentary authorisation to access public money.

Australian Constitution

Section 81 Consolidated Revenue Fund

All revenues or moneys raised or received by the Executive Government of the Commonwealth shall form one Consolidated Revenue Fund, to be appropriated for the purposes of the Commonwealth in the manner and subject to the charges and liabilities imposed by this Constitution.

Section 83 Money to be appropriated by law

No money shall be drawn from the Treasury of the Commonwealth except under appropriation made by law.

Initiating money Bills

Section 53 provides that Bills appropriating funds from the Consolidated Revenue Fund or imposing taxation cannot originate in the Senate. In other words, money Bills must originate in the popularly elected House of Representatives.

Australian Constitution

Section 53 Powers of the Houses in respect of legislation

Proposed laws appropriating revenue or moneys, or imposing taxation, shall not originate in the Senate. But a proposed law shall not be taken to appropriate revenue or moneys, or to impose taxation, by reason only of its containing provisions for the imposition or appropriation of fines or other pecuniary penalties, or for the demand or payment or appropriation of fees for licences, or fees for services under the proposed law.

The Senate may not amend proposed laws imposing taxation, or proposed laws appropriating revenue or moneys for the ordinary annual services of the Government.

The Senate may not amend any proposed law so as to increase any proposed charge or burden on the people.

The Senate may at any stage return to the House of Representatives any proposed law which the Senate may not amend, requesting, by message, the omission or amendment of any items or provisions therein. And the House of Representatives may, if it thinks fit, make any of such omissions or amendments, with or without modifications.

Except as provided in this section, the Senate shall have equal power with the House of Representatives in respect of all proposed laws.

Section 54 Appropriation Bills

The proposed law which appropriates revenue or moneys for the ordinary annual services of the Government shall deal only with such appropriation.

The High Court has held that section 53 is not justiciable. The courts will not entertain an argument that a law appropriating funds or imposing taxation is invalid merely because the Bill for the law originated in the Senate. Section 53 provides direction as to the internal proceedings in Parliament, which as a general rule are not justiciable.

Osborne v Commonwealth (1911) 12 CLR 321

Griffith CJ

[Sections] 53 and 54 deal with "proposed laws" - that is, Bills or projects of law still under consideration and not assented to - and they lay down rules to be observed with respect to proposed laws at that stage. Whatever obligations are imposed by these sections are directed to the Houses of Parliament whose conduct of their internal affairs is not subject to review by a Court of law.

Barton J

No lawyer, still less one who has any acquaintance with the practice of Parliaments, can doubt that in legislation a "proposed law" is what is known as a Bill, and a "law" is what is known as an Act or Statute. The one is a *projet de loi*, not necessarily passed even by one House of Parliament, the other an actual law made effective by passage through both Houses, and by the Royal assent. Up to the moment of that assent there is only a proposed law or Bill ... [Sections] 53 and 54 relate, as is clear, only to the order of business between the two Houses in dealing with the progress of Bills, and are therefore, and from the necessity of the thing, merely directory ...

Western Australia v Commonwealth ('Native Title Act Case') (1995) 183 CLR 373

Mason CJ, Brennan, Deane, Toohey, Gaudron and McHugh JJ

Section 53 is a procedural provision governing the intra-mural activities of the Parliament. The traditional view is that this Court does not interfere in those activities. That view was stated by

Mason CJ, Deane, Toohey and Gaudron JJ in *Northern Suburbs General Cemetery Reserve Trust v Commonwealth* ((1993) 176 CLR 555 at 578) in reference to s 54 of the Constitution:

> a failure to comply with the dictates of a procedural provision, such as s 54, dealing with a 'bill' or a 'proposed law' is not contemporaneously justiciable and does not give rise to invalidity of the resulting Act when it has been passed by the two Houses of the Parliament and has received the royal assent.

The traditional view accords both with the text of s 53, which speaks of "proposed laws" rather than "laws" (*Osborne v Commonwealth* (1911) 12 CLR 321 at 336, 352, 355) and with the intention manifested in the Convention Debates (*Official Report of the National Australasian Convention Debates*, (Adelaide) 13 April 1897 at 472–473.).

Wilkie v Commonwealth (2017) 349 ALR 1

Kiefel CJ, Bell, Gageler, Keane, Nettle, Gordon and Edelman JJ

Each of ss 53, 54 and 56 of the *Constitution* is a "procedural provision governing the intra-mural activities of the Parliament" in respect of which "this Court does not interfere". A failure to comply with any one or more of them "is not contemporaneously justiciable and does not give rise to invalidity of the resulting Act when it has been passed by the two Houses of the Parliament and has received the royal assent".

Appropriations

An appropriation is an 'ear-marking' of funds for a particular purpose.

Victoria v Commonwealth and Hayden ('AAP Case') (1975) 134 CLR 338

Jacobs J

The appropriation is no more than an earmarking of the money, which remains the property of the Commonwealth. All it does is to disclose that the Parliament assents to the expenditure of the moneys appropriated for the purposes stated in the appropriation.

Section 81 provides that an appropriation must be 'for the purposes of the Commonwealth'.

In the ***First Pharmaceutical Benefits Case***, the High Court held that the words 'purposes of the Commonwealth' have the consequence of imposing a requirement that appropriations cannot be made in blank. In other words, appropriations must be made for a designated purpose.

The case is also the origin of the now-rejected idea that section 81 authorises the Federal Executive Government to spend any money validly appropriated. The legislation under consideration in this case was struck down because it went beyond appropriating funds and authorising their expenditure and purported to regulate a subject-matter unrelated to any head of legislative power. Some judges also suggested that, because appropriations must be made by law, it was for Parliament as law-maker to determine whether a purpose is 'for the purposes of the Commonwealth'.

Attorney-General (Vic) ex rel Dale v Commonwealth ('First Pharmaceutical Benefits Case') (1945) 71 CLR 237

This case was decided before paragraph (xxiiiA) was inserted into section 51, adding as a head of power: the provision of maternity allowances, widows' pensions, child endowment, unemployment, pharmaceutical, sickness and hospital benefits, medical and dental services (but not so as to authorise any form of civil conscription), benefits to students and family allowance.

Latham CJ

The statement of claim alleges the enactment of the *Pharmaceutical Benefits Act 1944*, which provides for the granting of pharmaceutical benefits to all persons ordinarily resident in the Commonwealth without payment by such persons for such benefits, and for the payment by the Commonwealth to approved pharmaceutical chemists at rates to be prescribed under the Act for the supplying of the said pharmaceutical benefits. The payments to be made by the Commonwealth to the chemists are, according to the Act, to be made out of a trust account established under the *National Welfare Fund Act 1943*. The plaintiff alleges that the provisions of the Constitution do not authorize the enactment of the *Pharmaceutical Benefits Act* or the appropriation of public moneys for the purposes of the Act ...

[I]n the case of the words "for the purposes of the Commonwealth." These words can be interpreted as providing that all appropriations (which must be "made by law" – s 83) must be for purposes which can be shown to be purposes of the Commonwealth. In other words, there cannot be appropriations in blank, appropriations for no designated purpose, merely authorizing expenditure with no reference to purpose. An Act which merely provided that a minister or some other person could spend a sum of money, no purpose of the expenditure being stated, would not be a valid appropriation Act.

But this statement only raises the question: What are purposes of the Commonwealth within the meaning of the section?

I approach the consideration of this question with the prima facie opinion that the words "purposes of the Commonwealth" (which plainly *include* purposes "in respect of which the Parliament has power to make laws") are not identical in meaning with the latter words I have already stated my opinion that each such power includes a power to authorize the expenditure of money. A meaning is given to the words "to be appropriated for the purposes of the Commonwealth" if they are read as intended to show positively that there may be other Commonwealth purposes than those in respect of which power to make laws is given elsewhere in the Constitution. Otherwise the words have no legal effect whatever.

What then is the authority which can determine what purposes are purposes of the Commonwealth? As the appropriation is to be made by law (s 83), the natural answer is – the authority which makes Commonwealth laws, that is, the Commonwealth Parliament, not the executive authority which administers laws when made, nor the judicial authority which interprets and applies the laws. Thus, in my opinion, the Commonwealth Parliament has a general, and not a limited, power of appropriation of public moneys. It is general in the sense that it is for the Parliament to determine whether or not a particular purpose shall be adopted as a purpose of the Commonwealth ...

For these reasons, in my opinion, the provisions of s 81 can fairly be read as intended to mean that it is the Commonwealth Parliament, and not any court, which is entrusted with the power, duty and responsibility of determining what purposes shall be Commonwealth purposes, as well as of providing for the expenditure of money for such purposes.

This conclusion, however, relates only to laws providing for the expenditure of money. It does not follow that the Commonwealth Parliament, because it can, as it were, subscribe towards the support of what it considers to be worthy objects, can take legislative control of matters relating to any such objects in respect of which there is no other grant of legislative power. A company may have power to subscribe to a hospital or a football club without having power to conduct a hospital or to organize and control a football club ...

The question therefore is whether the *Pharmaceutical Benefits Act* falls within the sphere of Commonwealth legislative power. If it is an Act for the appropriation of money, s 51(xxxix) of the *Constitution* would authorize the inclusion in the Act of provisions to prevent the use of the money for purposes other than those declared by Parliament. But the power to make laws for the appropriation of money can go no further than this. If the Act can properly be described as an Act for the appropriation of money with safeguards against wrongful expenditure of the money, it is in my opinion valid. If, on the other hand, it is an Act which, though it appropriates money, is really an Act for the control of doctors, chemists, sale of drugs and the conduct of persons who deal with doctors and chemists, then in my opinion it is invalid, for the reason that the Act is an Act with respect to subjects which are not committed to the Federal Parliament ...

Dixon J

But the claim is made that, under ss. 81 and 83, the Parliament has power to authorize the expenditure of money without any limitation of purpose. The claim means that, though the Commonwealth is a government of defined and enumerated powers, the power to spend money is independent of the limitations which affect the other powers of the Commonwealth and is not to be restricted by reference to the purposes for which, otherwise, the Commonwealth is conceived to have been established. There has not been wanting support for this view among those who have written about the Constitution, though I think the more general opinion has been against it.

But I cannot see that this case requires us to choose between the two views. If it be conceded to the full that the power of appropriation authorizes the expenditure of money on any purpose the Parliament may think fit without restriction as to subject matter, it nevertheless appears to me to be a proposition that has little or no relevance to this case. It is certainly not one that can support the *Pharmaceutical Benefits Act* as a whole. If it were true that the Act was primarily an appropriation for expenditure and that it did not appear impossible to sever the provisions which went beyond what is incidental to such an appropriation, it would be then necessary to consider how much could be supported under s. 81 and how much of the rest could be stripped from the enactment without changing its essential character. But the fact is that under the *Pharmaceutical Benefits Act* appropriation of money is the consequence of the plan; the plan is not consequential upon or incidental to the appropriation of money ...

McTiernan J

The words "for the purposes of the Commonwealth" in s 81 are general words and no limitation on them is expressed. They are not convertible into such a phrase as "for purposes in respect of which the Parliament is given the powers of legislation contained in s 51 or any other section," or into such a phrase as "for the purposes of the Constitution." The purposes of the Commonwealth are, I think, such purposes as the Parliament determines. This view of the meaning of the words "the purposes of the Commonwealth" is consistent with the union of the people of the States in a Commonwealth.

Any purpose for which the elected representatives of the people of the Commonwealth determine to appropriate the revenue is a purpose of the Commonwealth. If it were otherwise, judicial scrutiny of a purpose for which Parliament appropriated revenue could take place in order to determine whether the purpose was lawful or not. The Constitution puts the power of the purse in the hands of Parliament, not in the hands of the Courts. I think that the object of s 81 is to put this power in the hands of Parliament ...

In the ***AAP Case***, there was again a division of opinion in the High Court as to the meaning of the words 'purposes of the Commonwealth'. The majority – McTiernan, Mason and Murphy JJ – held that it was for Parliament to determine what purposes are Commonwealth purposes.

Victoria v Commonwealth and Hayden ('AAP Case') (1975) 134 CLR 338

This case concerned funding of a government policy called the 'Australian Assistance Plan', which involved the Federal Government giving funds to local councils for various spending initiatives.

Mason J

The first question for decision is whether the power of the Commonwealth Parliament to appropriate by statute moneys standings to the credit of Consolidated Revenue is unlimited and extends to any purpose which the Parliament may select as a purpose of the Commonwealth (the view taken by Latham CJ and McTiernan J in the *Pharmaceutical Benefits Case* (1945) 71 CLR 237) or whether it is more narrowly confined to purposes conforming to the powers and functions entrusted to the Commonwealth as a national government under the Constitution (the view which, subject to some variations, was taken by the other members of the Court in the same case) … In ascertaining the meaning of "for the purposes of the Commonwealth", which is the critical expression in s 81, it is necessary to keep in mind the function and purpose of an Appropriation Act … An Appropriation Act has a twofold purpose. It has a negative as well as a positive effect. Not only does it authorize the Crown to withdraw moneys from the Treasury, it "restrict(s) the expenditure to the particular purpose", as Isaacs and Rich JJ observed in *Commonwealth v Colonial Ammunition Co Ltd* (1924) 34 CLR 198, at p 224 …

Their Honours, after noting that an Appropriation Act is "financial, not regulative", continued: "It … neither betters nor worsens transactions in which the Executive engages within its constitutional domain, except so far as the declared willingness of Parliament that public moneys should be applied and that specified funds should be appropriated for such a purpose is a necessary legal condition of the transaction." An Appropriation Act therefore is something of a *rara avis* in the world of statutes; its effect is limited in the senses already explained; apart from this effect it does not create rights, nor does it impose duties …

I would give to the words "for the purposes of the Commonwealth" in s 81 the meaning ascribed to them by Latham CJ in the *Pharmaceutical Benefits Case* (1945) 71 CLR, at p 256, that is, for such purposes as Parliament may determine.

But this is not to say that the Commonwealth has an unlimited executive power or that a statutory appropriation provides lawful authority for the engagement by the Commonwealth in particular activities. An appropriation, as I have explained, has a limited effect. It may provide the necessary parliamentary sanction for the withdrawal of money from Consolidated Revenue and the payment or subscription of money to a particular recipient or for a particular purpose but it does not supply legal authority for the Commonwealth's engagement in the activities in connexion with which the moneys are to be spent. Whether the Commonwealth can engage in any specific activities depends upon the extent of the Commonwealth's legislative, executive and judicial powers …

In the light of what I have already said as to the extent of the appropriation power, the Appropriation Act, in so far as it relates to item 530.4, the item in question, is a valid exercise of that power conferred by s 81. However, in my view the activities which call for the expenditure of this money, the elements which comprise the scheme known as the Australian Assistance Plan, stand largely, if not wholly, outside the boundaries of the executive power of the Commonwealth …

The minority – Barwick CJ and Gibbs J – took the position that such a broad interpretation would undermine the distribution of powers between the Commonwealth and States.

Victoria v Commonwealth and Hayden ('AAP Case') (1975) 134 CLR 338

Barwick CJ

In my opinion, the words "for the purpose of the Commonwealth" were intended to and do limit the legislative power of the Commonwealth to appropriate and authorize the expenditure of the Consolidated Revenue Fund. They must be construed and applied in the light of the circumstances and constitutional provisions to which I have referred. It follows inevitably, in my opinion, that they cannot be writ out of the Constitution by deciding that any purpose which the Parliament considers to be a Commonwealth purpose is an authorized purpose. That is but an example of "words meaning what I say they mean", a notion more likely to be found in fantasy than in constitutional law ...

What then are purposes of the Commonwealth within s 81? The Commonwealth is a polity of limited powers, its legislative power principally found in the topics granted by ss 51 and 52: its executive power is described as extending to the execution and maintenance of the Constitution and of the laws of the Commonwealth. No doubt some powers, legislative and executive, may come from the very formation of the Commonwealth as a polity and its emergence as an international state. Thus it may be granted that in considering what are Commonwealth purposes, attention will not be confined to ss 51 and 52 ...

In my opinion, the expression in s 51(xxxi) of the Constitution "for any purpose in respect of which the Parliament has power to make laws;" is a reasonable synonym for the expression "the purposes of the Commonwealth" in s 81 ...

In my opinion, no power resides in the Commonwealth to implement and carry out a social welfare plan such as the Australian Assistance Plan. It follows, in my opinion, that that Plan is not a purpose of the Commonwealth within the meaning of the language of s 81 ...

The debate about what purposes are Commonwealth purposes is now of limited significance. The High Court has held that to spend money not only must funds be appropriated but another law must authorise the actual spending of appropriated funds (see 'Power to spend appropriated funds' in this chapter).

Nevertheless, an appropriation must be for a purpose rather than in blank (in the sense of being without any limitation as to the purpose of the appropriation). However, that purpose need not be articulated with any great degree of particularity. ***Combet's Case*** demonstrates that the purpose of an appropriation can be expressed at a very high level of generality.

Combet v Commonwealth (2005) 224 CLR 494

The Appropriation Act (No 1) 2005–2006 (Cth) *appropriated money, among other purposes, to achieve outcomes described as 'efficient and effective labour market assistance', 'higher productivity, higher pay workplaces' and 'increased workforce participation'. Section 7(2) provided:*

> *An amount issued out of the Consolidated Revenue Fund for a departmental item for an entity may only be applied for the departmental expenditure of the entity.*

Section 8(2) provided:

> *An amount issued out of the Consolidated Revenue Fund for an administered item for an outcome of an entity may only be applied for expenditure for the purpose of carrying out activities for the purpose of contributing to achieving that outcome.*

A majority of the High Court held that funding for an advertising campaign to promote proposed new industrial relations laws fell within these appropriations.

Gleeson CJ

The *Constitution*, consistently with the background of constitutional history and parliamentary practice with which the framers were familiar, reserves to the Parliament, and especially the House of Representatives, the power associated with control of funding through appropriation. It is for Parliament, consistently with the *Constitution*, to decide how it exercises that control. One factor of practical significance is the degree of specificity with which appropriations are made. Section 81 of the *Constitution* provides for the Consolidated Revenue Fund "to be appropriated for the purposes of the Commonwealth". It is for the Parliament, in making appropriations, to determine what purposes are purposes of the Commonwealth. It is also for the Parliament to determine the degree of specificity with which such purposes are expressed. "Provided that purposes are stated it is a matter for the Parliament how minute and particular shall be the expression of purposes in any particular case." "The purpose of any appropriation may be indicated generally. 'One-line' appropriations are valid."

Gummow, Hayne, Callinan and Heydon JJ

The plaintiffs' contention that expenditure of public money on advertising about the reform package is unlawful was a contention about the proper construction of the *Appropriation Act (No 1)* 2005–2006. They did not contend that there could be no appropriation for payment for government advertising as a purpose of the Commonwealth within the meaning of s 81 of the *Constitution*. Given the reasoning in *New South Wales v Bardolph*, that is unsurprising. Their contention was there *was no appropriation*, not there could never be an appropriation ...

It is for the Parliament to identify the degree of specificity with which the purpose of an appropriation is identified. It may readily be accepted that the constitutional provisions examined earlier in these reasons are to be understood as providing for what, in 1903, was said in relation to the House of Commons to be "a comprehensive and continuous guardianship over the whole finance" of the Commonwealth. But the manner of exercising that guardianship, within the relevant constitutional limits, is to be determined by the Parliament. In that regard it is essential to recall, as Mason J pointed out in *Victoria v The Commonwealth and Hayden*, that:

> It has been the practice, born of practical necessity, in this country and in the United Kingdom, to give but a short description of the particular items dealt with in an Appropriation Act. No other course is feasible because in many respects the items of expenditure have not been thought through and elaborated in detail.

What is apparent from consideration of past practice is that at least since the mid-1980s the chief means of limiting expenditures made by departments of State that has been adopted in annual appropriation Acts has been to specify the *amount* that may be spent rather than further define the purposes or activities for which it may be spent. There is, therefore, nothing in the relevant constitutional framework or in past parliamentary practices which suggests some construction of the *Appropriation Act (No 1)* 2005–2006 different from the construction required by its text ...

The question posed by the plaintiffs is whether expenditure on advertising the Government's reform package falls within the figure of $140,131,000 appearing in that part of Sched 1 to the *Appropriation Act (No 1)* 2005–2006 which relates to the Department of Employment and Workplace Relations. That figure is in the "Departmental Outputs" column against Outcome 2 – "Higher productivity, higher pay workplaces". The answer is in the affirmative for the following reasons.

1. That figure is an integer in the total amount of $1,447,552,000 set out in Sched 1 in relation to the Department under the heading "Departmental Outputs".
2. Therefore that total amount of $1,447,552,000 is a "departmental item". It is not an "administered item", because it is not set out opposite an outcome under the heading "Administered Expenses".
3. Section 7(2) restricts the application of that departmental item of $1,447,552,000: it may only be applied "for the departmental expenditure" of the Department. But the Act imposes no narrower restriction on the scope of the expenditure.
4. In this respect s 7(2) is in contrast with the restriction imposed by s 8(2) on an administered item: an administered item may only be applied "for expenditure for the purpose of carrying out activities for the purpose of contributing to achieving" the outcome to which the amount is attributed.
5. Therefore it does not matter whether any part of the $140,131,000 (or the $1,447,552,000) is spent otherwise than on activities leading to higher productivity or higher pay workplaces (or activities forming part of either of the other two outcomes), so long as it is "departmental expenditure".
6. That conclusion is supported by the terms of the note to the definition of "departmental item".
7. The plaintiffs did not contend that expenditure of either $140,131,000 or $1,447,552,000 on advertising the reform package was not "departmental expenditure" ...

Justice Kirby gave a strong dissent. He argued that the majority's interpretation undermined the constitutional requirement that appropriations be for a designated purpose and the principle of parliamentary control of government spending.

Combet v Commonwealth (2005) 224 CLR 494

Kirby J (dissenting)

In *Brown v West* this Court approved the remarks of Mason J in the *AAP Case* when his Honour said:

> Section 83 in providing that 'No money should be drawn from the Treasury of the Commonwealth except under appropriation made by law', gives expression to the established principle of English constitutional law enunciated by Viscount Haldane in *Auckland Harbour Board v The King*: 'no money can be taken out of the consolidated Fund into which the revenues of the State have been paid, excepting under a distinct authorization from Parliament itself'. An Appropriation Act has a twofold purpose. It has a negative as well as a positive effect. Not only does it authorize the Crown to withdraw moneys from the Treasury, it 'restrict(s) the expenditure to the particular purpose', as Isaacs and Rich JJ observed in *Commonwealth v Colonial Ammunition Co Ltd*.

This Court also upheld a principle that had been stated by Latham CJ in *Attorney-General (Vict) v Commonwealth*:

> [T]here cannot be appropriations in blank, appropriations for no designated purpose, merely authorizing expenditure with no reference to purpose.

And the Court gave effect to what Isaacs J had said still earlier in *New South Wales v Commonwealth* ("the *Surplus Revenue Case*"):

> 'Appropriation of money to a Commonwealth purpose' means legally segregating it from the general mass of the Consolidated Fund and dedicating it to the execution of *some purpose which either the Constitution has itself declared, or Parliament has lawfully determined*, shall be carried out.

...

The criterion, thus endorsed by this Court, is one of "distinct authorization from Parliament itself" ... To conclude otherwise would be to depart from the principles endorsed in *Brown v West*. This Court should not retreat from the clear rule expressed in that case. Behind it stands a principle of comparative strictness required by the text of our Constitution, by centuries of history and by policies of good governance to which that text gives effect ...

The parliamentary appropriation for the Executive Government's advertising campaign challenged by the plaintiffs was not made. The "distinct authorization from Parliament itself" was not given for the appropriation propounded in this case.

However much the requirement of specificity and distinctiveness of appropriations is blunted by Executive Government practice, and even parliamentary acquiescence, it cannot be denuded of meaning in Australia, given the constitutional provision that requires that appropriations must be for designated purposes. Parliamentary appropriations cannot be given in blank or with no reference to a purpose. The purpose must either be declared in the *Constitution* itself or lawfully determined by the Parliament. In the exigencies of modern government, it may be accepted that such purpose can be declared at a level of generality. However, that generality cannot be so vague and meaningless as to negate the significant constitutional consequences that attach to the designation of the appropriation and its purpose. Were this Court to permit a departure from this rule it would turn its back on the constitutional text, ignore the long struggles that preceded it, impermissibly diminish the role of the Senate, undermine transparency in government, diminish the real accountability of the Parliament to the electors and frustrate the steps taken by successive governments and Parliaments to enhance good governance in the legislative (and specifically financial) processes of the Parliament ...

This Court should make it clear that, if such an advertising campaign is ever to be permitted in such a case, using money drawn from the Treasury of the Commonwealth, it cannot occur "except under a distinct authorization from Parliament itself". And that was missing in this instance.

Wilkie confirms that it is for Parliament to determine the specificity of the purpose of an appropriation. ***Wilkie*** held an appropriation for the purpose of expenditure that the Finance Minister considers to be 'urgent' and 'unforeseen' was valid.

Wilkie v Commonwealth (2017) 349 ALR 1

The Federal Executive Government instructed the Australian Bureau of Statistics to exercise its statutory power of statistics collection to conduct a postal survey of the views of Australian adults about whether the law should permit same sex couples to marry. One question for the High Court was whether there was a valid appropriation of funds to pay for the survey to be conducted.

Kiefel CJ, Bell, Gageler, Keane, Nettle, Gordon and Edelman JJ

Section 10 of *Appropriation Act No 1 2017–2018*, which was the central focus of the challenge in each proceeding, is headed "Advance to the Finance Minister". Section 10 provides:

> **(1)** This section applies if the Finance Minister is satisfied that there is an urgent need for expenditure, in the current year, that is not provided for, or is insufficiently provided for, in Schedule 1:
>
> **(a)** because of an erroneous omission or understatement; or
>
> **(b)** because the expenditure was unforeseen until after the last day on which it was practicable to provide for it in the Bill for this Act before that Bill was introduced into the House of Representatives.
>
> **(2)** This Act has effect as if Schedule 1 were amended, in accordance with a determination of the Finance Minister, to make provision for so much (if any) of the expenditure as the Finance Minister determines.
>
> **(3)** The total of the amounts determined under subsection (2) cannot be more than $295 million ...

Section 12 of *Appropriation Act No 1 2017–2018* provides:

> The Consolidated Revenue Fund is appropriated as necessary for the purposes of this Act, including the operation of this Act as affected by the *Public Governance, Performance and Accountability Act 2013*.

... [An] appropriation can only be for a purpose which Parliament has determined. The need for such a determination of purpose is reflected in the language of ss 56 and 81 of the Constitution and is inherent in the nature of an appropriation:

> 'Appropriation of money to a Commonwealth purpose' means legally segregating it from the general mass of the Consolidated Fund and dedicating it to the execution of *some purpose which either the Constitution has itself declared, or Parliament has lawfully determined*, shall be carried out.

Together with the prohibition in s 83 of the Constitution, the requirement for an appropriation to be for a legislatively determined purpose results in an appropriation serving a dual function:

> Not only does it authorize the Crown to withdraw moneys from the Treasury, it 'restrict(s) the expenditure to the particular purpose', as Isaacs and Rich JJ observed in *The Commonwealth v Colonial Ammunition Co Ltd*.

"[T]here cannot be appropriations in blank, appropriations for no designated purpose, merely authorizing expenditure with no reference to purpose", just as "[t]here can be no appropriation in gross, authorizing the withdrawal of whatever sum the Executive Government may decide in the exercise of an unfettered discretion". An appropriation must always be for a purpose identified by the Parliament, albeit that "[i]t is for the Parliament to identify the degree of specificity with which the purpose of an appropriation is identified".

The plaintiffs in the Wilkie proceeding argued that, in enacting s 10 of *Appropriation Act No 1 2017–2018*, Parliament transgressed that constitutional limitation, abdicated its legislative responsibility and impermissibly delegated its power of appropriation to the Finance Minister. ...

The argument was that s 10 of *Appropriation Act No 1 2017–2018* purported to confer power on the Finance Minister to alter *Appropriation Act No 1 2017–2018* so as to supplement "by executive fiat" the amount appropriated by Parliament in Sched 1.

The argument was based on a fundamental misconstruction. The provision of *Appropriation Act No 1 2017–2018* which appropriates the Consolidated Revenue Fund is s 12 ...

Section 12 operated on and from the commencement of *Appropriation Act No 1 2017–2018* as an immediate appropriation of money from the Consolidated Revenue Fund for the totality of the purposes of the Act. Section 12 so operated as an immediate appropriation of the amount of $295 million specified in s 10(3) ...

The power of the Finance Minister to make a determination under s 10(2) of *Appropriation Act No 1 2017–2018* is not a power to supplement the total amount that has otherwise been appropriated by Parliament. The power is rather a power to allocate the whole or some part of the amount of $295 million that is already appropriated by s 12 operating on s 10(3).

Nor is the power of the Finance Minister to make a determination under s 10(2) of *Appropriation Act No 1 2017–2018* at large if the precondition to the exercise of that power set out in s 10(1) is met ...

Passing scepticism has from time to time been expressed academically, in the Senate and in this Court as to how the Advance to the Finance Minister or the Treasurer in the form in which it existed in the century before enactment of *Appropriation Act No 1 1999–2000* could be reconciled with the constitutional requirement for an appropriation to be for a legislatively determined purpose. The reconciliation lies in recalling that the degree of specificity of the purpose of an appropriation is for Parliament to determine.

The constitutional requirement for Parliament to determine the purpose of an appropriation cannot be so constraining of legislative options as to ignore "practical necessity" ...

To appropriate by s 12 of *Appropriation Act No 1 2017–2018* the amount specified in s 10(3) to be applied, relevantly under s 7, in accordance with a direction under s 10(2) if the precondition in s 10(1) is met is to appropriate that amount for a purpose which Parliament has lawfully determined may be carried out.

The constitutional challenge of the plaintiffs in the Wilkie proceeding, for those reasons, failed.

21.3 Power to spend appropriated funds

In ***Pape v Commissioner of Taxation***, the High Court unanimously held that sections 81 and 83 do *not* authorise the Federal Executive Government to spend money that has been validly appropriated. In order for the Federal Executive Government to spend public money, two things are necessary:

1. Funds must be appropriated by law from the Consolidated Revenue Fund.
2. The expenditure of appropriated funds for the designated purpose must be authorised by some law.

The law authorising the expenditure will be either a statute enacted under a head of federal legislative power or a constitutional provision such as section 61. The consequence of this view is that the precise scope of the expression 'for the purposes of the Commonwealth' is now of lesser importance. The purposes pursued under a statute enacted under a head of federal legislative power or a constitutional provision such as section 61 are necessarily Commonwealth purposes.

Pape v Commissioner of Taxation (2009) 238 CLR 1

In this case there was an appropriation of funds, and the law authorising the expenditure of those funds was section 61 of the* Constitution *(as an exercise of the 'nationhood' power).

French CJ

In my opinion, the history, the text and the logic underlying the operation of ss 81 and 83 are inconsistent with their characterisation as the source of a "spending" or "appropriations" power, notwithstanding their description as such in some of the judgments of Justices of this Court. There is no clear indication in the judgments of a majority consensus in support of a contrary view. The clearest statement of the character of ss 81 and 83 in this regard, with which I respectfully agree, is that of McHugh J in the passage quoted above from *Northern Suburbs General Cemetery Reserve Trust*. Neither provision confers power. Section 81 directs all revenues or moneys made by the Executive Government into the Consolidated Revenue Fund. Such moneys are only to be appropriated from that Fund for "the purposes of the Commonwealth". By virtue of s 83 no money can be drawn from the Fund absent such an appropriation by law, that is to say by statute.

Substantive power to spend the public moneys of the Commonwealth is not to be found in s 81 or s 83, but elsewhere in the Constitution or statutes made under it. That substantive power may be conferred by the exercise of the legislative powers of the Commonwealth. It may also be an element or incident of the executive power of the Commonwealth derived from s 61, subject to the appropriation requirement and supportable by legislation made under the incidental power in s 51(xxxix).

Gummow, Crennan and Bell JJ

Once the nature of the process of parliamentary appropriation is appreciated, the sections of the Constitution which provide for it do not serve as sources of a "spending power" by the width of which is determined the validity of laws which create rights and impose obligations or otherwise utilise the supply approved by an appropriation ...

[T]he inclusion in s 83 of the Constitution of the words "by law" served, as Harrison Moore wrote:

> [to exclude] the once popular doctrine that money might become legally available for the service of Government upon the mere votes of supply by the Lower House.

Thus s 83 affirms that a vote or resolution of either chamber cannot suffice. Where, for the purposes of the Constitution, a resolution rather than a law will suffice, as it does for the exception as to bounties made by s 91, the Constitution expressly so provides. Further, the phrase "by law" is apt also to include those appropriations, such as for the salaries of the Governor-General (s 3), and Ministers (s 66), which are made by force of the Constitution itself.

In the *Pharmaceutical Benefits Case*, however, Dixon J went further. He said that:

> s 83, in using the words 'by law' limits the power of appropriation to what can be done by the enactment of a valid law.

Section 83 thus provided the path by which Dixon J responded to the Commonwealth's submission as to the width of "the power to spend" and in doing so his Honour reached the point which the plaintiff seeks by fixing upon the phrase "the purposes of the Commonwealth" in s 81. For the reasons that have been given above respecting the place of appropriation in the scheme of the Constitution, neither construction of s 81 and s 83 should be accepted. Nor, as explained above, should that broad, and reiterated, submission by the Commonwealth respecting the "spending power".

Hayne and Kiefel JJ

[T]he premise for the Commonwealth's argument in the *Pharmaceutical Benefits Case*, that s 81 gives a power to spend, should not be accepted. Section 81 does not provide for spending; it regulates the relationship between the Executive and the Parliament. Section 81 provides for control by the Parliament over the *purposes* to which the Consolidated Revenue Fund may be applied and s 83 regulates withdrawal of money from the Treasury of the Commonwealth. The power to spend lies elsewhere.

...

Heydon J

That conclusion – that ss 81 and 83 do not create a grant of legislative power to authorise expenditure – is supported by the following parts of the Constitution. Chapter I Pt V is headed "Powers of the Parliament". It would be expected that the grants of legislative power are to be found in that Part. In that Part, ss 51 and 52 set out many legislative powers, and the succeeding sections set out various powers and restrictions on powers of the Parliament and its two Houses. The defendants submitted that that was not conclusive, since powers could also be found in the Chapter in which ss 81 and 83 were placed, namely Ch IV, which is headed "Finance and Trade". They gave ss 94 and 96 as examples. But the power to provide in the manner described in s 96 is actually found in Ch I Pt V, particularly s 51(xxxvi). Section 94 is not, or at least not primarily, a power to legislate. And in other parts of their argument the defendants treated s 94 as obsolete. Further, the defendants' argument does not confront the difficulty that the only words which can support a power in s 81 are the words "to be appropriated". Even if those words confer a power, it must be limited to a power of appropriation. But the authorities say that an appropriation of money is simply the earmarking or segregating of it from the Consolidated Revenue Fund. Hence, at most, s 81 could confer a power so to earmark or segregate.

Conclusion. Section 81 does not create a "legislative power" to confer on the Executive the power to spend what is appropriated.

In ***Williams (No 2)***, the High Court reaffirmed the decision in ***Pape*** that sections 81 and 83 do not authorise the Federal Executive Government to spend funds that have been validly appropriated.

Williams v Commonwealth (No 2) (2014) 252 CLR 416

French CJ, Hayne, Kiefel, Bell and Keane JJ

In *Pape*, all members of the Court concluded that ss 81 and 83 of the Constitution do not confer a substantive spending power. All members of the Court agreed that the power to spend appropriated moneys must be found elsewhere in the Constitution or in statutes made under it. The majority of the Court held that the determination of the Executive Government that there was a need for an immediate fiscal stimulus to the national economy enlivened legislative power under s 51(xxxix) to enact the impugned law as a law incidental to that exercise of the executive power. But the division of opinion about this more particular issue should not be permitted to obscure the importance of the conclusions about location of the power to spend. It is those conclusions which underpinned the decision in *Williams (No 1)*...

No doubt, as the Solicitor-General of the Commonwealth pointed out in the course of the argument of this case, differences can be identified in the reasons given in *Williams (No 1)* for the conclusions reached in that case. But of more immediate relevance than the differences in reasoning which can be identified in *Williams (No 1)* are the premises which underpinned the decision. Those premises were established in *Pape*. They are, first, that the appropriation of moneys in accordance with the requirements of ss 81 and 83 of the Constitution does not itself confer a substantive spending power and, second, that the power to spend appropriated moneys must be found elsewhere in the Constitution or in statutes made under it ...

To hold that the Parliament may make a law authorising the expenditure of any moneys lawfully appropriated in accordance with ss 81 and 83, no matter what the purpose of the expenditure may be, would treat outlay of the moneys as incidental to their ear-marking. But that would be to hold, contrary to *Pape*, that any and every appropriation of public moneys in accordance with ss 81 and 83 brings the expenditure of those moneys within the power of the Commonwealth.

The legislative response to *Williams (No 1)* (2012) 248 CLR 156 (which was examined in Chapter 20 in the context of the power of the Federal Executive Government to enter into contracts) was the enactment of legislation purporting to authorise government expenditure on a large range of programs then in existence and that might in future be added to the list by executive determination. Many of the spending items appear to have no connection with a head of federal legislative power. *Williams (No 2)* held that one of those spending items – funding for the school chaplains program – was invalid because it did not fall within the scope of any head of federal legislative power.

Senate Standing Committee on Regulations and Ordinances, *Parliamentary Scrutiny of Delegated Legislation* (Report, June 2019)

The Commonwealth's response to this decision [that is, *Williams (No 1)*] was to introduce legislation in 2012 (*Financial Framework Legislation Amendment Act (No 3) 2012* (Cth)) that retrospectively provided legislative support for over 400 non-statutory funding schemes. That legislation also empowered the executive to authorise expenditure on future grants or programs by specifying the program in delegated legislation. Specifically, section 32B of the *Financial Framework (Supplementary Powers) Act 1997* authorises expenditure on grants or programs which are specified in regulations made under that Act.

The *Industry Research and Development Act 1986* similarly provides authority for Commonwealth expenditure in relation to industry, innovation, science and research programs. The programs on which expenditure is authorised are prescribed by legislative instruments made under that Act ...

New programs for expenditure are routinely added to the Financial Framework (Supplementary Powers) Regulations 1997 and prescribed by instruments made under the *Industry Research and Development Act 1986*.

Senate Standing Committee for the Scrutiny of Delegated Legislation, 'Scrutiny of Commonwealth Expenditure', *Consolidated Guidelines* (February 2022)

Senate standing order 23(3)(b) requires the committee to scrutinise each instrument as to whether it appears to be supported by a constitutional head of legislative power and is otherwise constitutionally valid.

Accordingly, explanatory statements to instruments specifying Commonwealth expenditure should:

- clearly identify each constitutional head of power that is relied on to support expenditure on the relevant grant or program; and
- explain how each identified head of legislative power supports the grant or program, drawing on relevant jurisprudence where appropriate.

Where numerous heads of power are relied upon, the explanatory statement should include sufficient information to establish how the identified heads of legislative power provide authority for the whole of the relevant grant or program.

21.4 Grants to States

Laws authorising the Federal Executive Government to spend appropriated funds may be enacted under any head of federal legislative power. An important source of power to enact laws authorising the spending of money is section 96. Section 96 gives Parliament a broad power to authorise the Federal Executive Government to grant money to States on terms and conditions.

Australian Constitution

Section 96 Financial assistance to the States

During a period of ten years after the establishment of the Commonwealth and thereafter until the Parliament otherwise provides, the Parliament may grant financial assistance to any State on such terms and conditions as the Parliament thinks fit.

In practice, the Commonwealth regularly uses this power to implement its policies in areas such as education in which it cannot legislate directly. The Commonwealth grants funds to the States on condition that the States implement the Commonwealth's preferred policies.

The ***Federal Roads Case*** demonstrates how the Commonwealth can use section 96 grants to induce the States to exercise their powers in ways the Commonwealth wants. In this case, the Commonwealth gave the States money to build roads.

Victoria v Commonwealth ('Federal Roads Case') (1926) 38 CLR 399

The Federal Aid Roads Act 1926 *(Cth) empowered the Commonwealth to enter into agreements with each of the States to provide funds to the States for the construction of roads, subject to the terms and conditions the Federal Executive Government chose to include in the agreement. Victoria argued the Act was invalid for the following reasons:*

1. *It permitted terms and conditions for the funding outside the scope of section 51 heads of power.*
2. *It might lead to only one State agreeing to accept funding with the result that the Commonwealth would be giving preference to that one State contrary to section 99 of the Constitution.*
3. *It was really an Act with respect to roads rather than an Act about grants to States.*

The full judgment of the High Court – consisting of only three sentences – is set out below.

Knox CJ, Isaacs, Higgins, Gavan Duffy, Powers, Rich and Starke JJ

The Court is of opinion that the *Federal Aid Roads Act No 46 of 1926* is a valid enactment.

It is plainly warranted by the provisions of s 96 of the *Constitution*, and not affected by those of s 99 or any other provisions of the *Constitution*, so that exposition is unnecessary.

The action is dismissed.

Deputy Federal Commissioner of Taxation v WR Moran Pty Ltd demonstrates three important points about the operation of section 96. First, the Commonwealth can use the States as mere conduits, granting funds to the States on condition that the entirety of the funds granted be passed onto some other person or entity. Secondly, the case also shows that there is nothing in section 96 prohibiting the Commonwealth from discriminating in favour of or against particular States when granting money. Thirdly, the case demonstrates that legislation enacted under section 96 can authorise the Federal Executive Government to decide the conditions attached to grants; the conditions need not be specified in the legislation.

Deputy Federal Commissioner of Taxation (NSW) v WR Moran Pty Ltd ('Flour Tax Case') (1939) 61 CLR 735

Section 51(ii) prohibits taxation laws that discriminate between States. Tasmania argued that a law that gave grants to States using funds raised by a federal tax was a law with respect to taxation that had the effect of discriminating against Tasmania. A majority of the High Court disagreed because section 51(ii) applies only to taxation laws and not to laws enacted under section 96.

Latham CJ

The result of this whole scheme of Federal and State legislation is that a Federal excise duty is imposed upon flour which is paid upon the same basis by persons in all States. The proceeds of the duty go into the Federal consolidated revenue. An equivalent sum is then taken from the consolidated revenue and is paid by the Commonwealth by way of financial assistance to the States of the Commonwealth, upon condition that the States apply the moneys in the assistance and relief of wheat growers. In the case of Tasmania, however, a special grant is made by the Commonwealth which is not subject to any Federal statutory conditions, but which, in fact, is applied, and which it was known would be applied, by the Government of Tasmania in paying back to Tasmanian millers and others nearly the whole of the flour tax paid by them in respect of flour consumed in Tasmania ...

The grants made by the *Wheat Industry Assistance Act* are made by virtue of the power conferred on the Commonwealth Parliament by s 96 of the *Constitution* ... The words of this section show that Parliament may grant financial assistance to a single State under this power and may therefore discriminate between States in making grants. They also show that the Parliament has the fullest power of fixing the terms and conditions of any grant made under the section. Parliament does fix the terms and conditions of the grant if, by legislation, it authorizes a Minister to determine such terms and conditions ...

Further, the case of *Victoria v Commonwealth* (the *Roads Case*) is conclusive against the defendant upon this point. It was there held, by a court of seven justices, that the *Federal Aid Roads Act 1926* was a valid enactment, "being plainly warranted by the provisions of s 96 of the Constitution, and not affected by those of s 99 or any other provisions of the Constitution". The *Federal Aid Roads Act* approved agreements between the Commonwealth and the States for making roads under which payments were made to the States "in such amounts at such times and subject to such conditions as the Minister may from time to time determine." Other provisions of the agreements required the Minister to be satisfied as to various matters before he was bound to make payments. It was argued that "the terms and conditions referred to in s 96 must be terms and conditions imposed by the Parliament itself and not terms and conditions fixed by executive authority". This argument was rejected, and it must again be rejected in the present case ...

On appeal, the Privy Council agreed with the High Court's decision.

WR Moran Pty Ltd v Deputy Federal Commissioner of Taxation (NSW) (1940) 63 CLR 338

Viscount Maugham, Lord Atkin, Lord Russell of Killowen, Lord Wright, Lord Porter

We must now consider s 96 ... There are no restrictions whatever in this section, and it is clear that while the section remains in operation, the Parliament – apart from the restrictions contained in s 51 which must be considered in a moment – may in the matter of financial assistance discriminate between States as much as it thinks fit ...

In coming to this conclusion their Lordships wish to make it clear that, as at present advised, they do not take the view that the Commonwealth Parliament can exercise its powers under s 96 with a complete disregard of the prohibition contained in s 51(ii), or so as altogether to nullify that constitutional safeguard. The prohibition is of considerable importance; and the Constitution should be construed bearing in mind that it is the result of an agreement between six high contracting parties with in some respects very different needs and interests. Cases may be imagined in which a purported exercise of the power to grant financial assistance under s 96 would be merely colourable. Under the guise or pretence of assisting a State with money, the real substance and purpose of the Act might simply be to effect discrimination in regard to taxation. Such an Act might well be *ultra vires* the Commonwealth Parliament. Their Lordships are using the language of caution because such a case may never arise, and also because it is their usual practice in a case dealing with constitutional matters to decide no more than their duty requires ...

The ***First Uniform Tax Case*** demonstrates that the Commonwealth can use section 96 to induce a State to abstain from exercising it powers. In this case, federal legislation made generous grants to the States on condition that they stopped levying State income taxes. The High Court emphasised that section 96 cannot be used to legally compel States to accept a grant of funds and the attached conditions. There is no compulsion provided a State is legally free to decline to accept the grant of funds and the attached conditions, even if for practical and economic reasons the State is unable to refuse.

South Australia v Commonwealth ('First Uniform Tax Case') (1942) 65 CLR 373

Both the Commonwealth and States have power to impose income taxes. The Commonwealth implemented a legislative scheme designed to stop the States imposing income taxes. Federal taxation statutes imposed a high rate of federal income tax and provided that every taxpayer must pay their federal income tax before paying any State income tax. The effect was that taxpayers would not have sufficient funds to pay their State income taxes, making it practically impossible for a State to levy income tax. The* States Grants (Income Tax Reimbursement) Act 1942 (Cth) *gave funds to States on condition that the States did not impose income tax.

Latham CJ

The plaintiffs contend that these Acts constitute a scheme for the purpose of compelling the States to abandon their constitutional right to impose taxation on incomes ...

The *Tax Act* imposes a tax at rates such that there is left little practical room for State income tax. The *Grants Act* shows the intention of the Commonwealth Parliament that the Parliaments of the States should cease to tax income ...

The Commonwealth may properly induce a State to exercise its powers (eg the power to make roads: See *Victoria v Commonwealth*) by offering a money grant. So also the Commonwealth may properly induce a State by the same means to abstain from exercising its powers. For example, the Commonwealth might wish to exercise the powers given by the Constitution, s 51 (xiii) and (xiv) to legislate with respect to banking, other than State banking, and insurance, other than State insurance. The Commonwealth might wish to set up some Federal system of banking or insurance without any State competition. If the States were deriving revenue from State banking or State insurance, they might be prepared to retire from such activities upon receiving what they regarded as adequate compensation. The Commonwealth could properly, under Commonwealth legislation, make grants to the States upon condition of them so retiring. The States could not abdicate their powers by binding themselves not to re-enter the vacated field, but if the Commonwealth, aware of this possibility, was prepared to pay money to a State which in fact gave up its system of State banking or insurance, there could be no objection on this ground to the validity of the Commonwealth law which authorized the payment.

But the position is radically different, it is urged, if the so-called inducement practically amounts to coercion. Admittedly the Commonwealth Parliament could not pass a law compelling a State to surrender the power to tax incomes or prohibiting the exercise of that power by a State. Equally, it is said, the Commonwealth cannot lawfully make an offer of money to a State which, under the conditions which actually exist, the State cannot, on political or economic grounds, really refuse.

This identification of a very attractive inducement with legal compulsion is not convincing. Action may be brought about by temptation – y offering a reward – or by compulsion. But temptation is not compulsion. A person whose hand is physically propelled by another person against his will so that it strikes a blow is not guilty of assault. But it would be no defence to allege that he really could not help striking the blow because he was offered £1,000 for doing it ...

The *Grants Act* does not compel the States to abandon their legislative power to impose a tax upon incomes. States which do not abstain from imposing income tax cannot be said to be acting unlawfully. There is no command that they shall not impose such a tax ...

Conclusion as to Tax Act and Grants Act. – Thus the objections to the *Tax Act* and the *Grants Act* fail, whether those Acts are considered separately or as part of a scheme to bring about the abandonment by the States of the raising of revenue by taxation of incomes.

...

Starke J (dissenting)

In my opinion, the object of the Act is not merely to grant financial assistance to the States, but there is linked up in it an object and an end that is inconsistent with the limited grant of power given by s 96 to the Commonwealth, namely, making the Commonwealth the sole effective taxing authority in respect of incomes and compensating the States for the resulting loss in income tax. The argument that the *States Grants Act* leaves a free choice to the States, offers them an inducement but deprives them of and interferes with no constitutional power, is specious but unreal. And it does not meet the substance of the States' position that the condition of the Act relates to a matter in respect of which the Commonwealth has no constitutional power whatever, and yet by force of the condition and not as a consequence of the exercise of any power conferred upon the Commonwealth, the grant of assistance to the States is withdrawn unless they comply with its terms. The real object of the condition is that already stated, and it is in my judgment neither contemplated by nor sanctioned by the Constitution, and in particular by s 96 thereof. As I have said, all State legislation and functions might ultimately be so controlled and supervised.

The ***Second Uniform Tax Case*** reaffirmed that section 96 can be used to induce a State to abstain from exercising its powers. Chief Justice Dixon expressed doubts about the reasoning in the ***Flour Tax Case*** and the ***First Uniform Tax Case*** but declined to overrule those cases.

Victoria v Commonwealth ('Second Uniform Tax Case') (1957) 99 CLR 575

Dixon CJ

[T]he Court is now invited to depart from the decision in *South Australia v Commonwealth*, either by treating it as wrongly decided or by distinguishing it as a decision resting in an essential degree on the scope of the defence power in time of war. Having regard to the lapse of time in which no State has taken proceedings seeking judicial relief against the statutes, to overrule the decision or even so to distinguish it must involve a grave judicial responsibility ...

There has been what amounts to a course of decisions upon s 96 all amplifying the power and tending to a denial of any restriction upon the purpose of the appropriation or the character of the condition. The first case decided under s 96 was *Victoria v Commonwealth* ... [T]he power conferred by that provision is well exercised although

(1) the State is bound to apply the money specifically to an object that has been defined, (2) the object is outside the powers of the Commonwealth, (3) the payments are left to the discretion of the Commonwealth Minister, (4) the money is provided as the Commonwealth's contribution to an object for which the State is also to contribute funds. Road-making no doubt may have been conceived as a function of the State so that to provide money for its performance must amount to financial assistance to the State. But only in this way was there "assistance".

In *Deputy Federal Commissioner of Taxation (NSW) v WR Moran Pty Ltd*, one of the matters decided was the validity of s 6 of the *Wheat Industry Assistance Act 1938* ... Now it might have been thought that these provisions were outside s 96 because they gave no assistance to the State as a body politic but used it only as a conduit or an agency by which the moneys would be distributed among the wheat growers of the State ...

The decision, which was affirmed in the Privy Council, without express reference to this use of s 96, must mean that s 96 is satisfied if the money is placed in the hands of the State notwithstanding that in the exercise of the power to impose terms and conditions the State is required to pay over the money to a class of persons in or connected with the State in order to fulfil some purpose pursued by the Commonwealth and one outside its power to effect directly. I should myself find it difficult to accept this doctrine in full and carry it into logical effect, but the decision shows that the Court placed no limitation upon the terms or conditions it was competent to the Commonwealth to impose under s 96 and regarded the conception of assistance to a State as going beyond and outside subventions to or the actual supplementing of the financial resources of the Treasury of a State ...

In the present attack upon the validity of the *Tax Reimbursement Act 1946–1948* the two States that are plaintiffs naturally rest heavily upon the argument that the Act is a law for the restriction or control of the States in the exercise of their taxing powers, that on its face the purpose appears of compelling the States to abstain from imposing taxes upon income. If s 96 came before us for the first time for interpretation, the contention might be supported on the ground that the true scope and purpose of the power which s 96 confers upon the Parliament of granting money and imposing terms and conditions did not admit of any attempt to influence the direction of the exercise by the State of its legislative or executive powers. It may well be that s 96 was conceived by the framers as (1) a transitional power, (2) confined to supplementing the resources of the Treasury of a State by particular subventions when some special or particular need or occasion arose, and (3) imposing terms or conditions relevant to the situation which called for special relief of assistance from the Commonwealth. It seems a not improbable supposition that the framers had some such conception of the purpose of the power. But the course of judicial decision has put any such limited interpretation of s 96 out of consideration. In any case it must be borne in mind that the power conferred by s 96 is confined to granting money and moreover to granting money to governments ...

Once the interpretation is accepted in full which the decisions in *Victoria v Commonwealth* and in *Moran's Case* combine to place upon the section it becomes difficult indeed to find safe ground for saying that the condition of the grant of financial assistance may not be that a particular form of tax shall not be imposed by the State. The interpretation flowing from these two decisions is not consistent with the view that there must be a need for relief or a reason for giving assistance which is not itself created by the Commonwealth legislation connected with the grant. It is inconsistent with the view that the terms or conditions cannot require the exercise of governmental powers of the State and require the State to conform with the desires of the Commonwealth in the exercise of such powers. It seems a short step from this to saying that the condition may stipulate for the exercise or non-exercise of the State's general legislative power in some particular or specific respect ...

In short the result of my consideration of the two prior decisions upon s 96 has been to convince me that the decision of the majority of the Court with respect to the Tax Reimbursement Act in *South Australia v Commonwealth* was but an extension of the interpretation already placed upon s 96 of the Constitution. The three decisions certainly harmonise and they combine to give to s 96 a consistent and coherent interpretation and they each involve the entire exclusion of the limited operation which might have been assigned to the power as an alternative ...

I therefore think that the validity of that Act must be upheld.

Section 96 can be used by the Commonwealth to give effect to policies the Commonwealth lacks the legislative power to bring about directly. An absence of power is different from a prohibition on power. Cases like the ***DOGS Case*** and ***ICM Agriculture*** demonstrate that laws enacted under section 96 are subject to limitations on power found elsewhere in the *Constitution*. A law enacted under section 96 that breaches a limitation on power will be invalid.

Attorney-General (Vic) ex rel Black v Commonwealth ('DOGS Case') (1981) 146 CLR 559

The Commonwealth granted funds to the States under section 96 on condition that the funds be distributed to non-government schools including schools operated by religious groups. The plaintiff argued that these laws were laws 'for establishing any religion' contrary to section 116. A preliminary issue was whether section 96 was limited by section 116.

Barwick CJ

Section 116 in terms applies to all laws, in my opinion, without exception. The Parliament "shall not make any law for establishing any religion". I can find no acceptable reason for excluding from this universality an Appropriation Act or an Act granting money to a State pursuant to s 96.

Gibbs J

The question is whether if the conditions of a grant of financial assistance require the State to which the grant is made to establish a religion within the meaning of that section, the Act by which the grant is authorized is invalid as contrary to s 116 ... I consider that the ordinary rules of statutory construction should be applied, and that ss 96 and 116 should be read together, the result being that the Commonwealth has power to grant financial assistance to any State on such terms and conditions as the Parliament thinks fit, provided that a law passed for that purpose does not contravene s 116. It is one thing to say that the Parliament, by a condition imposed under s 96, could achieve a result which it lacks power to bring about by direct legislation, but quite another to say that the Parliament can frame a condition for the purpose of evading an express prohibition contained in the Constitution.

Wilson J

Let me assume, for the purpose of the argument, that the Parliament sought to establish a religion, and proceeded to enact laws pursuant to s 96 and provide funds pursuant to s 81 as part of a scheme to achieve that result. As at present advised, and with great respect to those who think differently, I am unable to see why those laws would not offend s 116.

ICM Agriculture Pty Ltd v Commonwealth (2009) 240 CLR 140

Section 51(xxxi) authorises laws with respect to 'the acquisition of property on just terms from any State or person for any purpose in respect of which the Parliament has power to make laws'. One issue in this case was whether the Commonwealth could enact a law under section 96 that could also be characterised as a law with respect to section 51(xxxi).

French CJ, Gummow and Crennan JJ

[T]he legislative power of the Commonwealth conferred by s 96 and s 51(xxxvi) does not extend to the grant of financial assistance to a State on terms and conditions requiring the State to acquire property on other than just terms.

Heydon J

It was a necessary step in the achievement of that goal that the plaintiffs' licences be cancelled. That was effectuated partly by Commonwealth legislation – the *National Water Commission Act 2004* – which authorised the supply of funding to New South Wales pursuant to s 96 of the *Constitution*. And it was effectuated partly by New South Wales legislation – the Amendment Regulation made pursuant to the *Water Management Act 2000* ...

Section 51(xxxi) prevented the *National Water Commission Act 2004* from being validly enacted in terms as wide as it was because it was legislation providing for the acquisition by New South Wales of property otherwise than on just terms. The Act was therefore invalid.

21.5 DISCUSSION QUESTIONS

1. What does section 53 require? Why is that provision not justiciable?
2. What is an appropriation? What are the requirements for a valid appropriation?
3. What is the difference between appropriating funds from the Consolidated Revenue Fund and authorising the expenditure of those funds?
4. What does section 96 permit the Commonwealth to do? Are there any limits?
5. Problem question: Consider the following hypothetical legislation and scenario. The Commonwealth Parliament enacts a statute with a single provision stating:

> The Minister for Finance shall pay the amount of $100 million to the State of South Australia on condition that the State of South Australia takes possession of the lands specified in the first schedule to this Act and constructs a sports facility on those lands.

The South Australian Parliament enacts a statute authorising the Treasurer of South Australia to issue a declaration specifying that from a particular date ownership of lands specified in the federal statute, which includes a number of residential properties, transfers to the South Australian Government. The South Australian statute also provides that each affected land owner shall be paid $10 000 in compensation for the loss of their property, which is considerably below market value.

The Treasurer of South Australia is considering whether to issue a declaration. Affected landowners believe that if South Australia does not receive the federal money, the Treasurer of South Australia will decide to not issue a declaration and their properties will be saved.

What constitutional arguments might there be for preventing the Commonwealth Minister for Finance from paying the money to South Australia?

PART

7

FEDERALISM

INCONSISTENCY BETWEEN FEDERAL AND STATE LAWS

22

22.1 Overview

This chapter examines the way in which the *Australian Constitution* resolves inconsistencies between federal and State laws. The *Constitution* enables the Commonwealth to legislate concurrently with the States on many subject-matters. This means that both federal and State laws may apply to the same situation. Section 109 of the *Constitution* has the effect that where such federal and State laws are inconsistent the federal law prevails and the State law is inoperative to the extent of the inconsistency.

Australian Constitution

Section 109 Inconsistency of laws

When a law of a State is inconsistent with a law of the Commonwealth, the latter shall prevail, and the former shall, to the extent of the inconsistency, be invalid.

Inconsistency arises where a State law would alter, impair or detract from the operation of a federal law. Inconsistency may arise where it is impossible to obey both the federal and State laws, where the State law prohibits the exercise of a right granted by federal law, or where a State law purports to operate on a subject-matter on which a federal law has evinced an intention to cover exclusively. To the extent of any such inconsistency, State laws are inoperative.

Key concepts considered in this chapter include:

- invalid
- inoperative
- inconsistency
- impossibility of simultaneous obedience
- inconsistent rights and duties
- cover the field
- manufacturing inconsistency
- manufacturing consistency.

22.2 The meaning of 'invalid to the extent of the inconsistency'

In many instances, federal laws and State laws on the same subject-matter are able to operate concurrently. Where a federal law and a State law on the same subject-matter are unable to operate concurrently, section 109 of the *Constitution* resolves the conflict. Section 109 provides that the federal law prevails and that the State law is invalid to the extent of the inconsistency.

Where a federal law and a State law are inconsistent, it is section 109 of the *Constitution* that produces the invalidity of the State law. Federal laws do not of their own force invalidate inconsistent State laws. The word 'invalid' in section 109 does not mean invalid in the usual sense of 'void'. 'Invalid' in this context means 'inoperative'.

Western Australia v Commonwealth ('Native Title Act Case') (1995) 183 CLR 373

Mason CJ, Brennan, Deane, Toohey, Gaudron and McHugh JJ

If, by reason of inconsistency with a law of the Commonwealth, a State law is to the extent of the inconsistency "invalid" – that is "suspended, inoperative and ineffective" (*Butler v Attorney-General (Vic)* (1961) 106 CLR 268 at 286 per Windeyer J) – the effect on the State law is not produced directly by operation of the Commonwealth law but by s 109 of the Constitution, the operation of which is attracted by the inconsistency ...

It was an inevitable consequence of the constitutional distribution of specific legislative powers to the Commonwealth and residual legislative powers to the States that there would be cases of inconsistency between the legislative provisions governing the same act, matter or thing. Section 109 of the Constitution prescribes which law should prevail and which should be "invalid". But the effect of s 109 on a State law that is inconsistent with a law of the Commonwealth is not to impose an absolute invalidity. On the contrary, the State law remains valid though it is rendered inoperative to the extent of the inconsistency, but only for so long as the inconsistency remain ... The extent of the inconsistency depends on the text and operation of the respective laws ...

The non-literal meaning of 'invalid' has important practical consequences. The federal law with which the State law is inconsistent might in future be repealed or cease operation for some other reason. Were that to happen there would no longer be any inconsistency and the State law would 'revive' and become operative.

Butler v Attorney-General (Vic) provides an example of a State law reviving after a period of inconsistency. Certain provisions of a Victorian statute were inconsistent with federal legislation enacted under the defence power in section 51(vi). The federal legislation later ceased operation because the High Court decided the federal legislation was no longer supported by the defence power. The High Court held that from the point in time that the federal legislation ceased operation the provisions of the Victorian statute became operative.

Butler v Attorney-General (Vic) (1961) 106 CLR 268

Fullagar J

In *Wenn v Attorney-General (Vic)* (1948) 77 CLR 84 it was held that ss 4, 7, 9 and 10 of the Victorian Act were inconsistent, within the meaning of s 109 of the Constitution, with the provisions of Pt II of the Commonwealth Act, and were therefore invalid. *Wenn's Case* 84 was decided on 20th August 1948. The Commonwealth Act had, of course, been enacted as an exercise of the defence power, and on 16th April 1959 this Court decided in *Illawarra District County Council v Wickham* (1959) 101 CLR 467 that Pt II thereof could no longer be supported as an exercise of that power. It was never suggested that it could be supported under any other constitutional power. It follows from *Wickham's* that, at the time which is material in the present case, Pt II of the Commonwealth Act had ceased to be in force as a law of the Commonwealth.

It is on the facts so far stated that the first question arises. That question is whether ss 4, 7, 9 and 10 of the Victorian Preference Act acquired the force of law when the Commonwealth Act ceased to have the force of law. It is quite clear, in my opinion, that this question must be answered in the affirmative. The Victorian Act was not unconstitutional. It was a valid law of the State, and it was fully operative as a law of the State from 21st March 1944 to 27th August 1945. On the latter date it ceased to operate as such a law. But that was not because of any inherent vice. It was merely because the "field" was temporarily occupied by valid Commonwealth legislation. It remained on the statute book and was never repealed by the State Parliament. When the Commonwealth legislation expired, the only obstacle to its operation as a valid law of the State was removed, and it resumed the full force and effect which it had had before 27th August 1945 ...

Taylor J

[I]t seems to me that the words "to the extent of the inconsistency" must be taken to have a temporal as well as a substantive connotation. Indeed the scheme of the section is consistent only with this view. The Federal Act can "prevail" only whilst it remains in force and invalidity of the State Act is produced only as the counterpart of the "supremacy" of the Federal Act ...

Windeyer J

The preference provisions of the Re-establishment and Employment Act 1954 (Cth) ceased to have validity when they could no longer be sustained by the defence power. Thereupon the Discharged Servicemen's Preference Act 1943 (Vic) came again into operation. It had never lost its place in the Victorian statute book. It had merely been, for the time, invalid - that is to say, suspended, inoperative and ineffective - because the Commonwealth statute had entered into occupation of the whole field ...

Section 109 inconsistency can arise only if the federal and State laws in issue are otherwise valid. If the two laws are not otherwise valid, there cannot be any inconsistency.

22.3 Inconsistency

As a general definition, inconsistency arises where a State law would alter, impair or detract from the operation of a federal law. The case law often groups cases of inconsistency into categories:

- direct inconsistency where it is impossible to obey both the federal and State laws
- direct inconsistency where the State law prohibits the exercise of a right granted by federal law (sometimes also called 'inconsistent rights and duties inconsistency'), and
- indirect inconsistency where a State law purports to operate on a subject-matter which a federal law has evinced an intention to cover exclusively.

Jemena Asset Management (3) Pty Ltd v Coinvest Ltd (2011) 244 CLR 508

French CJ, Gummow, Heydon, Crennan, Kiefel and Bell JJ

Applicable principles have been reiterated in the joint reasons of the whole Court in *Dickson v The Queen* (2010) 241 CLR 491 at 502: The statement of principle respecting s 109 of the Constitution which had been made by Dixon J in *Victoria v Commonwealth* (*"the Kakariki Case"*) (1937) 58 CLR 618 at 630 was taken up in the joint reasons of the whole Court in *Telstra Corporation Ltd v Worthing* (1999) 197 CLR 61 at 76 as follows:

> In *Victoria v Commonwealth* (1937) 58 CLR 618 at 630, Dixon J stated two propositions which are presently material. The first was: 'When a State law, if valid, would alter, impair or detract from the operation of a law of the Commonwealth Parliament, then to that extent it is invalid.' The second, which followed immediately in the same passage, was: 'Moreover, if it appears from the terms, the nature or the subject matter of a Federal enactment that it was intended as a complete statement of the law governing

> a particular matter or set of rights and duties, then for a State law to regulate or apply to the same matter or relation is regarded as a detraction from the full operation of the Commonwealth law and so as inconsistent.' ...

The first proposition is often associated with the description "direct inconsistency", and the second with the expressions "covering the field" and "indirect inconsistency".

The expression "cover the field" means "cover the subject matter", which was the description used and explained by Dixon J in *Ex parte McLean* (1930) 43 CLR 472 at 483–486. From the outset the aspect of inconsistency associated with the expression "covering the field" has not been free from criticism. There can be little doubt that indirect inconsistency involves "more subtle ... contrariety" than any "textual" or "direct collision" between the provisions of a Commonwealth law and a State law.

The crucial notions of "altering", "impairing" or "detracting from" the operation of a law of the Commonwealth have in common the idea that a State law conflicts with a Commonwealth law if the State law undermines the Commonwealth law. Therefore any alteration or impairment of, or detraction from, a Commonwealth law must be significant and not trivial.

Although the utility of accepted tests of inconsistency, based on recognising different aspects of inconsistency for the purposes of s 109, is well established as Mason J observed in *Ansett Transport Industries (Operations) Pty Ltd v Wardley* (1980) 142 CLR 237 at 260, it is not surprising that different tests of inconsistency directed to the same end are interrelated and in any one case more than one test may be applied in order to establish inconsistency for the purposes of s 109. All tests of inconsistency which have been applied by this Court for the purpose of s 109 are tests for discerning whether a "real conflict" exists between a Commonwealth law and a State law.

Bell Group NV (in liq) v Western Australia (2016) 260 CLR 500

French CJ, Kiefel, Bell, Keane, Nettle and Gordon JJ

Where there is an alleged conflict between a Commonwealth law and a State law, "s 109 requires a comparison between any two laws which create rights, privileges or powers, and duties or obligations, and s 109 resolves conflict, if any exists, in favour of the Commonwealth".

A conflict may arise in a number of ways. The State law, if valid, might "alter, impair or detract from the operation of a law of the Commonwealth Parliament". If so, then to that extent it will be invalid because of what sometimes is described as "direct inconsistency". As the Court said in *Jemena Asset Management (3) Pty Ltd v Coinvest Ltd*:

> The crucial notions of 'altering', 'impairing' or 'detracting from' the operation of a law of the Commonwealth have in common the idea that a State law conflicts with a Commonwealth law if the State law undermines the Commonwealth law. (emphasis added)

The conflict may also arise from the laws' legal operation or from their practical effect. "[A] ny alteration or impairment of, or detraction from, a Commonwealth law must be significant and not trivial". The question of whether any alteration or impairment of, or detraction from, a Commonwealth law is significant is "always one of fact and degree". The starting point is an analysis of the laws in question and their true construction. The extent of the inconsistency "depends on the text and operation of the respective laws" ...

Direct and indirect inconsistency are not mutually exclusive categories. What really matters is not identifying categories of inconsistency but identifying the nature and extent of inconsistency arising in a particular case. The various categories of inconsistency are simply analytical tools to assist that process.

Ansett Transport Industries (Operations) Pty Ltd v Wardley (1980) 142 CLR 237

Mason J

"Direct inconsistency" is a description which has always been applied to cases in which it is impossible to obey both laws (*R v Licensing Court of Brisbane; Ex parte Daniell*). It is also a description which has been applied to cases in which the Commonwealth law grants a permission or a right and the State law prohibits that which is permitted or prohibits the exercise of the right (*Colvin v Bradley Brothers Pty Ltd*). Cases of this kind have sometimes been treated as a separate head of inconsistency though even when so treated they have generally been related to the "cover the field" test, apparently on the ground that direct inconsistency is confined to a situation in which simultaneous obedience to both laws is impossible.

As the various tests which have been applied by the Court are all designed to elucidate the issue of inconsistency it is not surprising that they are interrelated and that in a given case more than one test is capable of being applied so as to establish inconsistency. Especially is this so when it is the giving of a permission or the grant of a right by Commonwealth law that is the foundation of a claim of inconsistency. If, according to the true construction of the Commonwealth law, the right is absolute, then it inevitably follows that the right is intended to prevail to the exclusion of any other law. A State law which takes away the right is inconsistent because it is in conflict with the absolute right and because the Commonwealth law relevantly occupies the field. So also with a Commonwealth law that grants a permission by way of positive authority. The Commonwealth legislative intention which sustains the conclusion that the permission is granted by way of positive authority also sustains the conclusion that the positive authority was to take effect to the exclusion of any other law. Again it produces inconsistency on both grounds ...

Direct inconsistency

The case law demonstrates that direct inconsistency arises in two key ways:

1. where it is impossible to simultaneously obey both the federal and State laws, and
2. where a State law prohibits the exercise of a right granted by federal law.

Where it is impossible to simultaneously obey both a State law and a federal law, the State law alters, impairs or detracts from the operation of the federal law. ***R v Licensing Court of Brisbane; Ex parte Daniell*** provides a clear example of a State law requiring what a federal law forbids. The case concerned a federal law providing that a State referendum could not be held on the same day as a Senate election, and a State law that set the date for a State referendum on liquor trading hours for the day of a Senate election. The High Court held that the State law was inconsistent with the federal law.

R v Licensing Court of Brisbane; Ex parte Daniell (1920) 28 CLR 23

Knox CJ, Isaacs, Gavan Duffy, Powers, Rich and Starke JJ

There arises upon that construction a conflict, or inconsistency, between the State Act authorizing and commanding the vote on that day and the Commonwealth Act, assumedly competently made, forbidding the vote on that day. Then s 109 of the Constitution enacts that in such a case the State law, to the extent of the inconsistency, is invalid ...

Australian Mutual Provident Society v Goulden provides another example of inconsistency arising due to the impossibility of simultaneous obedience. The *Life Insurance Act 1945* (Cth) required insurance companies to take the existence of disabilities into account when calculating life insurance premiums. However, the *Anti-Discrimination Act 1977* (NSW) prohibited companies discriminating against people with disabilities by treating them less favourably than people without disabilities. The High Court held that since it was impossible for the life insurance company to obey both laws the State law was inconsistent with the federal law.

Australian Mutual Provident Society v Goulden (1986) 160 CLR 330

Gibbs CJ, Mason, Brennan, Deane and Dawson JJ

[T]he [federal] Act should be understood as giving expression to a legislative policy that the protection of the interests of policy holders is to be achieved by allowing a registered life insurance company to classify risks and fix rates of premium in its life insurance business in accordance with its own judgement founded upon the advice of actuaries and the practice of prudent insurers. In the words of Dixon J in *Victoria v Commonwealth* (1937) 58 CLR 618, at p 630, it would alter, impair or detract from the Commonwealth scheme of regulation established by the Act if a registered life insurance company was effectively precluded by the legislation of a State from classifying different risks differently, from setting different premiums for different risks or from refusing to insure risks which were outside the class of risk in respect of which it wished to offer insurance.

In particular, State legislation which, either absolutely or subject to qualifications and exceptions, made it generally unlawful for a life insurance company to take account of physical impairment in determining whether it would or would not accept a particular proposal or the terms upon which it would grant insurance cover would be inconsistent with the essential scheme of the provisions of the Act regulating the issue of policies and the fixing of premiums. Indeed, such legislation would undermine and, to a significant extent, negate the legislative assumption of the underlying ability of a registered life insurance company to classify risks and fix rates of premium in accordance with its own judgement based upon actuarial advice and prudent insurance practice upon which, as has been mentioned, the stringent controls and requirements which the Act imposes in respect of life insurance business of registered life insurance companies are predicated ...

Direct inconsistency also arises where State and federal laws confer inconsistent rights or duties, such as where a federal law grants a right and a State law prohibits the exercise of that right. In such cases, it remains possible to obey both laws by not exercising the right, since the grant of a right is a not a command to do anything. Nevertheless, the State law alters, impairs or detracts from the federal law because by granting a right the federal law intends the right be capable of exercise. This was the situation in ***Colvin v Bradley Brothers Pty Ltd.***

Colvin v Bradley Brothers Pty Ltd (1943) 68 CLR 151

New South Wales legislation prohibited the employment of women to work on milling machines. The terms of an industrial award made under federal legislation permitted the owner of a factory with milling machines to employ women to work on milling machines. The High Court held that the State law was inconsistent with the operation of the federal law.

Latham CJ

It was contended that the terms of the clause should be construed so as to preserve the operation of general State legislation directed towards the general health and well-being and safety of members of the community, including employees.

In my opinion there are two answers to this contention. In the first place the words used are not reasonably capable of being read as leaving room for the operation of State legislation generally. Express mention is made of the National Security Act and regulations thereunder and no mention is made of State legislation. State legislation is left to operate only "subject to this award." Secondly, express reference is made to certain State legislation relating to dangerous machinery, dust-extracting appliances, and the lifting of heavy weights. The operation of this legislation is expressly preserved. It is therefore difficult to argue that State legislation in general is preserved in operation ...

In this case there is an express prohibition by a State authority of the employment of females on a milling machine. There is an express permission by a Commonwealth authority to employ females on work which is admitted to include work on a milling machine unless such work is declared by a Board of Reference to be unsuitable. There has been no such declaration by a Board of Reference. Therefore there is an express prohibition by the State authority of that which is permitted by the Commonwealth authority ... In this case there is, in my opinion, a clear inconsistency, and therefore the Commonwealth award prevails ...

The case law makes clear that the grant of a mere right or permission by federal law will not necessarily render relevant State laws inoperative. On its proper construction, the federal law may actually be granting a right or permission intended to be exercisable subject to the general law, including any applicable State laws. ***Ansett v Wardley*** provides an example.

Ansett Transport Industries (Operations) Pty Ltd v Wardley (1980) 142 CLR 237

Wardley was refused employment as a pilot in accordance with Ansett's male pilots only policy. Wardley succeeded in an action against Ansett under Victorian anti-discrimination law, which prohibited discrimination on the ground of sex in hiring and dismissal decisions. Ansett argued that the Victorian anti-discrimination law was inconsistent with a clause of its pilots agreement that was binding under federal industrial relations legislation allowing Ansett to dismiss pilots with less than six months service without cause with seven days' notice in writing. Ansett intended to employ Wardley in order to comply with orders against it made under the Victorian anti-discrimination legislation and then immediately dismiss her. The High Court held that the federal law did not evince an intention to operate to the exclusion of any applicable State laws.

Stephen J

Ansett contends that the Agreement, by cl 6B, gives it an unqualified right to dismiss its pilots on any ground, either on written notice of appropriate duration or on payment in lieu of notice; on the other hand, the Act, by s 18 (2)(b), makes it unlawful for it to dismiss a pilot on the ground that she is a woman, the very ground upon which Ansett wishes to dismiss Mrs Wardley. Therein, it is said, lies the immediate point of inconsistency; direct collision occurs because what is permitted by the Commonwealth law is forbidden by the State law ...

In my view there is in this case no inconsistency within the meaning of s 109 of the *Constitution*. I regard the right of termination of the contract of employment which cl 6 of the Agreement confers as no absolute right, such as that for which Ansett contends. The right which it confers is not one which is capable of exercise regardless of the unlawfulness under State law of the ground for its exercise. On the contrary it is a right the nature of which is to be understood against the background to its operation which general laws of the land, whether State or federal in origin, provide ...

In my view there is in this case no inconsistency within the meaning of s 109 of the *Constitution*. I regard the right of termination of the contract of employment which cl 6 of the Agreement confers as no absolute right, such as that for which Ansett contends. The right which it confers is not one which is capable of exercise regardless of the unlawfulness under State law of the ground for its exercise. On the contrary it is a right the nature of which is to be understood against the background to its operation which general laws of the land, whether State or federal in origin, provide ...

The question as a whole resolves itself, in the end, into a search for legislative intent.

Mason J

I should point out that the major thrust of Ansett's case is to establish the existence of what has been called "direct inconsistency", that is, the disconformity which is created by the presence of an absolute right to dismiss for any reason whatsoever, which Ansett finds in the Agreement, and the presence in the State Act of a prohibition against dismissal for the prescribed reasons ...

If, according to the true construction of the Commonwealth law, the right is absolute, then it inevitably follows that the right is intended to prevail to the exclusion of any other law. A State law which takes away the right is inconsistent because it is in conflict with the absolute right and because the Commonwealth law relevantly occupies the field. So also with a Commonwealth law that grants a permission by way of positive authority. The Commonwealth legislative intention which sustains the conclusion that the permission is granted by way of positive authority also sustains the conclusion that the positive authority was to take effect to the exclusion of any other law ...

From my examination of the Agreement as a whole, I conclude that it should not be viewed as a general industry award which seeks to determine exhaustively the respective rights of employer and employee. Although the Agreement does deal with many of the matters usually found in an award, such as pay, hours of work and leave, its emphasis is on setting out in exact detail the manner and procedure governing the advancement of a pilot in terms of seniority and rights dependent thereon. Clause 6B does not deal with the substantive right of dismissal. Instead, its opening words assume the right of the employer under the general law to terminate the employment of a pilot and the import of the clause as laid down in pars 1, 2, 3 and 4 is to prescribe the procedure and regulate the means whereby the right to terminate may be effected ...

Commercial Radio Coffs Harbour v Fuller provides another example of a right or permission granted under federal law being exercisable subject to the operation of applicable State laws. In that case, the grant of a licence under federal legislation to engage in radio broadcasting on condition that certain types of broadcast antennae were constructed did not mean that the licensee could construct the antennae in breach of State planning laws.

Commercial Radio Coffs Harbour v Fuller (1986) 161 CLR 47

Gibbs CJ and Brennan J

On behalf of the applicant it is argued that, if the planning laws of New South Wales make it unlawful for the holder of a licence to do what has to be done in order to comply with the conditions of the licence and to commence the licensed service on the specified date, then simultaneous obedience to both the Commonwealth Act and the State planning laws is impossible and there is inconsistency between them.

The answer to this argument is to be found in the nature and purpose of the relevant provisions of the Commonwealth Act. Part IIIB of the Act provides for exemptions from the general prohibition of operation of transmitters for broadcasting and television enacted by Part IA. The purpose of Part IIIB is simply to provide the machinery for the granting of licences and to prescribe what the holders of licences must do to comply with the licensing regime. Part IIIB does not purport to confer powers or authorities on the holders of licences. If a duty imposed on the holder of a licence cannot be performed without contravening another law, Part IIIB gives no authority to contravene the other law ...

Ordinarily, a provision which imposes a duty under penalty to do a thing specified in the provision would be construed as conferring on the person on whom the duty is imposed a power or authority to do that thing: *Fenton v Hampton* [1858] 14 ER 727, at p 732). But an alternative construction may be warranted. If it is impossible to do the thing specified in the provision without contravening another law, the provision may be construed either as authorizing the doing of that thing (so that it is inconsistent with the other law) or as imposing a qualified duty which stops short of requiring contravention of the other law ...

Wilson, Deane and Dawson JJ

In the present case, our construction of the Commonwealth Act leads us to conclude that it does not purport to state exclusively or exhaustively the law with which the operation of a commercial broadcasting station must comply. The Act prohibits broadcasting without a licence. The prohibition is removed upon the grant of a licence, subject to certain conditions. Failure to comply with the conditions may result in a revocation or suspension of the licence thereby reinstating the prohibition. The licence confers on the grantee a permission to broadcast. There is nothing in the Act which suggests that it confers an absolute right or positive authority to broadcast so that the grantee, because he has a licence, is immune or exempt from compliance with State laws. On the contrary, in concentrating on the technical efficiency and quality of broadcasting services, the Act leaves room for the operation of laws, both State and Commonwealth, dealing with other matters relevant to the operation of such services ...

The Act does not purport to lay down the whole legislative framework within which the activity of broadcasting is to be carried on. It is intended to operate within the setting of other laws with which the grantee of a licence will be required to comply.

In ***APLA Ltd v Legal Services Commissioner (NSW)*** the High Court rejected an argument that State laws banning certain types of advertising by lawyers were inconsistent with the rights, duties, remedies and jurisdiction conferred, regulated or provided for by various federal statutes. The argument was that if lawyers could not advertise their services people would not be able to exercise their rights under the federal laws. The State laws were held to impose no burden on the operation of any federal law. A State law prevents the exercise of a right or permission under federal law only if the State law has the effect of precluding, overriding or rendering ineffective the federal law's grant of a right or permission.

APLA Ltd v Legal Services Commissioner (NSW) (2005) 224 CLR 322

Gleeson CJ and Heydon J

Preventing lawyers from advertising does not impair the federal legislation referred to in the case stated. Indeed, most of the legislation was originally enacted at a time when restriction on advertising by lawyers was the generally accepted professional standard. None of the federal legislation depends for its efficacy upon the unrestricted promotion of legal services. The rights, powers, and jurisdictions created have full legal effect and operation regardless of whether, at any given time, the States or Territories permit or restrict advertising by lawyers ...

Callinan J

The notion that a restriction upon advertising by solicitors soliciting personally injured or other clients, alters, impairs or detracts from the pursuit of remedies made available under federal legislation is, I think, far-fetched. People pursuing them are in no way impeded from doing so because lawyers may be subject to State rules about the way in which they may promote themselves or offer their services ... Whether lawyers can or cannot communicate that they wish to undertake the pursuit of claims under these enactments does not alter, impair or detract from the operation or objects of them, or the pursuit of federal claims or rights to which they give rise ...

[A] slight or marginal or insignificant impact of a State law upon a federal law will not give rise to a constitutional inconsistency. The impact must be one of some significance and such as would have the effect, if the State law were valid, of precluding, overriding or rendering ineffective an actual exercise of federal jurisdiction. But as I have said, I do not think that even a marginal impact is made here by the contested provisions ...

Direct inconsistency can also arise in the context of criminal laws. ***Dickson v The Queen*** demonstrates that direct inconsistency arises where a State law criminalises conduct that federal law intends should not be criminal. In this case, the High Court found that a federal offence of conspiracy to steal Commonwealth property was intended to operate only in narrow circumstances. The concurrent operation of a much broader State general conspiracy to steal property offence therefore criminalised conduct that the federal law intended should not be unlawful, and therefore altered, impaired and detracted from the operation of the federal law. In effect, the federal law had granted permission to engage in conduct that the State law then prohibited.

Dickson v The Queen (2010) 241 CLR 491

French CJ, Gummow, Hayne, Heydon, Crennan, Kiefel and Bell JJ

Shortly expressed, the appeal to this Court is brought on the ground that conspiracy to steal the cigarettes was not an offence against the law of Victoria so that the presentment preferred against the appellant should have been quashed. This conclusion is said to follow because (a) the cigarettes referred to in the presentment were property belonging to the Commonwealth to which the theft provision in s 131.1 of the *Criminal Code* (Cth) ("the Commonwealth Criminal Code") applied, in respect of which the conspiracy provision in s 11.5 attached; and (b) by operation of s 109 of the *Constitution*, the relevant provisions of the Victorian Crimes Act were pro tanto invalid in the sense of "suspended, inoperative and ineffective" ...

For the reasons which follow the submissions as to "direct inconsistency" which were made by the appellant should be accepted and the appeal allowed ...

[T]he case for inconsistency between the two conspiracy provisions with which this appeal is concerned is strengthened by the differing methods of trial the legislation stipulates for the federal and State offences, particularly because s 80 of the *Constitution* would be brought into operation. In the present case, the jury trial provided by the law of Victoria under s 46 of the Juries Act did not require the unanimity which, because s 4G of the Commonwealth Crimes Act would have stipulated an indictment for the federal conspiracy offence, s 80 then would have mandated at a trial of the appellant ...

The direct inconsistency in the present case is presented by the circumstance that s 321 of the Victorian Crimes Act renders criminal conduct not caught by, and indeed deliberately excluded from, the conduct rendered criminal by s 11.5 of the Commonwealth Criminal Code. In the absence of the operation of s 109 of the *Constitution*, the Victorian Crimes Act will alter, impair or detract from the operation of the federal law by proscribing conduct of the appellant which is left untouched by the federal law. The State legislation, in its application to the presentment upon which the appellant was convicted, would undermine and, to a significant extent, negate the criteria for the existence and adjudication of criminal liability adopted by the federal law. No room is left for the State law to attach to the crime of conspiracy to steal property in the possession of the Commonwealth more stringent criteria and a different mode of trial by jury. To adapt remarks of Barwick CJ in *Devondale Cream*, the case is one of "direct collision" because the State law, if allowed to operate, would impose upon the appellant obligations greater than those provided by the federal law ...

Section 11.5 of the Commonwealth Criminal Code received detailed consideration by this Court in *R v LK*. The extrinsic material considered in *R v LK* indicated that the narrower scope of s 11.5 reflects a deliberate legislative choice influenced by the work of what in *R v LK* were identified as the Gibbs Committee and the Model Criminal Code Officers Committee.

What is immediately important is the exclusion by the federal law of significant aspects of conduct to which the State offence attaches. There are significant "areas of liberty designedly left [and which] should not be closed up", to adapt remarks of Dixon J in *Wenn v Attorney-General (Vic)* ...

The result in the present case is that in its concurrent field of operation in respect of conduct, s 321 of the Victorian Crimes Act attaches criminal liability to conduct which falls outside s 11.5 of the Commonwealth Criminal Code and in that sense alters, impairs or detracts from the operation of the federal legislation and so directly collides with it ...

Indirect inconsistency

Indirect inconsistency is sometimes called 'cover the field' inconsistency. Where a federal law is intended to be a complete statement of the law on a particular subject-matter, that federal law has 'covered the field' and excluded the possibility of any State law operating within the same field. Inconsistency necessarily arises if a State law seeks to operate in the same field.

Clyde Engineering Co Ltd v Cowburn and ***Ex parte McLean*** provide early examples of indirect inconsistency. Both cases demonstrate the importance of the need to carefully: (1) identify the precise field the federal law occupies; and (2) determine whether the federal law evinces an intention to occupy that field to the exclusion of any State law.

Clyde Engineering Co Ltd v Cowburn (1926) 37 CLR 466

A new industrial award made under federal legislation set standard full-time hours at 48 hours per week. State legislation required that overtime penalty rates be paid to any worker working more than 44 hours per week. It was possible to comply with both laws by an employee working 48 hours and the employer paying overtime rates for four hours. The High Court held that the federal law was intended to exclude the possibility of any State law operating concurrently on the subject-matter of hours of work.

Isaacs J

But surely the vital question would be: Was the [federal] Act on its true construction intended to cover the whole ground and, therefore, to supersede the [State Act]? If it was so intended, then the inconsistency would consist in giving any operative effect at all to the [State] Act, because the [federal Act] was intended entirely to exclude it.

The suggested test, however useful a working guide it may be in some cases or, in other words, however it may for some cases prove a test, cannot be recognized as the standard measuring rod of inconsistency. If, however, a competent legislature expressly or impliedly evinces its intention to cover the whole field, that is a conclusive test of inconsistency where another legislature assumes to enter to any extent upon the same field ...

If such a position as I have postulated be in fact established, the inconsistency is demonstrated, not by comparison of detailed provisions, but by the mere existence of the two sets of provisions ...

There is manifest inconsistency from the standpoint of totality dependent, however, entirely on the view taken as to the effect of establishing a minimum wage or maximum hours ...

Ex parte McLean (1930) 43 CLR 472

Federal legislation prescribed a penalty for any worker who was employed under a federal industrial award who failed to work with due care and skill. State legislation prescribed a different penalty for any worker who failed to work with due care and skill. The High Court held the State law was inconsistent with the federal law.

Dixon J

The same acts or omissions were therefore made subject to the penal sanctions of the Federal enactment and the somewhat different penal sanctions of the State enactment.

When the Parliament of the Commonwealth and the Parliament of a State each legislate upon the same subject and prescribe what the rule of conduct shall be, they make laws which are inconsistent, notwithstanding that the rule of conduct is identical which each prescribes, and s 109 applies. That this is so is settled, at least when the sanctions they impose are diverse.

But the reason is that, by prescribing the rule to be observed, the Federal statute shows an intention to cover the subject matter and provide what the law upon it shall be. If it appeared that the Federal law was intended to be supplementary to or cumulative upon State law, then no inconsistency would be exhibited in imposing the same duties or in inflicting different penalties. The inconsistency does not lie in the mere coexistence of two laws which are susceptible of simultaneous obedience. It depends upon the intention of the paramount Legislature to express by its enactment, completely, exhaustively, or exclusively, what shall be the law governing the particular conduct or matter to which its attention is directed. When a Federal statute discloses such an intention, it is inconsistent with it for the law of a State to govern the same conduct or matter ...

But, in this case, the State law, s 4 of the *Masters and Servants Act 1902*, deals directly with the relation of employer and employed, and in virtue of that industrial relation makes penal the very default which the Federal law punishes somewhat differently in the regulation of the same relation.

The ***Mining Act Case*** provides an example of the High Court finding that a federal law did not evince an intention to cover a particular field. In this case, a federal law prescribed only some of the rights and duties of private persons in respect of certain private land used for defence training purposes. By contrast, the federal law prescribed all of the rights and duties of the Commonwealth with respect to the use of that land. The High

Court held that the incomplete statement of private persons' rights and duties evinced an intention to not cover the field of private persons' rights and duties in respect of the land. It followed that State mining legislation authorising the grant of mining licences in respect of the same land was not invalid for indirect inconsistency. However, the High Court noted the possibility that particular exercises of the rights conferred by the State legislation might give rise to direct inconsistency.

Commonwealth v Western Australia ('Mining Act Case') (1999) 196 CLR 392

Gleeson CJ and Gaudron J

To say that a Commonwealth law "covers the field" is simply to say that there is to be discerned an intention on the part of the Parliament of the Commonwealth that its legislation should be an exclusive and exhaustive statement of the law on the topic with which it is concerned. In this case, the question is whether the Defence Regulations evince such an intention with respect to private land included in a defence practice area ...

It is clear that the regulations to which reference has been made constitute an exhaustive statement of the Commonwealth's rights and obligations with respect to private land in a defence practice area. However, they make limited provision as to the rights and obligations of other persons. Save to that limited extent, their rights and obligations are left to the general law. Accordingly, it cannot be said that the Defence Regulations manifest an intention to "cover the field" with respect to the rights and obligations of persons other than those acting for or on behalf of the Commonwealth in relation to the perimeter area.

Nor, in our view, can it be said that any provision of the Mining Act would, if valid, alter, impair or detract from the operation of the Defence Regulations or that the Act is otherwise inconsistent with the Regulations because, for example, the Act and the Regulations cannot be obeyed simultaneously or one takes away what the other confers. That is because the Mining Act does not confer rights to enter upon or use land in the perimeter area. Rather, it simply allows that authority may be granted to persons to enter or conduct mining operations on that land.

The Defence Regulations do not operate to prevent entry or activity on the perimeter area, except if a defence operation or practice has been authorised by a chief of staff pursuant to reg 51(1). It would seem clear that, were authority to be granted pursuant to the Mining Act to enter upon or conduct mining activities on land in the perimeter area at a time or times specified in an authorisation under reg 51(1) for the conduct of a defence operation or practice, there would be direct inconsistency between that authorisation and the authority granted under the Mining Act. That inconsistency would result from the inconsistent operation in the particular circumstances of the Mining Act and the Defence Regulations – "operational inconsistency", as it is called.

Section 109 of the *Constitution* operates to render a State law inoperative only to the extent of its inconsistency with a law of the Commonwealth and only for so long as the inconsistency remains. Although there may be "operational inconsistency" between the Mining Act and the Defence Regulations in the event and to the extent that authority is conferred pursuant to the former to enter upon or engage in activities on land in the perimeter area at a time when a defence operation or practice is authorised under reg 51(1) of the Defence Regulations, that situation has not yet arisen. Thus, at the present time, there is no inconsistency between the Mining Act and the Defence Regulations ...

22.4 Manufacturing inconsistency

The Commonwealth Parliament can deliberately legislate to exclude or override the operation of State laws. This is sometimes called 'manufacturing inconsistency'.

Bayside City Council v Telstra provides an example of a federal law granting an immunity from the operation of certain State laws. The High Court held that, provided the federal law can be characterised as a law with respect to a head of federal legislative power, a federal law can expressly exclude the operation of State laws. In this case, a federal law provided that telecommunications carriers were immune from having to pay State taxes that discriminated against the carriers. It followed that State laws imposing such taxes on telecommunications carriers were directly inconsistent with the federal law.

Bayside City Council v Telstra Corporation Ltd (2004) 216 CLR 595

Federal telecommunications legislation provided that 'a law of a State or Territory has no effect to the extent to which the law discriminates, or would have the effect (whether direct or indirect) of discriminating, against a particular carrier, against a particular class of carriers, or against carriers generally'.

Gleeson CJ, Gummow, Kirby, Hayne and Heydon JJ

The power conferred by s 51(v) of the *Constitution*, to make laws with respect to postal, telegraphic, telephonic and other like services, includes a power to make laws with respect to telecommunications services. So far as presently relevant, it extends to making laws regulating the terms and conditions upon which such services may be provided, the licensing of carriers, their conduct as licensees, and the conferring upon them of powers and immunities in connection with the activities undertaken by them pursuant to the chosen regulatory framework. The federal object of promoting the development of the telecommunications industry, and ensuring that telecommunications services would be provided to meet the needs of the Australian community, falls within a head of the legislative power of the Parliament of the Commonwealth. Conferring upon carriers an immunity from discriminatory burdens imposed upon them by State or Territory laws in their capacity as carriers has a direct and substantial connection with the power ...

Telstra and Optus contend that, if and to the extent to which the provisions of the Local Government Acts of New South Wales and Victoria, pursuant to which the charges and rates in question were imposed or levied, fall within the description of laws which discriminate, or would have the effect (whether direct or indirect) of discriminating, against carriers generally, then they are inconsistent with the Telco Act and invalid ...

It appeared to Wilcox J that, in the application of s 109, there is a material difference between a Federal law which provides, for example, that a carrier shall not be liable to any State tax, and a law which provides that a carrier shall not be liable to any discriminatory State tax. If the difference is thought to be that a law of the second kind is a law with respect to discrimination and not a law within s 51(v), then the answer to that is given above. Beyond that, the difference is elusive. If protecting carriers against the imposition of burdens, such as taxation, by State law has a sufficient connection with the power confined by s 51(v), then it is difficult to understand why protecting carriers against discriminatory burdens does not have the same connection with the power. Nor does such a limited protection become a bare attempt to exclude State power upon a subject as to which the Parliament has not chosen to legislate exhaustively ...

As a matter of power, the narrower immunity is as easily sustained as a wider immunity. The enactment of a valid Federal law pursuant to the power engages s 109 ...

Federal legislation can also simply list the State laws it intends should not operate. Provided that the federal law can be characterised as being with respect to a head of federal legislative power, section 109 will operate to render the listed State laws inoperative. This is what happened in the ***WorkChoices Case***. The High Court explained that when a federal law lists State laws it intends should not operate, the federal law is defining the field in which it operates to the exclusion of State laws.

New South Wales v Commonwealth ('WorkChoices Case') (2006) 229 CLR 1

Section 16 of the Workplace Relations Amendment (Work Choices) Act 2005 *(Cth) provided:*

> *(1) This Act is intended to apply to the exclusion of all the following laws of a State or Territory so far as they would otherwise apply in relation to an employee or employer:*
> *(a) a State or Territory industrial law;*
> *(b) a law that applies to employment generally and deals with leave other than long service leave;*
> *(c) a law providing for a court or tribunal constituted by a law of the State or Territory to make an order in relation to equal remuneration for work of equal value (as defined in section 623);*

> *(d) a law providing for the variation or setting aside of rights and obligations arising under a contract of employment, or another arrangement for employment, that a court or tribunal finds is unfair;*
>
> *(e) a law that entitles a representative of a trade union to enter premises.*
>
> ...
>
> *(4) This Act is intended to apply to the exclusion of a law of a State or Territory that is prescribed by the regulations for the purposes of this subsection.*

Gleeson CJ, Gummow, Hayne, Heydon and Crennan JJ

Western Australia submitted that s 16, since it is aimed at preventing the exercise of State legislative power on various matters rather than preserving the operation of Commonwealth legislation on those matters, is not "a law of the Commonwealth" within the meaning of s 109, and cannot prevail over State legislation passed in exercise of its concurrent power. It is true that on the construction of s 16(1) which was accepted above, provisions like s 16(1)(d) and (e) only apply to circumstances involving employees and employers as defined in ss 5(1) and 6(1), and hence to circumstances where, subject to the present controversy, Commonwealth power exists. But even on that construction, Western Australia contended that there was an area – relatively narrow, perhaps, but still an area – where the Commonwealth had refused to legislate positively and had used s 16 to prevent the States from doing so. That is, the Commonwealth had effectuated a bare exclusion of State law ...

The Commonwealth contended rather that it was open to the Commonwealth Parliament to indicate the relevant field it intended to cover to the exclusion of State law, that s 109 would then operate even though the Commonwealth had not made its own detailed provisions about every matter within that field which State law dealt with, and that it sufficed for the Commonwealth to have some provisions dealing with aspects of the field, leaving others unregulated. The Commonwealth submitted that the relevant field was to be identified, not by reference to the areas regulated by State law, but by reference to the terms of the Commonwealth law ...

The Commonwealth's submissions are to be preferred. Western Australia pointed to nothing in s 109 itself or in the case law on s 109 suggesting that s 109 will not cause Commonwealth law to prevail over an inconsistent State law and render it invalid to the extent of the inconsistency unless the Commonwealth law provides some regime for regulating each particular aspect of the topics dealt with by the State law ...

Section 109 may operate where the Commonwealth chooses to enact a scheme involving a more detailed form of regulation than State law provides. Equally, s 109 may operate where the Commonwealth creates a scheme involving less detailed regulation than State law provides. And s 109 may operate where the Parliament has done what it has in the new Act – to provide a more detailed scheme than State law in some respects and a less detailed scheme in other respects ...

Although the Commonwealth can manufacture inconsistency, the Commonwealth cannot prohibit the States from enacting inconsistent laws. It is beyond the scope of federal legislative power to deprive the States of their legislative powers. Section 109 is only enlivened where there is a valid federal law. In other words, the Commonwealth Parliament can legislate to exclude the operation of particular State laws or particular types of State laws but it cannot legislate to stop the States enacting those laws in the first place.

Western Australia v Commonwealth ('Native Title Act Case') (1995) 183 CLR 373

Brennan J

Section 107 of the *Constitution* confers on or confirms to the Parliaments of the respective States the powers vested in those Parliaments as at the establishment of the Commonwealth except to the extent that any power is "exclusively vested in the Parliament of the Commonwealth or withdrawn from the Parliament of the State". It is beyond the power of the Parliament of the Commonwealth to enact a law that is inconsistent with s 107. It is therefore beyond the legislative power of the Commonwealth Parliament to withdraw from any State Parliament a legislative power that is conferred on or confirmed to that Parliament by s 107. Nor does the Parliament of the Commonwealth have power directly to control the content of a State law. By virtue of s 107 of the *Constitution*, a valid law of a State operates according to its tenor except to the extent, if any, that s 109 of the *Constitution* renders the State law "invalid". In *Gerhardy v Brown* ((1985) 159 CLR 70 at 121; see *Mabo (No 1)* (1986) 166 CLR at 196–197, 203, 216, 243), Brennan J said:

> It is ... outside the powers of the Commonwealth Parliament to prohibit the Parliament of a State from exercising that Parliament's powers to enact laws, whether discriminatory or not, with respect to a topic within its competence. It is not to the point that a law, if enacted by the State Parliament, will be invalid by reason of its inconsistency with a Commonwealth law. A Commonwealth law purporting to prohibit a State Parliament from enacting a law finds no support in s 109 of the *Constitution*; rather, s 109 operates on a law that a State Parliament has lawfully enacted.

...

22.5 Manufacturing consistency

The Commonwealth Parliament can also deliberately legislate to preserve the operation of State laws or avoid inconsistency. This is sometimes called 'manufacturing consistency'.

Direct inconsistency can be avoided by drafting the federal legislation so that it does not apply or operate in circumstances where State legislation operates. Indirect inconsistency can be avoided by the federal law expressly stating that it intends for State laws to operate concurrently.

Avoiding direct inconsistency

Direct inconsistency can be avoided by drafting the federal legislative scheme in such a way that it does not apply where State law applies. One technique the Commonwealth uses to preserve the operation of State laws is the use of 'roll back' provisions, such as was used in the legislative scheme at issue in ***Momcilovic***. In simple terms, a 'roll back' provision has the effect that a federal law will not apply in circumstances where a State law applies.

Momcilovic concerned federal and State drug trafficking offences. Unlike in ***Dickson***, the State criminal offence under consideration in *Momcilovic* did not criminalise conduct that federal law intended should not be unlawful. Further, unlike in ***Ex parte McLean***, the federal offence under consideration in *Momcilovic* had operation only if the State offence was not prosecuted. It followed that in operation there could be no direct inconsistency between the federal and State offence provisions.

Momcilovic v The Queen (2011) 245 CLR 1

Momcilovic was charged with a drug trafficking offence under section 71AC of the **Drugs, Poisons and Controlled Substances Act 1981** *(Vic). Momcilovic argued that section 71AC was inconsistent with the similar federal offence found in section 302.4 of the* **Criminal Code** *(Cth), which had a different maximum penalty and some differences in the elements of the offence. Another provision of the* **Criminal Code**, *section 300.4, provided that the* **Criminal Code** *was 'not intended to exclude or limit the concurrent operation of any law of a State'. Further section 4C(2) of the* **Crimes Act 1914** *(Cth) provided that where a person has been punished under a State law for an act that also constitutes a federal crime, the person is not liable to be prosecuted for the federal crime.*

Gummow J

If, as in the present case, the federal and State penalty provisions each specify a maximum penalty, and that maximum differs, the provisions thereby confer a judicial discretion or power to be exercised within those respective limits and in the circumstances of the particular case. Conflict may arise, but only upon the exercise of those powers.

However, the Crimes Act diminishes the occasions for that conflict. Where "an act or omission" constitutes an offence under both a federal law and that of a State, and "the offender has been punished for that offence under [State law]", the offender "shall not be liable to be punished for the offence under [federal law]". Section 4C(2) of the Crimes Act so provides ...

Section 4C(2) of the Crimes Act is designed to avoid the injustice of exposure to double punishment in cases where the doing of a single act may involve the actor in the commission of an offence against federal and State law. Its effect, when the occasion for its operation arrives, is to achieve what has been called a "roll-back" of the federal criminal law, or its "withdraw[al] pro tanto".

With respect to the appellant in this case, there has been no prosecution of the federal offence and no occasion of operational inconsistency has arisen with respect to the application of the penalty provisions of the federal and State laws. If the occasion had arisen, s 4C(2) would have removed the occasion for any "direct" inconsistency ...

The appellant submitted that her case and *Dickson v The Queen* were in pari materia. But it should be noted that the law of Victoria creating the crime of conspiracy which was at stake in *Dickson* rendered criminal conduct deliberately excluded from the federal offence ...

[Section] 71AC is less stringent than the provisions of the Code; the federal law cannot be said upon its proper construction designedly to have left a liberty which the operation of s 109 does not permit by the State law to be "closed up" ...

Avoiding indirect inconsistency

Indirect inconsistency can be avoided by the federal law expressly stating that it intends for State laws to operate concurrently. In other words, the federal law can state an intention not to cover the field. The ***GMAC Case*** holds that this technique is effective to avoid indirect (or 'cover the field') inconsistency arising. That case also points out that the technique cannot avoid direct inconsistency.

R v Credit Tribunal; Ex parte General Motors Acceptance Corporation ('GMAC Case') (1977) 137 CLR 545

Section 75(1) of the Trade Practices Act 1974 *(Cth) provided: 'Except as provided by sub-section (2), this Part is not intended to exclude or limit the concurrent operation of any law of a State or Territory.'*

Mason J

[A]lthough a provision in a Commonwealth statute which attempts to deny operational validity to a State law cannot of its own force achieve that object, it may nevertheless validly evince an intention on the part of the statute to make exhaustive or exclusive provision on the subject with which it deals, thereby bringing s 109 into play. Equally a Commonwealth law may provide that it is not intended to make exhaustive or exclusive provision with respect to the subject with which it deals, thereby enabling State laws, not inconsistent with Commonwealth law, to have an operation. Here again the Commonwealth law does not of its own force give State law a valid operation. All that it does is to make it clear that the Commonwealth law is not intended to cover the field, thereby leaving room for the operation of such State laws as do not conflict with Commonwealth law.

It is of course by now well established that a provision in a Commonwealth statute evincing an intention that the statute is not intended to cover the field cannot avoid or eliminate a case of direct inconsistency or collision, of the kind which arises, for example, when Commonwealth and State laws make contradictory provision upon the same topic, making it impossible for both laws to be obeyed ... But where there is no direct inconsistency, where inconsistency can only arise if the Commonwealth law is intended to be an exhaustive and exclusive law, a provision of the kind under consideration will be effective to avoid inconsistency by making it clear that the law is not intended to be exhaustive or exclusive.

It is against this background of settled constitutional interpretation that s 75 is to be construed. In the light of what has already been said, the terms of s 75 (1) are open to the objection that they refer to the concurrent operation of State laws; they do not speak of the extent of the intended operation of the Commonwealth law. None the less, there is to be gathered from the sub-section a very clear expression of intention that the *Trade Practices Act* is not an exhaustive enactment on the topics with which it deals and that it is not intended to operate to the exclusion of State laws on those topics. As such it does not avoid any instance of direct inconsistency which may occur between the *Trade Practices Act* and the two South Australian Acts, but in accordance with all that I have said, it eliminates any suggestion of inconsistency otherwise arising ...

Inability to manufacture consistency retrospectively

An important limitation on the Commonwealth's ability to manufacture consistency is the inability to manufacture consistency retrospectively. ***Metwally*** explains that an attempt to manufacture consistency retrospectively is really an attempt to deprive section 109 of its operation. No Parliament possesses power to deprive the *Constitution* of its operation. The Commonwealth can manufacture consistency only prospectively. In other words, the Commonwealth can prevent inconsistency arising in the future but it cannot undo past inconsistency.

University of Wollongong v Metwally (1984) 158 CLR 447

Viskauskas v Niland *(1983) 153 CLR 280 held that the* **Racial Discrimination Act 1975** *(Cth) had covered the field of racial discrimination with the result that the racial discrimination provisions of the* **Anti-Discrimination Act 1977** *(NSW) were invalid. In response to that case, the Commonwealth Parliament inserted a new provision into the federal statute providing: 'This Act is not intended, and shall be deemed never to have intended, to exclude or limit the operation of a law of a State or Territory that furthers the object of the Convention and is capable of operating concurrently with this Act.'*

Gibbs CJ

It was submitted that since the Commonwealth Parliament has power to make its enactments retrospective, it could retrospectively amend the Commonwealth Act, so as to indicate an intention not to exclude the operation of the State law, and thereby cause the Anti-Discrimination Act to have a valid operation from its inception, notwithstanding that in truth it was inconsistent with the Commonwealth Act at all times before the Amendment Act was passed.

The acceptance of this argument would mean that the Commonwealth Parliament could enact a law which would retrospectively deprive s 109 of the Constitution of its operation. If, at a particular time, a State law was inconsistent with a law of the Commonwealth, s 109, applied at that time, would have resulted in the invalidity of the State law. If, on the other hand, the State law was not inconsistent with that law of the Commonwealth, s 109 would not render it invalid.

If the respondents' argument were correct, the Commonwealth Parliament could retrospectively reveal that the Commonwealth law had an intention, which it lacked at the earlier time, either to cover, or not to cover, the whole field, with the result that the State law would be retrospectively invalidated or validated. In other words, the Commonwealth law itself could vary the effect which s 109 had produced at the relevant time; it could give to a State law a valid operation as at a time when s 109 had rendered it invalid. But Commonwealth statutes cannot prevail over the Constitution ...

22.6 DISCUSSION QUESTIONS

1. Why does 'invalid' in section 109 have a non-literal meaning?
2. Provide an example of each of the following categories of inconsistency:
   a. impossibility of simultaneous obedience inconsistency
   b. inconsistent rights and duties inconsistency
   c. cover the field inconsistency.
3. What does 'manufacturing inconsistency' mean?
4. What does 'manufacturing consistency' mean?
5. Problem question: Consider the following hypothetical legislation and scenario. The Commonwealth Parliament enacted the *Student Benefits Act 2020*, which sets out various benefits and discounts university and TAFE students may receive. Section 10 of the Act states: 'The benefits set out in this Act are the only benefits a university or TAFE student may receive in connection with their status as a student.'

   The Queensland Parliament had previously enacted the *Benefits for Students Act 2010*, which provided for various benefits to university and TAFE students in Queensland that are not included in the federal Act. In 2022, as a budget savings measure, the *Student Benefits Act 2020* was repealed.

   A Queensland university student seeks your advice as to whether a full-time university student may receive benefits under the Queensland Act in: (1) 2019; (2) 2021; and (3) 2023. Advise.

   (You may assume that the Commonwealth Act is supported by section 51(xxiiiA) of the *Constitution*.)

INTERGOVERNMENTAL IMMUNITIES

23

23.1 Overview

This chapter examines an implied limitation on the legislative powers of the Commonwealth and the States known as the 'intergovernmental immunities doctrine'. The doctrine arises from the fact that the *Australian Constitution* establishes a Commonwealth government and a series of separately organised State governments and requires their continued existence as independent or separate entities.

The intergovernmental immunities doctrine does not create a general immunity of the Commonwealth from State laws or a general immunity of the States from federal laws. Rather, the intergovernmental immunities doctrine gives rise to: (1) State immunity from federal laws which operate to destroy or curtail the continued existence of the States or their capacity to function as governments; and (2) Commonwealth immunity from State laws which operate to destroy or curtail the continued existence of the Commonwealth or its capacity to function as a government. Whether a law contravenes the intergovernmental immunities doctrine requires an evaluative assessment of a range of factors.

Key concepts considered in this chapter include:

- implied immunity of instrumentalities
- intergovernmental immunities
- executive capacities
- destroy or curtail the continued existence of the States or their capacity to function as governments

- alter or abolish the capacities of the Federal Executive Government
- regulate the exercise of federal executive capacities.

23.2 The former doctrine of implied immunity of instrumentalities

Until 1920, the High Court applied a doctrine known as 'implied immunity of instrumentalities'. The basic idea was that the Commonwealth could not be subject to State laws and the States could not be subject to Commonwealth laws.

The doctrine had its origins in ***D'Emden v Pedder***. In that case, the High Court held that State laws that attempted to control the exercise of federal powers, even by imposing taxes on the salaries of federal officials, were necessarily invalid.

D'Emden v Pedder (1904) 1 CLR 91

A Tasmanian law imposed a tax on certain salaries. A federal government official refused to pay the tax and was charged for failing to pay the tax. The High Court held that State laws could not apply to the Commonwealth or to Commonwealth officials.

Griffith CJ

It follows that when a State attempts to give to its legislative or executive authority an operation which, if valid, would fetter, control, or interfere with, the free exercise of the legislative or executive power of the Commonwealth, the attempt, unless expressly authorized by the Constitution, is to that extent invalid and inoperative. And this appears to be the true test to be applied in determining the validity of State laws and their applicability to federal transactions ...

The justification for this doctrine was that the *Constitution* established the Commonwealth and the States as independent sovereign entities. External interference with, or control of, a sovereign entity's powers would be inconsistent with sovereign status.

Baxter v Commissioners of Taxation (NSW) (1907) 4 CLR 1087

Griffth CJ, Barton and O'Connor JJ

The purpose of the Constitution was the creation of a new State, the Commonwealth, intended to take its place amongst the free nations, with all such attributes of sovereignty as were consistent with its being still "under the Crown." It is essential to the attribute of sovereignty of any Government that it shall not be interfered with by any external power. The only interference, therefore, to be permitted is that prescribed by the Constitution itself. A similar consequence follows with respect to the constituent States. In their case, however, the Commonwealth is empowered to interfere in certain prescribed cases. But under the scheme of the Constitution there is a large number of subjects upon which the legislative powers of both the Commonwealth and the State may be exercised ... it follows that a grant of sovereign powers includes a grant of a right to disregard and treat as inoperative any attempt by any other authority to control their exercise ...

The ***Engineers' Case***, as well as abolishing the reserved State powers doctrine, abolished the implied immunities of instrumentalities doctrine. The High Court explained that the implied immunities of instrumentalities doctrine was flawed because it asked what sovereignty requires rather than asking what the *Constitution* requires.

Amalgamated Society of Engineers v Adelaide Steamship Co Ltd ('Engineers' Case') (1920) 28 CLR 129

Section 51(xxxv) gives the Commonwealth Parliament power to legislate with respect to certain types of industrial disputes. The question for the High Court in this case was whether a law made under this power could apply to industrial disputes involving a State. The answer would be in the negative if the implied immunity of instrumentalities doctrine was applied. The High Court overruled the implied immunity of instrumentalities doctrine, explaining that it had no basis in the Constitution.

Knox CJ, Isaacs, Rich and Starke JJ

The Commonwealth Constitution as it exists for the time being, dealing expressly with sovereign functions of the Crown in its relation to Commonwealth and to States, necessarily so far binds the Crown, and laws validly made by authority of the Constitution, bind, so far as they purport to do so, the people of every State considered as individuals or as political organisms called States—in other words, bind both Crown and subjects.

The grant of legislative power to the Commonwealth is ... within the prescribed limits of area and subject matter, the grant of an "authority as plenary and as ample ... as the Imperial Parliament in the plenitude of its power possessed and could bestow," ... "The nature and principles of legislation" (to employ the words of Lord Selborne in *Burah's Case*), the nature of dominion self-government and the decisions just cited entirely preclude, in our opinion, an à priori contention that the grant of legislative power to the Commonwealth Parliament as representing the will of the whole of the people of all the States of Australia should not bind within the geographical area of the Commonwealth and within the limits of the enumerated powers, ascertained by the ordinary process of construction, the States and their agencies as representing separate sections of the territory ...

Applying these principles to the present case, the matter stands thus: s 51(xxxv) is in terms so general that it extends to all industrial disputes in fact extending beyond the limits of any one State, no exception being expressed as to industrial disputes in which States are concerned ...

The doctrine of "implied prohibition" finds no place where the ordinary principles of construction are applied so as to discover in the actual terms of the instrument their expressed or necessarily implied meaning. The principle we apply to the Commonwealth we apply also to the States, leaving their respective acts of legislation full operation within their respective areas and subject matters ...

We therefore hold that States, and persons natural or artificial representing States, when parties to industrial disputes in fact, are subject to Commonwealth legislation under pl xxxv of s 51 of the Constitution, if such legislation on its true construction applies to them ...

It is settled law that there is no blanket rule – as the implied immunity instrumentalities doctrine had laid down – that the Commonwealth is immune from State laws and that the States are immune from Commonwealth laws.

23.3 The conceptual basis for intergovernmental immunities

Contrary to what the implied immunities of instrumentalities doctrine had asserted, what the *Constitution* does is establish a Commonwealth government and a series of separately organised State governments. The *Constitution* is predicated upon their continued existence as independent or separate entities. Any law that would prevent one of these governments from continuing to exist in the form the *Constitution* contemplates is inconsistent with the *Constitution.* This is the conceptual basis for the modern immunities of the Commonwealth from certain types of State laws and of the States from certain types of Commonwealth laws.

The conceptual basis for intergovernmental immunities is usually traced to the ***Melbourne Corporation Case***, and in particular to Dixon J's judgment.

Melbourne Corporation v Commonwealth ('Melbourne Corporation Case') (1947) 74 CLR 31

Rich J

The view once prevailed that any legislative or executive act of the Commonwealth which would, if valid, interfere with the free exercise by a State or its instrumentalities of their legislative or executive powers was *pro tanto* invalid. At a very early stage, however, there were decisions inconsistent with this view, and it was finally exploded by the *Engineers' Case.* There is no general implication in the framework of the Commonwealth Constitution that the Commonwealth is restricted from exercising its defined constitutional powers to their fullest extent by a supposed reservation to the States of an undefined field of reserved powers beyond the scope of

Commonwealth interference. But this is always subject to the provisions of the Commonwealth Constitution itself.

That Constitution expressly provides for the continued existence of the States. Any action on the part of the Commonwealth, in purported exercise of its constitutional powers, which would prevent a State from continuing to exist and function as such is necessarily invalid because inconsistent with the express provisions of the Constitution, and it is to be noted that all the powers conferred by s 51 are conferred "subject to this Constitution."

Starke J

The federal character of the Australian Constitution carries implications of its own. As I have said before, "the government of Australia is a dual system based upon a separation of organs and of powers. The maintenance of the States and their powers is as much the object of the Constitution as the maintenance of the Commonwealth and its powers. Therefore it is beyond the power of either to abolish or destroy the other" ...

So we may start from the proposition that neither federal nor State governments may destroy the other.

Dixon J

I do not think that either under the *Constitution of the United States* or the *British North America Act* or the *Commonwealth Constitution* has countenance been given to the notion that the legislative powers of one government in the system can be used in order directly to deprive another government of powers or authority committed to it or restrict that government in their exercise, notwithstanding the complete overthrow of the general doctrine of reciprocal immunity of government agencies and the discrediting of the reasoning used in its justification ... It is but a consequence of the conception upon which the *Constitution* is framed. The foundation of the *Constitution* is the conception of a central government and a number of State governments separately organized. The Constitution predicates their continued existence as independent entities ...

The High Court affirmed in ***Henderson*** that the justification given in the ***Melbourne Corporation Case*** is the basis for the immunity of the Commonwealth from certain types of State laws.

Re Residential Tenancies Tribunal of New South Wales v Henderson; Ex parte Defence Housing Authority (1997) 190 CLR 410

The issue for the High Court in this case was whether a federal government agency that was the lessor of residential properties was subject to State legislation governing residential tenancies.

Dawson, Toohey and Gaudron JJ

The fundamental principle which lies behind those observations is that which was recognised in *Melbourne Corporation v Commonwealth*, namely, that the Constitution is predicated upon the continued separate existence of the Commonwealth and the States, not only in name, but as bodies politic to which the Constitution proceeds to distribute powers of government ...

The High Court affirmed in ***Clarke*** that the justification given in the ***Melbourne Corporation Case*** is the basis for the immunity of the States from certain types of Commonwealth laws.

Clarke v Federal Commissioner of Taxation (2009) 240 CLR 272

This case concerned the validity of federal legislation imposing special taxation rules on the pensions of State parliamentarians.

French CJ

Under the authority conferred upon it by the Constitution the Parliament of the Commonwealth can make laws affecting the States and their agencies. It cannot, however, make laws which destroy or significantly burden, curtail or weaken either the capacity of the States to carry out their proper legislative, executive and judicial functions or their exercise of those functions ...

The Constitution assumes the continuing existence of the States, their co-existence as independent entities with the Commonwealth, and the functioning of their governments. This assumption is readily inferred from the reference to "one indissoluble Federal Commonwealth" in the Preamble and the terms of ss 3, 5 and 6 of the *Commonwealth of Australia Constitution Act 1900* (Imp) and the provisions of Ch V of the *Constitution* itself. It underpins an implied limitation on Commonwealth power to make laws affecting the States ...

Hayne J

The root of the relevant principle is found in the proposition, often quoted from the reasons of Dixon J in *Melbourne Corporation*, that "[t]he foundation of the Constitution is the conception of a central government and a number of State governments separately organised. The Constitution predicates their continued existence as independent entities." This proposition, and particularly the reference to the continued existence of independent polities, must be understood in the context of the reasons as a whole.

Spence v Queensland resolved some uncertainty as to whether Commonwealth immunity from State laws was symmetrical with State immunity from federal laws. A majority of the High Court held that the intergovernmental immunities doctrine was symmetrical and reciprocal such that Commonwealth immunity from State laws can be understood as a 'reverse' *Melbourne Corporation* doctrine.

Spence v Queensland (2019) 268 CLR 355

Kiefel CJ, Bell, Gageler and Keane JJ

The Commonwealth and the States reciprocally have the benefit of the structural implication recognised in the *Melbourne Corporation Case*. The reciprocal application of that structural implication has been, and should remain, constitutional doctrine ...

Edelman J

The implication established in *Melbourne Corporation* derives from the assumption implicit in the text and structure of the *Constitution* that the Commonwealth and State governments will continue to co-exist as separate entities. There are, therefore, statements in *Melbourne Corporation* that support the symmetrical application of the implication both to protect the States from laws of the Commonwealth or other States, and to protect the Commonwealth from laws of the States ... The symmetry of this underlying assumption has been repeated in subsequent decisions in this Court.

In practice, the Commonwealth has a greater ability to interfere with the States than the States do with the Commonwealth. This is a result of section 109 of the *Constitution* (considered in Chapter 22), which provides that federal laws prevail over inconsistent State laws. In other words, assuming a relevant head of power exists, the Commonwealth can legislate to 'manufacture inconsistency' if it wishes to ignore particular State laws. This is quite separate from the intergovernmental immunities doctrine.

Spence v Queensland (2019) 268 CLR 355

Kiefel CJ, Bell, Gageler and Keane JJ

To observe that the constraint imposed by the structural implication recognised in the *Melbourne Corporation Case* has greater practical significance in its application to a Commonwealth law because of the force that s 109 of the *Constitution* gives to a Commonwealth law that is used as a sword against a State, however, is not to show that the constraint imposed by the structural implication is of no practical significance in its application to a State law that is used as a sword against the Commonwealth. The reciprocal operation of the structural implication is not displaced merely because s 109 allows a Commonwealth law to be used as a shield.

23.4 Methodology for applying the intergovernmental immunities doctrine

The *Constitution* empowers the Commonwealth to make laws that apply to and regulate the States. That is, various heads of federal legislative power are wide enough to support laws that apply to the States. As explained in Chapter 3, whether a federal law is supported by a head of legislative power depends on whether the law can be characterised as being with respect to that head of federal legislative power. Equally, State legislative power is broad enough to impact the Commonwealth's activities. For example, in *Pirrie v McFarlane* (1925) 36 CLR 170 the High Court held that Commonwealth officials were subject to State road rules just like anyone else when driving on public roads in the course of their official duties.

This general proposition is limited by the intergovernmental immunities doctrine, which operates as a limitation on legislative power. A federal law that is supported by a head of federal legislative power will be invalid if it breaches the intergovernmental immunities doctrine. Equally, a State law that is otherwise within State legislative power will be invalid if it breaches the intergovernmental immunities doctrine.

That part of the intergovernmental immunities doctrine concerned with State immunity from federal laws is often referred to as the '***Melbourne Corporation*** doctrine', after the name of the leading case. The reverse *Melbourne Corporation* doctrine protecting the Commonwealth against State laws that impermissibly burden the capacity of the Commonwealth to function as an independent government is sometimes referred to as the '***Cigamatic*** doctrine', after the name of a leading case.

The ***Melbourne Corporation*** doctrine was long understood to consist of two limbs:

1. a prohibition against discrimination which involves the placing on States of special burdens or disabilities, and
2. a prohibition against laws of general application which operate to destroy or curtail the continued existences of the States or their capacity to function as governments.

The two-limbed version of the doctrine has been abolished. In the 2003 case of ***Austin,*** the High Court held that the ***Melbourne Corporation*** doctrine consists of a single limb: a prohibition against laws which operate to destroy or curtail the continued existence of the States or their capacity to function as governments.

Austin did not overrule cases decided under the previous discrimination limb. *Austin* explained that the discrimination limb was really just a subset of the single, broad limb. It follows that pre-*Austin* discrimination limb cases are still good law.

Austin v Commonwealth (2003) 215 CLR 185

Gleeson CJ

Discrimination is an aspect of a wider principle; and what constitutes relevant and impermissible discrimination is determined by that wider principle ... A law which singles out a State or State agency may have as its object to restrict, burden or control State activity. Or a law of general application may so interfere with or impede State activity as to impose an impermissible burden on the exercise of its functions. It is not possible to state exhaustively every form of exercise of Commonwealth legislative power that might be contrary to the general proposition stated above ...

Gaudron, Gummow and Hayne JJ

Because the limitation on power is derived from the federal structure, it is difficult, if not impossible, to articulate it except in negative terms which are cast at a high level of abstraction – that the Commonwealth's legislative powers do not extend to making a law which denies one of the fundamental premises of the Constitution, namely, that there will continue to be State governments separately organised ...

There is, in our view, but one limitation, though the apparent expression of it varies with the form of the legislation under consideration. The question presented by the doctrine in any given case requires assessment of the impact of particular laws by such criteria as "special burden" and "curtailment" of "capacity" of the States "to function as governments". These criteria are to be applied by consideration not only of the form but also "the substance and actual operation" of the federal law ...

Kirby J

[T]he two aspects of the implied limitation upon federal legislative power, noted in past decisions, are essentially manifestations of the one constitutional implication. Both are referable to the underlying conception concerning the nature of the Australian federation. I share the view that each identified defect is to be determined by reference to the effect of the impugned legislation on the continuing existence of the States, and whether there is an impermissible degree of impairment of the State's constitutional functions. The presence of discrimination against a State may be an indication of an attempted impairment of its functions as the Constitution envisaged them. But any discrimination against States must be measured against that underlying criterion. It affords the touchstone of the implied limitation explained in the Court's decision in *Melbourne Corporation* ...

Clarke confirms that the ***Melbourne Corporation*** doctrine consists of a single limb. *Clarke* also emphasises that application of the *Melbourne Corporation* doctrine is an evaluative process.

Clarke v Federal Commissioner of Taxation (2009) 240 CLR 272

French CJ

In their joint judgment in *Austin*, Gaudron, Gummow and Hayne JJ identified "but one limitation" requiring the assessment in any given case of "the impact of particular laws by such criteria as 'special burden' and 'curtailment' of 'capacity' of the States 'to function as governments'". These criteria required consideration of the form, substance and actual operation of the relevant federal law. They would involve "matters of evaluation and degree and of 'constitutional facts' which are not readily established by objective methods in curial proceedings". Kirby J expressed a similar view. Gleeson CJ, in like vein, put it thus:

> Discrimination is an aspect of a wider principle; and what constitutes relevant and impermissible discrimination is determined by that wider principle.

Gleeson CJ referred back to the identification by Mason J in the *Queensland Electricity Commission Case* of the foundation for the implied limitation in the "constitutional conception of the Commonwealth and the States as constituent entities of the federal compact having a continuing existence reflected in a central government and separately organised State governments". The identification in *Austin* of a generally stated implied limitation, variously manifested, is consistent with the origins and evolution of the implication through decisions of this Court after the *Engineers Case* ...

The application of the implied limitation is evaluative. It has always been thus. There is a normative element in the criterion of "significance" by which the adverse effects of a Commonwealth law on State capacities or functions must be characterised, before such a law will be held to be invalid. Whether the effects of a law upon the capacities or functions of the States are "significant" is to be judged qualitatively and also, but not only, by reference to its practical effects ...

In my opinion, the application of the implied limitation requires a multifactorial assessment. Factors relevant to its application include:

1. Whether the law in question singles out one or more of the States and imposes a special burden or disability on them which is not imposed on persons generally.
2. Whether the operation of a law of general application imposes a particular burden or disability on the States.
3. The effect of the law upon the capacity of the States to exercise their constitutional powers.
4. The effect of the law upon the exercise of their functions by the States.
5. The nature of the capacity or functions affected.
6. The subject matter of the law affecting the State or States and in particular the extent to which the constitutional head of power under which the law is made authorises its discriminatory application.

None of these factors, considered separately, will necessarily be determinative of the application of the limitation. The decisions of this Court indicate that the fact that a law singles out the States or a State will be of considerable significance, to be weighed together with the effects of such a law on their capacities and functions. The fact that a law is of general application may make it more difficult to demonstrate, absent operational discrimination in its impact upon the States, that it transgresses the limitation.

Gummow, Heydon, Kiefel and Bell JJ

[I]n *Austin*, a majority of the Court, Gleeson CJ and Gaudron, Gummow and Hayne JJ, concluded that the notion of "discrimination" by federal law against a State is but an illustration of a law which impairs the capacity of the State to function in accordance with the constitutional conception of the Commonwealth and States as constituent entities of the federal structure ...

In ***Spence v Queensland***, Edelman J explained that the evaluative process required for applying the intergovernmental immunities doctrine can be understood as involving factors of breadth and depth.

Spence v Queensland (2019) 268 CLR 355

Edelman J

All of these formulations can be reduced to a consideration of the magnitude of the burden upon the other polity's capacity to function as a government. That assessment will be one of 'evaluation and degree'. The magnitude of a burden has dimensions of both breadth and depth. A burden will be more deeply felt the more that it is targeted at the other polity and the more essential the governmental function that it curtails is to that other polity ...

A burden will be wider the more that it curtails the operation of the governmental functions of the other polity. The curtailing of the governmental functions of the other polity might arise merely by curtailing the range of legislative policy choices of the other polity. Even more significantly, it might curtail the operation of key governmental institutions of the other polity.

If the magnitude of the burden on the other polity's capacity to function as a government is relevant then it should also be relevant to consider the significance of the law for the capacity of the polity enacting it to govern.

23.5 State immunity from Commonwealth laws

The nature of State immunity from Commonwealth laws can be understood by reference to the cases providing examples of permissible and impermissible burdens on the capacity of States to function as independent governments.

Examples of impermissible burdens on the capacity of States to function as independent governments

Melbourne Corporation concerned legislation that prohibited banks from doing the banking business of any State or any local governing authority established by a State without the written consent of the federal Treasurer. The purpose of the law was to effectively force the States to bank with the Commonwealth Bank of Australia, which at the time was owned by the Commonwealth. The High Court held that the law was invalid because its effect was to discriminate against the States or single them out in order to curtail their freedom in the execution of their constitutional powers (namely, management of State finances).

Melbourne Corporation v Commonwealth ('Melbourne Corporation Case') (1947) 74 CLR 31

Rich J

I think while power in a State and in its essential agencies to carry on the business of banking cannot be impaired, the power freely to use the facilities provided by banks, under modern conditions, must be regarded as essential to the efficient working of the business of government, and that power also cannot be impaired. Accordingly, whatever meaning may be given to "State banking," s 48 must be considered as wholly invalid ...

Starke J

The management and control by the States and by local governing authorities of their revenues and funds is a constitutional power of vital importance to them. Their operations depend upon the control of those revenues and funds. And to curtail or interfere with the management of them interferes with their constitutional power. Yet the Commonwealth by its legislation prescribes that, except with the consent in writing of the Treasurer, no bank shall conduct any banking business for a State, including any local governing authority. It operates to prevent the States and local governing authorities from dealing with their old and tried bankers except with the consent in writing of the Treasurer. The object is, of course, to compel the States and the local governing authorities to bank with the Commonwealth Bank, which is a Central Bank. And it was said that the handling of public funds is the appropriate function of a central bank. But that does not establish any constitutional power in the Commonwealth to compel the States so to bank. The States and the local governing authorities, and not the Commonwealth, have the power and the duty of administering, controlling and banking their revenues and funds ...

Dixon J

State and federal governments are separate bodies politic and prima facie each controls its own moneys.

There is thus a law directly operating to deny to the States banking facilities open to others, and so to discriminate against the States or to impose a disability upon them. The circumstance that the primary prohibition is laid upon the banks and not upon the States does not appear to me to be a material distinction. It is just as effectual to deny to the States the use of the banks and that is its object ...

At bottom the principle upon which the States become subject to Commonwealth laws is that when a State avails itself of any part of the established organization of the Australian community it must take it as it finds it. Except in so far as under its legislative power it may be able to alter the legal system, a State must accept the general legal system as it is established. If there be a monopoly in banking lawfully established by the Commonwealth, the State must put up with it.

But it is the contrary of this principle to attempt to isolate the State from the general system, deny it the choice of the machinery the system provides and so place it under a particular disability. Whether the right to exercise such a choice is of great or of small importance to the States is not a material matter for inquiry. It is enough that it forms part of the functions of the Executive Government of the States in administering the finances of the States ...

In my opinion s 48 of the Banking Act is void because an inseverable part of it is directed to control or restrict the Executive Government of the States in the use of banks for the conduct of their banking business ...

Queensland Electricity Commission v Commonwealth holds that isolating one State or all States from the operation of the general law in a way that restricts or burdens the exercise of their constitutional powers violates the ***Melbourne Corporation*** doctrine. This case involved legislation enacted under the arbitration of industrial disputes power in section 51(xxxv) that created a special set of rules and procedures in the Australian Conciliation and Arbitration Commission for one particular industrial dispute between a union and a Queensland government entity. The High Court held that the federal law burdened the State by providing special rules to govern decisions about the relationship between agencies of the State and their employees.

The High Court also explained that the ***Melbourne Corporation*** doctrine protects the agencies created by the States as well as the States themselves.

Queensland Electricity Commission v Commonwealth (1985) 159 CLR 192

Gibbs CJ

The laws forbidden by this principle are those which discriminate against all the States or any one of them by subjecting them or it to a burden or disability which is not imposed on persons generally, a law whose very object is to restrict, burden or control an activity of the States or of one of them. Further, notwithstanding the reference by Dixon J in the passage cited from *Melbourne Corporation v Commonwealth*, at p 83, and elsewhere, to "the restriction or control of a State in the exercise of its executive authority", there is no reason to limit the doctrine to laws which interfere only with the executive power of a State. A Commonwealth law which is directed at the exercise by a State of any of its governmental powers – legislative, executive or judicial – will fall within the ban.

The limitation prevents the Commonwealth from making laws directed at agencies of the States as well as at the States themselves; otherwise the principle would be a futility. There is simply no reason to hold that the agencies of the States, for this purpose, are restricted to agencies which represent the Crown or the State; the reason for the limitation is not to protect an exercise of the prerogative, but to protect the integrity of the States ...

I have already said that the provisions of the Act are directed at the electricity authorities of Queensland; the Act singles them out for attention and subjects them to disabilities to which other employers are not subjected. The electricity authorities are agencies of the State of Queensland – they perform public functions, under the authority of legislation of the State, and are substantially controlled by the Government of the State in the performance of their functions ...

The purpose of the Act in the present case is to place the electricity authorities of Queensland, which are agencies of that State, under special disabilities. For that reason it is unconstitutional ...

Mason J

Three comments should be made in relation to the prohibition as it has been expressed. First, the principle prohibits discrimination against a particular State as well as against the States generally. Discrimination against a particular State, at least so long as it involves the imposition of a special burden or disability on that State, by isolating it from the general law applicable to others, including other States, falls squarely within the principle. Secondly, ... the principle, as Stephen J indicated in *Koowarta*, protects legislatures as well as executive governments. Thirdly, it does not follow that every law which deprives a State of a right, privilege or benefit which it enjoys will amount to discrimination in the sense already discussed. A law which deprives a State of a right, privilege or benefit not enjoyed by others, so as to place the State on an equal footing with others, is not a law which isolates the State from the general law ... The object of the implied prohibition is to protect the State in the exercise of its functions from the operation of discriminatory laws whether the functions are discharged by the executive government or by an authority brought into existence by the State to carry out public functions even if the authority acts independently and is not subject to government direction and even if its assets and income are not property of the State. And it is significant that s 48 of the Banking Act, held to be invalid in *Melbourne Corporation*, was directed not only to a State but also to an "authority of a State, including a local governing authority". Accordingly, it is of no moment whether the plaintiffs in the first action, other than the Queensland Electricity Commission, represent the Crown in right of the State of Queensland. It is enough that they are agencies of the State, brought into existence for a public purpose ...

But when the Parliament singles out disputes in the electricity industry to which agencies of the State of Queensland are parties and subject them to special procedures which differ from those applying under the Principal Act to the prevention and settlement of industrial disputes generally, and of industrial disputes in the electricity industry in particular, it discriminates against the agencies of the State by subjecting them to a special disability in isolating them from the general law contained in the Principal Act ...

This regime is tailored for Queensland authorities, as distinct from the authorities of other States, and, what is more important, from the general run of employers in the industry ...

Laws of general application applying equally to the States and to others may breach the ***Melbourne Corporation*** doctrine. ***Re Australian Education Union*** considered the extent to which federal laws of general application prescribing minimum employment conditions can apply to the employees of States. The High Court held that a federal law of general application enacted under the arbitration of industrial disputes power in section 51(xxxv) prescribing minimum wages and employment conditions applicable to the vast majority of State employees would not impair the capacity of the States to function as governments. However, the High Court explained that a federal law would be invalid if: (1) it had the effect of prescribing the number and identity of a State's employees; or (2) it sought to prescribe the employment conditions of higher level officials such as Ministers, department heads, and judges.

Re Australian Education Union; Ex parte Victoria ('AEU Case') (1995) 184 CLR 188

Mason CJ, Brennan, Deane, Toohey, Gaudron and McHugh JJ

The fact is that the existence of the States and their Constitutions and their capacity to function as governments would not be impaired by the operation of federal awards made in respect of the vast majority of the employees sought to be covered by the logs of claims, at any rate if the award provisions were confined to minimum wages and working conditions which take appropriate account of any special functions or responsibilities which attach to them. The freedom of State governments to determine terms and conditions of employment of employees would be restricted but that is a consequence of the application of the arbitration power to States. Whether the making of a comprehensive award would result in a relevant impairment is another question which we leave for later discussion ... At this point it is convenient to consider South Australia's argument based on impairment of a State's "integrity" or "autonomy". Although these concepts as applied to a State are by no means precise, they direct attention to aspects of a State's functions which are critical to its capacity to function as a government. It seems to us that critical to that capacity of a State is the government's right to determine the number and identity of the persons whom it wishes to employ, the term of appointment of such persons and, as well, the number and identity of the persons whom it wishes to dismiss with or without notice from its employment on redundancy grounds. An impairment of a State's rights in these respects would, in our view, constitute an infringement of the implied limitation. On this view, the prescription by a federal award of minimum wages and working conditions would not infringe the implied limitation, at least if it takes appropriate account of any special functions or responsibilities which attach to the employees in question. There may be a question, in some areas of employment, whether an award regulating promotion and transfer would amount to an infringement. That is a question which need not be considered. As with other provisions in a comprehensive award, the answer would turn on matters of degree, including the character and responsibilities of the employee.

In our view, also critical to a State's capacity to function as a government is its ability, not only to determine the number and identity of those whom it wishes to engage at the higher levels of government, but also to determine the terms and conditions on which those persons shall be engaged. Hence, Ministers, ministerial assistants and advisers, heads of departments and high level statutory office holders, parliamentary officers and judges would clearly fall within this group. The implied limitation would protect the States from the exercise by the Commission of power to fix minimum wages and working conditions in respect of such persons and possibly others as well. And, in any event, Ministers and judges are not employees of a State ...

The rejection of the arguments put forward by the prosecutor and the intervening States - arguments which would have given the implied limitation a wide-ranging operation - means that the Commission has power to make awards binding the States and their agencies in relation to minimum wages and working conditions which take account of the special functions and responsibilities, if any, of a broad range of public servants and employees, including many members of the SPSF. On the other hand, as we have indicated, the operation of the implied limitation would preclude the Commission from making an award binding the States in relation to qualifications and eligibility for employment, term of appointment and termination of employment, at least on the ground of redundancy. It would also preclude the Commission from making an award binding the States in relation to the terms and conditions of employment or engagement of persons such as Ministers, ministerial assistants and advisers, heads of department and senior office holders - as well as parliamentary officers and judges ...

Austin involved federal legislation enacted under the taxation power in section 51(ii) imposing a special tax on recipients of State judicial pensions (that is, retired State judges). State judicial pensions are paid like salaries from the State Consolidated Revenue Funds and not from a superannuation fund to which contributions have been made. The federal tax was intended to treat retired judges like other high-income earners who were liable to pay a surcharge on superannuation contributions.

The High Court held that the federal legislation was invalid in its application to the retired State judges. The legislation sought to regulate the remuneration of high-level State officials contrary to ***Re Australian Education Union***. In doing so, the law significantly interfered with the capacity of the States to function as governments by impairing the States' choice of the nature of remuneration benefits for their judges and thereby the recruitment and retention of State judges.

Austin v Commonwealth (2003) 215 CLR 185

Gleeson CJ

That the Acts treat the first plaintiff, and other State judges, differently from the manner in which other "high-income earners" generally are treated for the purpose of taxing the value of the annual increases in the liability of their superannuation providers, and differently again from the manner in which Federal judges are treated, is not in dispute ...

Non-discriminatory federal taxes which applied to the States in their capacity as employers were held valid in *Victoria v Commonwealth* (pay-roll tax) and *State Chamber of Commerce and Industry v Commonwealth* (fringe benefits tax) ...

[T]he Parliament's power to make laws with respect to taxation does not extend to enable it to legislate to single out State judges for the imposition of a special fiscal burden. Judges, like other citizens, are subject to general, non-discriminatory taxation, and the mere fact that the incidence of taxation has a bearing upon the amount and form of remuneration they receive does not mean that federal taxation of State judges is an interference with State governmental functions. It is otherwise when, as here, a federal law with respect to taxation treats State judges differently from the general run of high income earners and federal judges, and to their practical disadvantage. That differential treatment is constitutionally impermissible, not because of any financial burden it imposes upon the States, but because of its interference with arrangements made by States for the remuneration of their judges. The practical manifestation of that interference is in its capacity to affect recruitment and retention of judges to perform an essential constitutional function of the State ...

Gaudron, Gummow and Hayne JJ

It is the character in constitutional law of what was done, as it bears upon the plaintiffs and the States of whose courts they are members, which is in issue. What resort to arguments of *economic* equivalence does reveal is that the impugned legislation is *legally* different from other, generally applicable legislation providing for the taxation of other pension and superannuation entitlements. That is, the impugned legislation subjects the plaintiffs, as State judicial officers, to special and legally different taxation arrangements from those generally applicable to persons eligible for, or in receipt of, pensions or superannuation ...

In the present case, the question thus becomes whether the two laws with respect to taxation, the Protected Funds Imposition Act and the Protected Funds Assessment Act, restrict or control the States, in particular New South Wales and Victoria, in respect of the working of the judicial branch of the State government ...

The Protected Funds Imposition Act and the Protected Funds Assessment Act are invalid in their application to the first plaintiff ...

As a general proposition, it is for the State of New South Wales, as for the other States, to determine the terms and conditions upon which it appoints and remunerates the judges of its courts. The concept of remuneration includes provision of retirement and like benefits to judges, spouses and other dependants ... The State of New South Wales chose to discharge its responsibilities for the establishment and maintenance of its judicial branch by providing the unfunded and non-contributory scheme in the NSW Pensions Act ...

Views may vary from time to time as to the relevant importance of these considerations and the measures to give effect to them. But in the constitutional framework in this country these are matters, respecting State judges, for determination by State legislatures. That constitutional framework also constrains those legislatures, in particular, by requiring them to take as they find federal laws of "general application" as part of the system enjoyed by the whole community ...

In its application to the first plaintiff, question 2(a) of the case stated asks whether either or both the Protected Funds Imposition Act and the Protected Funds Assessment Act are invalid on the ground that they so discriminate against New South Wales or so impose a particular disability or burden upon the operations and activity of that State as to be beyond the legislative power of the Commonwealth. That issue may be narrowed by asking whether that result comes about by a sufficiently significant impairment of the exercise by the State of its freedom to select the manner and method for discharge of its constitutional functions respecting the remuneration of the judges of the courts of the State ...

The circumstances that judicial pensions do not require contributions but are fixed as a proportion of the remuneration of a serving judge and are to be paid at the full rate only upon a substantial period of service as well as attainment of a minimum age, indicates the importance attached by legislatures to such schemes in the remuneration of the judicial branch.

There then is posed the "practical question" identified by Starke J in *Melbourne Corporation*. This, in the end, is whether, looking to the substance and operation of the federal laws, there has been, in a significant manner, a curtailment or interference with the exercise of State constitutional power ...

However, one tendency of the federal laws readily apparent from their legal operation is to induce the State to vary the method of its judicial remuneration. The liberty of action of the State in these matters, that being an element of the working of its governmental structure, thereby is impaired. No doubt there is no direct legal obligation imposed by the federal laws requiring such action by the State. But those laws are effectual to do so, as was the Banking Act [in the *Melbourne Corporation case*].

Clarke considered the same legislation in its application to retired State parliamentarians. The High Court reached the same result. The legislation sought to regulate the remuneration of high-level State officials contrary to ***Re Australian Education Union.*** In doing so, the law significantly interfered with the capacity of a State to function as a government by impairing the States' choice of the nature of remuneration benefits for their parliamentarians and thereby the recruitment and retention of State parliamentarians.

Clarke v Federal Commissioner of Taxation (2009) 240 CLR 272

French CJ

In the present case, the factors relevant to the validity of the CPSF Assessment and Imposition Acts in their application to members of the South Australian Parliament are:

1. The State is singled out by reference to benefits and funds established by State laws which are specifically designated by the Commonwealth laws.
2. The laws, in so far as they relate to the PS Scheme, impose a tax specifically upon persons holding office as members of the Parliament of the State.
3. The laws effectively and specifically burden the pension and superannuation benefits able to be enjoyed by members of the State Parliament.
4. Unlike income tax laws and other tax laws of general application, the impugned laws are specifically aimed at the remuneration arrangements between the State and members of its legislature.
5. The significance of the effects of the surcharge upon State legislators was reasonably evidenced by the amendment which the State made to the commutation provisions affecting pension and superannuation entitlements.

In my opinion, when these factors are taken together, the CPSF Assessment and Imposition Acts, read with their specific application to funds designated in reg 177 of the Income Tax Regulations 1936 (Cth), significantly interfered with the remuneration arrangements made between the State and its legislators and, to that extent, significantly burdened the exercise by the State of its powers and functions in fixing the remuneration of its legislators ...

Gummow, Heydon, Kiefel and Bell JJ

[T]he emphasis placed in *Austin* upon both the reference in s 5 of the Assessment Act to "high-income members of constitutionally protected superannuation funds" and the different taxation regime applicable to other superannuation funds as indicative that the Imposition Act and the Assessment Act are not laws of "general application" which the States must take as they find them as part of the system governing the whole community. In *Austin* Gleeson CJ pointed out, as instances of federal laws of "general application" that validly had been imposed on the States, along with taxpayers generally, pay-roll tax and fringe benefits tax ...

[M]embers of a State legislature are within that class of persons "at the higher levels of government" in respect of whom it is critical to the State's capacity to function as a government that it retain the ability to fix the terms and conditions under which they serve upon election to the Parliament of the State in question ...

The practical operation of the Imposition Act and the Assessment Act with respect to State parliamentarians, as much as to State judges in the position of Justice Austin, is to create an obligation on their part to pay a deferred compounding tax when leaving office. An occasion for the imposition of that obligation upon the appellant was his membership of the PSS, which was an incident of his service as a member of the House of Assembly ...

But the interest of the State in attracting, by the making of suitable remuneration, competent persons to serve as legislators, and thus as potential Ministers, is a long-standing constitutional value ... The fixing of the amount and terms of that remuneration is a critical aspect of the capacity of a State to conduct the parliamentary form of government. Numerous provisions of the Constitution assume the continued operation of that form of government in the States ...

Examples of laws that do not impermissibly burden the capacity of States to function as independent governments

Not all federal laws that apply to and regulate the States breach the ***Melbourne Corporation*** doctrine.

The ***Industrial Relations Act Case*** involved a federal minimum wage law that was expressed to cover employees generally. To avoid violating the principles set out in ***Re Australian Education Union***, the High Court read down the statute so that: (1) it did not apply to high-level State officials; and (2) it did not apply to the States in respect of determining the number of persons the States wish to employ, the terms of their appointment, and the number and identity of those they wish to dismiss on redundancy grounds.

Victoria v Commonwealth ('Industrial Relations Act Case') (1996) 187 CLR 416

Brennan CJ, Toohey, Gaudron, McHugh and Gummow JJ

The second argument with respect to the provisions of Div 1 of Pt VIA of the Act is based on the holding in *Re Australian Education Union* that the Commonwealth may not legislate to prevent a State from determining the rights and conditions of those employed at the higher levels of government. According to the argument, the power conferred on the Commission by ss 170AE and 170AH is conferred in terms wide enough to include such employees and, thus, the provisions of Div 1 of Pt VIA are, to that extent, invalid ...

In other words, s 6 can be read as binding the States to the extent that the provisions of the Act do not prevent them from determining the number of persons they wish to employ, the term of their appointment, the number and identity of those they wish to dismiss on redundancy grounds and the terms and conditions of those employed at the higher levels of government.

If s 6 is read down as indicated, the operation of the substantive provisions of the Act is correspondingly limited but their operation is otherwise unaffected. Thus, if any provision of the Act would otherwise operate to prevent the States from determining for themselves any of those matters which were held in *Re Australian Education Union* to be beyond the legislative power of the Commonwealth, the reading down of s 6 precludes invalidity for infringing the limitation on Commonwealth legislative power ...

The ***Melbourne Corporation*** doctrine is about protecting the continuing existence and functioning of the States *as independent governments*. The High Court has emphasised a number of times that the immunity does not protect every activity or function in which a State chooses to engage.

Austin v Commonwealth (2003) 215 CLR 185

Gaudron, Gummow and Hayne JJ

Some guidance as to the content of the limited State immunity is provided by the later decisions in this Court. In *The Tasmanian Dam Case*, Mason J and Brennan J pointed out that the concern was with the capacity of a State to function as a government rather than interference with or impairment of any function which a State government may happen to undertake. Later, in the *Native Title Act Case*, it was said in the joint judgment of six members of the Court that the relevant question for the application of the *Melbourne Corporation* doctrine was not whether Commonwealth law effectively restricted State powers or made their exercise more complex or subjected them to delaying procedures. Their Honours continued:

> The relevant question is whether the Commonwealth law affects what Dixon J called the 'existence and nature' of the State body politic. As the Melbourne Corporation

> Case illustrates, this conception relates to the machinery of government and to the capacity of its respective organs to exercise such powers as are conferred upon them by the general law which includes the Constitution and the laws of the Commonwealth. A Commonwealth law cannot deprive the State of the personnel, property, goods and services which the State requires to exercise its powers and cannot impede or burden the State in the acquisition of what it so requires.

Later in that judgment, their Honours distinguished between a federal law which impaired capacity to exercise constitutional functions and one which merely affected "the ease with which those functions are exercised" ...

In ***Fortescue***, the High Court rejected an argument that a federal tax on mining profits breached the ***Melbourne Corporation*** doctrine. The argument was that the mining tax: (1) reduced the economic viability of the States deciding to set up favourable royalties schemes to attract mining investment in their States; and (2) thereby burdened the States' ability to raise revenue and promote economic development. The High Court held that, even if that was the effect of the federal mining tax, it did not amount to a burden on any State in the exercise of its constitutional functions.

Fortescue Metals Group Ltd v Commonwealth (2013) 250 CLR 548

Hayne, Bell and Keane JJ

Western Australia submitted that it is "central to the capacity of [the] State to function as a government under the Constitution that it have the power to determine the most appropriate means of financing the development of communities in Western Australia". This submission bore a striking resemblance to arguments advanced by that State, and rejected, in *Western Australia v Commonwealth* (*Native Title Act Case*) (1995) 183 CLR 373. Western Australia alleged, in the *Native Title Act Case*, that, because the "capacity and power to grant, regulate and otherwise deal with land and other resources in Western Australia ... is a fundamental sovereign function of the Government of Western Australia as a State", provisions of the *Native Title Act 1993* (Cth) were invalid. But as the plurality held in that case:

> The [Native Title Act] does not purport to affect the machinery of the government of the State. The constitution of the three branches of government is unimpaired; the capacity of the State to engage the servants it needs is unaffected; the acquisition of goods and services is not impeded; nor is any impediment placed in the way of acquiring the land needed for the discharge of the essential functions of the State save in one respect, namely, the payment of compensation. The Act does not impair what Dawson J described [in *Queensland Electricity Commission v Commonwealth*] as 'the capacity to exercise' constitutional functions though it may affect the ease with which those functions are exercised.

If the [Mining Resources Rent Tax] Legislation does affect the States' control over land and resources, the effect is less direct and more speculative than the effect of the Native Title Act. If, then, the MRRT Legislation does diminish the choices available to the executive governments of the States, that diminution does not engage the *Melbourne Corporation* principle.

In *Austin* and *Clarke*, the perceived vice of the Commonwealth law in question lay in its impact upon the capacity of a State to fix the terms of its relationships with its judiciary and legislature as branches of the government of that State. As had previously been pointed out, in *Re Australian Education Union; Ex parte Victoria*, "critical to a State's capacity to function as a government is its ability, not only to determine the number and identity of those whom it wishes to engage at the higher levels of government, but also to determine the terms and conditions on which those persons shall be engaged".

The legislation held invalid in *Queensland Electricity Commission* was directed only at a State. It provided a special set of rules concerning the resolution of an industrial dispute between certain Queensland State electricity authorities and the Electrical Trades Union, which represented employees of those authorities. That is, the law sought to burden the State by providing special rules to govern decisions about the relationship between agencies of the State and their employees. By contrast, in the *Pay-roll Tax Case* (1971) 122 CLR 353, legislation imposing payroll tax on all employers (including the States) was held to be valid even though, of course, it placed a burden on the States.

The MRRT Legislation is not aimed at the States or their entities as was the legislation considered in each of *Melbourne Corporation, Queensland Electricity Commission, Austin* and *Clarke*. The MRRT Legislation does not impose any special burden or disability on the exercise of powers and fulfilment of functions of the States which curtails their capacity to function as governments. The MRRT Legislation does not deny the capacity of any State to fix the rate of royalty for minerals extracted by miners, and no burden upon a State attaches to any decision by the State to raise or lower that rate. If, as the plaintiffs asserted, the MRRT Legislation affects the States' ability to use a reduction in royalty rate as an incentive to attract mining investment in the State, the MRRT Legislation does not impose any limit or burden on any State in the exercise of its constitutional functions ...

23.6 Commonwealth immunity from State laws

The nature of Commonwealth immunity from State laws can be understood by reference to the cases providing examples of permisible and impermissible burdens on the capacity of the Commonwealth to function as an independent government.

Examples of impermissible burdens on the capacity of the Commonwealth to function as an independent government

Cigamatic involved State legislation governing the priority of creditors in the winding-up of a company. Priority concerns the order in which creditors get paid when a corporation is wound up. Lower priority creditors are at risk of insufficient funds being available to pay them. At common law, the Crown always has first priority. New South

Wales legislation prescribed an order of priority in which the Crown in right of the Commonwealth (that is, the Federal Executive Government) did not have first priority. The High Court held that the law was invalid because there is no grant to the States of any power that could authorise State laws regulating the rights and capacities of the Federal Executive Government.

Explained in more modern terms, the Crown's priority is a right forming part of the rights and powers granted to the Federal Executive Government by section 61 of the *Constitution*. There is no grant of power to the States that would allow the States to regulate the scope of federal executive power. State laws attempting to regulate the scope of federal executive power contradict the *Constitution* and impair the separate existence of the Commonwealth as a body politic to which the *Constitution* has distributed certain powers of government.

Commonwealth v Cigamatic Pty Ltd (in liq) (1962) 108 CLR 372

Dixon CJ

In the first instance the Commonwealth rests its claim on the right at common law of the Crown to priority of payment when in any administration of assets debts of equal degree due to the Crown and due to subjects of the Crown come into competition. This right arose from the sovereignty of the Crown and was accordingly expressed in terms of prerogative but it is today one of the fiscal rights of government and of course it clearly attaches to the Commonwealth. The claim of the Commonwealth in the present case resting on this right is, however, denied on the ground that by force of the State Companies Act it is excluded ...

It is not a question, as it appears to me, of interpreting some positive power of the State over a given subject matter. It is not a question of making some implication in favour of the Commonwealth restraining some acknowledged legislative power of the State. If you express the priority belonging to the Commonwealth as a prerogative of the Crown in right of the Commonwealth, the question is whether the legislative powers of the States could extend over one of the prerogatives of the Crown in right of the Commonwealth.

If, as in modern times I think it is more correct to do, you describe it as a fiscal right belonging to the Commonwealth as a government and affecting its Treasury, it is a question of State legislative power affecting to control or abolish a federal fiscal right. It is not a question of the authority of the power of a State to make some general law governing the rights and duties of those who enter into some description of transaction, such as the sale of goods, and of the Commonwealth in its executive arm choosing to enter into a transaction of that description. It is not a question of the exercise of some specific grant of power which according to the very meaning of the terms in which it is defined embraces the subject matter itself: for it is not the plan of the Constitution to grant specific powers to the States over defined subjects

...

Examples of laws that do not impermissibly burden the capacity of States to function as independent governments

The scope of the ***Cigamatic*** doctrine was expressed more clearly in ***Henderson's Case***. The High Court held that State laws cannot alter or abolish the capacities of the Federal Executive Government, because to do so would contradict the *Constitution*. The capacities of the Federal Executive Government are granted by the *Constitution*. However, State laws can regulate the exercise of the capacities of the Federal Executive Government. The key distinction is between the *existence* of Commonwealth capacities and the *exercise* of Commonwealth capacities. State laws cannot regulate the *existence* of Commonwealth capacities but can regulate the *exercise* of Commonwealth capacities provided that the regulation does not impermissibly burden the capacity of the Commonwealth to function as an independent government.

Henderson's Case holds that subjecting federal agencies to ordinary State tenancy laws applicable to all landlords when they own and lease out real estate in the course of their operations does not impermissibly burden the capacity of the Commonwealth to function as an independent government.

Re Residential Tenancies Tribunal of New South Wales v Henderson; Ex parte Defence Housing Authority ('Henderson's Case') (1997) 190 CLR 410

In this case, federal legislation established an agency with the function of owning residential properties and leasing them to defence personnel. The High Court held that State residential tenancies legislation was binding on that agency. The State legislation did not purport to alter, abolish or affect the existence of any capacity or function of the federal agency. The legislation was a law of general application with the effect of regulating the exercise of the federal agency's function.

Brennan CJ

I would draw a distinction between the capacities and functions of the Crown in right of the Commonwealth and the transactions in which that Crown may choose to engage in exercise of its capacities and functions. By "capacities and functions" I mean the rights, powers, privileges and immunities which are collectively described as the "executive power of the Commonwealth" in s 61 of the Constitution. The executive power of the Commonwealth, being vested in the Queen and exercisable by the Governor-General, derives its content mediately or immediately from the Constitution. Executive power may be conferred by a law of the Commonwealth or it may be the power which, at least in earlier times, was seen as part of the Royal prerogative. The executive power of the Commonwealth may be modified by valid laws of the Commonwealth but it is beyond the legislative reach of the States. The States have no legislative power that can modify a grant of power to the Crown in right of the Commonwealth by a law of the Commonwealth nor any legislative power that can modify a prerogative power conferred by the Constitution ...

A State law which purports on its face to impose a burden on the Crown in right of the Commonwealth fails for one of two reasons. If the burden falls on the enjoyment of the Commonwealth prerogative, the law would be offensive to s 61 of the Constitution; if it falls on the enjoyment of a statutory power, it would be inconsistent with the Commonwealth law conferring the power and would be invalid by reason of s 109 ...

However, there is no reason why the Crown in right of the Commonwealth should not be bound by a State law of general application which governs transactions into which the Crown in right of the Commonwealth may choose to enter. The executive power of the Commonwealth, exercised by its choice to enter the transaction, is not affected merely because the incidents of the transaction are prescribed by a State law. That, I understand, was the view which Dixon CJ was expressing in the passage cited from his Honour's judgment in *Cigamatic* ...

Dawson, Toohey and Gaudron JJ

It is necessary at the outset to observe a distinction between the capacities of the Crown on the one hand, by which we mean its rights, powers, privileges and immunities, and the exercise of those capacities on the other ...

The purpose in drawing a distinction between the capacities of the Crown and the exercise of them is to draw a further distinction between legislation which purports to modify the nature of the executive power vested in the Crown – its capacities – and legislation which assumes those capacities and merely seeks to regulate activities in which the Crown may choose to engage in the exercise of those capacities.

In *Cigamatic* it was held that a State legislature had no power to impair the capacities of the Commonwealth executive, but at the same time it was recognised that the Commonwealth might be regulated by State laws of general application in those activities which it carried on in common with other citizens ...

[T]he Constitution is predicated upon the continued separate existence of the Commonwealth and the States, not only in name, but as bodies politic to which the Constitution proceeds to distribute powers of government. In the application of the principle, however, it is necessary to differentiate between the Commonwealth on the one hand and the States on the other.

For the Commonwealth is given enumerated legislative powers which by reason of their content, context or subject matter may authorise it to affect the executive capacities of a State. Where that is so, the basic principle does not afford the State any protection from an exercise of Commonwealth legislative power having that effect ...

The States, on the other hand, do not have specific legislative powers which might be construed as authorising them to restrict or modify the executive capacities of the Commonwealth. The legislative power of the States is an undefined residue which, containing no such authorisation, cannot be construed as extending to the executive capacities of the Commonwealth. No implication limiting an otherwise given power is needed; the character of the Commonwealth as a body politic, armed with executive capacities by the Constitution, by its very nature places those capacities outside the legislative power of another body politic, namely a State, without specific powers in that respect. Having regard to the fundamental principle recognised in *Melbourne Corporation v Commonwealth*, only an express provision in the Constitution could authorise a State to affect the capacities of the Commonwealth executive and there is no such authorisation ...

But the fundamental point made in *Cigamatic* is that in the absence of a like power being conferred upon the States, the priority of the Crown in right of the Commonwealth in the payment of debts is not something over which the States have legislative power ...

The principle that a State law cannot affect the capacities of the Commonwealth executive clearly extends beyond those rights, powers, privileges or immunities which might be described as having their origin in the prerogative ...

Both in *Uther* and *Cigamatic* a distinction is drawn between State laws affecting Commonwealth executive capacities and State laws of general application regulating activities carried on by the Crown in the exercise of those capacities in the same manner as its subjects ...

In that passage Dixon CJ spoke of the legal rights of the Commonwealth in relation to its subjects. Sometimes that relationship will be one of equality: for example, the capacity of the Crown to enter into contracts is no more or less than that of its subjects. Sometimes the relationship will be one of privilege or immunity on the part of the Crown alone: for example, the right to the payment of debts in priority to others. Where the relationship is one of privilege or immunity it is immediately apparent that any diminution of the privilege or immunity will alter the relationship of the Crown with its subjects. But it is equally so when the relationship is one of equality and the Crown is singled out and treated differently, for the relationship then ceases to be one of equality.

When Dixon CJ spoke of general laws he meant laws of general application which bind the Crown and its subjects alike. Such laws are laws which do not have an impact upon any relationship of equality. But a State law which discriminates against the Commonwealth government and imposes a disability upon it will have an impact upon such a relationship and will constitute an interference with its executive capacities ...

Applying these principles to the facts of this case led to the conclusion that the State legislation did not breach the ***Cigamatic*** doctrine.

Re Residential Tenancies Tribunal of New South Wales v Henderson; Ex parte Defence Housing Authority (1997) 190 CLR 410

Dawson, Toohey and Gaudron JJ

Nothing has emerged in this case to indicate any purported alteration or denial of the executive capacity of the Crown in right of the Commonwealth by the provisions of the *Residential Tenancies Act*. The DHA is the creature of the *Defence Housing Authority Act* and that Act is predicated upon the existence of a legal system of which the *Residential Tenancies Act* forms a part. The latter Act does nothing to alter or deny the function of the DHA, notwithstanding that it regulates activities carried out in the exercise of that function in the same way as it regulates the same activities on the part of others. If, and to the extent that, the DHA in carrying out its functions is acting in the exercise of the executive capacity of the Commonwealth, the *Residential Tenancies Act* neither alters nor denies that capacity notwithstanding that it regulates its exercise ...

Spence v Queensland rejected an argument that a State ban on certain categories of people making political donations to State political parties impermissibly burdened the ability of the Commonwealth to conduct federal elections. The case reinforces the idea that the intergovernmental immunities doctrine does not operate to ensure that the Commonwealth can go about its activities entirely untouched by the operation of State laws. After all, the *Constitution* envisages that Australian society is to be governed by a combination of federal and State laws.

Spence v Queensland (2019) 268 CLR 355

One issue in this case concerned an argument by a property developer that Queensland laws prohibiting property developers making political donations to Queensland political parties and candidates for State and local government elections contravened the intergovernmental immunities doctrine. The idea underlying the argument was that the money donated for State and local political purposes would nevertheless have an impact on federal politics and campaigns.

Kiefel CJ, Bell, Gageler and Keane JJ

[I]nsofar as it imposes a limitation on the exercise of State legislative power, application of the doctrine requires consideration of whether an impugned State law is directed at the Commonwealth so as to impose some special disability or burden on the exercise of powers and fulfilment of functions of the Commonwealth which curtails the capacity of the Commonwealth to function as a government.

The nature of the requisite enquiry need only be stated for its non-application in the present case to be apparent. Subdivision 4 of Div 8 of Pt 11 of the *Queensland Electoral Act* and Div 1A of Pt 6 of the *Queensland Local Government Electoral Act* are not directed to the Commonwealth or to any persons or bodies who are uniquely or even primarily participants in a federal governmental process. They do not impose a special disability or burden on the Commonwealth. They do not deny to the Commonwealth the capacity to regulate its own elections. The most that can be said of them is that they deny to some persons and bodies who are participants in federal electoral processes a source of funds that would otherwise be available to be used in such a process.

23.7 DISCUSSION QUESTIONS

1. What is the rationale for the intergovernmental immunities doctrine?
2. What is the methodology for determining whether a law contravenes the intergovernmental immunities doctrine?
3. What sort of laws applying to low-level state officials does ***Re Australian Education Union*** prohibit the Commonwealth from making?
4. How does the intergovernmental immunities doctrine interact with section 109 of the *Constitution*?

5. Problem question: Consider the following hypothetical legislation and scenario. Relying on the corporations power in s 51(xx) of the *Constitution*, the Commonwealth enacts the *Mining Companies (Liquidation Rules) Act 2023*. Section 4 of the Act provides: 'The Crown in each of its capacities has last priority as between the unsecured creditors of any mining company.'

   Western Australia enacts the *Logistics Companies (Liquidation Rules) Act 2023*. Section 7 of the Act provides: 'The Crown in each of its capacities has last priority as between the unsecured creditors of any logistics company.'

   Advise whether section 4 of the Commonwealth Act and section 7 of the State Act breach the intergovernmental immunities doctrine.

RIGHTS OF OUT-OF-STATE RESIDENTS

24

24.1 Overview

This chapter examines section 117 of the *Australian Constitution*, which prohibits States from discriminating against residents in other States.

Australian Constitution

Section 117 Rights of Residents in States

A subject of the Queen, resident in any State, shall not be subject in any other State to any disability or discrimination which would not be equally applicable to him if he were a subject of the Queen resident in such other State.

Section 117 is a peculiar provision. It is not a limitation on power that invalidates offending laws: it confers an immunity on some individuals (namely, those who are Australians resident in a State, but not those who are non-Australians resident in a State or anyone resident in a territory or overseas) from offending laws. The basic methodology for determining whether section 117 applies involves a comparison of the position of the plaintiff in two scenarios. The first scenario is the actual situation of a plaintiff. The second scenario is the hypothetical situation of the plaintiff being a resident in the State alleged to have discriminated against the plaintiff. If the treatment of the plaintiff in both scenarios by the State would be the same, then there is no discrimination and section 117 does not apply. If the treatment of the plaintiff in both scenarios would be different, then there is discrimination on the ground of State residency and section 117 renders the plaintiff immune from the offending law.

Key concepts addressed in this chapter include:

- immunity
- subject of the Queen
- resident in a State
- discrimination.

24.2 Section 117 as an immunity rather than limitation on power

Section 117 is generally understood to serve national unity purposes.

Street v Queensland Bar Association (1989) 168 CLR 461

Mason CJ

This section is one of the comparatively few provisions in the Constitution which was designed to enhance national unity and a real sense of national identity by eliminating disability or discrimination on account of residence in another State ...

Brennan J

[T]he object of s 117 is to secure equal treatment for the individuals whom it protects ...

Toohey J

But underlying the section is the notion to which reference has already been made that Australia is a commonwealth and its laws are to apply equally to all its citizens ...

Dawson J

Reference to the Convention Debates makes it clear enough that the inspiration for s 117 was Art IV, s 2 of the *United States Constitution* which, so far as is relevant, provides that "The Citizens of each State shall be entitled to all Privileges and Immunities of Citizens in the several States." The use of the words "privileges and immunities" occasioned some uncertainties in an Australian context. To overcome this difficulty the provision was recast in a negative form prohibiting the imposition of any disability or discrimination upon the basis of residence in another State. Nevertheless, the fundamental purpose of s 117 is the same as that of Art IV, s 2 ... That purpose is a federal one, both provisions being designed to ensure that persons from one State are treated in another as citizens of the one nation, not as foreigners ...

Section 117 is not expressed as a limitation on power. Rather, section 117 is expressed as an immunity belonging to individuals. In this sense, it is one of the few provisions of the *Constitution* that might be described as being about individual rights.

The consequence of section 117 being expressed as an individual immunity rather than a limitation on power is that section 117 does not operate to invalidate laws. It operates to confer an immunity on an individual from laws that operate contrary to section 117 in respect of that individual, whilst leaving those laws valid and otherwise operative.

Street v Queensland Bar Association (1989) 168 CLR 461

Mason CJ

Its form and language indicate that s 117 is directed towards individuals and their protection from disability or discrimination of the kind contemplated by the section, and that it is not, except to that extent, a restriction on State or Commonwealth legislative power. So a person not subjected to any relevant disability or discrimination by a particular law could not have that law held invalid by establishing that it subjects a third person to such a disability or discrimination; that circumstance would not lead to a striking down of the offending law. Conversely, a person who would, but for s 117, be so affected by the law is immune from its operation in so far as it subjects him to impermissible disability or discrimination, though the law itself remains valid in its application to persons who would not be so affected. Perhaps an enactment might be rendered wholly invalid by s 117 if it depended for its operation upon the imposition of a prohibited form of disability or discrimination, but that is not a question which I need to examine ...

Brennan J

[Section] 117 does not restrict legislative or other power; it does not operate by invalidating the law or the governmental act by or under which the disability or discrimination is imposed. It confers an immunity on individuals or, if we choose to employ the rhetoric of rights, confers a constitutional right not to be subjected to a certain disability or discrimination ...

Section 117 is a singular provision. It does not purport to limit the grant of legislative power to the Commonwealth, to restrict the scope of any power of a State, to afford any protection against the subjection of a person in a State to a disability or discrimination imposed by or under a valid law if that person is not a subject of the Queen resident in another State or to afford any protection against disability or discrimination imposed on any person in a Territory. It is not in terms directed either to the Commonwealth or the States ...

Section 117 makes the persons within the class it describes immune from ("shall not be subject ... to") an impermissible disability or discrimination however imposed ...

Section 117 cuts across the exercise of all governmental power, conferring immunity directly on individuals; their immunity is not a consequence of a limitation on a power. A law which imposes an impermissible disability or discrimination on a protected person is not invalid; it remains in full force and, except in relation to protected persons, in full effect. Uniquely in the Constitution, s 117 carves out an area of personal immunity which cannot be breached by law, executive action or judicial order. It is a constitutional guarantee to each person within the protected class that no law or act of government will subject her or him to a certain kind of disability or discrimination ...

The fact that section 117 is not a limitation on power but confers an individual immunity gives rise to at least two key questions about the scope of section 117. First, does section 117 confer an immunity against executive and judicial action, as well as against legislation? Secondly, does section 117 confer an immunity against federal as well as State laws (and executive and judicial action)? The High Court has not authoritatively answered either question.

There is *dicta* in ***Street*** suggesting that section 117 confers an immunity against offending executive and judicial action as well as against offending legislation.

Street v Queensland Bar Association (1989) 168 CLR 461

Brennan J

Section 117 makes the persons within the class it describes immune from ("shall not be subject ... to") an impermissible disability or discrimination however imposed. Thus the immunity extends to disability or discrimination arising by exercise of executive or judicial, as well as legislative, power. The section does not purport to restrict the immunity it confers to disability or discrimination imposed directly by a law.

An impermissible disability or discrimination may be imposed as well by executive or judicial act as by law. The exercise of an executive discretion against a protected person on the ground that she or he is not a resident in the relevant State ("out-of-State residence") subjects that person' to a relevant discrimination ...

There is also *dicta* in ***Street*** suggesting that section 117 applies in respect of federal, as well as State, laws and governmental action.

Street v Queensland Bar Association (1989) 168 CLR 461

Mason CJ

Notably, it relates not to a State or the Commonwealth, but to a "subject of the Queen". Its form and language indicate that s 117 is directed towards individuals and their protection from disability or discrimination of the kind contemplated by the section, and that it is not, except to that extent, a restriction on State or Commonwealth legislative power ...

Brennan J

It is not in terms directed either to the Commonwealth or the States. It is found in Ch V – "The States" – but its mere presence in Ch V does not mean that it has no operation when a disability or discrimination is imposed by or under a law of the Commonwealth ...

Dawson J

It does not require the uniformity of laws throughout the land. It does, however, require the States, and perhaps the Commonwealth, to recognize in the discharge of their responsibilities that there is but one nation and that the citizens of that nation carry their citizenship with them from State to State. To this end, s 117 does not permit a citizen to be subjected in a State to any disability or discrimination the basis of which is, not the ordinary and proper administration of the affairs of that State, but his residence in another State ...

In ***Leeth***, the High Court avoided deciding whether section 117 applies to federal laws and governmental action, although there is *dicta* in the case in favour of the proposition.

Leeth v Commonwealth (1992) 174 CLR 455

Federal legislation provided that a court sentencing a person for a federal criminal offence should apply the rules of the State or Territory in which the court is sitting concerning minimum non-parole periods. Those rules varied between jurisdictions such that the minimum non-parole period a federal offender might receive would vary based on the location of the court in which the offender was sentenced.

Mason CJ, Dawson and McHugh JJ

And s 117 provides that a subject of the Queen, resident in any State, shall not be subject in any other State to any disability or discrimination which would not be equally applicable to him if he were a subject of the Queen resident in such other State. The Commonwealth contends that s 117 has no application to it but that is a question which remains to be decided ...

Deane and Toohey JJ

The main strength of the argument that the immunity of s 117 applies only in respect of State laws and actions lies in the fact that its terms, which are confined to discrimination or disability on a State-based comparison, are more obviously appropriate for application to State laws or actions than to the laws or governmental actions of the Commonwealth ...

On the other hand, the section is plainly capable of being applied to laws or actions of the Commonwealth and there is some support for this in more recent judgments in this Court: see

Henry v Boehm (1973) 128 CLR 482, at p 495; *Koowarta v Bjelke-Petersen* (1982) 153 CLR 168, at pp 213, 250; *Street v Queensland Bar Association* (1989) 168 CLR, at pp 486, 503–504. The question whether the injunction of s 117 is directed to the Commonwealth as well as the States was not, however, fully canvassed in argument and it is unnecessary to determine it for the purpose of resolving the present case ...

24.3 Who is a 'subject of the Queen'?

Section 117 confers an immunity on subjects of the Queen resident in States. The High Court has made clear that section 117 confers an immunity only on natural persons who are Australian. Section 117 does not confer an immunity on corporations or on non-Australians.

In ***Nolan***, the High Court explained that constitutional references to 'the Queen' are references to the Queen of Australia rather than to the Queen of the United Kingdom or other any other Commonwealth realm. As Chapter 1 explained, constitutional references to 'the Queen' should be read as referring to the reigning monarch.

Nolan v Minister for Immigration and Ethnic Affairs (1988) 165 CLR 178

This case concerned the Commonwealth's power in section 51(xix) to make laws with respect to 'aliens' but required the Court to consider the meaning of a 'subject of the Queen'.

Mason CJ, Wilson, Brennan, Deane, Dawson and Toohey JJ

We would add that, to the extent that there would otherwise be inconsistency in the use of the words "subject of the Queen" in the Constitution, it should be resolved by treating those words as referring, in a modem context, to a subject of the Queen in right of Australia ...

In ***Street***, the High Court explained that the consequence of 'the Queen' being a reference to the Queen of Australia is that section 117 confers immunity only on Australian citizens. Citizens of other Commonwealth realms, including British citizens, who are not also Australian citizens are not protected by section 117 even if they happen to reside in Australia.

Street v Queensland Bar Association (1989) 168 CLR 461

Deane J

The reference in s 117 to a "subject of the Queen" must be understood, in contemporary circumstances, as a reference to a subject of the Queen of Australia, that is to say, as a reference to an Australian citizen (see *Nolan v Minister for Immigration and Ethnic Affairs*) ...

Dawson J

The phrase "subject of the Queen" in s 117 must now be taken to refer to a subject of the Queen in right of Australia and hence to an Australian citizen: *Nolan v Minister for Immigration and Ethnic Affairs* ...

Toohey J

"Subject of the Queen" is now to be understood as referring to the Queen in right of Australia: *Nolan v Minister for Immigration and Ethnic Affairs* ...

Gaudron J

Within our federal framework it is the status of being a "subject of the Queen" (those words being understood to refer to a subject of the Queen in right of Australia: see *Nolan v Minister for Immigration and Ethnic Affairs*) and residence within a State which together signify membership of the body politic constituting that State ...

Following the decision in *Love v Commonwealth* (2020) 270 CLR 152 about non-citizen non-aliens (considered in Chapter 7), it is possible that section 117 confers an immunity on non-aliens (which is a slightly broad category than Australian citizens) resident in any State. While the issue may never arise in practice (because there are very few such people) and therefore require consideration by the High Court, it is difficult to see why a non-citizen, non-alien Aboriginal or Torres Strait Islander person should not be considered a subject of the monarch.

Section 117 does not confer an immunity on corporations. Since 'subject of the Queen' means 'Australian citizen' (or perhaps non-alien), it follows that section 117 confers an immunity only on natural persons. Corporations cannot be subjects of the Queen because they are not natural persons.

Street v Queensland Bar Association (1989) 168 CLR 461

Brennan J

Section 117 is expressed to protect the persons whom the section mentions: "A subject of the Queen, resident in any State." It gives no protection to those who are subjects of the Queen but who are not residents in a State; nor does it give protection to those who are residents in a State who are not subjects of the Queen; nor, of course, does it give protection to those who possess neither qualification. Its protection is limited to natural persons ...

Sweedman v Transport Accident Commission (2006) 226 CLR 362

Gleeson CJ, Gummow, Kirby and Hayne JJ

It is not suggested that a corporation may be a subject of the Queen within the meaning of s 117 ...

24.4 Disability or discrimination not equally applicable to a person if they were resident in another State

To determine whether a person has been subject to a disability or discrimination which would not be equally applicable to that person if the person were resident in another State requires a comparison. Early case law adopted a very formalistic approach to the required comparison. Modern case law takes a more practical approach to the required comparison.

The modern approach to the comparison required by section 117 is usually traced to Stephen J's dissent in ***Henry v Boehm***. In that case, a majority of the High Court held that South Australian rules requiring a person to reside continuously for three months in South Australia before being eligible to practise as a lawyer in South Australia and then for a further 12 months in order to practise unconditionally did not discriminate or impose a disability on lawyers resident in other States. The majority held that the rule applied equally to everyone and for that reason could not be in breach of section 117. The majority also held that 'resident in' a State means 'permanent resident of' a State.

Justice Stephen dissented. He held that 'resident *in* [a] State' is a much broader concept than permanent resident *of* a State. Justice Stephen explained that section 117 requires a comparison between a plaintiff's actual situation and the hypothetical situation of the plaintiff personally being resident in the State alleged to be engaging in discrimination or imposing a disability. The comparison required is *not* between the situation of the plaintiff and the situation of other people resident in the respondent State.

The hypothetical comparison of a plaintiff's personal position is required by section 117's use of the words '*if he were* a subject of the Queen resident in such other State'. In this case, undertaking the individual-focused comparison led Stephen J to the conclusion that the admission rules subjected the plaintiff to a disability or discrimination that would not have been equally applicable to him if he resided in South Australia.

Henry v Boehm (1973) 128 CLR 482

Stephen J (dissenting)

[F]or the section to apply it must appear that were the particular subject of the Queen resident in the legislating State this fact would of itself either wholly remove the disability or discrimination or else so affect its application to him as to cause it no longer to be equally as applicable to him as it in fact is having regard to his actual circumstances of residence ...

The question is, then, whether the present Admission Rules impose a relevant disadvantage by reference to circumstances of residence ...

The present plaintiff, a Victorian practitioner residing and practising in Melbourne, will thus have to reside continuously in South Australia for three months before becoming eligible to apply for admission and then for a further period of one year after his conditional admission before he can be granted absolute admission as a practitioner in that State ...

The practical effect of these requirements of residence in South Australia will no doubt be, in all but very exceptional cases, to compel an inter-State practitioner to give up his practice in that other State if he is to be admitted to practice in South Australia.

How then does s 117 bear upon the requirements of these rules; do they subject the plaintiff to any disability or discrimination which would not be equally applicable to him if he were resident in South Australia? To answer this question the process of comparison which the section calls for must be undertaken, the plaintiff's actual situation must be contrasted with a hypothetical one which differs from actuality only because it assumes the plaintiff to be a resident of South Australia; in making the comparison called for by s 117 no departure from actuality is to be made other than this one, relating to the plaintiff's residence. Being thus resident in South Australia but having previously been admitted to practice in Victoria, his position when wishing to use that qualification in order to gain admission to practice in South Australia is to be contrasted with his position as it is in fact.

The obvious difference between that hypothetical situation and the situation with which the plaintiff is in fact confronted is that were he already resident in South Australia he would not have to abandon his existing Victorian abode so as to reside continuously in South Australia, first for three months and then for a further twelve months. This difference arises because of the express requirements of the rules. If this may be said to be a "disability or discrimination" to which the plaintiff is subject by reason of his being "resident" in Victoria, using these words in the sense which they bear in s 117, then that section will apply ...

[Section] 117 does not concern itself with the making of any comparison between the situation of the plaintiff were he a resident of South Australia and the situation of other residents of that State. What s 117 calls for is, instead, a comparison between the plaintiff's situation as it is in fact and as it would be were he a resident of South Australia ...

In the present case, it is both unnecessary and undesirable to seek to define in advance the precise breadth of meaning of "resident" in s 117; it suffices to conclude, as I do, that the residence provisions of the Admission Rules do involve the imposition of a disadvantage by reference to the circumstance of being resident in a State, within the meaning of s 117. The requirement of r 27(1), continuous residence for at least three months, and of r 28(1), continuous residence for a further twelve months, each prescribes a condition of living in South Australia for a substantial and unbroken period of time which readily conforms to one of the ordinary meanings of "resident", a meaning unconfined by concepts of permanency or of the location of the permanent home.

I also conclude that these two rules do subject the plaintiff, resident in Victoria, to a disability or discrimination which would not be equally applicable to him if he were resident, in the sense indicated above, in South Australia. They require him to leave his established home in Victoria and to live continuously in South Australia for considerable periods of time. Were he resident, in the sense indicated above, in South Australia the requirement of the rules would bear quite differently and less onerously upon him; their precise effect in such a hypothetical situation cannot be predicated but at least it is clear that were he resident in South Australia the disability involved in lengthy residence away from Victoria would either be wholly absent or be substantially mitigated ...

The leading case on section 117 is ***Street v Queensland Bar Association***. The High Court overruled ***Henry v Boehm*** and adopted Stephen J's approach. The case concerned Queensland legal profession admission rules that: (1) allowed barristers admitted in other States to practise in Queensland only if they intended to practise principally in Queensland; and (2) imposed a one-year conditional practice admission period during which the barrister had to prove he or she practised principally in Queensland. The High Court held that Street, a barrister resident in New South Wales, was immune from these rules by reason of section 117.

The High Court in ***Street*** agreed with Stephen J's approach of comparing a plaintiff's position with the hypothetical situation of the plaintiff being resident in the respondent State. The High Court also agreed with Stephen J that residency in a State is a broader concept than permanent residency. The judgments of Mason CJ and Brennan J typify the reasoning of the High Court.

Street v Queensland Bar Association (1989) 168 CLR 461

Mason CJ

Mr Street claims that he is unable to comply with the amended Rules without foregoing his place of residence in Sydney and his practice as a barrister in New South Wales. He contends that the amended Rules are in contravention of ... s 117 of the Constitution ... I favour the "distributive" interpretation adopted by ... Stephen J in *Henry v Boehm* in preference to that taken by the majority ... The assimilation of "resident" in s 117 to "permanent resident" is arbitrary in the sense that the word is capable of a variety of shades of meaning and there is nothing in the context to support the selection of a meaning which works the greatest restriction in the operation of the section ...

It seems to me that for s 117 to apply it must appear that, were the person a resident of the legislating State, that different circumstance would of itself either effectively remove the disability or discrimination or, for practical purposes in all the circumstances, mitigate its effect to the point where it would be rendered illusory.

A disability or discrimination is rendered illusory if the fact of residence would substantially deprive it of its onerous nature. A requirement of continuous residence for a certain period would in my view be an example of a law whose onerous effect on non-residents would be rendered illusory under this test ...

I would apply the principle, along the lines mentioned above, that s 117 renders a disability or discrimination invalid if the notional fact of residence within the legislating State would effectively remove the disability or discrimination or substantially deprive it of its onerous nature.

Applying this test to Mr Street's appeal, it is clear that a requirement that he cease to practise outside Queensland would be less onerous were he to live in Queensland, although it would still be a significant imposition ...

If Mr Street were a resident of Queensland, a requirement that he cease practice outside Queensland would still permit him to practise in the State in which he resided. This stands in marked contrast to the actual position, which requires Mr Street to practise only in a State in which he does not reside. The disability is one imposed upon residents and non-residents alike, but in the case of a resident its effect is mitigated to a very substantial extent. Only a non-resident is prohibited from practising where he resides. The inconvenience suffered by a resident as a result of compliance with the requirement pales in significance beside the onerous and in many cases impossible burden imposed upon a non-resident ...

Brennan J

When a protected person alleges that he is subject to a disability or discrimination in a State other than his State of residence, a comparison must be made between the disability or discrimination to which the person is purportedly subjected in the other State and the disability or discrimination, if any, to which he would be subjected "if he were a subject of the Queen resident in such other State." The actual position of the protected person must be compared with the hypothetical position. The starting point is to identify the disability or discrimination to which the protected person is purportedly subject; the next enquiry is whether, if that person were resident in the State in which she or he is purportedly subject to the disability or discrimination, she or he would be subject to it to the same extent ("equally applicable"). Section 117 is focussed on the individual and looks to the actual benefit withheld or the actual burden imposed on the individual ("applicable to him"), not to the means by which the protected person is subjected to it. For the purposes of s 117, it is not the indifferent application of a law to in-State and out-of-State residents which is material, but the actual impact on a protected person of a law or governmental act in comparison with the impact it would have if that person were an in-State resident ...

The proposition that for a subject of the Queen to be "resident in a State" there must be a degree of permanency can be accepted only to the extent that it is relevant to distinguish residence from a mere sojourn or transient presence in a State. Otherwise "resident" imports no particular degree of permanence ...

To require residence in Queensland and cessation of practice in New South Wales as conditions of admission in Queensland of New South Wales barristers who are otherwise qualified to be admitted in Queensland is to discriminate against those who do not reside in Queensland on the ground of out-of-State residence. An applicant qualified for admission who resides in New South Wales must give up the barrister's place of residence and must cease to practise in the State of actual residence but if the barrister were resident in Queensland the place of residence could be retained and practice in the State of residence could be carried on ...

Goryl v Greyhound Australia confirms that the comparison required by section 117 is between a plaintiff's actual position and the hypothetical position of that same plaintiff being resident in the respondent State. A New South Wales resident was injured in New South Wales during a bus trip from Brisbane to the New South Wales central coast town of Wyong. The injured person sued the bus company for damages in a Queensland court. Queensland legislation limited the damages recoverable by non-residents to the damages recoverable in that person's State of residence, which in this case was significantly lower than the damages recoverable under Queensland law. The High Court found that this law discriminated against the injured person merely because she was a non-resident. It followed that the injured person was immune from that law by reason of section 117 and therefore entitled to recover the larger quantum of damages.

Goryl v Greyhound Australia Pty Ltd (1994) 179 CLR 463

Dawson and Toohey JJ

It is only s 20 which imposes a disability upon a person whose principal place of residence is not Queensland. It does so by preventing him from recovering in Queensland an amount of damages for bodily injury sustained in a motor accident which is greater than he might have recovered under the law of the State or Territory in which he had his principal place of residence. Section 20 applies irrespective of whether the accident occurred within or outside Queensland and regardless of whether the vehicle or vehicles involved were insured in Queensland ...

Where the damages recoverable in the claimant's principal place of residence are less than those recoverable in Queensland, s 20 must operate to the disadvantage of the claimant. It is common ground that the damages recoverable in New South Wales are, because of restrictions imposed by the *Motor* Accidents Act 1988 (NSW), less than those recoverable in Queensland ...

In applying s 117, the comparison to be made is between a non-resident in the position of the plaintiff and the position she would be in if she were resident in Queensland. Quite clearly the plaintiff is, upon such a comparison, subject both to a disability and to discrimination. She can only recover damages at a lesser rate than if she were resident in Queensland. And there is no difference in the plaintiff's position which would justify the distinction which is drawn. It is not because she claims the benefit of any welfare or insurance scheme established for and financed by Queensland residents. The disability imposed upon the plaintiff is imposed regardless of any indemnity available to the respondent under the statutory insurance scheme. It is simply a case of a non-resident being afforded under Queensland law different and less advantageous treatment than she would be afforded if she were a resident of Queensland. In our view, s 117 applies to relieve the plaintiff from that disability or discrimination so that she is entitled to recover the full amount of damages recoverable in Queensland at common law ...

Palmer v Western Australia (No 2) provides a straightforward example of the methodology. Western Australian legislation was argued to single out Palmer, a resident of Queensland and the owner of a mining company in dispute with the West Australian government, for the imposition of certain legal disabilities. Those disabilities would apply to Palmer regardless of his State of residency, including if he lived in Western Australia. Accordingly, section 117 was not triggered.

Palmer v Western Australia (No 2) [2021] HCA 31

Kiefel CJ, Gageler, Keane, Gordon, Steward and Gleeson JJ

First, the plaintiff argued that the Amending Act singles him out for a "disability" or "discrimination" of a kind forbidden by s 117 of the *Constitution*. Plainly, it does not. The prohibition in s 117 is against subjecting an Australian citizen resident in one State to a disability or discrimination in another State which would not be equally applicable to that Australian citizen if the Australian citizen were resident in that other State. Even if the Amending Act could be characterised as singling the plaintiff out for a disability or discrimination, that disability or discrimination could not be characterised as being of a kind forbidden by s 117 of the *Constitution*. Neither the legal operation nor the practical operation of the whole or any part of the Amending Act would be any different if the plaintiff were resident in Western Australia instead of being resident in Queensland.

In ***Sweedman v Transport Accident Commission***, the High Court distinguished the facts of ***Goryl***. The case highlights the need to examine carefully whether the differential treatment complained of involves discrimination based on residency in another State or discrimination based on some other ground. Section 117 applies only where discrimination is based on residency in another State. In this case, the differential treatment was held to be a function of whether or not contributions had been paid into a fund rather than a function of residency.

Sweedman v Transport Accident Commission (2006) 226 CLR 362

Sweedman, a New South Wales resident driving a New South Wales registered car, was the at-fault driver in a car accident that happened in New South Wales involving a Victorian registered car with Victorian residents Mr and Mrs Sutton as driver and passenger. The Victorians were compensated for their injuries by the Victorian Transport Accident Commission ('TAC') in accordance with Victorian legislation, using funds contributed by Victorian car registration charges. The Victorian legislation allowed the TAC to recover the money it pays to victims from at-fault drivers, unless the at-fault driver is also covered by the TAC indemnity fund.

Sweedman argued that her liability to the TAC breached section 117 because had she been a Victorian resident her car would have been registered in Victoria and therefore she would also have been covered by the TAC indemnity fund. The High Court held that the differential treatment was not a function of State residency. The differential treatment was a function of whether contributions had been paid to the TAC fund. The comparison required was between

Sweedman as a New South Wales resident driving a car registered in New South Wales and Sweedman as a Victorian resident driving a car registered in New South Wales. In both scenarios, Sweedman would not have been covered by the TAC indemnity fund. Therefore, there was no discrimination based on residency.

Gleeson CJ, Gummow, Kirby and Hayne JJ

The appellant is a subject of the Queen resident in New South Wales and contends that she is exposed in Victoria to a disability or discrimination, amenability to a s 104(1) claim by the Commission, which would not be equally applicable to her were she a resident of Victoria ...

[U]nlike the Queensland statute considered in *Goryl*, the operation of s 94 of the Victorian Act is not conditioned by residence. Rather, it is conditioned by payment for the relevant period of the "transport accident charge" for the registered motor vehicle in question. Section 94 would have obliged the Commission to indemnify Mr Sutton as driver of a motor vehicle registered in Victoria in respect of any liability in respect of an injury to or death of a person arising out of its use in Victoria or in another State or Territory, but not in respect of any period where the transport accident charge had not been paid. Payment of that charge to the Commission is required by s 109 and receipts are paid by the Commission into the Fund established under s 27. The obligation of payment of the charge is imposed upon the owner of a "registered motor vehicle" (s 109(1)). That expression has a detailed definition in s 3 which refers to the *Road Safety Act 1986* (Vic) and the regulations made thereunder. The upshot is that a vehicle may be registered in Victoria even though its owner or user or both ordinarily reside outside that State, and a person must not use a vehicle on a highway in Victoria unless registered under that statute or exempted under the regulations.

On the other hand, the effect of s 111 of the Victorian Act is that the owner of the car driven by the appellant, being insured under the third-party system in New South Wales, would not have been required, while in Victoria, to have paid the transport accident charge.

The words in brackets in s 104(1), namely "other than a person who is entitled to be indemnified under section 94", reflect the circumstance that the entitlement against the Commission under s 94 is, in a practical if not also legal sense, the consideration for payment of the transport accident charge. Without the exception to s 104(1), the benefit under s 94 conferred by payment of the transport accident charge required by s 109 would have been rendered nugatory.

The appellant is exposed to the claim by the Commission to indemnity under s 104(1). She is not exempted. But that is because she was not required to have paid the charge levied under the Victorian scheme.

There is no differential treatment in s 94 attributable to residence so as to attract s 117 of the Constitution. A non-Victorian resident who owned or drove a registered motor vehicle in respect of which the s 109 charge had been paid would have the benefit of the exception to s 104(1); a Victorian resident who had failed to pay the charge would not have the benefit of the exception.

By its terms, s 117 of the Constitution is addressed to protecting a "subject of the Queen" from disability or discrimination in the form of laws and governmental actions or policies. It is therefore necessary in each case where s 117 is invoked to examine the operation of the impugned law, action or policy, to decide whether the discrimen it chooses concerns the State residence of the person who invokes its provisions ...

24.5 The nature of discrimination and disability

Discrimination includes both legal and practical discrimination. ***Street*** explains that discrimination and disability are concepts concerned as much with practical effects as with legal form. Discrimination and disability may be imposed directly (where residency in another State is the criterion for differential treatment) or indirectly (where the practical effect of the law or policy has differential effect on out-of-State residents).

The law at issue in ***Street*** involved indirect discrimination, because the law did not, in express terms, single out out-of-State residents for differential treatment but nevertheless had that practical effect. The law at issue in ***Goryl*** involved direct discrimination, because the law singled out out-of-State residents for differential treatment.

Street v Queensland Bar Association (1989) 168 CLR 461

Mason CJ

In terms, the section applies when a subject of the Queen, being an out-of-State resident, is subject to a disability or discrimination under State law. The section is not concerned with the form in which that law subjects the individual to the disability or discrimination. It is enough that the individual is subject to either of the two detriments, whatever the means by which this is brought about by State law. This approach to the interpretation of the section accords with the approach generally adopted in connection with statutes proscribing particular kinds of discrimination ...

In terms, the section applies when a subject of the Queen, being an out-of-State resident, is subject to a disability or discrimination under State law. The section is not concerned with the form in which that law subjects the individual to the disability or discrimination. It is enough that the individual is subject to either of the two detriments, whatever the means by which this is brought about by State law. This approach to the interpretation of the section accords with the approach generally adopted in connection with statutes proscribing particular kinds of discrimination ...

It would make little sense to deal with laws which have a discriminatory purpose and leave untouched laws which have a discriminatory effect.

Once this is recognized, it becomes all the more difficult to accept that the fact that a requirement as to residence is universal in its application is necessarily an answer to the operation of s 117. Such a requirement may have a discriminatory effect in relation to an out-of-State resident for the simple reason that it may apply unequally by subjecting him to a greater burden or disadvantage than that imposed on a resident of the legislating State. So to forbid all persons from wearing a turban is on its face a prohibition applicable to all persons without distinction, but in effect is a discrimination based upon religious grounds because its only impact will fall upon adherents of a creed or religion which requires the wearing of turbans: *Mandla v Dowell Lee; Bhinder v Canadian National Railway Company* (1985) 2 SCR 561. An examination of the effect of the relevant law is both necessary to avoid depriving s 117 of practical effect and consistent with its emphasis upon the position of the individual ...

Brennan J

To determine the impact of a measure on an individual, it is necessary to take account of the particular circumstances of the individual. In other words, s.117 is concerned not only with legal rights and liabilities but also with the actual effect on the individual of legal rights and liabilities produced by a law or other governmental action ...

Discrimination of the relevant kind may be imposed on a ground which is expressed in another way. A governmental measure which is expressed to discriminate on a ground which is a natural or ordinary concomitant of out-of-State residence may single out protected persons for differential treatment as surely as if out-of-State residence were the ground expressed. In such a case, a protected person who is singled out for differential treatment or who is at a disadvantage in comparison with a notional in-State counterpart is subject to discrimination which "would not be equally applicable to him if he were a subject of the Queen resident in such other State." The facts in *Mandla v Dowell Lee* (1983) 2 AC 548 furnish an example ...

[D]iscrimination on a prohibited ground may be effected, albeit indirectly, when the expressed ground is a natural or ordinary concomitant of the prohibited ground ...

Deane J

[Section] 117 protects a non-resident from being subjected to disability or discrimination of the type to which it refers regardless of whether the disability or discrimination is directly imposed or is the indirect result of the operation of the relevant legislative provisions (eg the confinement of a benefit or advantage to a class which excludes a non-resident). If the substance of what is involved is disability or discrimination of the type referred to in s 117, mere differences in the form of the relevant legislation will not be effective to take it beyond the reach of the constitutional guarantee ...

Gaudron J

[T]he protection of s 117 extends to indirect discrimination or different treatment which is revealed by the disparate impact of the matter in complaint ...

McHugh J

Section 117 does not say, however, that the offending law must select residence as the criterion of disability or discrimination. The section requires that a subject of the Queen resident in any State "shall not be subject in any other State to any disability or discrimination which would not be equally applicable to him if he were a subject of the Queen resident in such other State". But in the language of modern anti-discrimination law, a law may have a discriminatory operation or a discriminatory impact. A person resident in another State may be subject to disability or discrimination on the ground of his residence not only from the direct operation of a law but also from its factual impact ...

There is no reason why the terms "discrimination" and "disability" in s 117 should be given a meaning which excludes disability or discrimination arising from the factual operation of the law. If the interstate resident is subject to a disability or discrimination because of his residence, it cannot matter whether that result is produced because the law selects interstate residence as the basis of discrimination or the imposition of the disability, or because the law selects some other criterion which operates so as to give rise in fact to a disability or discrimination on the ground of interstate residence. Discrimination can arise just as readily from a law which treats as equals those who are different as it can from a law which treats differently those whose circumstances are not materially different ...

The plaintiff in ***Sweedman*** made her argument on the ground of indirect discrimination. Her essential argument was that contributing to the TAC fund through car registration fees was part and parcel of being a Victorian resident. The High Court accepted that indirect discrimination would give rise to section 117 immunity, but held that there was no indirect discrimination in this case.

Sweedman v Transport Accident Commission (2006) 226 CLR 362

Gleeson CJ, Gummow, Kirby and Hayne JJ

The appellant urged consideration of the reality of the situation as that to which s 117 is directed. That emphasis upon substance and practical operation of laws impugned for contravention of a constitutional limitation or restriction on power may be accepted ...

There is no differential treatment in s 94 attributable to residence so as to attract s 117 of the Constitution. A non-Victorian resident who owned or drove a registered motor vehicle in respect of which the s 109 charge had been paid would have the benefit of the exception to s 104(1); a Victorian resident who had failed to pay the charge would not have the benefit of the exception ...

24.6 When discrimination against out-of-State residents is not prohibited

It has always been accepted that section 117 does not require States to afford residents in other States equality of treatment in all respects. An obvious example is voting rights. Section 117 does not require any State to permit out-of-State residents to vote in elections for its State Parliament.

High Court judges have not agreed on the explanation as to why section 117 does not require States to afford residents in other States equal treatment in all respects. Some judges explain that this result is a consequence of overriding concepts and structures of the *Constitution*, such as the existence of the States as autonomous entities within the federation. Some judges explain that this result is a consequence of the fact that differential treatment that is appropriate to any actual difference in a person's position does not amount to discrimination. Some judges combine the two explanations.

The judgments in ***Goryl*** summarise the differing approaches to this issue offered in ***Street***. The joint judgment of Dawson and Toohey JJ in ***Goryl*** suggests the different explanations are unlikely to lead to any practical difference in the outcome of particular cases. However, given the limited case law on section 117, it remains to be seen whether that is true.

Goryl v Greyhound Australia Pty Ltd (1994) 179 CLR 463

Deane and Gaudron JJ

It was acknowledged by all members of the Court in *Street v Queensland Bar Association* that not every instance of different treatment in a State of a resident of another State involves a disability or discrimination for the purposes of s 117 of the Constitution. The acknowledgements to that effect were based on different constitutional considerations. Mason CJ based his acknowledgement on the need to preserve "the autonomy of the States", while Dawson and Toohey JJ referred respectively to a disability or discrimination arising out of or in consequence of "the ordinary and proper administration of the affairs of that State" and "the capacity of the States to regulate their own affairs within a federal system". A different approach was taken by Brennan J and McHugh J, their Honours allowing only that s 117 was subject to implications necessarily drawn from the Constitution. Deane J acknowledged that a disability flowing "naturally from the structure of the particular State, the limited scope of its legislative powers or the nature of the particular right, privilege, immunity or other advantage or power to which it relates" is outside s 117, a view which does not differ greatly in substance from the view Gaudron J expressed, namely, that there is no disability or discrimination involved if different treatment proceeds from and is appropriate to a genuine difference ...

Dawson and Toohey JJ

In *Street v Queensland Bar Association* all members of the Court were of the view that not every kind of differential treatment by a State of a resident of another State amounts to the imposition of a disability or to discrimination within the meaning of s 117. Whether this is because the very nature of the federation, predicated as it is upon government State by State with the inevitable consequence that laws will differ from State to State, requires limits to be placed upon s 117 or whether it is because some kinds of differential treatment, properly viewed, cannot be described as imposing a disability or a discrimination, is probably a difference in approach rather than principle ...

The most obvious example of differential treatment which lies outside s 117 is the exclusion of non-residents from voting in a State election ...

No doubt difficulties may be encountered when one proceeds beyond the more obvious examples of differential treatment which are not prohibited by s 117. Guidance is then to be found in the object of s 117 which is to foster the concept of Australian nationhood, recognizing at the same time the capacity of the States to govern their own communities which is an essential feature of the federation.

McHugh J

However, s 117 has to be construed in the context of the constitutional premise that the States are autonomous entities in the federation. That premise requires an interpretation of s 117 that recognises the special relationship between a State and its people and the special responsibilities of a State to its people. Consequently, some subject-matters are the sole concern of a State and fall outside the scope of s 117. State elections provide a ready example ...

Apart from these necessary exceptions to s 117, which are derived from the assumptions and structure of the Constitution itself, no reason exists for narrowing the scope of that section. In particular, there is no ground for reading into the provision a requirement that the disability or discrimination must be "unjustifiable", "unreasonable" or "disproportionate to a legitimate State objective" ...

24.7 DISCUSSION QUESTIONS

1. Why is a law that breaches section 117 not invalid?
2. Why can States discriminate against out-of-State corporations?
3. What is the methodology for determining whether a law has discriminated against a person based on the person being an out-of-State resident?
4. When can a State discriminate against people based on out-of-State residency?
5. Problem question: Consider the following hypothetical scenario. The New South Wales Department of Health introduces a new selection process for medical internships for Bachelor of Medicine graduates. There are two application rounds. Applications are made approximately six months before students complete their medical degrees. In round one, only students enrolled in an accredited medical degree offered by a university located in New South Wales may apply. In round two, students enrolled in any accredited medical degree may apply. There are usually very few places left after round one.

   A medical student enrolled in an accredited degree at a university in Queensland seeks your advice as to whether she may apply in round one.

APPENDIX: THE AUSTRALIAN CONSTITUTION

Commonwealth of Australia Constitution Act 1900

Incorporating alterations of the Constitution made by

- *Constitution Alteration (Senate Elections) 1906*
- *Constitution Alteration (State Debts) 1909*
- *Constitution Alteration (State Debts) 1928*
- *Constitution Alteration (Social Services) 1946*
- *Constitution Alteration (Aboriginals) 1967*
- *Constitution Alteration (Senate Casual Vacancies) 1977*
- *Constitution Alteration (Retirement of Judges) 1977*
- *Constitution Alteration (Referendums) 1977*

An Act to constitute the Commonwealth of Australia

[9th July 1900]

WHEREAS the people of New South Wales, Victoria, South Australia, Queensland, and Tasmania, humbly relying on the blessing of Almighty God, have agreed to unite in one indissoluble Federal Commonwealth under the Crown of the United Kingdom of Great Britain and Ireland, and under the Constitution hereby established: And whereas it is expedient to provide for the admission into the Commonwealth of other Australasian Colonies and possessions of the Queen: Be it therefore enacted by the Queen's most Excellent Majesty, by and with the advice and consent of the Lords Spiritual and Temporal, and Commons, in this present Parliament assembled, and by the authority of the same, as follows:

1 Short title

This Act may be cited as the Commonwealth of Australia Constitution Act.

2 Act to extend to the Queen's successors

The provisions of this Act referring to the Queen shall extend to Her Majesty's heirs and successors in the sovereignty of the United Kingdom.

3 Proclamation of Commonwealth

It shall be lawful for the Queen, with the advice of the Privy Council, to declare by proclamation that, on and after a day therein appointed, not being later than one year after the passing of this Act, the people of New South Wales, Victoria, South Australia, Queensland, and Tasmania, and also, if Her Majesty is satisfied that the people of Western Australia have agreed thereto, of Western Australia, shall be united in a Federal Commonwealth under the name of the Commonwealth of Australia. But the Queen may, at any time after the proclamation, appoint a Governor-General for the Commonwealth.

4 Commencement of Act

The Commonwealth shall be established, and the Constitution of the Commonwealth shall take effect, on and after the day so appointed. But the Parliaments of the several colonies may at any time after the passing of this Act make any such laws, to come into operation on the day so appointed, as they might have made if the Constitution had taken effect at the passing of this Act.

5 Operation of the Constitution and laws

This Act, and all laws made by the Parliament of the Commonwealth under the Constitution, shall be binding on the courts, judges, and people of every State and of every part of the Commonwealth, notwithstanding anything in the laws of any State; and the laws of the Commonwealth shall be in force on all British ships, the Queen's ships of war excepted, whose first port of clearance and whose port of destination are in the Commonwealth.

6 Definitions

The Commonwealth shall mean the Commonwealth of Australia as established under this Act.

The States shall mean such of the colonies of New South Wales, New Zealand, Queensland, Tasmania, Victoria, Western Australia, and South Australia, including the northern territory of South Australia, as for the time being are parts of the Commonwealth, and such colonies or territories as may be admitted into or established by the Commonwealth as States; and each of such parts of the Commonwealth shall be called ***a State***.

Original States shall mean such States as are parts of the Commonwealth at its establishment.

7 Repeal of Federal Council Act

The Federal Council of Australasia Act, 1885, is hereby repealed, but so as not to affect any laws passed by the Federal Council of Australasia and in force at the establishment of the Commonwealth.

Any such law may be repealed as to any State by the Parliament of the Commonwealth, or as to any colony not being a State by the Parliament thereof.

8 Application of Colonial Boundaries Act

After the passing of this Act the Colonial Boundaries Act, 1895, shall not apply to any colony which becomes a State of the Commonwealth; but the Commonwealth shall be taken to be a self-governing colony for the purposes of that Act.

9 Constitution

The Constitution of the Commonwealth shall be as follows:

The Constitution

This Constitution is divided as follows:

Chapter I – The Parliament

Part I – General

1 Legislative power

The legislative power of the Commonwealth shall be vested in a Federal Parliament, which shall consist of the Queen, a Senate, and a House of Representatives, and which is hereinafter called ***The Parliament***, or ***The Parliament of the Commonwealth***.

2 Governor-General

A Governor-General appointed by the Queen shall be Her Majesty's representative in the Commonwealth, and shall have and may exercise in the Commonwealth during the Queen's pleasure, but subject to this Constitution, such powers and functions of the Queen as Her Majesty may be pleased to assign to him.

3 Salary of Governor-General

There shall be payable to the Queen out of the Consolidated Revenue fund of the Commonwealth, for the salary of the Governor-General, an annual sum which, until the Parliament otherwise provides, shall be ten thousand pounds.

The salary of a Governor-General shall not be altered during his continuance in office.

4 Provisions relating to Governor-General

The provisions of this Constitution relating to the Governor-General extend and apply to the Governor-General for the time being, or such person as the Queen may appoint to administer the Government of the Commonwealth; but no such person shall be entitled to receive any salary from the Commonwealth in respect of any other office during his administration of the Government of the Commonwealth.

5 Sessions of Parliament. Prorogation and dissolution

The Governor-General may appoint such times for holding the sessions of the Parliament as he thinks fit, and may also from time to time, by Proclamation or otherwise, prorogue the Parliament, and may in like manner dissolve the House of Representatives.

Summoning Parliament

After any general election the Parliament shall be summoned to meet not later than thirty days after the day appointed for the return of the writs.

First session

The Parliament shall be summoned to meet not later than six months after the establishment of the Commonwealth.

6 Yearly session of Parliament

There shall be a session of the Parliament once at least in every year, so that twelve months shall not intervene between the last sitting of the Parliament in one session and its first sitting in the next session.

Part II – The Senate

7 The Senate

The Senate shall be composed of senators for each State, directly chosen by the people of the State, voting, until the Parliament otherwise provides, as one electorate.

But until the Parliament of the Commonwealth otherwise provides, the Parliament of the State of Queensland, if that State be an Original State, may make laws dividing the State into divisions and determining the number of senators to be chosen for each division, and in the absence of such provision the State shall be one electorate.

Until the Parliament otherwise provides there shall be six senators for each Original State. The Parliament may make laws increasing or diminishing the number of senators for each State, but so that equal representation of the several Original States shall be maintained and that no Original State shall have less than six senators. The senators shall be chosen for a term of six years, and the names of the senators chosen for each State shall be certified by the Governor to the Governor-General.

8 Qualification of electors

The qualification of electors of senators shall be in each State that which is prescribed by this Constitution, or by the Parliament, as the qualification for electors of members of the House of Representatives; but in the choosing of senators each elector shall vote only once.

9 Method of election of senators

The Parliament of the Commonwealth may make laws prescribing the method of choosing senators, but so that the method shall be uniform for all the States. Subject to any such law, the Parliament of each State may make laws prescribing the method of choosing the senators for that State.

Times and places

The Parliament of a State may make laws for determining the times and places of elections of senators for the State.

10 Application of State laws

Until the Parliament otherwise provides, but subject to this Constitution, the laws in force in each State, for the time being, relating to elections for the more numerous House of the Parliament of the State shall, as nearly as practicable, apply to elections of senators for the State.

11 Failure to choose senators

The Senate may proceed to the despatch of business, notwithstanding the failure of any State to provide for its representation in the Senate.

12 Issue of writs

The Governor of any State may cause writs to be issued for elections of senators for the State. In case of the dissolution of the Senate the writs shall be issued within ten days from the proclamation of such dissolution.

13 Rotation of senators

As soon as may be after the Senate first meets, and after each first meeting of the Senate following a dissolution thereof, the Senate shall divide the senators chosen for each State into two classes, as nearly equal in number as practicable; and the places of the senators of the first class shall become vacant at the expiration of ~~the third year~~ **three years**, and the places of those of the second class at the expiration of ~~the sixth year~~ **six years**, from the beginning of their term of service; and afterwards the places of senators shall become vacant at the expiration of six years from the beginning of their term of service.

The election to fill vacant places shall be made ~~in the year at the expiration of which~~ **within one year before** the places are to become vacant.

For the purposes of this section the term of service of a senator shall be taken to begin on the first day of ~~January~~ **July** following the day of his election, except in the cases of the first election and of the election next after any dissolution of the Senate, when it shall be taken to begin on the first day of ~~January~~ **July** preceding the day of his election.

14 Further provision for rotation

Whenever the number of senators for a State is increased or diminished, the Parliament of the Commonwealth may make such provision for the vacating of the places of senators for the State as it deems necessary to maintain regularity in the rotation.

~~15 Casual vacancies~~

~~**If the place of a senator becomes vacant before the expiration of his term of service, the House of Parliament of the State for which he was chosen shall, sitting and voting together, choose a person to hold the place until the expiration of the term, or until the election of a successor as hereinafter provided, whichever first happens. But if the Houses of Parliament of the State are not in session at the time when the vacancy is notified, the Governor of the State, with the advice of the Executive Council thereof,**~~

~~may appoint a person to hold the place until the expiration of fourteen days after the beginning of the next session of the Parliament of the State, or until the election of a successor, whichever first happens.~~

~~At the next general election of members of the House of Representatives, or at the next election of senators for the State, whichever first happens, a successor shall, if the term has not then expired, be chosen to hold the place from the date of his election until the expiration of the term.~~

~~The name of any senator so chosen or appointed shall be certified by the Governor of the State to the Governor-General.~~

If the place of a senator becomes vacant before the expiration of his term of service, the Houses of Parliament of the State for which he was chosen, sitting and voting together, or, if there is only one House of that Parliament, that House, shall choose a person to hold the place until the expiration of the term. But if the Parliament of the State is not in session when the vacancy is notified, the Governor of the State, with the advice of the Executive Council thereof, may appoint a person to hold the place until the expiration of fourteen days from the beginning of the next session of the Parliament of the State or the expiration of the term, whichever first happens.

Where a vacancy has at any time occurred in the place of a senator chosen by the people of a State and, at the time when he was so chosen, he was publicly recognized by a particular political party as being an endorsed candidate of that party and publicly represented himself to be such a candidate, a person chosen or appointed under this section in consequence of that vacancy, or in consequence of that vacancy and a subsequent vacancy or vacancies, shall, unless there is no member of that party available to be chosen or appointed, be a member of that party.

Where:

(a) in accordance with the last preceding paragraph, a member of a particular political party is chosen or appointed to hold the place of a senator whose place had become vacant; and

(b) before taking his seat he ceases to be a member of that party (otherwise than by reason of the party having ceased to exist);

he shall be deemed not to have been so chosen or appointed and the vacancy shall be again notified in accordance with section twenty-one of this Constitution.

The name of any senator chosen or appointed under this section shall be certified by the Governor of the State to the Governor-General.

If the place of a senator chosen by the people of a State at the election of senators last held before the commencement of the *Constitution Alteration (Senate Casual Vacancies) 1977* became vacant before that commencement and, at that commencement, no person chosen by the House or Houses of Parliament of the State, or appointed by the Governor of the State, in consequence of that vacancy, or in consequence of that vacancy and a subsequent vacancy or vacancies, held office, this section applies as if the place of the senator chosen by the people of the State had become vacant after that commencement.

A senator holding office at the commencement of the *Constitution Alteration (Senate Casual Vacancies) 1977*, being a senator appointed by the Governor of a State in consequence of a vacancy that had at any time occurred in the place of a senator

chosen by the people of the State, shall be deemed to have been appointed to hold the place until the expiration of fourteen days after the beginning of the next session of the Parliament of the State that commenced or commences after he was appointed and further action under this section shall be taken as if the vacancy in the place of the senator chosen by the people of the State had occurred after that commencement.

Subject to the next succeeding paragraph, a senator holding office at the commencement of the *Constitution Alteration (Senate Casual Vacancies) 1977* who was chosen by the House or Houses of Parliament of a State in consequence of a vacancy that had at any time occurred in the place of a senator chosen by the people of the State shall be deemed to have been chosen to hold office until the expiration of the term of service of the senator elected by the people of the State.

If, at or before the commencement of the *Constitution Alteration (Senate Casual Vacancies) 1977*, a law to alter the Constitution entitled "*Constitution Alteration (Simultaneous Elections) 1977*" came into operation, a senator holding office at the commencement of that law who was chosen by the House or Houses of Parliament of a State in consequence of a vacancy that had at any time occurred in the place of a senator chosen by the people of the State shall be deemed to have been chosen to hold office:

(a) **if the senator elected by the people of the State had a term of service expiring on the thirtieth day of June, One thousand nine hundred and seventy-eight – until the expiration or dissolution of the first House of Representatives to expire or be dissolved after that law came into operation; or**
(b) **if the senator elected by the people of the State had a term of service expiring on the thirtieth day of June, One thousand nine hundred and eighty-one – until the expiration or dissolution of the second House of Representatives to expire or be dissolved after that law came into operation or, if there is an earlier dissolution of the Senate, until that dissolution.**

16 Qualifications of senator

The qualifications of a senator shall be the same as those of a member of the House of Representatives.

17 Election of President

The Senate shall, before proceeding to the despatch of any other business, choose a senator to be the President of the Senate; and as often as the office of President becomes vacant the Senate shall again choose a senator to be the President.

The President shall cease to hold his office if he ceases to be a senator. He may be removed from office by a vote of the Senate, or he may resign his office or his seat by writing addressed to the Governor-General.

18 Absence of President

Before or during any absence of the President, the Senate may choose a senator to perform his duties in his absence.

19 Resignation of senator

A senator may, by writing addressed to the President, or to the Governor-General if there is no President or if the President is absent from the Commonwealth, resign his place, which thereupon shall become vacant.

20 Vacancy by absence

The place of a senator shall become vacant if for two consecutive months of any session of the Parliament he, without the permission of the Senate, fails to attend the Senate.

21 Vacancy to be notified

Whenever a vacancy happens in the Senate, the President, or if there is no President or if the President is absent from the Commonwealth the Governor-General, shall notify the same to the Governor of the State in the representation of which the vacancy has happened.

22 Quorum

Until the Parliament otherwise provides, the presence of at least one-third of the whole number of the senators shall be necessary to constitute a meeting of the Senate for the exercise of its powers.

23 Voting in the Senate

Questions arising in the Senate shall be determined by a majority of votes, and each senator shall have one vote. The President shall in all cases be entitled to a vote; and when the votes are equal the question shall pass in the negative.

Part III - The House of Representatives

24 Constitution of House of Representatives

The House of Representatives shall be composed of members directly chosen by the people of the Commonwealth, and the number of such members shall be, as nearly as practicable, twice the number of the senators.

The number of members chosen in the several States shall be in proportion to the respective numbers of their people, and shall, until the Parliament otherwise provides, be determined, whenever necessary, in the following manner:

(i) a quota shall be ascertained by dividing the number of the people of the Commonwealth, as shown by the latest statistics of the Commonwealth, by twice the number of the senators;

(ii) the number of members to be chosen in each State shall be determined by dividing the number of the people of the State, as shown by the latest statistics of the Commonwealth, by the quota; and if on such division there is a remainder greater than one-half of the quota, one more member shall be chosen in the State.

But notwithstanding anything in this section, five members at least shall be chosen in each Original State.

25 Provision as to races disqualified from voting

For the purposes of the last section, if by the law of any State all persons of any race are disqualified from voting at elections for the more numerous House of the Parliament of the State, then, in reckoning the number of the people of the State or of the Commonwealth, persons of that race resident in that State shall not be counted.

26 Representatives in first Parliament

Notwithstanding anything in section twenty-four, the number of members to be chosen in each State at the first election shall be as follows:

New South Wales	twenty-three;
Victoria	twenty;
Queensland	eight;
South Australia	six;
Tasmania	five;

Provided that if Western Australia is an Original State, the numbers shall be as follows:

New South Wales	twenty-six;
Victoria	twenty-three;
Queensland	nine;
South Australia	seven;
Western Australia	five;
Tasmania	five.

27 Alteration of number of members

Subject to this Constitution, the Parliament may make laws for increasing or diminishing the number of the members of the House of Representatives.

28 Duration of House of Representatives

Every House of Representatives shall continue for three years from the first meeting of the House, and no longer, but may be sooner dissolved by the Governor-General.

29 Electoral divisions

Until the Parliament of the Commonwealth otherwise provides, the Parliament of any State may make laws for determining the divisions in each State for which members of the House of Representatives may be chosen, and the number of members to be chosen for each division. A division shall not be formed out of parts of different States.

In the absence of other provision, each State shall be one electorate.

30 Qualification of electors

Until the Parliament otherwise provides, the qualification of electors of members of the House of Representatives shall be in each State that which is prescribed by the law of the State as the qualification of electors of the more numerous House of Parliament of the State; but in the choosing of members each elector shall vote only once.

31 Application of State laws

Until the Parliament otherwise provides, but subject to this Constitution, the laws in force in each State for the time being relating to elections for the more numerous House of the Parliament of the State shall, as nearly as practicable, apply to elections in the State of members of the House of Representatives.

32 Writs for general election

The Governor-General in Council may cause writs to be issued for general elections of members of the House of Representatives.

After the first general election, the writs shall be issued within ten days from the expiry of a House of Representatives or from the proclamation of a dissolution thereof.

33 Writs for vacancies

Whenever a vacancy happens in the House of Representatives, the Speaker shall issue his writ for the election of a new member, or if there is no Speaker or if he is absent from the Commonwealth the Governor-General in Council may issue the writ.

34 Qualifications of members

Until the Parliament otherwise provides, the qualifications of a member of the House of Representatives shall be as follows:

(i) he must be of the full age of twenty-one years, and must be an elector entitled to vote at the election of members of the House of Representatives, or a person qualified to become such elector, and must have been for three years at the least a resident within the limits of the Commonwealth as existing at the time when he is chosen;

(ii) he must be a subject of the Queen, either natural-born or for at least five years naturalized under a law of the United Kingdom, or of a Colony which has become or becomes a State, or of the Commonwealth, or of a State.

35 Election of Speaker

The House of Representatives shall, before proceeding to the despatch of any other business, choose a member to be the Speaker of the House, and as often as the office of Speaker becomes vacant the House shall again choose a member to be the Speaker.

The Speaker shall cease to hold his office if he ceases to be a member. He may be removed from office by a vote of the House, or he may resign his office or his seat by writing addressed to the Governor-General.

36 Absence of Speaker

Before or during any absence of the Speaker, the House of Representatives may choose a member to perform his duties in his absence.

37 Resignation of member

A member may by writing addressed to the Speaker, or to the Governor-General if there is no Speaker or if the Speaker is absent from the Commonwealth, resign his place, which thereupon shall become vacant.

38 Vacancy by absence

The place of a member shall become vacant if for two consecutive months of any session of the Parliament he, without the permission of the House, fails to attend the House.

39 Quorum

Until the Parliament otherwise provides, the presence of at least one-third of the whole number of the members of the House of Representatives shall be necessary to constitute a meeting of the House for the exercise of its powers.

40 Voting in House of Representatives

Questions arising in the House of Representatives shall be determined by a majority of votes other than that of the Speaker. The Speaker shall not vote unless the numbers are equal, and then he shall have a casting vote.

Part IV – Both Houses of the Parliament

41 Right of electors of States

No adult person who has or acquires a right to vote at elections for the more numerous House of the Parliament of a State shall, while the right continues, be prevented by any law of the Commonwealth from voting at elections for either House of the Parliament of the Commonwealth.

42 Oath or affirmation of allegiance

Every senator and every member of the House of Representatives shall before taking his seat make and subscribe before the Governor-General, or some person authorised by him, an oath or affirmation of allegiance in the form set forth in the schedule to this Constitution.

43 Member of one House ineligible for other

A member of either House of the Parliament shall be incapable of being chosen or of sitting as a member of the other House.

44 Disqualification

Any person who:

(i) is under any acknowledgment of allegiance, obedience, or adherence to a foreign power, or is a subject or a citizen or entitled to the rights or privileges of a subject or a citizen of a foreign power; or

(ii) is attainted of treason, or has been convicted and is under sentence, or subject to be sentenced, for any offence punishable under the law of the Commonwealth or of a State by imprisonment for one year or longer; or

(iii) is an undischarged bankrupt or insolvent; or

(iv) holds any office of profit under the Crown, or any pension payable during the pleasure of the Crown out of any of the revenues of the Commonwealth; or

(v) has any direct or indirect pecuniary interest in any agreement with the Public Service of the Commonwealth otherwise than as a member and in common with the other members of an incorporated company consisting of more than twenty-five persons;

shall be incapable of being chosen or of sitting as a senator or a member of the House of Representatives.

But subsection (iv) does not apply to the office of any of the Queen's Ministers of State for the Commonwealth, or of any of the Queen's Ministers for a State, or to the receipt of pay, half pay, or a pension, by any person as an officer or member of the Queen's navy or army, or to the receipt of pay as an officer or member of the naval or military forces of the Commonwealth by any person whose services are not wholly employed by the Commonwealth.

45 Vacancy on happening of disqualification

If a senator or member of the House of Representatives:

(i) becomes subject to any of the disabilities mentioned in the last preceding section; or

(ii) takes the benefit, whether by assignment, composition, or otherwise, of any law relating to bankrupt or insolvent debtors; or

(iii) directly or indirectly takes or agrees to take any fee or honorarium for services rendered to the Commonwealth, or for services rendered in the Parliament to any person or State;

his place shall thereupon become vacant.

46 Penalty for sitting when disqualified

Until the Parliament otherwise provides, any person declared by this Constitution to be incapable of sitting as a senator or as a member of the House of Representatives shall, for every day on which he so sits, be liable to pay the sum of one hundred pounds to any person who sues for it in any court of competent jurisdiction.

47 Disputed elections

Until the Parliament otherwise provides, any question respecting the qualification of a senator or of a member of the House of Representatives, or respecting a vacancy in either House of the Parliament, and any question of a disputed election to either House, shall be determined by the House in which the question arises.

48 Allowance to members

Until the Parliament otherwise provides, each senator and each member of the House of Representatives shall receive an allowance of four hundred pounds a year, to be reckoned from the day on which he takes his seat.

49 Privileges etc. of Houses

The powers, privileges, and immunities of the Senate and of the House of Representatives, and of the members and the committees of each House, shall be such as are declared by the Parliament, and until declared shall be those of the Commons House of Parliament of the United Kingdom, and of its members and committees, at the establishment of the Commonwealth.

50 Rules and orders

Each House of the Parliament may make rules and orders with respect to:

(i) the mode in which its powers, privileges, and immunities may be exercised and upheld;

(ii) the order and conduct of its business and proceedings either separately or jointly with the other House.

Part V – Powers of the Parliament

51 Legislative powers of the Parliament

The Parliament shall, subject to this Constitution, have power to make laws for the peace, order, and good government of the Commonwealth with respect to:

(i) trade and commerce with other countries, and among the States;

(ii) taxation; but so as not to discriminate between States or parts of States;

(iii) bounties on the production or export of goods, but so that such bounties shall be uniform throughout the Commonwealth;

(iv) borrowing money on the public credit of the Commonwealth;

(v) postal, telegraphic, telephonic, and other like services;

(vi) the naval and military defence of the Commonwealth and of the several States, and the control of the forces to execute and maintain the laws of the Commonwealth;

(vii) lighthouses, lightships, beacons and buoys;

(viii) astronomical and meteorological observations;

(ix) quarantine;

(x) fisheries in Australian waters beyond territorial limits;

(xi) census and statistics;

(xii) currency, coinage, and legal tender;

(xiii) banking, other than State banking; also State banking extending beyond the limits of the State concerned, the incorporation of banks, and the issue of paper money;

(xiv) insurance, other than State insurance; also State insurance extending beyond the limits of the State concerned;

(xv) weights and measures;

(xvi) bills of exchange and promissory notes;

(xvii) bankruptcy and insolvency;

(xviii) copyrights, patents of inventions and designs, and trade marks;

(xix) naturalization and aliens;

(xx) foreign corporations, and trading or financial corporations formed within the limits of the Commonwealth;

(xxi) marriage;

(xxii) divorce and matrimonial causes; and in relation thereto, parental rights, and the custody and guardianship of infants;

(xxiii) invalid and old-age pensions;

(xxiiiA) **the provision of maternity allowances, widows' pensions, child endowment, unemployment, pharmaceutical, sickness and hospital benefits, medical and dental services (but not so as to authorize any form of civil conscription), benefits to students and family allowances;**

(xxiv) the service and execution throughout the Commonwealth of the civil and criminal process and the judgments of the courts of the States;

(xxv) the recognition throughout the Commonwealth of the laws, the public Acts and records, and the judicial proceedings of the States;

(xxvi) the people of any race, ~~other than the aboriginal race in any State~~, for whom it is deemed necessary to make special laws;

(xxvii) immigration and emigration;

(xxviii) the influx of criminals;

(xxix) external affairs;

(xxx) the relations of the Commonwealth with the islands of the Pacific;

(xxxi) the acquisition of property on just terms from any State or person for any purpose in respect of which the Parliament has power to make laws;

(xxxii) the control of railways with respect to transport for the naval and military purposes of the Commonwealth;

(xxxiii) the acquisition, with the consent of a State, of any railways of the State on terms arranged between the Commonwealth and the State;

(xxxiv) railway construction and extension in any State with the consent of that State;

(xxxv) conciliation and arbitration for the prevention and settlement of industrial disputes extending beyond the limits of any one State;

(xxxvi) matters in respect of which this Constitution makes provision until the Parliament otherwise provides;

(xxxvii) matters referred to the Parliament of the Commonwealth by the Parliament or Parliaments of any State or States, but so that the law shall extend only to States by whose Parliaments the matter is referred, or which afterwards adopt the law;

(xxxviii) the exercise within the Commonwealth, at the request or with the concurrence of the Parliaments of all the States directly concerned, of any power which can at the establishment of this Constitution be exercised only by the Parliament of the United Kingdom or by the Federal Council of Australasia;

(xxxix) matters incidental to the execution of any power vested by this Constitution in the Parliament or in either House thereof, or in the Government of the Commonwealth, or in the Federal Judicature, or in any department or officer of the Commonwealth.

52 Exclusive powers of the Parliament

The Parliament shall, subject to this Constitution, have exclusive power to make laws for the peace, order, and good government of the Commonwealth with respect to:

(i) the seat of government of the Commonwealth, and all places acquired by the Commonwealth for public purposes;

(ii) matters relating to any department of the public service the control of which is by this Constitution transferred to the Executive Government of the Commonwealth;
(iii) other matters declared by this Constitution to be within the exclusive power of the Parliament.

53 Powers of the Houses in respect of legislation

Proposed laws appropriating revenue or moneys, or imposing taxation, shall not originate in the Senate. But a proposed law shall not be taken to appropriate revenue or moneys, or to impose taxation, by reason only of its containing provisions for the imposition or appropriation of fines or other pecuniary penalties, or for the demand or payment or appropriation of fees for licences, or fees for services under the proposed law.

The Senate may not amend proposed laws imposing taxation, or proposed laws appropriating revenue or moneys for the ordinary annual services of the Government.

The Senate may not amend any proposed law so as to increase any proposed charge or burden on the people.

The Senate may at any stage return to the House of Representatives any proposed law which the Senate may not amend, requesting, by message, the omission or amendment of any items or provisions therein. And the House of Representatives may, if it thinks fit, make any of such omissions or amendments, with or without modifications.

Except as provided in this section, the Senate shall have equal power with the House of Representatives in respect of all proposed laws.

54 Appropriation Bills

The proposed law which appropriates revenue or moneys for the ordinary annual services of the Government shall deal only with such appropriation.

55 Tax Bill

Laws imposing taxation shall deal only with the imposition of taxation, and any provision therein dealing with any other matter shall be of no effect.

Laws imposing taxation, except laws imposing duties of customs or of excise, shall deal with one subject of taxation only; but laws imposing duties of customs shall deal with duties of customs only, and laws imposing duties of excise shall deal with duties of excise only.

56 Recommendation of money votes

A vote, resolution, or proposed law for the appropriation of revenue or moneys shall not be passed unless the purpose of the appropriation has in the same session been recommended by message of the Governor-General to the House in which the proposal originated.

57 Disagreement between the Houses

If the House of Representatives passes any proposed law, and the Senate rejects or fails to pass it, or passes it with amendments to which the House of Representatives will not agree, and if after an interval of three months the House of Representatives, in the same or the next session, again passes the proposed law with or without any amendments which have been made, suggested, or agreed to by the Senate, and the Senate rejects or fails to pass it, or passes it with amendments to which the House of Representatives will not agree, the Governor-General may dissolve the Senate and the House of Representatives simultaneously. But such dissolution shall not take place within six months before the date of the expiry of the House of Representatives by effluxion of time.

If after such dissolution the House of Representatives again passes the proposed law, with or without any amendments which have been made, suggested, or agreed to by the Senate, and the Senate rejects or fails to pass it, or passes it with amendments to which the House of Representatives will not agree, the Governor-General may convene a joint sitting of the members of the Senate and of the House of Representatives.

The members present at the joint sitting may deliberate and shall vote together upon the proposed law as last proposed by the House of Representatives, and upon amendments, if any, which have been made therein by one House and not agreed to by the other, and any such amendments which are affirmed by an absolute majority of the total number of the members of the Senate and House of Representatives shall be taken to have been carried, and if the proposed law, with the amendments, if any, so carried is affirmed by an absolute majority of the total number of the members of the Senate and House of Representatives, it shall be taken to have been duly passed by both Houses of the Parliament, and shall be presented to the Governor-General for the Queen's assent.

58 Royal assent to Bills

When a proposed law passed by both Houses of the Parliament is presented to the Governor-General for the Queen's assent, he shall declare, according to his discretion, but subject to this Constitution, that he assents in the Queen's name, or that he withholds assent, or that he reserves the law for the Queen's pleasure.

Recommendations by Governor-General

The Governor-General may return to the house in which it originated any proposed law so presented to him, and may transmit therewith any amendments which he may recommend, and the Houses may deal with the recommendation.

59 Disallowance by the Queen

The Queen may disallow any law within one year from the Governor-General's assent, and such disallowance on being made known by the Governor-General by speech or message to each of the Houses of the Parliament, or by Proclamation, shall annul the law from the day when the disallowance is so made known.

60 Signification of Queen's pleasure on Bills reserved

A proposed law reserved for the Queen's pleasure shall not have any force unless and until within two years from the day on which it was presented to the Governor-General for the Queen's assent the Governor-General makes known, by speech or message to each of the Houses of the Parliament, or by Proclamation, that it has received the Queen's assent.

Chapter II - The Executive Government

61 Executive power

The executive power of the Commonwealth is vested in the Queen and is exercisable by the Governor-General as the Queen's representative, and extends to the execution and maintenance of this Constitution, and of the laws of the Commonwealth.

62 Federal Executive Council

There shall be a Federal Executive Council to advise the Governor-General in the government of the Commonwealth, and the members of the Council shall be chosen and summoned by the Governor-General and sworn as Executive Councillors, and shall hold office during his pleasure.

63 Provisions referring to Governor-General

The provisions of this Constitution referring to the Governor-General in Council shall be construed as referring to the Governor-General acting with the advice of the Federal Executive Council.

64 Ministers of State

The Governor-General may appoint officers to administer such departments of State of the Commonwealth as the Governor-General in Council may establish.

Such officers shall hold office during the pleasure of the Governor-General. They shall be members of the Federal Executive Council, and shall be the Queen's Ministers of State for the Commonwealth.

Ministers to sit in Parliament

After the first general election no Minister of State shall hold office for a longer period than three months unless he is or becomes a senator or a member of the House of Representatives.

65 Number of Ministers

Until the Parliament otherwise provides, the Ministers of State shall not exceed seven in number, and shall hold such offices as the Parliament prescribes, or, in the absence of provision, as the Governor-General directs.

66 Salaries of Ministers

There shall be payable to the Queen, out of the Consolidated Revenue Fund of the Commonwealth, for the salaries of the Ministers of State, an annual sum which, until the Parliament otherwise provides, shall not exceed twelve thousand pounds a year.

67 Appointment of civil servants

Until the Parliament otherwise provides, the appointment and removal of all other officers of the Executive Government of the Commonwealth shall be vested in the

Governor-General in Council, unless the appointment is delegated by the Governor-General in Council or by a law of the Commonwealth to some other authority.

68 Command of naval and military forces

The command in chief of the naval and military forces of the Commonwealth is vested in the Governor-General as the Queen's representative.

69 Transfer of certain departments

On a date or dates to be proclaimed by the Governor-General after the establishment of the Commonwealth the following departments of the public service in each State shall become transferred to the Commonwealth: posts, telegraphs, and telephones; naval and military defence; lighthouses, lightships, beacons, and buoys; quarantine.

But the departments of customs and of excise in each State shall become transferred to the Commonwealth on its establishment.

70 Certain powers of Governors to vest in Governor-General

In respect of matters which, under this Constitution, pass to the Executive Government of the Commonwealth, all powers and functions which at the establishment of the Commonwealth are vested in the Governor of a Colony, or in the Governor of a Colony with the advice of his Executive Council, or in any authority of a Colony, shall vest in the Governor-General, or in the Governor-General in Council, or in the authority exercising similar powers under the Commonwealth, as the case requires.

Chapter III - The Judicature

71 Judicial power and Courts

The judicial power of the Commonwealth shall be vested in a Federal Supreme Court, to be called the High Court of Australia, and in such other federal courts as the Parliament creates, and in such other courts as it invests with federal jurisdiction. The High Court shall consist of a Chief Justice, and so many other Justices, not less than two, as the Parliament prescribes.

72 Judges' appointment, tenure, and remuneration

The Justices of the High Court and of the other courts created by the Parliament:

(i) shall be appointed by the Governor-General in Council;
(ii) shall not be removed except by the Governor-General in Council, on an address from both Houses of the Parliament in the same session, praying for such removal on the ground of proved misbehaviour or incapacity;
(iii) shall receive such remuneration as the Parliament may fix; but the remuneration shall not be diminished during their continuance in office.

The appointment of a Justice of the High Court shall be for a term expiring upon his attaining the age of seventy years, and a person shall not be appointed as a Justice of the High Court if he has attained that age.

The appointment of a Justice of a court created by the Parliament shall be for a term expiring upon his attaining the age that is, at the time of his appointment, the maximum age for Justices of that court and a person shall not be appointed as a Justice of such a court if he has attained the age that is for the time being the maximum age for Justices of that court.

Subject to this section, the maximum age for Justices of any court created by the Parliament is seventy years.

The Parliament may make a law fixing an age that is less than seventy years as the maximum age for Justices of a court created by the Parliament and may at any time repeal or amend such a law, but any such repeal or amendment does not affect the term of office of a Justice under an appointment made before the repeal or amendment.

A Justice of the High Court or of a court created by the Parliament may resign his office by writing under his hand delivered to the Governor-General.

Nothing in the provisions added to this section by the *Constitution Alteration (Retirement of Judges) 1977* affects the continuance of a person in office as a Justice of a court under an appointment made before the commencement of those provisions.

A reference in this section to the appointment of a Justice of the High Court or of a court created by the Parliament shall be read as including a reference to the appointment of a person who holds office as a Justice of the High Court or of a court created by the Parliament to another office of Justice of the same court having a different status or designation.

73 Appellate jurisdiction of High Court

The High Court shall have jurisdiction, with such exceptions and subject to such regulations as the Parliament prescribes, to hear and determine appeals from all judgments, decrees, orders, and sentences:

(i) of any Justice or Justices exercising the original jurisdiction of the High Court;
(ii) of any other federal court, or court exercising federal jurisdiction; or of the Supreme Court of any State, or of any other court of any State from which at the establishment of the Commonwealth an appeal lies to the Queen in Council;
(iii) of the Inter-State Commission, but as to questions of law only; and the judgment of the High Court in all such cases shall be final and conclusive.

But no exception or regulation prescribed by the Parliament shall prevent the High Court from hearing and determining any appeal from the Supreme Court of a State in any matter in which at the establishment of the Commonwealth an appeal lies from such Supreme Court to the Queen in Council.

Until the Parliament otherwise provides, the conditions of and restrictions on appeals to the Queen in Council from the Supreme Courts of the several States shall be applicable to appeals from them to the High Court.

74 Appeal to Queen in Council

No appeal shall be permitted to the Queen in Council from a decision of the High Court upon any question, howsoever arising, as to the limits inter se of the Constitutional powers of the Commonwealth and those of any State or States, or as to the limits inter se of the Constitutional powers of any two or more States, unless the High Court shall certify that the question is one which ought to be determined by Her Majesty in Council.

The High Court may so certify if satisfied that for any special reason the certificate should be granted, and thereupon an appeal shall lie to Her Majesty in Council on the question without further leave.

Except as provided in this section, this Constitution shall not impair any right which the Queen may be pleased to exercise by virtue of Her Royal prerogative to grant special leave of appeal from the High Court to Her Majesty in Council. The Parliament may make laws limiting the matters in which such leave may be asked, but proposed laws containing any such limitation shall be reserved by the Governor-General for Her Majesty's pleasure.

75 Original jurisdiction of High Court

In all matters:

(i) arising under any treaty;
(ii) affecting consuls or other representatives of other countries;
(iii) in which the Commonwealth, or a person suing or being sued on behalf of the Commonwealth, is a party;
(iv) between States, or between residents of different States, or between a State and a resident of another State;
(v) in which a writ of Mandamus or prohibition or an injunction is sought against an officer of the Commonwealth;

the High Court shall have original jurisdiction.

76 Additional original jurisdiction

The Parliament may make laws conferring original jurisdiction on the High Court in any matter:

(i) arising under this Constitution, or involving its interpretation;
(ii) arising under any laws made by the Parliament;
(iii) of Admiralty and maritime jurisdiction;
(iv) relating to the same subject-matter claimed under the laws of different States.

77 Power to define jurisdiction

With respect to any of the matters mentioned in the last two sections the Parliament may make laws:

(i) defining the jurisdiction of any federal court other than the High Court;
(ii) defining the extent to which the jurisdiction of any federal court shall be exclusive of that which belongs to or is invested in the courts of the States;
(iii) investing any court of a State with federal jurisdiction.

78 Proceedings against Commonwealth or State

The Parliament may make laws conferring rights to proceed against the Commonwealth or a State in respect of matters within the limits of the judicial power.

79 Number of judges

The federal jurisdiction of any court may be exercised by such number of judges as the Parliament prescribes.

80 Trial by jury

The trial on indictment of any offence against any law of the Commonwealth shall be by jury, and every such trial shall be held in the State where the offence was committed, and if the offence was not committed within any State the trial shall be held at such place or places as the Parliament prescribes.

Chapter IV - Finance and Trade

81 Consolidated Revenue Fund

All revenues or moneys raised or received by the Executive Government of the Commonwealth shall form one Consolidated Revenue Fund, to be appropriated for the purposes of the Commonwealth in the manner and subject to the charges and liabilities imposed by this Constitution.

82 Expenditure charged thereon

The costs, charges, and expenses incident to the collection, management, and receipt of the Consolidated Revenue Fund shall form the first charge thereon; and the revenue of the Commonwealth shall in the first instance be applied to the payment of the expenditure of the Commonwealth.

83 Money to be appropriated by law

No money shall be drawn from the Treasury of the Commonwealth except under appropriation made by law.

But until the expiration of one month after the first meeting of the Parliament the Governor-General in Council may draw from the Treasury and expend such moneys as may be necessary for the maintenance of any department transferred to the Commonwealth and for the holding of the first elections for the Parliament.

84 Transfer of officers

When any department of the public service of a State becomes transferred to the Commonwealth, all officers of the department shall become subject to the control of the Executive Government of the Commonwealth.

Any such officer who is not retained in the service of the Commonwealth shall, unless he is appointed to some other office of equal emolument in the public service of the State, be entitled to receive from the State any pension, gratuity, or other compensation, payable under the law of the State on the abolition of his office.

Any such officer who is retained in the service of the Commonwealth shall preserve all his existing and accruing rights, and shall be entitled to retire from office at the time, and on the pension or retiring allowance, which would be permitted by the law of the State if his service with the Commonwealth were a continuation of his service with the State. Such pension or retiring allowance shall be paid to him by the Commonwealth; but the State shall pay to the Commonwealth a part thereof, to be calculated on the proportion which his term of service with the State bears to his whole term of service, and for the purpose of the calculation his salary shall be taken to be that paid to him by the State at the time of the transfer.

Any officer who is, at the establishment of the Commonwealth, in the public service of a State, and who is, by consent of the Governor of the State with the advice of the Executive Council thereof, transferred to the public service of the Commonwealth, shall have the same rights as if he had been an officer of a department transferred to the Commonwealth and were retained in the service of the Commonwealth.

85 Transfer of property of State

When any department of the public service of a State is transferred to the Commonwealth:

(i) all property of the State of any kind, used exclusively in connexion with the department, shall become vested in the Commonwealth; but, in the case of the departments controlling customs and excise and bounties, for such time only as the Governor-General in Council may declare to be necessary;

(ii) the Commonwealth may acquire any property of the State, of any kind used, but not exclusively used in connexion with the department; the value thereof shall, if no agreement can be made, be ascertained in, as nearly as may be, the manner in which the value of land, or of an interest in land, taken by the State for public purposes is ascertained under the law of the State in force at the establishment of the Commonwealth;

(iii) the Commonwealth shall compensate the State for the value of any property passing to the Commonwealth under this section; if no agreement can be made as to the mode of compensation, it shall be determined under laws to be made by the Parliament;

(iv) the Commonwealth shall, at the date of the transfer, assume the current obligations of the State in respect of the department transferred.

86 [Customs, excise, and bounties]

On the establishment of the Commonwealth, the collection and control of duties of customs and of excise, and the control of the payment of bounties, shall pass to the Executive Government of the Commonwealth.

87 [Revenue from customs and excise duties]

During a period of ten years after the establishment of the Commonwealth and thereafter until the Parliament otherwise provides, of the net revenue of the Commonwealth from duties of customs and of excise not more than one-fourth shall be applied annually by the Commonwealth towards its expenditure.

The balance shall, in accordance with this Constitution, be paid to the several States, or applied towards the payment of interest on debts of the several States taken over by the Commonwealth.

88 Uniform duties of customs

Uniform duties of customs shall be imposed within two years after the establishment of the Commonwealth.

89 Payment to States before uniform duties

Until the imposition of uniform duties of customs:

(i) the Commonwealth shall credit to each State the revenues collected therein by the Commonwealth;

(ii) the Commonwealth shall debit to each State:

   (a) the expenditure therein of the Commonwealth incurred solely for the maintenance or continuance, as at the time of transfer, of any department transferred from the State to the Commonwealth;

   (b) the proportion of the State, according to the number of its people, in the other expenditure of the Commonwealth;

(iii) the Commonwealth shall pay to each State month by month the balance (if any) in favour of the State.

90 Exclusive power over customs, excise, and bounties

On the imposition of uniform duties of customs the power of the Parliament to impose duties of customs and of excise, and to grant bounties on the production or export of goods, shall become exclusive.

On the imposition of uniform duties of customs all laws of the several States imposing duties of customs or of excise, or offering bounties on the production or export of goods, shall cease to have effect, but any grant of or agreement for any such bounty lawfully made by or under the authority of the Government of any State shall be taken to be good if made before the thirtieth day of June, one thousand eight hundred and ninety-eight, and not otherwise.

91 Exceptions as to bounties

Nothing in this Constitution prohibits a State from granting any aid to or bounty on mining for gold, silver, or other metals, nor from granting, with the consent of both Houses of the Parliament of the Commonwealth expressed by resolution, any aid to or bounty on the production or export of goods.

92 Trade within the Commonwealth to be free

On the imposition of uniform duties of customs, trade, commerce, and intercourse among the States, whether by means of internal carriage or ocean navigation, shall be absolutely free.

But notwithstanding anything in this Constitution, goods imported before the imposition of uniform duties of customs into any State, or into any Colony which, whilst the goods remain therein, becomes a State, shall, on thence passing into another State within two years after the imposition of such duties, be liable to any duty chargeable on the importation of such goods into the Commonwealth, less any duty paid in respect of the goods on their importation.

93 Payment to States for five years after uniform tariffs

During the first five years after the imposition of uniform duties of customs, and thereafter until the Parliament otherwise provides:

(i) the duties of customs chargeable on goods imported into a State and afterwards passing into another State for consumption, and the duties of excise paid on goods produced or manufactured in a State and afterwards passing into another State for consumption, shall be taken to have been collected not in the former but in the latter State;

(ii) subject to the last subsection, the Commonwealth shall credit revenue, debit expenditure, and pay balances to the several States as prescribed for the period preceding the imposition of uniform duties of customs.

94 Distribution of surplus

After five years from the imposition of uniform duties of customs, the Parliament may provide, on such basis as it deems fair, for the monthly payment to the several States of all surplus revenue of the Commonwealth.

95 Customs duties of Western Australia

Notwithstanding anything in this Constitution, the Parliament of the State of Western Australia, if that State be an Original State, may, during the first five years after the imposition of uniform duties of customs, impose duties of customs on goods passing into that State and not originally imported from beyond the limits of the Commonwealth; and such duties shall be collected by the Commonwealth.

But any duty so imposed on any goods shall not exceed during the first of such years the duty chargeable on the goods under the law of Western Australia in force at the imposition of uniform duties, and shall not exceed during the second, third, fourth, and fifth of such years respectively, four-fifths, three-fifths, two-fifths, and one-fifth of such latter duty, and all duties imposed under this section shall cease at the expiration of the fifth year after the imposition of uniform duties.

If at any time during the five years the duty on any goods under this section is higher than the duty imposed by the Commonwealth on the importation of the like goods, then such higher duty shall be collected on the goods when imported into Western Australia from beyond the limits of the Commonwealth.

96 Financial assistance to States

During a period of ten years after the establishment of the Commonwealth and thereafter until the Parliament otherwise provides, the Parliament may grant financial assistance to any State on such terms and conditions as the Parliament thinks fit.

97 Audit

Until the Parliament otherwise provides, the laws in force in any Colony which has become or becomes a State with respect to the receipt of revenue and the expenditure of money on account of the Government of the Colony, and the review and audit of such receipt and expenditure, shall apply to the receipt of revenue and the expenditure of money on account of the Commonwealth in the State in the same manner as if the Commonwealth, or the Government or an officer of the Commonwealth, were mentioned whenever the Colony, or the Government or an officer of the Colony, is mentioned.

98 Trade and commerce includes navigation and State railways

The power of the Parliament to make laws with respect to trade and commerce extends to navigation and shipping, and to railways the property of any State.

99 Commonwealth not to give preference

The Commonwealth shall not, by any law or regulation of trade, commerce, or revenue, give preference to one State or any part thereof over another State or any part thereof.

100 Nor abridge right to use water

The Commonwealth shall not, by any law or regulation of trade or commerce, abridge the right of a State or of the residents therein to the reasonable use of the waters of rivers for conservation or irrigation.

101 Inter-State Commission

There shall be an Inter-State Commission, with such powers of adjudication and administration as the Parliament deems necessary for the execution and maintenance, within the Commonwealth, of the provisions of this Constitution relating to trade and commerce, and of all laws made thereunder.

102 Parliament may forbid preferences by State

The Parliament may by any law with respect to trade or commerce forbid, as to railways, any preference or discrimination by any State, or by any authority constituted under a State, if such preference or discrimination is undue and unreasonable, or unjust to any State; due regard being had to the financial responsibilities incurred by any State in connexion with the construction and maintenance of its railways. But no preference or discrimination shall, within the meaning of this section, be taken to be undue and unreasonable, or unjust to any State, unless so adjudged by the Inter-State Commission.

103 Commissioners' appointment, tenure, and remuneration

The members of the Inter-State Commission:

- (i) shall be appointed by the Governor-General in Council;
- (ii) shall hold office for seven years, but may be removed within that time by the Governor-General in Council, on an address from both Houses of the Parliament in the same session praying for such removal on the ground of proved misbehaviour or incapacity;
- (iii) shall receive such remuneration as the Parliament may fix; but such remuneration shall not be diminished during their continuance in office.

104 Saving of certain rates

Nothing in this Constitution shall render unlawful any rate for the carriage of goods upon a railway, the property of a State, if the rate is deemed by the Inter-State Commission to be necessary for the development of the territory of the State, and if the rate applies equally to goods within the State and to goods passing into the State from other States.

105 Taking over public debts of States

The Parliament may take over from the States their public debts ~~as existing at the establishment of the Commonwealth~~, or a proportion thereof according to the respective numbers of their people as shown by the latest statistics of the Commonwealth, and may convert, renew, or consolidate such debts, or any part thereof; and the States shall indemnify the Commonwealth in respect of the debts taken over, and thereafter the interest payable in respect of the debts shall be deducted and retained from the portions of the surplus revenue of the Commonwealth payable to the several States, or if such surplus is insufficient, or if there is no surplus, then the deficiency or the whole amount shall be paid by the several States.

105A Agreements with respect to State debts

(1) **The Commonwealth may make agreements with the States with respect to the public debts of the States, including:**
  (a) **the taking over of such debts by the Commonwealth;**
  (b) **the management of such debts;**
  (c) **the payment of interest and the provision and management of sinking funds in respect of such debts;**
  (d) **the consolidation, renewal, conversion, and redemption of such debts;**
  (e) **the indemnification of the Commonwealth by the States in respect of debts taken over by the Commonwealth; and**
  (f) **the borrowing of money by the States or by the Commonwealth, or by the Commonwealth for the States.**

(2) **The Parliament may make laws for validating any such agreement made before the commencement of this section.**

(3) **The Parliament may make laws for the carrying out by the parties thereto of any such agreement.**

(4) **Any such agreement may be varied or rescinded by the parties thereto.**

(5) **Every such agreement and any such variation thereof shall be binding upon the Commonwealth and the States parties thereto notwithstanding anything contained in this Constitution or the Constitution of the several States or in any law of the Parliament of the Commonwealth or of any State.**

(6) **The powers conferred by this section shall not be construed as being limited in any way by the provisions of section one hundred and five of this Constitution.**

Chapter V - The States

106 Saving of Constitutions

The Constitution of each State of the Commonwealth shall, subject to this Constitution, continue as at the establishment of the Commonwealth, or as at the admission or establishment of the State, as the case may be, until altered in accordance with the Constitution of the State.

107 Saving of Power of State Parliaments

Every power of the Parliament of a Colony which has become or becomes a State, shall, unless it is by this Constitution exclusively vested in the Parliament of the Commonwealth or withdrawn from the Parliament of the State, continue as at the establishment of the Commonwealth, or as at the admission or establishment of the State, as the case may be.

108 Saving of State laws

Every law in force in a Colony which has become or becomes a State, and relating to any matter within the powers of the Parliament of the Commonwealth, shall, subject to this Constitution, continue in force in the State; and, until provision is made in that behalf by the Parliament of the Commonwealth, the Parliament of the State shall have such powers of alteration and of repeal in respect of any such law as the Parliament of the Colony had until the Colony became a State.

109 Inconsistency of laws

When a law of a State is inconsistent with a law of the Commonwealth, the latter shall prevail, and the former shall, to the extent of the inconsistency, be invalid.

110 Provisions referring to Governor

The provisions of this Constitution relating to the Governor of a State extend and apply to the Governor for the time being of the State, or other chief executive officer or administrator of the government of the State.

111 States may surrender territory

The Parliament of a State may surrender any part of the State to the Commonwealth; and upon such surrender, and the acceptance thereof by the Commonwealth, such part of the State shall become subject to the exclusive jurisdiction of the Commonwealth.

112 States may levy charges for inspection laws

After uniform duties of customs have been imposed, a State may levy on imports or exports, or on goods passing into or out of the State, such charges as may be necessary for executing the inspection laws of the State; but the net produce of all charges so levied shall be for the use of the Commonwealth; and any such inspection laws may be annulled by the Parliament of the Commonwealth.

113 Intoxicating liquids

All fermented, distilled, or other intoxicating liquids passing into any State or remaining therein for use, consumption, sale, or storage, shall be subject to the laws of the State as if such liquids had been produced in the State.

114 States may not raise forces. Taxation of property of Commonwealth or State

A State shall not, without the consent of the Parliament of the Commonwealth, raise or maintain any naval or military force, or impose any tax on property of any kind belonging to the Commonwealth, nor shall the Commonwealth impose any tax on property of any kind belonging to a State.

115 States not to coin money

A State shall not coin money, nor make anything but gold and silver coin a legal tender in payment of debts.

116 Commonwealth not to legislate in respect of religion

The Commonwealth shall not make any law for establishing any religion, or for imposing any religious observance, or for prohibiting the free exercise of any religion, and no religious test shall be required as a qualification for any office or public trust under the Commonwealth.

117 Rights of residents in States

A subject of the Queen, resident in any State, shall not be subject in any other State to any disability or discrimination which would not be equally applicable to him if he were a subject of the Queen resident in such other State.

118 Recognition of laws etc. of States

Full faith and credit shall be given, throughout the Commonwealth to the laws, the public Acts and records, and the judicial proceedings of every State.

119 Protection of States from invasion and violence

The Commonwealth shall protect every State against invasion and, on the application of the Executive Government of the State, against domestic violence.

120 Custody of offenders against laws of the Commonwealth

Every State shall make provision for the detention in its prisons of persons accused or convicted of offences against the laws of the Commonwealth, and for the punishment of persons convicted of such offences, and the Parliament of the Commonwealth may make laws to give effect to this provision.

Chapter VI - New States

121 New States may be admitted or established

The Parliament may admit to the Commonwealth or establish new States, and may upon such admission or establishment make or impose such terms and conditions, including the extent of representation in either House of the Parliament, as it thinks fit.

122 Government of territories

The Parliament may make laws for the government of any territory surrendered by any State to and accepted by the Commonwealth, or of any territory placed by the Queen under the authority of and accepted by the Commonwealth, or otherwise acquired by the Commonwealth, and may allow the representation of such territory in either House of the Parliament to the extent and on the terms which it thinks fit.

123 Alteration of limits of States

The Parliament of the Commonwealth may, with the consent of the Parliament of a State, and the approval of the majority of the electors of the State voting upon the question, increase, diminish, or otherwise alter the limits of the State, upon such terms and conditions as may be agreed on, and may, with the like consent, make provision respecting the effect and operation of any increase or diminution or alteration of territory in relation to any State affected.

124 Formation of new States

A new State may be formed by separation of territory from a State, but only with the consent of the Parliament thereof, and a new State may be formed by the union of two or more States or parts of States, but only with the consent of the Parliaments of the States affected.

Chapter VII - Miscellaneous

125 Seat of Government

The seat of Government of the Commonwealth shall be determined by the Parliament, and shall be within territory which shall have been granted to or acquired by the Commonwealth, and shall be vested in and belong to the Commonwealth, and shall be in the State of New South Wales, and be distant not less than one hundred miles from Sydney.

Such territory shall contain an area of not less than one hundred square miles, and such portion thereof as shall consist of Crown lands shall be granted to the Commonwealth without any payment therefor.

The Parliament shall sit at Melbourne until it meet at the seat of Government.

126 Power to Her Majesty to authorise Governor-General to appoint deputies

The Queen may authorise the Governor-General to appoint any person, or any persons jointly or severally, to be his deputy or deputies within any part of the Commonwealth, and in that capacity to exercise during the pleasure of the Governor-General such powers and functions of the Governor-General as he thinks fit to assign to such deputy or deputies, subject to any limitations expressed or directions given by the Queen; but the appointment of such deputy or deputies shall not affect the exercise by the Governor-General himself of any power or function.

~~127 Aborigines not to be counted in reckoning population~~

~~In reckoning the numbers of people of the Commonwealth, or of a State or other part of the Commonwealth, aboriginal natives shall not be counted.~~

Chapter VIII – Alteration of the Constitution

128 Mode of altering the Constitution

This Constitution shall not be altered except in the following manner:

The proposed law for the alteration thereof must be passed by an absolute majority of each House of the Parliament, and not less than two nor more than six months after its passage through both Houses the proposed law shall be submitted in each State **and Territory** to the electors qualified to vote for the election of members of the House of Representatives.

But if either House passes any such proposed law by an absolute majority, and the other House rejects or fails to pass it, or passes it with any amendment to which the first-mentioned House will not agree, and if after an interval of three months the first-mentioned House in the same or the next session again passes the proposed law by an absolute majority with or without any amendment which has been made or agreed to by the other House, and such other House rejects or fails to pass it or passes it with any amendment to which the first-mentioned House will not agree, the Governor-General may submit the proposed law as last proposed by the first-mentioned House, and either with or without any amendments subsequently agreed to by both Houses, to the electors in each State **and Territory** qualified to vote for the election of the House of Representatives.

When a proposed law is submitted to the electors the vote shall be taken in such manner as the Parliament prescribes. But until the qualification of electors of members of the House of Representatives becomes uniform throughout the Commonwealth, only one-half the electors voting for and against the proposed law shall be counted in any State in which adult suffrage prevails.

And if in a majority of the States a majority of the electors voting approve the proposed law, and if a majority of all the electors voting also approve the proposed law, it shall be presented to the Governor-General for the Queen's assent.

No alteration diminishing the proportionate representation of any State in either House of the Parliament, or the minimum number of representatives of a State in the House of Representatives, or increasing, diminishing, or otherwise altering the limits of the State, or in any manner affecting the provisions of the Constitution in relation thereto, shall become law unless the majority of the electors voting in that State approve the proposed law.

In this section, *Territory* means any territory referred to in section one hundred and twenty-two of this Constitution in respect of which there is in force a law allowing its representation in the House of Representatives.

Schedule

OATH

I, *A.B.*, do swear that I will be faithful and bear true allegiance to Her Majesty Queen Victoria, Her heirs and successors according to law.

SO HELP ME GOD!

AFFIRMATION

I, *A.B.*, do solemnly and sincerely affirm and declare that I will be faithful and bear true allegiance to Her Majesty Queen Victoria, Her heirs and successors according to law.

(NOTE: *The name of the King or Queen of the United Kingdom of Great Britain and Ireland for the time being is to be substituted from time to time.*)

INDEX

www.ingramcontent.com/pod-product-compliance
Lightning Source LLC
LaVergne TN
LVHW060008210926
848481LV00013B/3669
* 9 7 8 1 0 0 9 3 2 6 6 0 5 *